Zambesia, England's El Dorado in Africa ... An account of the Gold Fields of British South Africa. [With maps.]

Edward Peter Mathers

Zambesia, England's El Dorado in Africa ... An account of the Gold Fields of British South Africa. [With maps.]
Mathers, Edward Peter
British Library, Historical Print Editions
British Library
1891
vii. 480 p. ; 8°.
010096.ee.22.

GUIDE TO FOLD-OUTS, MAPS and OVERSIZED IMAGES

In an online database, page images do not need to conform to the size restrictions found in a printed book. When converting these images back into a printed bound book, the page sizes are standardized in ways that maintain the detail of the original. For large images, such as fold-out maps, the original page image is split into two or more pages.

Guidelines used to determine the split of oversize pages:

• Some images are split vertically; large images require vertical and horizontal splits.
• For horizontal splits, the content is split left to right.
• For vertical splits, the content is split from top to bottom.
• For both vertical and horizontal splits, the image is processed from top left to bottom right.

Yours faithfully
E. Mathers.

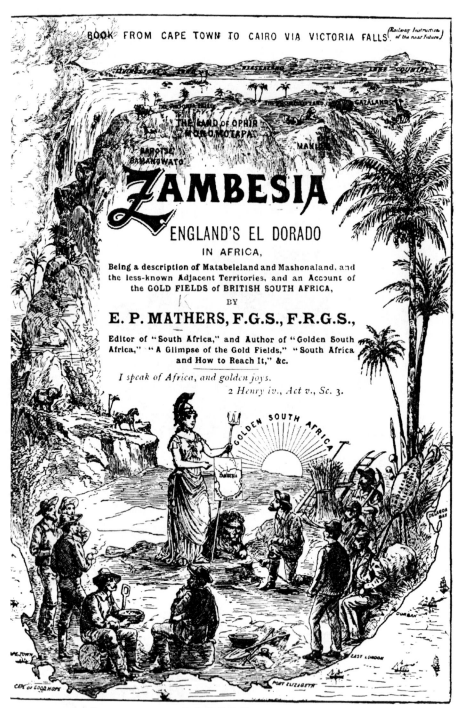

BOOK FROM CAPE TOWN TO CAIRO VIA VICTORIA FALLS (*Railway Instruction of the near Future.*)

ZAMBESIA

ENGLAND'S EL DORADO
IN AFRICA,

Being a description of Matabeleland and Mashonaland, and
the less-known Adjacent Territories, and an Account of
the GOLD FIELDS of BRITISH SOUTH AFRICA,

BY

E. P. MATHERS, F.G.S., F.R.G.S.,

Editor of "South Africa," and Author of "Golden South
Africa," "A Glimpse of the Gold Fields," "South Africa
and How to Reach It," &c.

I speak of Africa, and golden joys.

2 *Henry iv., Act v., Sc.* 3.

LONDON:
PUBLISHED BY KING, SELL, & RAILTON, LTD.,
GOUGH SQUARE & BOLT COURT, FLEET ST., E.C.

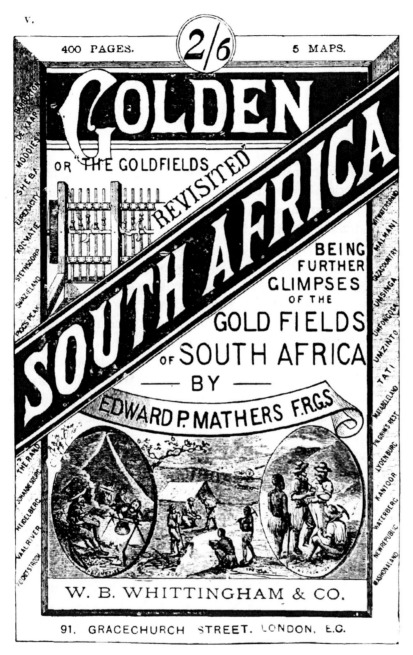

400 PAGES. **2/6** 5 MAPS.

GOLDEN

OR "THE GOLDFIELDS" REVISITED

SOUTH AFRICA

BEING
FURTHER
GLIMPSES
OF THE
GOLD FIELDS
OF SOUTH AFRICA
— BY —

EDWARD P. MATHERS F.R.G.S

W. B. WHITTINGHAM & CO.

91. GRACECHURCH STREET. LONDON, E.C.

A FEW OPINIONS OF THE PRESS.

" Full of interest."—*Daily Chronicle.*
" A very interesting volume."—*Truth.*
" Surpassing interest."—*Dundee Advertiser.*
" Charmingly written chapters."—*Engineering.*
" Best authority on the subject."—*Manchester Guardian.*

PREFACE.

IMMERSED as I am by my daily occupation in the chronicling and critical dissection of South African affairs, it seems to me as if it were hardly necessary to offer any explanation of the reason which has called this work into existence. It is as true to-day as when the ancient writer said it, that there is ever something new from Africa. The founding of Zambesia by a royally-chartered Company is the latest development in the advance of South Africa, and that development well merits the attention of the historian, however imperfectly, on account of partially-concealed tendencies, he may be able to fulfil his function. Though the mighty proportions of the Imperial edifice which is now being reared in South Africa will only be accurately gauged by a fuller distance of Time, a justification for the publication of this book may be found in the rapid northern expansion of British South Africa, and the consequent accompanying desire for information about the territory brought recently under the control and civilising influences of the colossal corporation which sways the fortunes of Zambesia. There is also possibly a special fitness in issuing this record at the conclusion of the prolonged negotiations with Portugal in respect of her claims to recognition as a South African Power. If the result of these negotiations has left much to be desired from one point of view, it may, at least, be welcomed as an indication of an aspiration on the part of Portugal to live at peace with her British neighbours in South Africa. Let her but infuse the same wish into the hearts and minds of her representatives on the borders of Zambesia, and the march of great events may now go on uninterruptedly. The acts of these representatives have handicapped Portugal heavily in her endeavours to arrive at an amicable understanding with Lord Salisbury, but it may be assumed, now that so much has been achieved towards a pacific partnership of progress, that she will answer honourably for these acts. However the concession to Portuguese aggrandisement in Northern Zambesia may be regarded, " we are a people yet," and the destiny of the Anglo-Saxon race to open up Africa from South to North may safely be left to the hereditary capacities of that race. I have used all due care in the preparation of these pages, which are necessarily, to a large extent, of a collatitious character, and I need only add my grateful acknowledgments to those who have ungrudgingly assisted me to produce the only effort of its kind.

23, Austin Friars, London, E.C.   THE AUTHOR.
          June, 1891.

CONTENTS.

MAPS.

CHAPTER I.

CHAPTER II.

CHAPTER III.

CHAPTER X.

CHAPTER XI.

CHAPTER XII.

CHAPTER XIII.

CHAPTER XIV.

CHAPTER XV.

CHAPTER XVI.

CHAPTER XVII.

CHAPTER XVIII.

CHAPTER XIX.

APPENDICES.

GOLDEN SOUTH AFRICA.

A FEW OPINIONS OF THE PRESS.

"Will remain of everlasting interest."—*Kokstad Advertiser.*

"Well written and easily comprehended."—*Stock Exchange Times.*

"A mine of information, and a treasury of reference."—*Public Opinion.*

"Throughout information of a practical character."—*Daily Telegraph.*

"Written in a most agreeable and entertaining manner."—*Barberton Herald.*

"Valuable work. . . . Pleasantly vivacious manner."—*Sheffield Daily Telegraph.*

"Than Mr. Mathers no better guide to South Africa could be got."—*Aberdeen Journal.*

"Mr. Mathers has done his work in his usual thorough style."—*Komatie Observer.*

"Mr. Mathers is a recognized authority on South African affairs."—*Pall Mall Gazette.*

"A very good survey of the country and its history, from a mining point of view."—*Daily News.*

"The book is one of the most interesting that has seen the light for many a day."—*Cape Argus.*

"The handbook amply informs all parties. It fully supplements the knowledge of the local man, and it is replete on every given point without exception, with all details which are required by the foreign inquirer."—*Natal Advertiser.*

"The Gold Fields are languishing for want of English capital, and if anything is calculated to either invite or repel the English investor, it is in this book. As a guide-book to the South African mining centres it is the best work extant."—*Natal Witness.*

"It is cram full of facts and information, which, so far as we are aware, can be obtained from no other published work. . . . Mr. Mathers believes in the new journalism, and his book, although invaluable to the mining interest, contains much that is as amusing and interesting as anything written by Lady Brassey."—*Financial Critic.*

"This very interesting volume consists of a series of sketches of the Transvaal Gold Fields from the pen of a distinguished Natal journalist. . . . Constitute a most graphic and complete account of the early history and present prospects of many auriferous spots in South Africa. . . . That admirable work."—*Weekly Bulletin.*

"In 'The Gold Fields Re-visited,' Mr. Edward P. Mathers, F.R.G.S., has revised and enlarged his valuable communications on the Gold Fields of South Africa . . . . The book contains much information and sound advice, and gives a correct view of the present condition of the South African gold-bearing regions."—*Morning Post.*

"This work is a laborious and conscientious attempt on the part of Mr. Mathers to put before the public a mass of useful information on the subject of the Gold Fields of South Africa. . . . The work is well written, and full of information. It should be read with care by all interested in the development of South Africa."—*Mining World.*

"Shareholders will learn more by a persual of this book than from the statements issued by the various companies, and will find themselves able to gauge pretty accurately the value of their property and the dividend it is likely to pay. . . . It is clear that Mr. Mathers has thoroughly mastered his subject, and he has the knack of interesting his readers in what to most would be a very dry subject."—*Financial World.*

Index to Illustrations.

INTRODUCTION.

WITH the formation of the British South Africa Company, and the founding of England's latest possession, Zambesia, the nations of the world—some of them with ill-concealed envy—saw a welcome new departure in the policy of the mother country towards South Africa. Albeit that it was taken at the eleventh hour, they witnessed a great step forward in the vitalisation of British centres of activity in South Africa, a re-quickening of that English national life which is to be all potent in fulfilling the Imperial destiny in that most interesting, most wealthy, and most romantic of all the continents of the earth. The successful march into, and peaceful occupation of, Mashonaland by the Pioneer Force of the royally-chartered Company mark yet another distinct epoch in the history of Africa south of the Equator—yet another landmark in the progressive journey when it will be convenient to again survey the scene behind, beneath, and before.

Events political, and developments industrial, have alike moved with wonderful rapidity in South Africa during the past lustrum. A mere five or six years ago, before the eyes of men had been turned to the northern territories, and before the more important proofs of those golden possibilities in the Transvaal Republic, of which I wrote a decade back, had been given, the political student in looking out over the various civilised territories of South Africa and casting the horoscope of their future, would have unhesitatingly given it as his opinion that English domination was diminishing year by year, and that an Anglo-Boer policy of a consolidation of the States of South Africa, under a Republican form of government, was swiftly reducing this dominion to a vanishing point. Since certain deplorable occurrences, which need not be further referred to here, had shocked the national *amour propre* and astounded the Empire by their disgracefulness, the policy of England and of English people in South Africa was largely that of drift. The policy of the Boers, and the Dutch generally, was, on the other hand, an active one. Their political keel was laid upon the lines of increasing the area of the Dutch Republics in all directions, and so minimising the chances of, and extinguishing the opportunities for, British expansion. The cry of a strong party, which got daily recruits, was "Africa for the Afrikander, from the Zambesi to Cape Town." It must not be forgotten that the conclusion of our supposititious studious seer would have been based to some extent on calculations showing the numerical preponderance of Boers or Dutch in South Africa over British-born subjects or their African-born descendants. In the Cape Colony alone, it was some five or six years ago estimated that of every three white people, two were Dutch; that in the Transvaal and Free State, out of every ten white people, nine were Boer or Dutch; and that in Natal alone was the scale weighed down in the other direction. There the estimated proportion was four English to one Dutch resident. The change came suddenly. The development of the gold industry in the Transvaal drew to that country comparatively great numbers of English-speaking people, whether from the mother land or the maritime colonies in South Africa. This fast-growing industry also attracted many millions of English capital, and this circumstance, in its turn, compelled thousands of Englishmen residing in England to take a new and deeper interest in South Africa. Swazieland also absorbed not a few hundreds of thousands of pounds in a similar way, and also drew the attention of more English shareholders to political events in South Africa.

These factors of industrial, commercial, and speculative enterprise indirectly influenced the tone of political feeling in South Africa. It rapidly became essentially English, and the turn of the drifting tide took place. Concurrently with this change in the hue of South African public affairs, Mr. Cecil Rhodes and his friends turned their attention to the great Native territories lying to the north of the Cape Colony and the South African Republic. Fortunately for the Empire, the position was swiftly realised. As if there had been some sudden and mightier revelation than before, it was seen that unless the blow was instantly struck to secure these territories for England, a few months would see them in the hands of republicans concentrated in Pretoria, to be used for the purposes of Boer aggrandisement, either with or without the co-operation of some alien European power. The effort was made, but not without difficulty, for a strong and strange struggle ensued, of which the Grobler incident gave an unmistakable clue. Luckily, however, the powers that rule in Downing Street became convinced that if British supremacy in South Africa was to be conserved, a determined stand must immediately be taken. It was taken, and the slight preliminary intimation given to South Africa in general, and to the Boers in particular, by Sir Charles Warren's expedition, was logically followed up and strengthened by a declaration of British rights, under various names and disguises, to the whole of the native territories lying to the north of the Cape Colony and the Transvaal. As I have said, a mere lustrum has served to change the whole position in South Africa. Whereas some five or six years ago the gathering force of Republicanism, which aimed at an independent United States of South Africa, was apparently on the eve of fruition, it has now become not only a vanished dream, but a political impossibility; and in its stead we find an almost universal aspiration to prosper under the protection of the Union Jack. We find the name of England once more in an honoured ascendant everywhere, and that, excluding malcontents, Boer Republicanism is discovering that the truest, and best development of Boer interests will be found in a cordial co-operation with an enlightened and non-bureaucratic British policy.

To Britishers generally this is a consummation to be greatly grateful for. As I have pointed out, two factors helped to it. One of these was the extraordinary and rapid development of the gold industry, and the other was the step taken in the north by Mr. Rhodes and his friends. To my mind the latter was the chief operating factor from a political point of view. The gold interests across the Limpopo might have been, and doubtless would have been, fostered under a Republican form of government, so that so far as these are concerned, the transfer of dominion or political sway from Dutch Republican to British Imperial need not necessarily have followed; but Mr. Rhodes and those associated with him, although nominally pursuing a commercial undertaking, in securing enormous rights in the native territories to the north, invariably enunciated the political gospel of British supremacy in their enterprise. The Union Jack was run up to the masthead, the word "British" figured as the first word in their title, the

B 2

imprimatur of the Privy Seal was placed upon their document of title, and a civilised-nineteenth-century letter of mark was issued to the Duke of Abercorn and others to carry ascendancy and Empire under the British name from the boundaries of the Cape Colony and the Transvaal to the Zambesi and beyond. Owing to the enterprise having been undertaken in this spirit, we find the reason for the full stop in the policy of English drift in South Africa, and for the reinstatement of British supremacy in that part of the continent. A great new English colony is being founded. Zambesia is hardly born, and already three railways are being planned to approach it from the south and east. A land that up to ten years ago was a sealed book to all but intrepid adventurers, to half-a-dozen men of the Selous stamp, will before long feel the splitting wedge of the locomotive, and it is safe to predict that ere the century closes it will be possible to take a tripper's ticket at Messrs. Cook and Son's bureau in London which will frank you to the Victoria Falls, *via* the Pungwe Railway on the East Coast, and carry you along the Central South African Railway to Cape Town, thence back to England within three months.

Not the least satisfactory and pleasing feature in the retrospect is that in the process of asserting this supremacy again for all time little or no violence has been done to any shade of national feeling. Despite the fact that Mr. Rhodes, the leader of the new departure, has always nailed the British colours to his mast, and has been in all things an ardent Imperialist, he has contrived to carry with him through all the phases of his colossal enterprise the stolid and invaluable support of the would-be Republican Boers and Dutch of the Cape Colony. And this following has been secured on this very logical basis—that the policy for the strongest and best development of South Africa must necessarily be one recognising Great Britain as the dominant power there, though there must be underlying that recognition the counter-recognition and affirmation that each State in South Africa has perfect freedom to govern itself in all local matters without interference from the Crown. Freedom from foreign interference, freedom from the muddling of Downing Street, were the aspirations which led thousands of men in South Africa to drift into a hesitating acceptance of uncongenial Republicanism, not from any wish to sever from England, but from a mere desire of self-protection and self-preservation. Granting the realisation of this longing, and the creation of this freedom, by a system which would not necessitate severance from England, and the rest naturally followed, and it was left to Mr. Rhodes to show as a part of his great scheme the way whereby this freedom and retention of the English tie could be combined.

In truth, it must be recalled that a certain amount of soreness has been evolved in the Transvaal. And naturally so. For the first time in the history of that country—in fact, for the first time in the history of Boerdom, the way to the north no longer exists. During a period of 250 years, the Dutch in South Africa have ever had the north as a direction in which to migrate should necessity demand, or choice dictate, and decade after decade through the centuries the Boers have steadily advanced from their original hamlet on the shores of the Cape peninsula till they have reached Mossamedes on the west coast, two thousand miles from their point of departure. This, however, is now all ended. There is no further north for the Boer to carve into according to his individual licence or liking. To the north the Boer may yet go, but it must be under restrictions imposed by British civilisation and British control. England is no longer content to penetrate Africa from the south, on the back of the Boer. The conditions are reversed. This feeling of soreness, however, is passing, and its ready cure is being found in the rapid Anglicisation of the South African Republic itself. Nominally, the Transvaal is a Boer Republic, and nominally the men who at present sway its destinies are Boers, and in some cases ultra-Boers; but practically the territory and the Government are swayed by a new set of needs, required and demanded by a great population of English-speaking people who have settled in that golden land. Thus it is we have it that the prospect lying now before South Africa is a consolidated dominion under the British flag, and thus it is that the retrospect founded on the facts I have been summarising prompts me unhesitatingly to largely give the credit for that prospect to the enterprise which found its inception and cause of being in the brain of Mr. Cecil Rhodes. "One people, one destiny," was the motto under which the Australian colonies recently took their first united step towards Federation, and it will be under that motto that the future Federation of South Africa will be accomplished. For the moment that Federation may seem far away, but the grand consummation is all the nearer through the founding of Zambesia. Has any one any doubt as to how the nationalities will compare in the near future in South Africa? He is answered when I say the British now outnumber the Boers in the Transvaal. Has he still any doubt? I would then say to him—go to the Paddington or Waterloo Railway Station on any Friday morning and see the crowds of well-to-do emigrants shoaling to the fair land which stretches its limitless expanse underneath the Southern Cross. While the Boer remains practically stagnant, the British population of South Africa is multiplying fast, and will soon multiply faster; and in course of time the former will merge in the latter in feeling, thought, language, and method. As I contemplate the course of current events in the great Northland of which Zambesia in its turn will but form the southern starting point in the ceaseless march of British progress through to the blue Mediterranean—

> I hear the tread of pioneers
> Of nations yet to be,
> The first low wash of human waves
> Where soon shall roll a sea.

CHAPTER I.

Ancient Africa.—Explorations to Date.—Gold the Lode-Star.
—The Zimbabye Ruins in Mashonaland.—Mysterious and
Massive Monuments of the Past.—How the Chartered
Company's Force Re-Discovered them.—Their Hoary Secrets.
—What were They and Who Built Them?—The Latest
Effort to Solve a Profound Problem.

BEFORE I proceed to describe Zambesia, as it is known
to-day, let us "look far back into other years" for
interesting and convincing evidence that the inheritance
of the British South Africa Company and the companies
which have joined fortunes with it is rich "beyond the dreams of
avarice." This I shall either compile from ancient records in
my possession, or cull from my own former writings or from
those of contemporary writers who have exercised the neces-

AFRICA AS KNOWN AT THE END OF THE 13TH CENTURY.

sary diligence and discretion to select the illustrative material I seek now to lay before my readers. Before the Portuguese circumnavigated Africa, much of the east coast was known

to Arab geographers, and in the fifth century before Christ,
Hanno, the Carthaginian, had crept down the west coast as far as
the Gulf of Guinea. Before the Christian era both Herodotus and
Eratosthenes showed familiarity with the broad features of African
geography. It was not, however, till toward the end of the
fifteenth century that an approximate idea of this geography was
obtained by the enterprise of Portuguese navigators. We have
such landmarks as the rounding of Cape Bojador in 1434; Cape
Blanco, 1441; Cape Verde, 1445; Fernando Po, 1471; the discovery of the mouth of the Congo by Diego Cao, 1484; the Cape
of Good Hope rounded by Dias, 1497 (this explorer passed the

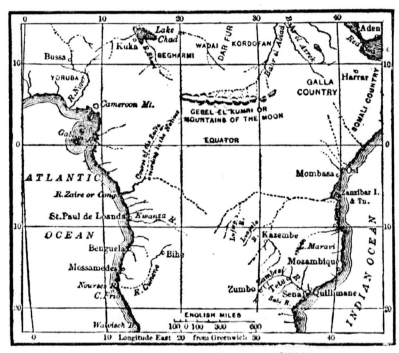

CENTRAL AFRICA AS KNOWN IN 1840.

Cape without seeing it in 1487); followed next year by Vasco Da
Gama at Natal, Quilimane, Mozambique, Mombasa, and Melinda.
Sofala and Kilwa were taken in 1505-6. From that time the
general outline of Africa has lain spread out before us in all its
amplitude. From that time, too, the interior—on the maps at
least—began to be rapidly filled up, until in the seventeenth and
beginning of the eighteenth centuries, Africa was generally represented in atlases and books as in Dapple's map of 1680. The
features are so fantastic that they look like a travesty of the truth.
From one great lake, named Zembre, three rivers take their rise,
no doubt representing the Nile, the Congo, and the Coanza.

That the crowd of features laid down on these old maps was the result of actual observation by European travellers is not to be believed, though no doubt Portuguese missionaries did penetrate for some distance into the interior. But the majority of the lakes and mountains and rivers with which the interior is filled were either due to the imagination of travellers and geographers, or were simply set down from vague and untrustworthy native report. As our own Swift had it—

> So geographers in Afric maps
> With savage pictures fill their gaps,
> And o'er unhabitable downs
> Place elephants instead of towns.

In short, the map of Africa seemed so whimsical a composition that the great French geographer, d'Anville, in the middle of last century, made a clean sweep, retaining only those features for the existence of which there was clear evidence, but leaving the great centre a complete blank. And so we may say it remained almost down to the time when Livingstone began his great work, and initiated what may be called the modern period of African exploration.

This will be a convenient place to divide the periods of exploratory work in Africa during the last hundred years.

1. Epoch 1790-1850. Periods of individual exploration in the north and south.
    (a) 1790-1830. Niger problem.
    (b) 1830-1850. Slow progress in Nile territories and in South Africa.
2. Epoch 1850-1890. Periods during which the explorations in Northern and Southern Equatorial Africa were connected with one another.
    (a) 1850-1862. Nile and Zambesi problems. Explorations in the Sahara Desert and in the Soudan.
    (b) 1862-1877. Congo problem. Connection between explorations in Eastern and Western Equatorial Africa.
    (c) 1877-1890. Filling in of details; the extension of colonisation in Tropical Africa; and the founding of Zambesia by the British South Africa Company.

Those who read these lines will probably be chiefly interested in an inquiry into the auriferous resources of the vast territory named in the latter part of sub-section c. I must again, therefore, hark back to the misty past. It is said that the use of gold is coeval with the advance in civilisation which dates from the discovery of the metals, and it has even been supposed that gold was the first metal which attracted the notice of man. Some historian has remarked, for instance, that when Brazil was discovered, the natives were found using fish-hooks of gold, but were unconscious of the value of the precious metal. It is interesting

in this connection to read the accounts of the voyages of the
Mediterranean races—the Phœnician, Egyptian, Etruscan, and
Greek—in search of gold. They travelled from Asia Minor,
Greece, Italy, and Africa, to Spain, Britain, and Ireland. Egypt,
Assyria, India, China, and Peru can each show "golden treasures"
dating from the earliest dawn of civilisation. Gold is said to have
been found in Cornwall, and it was probably the object of the
Phœnician and Roman expeditions, although tin was the chief
treasure found. In Wales and in Ireland there were also gold
mines before modern Pritchard-Morgans came on the scene ; while
in Hungary there are not wanting evidences of old workings. In

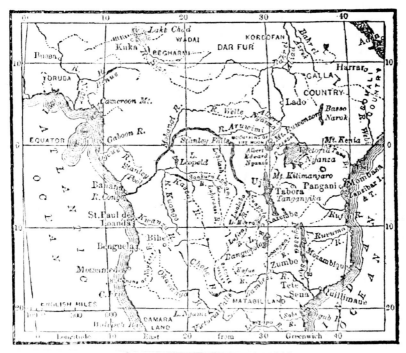

Central Africa as Known in 1890.

nearly every part of the world there are traces of old gold mines.
Gold seems to have been at all times a great impelling or attractive power, inducing men to start forth upon perilous enterprises
or hazardous journeys. It would be interesting to note the gain to
mankind in geographical knowledge and colonisation which has
accrued from the desire for gold. In modern times we have seen
how the gold mines of Mexico, of California, of Australia, and
though lastly, yet to prove themselves by no means least, of
South Africa, have been fruitful for good to mankind in general,
no matter how disappointing they have been to thousands of
individuals.

As far as the gold mines of South Africa are concerned, recent events have called attention to those both of an ancient and modern character. Those of these days I have amply described else- where. For the present we are to deal with those of medieval times, and a convenient introduction to them may be by an examina- tion of the stony monuments of a bygone age which have just been, as it were, re-discovered in Mashonaland, or what was at one period a part of the ancient kingdom of Monomotapa. Utilitarian and practical as were the objects of the march of the Pioneer Force of the British South Africa Company, some of its incidental results have not been without their interest for the archæologist and the student of ancient history. Among these was the sighting and the examination of the Zimbabye ruins—a remarkable collection of old remains which have excited no small amount of curiosity in England—curiosity alike as to their origin, and the purposes to which the buildings were devoted. As that erudite examiner of South African lore, Mr. John Noble, of Cape Town, recently pointed out in an excellent paper on the subject, there were misty legends in times past as to the existence of extensive buildings and ruins—supposed to be the relics of a very ancient civilisation—in certain parts of the interior of South Africa. These received some confirmation from the fact that the works of several of the old writers on Africa, two or three centuries ago, made mention of such prehistoric structures, generally associating them either with the ancient factories of the Queen of Sheba or King Solomon's mines. But for a long series of years, in the absence of any evidence as to their actual existence, the hazy and indefinite accounts given of them were classed among the fabulous stories which travellers were wont to tell. The first authentic information as to the survival of archæological remains, such as the old legends pointed to, was contributed by the German explorer, Carl Mauch, who, while travelling through the country between the Limpopo and Zambesi Rivers, in 1871, heard of what has since been known as the "Zimbabye Ruins," and also variously called by Baines the ruins of Zimbaoe and Mazimbaoe. Mauch located them in latitude 20° 15' 31" south, longitude 31° 37' 45" east, and 4200 feet above the level of the sea. Having, as will appear shortly, been told of the ruins by a local resident, he published an account of what he had seen, and so unexpected was it, and so marvellous did it appear that massive edifices, built of well-hewn stone, and forming a novel maze of circular walls and terraces extending over a large area of ground, should be found in the South African wilds, that there was a general impression the explorer had drawn upon the public credulity and greatly exaggerated what he had seen.

In a letter dated September, 1871, and addressed to the Rev. Mr. Gruetzner, he says: "The ruins may be divided into two parts; the one upon a granite rocky eminence of 400 feet in height, the other upon a somewhat elevated terrace. The two are separated by a gentle valley, their distance apart being about 300 yards. The rocky bluff consists of an elongated mass of granite, rounded in form, upon which stands a second block, and upon this again fragments smaller, but still many tons in weight, with fissures, chasms, and cavities. The western side of this mountain is covered from top to bottom by the ruins. As they are for the most part fallen in and covered with rubbish, it is at present impossible to determine the purpose the buildings were intended to serve; the most probable supposition is that it was a fortress impregnable in those times, and this the many passages—now, however, walled up—and the circular or zigzag plan of the walls would also indicate. All the walls, without exception, are built without mortar, of hewn granite, more or less about the size of our bricks. . . . Best preserved of all is the outer wall of an erection of rounded form, situated in the plain, and about 150 yards in diameter. It is at a distance of about 600 yards from the mountain, and was probably connected with it by means of great outworks, as appears to be indicated by the mounds of rubbish remaining. This oval has had but one entrance, which is three feet in width and five feet high, and upon the northern side, that is, facing the mountain. It had, however, been at one time built up, although subsequently in part fallen in again. The cause of this was probably the brittleness of the wooden cross-beams, which had too great a weight to carry. Inside, everything excepting a tower nearly thirty feet in height, and in perfect preservation, is fallen to ruin, but this, at least, can be made out, that the narrow passages are disposed in the form of a labyrinth. This tower consists of similar blocks of hewn granite, and is cylindrical to a height of ten feet, then upwards to the top conical in form. At the foot its diameter is fifteen feet, at the top eight feet, and it shows no trace of any entrance. It stands between the outer wall and another close to and parallel with it, the latter having had a narrow entrance. This entrance has, up to the height of a man, four double layers of quite black stone, alternating with double tiers of granite. The outer walls show an attempt at ornamenting the granite—it represents a double line of zig-zags between horizontal bands. This ornament is twenty feet from the ground, and is employed upon a third part of the south wall on each side of the tower, and only on the outside." Writing on the question of inscriptions, Mauch says: "On a hasty visit to the very widely-spread parts of these ruins I was not able (by the removal of rubbish and fragments of stone) to light upon any inscriptions. I picked up no implements which would enable one to determine the age of the ruins; many, indeed all that could be laid hands upon, had been consumed by the present occupants of the country." But it would seem that there is a common tradition of the existence of inscriptions, for the Rev. A. Merensky, the missionary who was sent to explore part of this country, wrote in 1871:

"Natives warned our people that in the attempt to push on to

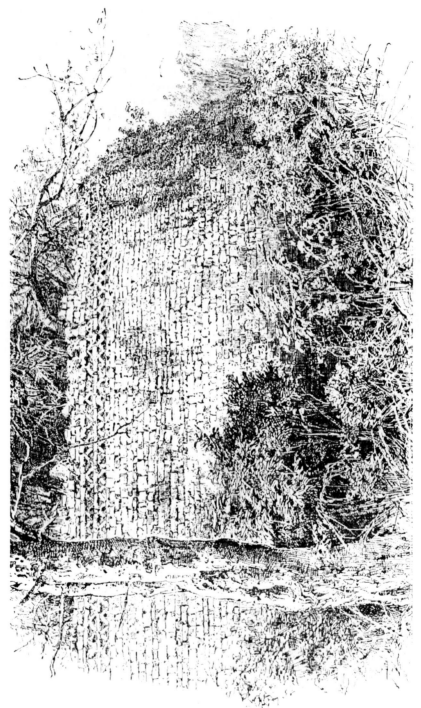

the ruins we should all be murdered, because the Makwapa were in
the habit of procuring different articles thence, and therefore kept
them concealed from other tribes. We could not, however, ascertain
what these articles were. A guide of the Banyai tribe told us much
about this mysterious spot, and thus we gathered that the Banyai
revere these ancient buildings; that no living creature may there
be put to death, no tree destroyed, since everything is considered
sacred. He also told us that a populous black tribe, acquainted
with the use of firearms, had formerly dwelt there, but about fifty
years before had gone northwards. We heard many details
regarding the form and construction of these ancient piles and the
inscriptions they bore, but I cannot answer for their truth."

Until quite recently, no European succeeded in following upon
Renders' and Mauch's footsteps to visit these ruins, although many
attempts were made, but unsuccessfully owing in some instances
to the opposition met with from the natives, and in others from
the unhealthiness of the climate at certain seasons. In the
winter of 1889, however, the locality was reached by two traders,
Messrs. Poselt, of Middelburg, South African Republic; and in
July of last year by the Rev. Mr. Helm, of the Dutch Reformed
Church Mission in Zoutpansberg, who received a request from the
Makalaka chief, Moghabi, to establish a mission among his
people, known as the Banyais, now living on the rocky eminence
where the ruins are. In the month of August last, some members
of the British South Africa Chartered Company's expedition to
Mashonaland turned aside from their route at Fort Victoria, to set
their eyes upon these interesting remains; and, after gazing in
wonderment upon them, they have testified that the description
given by Mauch was in all its main features exact and correct.
They have also taken sketches and photographs, and as they
appear reproduced here they clearly show the character of the
old buildings, as well as the thick jungle of vegetation and trees
nestling and burrowing among their foundations or overshadowing
their walls, bearing silent but conclusive testimony as to their
comparative antiquity. The modern discovery of the Zimbabye
Ruins has been usually attributed to Mauch, in consequence of
what Baines wrote on the subject; but there seems every reason
to believe, as I shall show further on, that their existence was
known of by, at least, one white man before Mauch visited the
locality.

As will also be seen later, a systematic effort is now to be
made by competent persons to wrest the secret of these ruins
which strew eastern Mashonaland. Measures have been taken
by Mr. Rhodes to preserve the remains and guard them from
injury, and in due time a careful excavation and examination of
the ground on which they stand will be made, in order to see if
anything can be recovered which may give a clue to their origin or
determine their age. All that Mauch found as an indicator of
these was a stone beam, ellipsoid in section and eight feet in length,

upon which ornamental figures, lozenge-shaped one within another, were engraved. Messrs. Poselt were more fortunate; notwithstanding the attempted resistance of the natives, they succeeded in abstracting two relics, which they have now in their possession at Middelburg. For a long time it was thought that one of them was the figure of a bird, about twelve inches in length, representing a species of parrot, sculptured on a greenish-tinted stone; the other there could be no doubt was a round stone, of the size of a Gouda

RELICS FROM ZIMBABYE.

cheese. Both of the curious specimens are now in the South African museum. Two photographs of them were taken recently, and by the courtesy of Mr. Rhodes one of these came into my possession, the other being sent to the British Museum. I reproduce the photograph, and some of my readers may be able to discover what the curious figures may mean. I think there can be little doubt that the one which was taken for a bird is that of some idol having suffered damage. To what race did it belong? That is what Mr. Bent is now trying to find out. Meanwhile let us pay an imaginary visit to the Zimbabye Ruins lying fifteen miles eastwards from Fort Victoria, which is in latitude 20° 85′, longitude 31° E.

Starting from our camp ere the morning mists have rolled away from the adjacent hills, we pass through an undulating country, beneath whose clayey surface slate rocks lie on edge, temptingly inviting the prospector to bide awhile, and scrutinise carefully their occasionally protruding sides, on the chance that he may light on gold-bearing quartz. Now the tall grass is to a great extent burnt away, partly with the object of more easily driving mice to their holes where they are caught by the Mashonas and eaten as a dainty dish, and partly to attract larger game when the verdant shoots shall appear amidst the black ashes. The stony clayey nature of the soil is shown by a " collo flower " putting forth its bloom before the springing up of the leaves, much as though it was in such a hurry to exhibit its beauty, that it could not afford to wait for the lagging greyish leaves, even though its loveliness would be enhanced by the contrast. Deep impressions, too, in the now dry soil show where herds of antelope and koodoo have crossed, and curled up layers of earth on the surface tell of the sun's evaporating influence. Soon we come to a wood, and here the tints of umber brown of varying intensity are precisely those of the autumn leaves, still ad-hering to the Mapani trees of the less elevated country. Spring is bedecking all the trees with their annual covering, and exquisitely delicate they look as we ride slowly under their tender shoots and gaze through them at the aasvogel soaring far aloft in the cloudless firmament. The wood-covered hill surmounted, we dismount and scramble down on the other side, through a growth strongly suggestive of an English coppice; but an ipomoea replaces the simple primrose, and instead of a lichen covering the boughs of the overhanging trees, long masses hang loosely down and wave to and fro in the cold morning breeze. Beneath our feet the boulders of a ferruginous conglomerate, recalling the " banket " of the Witwatersrand Gold Fields, and the dried-up depressions where water must have remained awhile after the last rains, show stains of iron. A little further on we pass over a hill of clay ironstone, and near this some small broken crucibles still containing ashes, and slag close by, show where the Mashonas have worked it, probably to make assegai blades and axes. Looking ahead, an extremely diversified country stretches out before us. In the distance bold granite hills with mighty boulders, visible for many miles, are piled up one behind the other to a far horizon in the southward, and again in another direction large hills of smoother outline, but far greater mass, bespeak an upheaved aqueous formation. Little masses of trees dotted here and there break up the long slopes and invite one to look for homesteads nestling beneath them, in the same way that the unburnt streaks of grass suggest the divisions of the civilised farmer. Here an unconsumed slope of pale ochreous grass ends in the frequent winding stream whose banks are eaten down deeply into the yielding soil, and whose waters babble over obstructions hidden beneath a fine evergreen tree, which loves to show its gratitude by sheltering its sustainer from the noontide glare of the sun. Beyond, a bed of reeds growing on the watery largesse, blocks its way, and insists on a temporary repose. There the lily, glad to find a placid resting place, raises its majestic leaves to the surface, and opens its petals of blue to contrast with the smiling sky above. We disturb a long-necked wading bird which wings away in clumsy flight; but the stately kingfisher takes no heed of our presence, and poises over the water or hurries like a strongly-impelled arrow to a new vantage spot, as though the white stranger existed not. Somewhat treacherous is the ground where the coarse grass is replaced by a finer and more needle-like variety, for it proves to be a bog, and our horses barely manage to flounder through it. Though distinctly on a slope, the water appears to remain on the surface, but so carefully hidden in the fine thick grass, that only the disturbing hoof can detect its presence. That difficulty over, we soon reach large masses of granite, which are just exposed above the surface, and are slippery from the convexity of their surface, whilst here and there is a boulder shedding concentric layers from its spherical mass as a tribute to disintegrating time, or perhaps the lightning flash of the tropical storm. Our guides now making the acquaintance of horses for probably the first time, have no idea of making their way other than in a bee line, and the valleys give us plenty of variety, in thick bush, bespattering bog, and smooth curved rocks, over which it is difficult to scramble without horse or man continually slipping. But they have the proverbial good trail-finding power, and the attendant keenness of vision, for whilst still miles away they point us out the ruins, which our field glasses confirm. With renewed energy we hasten on, glad to find that the indefinite rumour of their not being more than twenty miles or so away, is lessened by reality, and that we shall soon reach the goal of our hopes.

As we approach we pass over cultivated lands for the first time; but the millet and maize, the pumpkin and the pea-nut, are now safely harvested, and the agriculturist shows his knowledge of farming by commencing to break up his stubbles so as to give them the full benefit of the sun's powerful rays. On one field, what is known in Ireland as the lazy-bed system is in force; that is, the sod is turned over in lines upon the undisturbed sod on half the surface, raising it into a ridge, rotting the vegetation by smothering it, and giving the land the full benefit of the decaying plant as manure. The infrequent sight of a cavalcade, which has, no doubt, been espied long before by the outlook on the hill, has driven our dusky friends from their hoeing, and it is only on our

C

arrival at the base of the hill on which the inhabitants live, that
we come in contact with them.   Here we halt and unsaddle, and
partly by signs and partly by using the few Sechuana, Zulu, and
Setebele words which form the joint African linguistic stock of the
party, we succeed in inducing the head man and some dozen of
his henchmen to descend and palaver.   At first, things look bad,
for the necessity for bringing a present has not occurred to us,
being unaware of a resident population; we are informed before
anything can be done a suitable one must be given.   The proffer
of a knife is contemptuously refused, but a horse blanket meets
with acceptance, and the head man ascends the hill, informing us
that if we will wait, he will soon give us permission to ascend.
He also waives the unpleasant condition that we should go up
blindfolded, which he had at first insisted upon.   Whilst waiting,
we gaze at the dusky warriors, who appear to be much less interested in us than we in them, though enquiry elicits the fact that
only one or two white men have, prior to us, ever visited the spot.
Their clothes are the small loin skins which Kafir modesty demands, with an occasional waist-band, necklace, or bracelet of
coloured beads, wire, or neatly-woven hair, by way of ornament.
Their woolly locks are cut into a variety of fantastic shapes, such
as oblongs, tufts, and patches of different lengths, or if allowed to
grow, are made into tiny, shuttle-like masses, with some black,
unctuous compound.   As weapons, some of the party carry a fairly
strong bow, with a couple of arrows, the points being made
generally of barbed iron, the barbing varying widely in pattern.
The shafts of wood or cane, as the case may be, are tastefully
ornamented with neat designs, and when fitting the bowstring,
leave the two ends separated by a wedge, so that they project, and
serve the same purpose of steadying the flight as feathers.   Others
have assegais, one or two apiece, with broad blades neatly fastened
into handles, with plaited tendons or hide, and frequently counter-
poised by a circular piece of iron at the end of the shaft, which is
some five feet in length.   One or two carry trade muskets at full
cock, and capped in a careless fashion, as though heedless of the
danger incurred by their comrades.   But perhaps they know by
experience they are little to be dreaded.   After a few minutes have
been spent in waiting, shouts announce that we may ascend, and
a start is made over the bare boulders up the well-trodden path.
Turning a corner, our photographer pauses to take the first view
of what is the summit of a hill some three hundred feet in elevation.   Would that the brush of the artist could be called into
requisition to depict the brightly-coloured scene!   The granite
boulders are bright with tints of grey, intermingled with spots of
orange lichen, and climbing over them are masses of creepers of
the most vivid green.   Trees of fantastic shapes grow with un-
wonted luxuriance, and sheltered from the prevailing easterly
gales disport their strong limbs in all directions.   Dotted about to
enliven the masses of foliage, an ethrina bursts forth in masses of

flowers like bunches of pendent scarlet beaks, and the elegant castor-oil plant flourishes beneath. A solanum makes its presence conspicuous by its bright yellow ball fruits, and a jessamine exhales a perfume to compete in favour with a freely flowering purple and white composite, whose scent is that of a carnation. But though Nature's profusion crowns this beautiful scene, man's handiwork is there also, both of the primitive Banyai of to-day, and also of a race probably of a remote antiquity whose traces we have now to explore. While the hut of the modern man, with its walls of thin sticks and roof of thatch, may be seen to the left, a striking mass of walling may be noted on the right. We walk on to examine it more closely, and passing round by the huts, under the enormous granite boulders that shelter them, pause for a moment to turn and gaze at the summit of the hill round which we have just scrambled. Here the Banyai architecture is well represented; their little dwellings, just barely exceeding six feet in diameter, are to be seen scattered about on the bare rock, and are merely cylindrical baskets lined with clay. They are stoutly made, and often consist of several chambers, little cells holding a mere handful of corn, which is kept dry by a carefully-fitting lid or door. Little fowls, not larger than bantams, though of less sturdy build, are running around, and small cattle and no less small goats are kept on the hills in tiny kraals so that, excepting the people, who are well-built and of good size and physique, the crowded and climbing existence passed by these denizens of the bouldery hills seems conducive to littleness.

This habit of living on hill tops has been contracted by the Banyai, through fear of the raiding impis of their warlike neighbours, the fierce Matabele, for whom they keep a constant watch. It is with a strong sense of contrast that, passing through a wall which they have rudely built from the stone of their predecessors, we come on to a portion of the hill where the evidences of the toil of so different a people remain. First we reach what may be described as a bastion of massive structure, and beyond are two mighty walls rising some 20 ft. and about 10 ft. in thickness, which continue for a considerable distance round the hill and end where the base granite on which they are built is too precipitous to allow of a foothold. Scrambling up the breach, we enter a confused mass of ruins extending over hundreds of square yards, and consisting of massive walls upon walls, usually curved as though to form circular or oval chambers, some of them being probably 20 yards in diameter. Wherever the boulders with which the hill is so plentifully covered, permit, there is walling, and quite small spaces amongst the boulders are carefully filled in with courses of stone. On what is now the top of some of the walls long flake-like pieces of granite protrude to a length of eight or ten feet. On one part of a main outside wall two of these are some eight feet apart, and close to them are the remains of two solid circular columns of stone each about five feet in diameter. It would take a party

c 2

weeks to clear away the stones now fallen down sufficiently to take the measurements of the different chambers. Climbing plants, including, at least, two varieties of witicaceæ, one of which persistently stings when touched, and the other parting with the tiny thorns growing on its stems with unnecessary generosity, thwart anything like hasty measurements. Perplexed, filled with surprise, and regretting the shortness of the day, we reluctantly refrain from anything beyond a hasty scramble, and, warned by a friendly Banyai, turn our attention to the ruins beneath. To the westward, extending for fully half a mile round the base of the hill, are other extensive ruins of wall after wall, fairly visible in the long grass from our eyrie-like vantage ground, the furthest or outermost wall being some three hundred yards distant from the base, and other cross walls and portions of walls running in contours round the hill in varying lengths and at different heights.

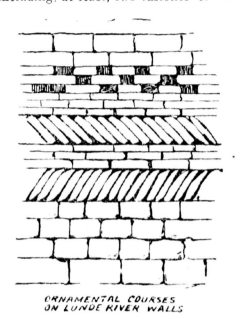

ORNAMENTAL COURSES
ON LUNDE RIVER WALLS

ORNAMENTAL COURSES ON THE WALLS AT ZIMBABYE

A ZIMBABYE CRYPTOGRAM

The comparatively level ground at the base of one wall and the top of the remains of the one immediately beneath it suggest terraces of the *débris* accumulated in excavating the stone, if quarried locally. Inside the outermost wall large depressions may have been reservoirs or baths for the use of the inhabitants when the place was occupied as a royal residence, as the name Zimbabye carries this significance elsewhere in Africa. But the most striking object of all in the magnificent panorama at our feet is a circular building, distant perhaps half-a-mile, and anxious to inspect it closely, we descend and follow the outer wall to the south-west.

This, on dying away, has its place taken by another some 30 yards inwards which would seem to have formed part of a sort of main entrance, with walls 15 ft. apart. The northernmost wall of these forms an oval chamber 60 yards in length and 25 yards in width, with a 2-ft. opening near its western extremity, built of carefully-cut stones, arranged so that the ends of the walls are rounded off. This seems to have been the only size and style of entrance to any of the buildings. Generally the walls are built on the bare, smooth granite of the surface, and boulders too massive to move remain in situ, both in the walls and in the centre of the enclosure. The outermost portion of the entrance is a maze, passages being blocked after running a short distance by cross walls. To the south the walls continue in a number of apparent partial circles and are numerous, the width of the raised ridge on which the buildings are most thickly erected being wider here than further to the north. Proceeding onward until we are south-west of the hill, and some 150 yards from the apparent entrance, we reach the main or most imposing ruin, an exceedingly massive circular structure of probably 80 yards in diameter. Externally, it appears to be merely a wall of imposing appearance, averaging some 25 ft. in height. Two breaches now exist in the walls, and one of these has been made at the eastward where a trace can be seen of a 2-ft. entrance already mentioned as the only form of doorway adopted by the builders, and this appears to have been the only spot at which ingress or egress was permitted. As the *débris* prevents access to the base of the walls, accurate measurements are impossible, but as near as can be ascertained, this wall is at this spot 30 ft. in height and 8 ft. in width at the top, 15 ft. at two-thirds from the top, and probably at least 18 ft. at the foundations some distance along.

Opposite a tower to be described later, the top of the wall narrows to 6 ft., and further round it is still narrower. Entering at this, the easternmost breach, one finds on looking southward, immediately inside the main wall, a second wall, also 30 ft. in height and 18 ft. thick. This, at first 8 ft. distant from the first wall, gradually curves to within 2½ ft. and then recedes again. A third wall now 20 ft. high is 5 ft. thick, and built to within 8 ft. of the second wall, and a fourth wall, 18 ft. high and some 4 ft. in thickness, follows 4 ft. distant. The effect of these high walls with variably narrow passages between them is most singular, and seen in the dim light which the thick foliage of grand trees spreading out above, grudgingly permits to penetrate, is weird in the extreme. Our movements are hampered by prickly and adhesive growths, long tendrils and creepers of many kinds, and by the masses of mixed stones and vegetable *débris* which check our every step.

It is only between the main and second walls that progress is easy, and passing between this massive masonry we proceed to where the walls have been blocked with extra stone, and to a 2-ft. doorway. Again we emerge into an irregular open space where stands a remarkable pillar. It is built of courses of well-wrought stone, similar to that of the best masonry of the ruins, and entirely without mortar; it is about 27 ft. in height and 6 ft. above the *débris* on the ground is 52 ft. in circumference. It has no signs of an opening, and its top, seen on climbing up, by the aid of the creeping plants which are slowly but surely dismantling it, was found to be solid. A second but smaller pillar is built to the

THE TOWER, BABY TOWER, AND CHAMBER AT ZIMBABYE   BETWEEN THE WALLS AT ZIMBABYE

south-east of this, being 5 ft. in diameter and now about 6 ft. in height. It is connected with walls circling away from the courtyard, and one of which has evidently been rebuilt by masons of less skill than the original builders, as, though following the same structure, the courses are irregular and of different sized stones. The remainder of the circle within the main wall is filled with other walls, generally of a circular tendency, though some are straight. No building exists to the south of this, but to the south-east and east many good walls are still standing to a height of several feet and extending over an area of several acres. The ornamentation of the main wall near its top is confined to that portion which faces between east and south. Whatever may be the date of the buildings the class of ornamentation used has been handed down from their builders to the Kafirs now residing around, whose arrow and bead work are designed with the same description of pattern.

The Times correspondent with the Pioneer Force of the British South Africa Company gave an interesting account of the ruins, some extracts from which may here be preserved :—

" The ruins themselves lie at the base of a striking and precipitous granite ' kopje,' inhabited by one of the Mashona tribes, under a chief called Moghabi. The first feature to be noticed on approaching the ' kopje ' is the existence of an outer wall, about 4 ft. high, running, apparently, right round the entire ' kopje ; ' but owing to the high grass and dense jungle-like undergrowth it was found impossible to trace this wall more than half a mile. Next come indications of a second and inner wall, which it was also impossible to trace for any distance for the same reasons. Then, amid a perfect labyrinth of remains of small circular buildings— a mighty maze, but not, apparently, without some plan—south-west of the ' kopje ' and 300 yards from its base, we find our-selves confronted with the startling and main feature of these remains—namely, a high wall of circular shape, from 30 ft. to 35 ft. high, forming a complete enclosure of an area of 80 yards in diameter. This wall (about 10 ft. in thickness at the base, and tapering to about 7 ft. or 8 ft. at the top) is built of small granite blocks, about twice the size of an ordinary brick, beautifully hewn and dressed, laid in perfectly even courses, and put together without the use of a single atom of either mortar or cement. This strange enclosure is entered on its eastern side by what at first sight appears to be a mere gap in the wall, but which closer examination reveals to be what was once evidently a well-defined, narrow entrance, as shown clearly by the rounded-off courses.

" Inside the building itself, which is most difficult to examine thoroughly, owing both to the dense undergrowth and presence of quantities of trees hundreds of years old, which conceal traces of, seemingly, a series of further circular or elliptical walls, and close to the entrance and outer wall, here 30 ft. high, stands a conical shaped tower, or turret, 35 ft. in height and 18 ft. in diameter at the base, built of the same granite blocks and consisting of solid masonry. Lastly, the remaining feature of this building to be touched upon in this brief account is that on the south-east front of the wall, and 20 ft. from its base, runs a double zigzag scroll, one-third of the distance round, composed of the same sized granite blocks placed in diagonal positions. On the ' kopje ' and hillside itself, too, there are numerous traces of remains of a similar character, circular buildings wedged in among boulders of rocks, walled terraces, at least nine in number ; and, built on the very summit, an enormous mass of granite blocks, to be used, apparently, as a fort, and which, owing to the complete absence of any disintegrating forces in this climate, is in an almost perfect state of preservation. The view obtained from the summit of the 'kopje' commands a panorama probably unrivalled in South African scenery. Its counterpart may, perhaps, be found in what is generally regarded as the gem of such scenery—the Marico district in the Transvaal.

"What may be the origin, history, and intention of these curious ruins, and, in particular, of the large circular building with its cone-shaped turret, is, as far as the members of the present expedition are concerned, a perfect mystery. The more scientific and learned element is mute in the presence of these prehistoric remains, and stand in silent amazement at their magnitude and solidity. No one, so far, has been bold enough to come forward and suggest some solution of the problem they present, or offer some explanation of the sermons they most infallibly preach. One thing is certain, however, that the area covered by the numerous walls and circular buildings points clearly to the existence at some time—perhaps 'before the ages'—of a large and semi-civilised population, at a time when slave labour was procurable to an unlimited extent.

"From the natives themselves, as is invariably the case with all South African natives in similar circumstances, we can glean no information whatever respecting these ancient relics, under whose very shadow they dwell; nor do they appear to entertain any superstitious reverence for them. They found them there, as did their forefathers, and there their interest in them and information about them begin and end. Perhaps upon the advent of the expected white population they will begin (and, judging from our own experience, the process seems to have already begun) to recognise their value as a medium for obtaining blankets, limbo, and beads, from the grateful and enthusiastic visitor. Then, at any rate, they will be led to regard them, at least from a practical and business-like point of view, much as the Egyptian Arab regards his pyramids, the Swiss peasant his glaciers, or the English verger his cathedral. It is satisfactory to learn that efficient steps have been taken to protect them both from the thoughtlessness of the visitor and the Philistinism of any prospector or adventurer. The Portuguese have suggested that these ruins form portions of the remains of the city and palace of the Queen of Sheba, 'in the land of Ophir.' Again, ancient Portuguese records refer repeatedly to a people in this part of south-east Africa, whom they found to be established long before their own arrival, and whom they represent to be working for gold in the far interior. To these people they give the name of Morisco (? Moors). With regard to the word itself—Zinbabye—its etymology and orthography, like most native names, it can be variously and equally correctly spelt Zinbâwe, Zinbaoe, and Zinbabye. The Portuguese traveller Lacerda, in his journey through the Zambesi region in 1798, speaks of a tribe,

Cazembe (near Lake Nyassa), who, in answer to his inquiries respecting the course of a certain river, described it as running close by their Zinbâwe, or royal residence. This fact, taken in conjunction with the existence of another Zinbabye in the Manica country, together with the ruins in this neighbourhood, would seem to fix the meaning of the word as palace or royal residence. Be this, however, as it may, whether these ruins are to be attributed to either Moorish or Phœnician origin, or whether the circular building was a temple or a palace, and the conical tower the Queen of Sheba's tumulus, are questions which only the skilled antiquary and those versed in such matters should presume to decide.

"In the meantime, many of us have been privileged to set eyes upon a spectacle which, with the exception of Mauch, as far as we know, no white man has ever hitherto been fortunate enough to behold. [As will be seen, the correspondent was not fully informed.— E. P. M.] I had almost omitted to add that remains of a similar character did exist within the knowledge of many, but on a far smaller scale, as far away as Tati, in Matabeleland. We ourselves, at the Lunde River, have come across similar remains, but, as compared with the Zimbabye ruins, only in their miniature. I have only now to say, in conclusion, that numerous photographs, drawings and measurements have been obtained, which will, no doubt, in course of time find their way home, and furnish ample employment for the archæologist and ruin hunter for many a long day to come."

Naturally the recent rediscovery of the Zimbabye ruins has led to a good deal of theorising on the subject of their origin. Says one writer : " The ruins are evidently those of a fortified camp or station, established, it can hardly be doubted, to control the enslaved population which worked the gold mines, and to protect the abler but scanty people which coerced and directed them, and took away, like the Spaniards in Peru, all transportable fruit of their labour. The choice of the knoll or headland ; the long and mighty walls at its feet, broad enough for archers to walk on ; the tall towers for observation ; the huge walled court or ' place of arms,' eighty yards in diameter, where the garrison exercised in safety,— all alike point to this object, the one on which, except their tombs and temples, the early conquerors spent most. Who they were may remain uncertain, but there is no reason which makes it peremptory that they should have been indigenous. The Hindoos who conquered and held Java for generations could just as readily have ascended the Zambesi, and organised some black tribe into a race of expert miners, and have guarded themselves in these buildings against their despair at their cruel and unending labour. So might the Malays who conquered Madagascar, and who remain to this day among the boldest and most adventurous of all maritime peoples. So might, and much more probably, the Arab people who founded the Sabæan Kingdom, who were certainly traders, and who would be drawn, as their descendants still are, by an irresistible attraction to the great and immensely wealthy continent just opposite their doors. And so, above all, might the Phœnicians. We do not know how far that adventurous and cruel race had searched southward along the coast of Africa; but we do know that Solomon's agents, who can only have been Phœnicians, brought back gold and ivory from some place which must have been in Africa, or 'India' in its large sense—the elephant not existing elsewhere—and we do know that the Phœnicians made voyages almost as distant and far more dangerous. They reached Cornwall and the Canary Islands, and may easily have reached Delagoa Bay. We know, too, that they were experienced metallurgists; that they hunted their world for profitable mines, in Sardinia, in Spain, and even in Britain; and that they kept the stories of their successes as strict trade secrets. They might have heard from some trader that there was gold in a country below the Zambesi, and so hearing would have followed up their clue for generations, as, ages after them, the merchant-nobles of Italy pursued their commercial adventures. With ships like theirs, which could carry but few adventurers and armed men, they must have worked their mines by indigenous slave-labour, and, cruel as they habitually were, would have needed, as they worked, just the fortifications we have found, from the top of which, it is mentioned, the whole country can be surveyed. Why they should have built with dressed stones, yet without mortar, with the use of which they must have been familiar, is not clear; but we may remark that this method admits of greater speed, and that the architects, whoever they were, made no blunder as to the strength and durability of their structures. There they are now, probably three thousand years after their erection, practically unhurt save by the jungle; while our scientifically constructed edifices in the tropics fade usually in three generations. It is a wonderful story, though not perhaps the pleasantest in the world for Englishmen, who have just taken the Phœnicians' place; but it is not wonder-exciting, like the dream that there once was in Mashonaland, in the very heart of Africa, a civilised indigenous race, which has for some unknown reason passed away. The negroes, or their race crossed with others, certainly never produced such a people, and who else can have inhabited Mashonaland?"

Another writer has the following reflections: "Who were they, these soldier-workmen of a vanished civilisation, and at whose bidding did they force their way into this barbarous place to dig for gold? . . . The country is dotted with strange broken relics of their work. The furnaces which they built to smelt the ore, the strong round keeps which they raised against the alarms of some besetting foe, the great stones on which they scored in undecipherable characters the record of their labours, perhaps the clue to their prize—these things remain and move the awe of the Matabele and his Mashona vassal. . . . 'And they came to Ophir, and fetched from thence gold, four hundred and twenty talents, and brought it to King Solomon.' 'Now the weight of gold that came to King Solomon in one year was six hundred threescore and six talents of gold.' The mysterious folk who have imprinted on Mashonaland the traces of an ancient quest for gold were none other, so the learned have conjectured, than those quick, adventurous Phœnicians who, in the days when the Red Sea was the Mediterranean of ancient commerce, and the Mediterranean its Atlantic, brought 'gold of Ophir, fine gold,' and 'great plenty of almug trees and precious stones' to the Oriental monarch whose magnificence is still a proverb upon modern lips. To-day, then, the Englishman is in the land of Ophir . . . opening afresh the treasure-house of antiquity, equipped with resources of which the deft Phœnician never dreamed. It may be that he will come upon such relics among the abandoned workings as will throw a new light upon the story of his predecessors, and re-write a page of the world's history. It may be even that he will stumble into chambers of subterranean wealth such as Mr. Haggard has imagined, secured with labyrinths like those of the Pyramids, with sliding stones, and all the appropriate witchcraft of an age when human life and human labour were of no account. At least, before many years are out, we may expect to see the image of Queen Victoria stamped on the gold with which King Solomon overlaid his ivory throne and wreathed the cedar pillars of his Temple."

. Mr. E. A. Maund, in the course of a paper on Matabeleland which he read to the Geographical Society last November, referred thus to the ruins : "The many and vast remains of ancient buildings all point, from their propinquity to old workings, to an extensive gold industry, when the means of extraction were crude as compared with modern appliances. There would be no lack of labour, for numbers of natives, who yearly went south to work, would gladly save themselves the 800 miles' tramp and work in the mines nearer home. With regard to the extensive ruins—not only at Zimbabye, but all over the country—which had so long puzzled the curious from their inaccessibility, the mystery surrounding their origin was now soon to be cleared up by competent archæologists, who were going out to investigate them. There could be little doubt that they were built for the smelting, and possibly the protection and storage of gold, copper, and other metals; but by whom? He heard one competent authority say they were probably, from the style of building, Phœnician ; another that they were Persian. Some Portuguese manuscripts and maps attributed them to the Moors, and they were certainly similar in style to old Moorish work in the northern hemisphere. The account of a voyage to Malabar and the coast of Africa by Barbosa, cousin of Magellan, conclusively proved that the Portuguese had nothing to do with the erection of these buildings. It showed, too, that the Moors had not then occupied the country. Why should not these brown Gentiles, with their partial civilisation and splendour, have been a decayed remnant of some old Phœnician State? It was evident that these buildings were connected with the mining of a people whose history we had lost. It was beside the question whether they were the famed mines of King Solomon, or whether the Queen of Sheba reigned there over a mighty and industrious population."

In the discussion which followed the reading of Mr. Maund's paper, Mr. Theodore Bent, the eminent archæologist, made some interesting remarks. His personal experience did not incline him, he said, to believe that the ruins were of Phœnician origin; indeed, they did not seem to bear the slightest resemblance whatsoever to Phœnician ruins. There could be no doubt that the Persians in the zenith of their power during the existence of the Sarsanian dynasty, possibly during the reign of the great King of that dynasty, Chosroes II., the Conqueror, had penetrated into Africa as far as Zanzibar, where Sir John Kirk had seen ruins undoubtedly Persian. This led Mr. Bent to the theory that it was possible the Persians had gone still further to Mashonaland, and that the ruins found there were Persian ruins. If the ruins were thoroughly dug out and investigated, perhaps some inscription might be found, and perhaps both Mr. Maund and he be found equally wrong in their theories.

Mr. Geo. Phillips, an old resident in Mashonaland, also took part in the discussion, and remarked that he had met Mauch near the ruins which had been described, and there was no doubt that there was a perfect line of them through the country. The most perfect ruins he had seen were some distance from those which had been described as at the Tati, in the walls of which there was a tree of large diameter which must have taken hundreds of years to grow.

Mr. Theodore Bent has now left England for South Africa to endeavour on behalf of science to solve the riddle to the propounding of, which I have thought it well to devote some considerable space. Before he left the country a representative of SOUTH AFRICA had a conversation with him on the subject of the ruins. In the course of this Mr. Bent said: "So far as I can judge from the photographs I have seen, and what I have read, I incline to the opinion that the ruins are of Persian origin, and that they belong to the period of the Sarsanian dynasty, and probably the reign of Chosroes II., who reigned between 590 A.D. and 620 A.D. History is clear upon the point that the Persians were in his time firmly established at Zanzibar, from which place they could easily, of course, have penetrated to the Mashona territory. Chosroes carried the Persian Empire all over Asia Minor, and into Africa. Sir John Kirk found Persian pottery and tiles at Zanzibar; but there is no evidence as to when the Persians left Africa. . . . I fancy they are the remains of walled-in kraals. The walls would give one that impression, while, of course, the forts on the hills had a definite object. In opening out the forts, I hope to come across some evidence that will throw light upon the subject. . . . I can scarcely say until we have opened it; but my belief is that the hermetically-sealed tower was a Zoroastian tower—a fire temple used for burning bodies, as practised by the fire-worshippers in Persia. Probably there will be traces of burnt bodies inside. . . . Of course I am speaking entirely in the dark, but we hope to reach Zimbabye during the second week in April, and if we find the work of excavation interesting we shall spend about two months over it. The British South Africa Company and the Royal Geographical Society have each made me a grant of £200 towards the expense, and I am in hopes of getting further assistance from other societies. I should very much like to go westward towards the kopjes, but everything will depend on how we find things when we get there. It is a fine country, and ought to be vigorously developed. The railway to the east coast would have to pass through the Portuguese territory; but there are so many rivers in Mashonaland that they ought to be made easy routes to Sofala—the Pungwe, if made neutral, would, in particular, give excellent access to the sea."

It is possible that, should Mr. Bent be baulked in his attempt to explore the ruins of Zimbabye, he may yet find something to elucidate their origin by turning his attention to old gold workings in the Transvaal. About a year ago there appeared in several of the Cape papers what purported to be a *fac simile* of an inscription found on a stone in one of these old workings. The matter has never been thoroughly investigated, and as Mr. A. W. Buckland points out, it may have been simply a practical joke like that perpetrated on the Society of Antiquaries, and engraved and published in Vol. ix. of the *Gentleman's Magazine;* but, if genuine, it would go far to bear out the long-cherished belief of antiquaries, that this is the land of Ophir, from which the gold for Solomon's Temple was procured, as the letters were undoubtedly Phœnician in character. Leaving, however, this inscription as too doubtful to be relied upon, it is yet certain that the old workings to be found in the Transvaal are worthy of scientific investigation; as a rule they can only be referred to the same people who opened those at Tati and Zimbabye, and for the protection of which the forts now in ruins were constructed. The original prospectus of that now discredited mining company, the Lisbon-Berlin, contained an illustration of old workings on the property, with an adjoining wall, which, in its construction of small blocks of hewn stone, would seem to resemble the Zimbabye ruins, whilst near by, we were told, was to be seen what appeared to be an ancient graveyard containing many pointed stones, upon which no inscription was visible.

Neither are these the only traces of a long-vanished race to be found in South Central Africa, for Mr. A. A. Anderson reports the discovery in the Marico district of circular stone kraals, built apparently like the ruins, of small hewn stones put together without mortar, with circular overlapping stone roofs closed by a single slab. The walls of these beehive huts are represented as nearly two feet thick, having also a stone door with lintels, sills, and door plates. Between each hut there is a straight stone wall five feet high, with doorways and lintels communicating with each square enclosure. " They were," he says, " I believe, erected by the same people who worked the gold mines, the remains of which we frequently find in the Transvaal and the Matabili, and beyond where so many of their forts still remain. In the Marico district there are two extensive remains of these stone towns, which must, from their extent, have occupied many years to complete. The outer wall that encloses the whole is six feet thick, and at the present time five feet high. Many large trees are growing out and through the roof of many of them . . . and they are so hidden by bush they are not seen until you are close upon them. Broken pieces of pottery are the only things I have discovered. The present natives know nothing of them ; they are shrouded in mystery." And here it must be observed that the Kafir tribes at present inhabiting this part of South Central Africa do not construct, and never have constructed, stone huts, and although they may sometimes pile stones together to form an enclosure, they certainly have never been known to hew stones and build them up systematically ; therefore these forts and walls, these huts and enclosures of hewn stone, scattered here and there over an immense district, and everywhere thickly overgrown with large trees and bushes, were certainly not the work of any known Kafir race; but whether their constructors were white or black has still to be determined.

An example of the native traditions concerning the ruins may be given. An old chief on the Zambesi River is reported to have said that " his father told him that his father's father of the tribe, many moons before, more dead moons than he can say, Abalunga (white people), with long hair, came to their country with strange animals, and much limbo (soft goods), and lived and made large kraals with stone roofs ; that these people were strong in war, making slaves of the tribes, and they made holes in the ground and got Tsipsi (gold) ; that these people made kraals as high as the trees, and lived many moons in the land, until the people in the land, and many people from the other side of the big river, grew strong again, and many people from the great salt places came and helped them, and they drove the white men to the great waters. And, to stop them coming back again, they pulled down their kraals, and filled up the holes in the earth. After many moons other people came from the great waters, and these were like white people. They brought long assegais, and much limbo and beads, and took away gold. After these people the Matabele came and killed their people, took their cattle and women, and made them slaves."

An erroneous impression that Mauch was the modern dis-coverer of the Zimbabye ruins has recently been removed. In the proceedings of the Royal Geographical Society for February there was published from the pen of Mr. E. A. Maund an important note regard-ing the remains which he obtained from Mr. Geo. Phillips in correc-tion and amplification of the remarks made by him at the meeting of the Society which I have noticed. The note ran as follows :—

" Mr. Phillips was all over that part of the country in 1866, and was with Mr. Hartley the year after, and saw many old gold diggings near the hill which then first got its name of Hartley Hill. In 1868 he and Mr. Westbeach crossed the Hanyani and went down the Mazoe. In October, 1871, he was hunting at the junction of the Ingwesi and Lunde Rivers, when a letter was brought to him from Herr Mauch. It was not signed, but the writer reminded him of an adventure they had had together with five lions on the Mahalapsi, so that he might identify him. Mauch said he was living with a man named Renders, and was in a bad plight, having been robbed of everything except his papers and gun. He begged him not to bring a Matabele with him, as they were living among the Mashonas. Phillips went and found Mauch and Adam Renders, an American, living on the top of a kopje, a few miles south-west of the ruins of Zimbabye. It was a pretty place ; a waterfall coming down from the ridges above fell into a pan by the hut, in which it disappeared, to come out again in a gushing fountain several hundred feet below—a cave of refuge being close by, with water flowing through it, to which they and their Mashona hosts could fly and barricade themselves in with a boulder of rock when Matabele raiding parties were afoot. Mauch told him of some ruins in the neighbourhood, and next day the party went to see them. It was really Renders who first discovered these ruins, three years before Mauch saw them, though Mauch and Baines first published them to the world; and they only described what the old Portuguese writers quoted by Mr. Maund talked of hundreds of years ago. Mauch, on their arrival at the Zimbabye ruins, asked what they thought of them. He (Phillips) confessed he was not greatly impressed, as they were exactly like several others he had seen in other parts of the country. There were the same zigzag patterns, and the mortarless walls of small hewn stones. Shortly before, when hunting in the mountains to the west of Zimbabye, he had come upon a regular line of such ruins, one of which must have been a very large place. It had three distinct gateways in the outer wall, which were at least 30 ft. thick at the base, and an immense ironwood tree, that would have taken hundreds of years to grow, had grown through a crevice in the wall and rent it asunder. On the side of a gateway were vast heaps of ashes with occasional potsherds about, the only evidence of the old inhabitants. He had found the same kind of ruins all over the country, very frequently on the summit of difficult kopjes. Those at Tati and Impakwe are good examples ; but the most perfect, perhaps, of all lies north-west of Tati. The tower there is about 60 ft. in length and breadth, and 80 ft. high, the walls about 15 ft. thick, and it is entered by a passage winding spirally to the top, which is so arranged as to be commanded by archers from the interior all the way, and is so narrow that it admits of the passage of one person only at a time."

As before indicated, ruins similar to those at Zimbabye are to be seen on a smaller scale further to the south on the Lunde River. The building, which, from the look of the stones and the trees growing within it, is, apparently, very ancient, is on a bare patch of granite, and measures some 53 ft. in diameter. What is apparently a terrace is found on the north side. There it is 6 ft. wide, but it gradually dwindles away in breadth, and merges into the outside wall on the southern side. Within this is a circular passage some 7½ ft. in width, surrounding a second thick, low wall, concentric with the other. In the midst of all is a hollow, now filled with ashes, and a little fusible slag, due, apparently, to the action of a fire of low power. The walls are formed of a hard porphyritic granite showing distinctly the mark of tools, and the outer wall is plastered inside. Who were the masons is, here as elsewhere, a matter for conjecture, as local tradition throws no light on the subject, even Tschibi, the chief of the district, confessing utter ignorance. He knows, however, of several similar structures in his dominions, and his people pay them fetish worship by placing sticks against the walls. The ornamentation only exists along a portion of the north-eastern wall; and along a few feet of it only the uppermost pattern of alternate stone and space is found, the rest of the ornamentation being suppressed.

We have seen that it is not possible to obtain from the natives living in and around these ruins any information as to who raised those wonderful buildings, or what purposes they were intended to serve. Moghabi, the Makalaka chief, declares "they found them there, as did their fathers before them," for the cradle of his people, he says, is further to the eastward. He informed the Rev. Mr. Helm that the native tradition from the olden time was, that these edifices were the work of Mozimo (the Supernatural or Supreme Being), but since some of his people have been to Kimberley, labouring in the diamond mines, and have told of the great stone buildings at that place, they are inclined to think that they may have been the work of white men in some remote period of which they have no knowledge. The records of Portuguese colonisation confirm the native tradition as to their antiquity. Early historians relate how, upon their first occupation of the country, at the beginning of the sixteenth century, the Portuguese learnt from the Arabs who were there before them, that there were structures of hewn stone, forming thick walls and round towers, like those now found at Zimbabye. At a later period, small forts and fortified positions were erected by the Portuguese at certain points along the Zambesi, and near to places where the search for gold was carried on in the interior; but Zimbabye was not one of these, nor has it ever been claimed as such. The solution of the problem of the origin of those ancient remains thus becomes limited to one or other of two suppositions. One is, that there may have once existed in South Africa a negroid race, which has long since passed away, among whom the con-

RUINS ON THE LUNDE RIVER.—GENERAL VIEW FROM THE NORTH-EAST.

structive faculty was so far developed that they were capable of designing and erecting those buildings.   The other, and the more probable one is, that some small colony or off-shoot of the early maritime races, carrying with them some knowledge of the arts, planted themselves for a time in that part of the country, and constructed at Zimbabye a fortified position, somewhat after the fashion of the many-walled Ecbatana, described by Herodotus, while they traded with the natives of the country or worked the gold in which it then abounded.   Whether these were Phœnicians, Egyptians, Arabians, Persians, Chinese, or some other partially-civilised race of a past age, will probably be determined by the archæological relics which may now be brought to light in the ruins themselves.

CHAPTER II.

Where the Queen of Sheba Lived.—The Gold of Ophir.—
King Solomon's Mines.—The Empire of Monomotapa.—What
Old Historians Wrote About It.—Golden South Africa
Long Ago.—A Huge Output with Primitive Appliances.—A
Vast Field Still to Work.

IT is a good many years since I joined those who have
come to the conclusion that the territory over which the
British South Africa Company now holds sway, contains the
veritable land of Ophir. A decade before latter-day chroniclers
had appeared on the scene to "enthuse" over freshly-learnt facts,
I bestowed attention on this absorbingly interesting subject.
I wrote in "Golden South Africa:" "It is generally agreed that
Ophir, whence Solomon is said to have drawn gold to the modern
value of £900,000,000, was situated in South-Eastern Africa, and
as I am of opinion that there is as good gold in this part of the
world as was ever taken out of it, some references to the past in
these regions may prove useful before proceeding to consider their
present and future." To me it is a striking fact, in this connection,
that, so far as I am aware, in no other part of Africa than in Zambesia and its environs is the rule of a woman permitted. In the
neighbourhood of Sofala and southwards there are five native queens,
and the destinies of Tongaland are swayed by a dusky female.
May not we have here a recognition of the fitness of women to hold
the sceptre handed down from the time of the Queen of Sheba?
In the book I have named I printed some remarkably interesting
testimony to the golden wealth of Zambesia, and I consider that
that information may well be amplified now that the country, part
of which was once known as Monomotapa, is being so rapidly
developed. Leaving a fuller perusal of the very earliest records of
them to the leisurely and studious specialist, it may be briefly stated
that the first settlements and ports of East Africa of which
there is any trace were those of Persians and Arabians. As regards
those of the former race Burton tells us there is now left nothing
but a name; but possibly Mr. Bent may prove otherwise shortly.
The Arabs (or Moors, as the Portuguese called them) had commercial connections with East Africa from a very remote time.
From the second century to the beginning of the sixteenth century

they were supreme along the coast from Aden on the north with Sofala in the south. And then Portugal came on the scene. In 1487 Sofala was visited by a Portuguese officer named Pedro de Covilham, who was despatched, *via* the Red Sea, by his king on a voyage of discovery. Ten years later Vasco da Gama followed up the information brought home by Covilham and rounded the Cape, making his famous discoveries. Wherever he touched on the East coast he conversed with Arabs, not much inferior in refinement to his own countrymen. Instead of the naked savages he had seen in the south he found the chiefs and principal inhabitants richly apparelled in silks and fine cottons, and their women adorned with ornaments of gold, silver, and pearls. Camoens, in his "Lusiad," gives expression to the pleasant surprise of the Portuguese at the first sight of these new-found friends, whom they soon after forcibly made subject to their rule:

> All Ethiopians are they, but it seems
> They have commune with some superior race,
>
> .   .   .   .
>
> They say that ships as long from stern to beak
> As ours, are wont to navigate their seas;
> That they go forth from eastern shores to seek
> The coast that southward broadens, and from there
> Back towards the birth-place of the sun they sail,
> Unto a land of men like us of feature pale.

Sofala was passed without being touched at by Vasco da Gama on his first voyage, but at Zanzibar he learnt that the Arab merchants traded largely with Sofala for gold, and with St. Lawrence (Madagascar) for silver. In the succeeding expedition, sent out under Alvarez de Cabral, two Arab vessels were overhauled, bound to Melinde with gold from the Sofala mines, and one of the ships of the fleet was afterwards specially despatched to find out the seaport of this gold-yielding region. In 1505, the Portuguese Commander, Pedro de Nhaya, took possession of it, and a year or two afterwards, under pretence of providing a magazine for the purposes of trade, he erected a fort near the town which the Arabs had founded there some two centuries before.

The gold-yielding region, now embraced in Zambesia, was then known as the "Empire of Monomotapa," vaguely described by the old writers as an "ample kingdom, lying inland from Sofala, and extending towards the Cape of Good Hope and Mozambique." Duarte Barbosa (whose account of the East Coast in 1512 is to be found in the Papers of the Hakluyt Society) informs us that the Emperor was "a great lord holding many other kings as his vassals," receiving no tribute but only services and gifts from them; that he had constantly with him a mighty army, amongst them being 6,000 women who bore arms and fought, like the Amazons of the present King of Dahomey, and that with these he went about subduing and pacifying his subjects throughout his empire. Other accounts say that once a year he sent out certain of his courtiers and servants to distribute new fire amongst his vassals, so as to cause the flame of loyalty to be kept alive, and those who failed to rekindle their fires by the king's torch were deemed rebels, and treated accordingly. The towns and villages throughout the empire were few, and the buildings were of wood and clay, covered with thatch; the nearest to Sofala, at a distance of one or two days, being known as Zimbahe (the court or " great place "), and six days' journey beyond that, another, named Benamotapa, where the king was wont to make his longest

From "Carte du Congo et du Pays des Cafres," by G. de l'Isle (circa) 1710

THE EMPIRE OF MONOMOTAPA.

residence, and whence the traders obtained the gold which they brought to the coast.

The name given to the country—*Monomotapa* (the *Muena Mutapa* of the Zambesian Portuguese)—has had many definitions given to it. I think it is a word of Zulu-Kafir derivation, and signifies the lord or man of the mine : *m'Tapa* literally translated is, " to empty a hole which was filled up with any substance ; " or " a person who makes a hole by taking the substance away." Probably the word Monomotapa was a native synonym for modern

"" digger," and was afterwards adopted as the title of the paramount chief or king. The inhabitants of the country were
undoubtedly tribes of the eastern branch of the A'Bantu family.
Their language, customs, and laws were of the familiar Zulu-
Kafir type; the king in his Zimbahe, or " great place," was only
approached by his subjects on their knees, prostrating themselves
before him, while with clapping of hands they *bonga'd* and extolled
him as " Lord of the Sun and Moon," or " Conqueror of his
enemies," &c.; and, as we shall shortly see, their greatest wealth"
" was in oxen and cows, which were with them more highly prized
than either gold or silver."

The Portuguese, in their early intercourse with the Arabs of
Sofala and the native gold-traders of Monomotapa, eagerly sought
for all information as to the particular localities where gold was
found; and from them they learnt that in the neighbourhood of
the *tracto do ouro* were buildings and ruins of ancient times.
Joao de Barros, the Portuguese historian of the epoch from 1496
to 1573, was the first to give a description of these. In his work,
De Asia (the earliest part of which was published at Lisbon
in 1552), he refers to Monomotapa and the kingdoms under
vassalage to its rulers, and says: " In the midst of the
plains in the kingdom of Batua, in the country of Toroe,
nearest the oldest gold mines, stands a fortress, square,
admirably built, inside and out, of hard stone. The blocks of
which the walls consist are put together without mortar, and are of
marvellous size. The walls are twenty-five spans in thickness;
their height is not so considerable compared with their breadth.
Over the gate of the building is an inscription, which neither
the Moorish traders (the Arabs of the coast) who were there, nor
others learned in inscriptions, could read, nor does anyone know in
what character it is written. On the heights around the edifice
stand others in like manner built of masonry without mortar;
among them a tower of more than twelve bracas (yards) in height.
All those buildings are called by the natives *Zimbahe*—that is the
royal residence or court, as are all royal dwellings in Monomotapa.
Their guardian, a man of noble birth, has here the chief command,
and is called Symbacao; under his care are some of the wives of
Monomotapa, who constantly reside here. When and by whom
these buildings were erected is unknown to the natives, who have
no written characters. They merely say they are the work of the
Devil (supernatural), because they are beyond their powers to
execute. Besides these, there is to be found no other mason work,
ancient or modern, in that region, seeing that all the dwellings of
the barbarians are of wood and rushes." De Barros further states
that when the Portuguese Governor of Sofala, Captain Vicente
Pegado, pointed to the masonry of the fort there, with a view to
comparison with the buildings at Toroe, the Moors (Arabs), who
had been at the ruins, observed that the latter structure was of such
absolute perfection that nothing could be compared to it; and they

gave their opinion that the buildings were very ancient, and erected for the protection of the neighbouring gold mines. From this De Barros inferred that the ruins must be the Agizymba of Ptolemy, and founded by some ancient ruler of the gold country, who was unable to hold his ground, as in the case of the city of Axium, in Abyssinia.

Herman Lopez de Castenhadas (1553), another Portuguese authority, whose work is epitomised in Astley's Collection of Travels, states that " the mines of Sofala were first possessed by the Moors of Magadoxa, afterwards by those of Quiloa, whose kings worked them till Yussen, one of the governors, rebelled and accepted the authority to himself ; " and he adds, " there are some buildings of wonderful structure, with inscriptions of unknown characters, but the natives know nothing of their foundation."

The late Mr. Thomas Baines, in his work, " The Gold Regions of South East Africa," writes : " The country of Monomotapa, a name which in itself signifies a place whence something valuable is derived, lies to the southward of the Zambesi, or, as Vasco da Gama called it, when he discovered it in 1498, the ' river of good signs.' It may be roughly stated as lying between the parallels of 16° to 19° south latitude, and the meridian of 30° to 35° east longitude. The country, according to the early historian, abounded in gold, which in great quantities was extracted from veins in many of the provinces, especially in the Kingdom of Torva, where also remained the ruins of ancient stone buildings, which for splendour and magnificence were reported to bear comparison with those of ancient Rome. The largest of these was traditionally supposed to have been the Queen of Sheba's palace, and the Moors of Sofala were said to have written testimony that Solomon derived all his gold from the Torvan mines." Again, in pointing out that several exploring parties were sent in search of rich countries in South Africa during the latter half of the seventeenth century, Mr. Baines says : " None of them succeeded in penetrating so far into the interior. The seaboard or coast region was known under the name it still bears, that of ' Sofala,' which signifies in Arabic a plain or low country. Sabia lies more inland behind Sofala, and is supposed by some authorities, including Josephus, and no less a personage than the author of the Koran, to be the ancient kingdom of the love-sick queen who visited Solomon when in all his glory, and of whom Mohammedan, Abyssinian, and Jewish writers relate such innumerable traditions. Several ruins of ancient buildings are found still in this region, which is drained by a river disemboguing on the east coast, still called ' Sabia.' The memory of the Queen of Sheba is still preserved amongst the Arabs of Sofala, as well as amongst the Habesh of Gondar in their scandalous chronicles. The site of the region of Ophir has from time immemorial been a bone of contention amongst archæologists, and vast learning has been uselessly expended to prove its locality, whether in Arabia Felix, or Arabia Petrea, Socotra, the Persian Gulf, India, the

Punjaub, Malacca, or the Moluccas of Spain. Such a weighty authority as Milton, who surely ought to know something on the subject, is in favour of Africa.

> ' Mombaza, Quiloa and Melind,
> And Sofala (thought Ophir) to the realm
> Of Congo and Angola furthest South.' "

It appears from De Faria's *Portuguese Asia* that Barreto, Governor of India, on his return to Lisbon, was nominated by the King for the Government of Monomotapa, with the additional title of Conqueror of the Mines there. The great inducement was the experience of the vast quantity of gold found, particularly at Manica. Barreto sailed from Lisbon in April, 1592, and having arrived at Mozambique, proceeded, by the advice of Francis de Monclaros, a Jesuit, up the River Cuama (Zambesi), and reached Sena, which is represented to be a town inhabited by Portuguese; but the expedition was unsuccessful, chiefly through the hostility of the native tribes, although the Emperor of Monomotapa had given Barreto permission to go on to the mines of Butua and Manchika. Vasco succeeded Barreto, and set out on another expedition by way of Sofala, and marched directly towards the mines of Manchika, in the kingdom of Chikanga, bordering on that of Quiteyve, the next in power to Monomotapa. From the opposition of the natives and the withdrawal of all provisions from the towns, the Portuguese suffered extreme want until they arrived at Zimbaoe, the court of the King of Quiteyve. Vasco burnt this place and marched on to Chikanga's. He afterwards went north to the silver mines of Maninnas; but he was misled by a stratagem of the natives, who scattered silver ore far enough away from the real mine; and, after fruitless digging, the expedition was abandoned. Vasco being gone, Cordosa (his captain) suffered himself again to be deceived by the Kafirs, who, leading him the way of death rather than that of the mines, killed him and his men. " This," says the chronicler, " was the end of the Government of Monomotapa, scarce begun sooner than ended, and possessed by two governors, who no sooner saw than they lost it; the first killed by rash words, the second expelled by a prudent, not barbarous, stratagem. However, the peace and trade with the Emperor of Monomotapa continued." De Faria says that the Cuama, or Zambesi, runs through Monomotapa, and falls into the sea by four mouths, and that the river is navigable to the town of Sena, "inhabited by Portuguese," and to Tete, also a colony of the Portuguese. The empire of Monomotapa was represented to be bounded on the north and partly on the west by the River Zambesi —Empondo, or Quama; on the remaining part of the western border and on the south by the country of the Hottentots and certain Kafirs, from which it was separated by the River Magnika, called also that of "Lorenzo Marques," and the "Holy Ghost." On the east Monomotapa was bounded by the Indian Ocean. The richest mines were said to be those of Massapa, called Afur or Fura, "where has been found a lump of gold worth twelve thousand ducats, and another of the value of four hundred thousand." The mines of Manchika and Butua were reported to be not much inferior. There is no evidence that the Portuguese themselves worked the mines. Throughout the record they are spoken of as "trading" for gold, and for this purpose they had a castle or fort at the mouth of the Quama, or Zambesi, and at Tete, further up the river, and 120 leagues from the sea. Three fairs or markets, whither they traded for gold, are named Luane, Buento, and Massapa; at the last station was a Portuguese magistrate, appointed by the commander of "Mozambik" to settle differences that might arise there. This appointment was made with the consent of the Emperor of Monomotapa, on condition that the officer did not go into the country without special leave. The gold was exchanged for cloth, glass beads, and silks, brought from Kambaya, and other articles of little value. The trade was carried on right across the continent, if we are to believe the Portuguese author, who says that the blacks of Butua, in the kingdom of Chikanga, carried the gold to Angola. At the trading stations Massapa and Luane were churches of the Dominicans, and De Lesle marks La Victorie, a convent of the Dominicans, near the Zambesi. In this old chronicle of Barreto's expedition in 1569, mention is made of the ruins of stately buildings, supposed to be palaces and castles, at Mount Afur or Fura, near Massapa; so that the "ancient structures, of great labour and singular architecture, built with stone, lime, and timber, the like whereof are not to be seen in all the provinces adjoining," were long antecedent to the period of Portuguese trade. The inhabitants of the Empire of Monomotapa are described as black in colour, and in number infinite; very courageous in war, of a middle stature, and swift of foot.

Bruce, who travelled in Abyssinia a hundred years ago, favoured the idea that the country about Sofala, near which the Limpopo empties itself in the ocean, is ancient Ophir. He took a great deal of trouble to investigate the matter now under consideration by consulting Portuguese records, and he framed a map which appeared in the book of plates which accompanied the earlier editions of his work, to show that the fleet of Solomon and Hiram would just take the time mentioned in Scripture as the length of the voyage in going to and returning from Sofala. Bruce states that "John dos Santos, a Dominican Friar, says that on the coast of Africa, in the kingdom of Sofala, the main land opposite Madagascar, there are mines of gold and silver, than which none can be more abundant. They bear the traces of having been wrought from the earliest ages. They were actually open and working when the Portuguese conquered that part of the peninsula, and were probably given up since the discovery of the New World, rather from political than other reasons." The friar says, "he landed at Sofala in the year 1586, that he sailed up the great River Cuama as far as the Tete, and from thence he penetrated for above 200 leagues into the country, and saw the gold mines there working at a mountain called Afura." From the friar mentioning Tete, it is probable that the river he sailed up, even though he should have landed at Sofala, which was then the name of the *kingdom*, was the Zambesi, one of the mouths of which is yet called Cuama. Bruce hazards the opinion, " It is probable, however, that the Gold Fields about the Limpopo and the Zambesi are of immense extent." Friar dos Santos, just referred to, says in his *Eastern Ethiopia :*—" Near to Mapassa, there is a great high hill called Fura, whence may be discerned a great part of the kingdom of Monomotapa. On the top of that hill are still standing pieces of old walls and ancient ruins, of lime and stone—a thing unknown in all Caphraria, for the king's houses are of wood, daubed with clay and covered with straw. The natives, and especially the Moors here, declare that these belonged to the service of the Queen of Sheba, which carried gold, &c., down the Cuama (Zambesi) to the sea, and thence along the coast of Ethiopia to the Red Sea."

For ages the extent and productiveness of the " sunny fountains which run down " the sand of " Golden South Africa " have been the fruitful theme of the geographer, the historian, and the romance writer. I have before me a very curious old work with the imprint " Londini, 1600." It is entitled " A Geographical Historie of Africa Written in Arabicke and Italian by John Leo and More borne in Granada and brought up in Barbarie." I learn from it that one of these old empires south of the Equator—that of Mohenemugi—was a veritable land of Goshen—at least it would have been a paradise to Mr. Goschen. Gold was so plentiful that it could not even be used for money, let alone held in reserve against pound notes. The Emperor traded with the coast princes for " cloth of silke " and other commodities, especially certain ornamental balls. " But among the rest, they " (the traders) " bring especially certaine little balles, of a red colour and in substance like unto glasse, being made in Cambaya of a kind of Bitumen or clammie claie, which balles they used to weare like beades about their necks. They serve also to them in stead of money, for gold they make none account of." But it is with Monomotapa that our present business lies. Let us see, then, what Leo had to say about it through his translator Pory. " Sofala, or Sefala, the fift and last generall part of Zanguebar, is a small kingdome lying vpon the sea-coast, betweene the rivers of Cuama and Manice, being so called after the name of a river running through it, in which river lyeth an Island, which is the head and principal place of the whole countrie. On this Island the Portugales have built a most strong forte, by meanes whereof they are become Lordes of the richest trade in all those parts. For (to say nothing of the Iuorie, Amber, and slaves which are hither brought) all the gold in a manner that is taken out of those manifolde and endlesse mines of Sofala and all the Inland-countries thereabouts, is here exchanged unto the Portugales for cotton-cloth, silkes, and other commodities of Cambaia : all which is thought yeerely to amount unto the summe of two millions of gold. This golden trade was first in the power of the Moores of Magadazo ; and afterward it befell to them of Quiloa. The inhabitants of Sofala are Mahumetans, being governed by a king of the same sect, who yeeldeth obedience to the crowne of Portugale, because hee will not be subject to the empire of Monomotapa. . . . . B E nomotapa, Benomotaxa, or Monomotapa is a large empire, so called after the name of the prince thereof, who in religion is a Gentile, and for extension of dominions, and military forces, a renowmed and mightie emperour ; in the language of whose subiects an emperour is signified by this word Monomotapa. This empire of his lyeth, as it were, in an Island which containeth in compasse seven hundred and fiftie, or (as some thinke) one thousand leagues, being limited on the northwest by the great lake whereout Nilus springeth ; on the south, by the river Magnice and the tributarie kingdome of Butua or Toroa ; on the east it hath the sea-coast and the kingdome of Sofala, which in very deed is a member thereof ; and the North part abutteth upon the river of Cuama, and the empire of Mohenemugi. That part of this great Island which lyeth betweene the mouth of Cuama, and the cape de los Corrientes, is a very pleasant, holesome, and fruitfull country. And from the said cape to the river of Magnice, the whole region aboundeth with beasts both great and small ; but it is cold by reason of the sharp brizes which come off the sea ; and so destitute of wood, that the people for fewel are constrained to use the dung of beasts, and they apparel themselves in their skinnes. Along the banke of the river Cuama are divers hilles and downes covered with trees, and vallies likewise watered with rivers, being pleasantly situate, and well peopled. Here are such plenty of Elephants, as it seemeth by the great quantitie of their teeth, that there are yeerely slaine betweene foure and five thousand. Their elephants are nine cubites high, and five cubites in thickness. They have long and broad eares, little eyes, shorte tailes, and great bellies : and some are of opinion, that Ethiopia yeeldeth as many elephants as Europe doth oxen. The townes and villages of this empire are very few, and their buildings are of wood and clay, covered with thatch. None may have doores to their houses but onelly great personages. Their principal cities are Zimbas, and Benamataza, the first whereof is one and twentie, and the second fifteene daies journey from Sofala. They serve this emperour at the table upon their knees : to sit before him, is all one, as with us for a man to stand upon his feete, neither may any presume to stand in his presence, but onely great lords. He is tasted unto, not before, but after he hath eaten and drunke. For his armes he hath a spade and two dartes. Tribute he taketh none, but onely certaine daies service and giftes presented unto him; without which there is no appearing in his sight. Hee carrieth, whithersoever he go, foure hundred dogs, as a most sure and trustie guard. Hee keepeth all the heires of his tributary princes, as vassals, and as pledges of their fathers loialtie. There are no prisons in al his empire: for sufficient testimonie being brought of the commission of any crime, justice is executed out of hand: and of all offences none are punished with greater severitie and rigour, then witchcraft, theft, and adulterie. His people are of a meane stature, blacke, and well proportioned. They are Gentiles in religion, having no idols, but worshipping one onely God whom they call Mozimo. They go apparelled in cloth of cotton, either made by themselves, or brought from other countries: howbeit the king will in no case weare any forrein cloth for feare of poison or such like trecherie: and the meaner sort of his subjects are clad in beasts skins. Among all the armies and legions of soldiers, which this emperour (for the defence of his great estate) is forced to maintaine, his Amazones or women warriers before mentioned are the most valiant, being indeed the very sinewes and chiefe strength of all his militarie forces. These women, after the manner of the ancient Scythish or Asiatike Amazones, so much spoken of in histories of former times, seare off their left paps, that they might not by an hinderance unto them in their shooting. They are most expert in warlike stratagems, and swift of foote. Their weapons are bowes and arrowes. At certaine times for generations sake they accompany with men; sending the male children home to their fathers but keeping their daughters unto themselves. They inhabite towards the west, not farre from the beginning of Nilus, in certaine places which themselves make choise of, and which are graunted unto them by the favour of the Emperour. This empire of Monomotapa comprehendeth not onely the foresaid great island, but stretcheth it selfe farther also toward the cape of Buena esperança, as farre as the kingdomes of Butua or Toroa, which being governed by particular lords, do acknowledge Monomotapa for their soveraigne. Throughout all this emperours dominions is found infinite quantitie of gold, in the earth, in the rockes, and in the rivers. The goldmines of this countrey neerest unto Sofala are those of Manica, upon a plaine environed with mountaines; and those also in the province of Matuca, which is inhabited by the people called Battonghi, and situate betweene the Equinoctiall line and the Tropique of Capricorne. These mines are distant from Sofala, betweene the space of 300 and sixe hundred miles: but those of the provinces of Boro and Quiticui are fifteene hundred miles distant towards the west. Others there are also in the kingdomes of Toroa or Batua: so that from hence or from Sofala, or from some other part of Monomotapa, some are of opinion, that *Salomons* gold for the adorning of the temple at Jerusalem, was brought by sea. A thing in truth not very unlikely: for here in Toroa, and in divers places of Monomotapa are till this day remaining manie huge and ancient buildings of timber, lime and stone, being of singular workemanship, the like whereof are not to be found in all the provinces thereabouts. Heere is also a mightie wall of five and twentie spannes thicke, which the people ascribe to the workemanship of the divell, being accounted from Sofala five hundred and ten miles the neerest way. All other houses throughout this empire (as is aforesaid) consist of timber, claie, and thatch. And heere I may boldly affirme, that the ancient buildings of this part of Africa, and along the coast of the east Indies, may not onely be compared, but even preferred before the buildings of Europe. The authors of which ancient monuments are unknown : but the later African buildings have beene erected by the Arabians. In the time of *Sebastian* king of Portugale, the emperour of Monomotapa and many of his nobles were baptised : howbeit afterward being seduced by certaine Moores, hee put *Gonsalvo Silua* to death, who converted him to the Christian religion. Whereupon *Sebastian* king of Portugall sent against him an armie of sixteene thousand, consisting for the most part of gentlemen and men of qualitie, under the conduct of *Francisco Barretto*. The Monomotapa being afraid of the Portugall forces, offered *Baretto* as good and acceptable conditions of peace as might be desired : but he not contented with reason, was quite overthrowne, not by his enimies, but by the unholesome aire of Ethiopia, and by the mainfold diseases which consumed his people." As showing what led up to Portugal sending Barretto on an expedition against the emperor; I may make a further extract from Leo's narrative :— "Not long time after, the emperour let *Gonsalvo* to understand that he and his mother were resolved to become Christians, and that therefore he should come to baptize them. But he to instruct them better in the faith, deferred it off for some daies. Finally five and twentie daies after his arrivall, with unspeakeable solemnity and preparation, he gave the water of baptisme to the king, and to his mother. He was called *Sebastian*, and shee *Maria*. And presently after, about three hundred of the principall in this emperours court were baptized. *Gonsalvo* for his wonderfull abstinence, charity, wisedome, and for many other his singular vertues was so reverenced and esteemed by those people, as if he had come downe from heaven among them. Now as matters proceeded thus prosperously, and with so desireable successe, behold, an horrible tempest arose which drowned the ship. There were in the court fower Mahumetans most deere unto the king. These men finding out some occasion, suggested unto him, that *Gonsalvo* was a Magician, who by witchcraftes and inchantments could turne kingdomes topsie turvie : and that he was come to prie into his estate, and to stir up his people to rebellion, and so by this means to bring his kingdome under subjection to the Portugals. With these and such like suggestions they brought the king (who was but a young man) to determine the death of *Gonsalvo*. The effect whereof was, that after long praier, reposing himselfe a little ; he was by eight of the kings servants slaine, and his body throwne into the river Mensigine.   Neere unto the same place, were with like violence put to death, fiftie new-converted Christians.   This rage and furie being over, the king was advertised by the principall of his kingdome, and then by the Portugals, of the excesse and outrage he had therein committed.   He excused himselfe the best he could, causing those Mahumetans to be slaine, who had seduced him ; and he sought out some others also who lay hid, to put them to death.   Whereupon it seemed that by the death of father *Gonsalvo*, the conversion of this great king, and of his empire, should have bin furthered, and no whit hindered, if the Portugals would rather have prevailed by the word of God, then by force of armes.   The which I say, bicause instead of sending new preachers into those countries, to preserve that which was alreadie gotten, and to make new conversions, they resolved to revenge themselves by warre. There departed therefore out of Portugall a good fleete, with a great number of noble Portugals therein, conducted by *Francisco Barretto*.   At the fame of this warre, mooved against him, the Monomotapa full of feare, sent to demaund peace of *Barretto*.   But he aspiring to the infinite mines of gold in that kingdome, contemned all conditions offered him.   The effect of this enterprise was, that this armie which was so terrible to a mightie Monarke, was in fewe daies consumed by the intemperature of the aire, which is there insupportable to the people of Europe."

In reading up history for my present special purpose I find one of the most curious books on my table at present to be one by Samuel Purchas.   It has a very long title, beginning, " Purchas his Pilgrimage on, &c.," and was printed in the year 1614 at London, and sold " at the Signe of the Rose," in St. Paul's Church Yard. The book deals in a dry way with everything that was known (and not known) in that day under the sun, moon, and stars, and naturally the wonderful Empire of Monomotapa attracts a considerable share of attention.   But very short excerpts from this work must suffice : "The Mines neerest to Sofala, are those of Manica, which are in wide champaines compassed with mountaines, ninetie myles in circuit.   The places where the Golde is, appear and are knowne by the drynesse and barrennesse of the soile, as if Nature itselfe could not hord up Gold in her spacious chest, but shee must needs prove bare and barren of her wonted good workes ; and how much lesse, unnaturall and degenerate Mankind ?   The Province is called Mutaca, the people Botonghi (which although they are betweene the Line and the Tropike) yet in Winter have such snowes in the mountaines, that if any abide there, they die frozen in them ; and in Sommer-time the aire in the tops of those hils is so cleare and pure that some of our men, which were then there, saw the new Moone, the same day that shee had kissed her bright and bountifull brother. . . . Sofala lieth betweene Cuama and Magnice, two Rivers.   Heere the Portugals have on a little Island (whence the whole Kingdome hath his name) a Fort and Factorie of a very rich Trade, the people bringing great quantitie of Golde (whereof they have pletifull Mines) for their Cloth and other commodities ; it is supposed that it amounteth to two millions yearely. Ortelius is of opinion, That this Cephala, or Sophala, is that which in Salomons time was called Ophir, from whence so great quantitie of golde was brought by his navie. . . . There are other Mines in the Provinces of Boro and Quiticui, in which and in the Rivers, is found Gold not so pure. The people are carelesse and negligent to get, and the Mores which traded with them, were faine to give their wares in trust, with promise by such a time to pay them in Gold, and the people would not faile in their word. Other Mines are in Toroa, wherein are those buildings which Barrius attributeth to some forren Prince, and I, for the reasons before alledged, to Salomon. It is a square fortresse, of stone ; the stones of marveilous greatnesse, without anie signe of morter or other matter to joyne them. The wall five and twentie spannes thicke, the height not holding proportion. Over the gate are letters, which learned Moores could neyther reade nor know what letters they were. The Moores which saw them, said the Portugals Castles were in no way to bee compared to them. They are five hundred and tenne myles from Sofala, West-ward, in one and twentie degrees of Southerly Latitude : in all which space is not found one building Ancient or later ; the people are rude, and dwell in Cottages of Timber. . . . The Captaine of Mosambique, in his three yeares governement, maketh three hundred thousand duckats gaine, especially by gold from Sofala."

In "Golden South Africa" I referred to that ponderous tome on "Africa," published in the year 1670, "illustrated with notes, and adorned with peculiar maps and proper sculptures by John Ogilby Esq., Master of His Majesties Revels in the Kingdom of Ireland." The book has much to say on my present subject, and as it lies open before me in all the plenitude of its quaint facts, the temptation is great to quote largely from it. But I shall content myself with a few brief selections. In the writer's description of the Empire of Monomotapa references to the gold of the country abound in every page. Certain "Hangings of divers colours" in the Emperor's palace are "cover'd over with plates of gold," and so common is it that "oxen and cowes" are "more highly es-teem'd than gold or silver." "The King bestows every day in perfumes two pound of gold which certain merchants furnish him with." "The wealth of this countrey consists in gold, found in Mines and Rivers ; which, though littel valu'd yet they narrowly search for, because they find it necessary for the purchase of out-landish merchandises." The method of finding the gold in Monomopata is thus described : "There are found several Gold mines in the Bowels of the Earth, and also in some of their Rivers, for which the Inhabitants dive in the Stream, and take it up with the bottom from the Mud, and so pick it out ; which Gold-diving they also practice in divers great lakes, spread far and near in this

kingdom; for which cause the King of Monomotapa is not without
reason call'd by the Portuguese The Golden King." I read,
" They have many rich Gold-Mines, whereof Boro, and Quitici are
the names of two, lying about a mile and a half from Sofala. . .
The city Fatuka boasts great abundance of gold, silver, and
Precious-Stones, beyond all her neighbors." In his long disser-
tation on the kingdom of Sofala Old Ogilby gives the names of a
number of rivers, " all which make their way through Monomotapa,
in many places casting up Grain-Gold." Again, " The Mines and
rivers afford abundance of Gold, which the Blacks gather in a kind
of little Purses, of no small quantity." Further on I come to
these passages : "The inhabitants relate that the Gold-Mines of
Sofala afford yearly two Millions of Metigals [Value £1,001,354.
E.P.M.], every Metigal accounted for a Ducket and one third
part ; and that the ships of Zidem, Meque, and many other places,
in times of Peace, have yearly fetch from thence two Millions of
Gold ; And, lastly, that this is the very true Ophir, from whence
King Solomon had his Gold. And, indeed, according to the writing
of Moguett, no place in Africa affords better and greater plenty of
this metal ; for the General of Mozambique, during his three years'
Service in the Wars, receiv'd more than three hundred thousand
esckusos, on Crouns in Gold, besides the Pay of the Souldiers, and
the third part answer'd to the King of Portugal. The Inhabitants
Trade with other Mahumetans, coming over Sea in small Ships
call'd Zambuko, and bringing thither Silk Stuffs and Ash-colour'd,
Yellow and Red Kambaian Beads, which they exchange for Gold ;
as those of Sofala barter these Wares again with them of Monomotapa for Gold, which they receive with out weight." It is
interesting to read this hoary authority's arguments in favour of
the land which the British South Africa Company now keeps watch
and ward over being the veritable land of Ophir. As thus : "And
now it coming just in our way, and seeing both Expositors of holy
Scripture and Geographers understand this Countrey of Sofala to be
the Golden Ophir, to which King Solomon sent a Fleet of Ships,
Man'd with the Servants of Hiram, King of Tyrus, from Ezion-
geber, a haven lying at the Red-Sea ; returning again after three
years' Voyage, loaden with Gold and Elephants Teeth. . . . Yet
divers make Ophir the same with Sofala because it has much gold
and ivory. And if all the main land (included between the rivers
Magnice, and Quama, and submitting unto Monomotapa) be all as
Barros, Calles, or Sofala, as well as the rest on the Sea-Coast, it
may with great reason be judg'd that this countrey can be no other
than the Golden Ophir of Solomon ; partly because of the Houses
there to be found, near the Gold-Mines ; not built after the manner
of the countrey, but seem the work of Foreigners ; and partly,
because of the Inscriptions in strange and unknown Letters.
Moreover, Thomas Lopez, in his Voyage to the Indies, affirms
that among the Inhabitants of this Countrey there remain Books
which shew that Solomon every three year had his Gold thence.

Besides, the Septuagint Interpreters have translated the word Ophir into the Greek word Sophira, which agrees very near with Sofala. And Josephus, the Jewish Historiographer, calleth it Indian-Ophir; adding, moreover, that in his time it was call'd The Gold Countrey." But I must take leave of Ogilby's fascinating folio. In view of the contention of the Portuguese that the natives have always loved and welcomed them it will be appropriate to make one further brief quotation. In his chapter on Mozambique Ogilby has this significant paragraph : " Their Riches consist in Gold, found in the Rivers, Ivory, Ebony, and Slaves ; yet are they so fearless of any attempts to be made upon them, that they debar no Foreigners to come into their Havens, the Portuguese onely excepted." How would the Lisbon Geographical Society, who are fond of bringing ancient documents to light, explain away that passage ?

I shall cite still another high authority, who favours the contention that Ophir lies between the Zambesi and the Limpopo. An address which Sir Roderick Murchison once delivered to the Royal Geographical Society was pregnant with subjects for reflection for the geologist, geographer, or gold prospector in the whilom realm of Monomotapa. It is a fitting time to republish the following from the address he delivered when Carl Mauch's statements were causing excitement. He said : " Having traversed and examined the Transvaal territory, of which he constructed a map, Mauch became acquainted with Mr. Hartley, an elephant hunter, who, in quest of ivory, had visited all the highest lands of the region which form the broad-backed lofty watershed between the Rivers Zambesi on the north and Limpopo on the south. Being informed by Hartley of the existence in these high and rocky lands of the relics of ancient metalliferous excavations, Mr. Carl Mauch explored them, hammer in hand, and in two separate localities—the one in S. lat. 20° 40″, and on an affluent of the Limpopo, the other on an affluent of the Zambesi, about 40 miles south of Tete—he discovered rich auriferous white quartz rocks, whether hard slate (probably Silurian) or various igneous rocks, including a great predominance of granite and diodorite. The loftiest parts of this elevated tract being 7000 ft. above the sea, and lying in S. lat 19° 50″, and E. long. 28° 35″, presents in parts great accumulations of these broken masses of granite to which my illustrious friend the late Leopold von Bush assigned the appropriate name of ' Felsen Meer,' or a sea of rocks. Many travellers have too often erroneously considered these to be boulders, while in fact they are simply the results of decomposition *in situ*, as seen in many granite countries. The auriferous quartz rock, in places still seen to rise a few feet above the surface, has, where rich in gold, been quarried down in open trenches to the depth of six feet or more. These works seem to have been abandoned simply from the influx of water, and in one spot the traveller detected the remains of smelting operations with slag and scoriæ, the relics of lead ore

E

being also observable. Of the auriferous localities described by Mr.
Mauch, that which lies to the north, on a tributary of the Zambesi,
is the most sterile, and this fact explains why the Portuguese have
never made much of it; Dr. Livingstone having spoken only of
small quantities of gold dust being washed down in the rivers
to the south of Tete. On the other hand, the existence of the
rich tract on the River Thati, or Tati, an affluent of the
Limpopo, and the proof of old works having been in operation
there, greatly favours the suggestion I am about to offer, that the
Ophir of Solomon was probably near the mouth of that great
stream. In the meantime the discoveries of Mr. Mauch have
awakened the interest of many of the colonists of Natal, and
doubtless the tract which seems to have been neglected for so many
centuries will be soon the scene of active operations of the miner.
This newly-discovered auriferous tract is, I may state, precisely in
that position in which, as a geologist, I should have expected to
find gold, i.e., in the elevated and ancient slaty quartzose rocks
(probably Silurian), with granite and greenstone, which form the
mountains in S. lat. 21 degrees that constitute the watershed
of some streams, tributaries of the Limpopo, to the south. From
the well-known fact that some of the rivers of Africa—particularly
the Niger and its affluents—contain gold dust, we may reasonably
expect that the other mountain tracts from which they flow will
eventually prove to be as auriferous as the upper region of the
Limpopo in the south-east of Africa; and thus with the spread of
enterprise the geological *nuclei* of Africa may prove remunerative
to searchers for the precious metal. This discovery of gold leads
us once more to consider a suggestion that the Ophir of Solomon
might, after all, have been situated in the country of the Limpopo.
He supported his view by mentioning some recent reports brought
by some missionaries of the existence on that stream of the ruins
of an ancient city. The Ophir of Scripture had from early times
been supposed to lie somewhere on the south-east coast of Africa.
It was this belief that led the Portuguese to send expeditions soon
after the voyage of Vasco da Gama, and subsequently to colonise
largely in these latitudes; the relics of churches built by the Jesuit
fathers being, it is said, still to be traced. But after all, the
Portuguese were never successful in finding any great gold field,
owing probably to their chief settlements being upon the Zambesi,
and to their having omitted to extend their researches southward
in the interior. The question as to the real site of the Ophir of
Solomon has long been a subject of dispute. My lamented friend
the late Mr. John Crawford, President of the Ethnological Society,
has, in his excellent work, ' The Descriptive Dictionary of the
Indian Islands,' analysed with great perspicuity and much knowledge the various hypotheses which have been suggested, and has
considered that Ophir cannot with any show of possibility be
placed in any part of India where the geographer Carl Ritter had
supposed it to be. Quite agreeing with my eminent friend that all

the commodities forming the exports from Ophir could not well
have been the native products of one and the same place, and that
Ophir may have been an emporium, we have yet to ascertain, by a
proper survey, whether the site of such an important place of trade
might not have been at or near the mouth of the great Limpopo
River, which flows from the above-mentioned gold mountains.
Looking to the great objection to the hypothesis of Ophir being in
India, inasmuch as the seamen of the days of Solomon could not
have made such long voyages, the learned author of the article
'Ophir,' in Smith's 'Dictionary of the Bible,' naturally preferred
Arabia as the country in which Ophir was situated, both from its
proximity to the Holy Land and as being within the bounds of the
earliest navigators. Although I at one time thought that Arabia
might possibly have been the auriferous region in question, I
abandon that idea when I ascertain that the mineral structure of
that peninsula was such as to render it most unlikely that at any
time it could have yielded gold. The absence of rivers and
seaports is also strongly against the Arabian hypothesis. Knowing, as we now do, from the structure of the adjacent countries,
that the traders from Tarshish, whether Tyrians or Jews, could
find no gold on either shore of the Red Sea, they would naturally
continue their coasting voyage along the east coast of Africa in
their endeavour to find it. In doing so, we further know, from
the mineral structure of the region north of the equator and the
fact that the Jub, Ozy, and other streams which traverse the
Somauli country, flow from tracts of sandstone and volcanic rocks,
and bring down gold-dust, that the old navigators could meet with
no success in those parallels. Neither is the country between
Zanzibar and the Zambesi auriferous. It is only on reaching the
latitude of 20 degrees S. that auriferous rock occurs in the mountains of the interior, in a region from which, as before said, the
waters flow to the Zambesi on the north, but chiefly to the
Limpopo on the south. I venture, therefore, to say, that of
all the sites hitherto suggested, the region which feeds these
streams was, according to our present knowledge, in all probability
the source which supplied the ancient Ophir. I have before stated
that this region, besides gold, is rich in ivory and ostrich feathers;
and if Hebrew scholars see no objection to the supposition that
Biblical writers might not clearly distinguish between the feather
of the peacock and those of the ostrich, another difficulty in
choosing this South African site vanishes. I would also add that
parts of this region are specially rich in ebony—so rich, indeed,
that according to Livingstone, great profit might be obtained by
bringing home cargoes of these valuable trees from the River
Rovuma. Now, may not these have been the famous almug trees
of which Solomon made pillars for the house of the Lord and the
King's house, as well as harps and psalteries for the singers?"

In the works of Dapper, and other authors of the seventeenth
century, we have very similar accounts to those I have been

E 2

reciting. But sufficient evidence is afforded, by the quotations
already given, that relics of an ancient civilisation,—corresponding
in almost every detail with those found at Zimbabye,—were
known to be in existence anterior to the Portuguese occupation of
the country, and even prior to the time of the Arab colony they
found at Sofala. The question of their actual age and origin,
however, still remains as much a puzzle as it was to De Barros
and his contemporaries 350 years ago!

I shall not further follow the Portuguese expeditions for the
conquest of Monomotapa and its mines, the rapid decay of
that Power, until they lost all hold upon the country, and its
subsequent conquest, during the first half of the present
century, by the Zulu adventurers, O'Nabe, Manicusse, and
Umzila, who established their supremacy over it. I shall briefly,
however, take up the thread of the history of Matabeleland from the
establishment of Mosilikatse's power over it. Meanwhile I am
reminded by Mr. John Noble that there is one historical link
between the Cape Colony and Monomotapa which should not be
forgotten. When Van Riebeck founded the first European settlement on the shores of Table Bay, he formed the idea of penetrating inland, and reaching as far as Monomotapa, in order to tap its
trade from the south, for the benefit of the Dutch East India
Company. He thought that if the inhabitants of Monomotapa once
became acquainted with the Hollanders, and compared their kind
treatment with the imperious domination of the Portuguese, they
might be induced to bring their "gold, ivory, and pearls" over-
land to the Cape, instead of to Sofala and Mozambique.
Encouraged by rewards offered by the Government, which
were to be in proportion to the distance travelled and the value of
the discoveries made, a party of 13 volunteers, under the leadership
of one Jan Danckerts, was organised and started from Cape Town on
November 12, 1660. They were provided with three oxen, to carry
their ammunition, provisions, and merchandise; and they were
enjoined, upon reaching any of the towns of Monomotapa, to
endeavour to induce some of the natives to return with them,
should they even leave some of their own party as voluntary
hostages. On the 4th of January, 1661, they came back to the
Cape—unsuccessful. They had only advanced northwards as
far as the Oliphant's River, when they returned, "partly from
the inability of some and the unwillingness of others to go
further, and from their leader being afraid of exercising his
authority in too absolute a manner." The journal of the expedition is preserved in the archives of the Cape Colony. Times are
changed since those in which Van Riebeck's infant settlement
thus attempted to extend the commercial operations of the Dutch
East India Company. The young Colony then planted has since
taken root in the soil, and developed into vigorous and lusty life.
Its sons, with an ever-expanding vitality, have spread from Table
Bay northwards to the Vaal and Limpopo Rivers; and in the

year of grace, one thousand eight hundred and ninety, they formed the main body of the Pioneer Force of the British South Africa Company, who, equipped with all the appliances of modern civilisation, have peacefully opened up and now occupy the high, healthy, and auriferous plateaux forming the watershed of the Zambesi River. The dreams of the first European settlers of the land have been more than realised; their descendants to-day —the Colonists of South Africa—are entering into possession of the ancient empire of Monomotapa.

CHAPTER III.

EARLY HISTORY OF MATABELELAND.—FOUNDING OF THE NATION.—
CAREER OF MOSILIKATSE.—HIS FIGHTS WITH THE BOERS.—MIS-
SIONARY WORK IN MATABELELAND.—VISITS TO MOSILIKATSE.
—THAT POTENTATE " AT HOME."

ALTHOUGH the *Pax Britannica* has been extended only at the
last hour, England has now in verity thrown her mantle
over the Matabeles, and consequently aught concerning
the early times of that people forms interesting reading.

The modern history of Matabeleland and Mashonaland, formerly
known as Monomotapa and now merged in Zambesia, begins with
the reign of the great chief—" the scourge of the Bechuanas," "the
Napoleon of South Africa "—Mosilikatse, father of Lo Bengula,
the present king. I have on my table the records of travellers
who came much in contact with Mosilikatse ; but the most interesting of all these are to be found in the reminiscences of the good
and famed Dr. Moffat, as edited and written by his son, the Rev.
J. S. Moffat, now the British representative at Lo Bengula's Court
at Bulawayo. In " The Lives of Robert and Mary Moffat," from
the pen of that gentleman, we get graphic sidelights on the character
of the dreaded Matabele king. The missionary shows us an aspect
of the potentate different from that generally known ; indeed Dr.
Moffat seems to have had considerable influence over Mosilikatse.
But I fear the effect of that influence lasted only while he was
with him on his occasional visits.

Mosilikatse's father was a chief whose country lay to the north-
east of Natal, but being attacked and totally defeated by a neighbouring tribe, he took refuge with Chaka, the Zulu tyrant (predecessor of Dingaan), with whom he remained till his death. The
young Mosilikatse succeeded in gaining the favour and confidence
of the despot, and in process of time was entrusted with the command of an important military post and the charge of a large
number of cattle. Seizing his opportunity he revolted and fled
with his people and the booty towards the north-west, " eating up " in
his progress several tribes, and soon becoming almost as formidable
as Chaka. His name inspired terror through a vast region, as he
completely subjugated or destroyed every tribe from whose opposition he had anything to dread. He was fought by Dingaan, but

always beat him off. For a time he settled down (about 1830) in the country near the sources of the Molopo and Mariqua Rivers. When the Boer emigrant farmers moved northwards they encountered Mosilikatse's warriors near the Vaal River. Twenty-eight of their number were killed, and their flocks and herds, and even some of their children, were carried off. Later on another party of Boers (twenty-five men and women) were massacred by the Matabeles and their wagons and property destroyed. The Boers collected themselves, and on the 29th of October, 1836, had from within their hastily constructed laager to defend themselves against a very large force of Matabeles. The natives, with great cries, stormed the little camp ferociously, but the colonists, being excellent marksmen, used their elephant guns with deadly effect. The little band of Boers won the day. They held their position and the Matabele retired. The main body of the emigrants resolved to take ample revenge for the massacre of their countrymen, and in January, 1837, about a hundred of them, under Gerrit Maritz, with native allies, advanced into Mosilikatse's territory, attacked his military town, Mosega, and recovered some of their stolen cattle. All the discipline and barbarian valour of the despot's warriors could not avail in a contest with the superior arms and tactics of the Boers. He soon retired northward, and was lost to all view in the depths of the then unknown interior. It has since appeared that he made his way straight to the Zambesi; but finding it impossible to cross his immense herds of cattle, he retraced his steps for some distance. He conquered all the tribes in the Matabele highlands, consisting of Makalakas and Mashonas, but ultimately settled down and occupied the elevated plateau upon which his son is now living. He no doubt chose the spot for sanitary reasons; for the country is very healthy. But Mosilikatse seems to have been a South African Alexander in his younger days. He still kept an eye beyond the Zambesi. One tale has it that he made up his mind to cross the river with an expedition, and carry fire and spear amongst the tribes on the north bank. The story goes that he arranged with a petty local chief called Wanki, who lived on the south bank, to ferry the Matabele force to the other side. Wanki took Mosilikatse and his men in boats to an island in the middle of the river, and left them there over night, promising to come in the morning and complete his task. This he did not do, but deserted to the north bank, and left Mosilikatse and his force to their fate. Many of them were drowned in attempting to cross to their own side; crocodiles destroyed many more; but Mosilikatse and some others finally managed to get back, and returned to their own country. The chief found that in his absence the tribe, believing him dead, had installed his eldest son, Kuruman, as king. Much annoyed, Mosilikatse put to death all the headmen who had connived at this, and, as the story has it, sent away Kuruman to live in a sort of genteel exile with Umbigo, a chief supposed to be devoted to the King. In 1868 Mosilikatse died, and Kuruman was sought for as his successor, but was not to be found; and his uncle, Umgombat, Mosilikatse's brother, then announced that Kuruman had been assassinated, and that he himself had taken part in the deed. The next heir was Lo Bengula, who, however, refused to reign, as he was not convinced of his brother's death. Finally, after repeated search, Lo Bengula yielded to the representations of the "indunas," and was crowned in 1870. Another tale has it that Kuruman was executed straight away, and that the sentence ran: "Not to stab him with an assegai, nor bruise him with a kerri, nor to strangle him with a reim, but to take his head between the hands, and kill him by twisting his neck." This, it is said, was effected, so that the body of a royal child might not be disfigured.

"Mosilikatse has," wrote the Rev. J. S. Moffat, "shown his genius in the success with which he has completely formed a people out of the most unpromising materials, and imbued them with his own martial spirit. There are three distinct classes among the Matabele; the original Zulus, with whom he emigrated, and their children. Of those who with him crossed the Drakensberg a mere handful of withered old men remain. They have but few children; for marriage as an institution was not recognised by the early discipline of Mosilikatse when he was fighting for existence. This upper or aristocratic class is small, but, of course, very influential. They are known as the Bezansi; that is to say, 'those who come from the low country on the coast.' The middle and a large class are men now in the prime of life, who were incorporated into the tribe in the early part of his career. They are mostly Basutos and Bechuanas, and can generally tell to what particular tribe they belonged, though they were captured mere children. They are as different from the Bechuanas, their compatriots, as can well be imagined. They are finer physically, and may show as perfect a discipline as the *old Zulus*. Anyone who doubts that the characteristics of a race may be modified or almost entirely changed in a single generation has only to go and compare the Bechuanas in their native haunts with their very relatives, who have been seized by Mosilikatse in childhood, and trained into bold and athletic warriors. This middle class is known as the ' Benhla,' that is, 'the people from the upper country.' They cannot pretend to the distinction of the ' Bezansi;' but they have the national spirit, and look down with contempt upon their brothers, the ' Basholo.' The third and lowest class, known as the ' Magole,' or ' bush-draggers,' are the slaves taken in the more recent wars of the Matabele from the Makalaka and Mashona. They are serving their apprenticeship, and in process of time become warriors like their predecessors. Even these lads, in a few months, after the bitterness of captivity is past, become Matabele heart and soul, and may be seen waving their knob-kerries as they follow the cattle to pasture, and singing the praises of Machobane. This mythical being is the father of Mosilikatse, and the tutelary deity of the Matabele."

As I have said that Dr. Robert Moffat supplies interesting data concerning Mosilikatse, let me summarise some of this from his own journal of his visit to the King.

"This records the first contact with the Matabele tribe under the chief Mosilikatse or Umziligazi, as he would be called in Zululand, whence he came, himself a fugitive from the tyranny of Chaka. He headed another wave of emigration which rolled westwards, and threw into terror and confusion the comparatively unwarlike Basuto and Bechuana tribes, who inhabited what is now the Transvaal. In the year 1829 two traders went into the interior to shoot elephants and to barter. Hearing from the Bahurutse that a tribe rich in cattle lay far eastward, they went on, and were well received by Mosilikatse, the King, who, however, allowed them to approach his town on horseback only. Before this, the Matabele or Mantotoana, as they were then called, had come in contact with the Bahurutse and had learned, through them, of the existence of the white people, especially those at Kuruman, with whom they were best acquainted. Mosilikatse, in quest of more extensive and particular knowledge of the white men, was led to send two of his headmen, charging them to inquire specially about the manners and teaching of those at the Kuruman. On their arrival here with three attendants, everything astonished and interested them, and they themselves were the objects of still greater astonishment to our people, who stared at them as though regarding another order of beings. They were shown every attention, and they in turn were full of gratitude. The order of worship and the singing arrested their attention, while the water-courses, gardens, houses, and blacksmith's forge kept their minds in constant exercise."

Dr. Moffat sets out on a visit to Mosilikatse, and this, in abridged form, tells in his own words of his meeting with the King. "Towards evening we came to the Oori River, a pretty large stream, in which sport the hippopotamus and the crocodile. At this place the river passes through a range of high hills, and flowing N.N.E. is joined by other streams, after which it is called the Limpopo. We crossed the hills by a pass, and halted on the banks of the Oori, where it enters the range, crossing next day and halting at a town where we were to await orders as to our future course. Next day we went on, and at length came within sight of the King's abode. Having preceded the wagons on horseback, we entered the large public cattle fold, where were ranged in a semi-circle about eight hundred warriors in full dress. About three hundred more sat concealed in ambush, perhaps for precaution or to try our courage. We proceeded to the centre of the fold, when they beckoned us to dismount. We had scarcely reached the ground, when those who were secreted at the entrance rushed in, shouting and leaping with the most fantastic gestures, so that our horses, unaccustomed to such fun, tried to break away from us. . . . . A profound silence followed for some ten minutes, then all commenced a war song, stamping their feet in time to the music.

No one approached, though all eyes were fixed upon us. Then all was silent, and Mosilikatse marched out from behind the lines with an interpreter, and with attendants following, bearing meat, beer, and other food. He gave us a hearty salutation, and seemed overjoyed. By this time the wagons were drawing near, and as he had never seen such things before, he desired to see them walk as he called it. We left the fold, the warriors maintaining their position in perfect silence. As the wagons drew near he seemed awe-struck, moving backward, and drawing me along with him. When they had halted, and the oxen were unyoked, he approached with great caution, grasping me with one hand, and holding the other on his mouth. He spoke little at first, but examined all minutely, especially the wheels, and when told of how many parts each wheel was composed his surprise seemed to reach its climax. He then returned to the fold, where he was received by his warriors with immense bursts of applause. . . . I had long conversations with him on these subjects. I took the opportunity of pointing out to him the horrors of war, and directed his attention to the depopulated country once swarming with inhabitants, who had lived in comparative peace and plenty. I told him how I had met with only a few wretched individuals, the remnant of all the multitudes that must have been either destroyed or scattered. I told him that though his cattle posts were numerous, they were lost in the immense and solitary region which was as a land that mourned, while innumerable bones that strewed the plains, seemed to call to Heaven for vengeance. He tried to lay the blame on Mantatees and others who had preceded him; but time would fail to tell of all the subjects on which we talked. I felt glad when the day came that I could return home. Short as my stay was, the varied instances of despotism and horrid cruelty made me feel as if I sojourned in the tents of Kedar. Everything I saw or heard filled me with melancholy. I had never before come in contact with such savage or degraded minds. Truly, the dark places of the earth are full of the habitations of cruelty. Let such as philosophise on the happiness enjoyed by man in his savage state, visit such scenes and hear the ten thousand sighs and groans which echo in these gloomy shades, and shudder at the innocent blood shed through the length and breadth of heathen lands—and then, if they can, tell the world that such are happy. Mosilikatse showed much anxiety to prolong my stay. My engagements at home made it impossible for me to delay. He often made me promise to visit him at some future time and to stay a year. I assured him I should not cease to remember him, and to pray for him and his people that God might send them teachers. As the time drew near for my departure his attachment seemed to increase, so much so that some of his people thought I had given him some kind of medicine which made him love me. He accompanied me a short distance from the town, when he took

my hand, and addressing me by name, said: 'Ramary, your
visit to me seems like a dream; my heart will follow you. Go
in peace to Kuruman, and when you come again bring Mamary
with you. Tell the White King I wish to live in friendship. He
must not allow the Batlaro and the Korrannas to come and
annoy me as they have done. Let the road to the Kuruman for
ever remain open.' As the wagons moved off he and his men

THE LATE DR. MOFFAT.

(By permission of Messrs. Elliott and Fry.)

sat down on the grass and chanted some dirge, and I walked away
musing on all the things I had seen, and on the deplorable
condition of the heathen world. His attention and kindness
have been unbounded."

In 1838 very little was known of Mosilikatse. Subsequent to
his disappearing to the north so little was heard of him that his

actual existence began to be doubted. After a long and laborious journey Dr. Moffat again visited the King, in 1854 ; but a change had come over him, and the missionary thus writes :—

" We entered an immense large fold, and following a headman were led to the opposite side, where sat some fifty or sixty warriors. The town seemed to be new, or half finished. There was nothing like the order or cleanliness I had seen before. We stood for some minutes at a door or opening in the fence leading to some premises behind. In the meantime Mosilikatse had been moved from his house to this doorway. On turning round there he sat—how changed ! The vigorous, active, and nimble chief of the Matabele, now aged, sitting on a skin, lame in the feet, unable even to walk or to stand. I entered ; he grasped my hand, gave an earnest look, and drew his mantle over his face. It would have been an awful sight for his people to see the hero of a hundred fights wipe from his eyes the falling tears. He spoke not, except to pronounce my name, Moshete, again and again. He looked at me again, his hand still holding mine, and he again covered his face. My heart yearned with compassion for his soul. Drawing a little nearer to the outside so as to be within sight of Mokumbate, his venerable counsellor, he poured out his joy to him." Mosilikatse was almost helpless with dropsy, but Dr. Moffat, who remained with him nearly three months, succeeded in effecting a satisfactory cure. The return journey of 700 miles to Kuruman was accomplished without notable event. Later on Mrs. Moffat wrote : " There is something very remarkable in the uncommonly strong attachment of the poor savage Mosilikatse to my husband—an attachment which has lasted twenty-three years—and we cannot help thinking that this circumstance is to be overruled for some great object." In 1857 Dr. Moffat again made a pilgrimage to Mosilikatse to try and induce him to allow missionaries to be established among his people. The failure of attempts in former years to found missions among his people had not left a good impression on the mind of the King, and even Mosilikatse and his people, we read, had a deep conviction that the opening of the country to white men to come and settle would be the beginning of the end. However, he consented to missionaries coming into his country, and 1860 saw a mission established there. In taking leave of this aspect of Matabele history I shall quote his son's description of Dr. Moffat's final farewell of Mosilikatse :—" On Sunday morning, the seventeenth of June, he walked up to the chief's kraal, for the purpose of speaking to Mosilikatse and his people, for the last time, on the great themes of life, death, and eternity. As we followed him along the narrow path, from our camp to the town, about a mile distant, winding through fields and around patches of the uncleared primeval forest, no step was more elastic and no frame more upright than his. In spite of unceasing toil amid tropical heats and miasmatic exhalations, in spite of cares and disappointments, his wonderful energy seemed un-

abated.   The old chief was, as usual, in his large courtyard, and
gave kindly greeting.   They were a strange contrast as they sat
side by side—the Matabele tyrant and his friend the messenger of
peace.   The word of command was given, the warriors filed in and
ranged themselves in a great semi-circle, sitting on the ground, the
women crept as near as they could, behind huts and other points
of concealment, and all listened in breathless silence to the last
words of ' Moshete.'   He himself knew that they were his last
words, and that his work in Matabeleland was now given over to
younger hands.   It was a solemn service, and closed the long
series of such, in which the friend of Mosilikatse had striven to
pierce the dense darkness of soul which covered him and his
people. . On the morrow there was the last leave-taking, and
Moffat started for his distant home.   That was twenty-four years
ago.   Of the three men whom he left in his work, one has passed
to his rest, another has retired, and the third, William Sykes,
is still at his post.   Mosilikatse, faithful to his promise, was
a steady friend to the new missionaries ; and in this respect
his son Lo Bengula has followed in his steps ; but the mission
has as yet been without visible success.   Time only will tell what
has been the meaning of this strange history.   It is more than
fifty years since Moffat first visited the Matabele.   In the meantime attempts have been made by the Paris missionaries and by
the American Board to establish missions among them, but in vain.
Sykes and those now associated with him, have been able to maintain a foothold in the country, but it is difficult to see any result
commensurate with the existence of a mission for twenty-five years.
The day will declare it ! "

Mention must be made here also of the interesting work from the
pen of the Reverend John Mackenzie, "Ten Years North of the
Orange River," an account of the author's mission labours among
South African natives.   Mr. Mackenzie also visited Mosilikatse, and
gives us a valuable sketch of his sojourn in the Matabele country in
1863.   He writes :—

A fire had been placed in the middle of the pen, and near to it,
seated in an old-fashioned arm-chair, the gift of Mr. Moffat, sat
Mosilikatse.   As we advanced, we got each a warm and rather lengthy
shake of the hand, the attendants shouting lustily, " Great king !
Man-eater ! " &c.   We took our places on the ground opposite the arm-
chair, and had a full view of its occupant, who was the object of this
abject praise.   We saw an old frail man, so frail that he could not
stand by himself or walk a single step.   His legs were paralysed,
his arms moved with difficulty, and in a spasmodic manner ; his head
was grey, and his face bore the wrinkles of old age.   The only clothing
of the chief at the time of our introduction to him consisted of an
English blanket brought loosely round his loins, and a naval officer's
cap on his head.   An old greatcoat, the original colour of which was
to me a matter of speculation, served as a footstool and was removed
with the chair when the chief desired to change his position.   I
sought in the countenance of Mosilikatse some explanation of his

bloody and successful career, but I cannot say that I found it in the face of the old man before me. He had a good head and large eyes, almost the largest I have seen in an African face. And if we were in the presence of one who could listen unmoved to the voice of justice and mercy, we had little to remind us of the fact. A bright-eyed child sat near the chief, and waited upon him. He was a captive, and his parents had no doubt been ruthlessly murdered. He sat beside the arm-chair of Mosilikatse like a favourite lap-dog, the chief occasionally taking notice of him, and smiling at his apparently happy looks. Strange to say, this little favoured captive boy did not like his position as spaniel or plaything to Mosilikatse. Although I never spoke to him, except, perhaps, by a kindly glance of the eye, I found after leaving the chief's camp, on my departure from the country, that this little fellow had forsaken the smiles and the dainties of Mosilikatse and secretly ensconced himself in one of my wagons. Poor boy! I could not let him stay. But it was with a heavy heart that I led him out, and delivered him to two soldiers to take back to his heathen master. Some of Mosilikatse's "wives," of whom I was told there were hundreds in the country, sat near to their lord, ready to obey his slightest wish. We were presented with boyalwa, or native beer, in a drinking vessel neatly woven of grass. The women held in their hands elegant spoons also made of grass for skimming away flies or other objects from the beer. No notice was taken of the two greatcoats which we had sent the day before as presents; but immediate application was made for additional "help," as the Matabele express it. However, our reception on the whole was gracious enough, as things go there. Mosilikatse seemed to lose sight of my connection with Sekhome, and recognised me as a missionary from England or Kuruman, the difference or distance between those two places not being understood by the Matabele. I have been amused to observe the hazy notions as to places and persons which prevail in the interior. Till the day of his death, Mosilikatse thought of his friend Mr. Moffat as chief of the traders and hunters who annually visited his country. An Englishman who never saw Mr. Moffat, and certainly never visited Kuruman, delivered every year at his first interview with Mosilikatse an improvised message to the chief, with which he said he had been intrusted by Mr. Moffat. Again, on leaving the country at the end of the season, this person went regularly to the chief to receive a message for his chief at Kuruman, his journey all the while leading him hundreds of miles away from that place. Then the people of Kuruman invariably gave themselves out in the interior as subjects of Moffat. "Mahure," they said, "was chief at Taung—Moffat was chief at Kuruman." This insured for them more consideration than they would otherwise have received. At Lake 'Ngami an English trader most gravely assured the chief that he could not again show face at Kuruman and answer to Moffat for the goods in his wagon, unless Lechulatebe gave him more ivory for them than he was then offering! And after all there was great reason for the current report that Mr. Moffat was the chief of Kuruman. As the land belonged to the Missionary Society, the kingly office of apportioning the gardens rested for fifty years with him. Then the residents on the stations belonged to different and sometimes distant tribes, and it was their custom to bring their quarrels to Mr. Moffat for settlement. And no chief in the country entertained strangers with more regularity and cheerfulness than this venerable missionary, the maize and the corn which the guests received for food being reaped in the gardens laid out and irrigated by his skill and industry . . . . . . Mosilikatse's admiration for Englishmen was very great, and could not possibly have long survived the advent of the "mixed" society which has recently found its way into his country. I have heard him say to his congregated officers and men, pointing to the Englishmen present, "These are the masters of the world. Don't you take notice how they sleep in the open country alone and unprotected, and are not afraid? They are in my country one day; they pass on to the towns of other chiefs; they go fearlessly, for they bear no malice, but are the friends of all. And when the great men in the white man's country send their traders for my ivory, do you think they give me beautiful things in exchange because they could not take the ivory by force? They could come and take it by force, and all my cattle also. And yet look at them! They are humble and quiet and easily pleased. The Englishmen are the friends of Mosilikatse, and they are the masters of the world."

In 1836 Captain William Cornwallis Harris, of the H.E.I. Company's Engineers, paid a visit to Mosilikatse's country, and has left a very interesting account of his adventures in his work, " The Wild Sports of Southern Africa, being the Narrative of a Hunting Expedition from the Cape of Good Hope, through the territories of the Chief Mosilikatse, to the Tropic of Capricorn." He visited the despot at his residence at Kapani near lat. 25°, long. 28°, and he devotes some chapters to describing affairs there as he saw them. Here is how he writes about his first introduction to the monarch :—" In the course of a few minutes, loud shouting and yelling announced his approach. He was attended by the spies that had accompanied us from Mosega, several of his chiefs, and most of the warriors who were not absent on the expedition I have alluded to, armed with shields and assegais. As he advanced, others rushed up with a shout, brandishing their sticks. A number of women followed with calabashes of beer on their heads; and two pursuivants cleared the way, by roaring, charging, prancing, and caricoling, as already described, flourishing their short sticks in a most furious manner and proclaiming the royal title in a string of unbroken sentences. As we advanced to meet him several of the crowd exclaimed 'Haiyah! Haiyah!' a shout of congratulation and triumph. Having shaken hands, we led him into the tent, and seated him on a chair; the courtiers and great men squatting themselves on their hams on the ground in semi-circular order on either side. He was particularly glad to see Andries, and shook him by the hand several times. The expression of the despot's features, though singularly cunning, wily, and suspicious, is not altogether disagreeable. His figure is rather tall, well turned, and active, but, through neglect of exercise, leaning to corpulency. Of dignified and reserved manners, the searching quickness of his eye, the point of his questions, and the extreme caution of his replies, stamp him at once as a man capable of ruling the wild and sanguinary spirits by which he is surrounded. He appeared about forty years of age, but being totally beardless, it was difficult to form a correct estimate of the years he had numbered. The elliptical ring on his closely-shorn scalp was decorated with three green feathers from the tail of the paroquet, placed horizontally, two behind and one in front. A single string of small blue beads encircled his neck; a bunch of twisted sinews encompassed his left ankle, and the usual girdle, dangling before and behind with leopard's tails, completed his costume. The interpreters, three in number, were ranged in front. After a long silence, during which the chieftain's eyes were far from inactive, he opened the conversation by saying he rejoiced we had come to give him news from his friends the white people. Mohanycom put this speech into Sichuana, Baba translated it into Dutch, and Andries endeavoured to render the meaning intelligible in English. To this we replied, that having heard of the King's fame in a distant land, we had come three moons across the great water to see him, and had brought for his acceptance a few trifles from our country which we thought might prove agreeable. He smiled condescendingly, and the Parsee immediately placed at his august feet the *duffel* great coat which I have already described as being lined and trimmed with scarlet shalloon; a coil of brass wire weighing fifty pounds; a mirror two feet square; two pounds of Irish *blackguard* snuff, and fifty pounds weight of blood-red beads. Hitherto the King had considered it beneath his dignity to evince the slightest symptom of astonishment—his manner had been particularly guarded and sedate, nor had it been possible to read in his countenance aught that had been passing in his bosom; but the sight of so many fine things at once threw his decorum off the balance, and caused him for the moment to forget what he owed to himself in the presence of so large an assembly. Putting his thumb between his teeth, and opening his eyes to their utmost limit, he grinned like a schoolboy at the sight of gingerbread, patting his breast, and exclaiming repeatedly, 'Monanti, monanti, monanti, monanti, tanta, tanta, tanta!' (Good, good, good, bravo, bravo, bravo, bravo!) Having particularly brought to his notice that the device of an uplifted arm grasping a javelin, on the clasps of a great coat, referred to his extensive conquests, of which all the world had heard, we placed before him a suit of tartan sent him by Mrs. Moffat, with a note which he requested me to read; and hearing his own name coupled with that of Ma-Mary, as he termed that lady, and the word 'tumerisho' (compliments), he grinned again, and clapped me familiarily on the back, exclaiming as before 'Tanta, tanta, tanta.' He now rose abruptly, big with some great conception, and made signs to the Parsee to approach, and assist him on with the coat; habited in which he strutted several times up and down, viewing his grotesque figure in the glass with much evident self-applause. He then desired Mohanycom to put it on and turn about, that he might see if it fitted behind; and this knotty point settled to his unqualified satisfaction, he suddenly cast off his tails, and appearing in *puris naturalibus*, commanded all hands to assist in the difficult undertaking of shaking him into the tartan trousers. It was indeed no easy work to perform, but once accomplished, his Majesty cut a noble figure. The Parsee wore a pair of red silk braces, which he presently demanded, observing that they would supply the place of those that Mrs. Moffat *had forgotten* to send. Shortly after this, he directed an attendant to take everything to his kraal; and resuming his solemnity and his seat, tea was brought in." As Captain Harris's stay with Mosilikatse became extended the despot threw off his reserve and gravity, "familiarly pulling our beards, of which the luxuriant growth elicited his admiration and surprise. He frequently asked us how many wives we had, and whether they also had beards." The writer's descriptions of the King's extreme covetousness of everything the travellers showed, and of the curious bargains effected, are highly amusing. His Majesty took all he could get from the party, and as a proof of the extent of his gratitude and the munificence of his nature, presented them with two of his worst oxen and a toothless cow. For a long time Mosilikatse would not consent to the travellers returning south by the Vaal River, his pretended motive being their safety, but his real one being that they should not hear of the massacre of the emigrant farmers.

The Rev. J. Smith Moffat tells us in Blue Book C. 4,588 that "In 1835 an expedition for scientific purposes under Dr. Andrew Smith visited Umziligazi, chief of the Matabele tribe. The Matabele then occupied the Marico and Rustenburg districts in the Transvaal. The expedition remained some weeks in the dominions of Mosilikatse, and so satisfactory were the relations of its members with Mosilikatse that Dr. Smith persuaded that Chief to send messengers to Cape Town. They were treated with great consideration, and returned to their master with presents and with a good impression of the character of the English people. It was a severe trial to the faith of the Chief and of his people, that the emigrant Boers were permitted by the Government to leave the Colony, and to encroach upon his territory and that of other Chiefs who, like him, had always sought to be on friendly terms with the English. . . . In 1859 a mission was commenced at Inyati by the London Missionary Society. This arose out of visits which had been previously paid to Mosilikatse by my father. I was a member of that mission, and lived at Inyati until 1865, when I was transferred to Kuruman. During the whole of my residence there, not only I myself, but all Englishmen, were treated with respect and goodwill. It was a strong national sentiment that the English and the Matabele were friends; a point was made of this on all public occasions, and in the national war songs. I have been away from that country for twenty years, and do not know whether the same goodwill has been preserved, though, from what I hear, I should judge that no Englishman who preserves his self-respect has ever met with anything but consideration from the Matabele and their Chief, that is Umziligaza, and his son Lo Bengula, who succeeded him about the year 1868." In that year Mosilikatse was gathered to his fathers at the age of 72.

F

CHAPTER IV.

THE BOERS AND MATABELELAND.—THEIR SCHEMES TO ANNEX THE
COUNTRY.—A REPUDIATED TREATY.—LO BENGULA FAVOURS THE
BRITISH.—A LONG FAREWELL TO BOER DREAMS.—THE GROBLER
INCIDENT.—SIR SIDNEY SHIPPARD'S VISIT TO LO BENGULA.—HIS
THRILLING ADVENTURES.—EXPERIENCES AT THE KING'S KRAAL.—
ALARMING CONDITION OF MATABELELAND.

WHEN in August, 1486, John II. of Portugal despatched
two ships southward on a voyage of exploration, he little
dreamt that the land they were to reach was to
come into the possession of the little island of Britain
that lay to the north of Europe, about which they
knew so little, and from which little indeed was expected.
Just as little did Vasco da Gama think as he doubled the Cape on
his way to India, some ten years afterwards, that he was laying down
a track which none would use so frequently as the inhabitants of
that same despised island. Yet so it has proved. The " Giant
Cape " which they sighted, the route they discovered, have been of
importance to none so much as the English. Time, indeed, elapsed
before the discoveries thus made were utilised. Two centuries
slipped away before the value of the Cape was fully understood;
three centuries before it passed into the hands of the nation which
has colonised and which governs it. Used for some time as a
station for ships, it remained free to all till, in 1652, the Dutch
East India Company took possession of it, in the hope of developing
some trade with the interior. In this, despite their system of perpetual restriction, they were successful; but it was not this success
that directed the attention of England to its importance to them.
That importance lay chiefly in the position it occupied on the way
to India; and so in natural sequence the formation of the Indian
Empire preceded the settlement of the English at the Cape. When
the former had been carried out, and when England, through the
vicissitudes of her struggle with America, found herself in hostile
relation with Holland, an expedition to seize the Cape was
planned. The fleet despatched for that purpose in 1781 met with
reverses, and the Dutch remained masters of this important position
till 1795, when the British Government, with the concurrence of the

Prince of Orange, then an exile from his country, took forcible possession of the colony. It was restored, indeed, in 1803, but only for a period of three years, for on the renewal of hostilities it was retaken by an armament under Sir David Baird. Since then it has been a part of the British Empire, the King of the Netherlands having ceded his rights in return for a pecuniary compensation a the peace in 1815.

For a long time but little progress took place in the new possession. There were difficulties to overcome, for in inheriting it the English had inherited the legacy of troubles which had been accumulating during the Dutch régime. On the frontier clustered the native tribes in a state of perpetual unrest, liable to be changed for an attitude of active animosity by any chance mishap. Each attack might be repulsed, but a repulse implied little more than a return into a condition of passive discontent. Within the colony itself there were difficulties of another kind. Not only was organisation wanting, not only was there a lack of the capital and labour necessary to progress, but within a very few years from the second capture of the Cape incidents occurred which showed what would be the future attitude of the Dutch inhabitants. It was no wonder, when the causes of trouble were so numerous, that little progress was made ; it is a testimony rather to the perseverance and ability of the various administrators that despite them the British supremacy was maintained, and so firmly established that it bore unmoved the two successive shocks of the Kafir war in 1824, and the discontent of the Boers at the promulgation of laws for ameliorating the condition of the slaves. The latter was perhaps a source rather of future than immediate danger. Unlike the Kafirs, who hurled themselves in vain against the lines of the British settlement, the Boers only sought means for escaping from the immediate dominion of their successors in rule and their conquerors. During 1835-37 this exodus went on. The number who thus voluntarily faced expatriation has been variously estimated at between 5000 and 10,000. They sold off their properties in haste, and with their wealth transformed into a portable form, set forth with their wives and children into the dim unknown regions beyond the Orange River. Nothing recalls the indomitable perseverance and the silent energies of their ancestors more than the boldness with which they thus dared adventure to seek freedom. Though I shall show how they tried to get Matabeleland I cannot here trace the interesting history of the Boers in South Africa. As I have pointed out, *ultima thule* has been reached by them in South Africa, that is so far as an independent existence is concerned. The timely granting of a royal charter to the British South Africa Company to bring the territories to the north and west of the South African Republic under the direct rule of the Company has served to show the Boers that the Limpopo is the last northern boundary they can hope to call their own. They had dreamed that, as their fathers had done before them, they would trek again to the north and (if they could not succeed by pacific methods) beat the soldiers of Lo Bengula, as they had beaten the warriors of his father fifty years ago. But for the fortunate circumstance of England arousing herself to a realisation of the situation, Zambesia might to-day have been jointly occupied by the Boers and the Germans. Long before the British South Africa Company was thought of, I wrote in "Golden South Africa": "It is said that one of Bismarck's ubiquitous emissaries recently saw Lo Bengula with a view to getting him to allow his country to come under German protection. If the German Chancellor succeeds in any such scheme he will deal a great blow at Anglo-Saxon enterprise in South Africa. England could have thrown her mantle over the Matabeles ere this if her present statesmen had had half the spirit of their forefathers and worked more for the State and less for party. Britain having neglected her opportunity, the Transvaal Government are now credited with carrying on secret negotiations with Lo Bengula to extend a ' friendly ' protection over his country. It is possible that Bismarck has been using Pretoria tools. Be that as it may, although this is scarcely the place to dwell upon the subject, there is little doubt that Germany, notwithstanding repeated specious explanations on the subject, is leaving no stone unturned to establish domination in South Africa. There is equally little doubt that the British Government view German intrigue south of the Equator with what may very easily prove to be a disastrous indifference."

Notwithstanding the fact that over half-a-century ago the Matabile ruler expressed a desire for friendship with Englishmen, it is, we see, but a year or two since the country through which the highway to the north must always run nearly passed into German hands. The following treaty should find a place among the historical documents concerning Matabeleland.

The King of the Abaqua Zooloo or Qua Machoban, Umsiligas, engages to be a faithful friend and ally of the Colony; to preserve order in his territory and to abstain from war unless forced thereto in self-defence; to protect all white men who may visit his country, and to defend and treat in a friendly manner all missionaries or other persons who may, with his consent, settle and reside in his territory, so long as they act in accordance with justice.

He engages to defend and assist all travellers or traders who may reach his country, either with the object of extending knowledge or otherwise benefiting mankind.

He engages not to interfere with the remnants of tribes resident in the vicinity of his country, unless in self-defence, and promises to permit them to enjoy, undisturbed, the advantages of religious instructors, should any such be disposed to settle amongst them; he engages to cultivate and encourage peace, and apprise the Colonial Government of any intended or actual hostile movements in the interior, and to act in concert with the said Government, in subduing whatever may be calculated to disturb the general peace, or retard the civilisation and prosperity of the native tribes of South Africa.

The Governor of the Cape Colony engages to regard Umsiligas and his subjects as friends, and will receive any of them as such when they visit the Colony.

That he will grant, in the first instance, as presents for Umsiligas, a variety of articles suitable to his present condition, and will continue supplies of the kind from time to time, so long as the terms agreed upon shall be strictly observed.

And in order to facilitate intercourse hereafter between Umsiligas and the Colony, the Governor will duly consider the request made for an individual of the Colony to be resident with the Abaqua Zooloo or Qua Machoban, and endeavour to obtain a missionary for that purpose, who will be most calculated to forward the views of the contracting parties.

(Signed)

      B. D'URBAN, Governor, (L.S.)

      UM 'NOMBATE, his X mark, (L.S.)

March 3rd, 1836.

MATABELE HEADDRESS

The fit of English indifference as to what became of South Africa, watched with anxiety by all truly desirous of the extension of the British Empire, passed away. The period of masterly inactivity in Downing Street came to an end, if not in time to prevent Germany absorbing a share of English Africa, at least in time to prevent the Boers accomplishing their long-cherished scheme of annexing Matabeleland. How perilously near the brink of the precipice the Imperial Government drove the coach of Empire in South Africa may be gathered from the conclusion to the admirable article the lamented Lord Carnarvon wrote in the *Fortnightly* of June, 1888, when he said:

We cannot here afford to lament another opportunity lost. It has been well pointed out how in the modern craving for colonial annexations the vast continent of Africa—lately unexplored, unoccupied, uncared for—has become in the eyes of European nations a lottery, in which territorial prizes may be drawn by lucky or daring adventurers. Never since the days of Cortes or Pizarro has there been a territorial scramble on so large a scale, and if the appropriations are conducted with greater humanity as regards the native inhabitants, self-interest and the hope of commercial advantage enter quite as largely into the policy of the matter now as formerly. France, Germany, Portugal, and England are the principal owners or claimants of this vast property, and their pretensions often over-lap and conflict with each other to an extent which may easily give rise, even in a near future, to dire trouble. But some considerable and important stretches of country are still undisposed of, and in the interests of England and her African Colonies, none perhaps are so important as the large tract lying immediately to the north of the Transvaal, and of our Bechuanaland territory. It is flanked on the west coast by the new German settlements, on the east by Delagoa Bay and the Portuguese possessions; and on the north it is bounded by the Zambesi. Were it to pass into the hands of another European Power, it would virtually

hem us in, and so alter the position and relations of every neighbouring
State as to disturb the whole balance of South African politics, the cost
of which disturbance can perhaps best be estimated by recent wars and
troubles in that part of the world. But this middle space which, unfortunately, can no longer remain a no-man's land, though its rulers have
readily engaged to accept no other sovereign, has never been formally declared British territory, and if now it were allowed to pass into foreign
hands the results would be simply disastrous. With it our colonies would
lose their right of way into the interior ; with it our traders would forfeit
the markets, which would soon be closed by hostile tariffs ; with it
England and her colonies alike would relinquish the free navigation of
the Zambesi—the great high road of Eastern Africa. It was both possible
and expedient, while the question did not press, to adjourn the decision ;
and were it possible to preserve the territory neutral and free to all
nations it would probably be wisest to accept such a solution ; but now
that this part of Africa has become the subject of foreign ambition or
enterprise, every one who knows anything of South African policy has
long known that our safety lies in the formal extension of our protectorate
up to the banks of the Zambesi. The time has now come. The Governments of Europe, for various reasons, are engaged in a tremendous race
of territorial annexation ; everywhere the void places of the earth are
being appropriated, though they cannot be filled up, and at this moment
the confiscation of a whole continent, larger than Europe itself, proceeds
with astonishing speed, though most of us at home are so ignorant, or so
indifferent, or so absorbed in local concerns, that we hardly give this new
and portentous phenomenon a second thought. The age in which our lot
is cast is a wonderful one, not more in what it does than it what it
leaves undone.

But it was the Boer who wanted Matabeleland first ; whether
he made terms afterwards with a European power was not of
initial consequence. He had been long trying to send his pioneer
force into the Land of Ophir, and we shall have to turn to
Blue Book history for a sequential account of his final and
unsuccessful efforts to realise his dream. Towards the end of 1887
it was freely asserted in the South African press, that a secret
understanding had been arrived at between Lo Bengula, the
Matabele monarch, and President Kruger of the Transvaal. It was
said about the same time that a geographer, having just constructed
a map of the territories beyond the Vaal River, submitted his draft
to President Kruger for approval. The customary distinctions of
colour had been observed in the work, the South African Republic,
as defined by the Convention of London, being of the symbolical
golden yellow, and the native territories invested in a sombre coat
of pigment. "Make those yellow too," said the President, pointing to Matabeleland and Swazieland. "But," remonstrated the
draftsman, "they are not included in the region which enjoys your
Honour's beneficent rule." The President did not argue the
question. "Make them yellow," he simply repeated ; "the land
is all of one colour." Some versions of the story were enriched
with remarks about the British Government and its most eminent
representative in South Africa, which would have been as superfluous as uncivil. It was not necessary, or even likely, that the

mere map-maker should be made acquainted with Mr. Kruger's opinion of the power or of the man from whom resistance to his plan might be reckoned upon in the event of an earnest assertion of English responsibility. The massive, unadorned, unqualified exhibition of intention and will is more picturesque, and more in accordance with the probability of the case, than any vulgar display of animosity or contempt. Mr. Kruger had mentally taken the measure of the forces to be reckoned with, the mere *sic volo sic jubeo, sit pro ratione voluntas* gave the most impressive statement of the result. For it was so. At that time President Kruger had but to will and to command, to give no reason for any of his acts, but merely signify that it was his pleasure that he should commit the acts. He, however, met his match in Mr. Rhodes, who " got round " both him and his country.

It was soon after the Boers had won back their independence from the British, that they thought they would put a scheme for possessing themselves of Matabeleland into operation. Early in 1882, a certain letter found its way to Lo Bengula's kraal. It was dated " Marico, S.A.R., March 9, 1882," and addressed to " The Great Ruler, the Chief Lo Bengula, Son of Umziligaze, the Great King of the Matabele nation." A portion of it is worth preserving : " Now you must have heard that the English took away our country, the Transvaal, or, as they say, annexed it. We then talked nicely for four years, and begged for our country. But no ; when an Englishman once has your property in his hands, then is he like to an ape that has its hands full of pumpkin-seeds. If you don't beat him to death, he will never let go. And thus all our nice talk for four years did not help us at all. Then the English commenced to arrest us, because we were dissatisfied ; and that caused the shooting and fighting. Then the English first found that it would be better to give us back our country. . . . And we will now once more live in friendship with Lo Bengula as we lived in friendship with Umziligaze ; and such must be our friendship that so long as there is one Boer and one Matabele living these must remain friends." There was an allusion to the good time coming, " when the stink which the Englishman brought with him is blown away altogether," and the letter concluded with the signature :—" The Commandant-General of the S.A. Republic, for the Government and Administration, P. J. Joubert." Of course Piet Joubert, like us all, has accumulated more wisdom since that time, and finds it is best for all parties to include the English in his bonds of " friendship."

Although, in the beginning of 1888, Lo Bengula emphatically denied having made any agreement with the South African Republic, a mass of correspondence took place on the subject between the Transvaal and Imperial Governments. In August of the year named, President Kruger wrote to the High Commissioner enclosing a copy of an alleged treaty, signed on the 30th July, 1887, and stating that it was the result of requests of Lo Bengula, in

1885 and 1886, that the South African Republic should renew two
treaties entered into between it and Mosilikatse in 1853. The
treaty was a very flimsy document, and w_s doubtless obtained to
allow the Transvaal Government to appoint Pieter Johannes
Grobler as their "Consul" in Matabeleland, a request which
Lo Bengula refused. It happened, however, that on February
11th, 1888, Lo Bengula entered into a treaty with the British
through the medium of Mr. J. S. Moffat, who was then Her
Majesty's Assistant Commissioner in Bechuanaland. A copy of that

SIR HERCULES ROBINSON, BART., G.C.M.G., P.C.

treaty will be found in the chapter which sketches the creation of
the British South Africa Company. In October, Mr. Moffat
secured from Lo Bengula a document repudiating the alleged
Transvaal treaty of the 30th July of the previous year, the King
saying : "They are not my words." The Transvaal Government
wrote strongly to the High Commissioner refusing to recognise
Mr. Moffat's treaty; but it does not seem necessary to follow their

contentions,- one of which was that Lo Bengula repudiated the
treaty made through the offices of Mr. Moffat.   To cut short a
one-sided wrangle, Sir Hercules Robinson wrote to Lord Knutsford
advising that the Transvaal Government be informed " that Her
Majesty's Government, whilst accepting the *bonâ fides* of the
Government of the South African Republic, are satisfied of the
validity of Mr. Moffat's agreement of February 11 last, and do not
consider it open to discussion."   In due course the Transvaal
Government were written to in these terms by the High
Commissioner, and the matter was amicably settled.   Sir Hercules
Robinson is certainly entitled to lasting credit for so conducting
negotiations with the South African Republic that its members
could finally submit gracefully to the inevitable and allow British
money and not the Boer rifle to subjugate Zambesia.   The farewell of the Boer to all his dreams of expansion to the North is well
worth preserving here in full in the following despatch :—

STATE SECRETARY, Pretoria, to His Excellency the GOVERNOR, Cape
Town.

(Translation.)

Government House, Pretoria,
April 3, 1889.

YOUR EXCELLENCY,

I am instructed to acknowledge the receipt of your Excellency's
despatches of 22nd and 23rd March last, which this Government has
noted with regret.

This Government considers it of importance immediately to give the
assurance that the subjects dealt with in your Excellency's said despatches
will not bring it to an unfriendly attitude towards Her Majesty's Government, and will give no cause for a rupture.   If these matters cannot be
settled to the satisfaction of both sides, either by correspondence or at a
conference, then this Government, sooner than let it come to a rupture,
will rather suffer under it.   The Government wishes readily to give the
assurance of this.

When this Government traces back the relations which have existed
between the British Empire and this Republic, then it feels that it may
not, and does not wish to let it come to a rupture on this subject.

Indeed, this Government does not wish to be ungrateful.   It has not
forgotten that England, though great and powerful, was not afraid to
make an end to our war of freedom, and to give back this land to us.
Subsequently, when circumstances made the addition, to this Republic,
of a piece of land in the south-east desirable, Her Majesty's Government
also offered no objection thereto.   Still more.   When certain persons
were opposing this State in its natural and lawful exertion to bring about
the Delagoa Railway, and when, wishing to work this Republic to their
own advantage, they expected the support of Her Majesty's Government
in it, Her Majesty's Government, at the request of this Government,
immediately declared that they would not grant that support.   Again,
when a legitimate regulation of the immigration of Arabs and Asiatics
was necessary, and the Convention of London stood in the way of that
regulation, Her Majesty's Government yielded and removed that
hindrance out of the way.

As already said, this Government, therefore, does not wish to, and may not, let it come to a rupture; but still it cannot omit to testify its regret at the manner in which the Republic is, as it were, repelled in your Excellency's despatches now under acknowledgment.

At the negotiations which, in London, in 1884, led to the conclusion of the Convention it was set forth to Lord Derby, by our deputation, how necessary it was for the Republic, in view of the preservation of order and peace on our borders, to have the liberty of concluding treaties and entering into agreements with the native races whose territory bordered on three sides of this State. This was yielded by Lord Derby only with the addition of the stipulation that as regards the east and west of this Republic these treaties and agreements should be subject to the approval of Her Majesty's Government, because, as Lord Derby expressed it, Her Majesty's Government had interests there. Thus the north remained free for this Republic. There the Republic can freely conclude treaties, and spread its influence. Only then, when those treaties caused an alteration of our boundary line, would Her Majesty's Government have to concur in them.

It was not the intention of Article 2 of the Convention of London to determine that the territory of this Republic could never be enlarged, but only that it would have to take place in agreement with Her Majesty's Government. This Government is of opinion that the Convention of London must be so interpreted that, not as little, but as much, freedom as possible is allowed to the Republic.

This Government is thus of opinion that it must abide by the same views as before expressed by it.

I have, &c.,

(Signed)   W. EDUARD BOK,
State Secretary.

His Excellency the High Commissioner,
     Cape Town.

What is known as the Grobler " incident," the fatal and unexpected termination to the efforts of the Transvaal Government to establish official connection with Matabeleland, should perhaps be briefly referred to here. The correspondence connected with it covers a hundred Blue Book pages, but the salient features can be summarised. Mr. Piet Grobler, who was an absconding debtor of Khama's, had, as we have seen, been appointed Consul for the Transvaal in Matabeleland. He proceeded to that country by means of a pont which he placed across the Limpopo into Khama's country without his authority, and was, when the collision, afterwards known as the " incident," took place, returning from Matabeleland to the Transvaal for the purpose, it is said, of fetching his wife. A party of Bamangwato had been ordered by the Chief Khama to stop all white men travelling over the new road between the Shashi and Macloutsie Rivers, and a section of that party met Mr. Grobler's return party, consisting of five white men, two women, some children, and five Matabele who were travelling to the Transvaal from Matabeleland. The Bamangwatos stopped Mr. Grobler's wagons, and a dispute took place, of which different accounts are given. The evidence, however, tends to show that Mr. Grobler, angry at being stopped, assaulted the natives, and took away their guns. Subsequently, on a reinforcement of Bamangwatos arriving under the Chief

Mokhuchwane, a conference took place, which resulted in an agreement being signed by the Chief, and the arms were restored to the natives. The agreement, which was put on paper, consisted in a promise on the part of the Bamangwatos to pay 250 head of cattle to Mr. Grobler, being the equivalent of about £1,500, as compensation for the few hours' detention of his wagons, and for an accident that had happened to one of his party whilst pursuing a Bamangwato. Such an agreement, on the face of it, was extravagant and preposterous. It had, however, been signed by the Chief, and a peaceful parley was arranged ostensibly to explain its provisions to the large body of natives present, both parties agreeing to come unarmed. The Boers left their rifles behind, but kept their revolvers, and the natives, who also left their guns at a distance, came partially armed. During the parley a preconcerted signal was given, and a treacherous attempt was made by the natives to seize the Boers, who defended themselves with their revolvers, and defeated the natives, capturing 33 rifles and 6 horses. In the conflict several were wounded on each side, and Mr. Grobler, who was shot in the leg, died 16 days later. During the night the natives again attacked the Boers in their wagons, firing ten shots, which were returned by three shots, but on this occasion no casualties resulted on either side, and the next day but one the Boers were met and escorted into the Transvaal by a party of friends who had been sent to meet them. Sir Sidney Shippard, the Deputy Commissioner in Bechuanaland, was despatched to make a full inquiry into the circumstances of the incident. This he did, and he gave it as his view that Grobler had been accidentally shot by one of his own men in the skirmish. A lengthened correspondence ensued between the British and Transvaal Governments as to compensation, and various suggestions from both sides as to arbitration came to nothing. Finally the British Government admitted that the collision took place in disputed territory, and on the ground of one of the claimants (Lo Bengula) who was the chief to whom Grobler had been accredited by his own Government, and was provoked by the men belonging to a chief (Khama) under British protection. The widow of Grobler was awarded on behalf of Khama an annuity of £200 a year, and one of the wounded white men (Lotrie) received a gratuity of £250. This offer was accepted by the South African Republic, who had already granted Mrs. Grobler a thousand a year, and the incident closed.

A visit was undertaken at this time by Sir Sidney Shippard, the Bechuanaland Deputy Commissioner, to Lo Bengula at his kraal, in response to His Majesty's invitation. After holding his inquiry into the Grobler affair Sir Sidney proceeded into Matabeleland to hold a parley with the King, and was thus enabled to send a confidential report on the state of the country to the British Government. He wrote a number of able despatches describing his journey to and from Bulawayo, and he and his party deserve all praise for their admirable behaviour under exceptionally perilous

and irritating conditions. Sir Sidney and his party left the Tati
on the 4th October, 1888, and reached a Makalaka village on the
Semokwe River on the 8th. Here they encountered a party of
probably more than four hundred Matabeles and Makalakas all
variously armed. When they had outspanned, an induna gravely
handed Sir Sidney a letter from the King and a superstitious busy-
body who was a spy of the King's caused general excitement by
spreading the report that the " Administrator is a magician possessing the most marvellous and deadly power, and that though coming
to visit Lo Bengula in the guise of friendship, he has behind him
an immense army destined for the conquest of Matabeleland, and
already advancing in three columns, one through the disputed

SIR SIDNEY SHIPPARD AND PARTY.

territory between the Shashi and the Macloutsie, the second by the
Tati, and the third from the north-east." The Induna informed
Sir Sidney that an impi had been sent to stop him unless he consented to go on accompanied by only four white men. He explained in vain that the men he had with him were only an escort
and not part of an " impi." He wrote a letter to Mr. Moffat at
the King's kraal, but the natives would not allow the orderlies to
proceed at first. They got away, but Sir Sidney and his party
were not only kept prisoners but had to submit to a series of hostile
demonstrations which might easily have ended gravely. A descrip-

tion of one of these will suffice to show the danger in which the Deputy Commissioner and those who accompanied him were placed.

On Tuesday, the 9th instant, another regiment, called the Impandine regiment, arrived. The only hostile demonstration we had noticed before their arrival, after an understanding had been arrived at with the Induna, was that in their war dances young warriors would rush towards our encampment with their shields and shake their assegais and knobkerries at us, but they had abstained from poising assegais or stabbing at us. The new comers went a good deal further. In passing our encampment

SIR SIDNEY G. A. SHIPPARD, K.C.M.G.

they jeered at us, taunting and insulting us, and in their war dances some of them ran out stabbing at us and poising assegais, shouting out that they would soon make an end of us when they came into our camp. The Matabele war dance is identical with that of the Zulus, and great allowance must be made for the vanity and bragging of these young savages ; but in this case there can be no doubt that they meant to convey to us threats, defiance, and a challenge to fight.

We hardly knew what to expect, and though resolved to give no provocation, and not to strike the first blow, we thought it as well to be prepared, and therefore had the spare arm chest unscrewed and the boxes of cartridges opened. We could count on 22 in all, and had more than sufficient Martini-Henry rifles for the whole party, even counting servants, drivers, and leaders, but unfortunately only 150 rounds of ammunition per man; as a good deal of the ammunition we brought up to Baines' Drift was given to Khama, and a large supply was left with Lieutenant Lockner's patrol.

The utmost we could have hoped to do in the event of an attack would have been to fight our way back to the mountain pass from which we had emerged below the Mangwe, and where, unless attacked by another impi from below, we might be able to keep the savages at bay.

Fortunately there are in my present small escort several crack marksmen who would rarely, if ever, waste a cartridge. Our men behaved throughout with admirable coolness, and looked at the dancing savages with the most stolid indifference. After this sort of thing had gone on for some time I saw the Induna in command of the newly-arrived Impandine regiment coming towards me with the village headman and the latter's two sons. One or two of the Impandine regiment, with their

weapons, followed the Induna, and two or three more, also armed, broke through every rule of native etiquette by coolly leaping over my slight fence into my "scherm." I took no notice of them, and looked at the Induna for an explanation. He was a middle-aged man, very strongly built, and dressed in a queer mixture of European and Matabele fashions. He looked at me steadily, and then sat down on the ground before me; all the others in the "scherm" immediately followed his example. I took a seat, and enquired through the interpreter what he wanted. He said he only wanted to see the white chief, about whom he had heard so much that he wanted to see with his own eyes. I asked whether he was aware of all that had taken place, and that I was now awaiting a letter from Lo Bengula. He said he was perfectly aware of it, and was about to proceed to the Tati to ascertain whether an impi is coming into Matabeleland by that way, as had been reported. To this I made no reply. Major Goold Adams then asked him whether any more of the Matabele regiments were coming to stop our party. He seemed much amused at the question, and then took leave in a rather more civil manner. He had hardly been gone three minutes when the whole of his regiment came marching down straight towards us, though they did not enter the enclosure. They danced, yelled, howled at us, and insulted us in every way they could, some of them going as far as to stab at me with their assegais close to my fence and within a few feet of me. One of them ran close up to my baggage wagon, where Trooper Querl (who is in charge of my wagonette) was standing with his arms folded, and went through the action of stabbing him with an assegai within a few inches of him. Querl, who is a very fine-looking man, stood perfectly quiet and never moved a muscle ; but Sergeant-Major Bodle, as he afterwards told me, thought they meant to kill me when they came rushing round my "scherm," and was on the point of ordering an escort to take their rifles and bandoliers when, by a happy inspiration, he paused, and the moment of danger passed. Neither Major Goold Adams, who was standing by me in the "scherm," nor I, thought for a moment that anything serious was intended by the Matabele, unless they could have provoked us to strike the first blow, and Major Goold Adams noticed that in rushing on, the Matabele, with few exceptions, held their assegais in the left hand, with the shield and only knobkerries in the right hand, while the Induna, who would certainly have been bound to lead an attack, was behind the regiment on horseback. This regiment consisted entirely of Matjaha (sometimes pronounced Matchaka), young unmarried soldiers, who are hardly to be controlled by the Indunas, or even by the Chief himself. They had evidently received orders not to attack us, though, if they could have succeeded in provoking any of our own men to commence a fight, they would have considered themselves justified in disobeying orders. They ultimately marched off, bellowing and roaring as they went along, followed by their Induna, who was civil enough to ride up to my "scherm" to say good-bye. Trumpeter Rowland replied, on my behalf, that I wished him and his men a pleasant journey.

The party remained in captivity several days, but finally the missive came which was to allow the British party to get past the natives who had been at that period, through their chiefs, praying for permission to kill all the whites in the country. They left the Makalaka village, but at the hands of further bodies of natives were subjected on their journey to further insolence similar to that already described. At length—

On the 15th instant, at about 4 p.m., we arrived at the Umguza River without any further hindrance, though our headman, whose man had gone on with my letters, was obliged to explain very often to Matabele along the road who we were and why we were travelling to the Chief's place. At the Umguza River Mr. Moffat rode out to meet me, and gave me a very bad account of the state of things here and throughout Matabeleland. It seems that it was only on that very morning that upwards of 1000 men of the Umbezweni regiment had left this place, after having spent the greater part of yesterday in trying to persuade Lo Bengula to let them massacre all the white men in Matabeleland. Their argument, as I was given to understand, was that though there are only about 80 white men here now, who, as they said, would be a mere breakfast for them, thousands may come hereafter unless these few are killed now, so as to frighten the others ; and they also clamoured to be led against the white men's towns. Lo Bengula listened in silence for a long time. At last he answered the Umbezweni regiment. After refusing point blank his permission to massacre the Europeans, or as the Matjaha said, " to give them all the white men now here," Lo Bengula is reported to have said, " The white men here are my guests. If you are really so anxious to fight white men, I will send you down to Kimberley in charge of the Indunas. From Kimberley the Indunas shall return to me, and you shall remain there and try to fight the white men, and then you will see what the white men can do to you," or words to that effect. Then Lo Bengula went inside his kraal, and the old Induna who commands the Umbezweni regiment was so alarmed at the Chief's wrath that he spent the rest of the afternoon in dancing before Lo Bengula's kraal and singing the Chief's praises in the most fulsome and abject terms in the hope of pacifying " the Great Elephant, the eater of men, the man of men, the stabber of the sun, &c." I have been credibly informed that a few days ago one of the young regiments asked permission to kill their present Indunas, who, they said, are old women and cowards, and to elect others who would not be afraid to lead them against white men.

To others who have urged him to murder all the English now in Matabeleland, Lo Bengula is said to have replied, " You want to drive me into the lion's mouth." From all I can gather, a great deal of mischief has been made by two or three Europeans who have lived long in Matabeleland, and are anxious to prevent the granting of mineral concessions to others ; and I have also been assured that certain men from the Transvaal, whose names have been mentioned to me, are doing their utmost to poison the minds of the Matabele against the English. These men are said to make no secret of their wish to see our throats cut.

At the King's kraal Sir Sidney was very well received by Lo Bengula, the King doing him the very exceptional honour of sending all his principal Indunas to greet him on his behalf. The spokesman was an old Induna and general, the same who commanded the expeditionary force sent with such disastrous results to Lake 'Ngami. The old general was most courteous, and asked how, according to English customs, he ought to salute Sir Sidney, and convey the Chief's greetings. He explained that the Chief Lo Bengula was then much occupied with business, but hoped in a few days to be able to fix a time for the interview. Sir Sidney's long descriptions of his experiences at the kraal are very interesting reading, but I must be content to give only a few extracts, and these only because they explain graphically the condition of Matabeleland at that time (October, 1888), and show how the later steps of the British Government were not taken a day too soon.

Shortly afterwards I received a visit from the great war doctor, an old Kafir from the Cape, dressed in European clothes, the same who " doctors " the spears and javelins of the Matabele before each of their atrocious raids, and purifies the returning warriors from the taint of bloodshed abroad before they enter the precincts of the royal kraal. No less than 13 Impis of Matabele have been sent on forays this year, and the desolation among the Mashona and Banyai villages, south of the Zambesi, and among the tribes for some distance on the north of that river, has, I am assured, been appalling. Bishop Knight Bruce, of Bloemfontein, whom I have been so fortunate as to meet here on his way down, and who has been four days' journey north of the Zambesi, and as far as Umzila's boundary on the east, gives a terrible picture of the results of a Matabele raid. He describes the ruins of a Mashonaland village destroyed this year, the burnt huts, and the little patches of garden ground fenced in and carefully cultivated by the industrious

Mashona, none of whom have lived to reap the fruits of their labour. Every man, woman, and infant in these villages had been killed by the spear or "stabbing assegai" of the Matabele Matjaka, except the old women, who are used as carriers as long as they are wanted, and then tied to trees, round which dry grass is heaped up and then set on fire, such holocausts of old Mashona women being regarded as a capital joke by the Matabele Matjaka. Of the children and girls who are driven here as slaves, those who survive the journey are afterwards fairly well treated. Lo Bengula allows the slave boys nothing but beef to eat, however great their craving for farinaceous food; the result being that all the weaker boys soon die of dysentery, while the survivors become very strong, and consequently fit to be incorporated, in due time, into a regiment of Matjaka of the requisite ferocity. I see great numbers of these slave boys here.

*　　*　　*　　*　　*　　*

Lo Bengula had, I was told, been painting himself all over in the most hideous manner, and been busily engaged in incantations, divinations, and witchery of all kinds to enable him to read my mind, discover the real intentions of the English, and fortify himself against the insidious arts of the Great Queen's magician. I could only hope that the results had proved satisfactory to the Royal mind. On arriving at the Chief's kraal I was at once ushered into the innermost enclosure. I was accompanied by the Right Reverend the Bishop of Bloemfontein, Mr. J. S. Moffat, Assistant Commissioner, Major Goold Adams, and the Reverend C. D. Helm, of the London Missionary Society, the Chief Missionary at Hopefountain, who very kindly undertook the onerous duty of interpreting for me. The Rev. D. Carnegie, Missionary at Hopefountain, was also present. I was careful to have seats carried in by my servants as I found that all Europeans here without exception are accustomed to sit on the ground before Lo Bengula, exactly as the natives do, some of the old white inhabitants, and even some of the new concession seekers actually grovelling before the Amandabele Chief with their hands on their knees and thus sidling up to their places in the circle in the crouching attitude of the natives who are fawning on him for boiled beef and Kafir beer. A few minutes after I had taken my seat near his wagon a curtain was drawn aside, and the great man appeared and deliberately stepped over the front box of his wagon and sat down on the board before the driver's seat. He was completely naked save for a very long piece of dark blue cloth rolled very small and wound round his body, which it in nowise concealed, and a monkey skin worn as a small apron and about the size of a Highland sporan. In person he is rather tall, though considerably shorter than Khama, and very stout, though by no means unwieldy. His countenance reminded me of Mr. George French Argus's portrait of the Zulu Chief 'Mpanda. His colour is a fine bronze, and he evidently takes great care of his person, and is scrupulously clean. He wears the leathern ring over his forehead as a matter of course. Altogether he is a very fine-looking man, and, in spite of his obesity, has a most majestic carriage.

Like all the Matabele warriors, who despise a stooping gait in a man, Lo Bengula walks quite erect with his head thrown somewhat back and his broad chest expanded, and as he marches along at a slow pace with his long staff in his right hand, while all the men around shout out his praises, he looks his part to perfection.

As he looked at me I rose and saluted him by lifting my helmet, after which I went up to his wagon, and he shook hands with me very cordially. His manner was extremely courteous, and appeared to me to betoken some familiarity with European customs. The interview, though comparatively brief, was highly satisfactory, and Lo Bengula asked me to return the following morning at about 7 a.m., so far as I could understand from his way of indicating the position of the sun. What passed between the Amandebele Chief and myself at this and subsequent interviews will form the subject of a separate and confidential despatch. Next morning (Friday, 19th instant) while I was preparing to start for the Chief's kraal, which is about a mile from my encampment on the Umguza River, the old Induna Lootche came to ask me to postpone my visit as one of Lo Bengula's children had died that morning at a kraal some distance off. I expressed my regret at Lo Bengula's loss, and fully expected that I should have no opportunity of again seeing him for some days, but was agreeably surprised by a message the same afternoon asking me to visit the Chief, who wished to see me. When I arrived he was engaged in the sacred duties of "medicine" or "mystery" of some kind in the holiest of his kraals—the goat or "buck" kraal—and I had to wait till he had washed off the paint and resumed his ordinary aspect. He did not keep me waiting long and received me in a very friendly manner and took me into a shady corner of his great kraal close to the place where he keeps all his meat and dried skins. To the olfactory nerves of a European invalid it was trying, but the Chief evidently meant the selection of this favourite spot to be regarded as a proof of goodwill. He asked me, when all were seated, that is to say, the two Indunas Lootche and Segombo, Mr. Moffat, the Rev. C. D. Helm (interpreter), and Major Goold Adams, to give him a complete account of what had occurred between Khama and the Transvaal Boers, which, of course, I did. The rest of the conversation, so far as material to British interests, will be found in the confidential despatch above referred to. At parting, Lo Bengula asked me to come again between 7 and 8 o'clock this morning (Saturday, 20th October), when he gave me his replies to all I had said. I need only say here that I left more than satisfied with the results of my interviews. He promised me two men to start with me on Tuesday morning, the 23rd instant, for the Tati. On Friday afternoon Lo Bengula expressed a wish to inspect my wagonette. I walked by his side on his right hand through his vast kraals both in going and returning, and I noticed a very large number of Matabele seated on the ground both in the outer kraal and outside it. As the Chief passed through their ranks the cheers and shouting of Lo Bengula's praises became general and very loud. I took this to be the invariable reception of the Amandebele Chief by his followers, but Mr. Moffat assured me that it was extraordinary, and had a certain significance. For upwards of 50 years the Amandebele had been taught to regard the English as their friends. Their confidence had been shaken by the recent scare and the false reports spread by emissaries from the Transvaal. The people had jumped to the conclusion of treachery on our part. Lo Bengula, though possessed of superior intelligence, had, of course, been obliged to redouble his incantations, but in the main he had stood firm against the popular delusion, and had decided on receiving the British Deputy Commissioner. Even his returning to examine my vehicle was in the eyes of the people a proof of his superiority of mind, or, at any rate, of the greater power of his own magic. The result has justified his faith and courage; our walking side by side was the visible proof of a cordial understanding, and hence the deafening cheers. Such, at least, was the impression I was led to form.

This afternoon (Saturday, October 20), at Lo Bengula's request, Major

Goold Adams put the men of the escort through their drill with rifles and bayonets, but of course without bandoliers. The Chief walked some distance in front of his outer kraal to witness it, and watched everything with the keenest interest. He asked whether the Martini-Henry rifles could be fired without breaking the bayonets, the construction and use of which were fully explained to him. The men managed their horses admirably, and Lo Bengula said he could perfectly understand what would be the effect of a large body of such men. Some bayonet exercise with a march past and salute wound up the little review, after which Lo Bengula said, " I have seen."

*   *   *   *   *   *

I regret to say that in spite of the present comparative calm Mr. Moffat remains firmly of opinion that a massacre of all white persons in Matabeleland is certain to take place sooner or later, and would in all probability follow immediately on the first attempt by Transvaal filibusters to effect a settlement or obtain any sort of footing north of the Limpopo. He appears to regard the danger as imminent, and in this Mr. S. H. Edwards, who has had a very long and intimate acquaintance with the Amandebele, entirely agrees with him. New comers affect to despise such warnings. Lo Bengula's power of restraining the Matjaha is said by those best acquainted with the country to be greatly diminished within the last few years. The older Indunas, the companions of his boyhood, are said to be still devoted to their Chief, but the younger regiments, many of which can boast of no Zulu blood, and consist entirely of Maghole, i.e., slave boys or captives taken in war, and trained up to become Matjaha, are said to be anything but loyal to Lo Bengula. It is impossible to forecast the future in such a country as this. A Matjaha rebellion, attempted revolution, and civil war, appear to me to be not unlikely.

*   *   *   *   *   *

Some of the older Matabele Indunas and Indodas are confessedly sick of carnage, and desire nothing so much as a peaceful government with a security for life and property, not to be obtained under the present regime; but the restless and bloodthirsty Matjaha are perpetually craving for the fresh slaughter of helpless victims, who attempt no resistance and make but feeble efforts to escape by flight or by betaking themselves to hiding places, and Lo Bengula dare not withstand the importunity of his troops, even if he would. The insatiable vanity and almost incredible conceit of the Matabele Matjaha seem to have much to do with the continuance of the raid system. The Matjaha, who has never met a foeman worthy of his steel, believes himself to be invincible, and is assured that the Matabele could conquer all the nations of the earth; and one of the principal reasons why he slaughters as many victims as possible is in order that at the great dance of the first fruits before the Chief and the women and girls of the tribe, he may be called upon to perform a *pas seul*, a saraband in which he may make in the air as many stabs with a stick (assegais before the Chief being prohibited), as he has taken human lives. For this purpose a baby at the breast and its mother would, of course, count for two.

*   *   *   *   *

After referring very briefly to the business which Mr. Moffat still has to complete with him, I informed Lo Bengula, apparently somewhat to his surprise, that in a few days Mr. Moffat would probably take leave of him for a time. Lo Bengula repeated over and over again how pleased and rejoiced he was that I had come to see him, and had told him so much that he wished to know ; he promised in the event of Mr. Moffat's absence to write to me through Mr. Helm, if anything occurred as to which he might need my advice, and especially to let me know at once about any attempt by filibusters from the Transvaal to invade his territory; and he wound up by expressing every good wish for my prosperous journey, and success in everything. It is hardly necessary to add that the demeanour of the Indunas and of all around the Chief was modelled in strict accordance with the Royal example. Mr. Helm told me afterwards that some of the Indunas, alluding to the recent scare, had said to him: "After all, we find that it was only a friendly visit from the Administrator to the King, and we Matabele feel that we made fools of ourselves in believing absurd stories about it."

Here I may conclude my extracts from Sir Sidney's vivid despatches, by stating that Lord Knutsford, in acknowledging them, bore testimony to the ability and caution shown by the party under the very trying circumstances. His lordship remarked—and all my readers will agree with him—"It is plain that on their journey up to Lo Bengula's place, they were for a great part of the time in imminent peril of their lives, and had not each member of the party behaved not only with courage and fortitude, but with self control and discretion, a catastrophe might have ensued."

CHAPTER V.

MOSILIKATSE'S SUCCESSOR.—LO BENGULA.—HIS DAILY LIFE.— MANNERS AND CUSTOMS AT HIS KRAAL.—SCENES OF A VANISHING BARBARISM.

WE have seen how Mosilikatse, the founder of Matabeleland, died in 1868, and how the heir to the throne, Kuruman, disappeared, most probably from the earth. I read, in Captain Harris' book, of Kuruman as being, in 1836, "an aristocratic and intelligent lad 14 or 15 years of age," but who had "the blood of a despotic sire flowing in his veins." After his father died search was made for two years by Umbate, the only surviving councillor of Mosilikatse, for Kuruman, Lo Bengula, the next heir, showing a strong aversion to ascending the throne, as long as there was a possibility of his brother being found. Lo Bengula's mother and Kuruman's were sisters. Almost immediately after Lo Bengula's accession, a man who went by the name of Kanda, but claiming to be Kuruman, was heard of in the Transvaal. The Matabele say that this man's name was also Kuruman, but that he was not the real heir, but a son of Mosilikatse by an inferior wife. When he grew up, he went into the Transvaal, where he was a servant to a Mr. Coetzee, of the Marico district. There he lost an eye in a quarrel, from a thrust with a sharpened stick. Afterwards he was in the service of Sir T. Shepstone, then Secretary for Native Affairs in Natal. After Lo Bengula's accession this man was induced to put himself forward as the real Kuruman, though it is said he had previously denied that he was so ; and returning into the Transvaal, he became chief of a small band of exiles or refugees from Matabeleland. He made frequent proposals to the Boers to take up his case on almost any terms ; and the Matabele people have said that had the Sikukuni war, which brought the Republic under Mr. Burgers to grief, not broken out, Kuruman's pretensions would have been made of use by the Transvaal to get a slice of the coveted Matabele country. In 1876 he was living at Pilansberg, in the Transvaal, as a *protégé* of Paul Kruger's, and having about 100 warriors. Such is the history of one Kuruman, who died some half-dozen years ago, and whom there seems little doubt we should regard as a mere pretender, but whose claims were beginning to furnish the restless element in the Transvaal with a most convenient pretext for entering Matabeleland, and commencing a career of annexation and slaughter.

Lo Bengula was declared King by the old councillor Umbate, and the headmen agreed to the succession. There were great rejoicings at the proclamation on the 25th January, 1870, fully ten thousand warriors, dressed in full fighting costume, attending at the head kraal to dance and shout themselves hoarse with praises of the new King. Like some other monarchs, however, Lo Bengula had to wade through blood to his throne. The town of Sokindaba and others would not recognise him, and a great three days' battle was fought. The new King's troops were several times repulsed, but in the end the rebel chiefs were defeated with great slaughter, it being computed that ten thousand men were slain. Mr. John Dalton, an Australian miner, who was in the country at the time, and who is now in the Transvaal, walked over the battlefield and says the bodies of the dead were in some parts of it piled six feet high, and that the veld seemed literally paved with them.

Of advanced ideas, Lo Bengula is nearing threescore years of age. Although what would be called fat among white men, the King is of a very dignified appearance and bearing. His conduct maintains his reputation. He is never to be seen in a rage; but when either administering justice or meeting foreign envoys always preserves a dignified composure and calm, cool demeanour. His costume consists of about four yards of blue calico twisted over his shoulders, and two or three tiger tails wound around his waist. Sometimes he wears a pair of boots (seventeens) and sometimes only socks. Occasionally he has been seen with two or three revolvers tied round his waist. His appetite is immense. He eats three meals a day, generally consisting of meat and beer. This is the Matabeles' food, it being considered childish to touch milk, poultry, or any such trifles considered dainty in more civilised communities. The King is extremely temperate and altogether abstains from spirits; beer he drinks, but when, as is not uncommon, traders make him a present of champagne he always gives it to his wives. His abstinence, however, does not save him from gout, from which he suffers greatly.

Before Lo Bengula ascended the throne he used European dress and was in the habit of travelling about the country with a trader called Philips, riding with him in his wagon everywhere. Since he has been King he has entirely discarded white men's clothes and appears with only his head sash, encouraging his people to consider him wholly severed from European influence. Life in a wagon, however, still charms him, and he continues always to dwell in his ox-cart as his palace, the wagon he now uses having been captured by his army in a raid at Lake 'Ngami. From time to time he moves his headquarters, inspanning his oxen and going off without any warning. If asked where he is going, he replies, " Follow my wheel tracks and see." This habit is probably partly due to an

idea that he will thus prevent combinations against him, partly to
an early habit, and partly to an imitation of his father, who did the
same before him.

There are 78 queens (his father had 500), of whom 10 are Royal
and the rest concubines, but by none of his Royal wives has the
King any son, and it is probable that when he dies there will be
fighting between the various sons of the other wives, each being
supported by the district from which his mother came.   The wives
are scattered over the country in the various kraals, and when a
Royal progress takes place the queens do not go with their lord
but await him at the kraal to which he is going.   The King takes
four new wives every year.

Bulawayo, the capital, situate about 120 miles from Tati, may

LOBENGULA "AT HOME" - AN INDABA.

be taken as a specimen of a large kraal.   In the centre is the
King's wagon and round it his wives' huts, all circular, built of mud
bricks and roofed with reeds.   His Majesty's slaves also occupy
the kraal, inside which there is a smaller division called the " buck-
kraal," into which his flocks of goats and sheep are driven at night
time.   During the day this buck-kraal is the *sanctum sanctorum*
of the King.   Round the central cluster of huts is an open space
of grass 400 yards wide, and round this space are the habitations
of the warriors—said to number 4000—and their families ; beyond
these, again, is the stockade, which is several miles in length.
Bulawayo means " The one that is slain," or " place of killing."
Gubulawayo is sometimes used, the prefix Gu, or Go, signifying *at*,
to, or *from*.   Bengula, the name of the King, means " defender,"
the prefix Lo signifying *the*.

If a stranger approaches he will probably find Lo Bengula, with
six of his Indunas, administering justice.   Cases are brought

from all parts of the country and are formally argued and judicially decided. The Indunas act as counsel for the parties and take technical points with an ingenuity which would do credit to a British Queen's Counsel, and discuss and debate the cases with great eagerness. Indeed in many ways the Matabele litigation is similar to our own ; for although the Indunas fiercely urge the claims of a client while the case lasts, their differences disappear the moment the King's decision is given. During the pendency of a case, moreover, the Indunas keep religiously away from the parties concerned and their friends ; but as soon as the case is over they approach the successful or defeated party as if there had been no dispute. The King very prudently draws his assessors in turn from various parts of the country, and does not allow any set of men from long habit to become his masters or too experienced advisers.

The white man who comes upon this scene will be kept waiting till the dispute is disposed of, and so hot is the sun that he will

MATABELE HEADDRESS

gladly avail himself even of the shade of the meat rack (for there are no trees), and try, by smoking, to avoid the flies which his shelter brings him. When he is well received the King will send him a bucket full of beer, which he is expected to drink, or, if beer is scarce, meat to the amount of 16 platefuls, which he must eat, unless the King's back is turned, when the traveller will hastily give portions to the black boys, who are ever ready. Lo Bengula's conduct to the traveller will be courteous, but he is not easily to be taken in, being very shrewd.

Whenever the King wishes to break up an interview, or objects to see anyone, he retires to the buck-kraal mentioned, and only a few privileged Europeans have the right of sending in a messenger intimating their wish to speak with him. On one side of the buck-kraal there is a stage or platform made of rough hewn logs. Every morning the flesh of four bullocks, the quantity required daily for the royal household, is placed on this stage. As may well be imagined, the constant dropping of blood from the meat on to the ground has collected millions of ants on that particular spot. While holding a conference, or granting an interview, the King is very fond of sitting on an old condensed-milk-box, and leaning against one of the posts of this stage. Lo Bengula is perfectly impervious to the attacks of the myriads of ants ; but the unfortunate white man who has the honour of conversing with the King does not enjoy the same immunity. In accordance with Matabele etiquette, the stranger or visitor must have his head at a lower elevation than the King's, and has therefore to sit on the ground. The result is that he is attacked by these insects in swarms, and the effect of their disagreeable attentions does not leave him for many days. The King sits the whole afternoon in his sanctum drinking Kafir beer, with five or six of his favourite wives seated in front of him. Behind and to his left are generally some twenty or thirty of his headmen. At every sentence uttered by the King, no matter how trivial may be the topic, these men shout the titles of their mighty monarch. Some of these titles are :—" Stabber of the Sun ; " " Mountain of Zulus ; " " Eater of men ; " " The man who owns all the Cattle," and, above all, the sacred word " Kumalo." This constant chorus of laudatory ejaculations has an extraordinary effect on those who first take part in such a scene ; but Lo Bengula pays not the slightest heed to his courtly attendants or their high-flown praises. The manner in which a Matabele ap-

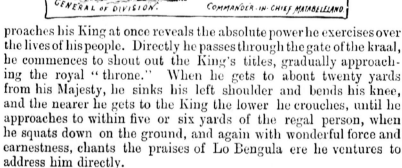

GENERAL OF DIVISION.   COMMANDER-IN-CHIEF MATABELELAND.

proaches his King at once reveals the absolute power he exercises over the lives of his people. Directly he passes through the gate of the kraal, he commences to shout out the King's titles, gradually approaching the royal " throne." When he gets to about twenty yards from his Majesty, he sinks his left shoulder and bends his knee, and the nearer he gets to the King the lower he crouches, until he approaches to within five or six yards of the regal person, when he squats down on the ground, and again with wonderful force and earnestness, chants the praises of Lo Bengula ere he ventures to address him directly.

Tall (nearly six feet), very black, and fat, the King has yet, as

we have seen, a nameless air of dignity about him.   Clad in all his
native simplicity (for, as we have said, he now scorns European
clothing), with a narrow apron of monkey skin before and behind,
he looks in his royal nakedness every inch a king ; and there are a
good many inches of him, both in length and breadth.   He has a
small head and face, but a very bulky person.   His weight must
be about 300 lbs., and his chest measurement is from fifty-five to
sixty inches.   His features are aquiline, but very coarse and
sensual, and in repose they exhibit great craft and cruelty.   But
his smile quite changes the character of his face, so childlike
and sweet is its expression.   His natural disposition is not cruel ;
but the continued exercise of almost unlimited power over the lives

LO BENGULA REVIEWING HIS WARRIORS.

(From an oil painting hanging for many years in his house, and given by him to
Mr. E. A. Maund.)

of others has grafted in it a love of bloodshed.   The annals of his
domestic policy are written in lines as bloody as are those of his
foreign conquests—brothers, sisters, nephews, nieces, friends, have
all fallen before his ruthless hand.   The King is one of the most
intelligent men in his nation.   His memory is prodigious, and,
when he chooses to exert it, he has great tact and natural politeness.   He has social qualities, too, and likes a good chat.   He
often unbends with his courtiers ; but they are ever on the *qui vive*

to say only what they know will please, and are careful never to contradict him. The duties of the King are no sinecure. He is the most hard-worked man in the nation. From morning till night

UMJAN CHIEF OF THE IMBIZU Reg.t

he is hearing reports from all parts of his dominions, arranging the settlement of difficult law cases, judging criminals, and transacting farm business. He is a farmer on a gigantic scale, for he has the

control and management of all the nation's cattle. Not being at
all particular about the truth, Lo Bengula is a clever diplomatist.
He takes absolutely no exercise, rarely indulges in walking, except
a few yards every day. His walk is most imposingly majestic; he
treads the ground in a manner which shows that he is conscious of
his absolute power. The great redeeming feature in Lo Bengula's
character is his great liking for white men. He has ever been a
firm and true friend to the whites, and during his long reign there
is no substantial proof that he has ever been privy to any act of
molestation of a white person. During recent years, any traveller
or trader who had been illtreated or robbed by Matabeles, has only
to report the matter to the King, and he will at once take steps to
discover and punish the offender.

The system of centralisation is carried out in Matabeleland
even to the smallest details. Everything emanates from the
King. Nobody possesses anything except the King. Mosilikatse,
when he organised his army into a nation, did so on the principle
of Louis XIV., "L'etat c'est moi;" this was the secret of his
power. The cloak of his power fell upon Lo Bengula, but it is
getting sadly worn out, and he may truly say, as Louis XV. did,
"Aprés moi le deluge." Apparently, he is looked upon by his
people as a sort of deity; in reality he is as much ruled by them
(ever fearing a violent death at their hands) as he himself is
feared. He is the centre from which everything radiates and to
which all things converge in Matabeleland. The destruction of an
impi, or the death of a calf at some cattle post are alike reported
to him with minutest details. Lo Bengula may be considered a
victim of circumstances; as I have hinted, he never wished to be
King, and was with difficulty persuaded to accept that dangerous office
when Kuruman was acknowledged to be dead. He is much more
suited to a farmer's life, and is only happy when he gets away
from the military kraal to one of his cattle posts. He has sufficient intuitive knowledge to despise many of the superstitions
of which, as chief rain-maker, he is the exponent. Though
not a Christian he has a great respect for the white man's creed,
and will tell you he himself believes God makes the rain, though
he may be coming straight from his medicine kraal, after being busy
there for hours brewing mystic potions, or "hell-broth," as
traders call it, for the purpose of making rain, or throwing bones
to discover some one accused of witchcraft, or to ferret out who is
to blame for the failure of an expedition, or for a trek ox falling lame.
As we have seen, he sits a great number of hours daily in his kraal
and hears the numerous reports, complaints, and charges, which
are all brought to him. When both sides have laid their case
before him, the King, who apparently has not been listening, puts
a few questions and then gives sentence. Death is the penalty for
bewitching, and the sentence once given, the delinquent is hurried
outside the kraal and quickly despatched with knobkerries. Belief
in witchcraft is a fearful scourge in the country, and is a convenient

way of getting rid of an enemy. The King's sister, Nui Nui, was the cause of a fearful number of deaths by this charge. At last, however, she accused a favourite fresh young wife of Lo Bengula's, of whom she was jealous ; but the King was sufficiently bewitched by the same person himself in another way to have his own sister made away with instead. One of the laws relating to marriage it is believed some men in England would be rather glad to see part of the national code, namely, that a mother-in-law may not enter her son-in-law's house, and, should they meet in the street, they must avert their gaze.

Among the many white visitors who have interviewed Lo Bengula, no one has yet been able to take his photograph. Like Umbandine, his cousin, and other native potentates, he has a rooted objection to being " shot at " by the camera. If any one could have succeeded in getting his picture in this way it would have been Mr. E. A. Maund, who is a great favourite with the King. Surgeon-Major Melladew was promised a " sitting " one morning, but the King had disappeared in the night. The military doctor followed him on horseback some miles, and then His Majesty's excuse was that no Matabele King could be photographed unless in full war paint, which he had not with him there. At another time he stated confidentially to Mr. Maund that it would never do for him to be photographed, as his people would think that part of him (his soul) had been taken away from him. To that gentleman he also said one day that he would allow him to use his pencil as Baines used to do.

Brief extracts from records of visits to Lo Bengula may here be given. The late Mr. Frank Oates, in his book on " Matabeleland and The Victoria Falls," says something about life at the royal kraal on his way to the north.

I called on Lo Bengula, accompanied by Fairbairn, the day I arrived here, and found him the picture of a savage king, just as one might have imagined, and coming quite up to standard. The day I first saw him he was nearly naked and lying on a skin inside his hut, to enter which you have to crawl on your hands and knees through a little aperture in the front ; in fact, it is like a beehive entrance. He took me by the hand and placed meat before me, and asked a few questions about my journey. I told him I should come again next day. Of course I had to make him a present, and I knew he would expect it next day, after which I should ask his leave and assistance to go through the country to the Victoria Falls if possible. I gave him a gun and ammunition, which pleased him very much, and he has done everything he could for me. . . . . Took Hans and went to King's. Dance going on, consisting of the men of two large kraals forming a circle, "marking time," and waving sticks, whilst the King, with rhinoceros-horn knobkerry, acted as bandmaster. There was also singing. Nini (the King's favourite sister) requested me to stand up and join, which I did. Every now and then a man rushes out into the space in the middle, shaking his shield and brandishing his assegai, enacts his fighting, and shows how many he has killed, whilst loud shouts are raised on all sides. The usual dress consists of a head-dress of black feathers, and a bunch of monkeys' tails round the loins, with white frills of ox-tails on the arms, and (in the case of veterans I suppose) a long solitary feather to top all, and a piece of fur round the head. The King had on a broad-brimmed black felt hat, a large bunch of monkeys' skins round his middle, and carried an Elcho sword bayonet (my present) and a rhinoceros-horn knobkerry. On this occasion Mr. Oates was greatly struck with the physique of the girls who staggered to the kraal under the weight of huge calabashes of beer, magnificent specimens of shapely young Kafir women; one tall handsome girl, who was a looker-on, presented a fine picture of a well-developed savage woman, and seemed fully aware of her own personal advantages. Mr. Oates had an opportunity of seeing more of these Court beauties. However, Thomson and I went to the kraal to see, and were well repaid. In the midst of a large circle formed by warriors, four wives of the King, dressed all alike and modestly covered, were dancing, or, rather, slowly pacing. Each had a checked print over her shoulders and a black skirt reaching low down. With them was a future wife, partially clad in gaily-coloured calicoes, but without skirt. The wives, Thomson says, are very nice women. As I went with him through the crowd I could not help seeing what respect is shown him, and how all make way for him. [Mr. Thomson was a missionary stationed at Hope Fountain, a short distance from the kraal.] Suddenly the royal sister appeared, and presented a most singular, not to say magnificent appearance. It was something like the appearance of the prima donna at the opera, or the leading spirit in some gorgeous pantomime. She is very stout and tremendously *embonpoint*, and her skin is of a coppery hue. She wore no dress, and the only covering above her waist was a number of gilded chains, some encircling her, some pendent. Round her arms were massive brazen bracelets. A blue and white Freemason's apron appeared in front, and looked strangely anomalous there, though really not unbecoming. From her waist also there hung down behind a number of brilliantly-coloured woollen neck wraps, red being the predominant colour. Under the apron was a sort of short black skirt, covering the thighs, made of wrought ox-hide. Her legs and feet were bare, but round her ankles were the circlets of bells worn by the women to make a noise when they dance. Her headdress was decidedly pretty— a small bouquet of artificial flowers in front, amongst the hair, standing in all directions, feathers of bee-eaters' tails. A small circular ornament, fashioned out of red clay, was on the back of her head. She put herself in posture for the dance, but did not move very much or energetically whilst keeping time; she suffered too much from adiposity. She held one of the large oval black and white ox-hide shields surmounted by a jackal's tail, such as are carried by the warriors. Poor Nini came to a sad end. She was very fond of white men and wished to marry a trader, who had left for a time hoping that he might find her a married woman on his return. It was not lawful, however, for Nini to be wedded before the King had taken a chief wife; and when the domestic household was completed by this step, the lady (one of Umzila's family) being jealous of Nini's influence over Lo Bengula compassed the death of that fleshy and amiable princess.

Later, in describing an incident of punishment which need not be further referred to, Mr. Oates writes :—" The scene, with the King sitting on his front-box, would make a picture—the setting sun ; the dark green trees beyond the kraal, and the green walls of the newly-erected kraal ; the yellow beehive-like huts ; the yellowish

A MATABELE GIRL.

trodden grass in the space ; the herds of goats and sheep, with lambs and kids, and pack of dogs, crowding round the King's wagon ; the group of natives, some all but naked, some adorned with feathers, some with a single article of European dress, as a hat, crouching on their haunches, forming the court of the black King ; tusks of ivory lying about. To complete the picture, a white trader or two should be introduced, not above crouching before his sable majesty, who sits there in his broad-brimmed black felt hat, pipe in mouth (a small briar-root, worth perhaps 2d. at home), cotton shirt not over clean, unbraced baggy trousers, and large clumsy shoes, a benignant smile generally on his black face."

Mr. Walter Montagu Kerr, in his entertaining book, " The Far Interior," hits off his visit to Lo Bengula very interestingly thus :—

Fairbairn, Selous, and myself went up to see old King Lo Bengula. I was very eager to know in what sort of humour was the old gentleman. A missionary, Mr. S——, who had had a quarter of a century of Christian effort in Matabeleland, and was able to know the character of the people had, when we met him in full retreat in Bechuanaland, given a dreadful account of the condition of affairs, saying that it was impossible to live in Matabeleland since the difficulty about the hippo-killing. The poor missionary's beard had been pulled, and he had to suffer other indignities which, as an apostle of divinity, he could not brook. But what special exemption could he expect ? Many observers note that after five-and-twenty years of missionary labour there are no converts to the faith of our fathers. After so long a period of profitless contention with a people who are both deaf and blind to persuasion, it could hardly be expected that Mr. S—— would find more sympathetic treatment than other whites. Fairbairn informed me that with the payment of all the fines the troubles about the sea-cow row, to which I have referred, had vanished, and that now the old man was in a very good humour. When we entered the King's kraal I could see him seated under his roof porch. A few of his people were around. All of us shook hands with him, and were received with more courtesy than might be expected from a savage king. We sat on the ground beside him, and his prettiest slave-girls brought in beer. Kneeling before us they would drink first, and then hand the liquor to us.

Lo-ben seemed very friendly, and evidently had quite forgotten the troublesome episode of the shooting of the sea-cow. When Selous asked permission to enter the hunting-veld, the monarch granted his request with a smile, remarking, " Selous is a young lion." Looking at me, he then asked what I was about to do. On being told that I was anxious to go through his country and subsequently through unexplored Mashona-land to the Zambesi, he simply remarked, " It is very far away."

A crowd of indunas began to assemble, and, as it was clear that a big talk was about to ensue, we departed without making a further attempt to gain the desired permission. Walking to the back of the house we saw numbers of hive-shaped huts, the houses of the queens, the housing of the royal harem.

Here was a novel scene! Upon grass mats, in front of the huts singly, or in bevies here and there, the queens of the Matabele reclined gracefully and with careless ease, basking their rather *embonpoint*, but yet symmetrical, figures like glossy seals lolling in the warmth of the sun. A strange and not unpleasant odour filled the air, for these queens are in the habit of scenting themselves with a perfume made from wild flowers and herbs rolled into balls about the size of small apples.

The picturesqueness of the figure grouping, however, was somewhat marred by the occupation of some of the royal ladies, who were imbibing copious quantities of beer, and eating largely of meat. Yet they were a happy-looking company, beaming with good nature, and all running to portliness, which evidently increased with years. They asked Fairbairn numerous questions about me, and with feminine curiosity seemed particularly anxious to know where my wives were, if I had any, and, if so, how many? One in a jesting humour called to some slave - girls who passed, and turning to me, said :—

"Now choose a wife from among them; which shall it be ?"

Fairbairn was well acquainted with all the queens. He seemed to have *entrée* into every part of the kraal. It is a very unusual privilege to be allowed to walk through the harem. Slaves of both sexes and of all ages and sizes were moving to and fro among the huts.

A new house was being erected for his Majesty, the material being bricks, and the builder an old British tar, a Yorkshireman, named Johnny, who years before, while cruising on the East coast, had suddenly left his ship of his own accord, and found his way to the happier and freer atmosphere of the far interior. Johnny was a genial soul, and a very funny old boy. There he stood slinging mud like a

THE LATEST STYLE IN WOOL.

Thames dredger, and yet in feeling as free and independent as an American senator. He has built the only houses that are worthy the name in Matabeleland.

Many of the Matabele queens were peeping in at the windows of the partially-finished house, and evidently made a good deal of fun of Johnny, who would turn round every now and then and give them the contents of his trowel.

I was astonished to see the interior of a queen's hut which had a cleanly black polished floor, and everything arranged in the tidiest manner. Floors are composed of ant-heaps, cow-dung, and ox-blood,

H

which, when set, becomes very hard. The occupant of this hut showed me how the floor was polished by means of a fine smooth, round pebble, which, held in both hands, was rubbed along the surface, the operator spitting every now and then to supply the necessary moisture. There was a rack on one side of the hut on which were placed numerous baskets and all sorts of little tricks, while against the wall, neatly folded up, were the cane mats on which the dwellers slept. A queen's mark of distinction is unique. All of them shave their heads, and wear at the top, and well at the back, a small inverted cup of about one and a half inches in diameter made of red beads. Round their waists they wear kilts of black ox-hide falling to the knees. The kraal was full of slaves who had been caught during war, and brought to the King by his fighting men.

Some days elapsed before we again visited Lo-ben, so that we had ample time to think over the plans which might be successfully adopted in approaching him with my request. The most feasible seemed to be to present him with a very elaborate silver-mounted sword-knife, and a fine bull.

The day arrived when we should visit the King. We had heard that he was suffering from gout, doubtless through over-indulgence in native beer. He would soon leave for one of his other towns, so Fairbairn and myself again approached, and found him encircled by a multitude of indunas. Preferring to await a favourable opportunity for our request, we sat down beside the monarch. Patience, however, entailed great personal inconvenience. For four weary hours we sat drinking beer, and trying to devour great chunks of beef handed to us upon the royal fork of his Majesty, who, while attending to the orations of his people, was busily engaged in gorging himself with a mass of meat which he held on a fork in his left hand, while with an enormous carving-knife he fanned off the swarming flies. Every now and then Fairbairn took a sly look at me to see what my powers of reception were in the beef-eating line.

Little slave boys, who had only recently been captured, and were nothing but skin and bone, crouched up beside us, and were glad to accept either morsels of beef or drops of beer that we did not want. Gladly enough would I have given them the whole lot, but I was well aware that the better I proved a capacity for eating and drinking the more would savage appreciation smile upon me and favour my designs. The reader therefore may be sure that I tried to be sufficiently omnivorous.

Evidently a case of no slight importance was being heard by Lo-ben. All eyes were riveted upon him, and the facial expressions showed how eager every hearer was to catch even an echo of the weighty words which fell from the monarch's mouth. Occasionally, as he conversed with the assembled indunas, Lo-ben would utter some transcendent expression of infallible wisdom which, when given forth, would get many responsive ejaculations of acquiescence and sympathy.

"Yebo, yebo, Kumalo!" cried the audience. "Ye, hay, hay!" (Yebo means yes. Kumalo is a courtesy title for the royal family. The other exclamations indicate approval.) An oppressive subjection was evident among the crowd. They sat willing, should the potentate so ordain, and without a word of remonstrance, to see their own brothers die the death, for here could be found the most vivid illustration of the axiom, "the King can do no wrong." It was strangely noticeable that all who passed the circle of royalty had to cower to the earth, crouching as though they were about to collapse altogether.

Sunset was approaching, and as everyone excepting those immediately connected with the royal household were bound to be outside by that time I was beginning to fear a further delay, but luckily the crowd dispersed, and as the monarch seemed to be in good humour, Fairbairn deftly put to him the momentous question. A frank permission was the response. I was to be allowed to travel freely through the country. After this I presented Lo-ben the sword-knife, giving him at the same time the promise of a fine bull, for the purchase of which I had already negotiated. "You may go through my country," he said, "but it is very far to the Zambesi."

I thanked him and bade him good-bye.

"Go well, Son of the Sea," was his reply.

I thought this parting benediction of old Lo-ben was far from being devoid of poetry, but strangely enough I soon had other examples of the exaltation in this respect which assuredly characterises this remarkable people.

As I walked along with Fairbairn the far-off western sky blazed resplendently across the heavens its fiery farewell. The reflected glow of its light gave a crimson richness to the dome-topped huts of the royal kraal, and gleamed softly through the jagged spaces of the primitive citadel. The departing sun told that it was time for us to take our leave, and make our way to the outer side of the encircling fence before the "young men" would let the saplings fall so as to unite the two horns of the fortress and make an endless line around the home of the monarch. We had almost reached the wide portals of the enclosure, when suddenly stentorian shouts rent the air, making us pause in our progress. The shouts proceeded from a young warrior who stood in an attitude which reminded one of Ajax defying the lightning, looking a gladiatorial figure shining red in the evening light.

"Inkosa miama!" (black king) he exclaimed, and then continued to shout the following praises which for convenience I will write in English, with the native equivalent :—

"Calf of a black cow!" (Inkoniama inkomo).

"Man eater" (Ihlama doda).

"Lion" (Siluana).

"Thou art as great as the world" (Uena ngaga gelizwe).

"Thou who appeared when men spoke confusedly" (Uvela be vungasa). In times of anarchy.

"Star that shot through the firmament in the day of Zuangandaba!" (Inkanyezi e ya tjega emini gwa Zuangandaba). Zuangandaba was the chief town of Lo-ben's enemies in the time of the civil war, and he conquered it.

"Thou art in the plains" (Uso bala). He did not hide.

"Black mystery" (Indaba emniama).

"Thou who pierceth the sky that is above!" (Ihlabe Zulu elipezulu).

"Calf of the terrible!" (Inkoniama gesilo).

"The letter destroyer" (Usa pula ngwalo).

The word *ngwalo* has reference to a correspondence of Lo-ben and his indunas with Sir T. Shepstone respecting Kuruman, the rightful heir.

"He crossed the great desert!" (Wa dabula Ihalihali).

"The black duck of Umzilagazi!" (Itata elimniama eliga Umzilagazi).

"The black calf of Bulawayo!" (Itoli elimniama la gwa Bulawayo).

Such were the pæans sung lustily at the gate. Fairbairn and myself waited a little to listen, but getting tired of the endless shouts we pushed on homewards, the vehemence of the shouts lessening and dying as we proceeded. At the time when I heard the interpretation of the sentences,

I could not help thinking how barbarously delightful was the poetry of this warlike race. Their songs in laudation of their King were disinterested songs of praise. Perhaps a new Utopia was here, in which love was true and loyalty unselfish.

I was particularly told that the people would come great distances to sing the praises of Lo-ben.

Was there any ulterior motive? The truly disinterested man cannot be found among us whites. Was devotion—so true an attribute of the blacks—and flattery at last sincere?

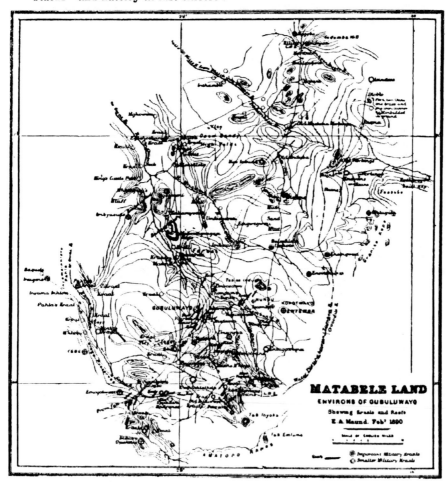

I asked Fairbairn about the matter.

"Oh," was his reply, "the old man gives them *uxuala*."

Bah! that was it. The poetry was gone. Vulgar beer! Not a spark of the divinity of poetry! Henceforth I would not believe in exceptional blacks, but would regard them as ordinary mortals, as plain, practical men, with common cravings, and with modes of gratifying them similar to those of the human family generally.

*   *   *   *   *   *

The kraal or town of Bulawayo is situated on the outer side of a great elliptic enclosure of about half a mile in length, which is entirely occupied by royalty, its adherents, and belongings. Once a year in this immense enclosure a great dance—Inxwala—takes place. It is a national event, and is considered the first and most martial sight in South Africa. The King stands in the centre of his 6000 warriors, who are bedecked with ostrich feather capes and otter skin turbans, their arms being the assegai and the shield. Various warlike evolutions are gone through, such as darting their glistening weapons swift through the air, as all the warriors join, and together tap their shields with rhythmic beat, shouting and singing the while the song of the assegai, and the praises of the great black King.

> "Come and see at Majobana's; come and see!
> Here is the display, display of the assegai!
> Come and see at Majobana's; come and see!"

Then, stamping one foot and pointing the assegai towards the heavens, they exclaim in chorus, "Sh—Shu—Shu," which literally means, "We stamp out—we will conquer!" This they never tire of repeating.

I was told that year after year the number of warriors at this dance is diminishing. Opposing factions have assumed or are assuming proportions which forebode a troublesome future in the reign of the present King. The scions of royalty are not permitted to have very large kraals. Their conduct is often a source of danger. Three months previously to our visit Lo-ben put to death his uncle, Usikuana, and all his kraal, comprising about forty people, a doom which was brought on through the uncle exercising privileges which were only permitted in the royal circle to the King himself.

REGENT OF MATABELELAND

Another massacre which was found to be in order resulted in the merciless annihilation of a number of families. On the death of Umzilagazi, the father of Lo-ben, the body was buried with all the deceased's effects. His wagons and everything he had possessed were thrown into a cave called Ntumbani, which is the name for the grave of a king. Near to this last resting-place of royalty a kraal was erected, and the inhabitants were told to watch the sepulchre that it might not be disturbed. But on burning the high grass to clear the ground for harvest, an evil wind arose, turning the relentless flames towards the grave of the old conqueror until it was licked clean of everything, the ironwork alone remaining to tell the tale of destruction. For such neglect there could be but one punishment. So at early dawn the executioners fell upon the unfortunate watchers, closing their earthly career, and sending their spirits to the crocodile and hippo. Dogs and all were slain.

A writer in a Cape paper about five years ago had the following :—

We found old Lo Bengula sitting on a Zulu chair. The only garment he wore was the " staartriem," a rather diminutive article of dress. The old vagabond is as fat as a pig, and his stomachal region hangs over his knees. It is a sight to see him sit; he always lets his hands rest on his thighs, and sits with his legs wide apart. He was only a short way off from the dancing party, and took great interest in the martial movements of his Indunas. After we had looked with much interest on the scene for about half-an-hour, there suddenly leaped to the front from the ranks a tall yellow Induna, brandishing his spear and other arms about, and addressing the interpreter of the King in a loud voice said : "Ask the King what those white people have come here for !" Old Lo instructed the interpreter to tell him : " These white people have come here on their own authority, and they only come to look on." The excited Induna replied : " Tell the King that I say he lies ; let him leave these three whites to us for a few minutes, just to bathe our spears in their blood ; let him do this ; then we shall be convinced that he loves us more than the whites." Old Lo Ben was about to burst with anger, and it was a horrible sight to see his ugly eyes rolling about. He replied to the impudent Induna : " You may have those three whites (the correspondent, Grobler, and Mackenzie), but you must first go to the Gold Fields and Diamond Fields, and wash your spears in the blood of all the whites there, exterminate them every- where, and when you have finished your work you can have these three whites too." The malicious Induna did not say another word, and the dancing went on. If the King did not like whites, because he gets many presents from them, we would certainly have been killed. But I would not trust too much to the old chap, for he, too, is an old rascal, and it does not take much to set the lot aflame, as the Kafirs are ripe for mischief. In the olden days it was an easy matter to get on with that tribe. It hap- pened once that a Boer hunter, nicknamed Hans Dons, got amongst them, and was made to stay some time at the kraal of the then King, Mosilikatse, a very cruel tyrant. The natives were at that time not so familiar with firearms as they since have become, and by shooting a bullock for them now and then—for he was not over-supplied with ammunition—he passed for a very big warrior indeed. One evening the Kafirs were " amusing " themselves by throwing live coals at each other, which they took from a big fire round which they feasted. Mosilikatse asked Hans Dons if he could do the same. He said that he could do better, as he would throw the embers of the fire without using any hands, but merely by a *muti* (charm). So he took some of his scanty gun- powder, tied it up in a rag and dropped it in the fire. When it exploded it sent the embers and all the burning fuel flying in all directions over the Kafirs and huts, setting fire to a great many of the latter ; and as a reward for his superior witchcraft, Hans Dons was promoted to the post of Wizard-in-Chief to the King. He lived in clover, as it were, for some time, till he was one day called upon to furnish rain, it being a very dry season. Should he fail, his punishment was to marry an old hag of a Kafir woman ! Under pretence that he wanted a big water-maker's head he ordered the whole body guard of the King away to the Zambesi, and sent others, whom he did not fancy, in different northward directions. When the coast was clear he made tracks southward, ordering everything he wanted on his authority as Chief Wizard. The rain came whilst he was on his way to the Transvaal, and was doubtless ascribed by the natives to his intervention.

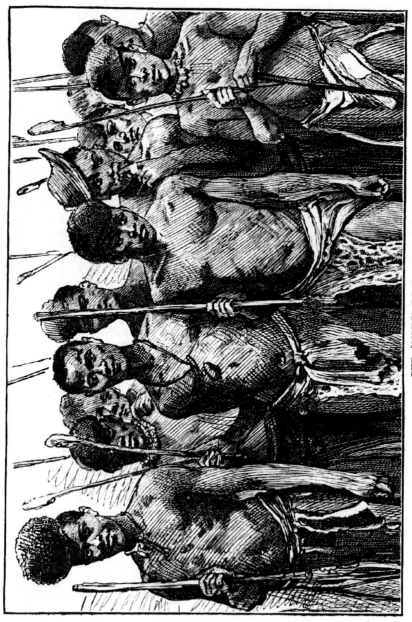

THE IMBEZI REGIMENT.

Mr. F. Johnson, in the course of a description of a visit to the King, once said: "Of course the whole of the Matabeles are very superstitious, and strongly believe in witchcraft and rain-making. The King has the reputation of being a remarkably good hand at making a thunderstorm, and in this he gives way to no man. I remember one day in June—the one month in the whole year in which you least expect rain—some natives had brought a large python into camp, and were singing some of their rain songs. It is sudden death to any native in Matabeleland who, if he sees a python, does not by some means or other manage to secure it and bring it in alive. The King took possession of the reptile, and said he must go and make rain. I laughed at this, and said I did not think he could do so, to which the King replied, 'You will see.' The python was skinned alive, its liver taken out and cooked, and the usual rain-making rites performed. Curiously enough, just before sundown the sky clouded over, and soon afterwards one of the heaviest thunderstorms I had ever seen broke over the place. Next morning the King asked me if a white man could make a thunderstorm like that? I said, 'No, King; if we could get you down amongst the farmers in the Karoo we could guarantee you a fortune.' Subsequently I found the key to this wonderful rain-making. The King has devoted much time and attention to watching the clouds and other forecasts of the weather, and has been well instructed in this by the old people. He never attempts to make rain unless he sees that it is pretty certain rain is about to come. For instance, if the wind veers round and blows three days from the west it is almost a certainty that there will be rain on the fourth day. The people do not know all this, but the King does, and accordingly succeeds in maintaining his reputation for skill in that particular art."

Mr. Thompson, who was with Mr. Maguire and Mr. Rudd at Lo Bengula's kraal obtaining the famous concession, was interviewed by a London pressman, and said some things about life at Lo Bengula's kraal which, whether they be truth or fiction, afford startling enough reading:—

"First, Mr. Thompson, give us a picture of Lo Bengula himself."

"Lo Bengula? You would not easily forget him if once you saw him. He stands six feet in his skin, and he is fat and big all over, and he weighs about twenty stone. In age he is forty-eight or fifty. He walks as I have seen no other man walk, before or since; moving his elephant limbs, and planting his feet one after the other as if he was planting them for ever; and rolling his shoulders from side to side, and looking round him in a way which is dreadful to see. He has great, bulging, blood-shot eyes, and when he rolls them to look you up and down, in his lordly sort of way, I tell you it's enough to scare a man off-hand. His palace, you must know, is a wagon that somebody has given him. There he used to sit, on a block of wood in the middle of a great pole stockade, surrounded by hundreds of sheep and goats. Every yard of the ground is covered with dung, layer over layer, and the whole place is filthily dirty. When you approach the King, of course you have to squat down on your haunches, and remain in that position during the whole of the interview."

* * * * * * * *

"He is a truculent fellow, King Lo Bengula, by all accounts?"

"I tell you he is deadly cruel. He will inflict torture or death on the slightest pretext. Matabele customs lend themselves to that sort of thing; the 'smelling out,' for instance, at the Nwalo—that's the big yearly dance in February. On the appearance of the new moon, the whole nation comes together, and thousands of warriors dance this dance for a whole afternoon, and also feast in detachments. There is a great slaughter of cattle for the occasion. The men dance in a long line, standing about six deep, and waving sticks and spears headed with cat-tails, which resemble waving maize. The women dance opposite them in another body. A weird, crooning chant goes on all the time, and now and again a warrior will step forward a little and stab with his assegai at the ground, representing any killing which he may have done that year. Amid deafening yells, he stabs and twists his weapon round in the body of his imaginary foe. To crown the performance, Lo Bengula stalks forth, and the warriors form into the famous Zulu horns, and throw themselves round their chief. Afterwards Lo Ben goes through a sort of cleansing—a purely ceremonial sort of cleansing, being solemnly bathed with a special sort of 'broth.' The next day is given up to beer drinking—and when the Matabele are drunk, I can tell you it's a pretty bad sight. They are not angels when sober; but when they reel about drunk——"

Words failed Mr. Thompson to describe the drunken Matabele.

"This is a great occasion," he went on presently, "for the 'smelling-out' performance. About four of the head doctors go through a hankey-pankey with 'the bones' (knuckles of all sorts of creatures, some human), in order to detect wizards. Wizards are people against whom they or the King have a grudge. And they sing to Lo Bengula, 'Oh, thou King of all kings, Father of the Sun, Ruler of the Skies and Rains, who will cause Rains to come or keep away—who so great a king?—and cattle to cover all the hills! O thou Son of the Black Cow! We konza (that is, bow) before Thee, to show what wizards have been at work to destroy Thy power!' Then it's short work with the wizards."

"Ah, yes, Lo Ben is cruel," pursued Mr. Thompson, meditatively. "I remember once, when I was waiting for an audience, I saw a man brought in who was guilty of having drunk some of the King's beer. It was at the time of the great dance, when for a month there is a special licence, and when anyone carrying beer about is liable to have it raided. But this man had levied toll on the King's beer, when it was being carried by the King's women. The poor wretch was brought before the King. He was horribly afraid. His eyes stuck out of his head, and his knees knocked together as he tried to make obeisance. The King bade them hold him fast, then he said, looking the culprit up and down, 'You have a nose and a mouth, and two ears, and two eyes. You have used your nose to smell King's beer—(turning to attendants)—cut off his nose!' They cut off the man's nose. 'You have used your mouth to drink King's beer: cut off his mouth!' They cut off the man's lips. He was a horrid sight. Lo Bengula waited a moment. Then he said deliberately: 'You have heard that it is not allowed to drink King's beer; but your ears are no good to you.' Off went the poor wretch's ears. He looked at the King with a look dreadful to see. 'Your eyes—cover up his eyes!' shouted the King. 'Put his forehead over his eyes that they may not see King's beer!' and they cut the forehead of the man, and turned down the flap of skin as a surgeon might turn it, so that it hung over his eyes. Then the King looked at the man for a few minutes, and the man grovelled before him in the dung; until suddenly the King fell into a rage—perhaps he was ashamed of himself—and bade them beat the man with logs of wood. They beat him within an inch of his life. Last, the poor wretch mustered strength to crawl away, like a broken snake, along the ground; and he went and lay under a wagon until nightfall. Then he crept down to the stream to bathe his wounds. He came close past my wagon, and you never saw such a ghastly sight as he was. The flap of skin hung over his eyes, but it was dried and stark."

But I prefer Mr. E. A. Maund as an authority on any question connected with Lo Bengula. This gentleman has several times visited Bulawayo on important missions, and as I have said, he is a great favourite with the King. He has been of much kindly assistance to me in the preparation of this work, and I may here give some of his statements bearing upon our present subject, and made in answer to questions put to him :—" Lieut. Haynes, R.E., and Lieut. Stokes, R.A., and I went up in 1885 to acquaint Lo Bengula with the protectorate that had been declared over his foe, the Bechuana chief Khama, as a rumour was about that he was coming down to attack Khama. We were to tell him to have hands off; he wrote a letter saying he would be friendly with Khama, and he has acted up to it. I have never seen Lo Bengula drunk. When a certain white man had been on the boose for a week, he said to me, ' Maundy, a man should never get drunk during the day, but wait for the night, and then get drunk in his hut with his women.' Lo Bengula is neither short nor tall; he looks shorter than he is, because of his great obesity. He is something of the proportions of Cetewayo, only not quite so big. He has got sore eyes, probably from the smoke in his hut, and I have often for weeks doctored them ; it is a sort of epidemic among the natives, and it is worse in the cold weather when they have fires than at any other time. This gives him what people call a cruel look, but on closer observation I believe it to be due to this weakness of the eyes."

" Is he personally a cruel man ? "

" No. You see, he has to rule by fear, and you can't have half measures with savages. He was made king rather against his will. Naturally, by instincts, he is a farmer, delighting in his cattle, and I believe he would sooner be leading a farmer's life than that of a king. He has got rid of men who were plotting, or whom he thought were doing so, against him. King Lo Bengula is by no means so black as he is painted (I mean in character). I must differ from those who say he is ' deadly cruel.' We must not judge him by our standard. He has to rule a turbulent people, who do not know the value of life. Speaking one day to me of killing, he said, ' You see, you white men have prisons, and can lock a man up safely. I have not. What am I to do ? When a man would not listen to orders, I used to have his ears cut off as being useless; but whatever their punishment they frequently repeated the offence.

Now I warn them—and then a knobkerried man never repeats his offence.' This, for a savage, was fairly logical. It may appear to us cruel ; but remember how short a time it is since we hanged for sheep-stealing, and certainly the savage execution with the knob-kerrie is not so revolting, and is less painful than a civilised execution refined with electricity. A blow on the back of the head, and all is over. Lo Bengula is very hospitable to white men, and likes them always about him. He is, in my opinion, much more adapted to a farmer's life—being very fond of his cattle—than to

MR. E. A. MAUND.

ruling the crew he does. As a young man, he was a keen sports-man, but is now too grossly fat to get on a horse. Though his head kraal has the sinister name of 'Gubulawayo,' or the 'place of killing,' yet all that sort of thing has much toned down, and one sees little of such horrors. Lo Bengula is far too refined to orna-ment the approach to his kraal with human heads, as chiefs do further removed from civilisation. Notwithstanding all the malicious reports to the contrary, the King and people have kept to their promises of friendship to the English, and acted up to their engagements. The Matabeles have great respect for the missionaries, who, though they have done very little in the way of conversion, yet by their example have done much in the way of teaching the natives house-building and to till their gardens, besides being of service as doctors. Like all native races the Matabele has great respect for the medicine man. On one occasion at Mabuquswai, a Matabele town of truculent fellows, the natives were somewhat rude to me in '88. I said I would be revenged, and when I returned with the Indunas, the young men came in hundreds to be doctored. To one and all I gave a good jalap pill. On again visiting the town I was received with great affection. But talking of the King, he has done very cruel acts undoubtedly, but kings' characters are to be judged by the policy they have been forced to pursue. His nation is a marauding one by instinct as well as tradition, killing those they have come in contact with for the sake of their cattle. I have now paid him three long visits at a very trying time, and I must say that throughout he has behaved splendidly to the white men. I only judge him by his acts. Constantly he used to send me oxen and sheep, keeping me supplied with them for months. Whenever any white man comes up to his kraal, there is always Kafir beer to be drunk, and very often he supplies them with rough bits of meat to eat."

" Would you call Lo Bengula a sincere man ? "

" He is not to be compared with Khama. They are as different as light from dark. Khama is in his way a charming man and also a Christian, but then he has had the benefits of education which the other man has not. He has lived with traders and missionaries who have had civilising influences over him. Lo Bengula is essentially a savage despot. He is all supreme—if he says a man has to die, he has to without a trial. His great idea in dealing with white men is to set them at variance in order to hear what they say about each other. From this, undoubtedly, he has got the name of being very insincere. There is no doubt he is grasping; he likes to get all he can out of the white men. He has not seen enough of the white men, and those he has had any connection with he looks upon not as food for plunder, but as being there for what they can get out of him. People are too rash in saying he is insincere, for he has been very considerate throughout with Englishmen, whom he admires as hunters and for their straightforwardness. He knows the difference between a Boer and an Englishman immediately. He has got the idea of getting the best out of everything. He cannot go by our laws as to what is upright, as to signing his name and so forth. I have seen men knocked on the head as witches; but that you cannot call cruelty, for we used to burn for witchcraft less than a hundred years ago. I attended a niece of the King, she having had a finger bitten off in a fight, and Lo Bengula had the woman who did it killed, as he did not believe it could have been cured else. Lo Bengula is like all natives and savages, whom you have to keep well in hand, and always before you to see that they do not do anything which they will chuckle over afterwards when they have got the best of you. I believe he is very sincere in his friendship to white men, and I daresay to his own natives. For instance, he promised to befriend us, and has never attacked Khama since '85, though he could have done so constantly. He promised to let the expedition go in, and he did so. It is difficult for a man in London to judge him; you must judge him by his surroundings and take into consideration his good sterling points, of which he has many. He has always behaved well to the white men."

CHAPTER VI.

BECHUANALAND.—THE BOERS AND THEIR WESTERN BORDER.—THE
DISPUTED TERRITORY.—KHAMA'S SUMMARY OF THE SITUATION.
—HIS DESCRIPTION OF HIS COUNTRY.—KHAMA AMONG HIS
PEOPLE.—A MODEL CHIEF.—PALAPYE.

AS it is through that country that the railway to Matabeleland
runs, some account of Bechuanaland, or, at least, of that
portion of the British Protectorate known as Khama's
country, should be given here. The progress of the Crown
Colony is described in the periodical reports of the Administrator.
Bechuanaland is a vast territory, with good vegetation, though
little surface water. As far north as Kanya it may be said to be
mountainless. There is a scarcity of water between the Orange
and Modder Rivers, but there is reason to believe that in
Bechuanaland a very good water supply lies below the sedimental
crust of limestone all over the country. It is a very fine grazing
land, farmers already doing well there, and recent reports speak
very favourably of its mineral deposits. Vryburg has, in consequence of Sir Charles Warren's report, become the centre of
Government for the district. Mafeking, to which the railway
is being pushed forward from Vryburg, was the headquarters
of Warren's forces. It was the chief town of Montsioa, and
the site of the Bethell fight and murder. Besides the native
town, which is extremely picturesque, there is a very thriving
white town, the headquarters of the Bechuanaland Police,
under Colonel Carrington. This town is doing a very good
trade, and when the Malmani Gold Fields were opened (not
twenty miles distant) affairs were very busy there. And, doubtless, they will be so again when the railway reaches the town
and it is once more opened up on a sound commercial basis.
Forty miles from Mafeking broken country is reached, and at Molopololo there is Sechele's town. There is a stretch of dryish
country extending across to the now deserted Shoshong, the
Molopololo having water only in pools during the dry season, and
the desert wells on the western route not serving for heavy transport purposes. There is undoubtedly plenty of water westward
in the Kalahari, but it is too far off the route to be of service on it.
Some correspondence took place between the Imperial Govern-

THE FIRST LOCOMOTIVE TO CROSS THE VAAL RIVER.

ment and the Government of the South African Republic respecting
the boundary line dividing the Transvaal and Bechuanaland. Its
nature may be gathered from one of the despatches, one from
Lord Knutsford to Sir Hercules Robinson :—

Downing Street, January 31, 1889.

SIR,—I have the honour to acknowledge the receipt of your despatch
of the 18th of December, enclosing a translation of a despatch from the
State Secretary of the South African Republic, in which exception is taken
to the intimation made by you to the Government of the Republic in
September and October, 1887, that the eastern limit of the Bechuanaland
Protectorate, to the northward of part of the territory of the South
African Republic, would be fixed at a line running from the Limpopo
River along the meridian 29·20 E. longitude, and it is stated that that
Government objects to acknowledge a British Protectorate eastward of
the 27th meridian E.

ON THE LIMPOPO.

The South African Republic considers itself entitled to object to the
extension of the Protectorate now under discussion beyond the 27th
meridian of east longitude on the same grounds as those on which it
considers that it is entitled to take exception to the recent declaration
that Matabeleland and Mashonaland are within the sphere of British
influence; and in the despatch which I have addressed to you, in reply
to your despatch of December 19, I have conveyed to you a general
expression of the views and policy of Her Majesty's Government, which
covers the present question of the boundary of the actual Protectorate as
well as the more general question of the extension of British influence to
the whole region lying northwards of the Transvaal. It should, however, be further observed to the Government of the South African
Republic that their objection to that part of the Protectorate which lies
to the eastward of longitude 27 as inclosing the Republic on a large
portion of its northern boundary might equally have been extended to
those parts of the Protectorate which lie east of the 26th meridian of

longitude, since those parts also lie to the northward of portions of the Transvaal Territory.

The existence of the Protectorate is, in fact, in no greater degree a bar to the prosecution, within the protected area, of lawful enterprise by burghers of the South African Republic, than is the extension of British influence to Matabeleland. Neither the Protectorate nor the sphere of influence has been declared in a spirit of unfriendliness to the South African Republic, nor from a desire to exclude its burghers from travelling or carrying on legitimate enterprise in those territories in common with British subjects and others, and after obtaining the consent of the native chiefs.

I agree with you, therefore, that, looking to the interval that has elapsed, as well as to the fact that the Protectorate has been explained · to the chiefs concerned, the present request of the Government of the South African Republic that the Bechuanaland Protectorate should be bounded to the eastward by the 27th meridian of east longitude, cannot be entertained.

I have, &c.,

(Signed)　　KNUTSFORD.

Needless to say, the " request " remained unfulfilled.

The country lying between the Shashi and Macloutsie Rivers is claimed both by Khama, as belonging to his country, and by Lo Bengula, as belonging to Matabeleland. For the moment it is known as the " Disputed Territory." As giving a very good insight into the questions in dispute between the neighbouring kings, and also as exhibiting his views on the drink question, I may here print a very interesting letter written by Khama to Sir Sidney Shippard, the Deputy Commissioner, Bechuanaland Protectorate :—

My Friend,

I beg to thank you for your letter of February 20th acknowledging mine of February 6th.

I was glad to find enclosed, for my information, a copy of a letter which, with sanction of his Excellency the High Commissioner, you had addressed to Messieurs J. G. Wood, Chapman, and Francis, and also of a Proclamation therein referred to.

It has made my heart very glad indeed to receive your Honour's assurance that the law will be rigorously enforced against all persons who attempt to stir up strife between Lo Bengula and myself on any pretext whatsoever, and that under no circumstances will Her Majesty's Government tolerate any renewal in the British Protectorate of the filibustering raids which were for so long the curse· of Bechuanaland.

It is easy for me most gladly to assure your Honour of my readiness to do anything that can reasonably be asked of me to preserve friendly relations with Lo Bengula or with any of my neighbours, because I do earnestly desire to live in peace. So very far from me is any hostile spirit towards Lo Bengula and his people that because of your Honour's request I have given my consent to Mr. Stromboom to go in with two wagons to the Matabele from the firm of Messrs. W. C. Francis and Clark, although it is well known to me that the larger part of these loads will be rifles and ammunition.

I am ready to do almost anything for the sake of keeping up peaceful

I

On the Limpopo River. admirable fishing here. Barbel Bream & Crocodiles.

relations with Lo Bengula, short of placing at risk the rights and possessions and lives of my people, but I should be guilty of wilfully sacrificing all these if I were willingly to give my consent to Lo Bengula's being allowed to extend the borders of his country all the way to the Macloutsie River.

Your Honour quite misunderstands the concession I have granted to Messrs. Johnson and Heany. I have not made any concession of debatable land. But I have given the right to Messrs. Johnson and Heany to prospect for gold throughout my country, at the same time making a distinct request privately that they would confine their search for the present, and until such time as might enable the Rev. J. R. Moffat to arrange with Lo Bengula a satisfactory boundary, to this side of the Macloutsie River. This they have promised to do.

I have been most wishful to avoid doing anything to cause complications or to give Lo Bengula unnecessary offence, and more especially not to embarrass the Rev. J. S. Moffat in his difficult mission to Lo Bengula. But it was Messrs. Wood, Chapman, and Francis who went to ask from Lo Bengula the Shashi and Macloutsie country, because they had asked it from me they say, and I have refused to have anything to say to them about it.

They neither hesitate to embarrass Mr. Moffat's mission nor to bring me into war with Lo Bengula. Then, again, I made an offer of my country to Sir Charles Warren in May, 1885, which your Honour informed me in March, 1886, Her Majesty's Government felt themselves unable to recommend the Queen to accept. Your Honour will permit me to point out that it is not the same thing to offer my country to

KHAMA.

Her Majesty to be occupied by English settlers, Her Majesty's subjects governed by Her Majesty's Ministers, and to allow men so worthless and unscrupulous in their characters as Messrs. Wood, Chapman, and Francis to come outside of all Governments and occupy my country and put up their drink canteens and flood my country with their drink after all the long struggle I have made against it, withstanding my people at the risk of my life, and just when they have themselves come to see how great a salvation my drink laws have proved to be. It were better for me that I should lose my country than that it should be flooded with drink.

Nothing has so startled me in your Honour's letter as your Honour's words about "the claims of the rival grantees." I admit no claims of rival grantees. Especially, on no account whatever will I admit or consent to hear of claims of Messrs. Wood, Chapman, and Francis.

Messrs. Johnson and Heany clearly understand that they are not at liberty to search for gold between Shashi and Macloutsie Rivers, until such time as the country has been acknowledged to belong to me. But then, when the righteousness of my claims have been acknowledged, they have my promise that they shall be allowed to make the first search in that portion also of my country, subject only to any advice or instructions which I might receive from His Excellency the High Commissioner.

Personally, I have nothing against Mr. F. P. Swinburne, but it is not right when Lo Bengula has flatly refused to give him any concession in the Matabele country, which he asked for distinctly, and distinctly named the Ramokwabane River, to accept in its place, and because he has lost the Tati, a gift from Lo Bengula of country which he well knew did not belong to that chief.

Perhaps I ought to explain to your Honour as I explained to Sir Charles Warren, that I am living upon the southern border of my country, not from choice, but because my troubles have hitherto prevented me from carrying out my purpose to remove my town to one of two places where there is an abundance of water for my people and our cattle. At present, with our town situated where it is, we depend entirely upon the rainfall for our gardens. At the Chwapong Hills, which lie east of the Matabele road and down the Macloutsie River, or again at Sernë, which lies west of the Matabele road and up the Macloutsie River, are the two places which we hope to remove to one or other of, and to allow Lo Bengula to come to Macloutsie would be like a man encouraging a lion to come and live among his cattle.

Then it is well known to me that the Matabele wish to leave their present country and cross the Zambesi River, and it is in their plan to make a great raid upon my cattle when they go.

The Matoka have prepared canoes for this purpose, and invite the Matabele to come and assist them against the Barutse.

Liwanika, the Chief of the Barutse, knows of this, and wrote to me last year to ask advice. He has just written to me again. He says: " I understand that you are now under the protection of the Queen of the English people. I do not know what it means. But they say there are soldiers living at your place, and some headman sent by the Queen to take care of you and protect you from the Matabele. Tell me all as a friend. Are you happy and quite satisfied? Are not the ways and laws of the white people burdensome to you? Tell me all. I am anxious that you should tell me very plainly, your friend, because I have a great desire to be received like you under the protection of so great a ruler as the Queen of England."

Your Honour has overlooked my request to put a notice in the press, warning the public against investing their money in Companies which promise great things in the country between Shashi and Macloutsie. It is my wish the public should be warned if your Honour sees no great objection to it. I enclose a signed notice for the press. If your Honour approves of it, will you kindly cause it to be forwarded for me to the *Diamond Fields Advertiser*, the *Cape Times*, and the *Cape Argus*, and to any other equally important papers you may think it is desirable to include with the above-named three, and I will pay the necessary expenses incurred in giving such notice,

Your Honour says, "If you agree so far as you and your people are concerned, to entrust to me the settlement of the whole question relating to the country between the Tati, the Shashi, and the Macloutsie Rivers, and will promise beforehand to abide by whatever I decide on, I will endeavour to come to a satisfactory understanding, both with the English concessionaires and with Lo Bengula."

We black people cannot take such a great step in the dark as that would be for me to take, without more knowledge of the likely results than I have, for I have absolutely none. What if I found you had given the whole country right up to the Macloutsie to the chief of the Matabele? That would be to bring the lion to the very door of my hut. My people would never forgive such an act of folly on my part, and they would never give their consent to my act. On the other hand, what if I found you had given Messrs. Wood, Chapman, and Francis the country, for they claim to have bought it all for ninety-nine years? Then I should be overwhelmed with drink.

I fear Lo Bengula less than I fear brandy.

I fought Lo Bengula when he had his father's great warriors from Natal, and drove him back, and he never came again, and God who helped me then would help me again.

Lo Bengula never gives me a sleepless night. But to fight against drink is to fight against demons, and not against men. I dread the white man's drink more than all the assegais of the Matabele, which kill men's bodies, and is quickly over, but drink puts devils into men, and destroys both their souls and their bodies for ever. Its wounds never heal.

I pray your Honour never to ask me to open even a little door to the drink, and Francis desires that, and always has desired it. That has been my constant battle with the firm of W. C. Francis and Clark.

       With greetings and good wishes, I remain, &c.,

               KHAMA, Chief of the Bamangwato.

NOTICE.

I, Khama, Chief of the Bamangwato tribe, at Shoshong, do hereby give notice that the tract of country between the Shashi and Macloutsie Rivers is debatable land, and the subject of negotiation between Lo Bengula, Chief of the Matabele, and myself, and that I protest against the action of all persons prospecting or commencing mining operations in that district, and will not hold myself responsible for any loss which may result from premature outlay, which it may be necessary eventually to disallow.   (Signed),   KHAMA.

Shoshong, March 7, 1888.

Some people consider that Lo Bengula's claim to the Disputed Territory is as unfounded as was the right of the Boers to the country up to the Zambesi, simply because they proclaimed it. On the other hand, competent authorities are of opinion that the Matabele Monarch's claim to the territory which forms the bone of contention is a good one. The report of the British Mission in 1885, to Lo Bengula, to discuss the question, said, "Lo Bengula acknowledged that he had no title to the country except that of Umsilikazi's conquest, and by saying, 'formerly Khama had no country,' he tacitly admits that now Khama has." The report also expressed the opinion that he, Lo Bengula, would have no objection to laying down the boundary, and conceding all Khama wants, if it was on the plea that Englishmen lived on the other side of the boundary. At the deliberations between himself and the British Mission, in 1885, Lo Bengula persisted that Khama had no country. Mr. Helm reminded the King of a letter he himself had written for him when Mr. Vermaark had appealed to him against Khama. At that time he practically acknowledged the Macloutsie River as the frontier. Mr. Vermaark had killed ostriches south of the Macloutsie River, and Khama, for the offence, took his horses and donkeys away. Vermaark said he had Lo Bengula's permission. On his appealing to Lo Bengula, the latter wrote (by Mr. Helm) to Khama for an explanation. Khama answered. "I punished him because the act was committed in my country." Lo Bengula then wrote, asking, "How far does that go?" Khama answered, "The country in which you live, if it comes to that." Lo Bengula took this answer in good part, treating it rather as a joke, and a sort of tacit understanding was come to that the Macloutsie River should be recognised as the boundary line. Lo Bengula remembered the letter, but said Khama only hunted and lived in that country on sufferance.

When Khama came under British Protectorate he described his country in a letter as follows :—

I, Khama, Chief of the Bamangwato, with my younger brothers and heads of my town, express my gratitude at the coming of the messengers of the Queen of England, and for the announcement to me of the Protectorate which has been established by the desire of the Queen, and which has come to help the law of the Bamangwato also. I give thanks for the words of the Queen, which I have heard, and I accept of (receive) the friendship and protection of the Government of England within the Bamangwato country.

Further I give to the Queen to make laws and to change them in the country of the Bamangwato, with reference to both black and white. Nevertheless I am not baffled in the Government of my own town, or in deciding cases among my own people according to custom ; but again I do not refuse help in these offices. Although this is so, I have to say that there are certain laws of my country which the Queen of England finds in operation, and which are advantageous for my people, and I wish that these laws should be established, and not taken away by the Government of England. I refer to our law concerning intoxicating drinks, that they should not enter the country of the Bamangwato whether among black people or white people. I refer further to our law which declares that the lands of the Bamangwatos are not saleable. I say this law also is good ; let it be upheld, and continued to be law among black people and white people.

My country has got known boundary lines :—

On the east the boundary line is that of the Transvaal going with the Limpopo until the Tolo River joins it. The Tolo is then the boundary ; but I come back to Makobe's Hill, and then go along the villages of the Malakala, who live between me and the Matabele ; from thence to the Gwai River till it falls into the Zambesi ; then I ascend the Zambesi till where it is joined by the Chobe ; then I go with the Chobe, and with the Malabi, and (with) Tamalakan and the Botlebi, till you come to Monomoato ; then the line crosses over and |makes for Gaina, and Selabi, and Monkatuse, and Goodiva, and Khami, and thence to Tsitle, which is between Lopepi and Boatlanami; then it makes for Lotlaka and Lelwala and Mogonono, including the grazing ground of these plains; thence it proceeds to the Limpopo, where the Ngotwane joins it. The word which I hear speaks about 22° as shown in maps ought to be taken away. I do not express thanks for it. It speaks of nothing which has existence. Boundary line there is none at 22°. It is to cut my country into two. But I say, is not this a word spoken before my boundaries were known? On account of matters of this description, and to make known to the Queen the largeness of the country which is now under her protection, I put in a map in which it is tried to show with correctness the boundaries of the Bamangwato. My people enjoy three things in our country; they enjoy their cultivated lands, and their cattle stations, and their hunting grounds. We have lived through these three things. Certainly the game will come to an end in the future, but at present it is in my country, and while it is still there I hold that it ought to be hunted by my people. I know that the help and protection of the Queen requires money, and I agree that that money should be paid by the country protected. I have thought how this can be done; I mean plans which can be thought out at the beginning so that the Queen's people may all be pleased—the black people and the white people. I propose that a certain country of known dimension should be mine and my people's for our cultivated fields and our cattle stations as I have shown in the map. Then I say, with reference to all the country that remains, I wish that the English people should come and live in it, that they should turn it into their cultivated fields and cattle stations. What I wish to explain is, that my people must not be prevented from hunting in all the country, except where the English shall have come to dwell. My people shall be stopped by cultivated lands and the cattle stations of the English inhabitants of the country. I speak this in effect inviting the English because it is a nation with which we have become acquainted, and with whose ways we have had pleasure. Then I request that the Queen's Government appoint a man to take charge of this matter, and let the protection of this country come from the English who will settle in it. I am of opinion that the country which I give over will exceed in value the cost of the Protectorate among the Bamangwato. But I feel that I am speaking to gentlemen of the Government of England. Shall I be afraid that they will requite me with witchcraft (deception leading to ruin)? Rather may I not hope that they may see both sides of the question of to-day, that they will regard the protection, and then regard also the country which I now say is theirs? That which I am also willing to contribute is to make due arrangements for the country of the lands and cattle stations of the Bamangwato, whether as to roads, or bridges, or schools, or other suitable objects. And further, I shall be ready along with my people to go out, all of us, to fight for the country alongside the English; to stop those who attack, or to go after them on the spoor of stolen stock. Further, I expect that the English people who come into the country shall protect it and fight for it, having provided themselves with horse and gun for this purpose. Having done this, without doubt, if there came a great difficulty, we would appeal for the help of our Queen in England. The right kind of English settler in the country will be seen by his doings on his place. Some may make themselves out to be settlers for a time only, while they are killing game, after which they would take their departure with what they had collected, having done nothing with their place. Therefore, I propose that it be enacted that the English settler who newly arrives should build his house and cultivate his lands, and show himself to be a true settler and worker, and not a travelling trader. Those who shall be received in the country, to become settlers in it, ought to be approved by the officer of the Queen appointed to this work; and I add, let us work together, let me also approve of those who are received.

Khama is recognised as paramount Chief over the whole of the Bamangwato tribe, except a small section. He rules the tribe more by kindness than severity. He is probably the best example of what a black man can become by means of a good disposition and early training in Christianity. The Bamangwatos are located in three large divisions. The first, till recently, lived at Shoshong and number 20,000. The position of the town had been chosen more for security against the Matabeles than for convenience. The water supply, which had been failing gradually for years, had become quite inadequate for the town. Crowds of women were to be seen all day and at night waiting for the precious fluid to trickle out of the sand. The town was overcrowded, dirty, and ill built; it was the largest native town in South Africa. Khama had 300 horsemen and 3,000 to 4,000 men for the defence of the place. He and his people have now removed to Palapye. The second division live in the Chopong Hills about 60 miles east of Shoshong. These are a large range stretching from the Palatchi Slopes to the Limpopo River. It is a most fertile and well-watered region. The Bachopong people are scattered over this large district in numerous towns, and very little is known of them. The third division is found on the Limpopo at Selika's town. Their numbers do not probably exceed 5,000.

The Bamangwatos have fought successfully against the Matabeles. Their weapon is the gun, with which they are badly armed. Their chief security from Matabele invasion has hitherto consisted in the dispersion of their enormous herds of cattle all over the country, where they lie hidden in the bush, and further in the secrecy with which they have concealed the existence of water along the road leading to Matabeleland.

Khama is a tall, thin, spare man, a little over fifty, completely clothed in European fashion, his features expressive of great refinement and intelligence, so much so, indeed, that he is a perfect type of a man who can indicate to us of what the South African native is capable in the shape of high racial development. Khama has the most remarkable history of any chief in South Africa. When quite a lad he was carefully trained by the Rev. Robert Moffat and his son, John Moffat, the missionaries, in the truths of Christianity. At 18 years of age he was commanded by his father, Sekomo, to take a second wife; but this, of course, was repugnant to the principles of the faith he had adopted, and he steadfastly refused to do so. He is greatly assisted in the government of his people by Mr. Hepburn, a very able Scotch missionary who has great influence over the King. Polygamy is not known in the country, the practices of witchcraft and smelling out have been abolished, as well as all other heathen customs; the system of trial by jury has been introduced, and even the poorest subject is not convicted of any offence charged against him unless the most convincing evidence is submitted by his accusers. All those of Khama's people who may be described as the middle and upper classes, are dressed like Europeans; they attend the Church services regularly, and conduct themselves in all the relations of life in as peaceable and orderly a fashion as any white civilised community. It is right to remember that much of the good work by the Rev. John Mackenzie in the country is to-day reflected in Khama's territory. Khama's *bête noir* is strong drink. Not only are his

KHAMA SENTENCING A NATIVE TO DEATH FOR MURDER.

subjects forbidden to taste, touch, or handle, but no white man living in his country is allowed to have any kind of intoxicating liquor in his possession.

Of the many laudatory and appreciative articles written about Khama, one from the pen of Mrs. Knight Bruce, in "Murray's Magazine," may be extracted from. It is partially based on Mr. Mackenzie's work, "Ten Years North of the Orange River."

"The wagons need not be watched now; we crossed into Khama's country last night, and none of his people will take anything."

The speaker was one of the Bechuanaland Border Police, and though our thoughts went off to traditions of a simple if a little mead-sodden England, we ourselves were standing by a struggling veld fire, near the 22nd parallel of south latitude, our wagons outspanned for the day at Selindia, the last water on our road before a trek of thirty-two miles into Shoshong. For a fortnight after leaving Mafeking, the frontier town of British territory, we had been slowly creeping north behind the undulating horns of an ox-team; our road a track of soft red sand, our outlook the immense grass-flats of Bechuanaland with their camel-thorn trees, mohatla bush and ant-heaps, the monotony broken here and there by strikingly beautiful, almost trossachs-like scenery.

From the tropical "River of Good Signs," as Vasco da Gama in his delight named the Zambesi, Bechuanaland reaches down to Griqualand West, and almost to the eminently European Diamond Fields.

To see Khama had been a reason for our journey. Coming nearer by many thousand miles to this African Chief, his reputation only gained; the Administrator and Sir Frederick Carrington (Commandant Bechuanaland Border Police), travellers, traders, and hunters all spoke of Khama with respect, some even with friendship. "Of Khama's splendid character," wrote one, "I cannot speak too highly."

Meanwhile he had become a more prominent man. He had extended English influence, he was ruling loyally to his new Suzerain a country that borders on our own and on the Transvaal, that is believed to contain gold-bearing strata, and through which pass the great trade-routes to the Zambesi and the north. Commercially and politically in the world of Africa, he had become an interesting figure; and he had emerged out of the dust storm that turns so much African history into a dull confusion dashed with a terrible red.

Khama is a radical reformer, who yet develops both himself and his people on the natural lines of the race; he has made himself into a character that can be spoken of as a "perfect English gentleman," but without losing for a moment his self-respect as an African; he has kept his position as a disciple, not a mimic of white civilisation, and he has shown how such a man can raise his nation. He has done it all, as he would tell us, because he is a Christian convert.

"For the interpretation of human life, an anecdote may be more valuable than a theory." A slight sketch of Khama may be evidence whether Islamism is indeed the force that can best raise the Africans.

At Selindia a little group of his people, the Bamangwato, stood round us for the first time, holding the quaintly-shaped white-wood pitchers in which they had brought milk—for sale, it must be confessed, in spite of a hospitable theory of Khama's that it is to be given to all strangers. The negro type was absent both in form and colour; indeed, one boy with a Roman contour of head, and a strikingly handsome face, we mutually and irresistibly named after a learned

Bishop of Hippo. These people, with the other Bechuana, belong
to the great Bantu race that may possibly be traceable to Syria,
and that has its own tradition of a descent from the north-west,
driving the aborigines southward or enslaving them. The race
comprises most of the better known nations, and whatever their
names—Zulu, Basuto, Fingoe, &c.—they retain three common
characteristics; they are skilful fighters, they have excellent
memories, and as a High Commissioner (who had much to do
with them) almost pathetically said : " They are born diplomatists."
The Bamangwato are a peaceful branch, feeding and clothing themselves by agriculture and hunting, though, as the big game is driven
farther north, " cotton goods " will sadly replace the old graceful,
exquisitely-sewn kaross. Their art-capacity reaches to fairly-shaped
articles of wood burnt with quaint patterns, often in zig-zag lines,
and to the general snuff-box ornamented prettily enough with inlaid
metal or ivory.

Leaving the too abundant waters of Selindia, hard trekking for
thirty-six hours brought us to the " gardens," or cultivated lands
surrounding Shoshong, Khama's capital, and the largest native
town in South Africa. For three or four miles the road passed
through the heavy crops of Kafir corn, and of maize " with his
garments green and yellow." We reached the out-span ground as
the sun rose over the mountains behind the town ; very grand the
massive granite range looked, every indentation marked with blue
shadow, while the mist slowly melted backwards up the deep gorge.
At the base of the hills were thousands of brown huts, in no
especial order, but divided into groups each enclosed with high
fencing that was here and there green with climbing gourds, a
welcome sight to English eyes weary of the primary reds and
yellows under the blue African sky. The gorge is the opening into
the pass leading north, and the source of the stream that now only
scantily supplies Shoshong with water; in former days it was a
river, but, with many of its comrades in this country, has either
dried up or found some more convenient channel underground.
Three miles to the south runs a parallel range of hills, chiefly
basaltic rock, and the oval-shaped plain lying between is one care-
fully-tended plough garden. The whole appearance of the place is
thoroughly African, but cultured and civilised. Plenty of life
goes on in the big town with its sixteen thousand inhabitants, its
resident traders and police, its visits of officers and hunters ; but its
main interest is still the chief.

Dates are a difficulty with natives ; but probably Khama was
born about 1830, one of the many sons of the many wives of
Sekhome, the then chief, but his legal heir. Two glimpses into a
wider world came to him as a boy ; he went for a hunting season
with Gordon Cumming, and he heard from a travelling native of
the new religion Dr. Moffat was teaching in the south. The next
to reach that then far interior town was a Lutheran missionary from
Germany, and Khama was soon afterwards baptised. Since then

the station at Shoshong has been in the charge of the London
Missionary Society, and from their missionaries Khama has received
further instruction.

Khama has been most resolute in repressing drink, both
the importation of spirits by traders and the inferior manufacture of a sufficiently stupefying liquor known as native
beer. The length of the struggle against the former, and the
persistent smuggling that has been detected, hardly reflect
credit on our white selves, or show that superiority one hears
of *ad nauseam* in countries where the races are intermingled.
Stopping the beer-making has been a more unpopular movement;
and with Khamane at hand to foster discontent, the chief has
undoubtedly put in jeopardy his own position. But in consequence
the quiet and order of Shoshong are striking; in spite of the
fifteen thousand inhabitants, it fulfils the dreams of Sir Wilfrid
Lawson, for to quote again from our Blue Book: " It would require
no police to manage the native part of the town. By his determination and courage Khama has put down strong drink among his
people, and prevented traders from bringing it into his country."
If Khama is thought too strict, it would not be by those who have
seen the state of other towns where there are large native populations,
and the canteen vote is valuable. Whatever white races may suffer
from unrestricted alcohol, the effects are worse on darker-skinned
peoples; physically they suffer to a greater extent, and morally
do not seem able to resist the craving for more until the stage of
madness and stupor is reached.

At sunrise every morning Khama is to be seen in his kotbla,
a scrupulously clean courtyard with mud walls, about ten feet
high, loop-holed and sharply cut. A curious assembly these walls
contain at times; outlying natives bringing in news, or what our
grand-parents might have considered news; a filibustering
expedition is hovering near the border; an ox has died mysteriously,
or a traveller's wagon has broken down; headmen (each in charge
of a section of the big population) waiting to lay difficulties or
accusations before the chief. A German traveller on his harmless
journey north for insects or game, sometimes with a single rifle;
or Major Goold-Adams, who has ridden up from Mafeking; or Mr.
Selous, full of gentle regret over the distance lions will keep; or a
missionary gaining hope from Khama's life for his work in a lonely
north. All alike, Khama greets with easy natural dignity, and
rather silent manner. " Your words are wise words," is the often
repeated answer to what he agrees with.

Sunday at Shoshong is a pretty, almost homelike day. Early in
the morning Khama goes up to the springs in the deep mountain
kloof, where hundreds of the women gather with their red or yellow
water-pots and calabashes; each as she passes the chief receives
his kindly greeting, " Good morning, my friend," or " my child."
Something of the same kind we saw when the large congregation
came out from the afternoon service, and Khama, with his kindly

face and sweet smile, walked up the wide road, patting the curly heads of the little brown children, and speaking to the elders. Later that day he was giving food to the old men of a regiment, for, as Lieutenant Haynes noticed, "Khama spends a great part of his revenue in acts of kindness to his people." The day had that beautiful stillness of Sunday, when the world is silent,

"To hear the angels sing."

Wagons are not forbidden to trek in, for the heavy roads are full

KHAMA AND HIS WIFE.

of difficulty, but Khama's strong wish against it is made known. He encourages his people to go to the outlying tribes to teach them, though he allows no pressure to be put on any one to join his own faith. Where heathen customs are harmless he does not forbid them, though he declared against them at once in all what might be called State functions. Every year he begins the digging season with a solemn meeting for public prayer instead of the old rites, and to the astonishment of the people the harvests continually increase. Unlike other interior chiefs, who either virtually or in plainest words demand presents from visitors as a payment for passing through their country, Khama refuses them if offered. He is indeed a most courteous host, as we had not only heard, but found during our stay in Shoshong.

To speak of Khama for a moment as a man, one is struck by what I can only call his winning personality. His Christianity, though so thorough, is in no way what the world is ready to condemn as morbid. He has remained the same keen hunter he was when a boy; his stud of horses is one even an Englishman might envy; his daily life is as simple and unaffected as possible. To his children he has been a most careful and loving father; his home remains completely African in its surroundings, but is full of refinement and courtesy. I shall always remember the pretty scene we shared in there our last evening in Shoshong; the large brown hut, its walls stencilled, the broad eaves covering the raised step that made a pleasant verandah; the wide, clean court shut in by loop-holed walls; the fire in one corner, with three little brown maidens, half-playing, half-cooking; the graceful figures of the girls carrying corn crossing the court at intervals; Khama's son, a bright gentlemanly boy, sitting near his mother, Mabisa, under the eaves; the daughters beside her; the little grandchildren running up to her; and among them all the tall slight man, his thin nervous face full of decision and of sweetness, who had won through endurance and peril the purity of that almost unique home among African chiefs.

"A Christian and a hero," was the description of Khama given by a soldier whose words carry weight in England and in Africa.

"It is not what people say of him," was the account given by a trooper in the Border Police, "it is what I know myself. I was quartered in Shoshong for eighteen months, and I call him a genuine Christian man. He does not make much fuss over it, but it is real."

There is, I know, a tendency to look on such a man as Khama much in the way in which we look on some freak of Nature, as of no weight in an argument. But there have been times when Science has found in so-called freaks of Nature evidence of her deepest laws. To those who believe in the power of Christianity to raise all native races alike, whether they were called Teutons in the past or Bantu in the present, Khama's life is but one of many that even here turn the walk by faith into the walk of sight. It has fulfilled that noblest test given to us in "Little Lord Fauntleroy:"

"It is better than everything else that the world should be a little better because a man has lived—even ever so little better, dearest."

Last October, Sir Henry Loch, the High Commissioner for South Africa, made an extended tour north, from Cape Town, going as far as Macloutsie on the border of Matabeleland, accompanied by Mr. Cecil Rhodes, Premier of the Cape Colony. It had been contemplated, if time permitted, to proceed as far as Bulawayo, to visit Lo Bengula, but it was found inconvenient to do so. Had the condition of political affairs necessitated the step, His Excellency would have gone on to meet the King, but finding Lo Bengula was faithfully carrying out his engagements, he turned back at Macloutsie. It had been imagined that Lo Bengula would

SIR H. B. LOCH, G.C.M.G., K.C.B.
High Commissioner for South Africa.
(From a Photograph by Messrs. Foster and Martin, Melbourne.)

journey as far as that to see Sir Henry, but those who thought this at all likely forgot the fact that the King is a very heavy man and travels only short distances. Besides that, it is doubtful if his Indunas would have allowed the King to so far forget his dignity as to travel to see anybody. Sir Henry Loch, however, contrived to view a great part of the first half of the future highway from Cape Town to Cairo. This route was described by newspaper specials who accompanied the Governor's party, and it will be convenient to draw upon them a little. I have said that Khama's town of Shoshong has now been deserted by him, and that he is now located with his people at Palapye. We often speak—like the Americans used to speak of Chicago—of Kimberley and Johannesburg as wonderful cities for their age. King Khama's Bechuana city of Palapye is a city not one whit less wonderful than either. Palapye is a native town covering some twenty square miles of ground, holding some thirty thousand inhabitants; yet, less than fifteen months ago, there was no such place as Palapye in existence. You walk through its broad avenues, you thread its well-trodden bridle-paths and footpaths, you admire its fine central square, on which a grand review might be held; you admire still more the comfortable red-clay thatched

TELEGRAPH STATION AT PALAPYE.

cottages—it seems sacrilege to write them down huts—with their neat enclosures, in which the "aboriginal," as they call him in Australia, may sit under his own vine and fig-tree, none daring to make him afraid; you enjoy gratefully the shade of the trees, the size of the oaks of Government Avenue, Cape Town, which everywhere screen the dwellings and paths from the sun, at the same time affording homes for thousands of chirping, twittering, and singing birds; you note on every hand neatness and comfort;

and a simple, innocent enjoyment of life; and you marvel at the native wisdom which has chosen such a model site for the town, on fine red sandy soil, with excellent and abundant water supply, the purest of air, and fine views on every hand. Here you find an immense store and outfitting establishment; there you find other stores; and round the corner a neat little galvanized office where, for five shillings, you may send a message in two minutes to your friends eighteen hundred miles away. ..Yet it was only in August and September of 1889 that the first dwellings were built in Palapye, and its inhabitants moved in a body, men, women, and picaninnies, old and young, from their homes at Shoshong. At this day, the well-known starting point for hunters and travellers, the great mart for poultry, Shoshong, or, as it was more commonly styled, Bamangwato or 'Mungwato, is a mere heap of charred ruins at the foot of the hills which its former inhabitants used as their fortress; and now we have in its place Palapye the Wondrous, all alive, healthy and beautiful. If we remember that this marvellous work, the Exodus from Shoshong and the re-housing at Palapye, was a work carried out by a native chief himself, without the slightest European assistance, we shall admit that Khama's fine city of Palapye is one of the most wondrous cities under the sun.

Not the least wonderful thing in Palapye is the great outfitting store of the Bechuanaland Trading Association, the sister Company of the Bechuanaland Exploration Company. There are two " old-established" traders besides the Company, viz., Messrs. Clark and Blackbeard, who are " doing well "; but, although the Trading Association holds no concession, and has no monopoly of the important and rapidly-increasing business of which Palapye is the centre, the shareholders must be able to congratulate themselves on the transactions at this store. The shop, an oblong building of solid masonry, is 60 feet long by 30 feet wide; but behind this is a large compound containing various warehouses stocked with goods; while near by is a large smithy and wheelwright's yard, where blacksmiths and carpenters are perpetually hard at work, repairing native and other wagons. Khama is planting an immense area with mealies, in order to meet the wants of the Europeans expected on their way to Mashonaland. In husbandry and cattle-rearing, growing mealies and native corn, and so on, Khama not only encourages his people, but sets them an excellent example. Fruit-growing, i.e., European fruit-growing, is being introduced on a small scale, and Mr. Gifford, of the Exploration Company, has done something to awaken the native mind to the merits of the potato. In the matter of secular as well as of religious education, Khama has shown himself an enlightened ruler by the hearty co-operation he has given to the missionary. Scattered in the divisions of Palapye are no fewer than nine or ten different schools, where the children are taught reading, writing, and the Scriptures by native teachers, trained

K

by Mr. Hepburn. The characteristic of the native scholars is their wonderful memory. Between 400 and 500 children, some not over ten years old, recently learnt by heart the whole, or nearly the whole, of St. John's Gospel in Sechuana, the incentive being prizes of Testaments in their own tongue, which well-won rewards were presented to them on the day of the young chief Sekgomo's wedding. Mr. Hepburn's native flock have just subscribed amongst themselves no less a sum than £3000 for the purpose of building a great new church. At present Palapye has no church, but every Sunday morning, at sunrise, an immense congregation, numbering sometimes nigh two thousand, assembles on the hill-side, near the missionary's house, for open-air service, followed in the afternoon, and sometimes in the evening also, by religious services conducted by Mr. Hepburn's native assistants in the various divisions of the town. As regards the bush people, the Bakalahari and the Masarwa, who were formerly the slaves of the Bechuanas, and who could be killed at pleasure by their masters, Khama's Christianity has had the very practical result of enabling them to live in peace and security, on equal terms with the people who used to persecute them, and encouraged to keep their own flocks of goats and sheep, and herds of cattle, instead of being forbidden to do so, and thereby forced often to subsist on roots, or starve. On the whole, Khama, as a native ruler, is as wonderful as is Palapye as a native town.

At Macloutsie, where a few months of hard work by the Imperial and the Chartered Company's police has caused quite a town of comfortable huts to spring up around the little pentagonal fort in the midst of the bush, we are, as it were, on the border line between the Land of the Rifle and the Land of the Assegai; Khama's men are now armed with the rifle, Lo Bengula's with the stabbing assegai, the consignment of rifles sent up last year being hardly yet given out, much less effectually practised with by the Majakas. Moreover, the Matabele seldom or never cross the Shashi, which is thirty-five miles away, the strip of country between the Rivers Shashi and Macloutsie, called, as we have seen, the Disputed Territory, forming with its long rugged chain of Lipokoli Hills a useful barrier between the boundaries of Khama's country and Lo Bengula's. Here, then, under the Union Jack of Great Britain and the flag also of the Chartered Company, with Khama and his rifle brigades as a well-trained and hitherto successful soldiery in case of need, the time has at last come to talk of the arts of peace. It is true that last October His Excellency the High Commissioner warned the members of the two police forces to be ready for any "emergency," as "complications" with the natives might at any moment arise; but on the principle that preparing for war is the best way to ensure peace, that is only another reason tending to the conclusion suggested. The country under Khama's rule possesses very considerable natural riches, were they but developed. Especially is this so with regard to the

THE BAOBAB.

K 2

country around Palapye, and to the north and north-east; while
the mountain district at the back of Shoshong, a district practically
unknown to Europeans, is said to be the very garden of the
country.   Along the Lotsani Valley, and under the Chopong Hills
are fine sites for farming, the land being not only well watered,
but being more loamy, clayey, and retentive of moisture than the
red sand of which most of the surface of Bechuanaland consists.
Yet here it is at present impossible to buy for love or money a
bundle of forage, a bag of mealies, or a sheep—here at a spot
where a farmer would make his whole farm a perfect garden !

A FLOOD ON THE LOTSANI RIVER.

From our camp, writes a correspondent, at the Pakwe River
I went with a member of the police force to the Heliograph Station
to see the instrument with which, by flashing an alphabet of " dots
and dashes," or rather short and long flashes, you can signal a
message by fifty-mile stages at the rate of over ten words a minute,
provided there is sun to shine on the mirror used.   On the way
through the bush our guide pointed out amongst other trees the
wild grape, the wild orange, the wild plum, and the baobab, all of
which yield fruit that is good eating when ripe ; suggesting the

thought that surely many fruit trees besides these might be
cultivated with profit on soil such as this by the Pakwe and elsewhere, under a tropical sun, and with water near at hand. On the
same short walk we came upon a baobab tree perhaps as large as
may be seen in these parts. The girth of its trunk at five feet
above the ground, measured by myself with a foot rule, was exactly
65 feet! Upon this tree were a number of the fruits, the size and
much the shape of rather small cocoanuts, and with a husk almost
as hard. Cracking one of these you find within it sections of a
dry powdery-looking substance like lumps of " cream of tartar,"
from which doubtless the tree gets its name of " cream of tartar "
tree. This substance, the taste of which is tart, and by no means
unpleasant, makes, when boiled, a drink of much value for its
cooling properties in fevers. The wood of the tree is very fibrous,
and the bark, when cut, bleeds gummy tears that dry blood-red.
You cannot call the baobab a good-looking tree; it looks too much
like the roots on a gigantic mangold-wurzel growing upside down;
—but, like the Lady Jane, it has the merit of being distinctly
" massive." There are many other trees not so thick-trunked but
taller, more shady, and far handsomer, on this land watered by the
Pakwe. From the signalling kopje we looked over a vast well-
wooded plain, bounded on one side by the hills and mountains of
the Matabeleland and Makalakaland border, on another by the
Waterberg and Zoutpansberg of the Transvaal, and on the third
by the heights in the neighbourhood of Palapye. It is a fine
stretch of country, and to look over it suggested other thoughts
besides the recollection that behind some of these heights lay the
blood-thirsty Matabele; behind others, the peaceful Bamangwato;
behind others, the busy miners; and behind others, the Chartered
Company's Land of Promise. Will this land of the Bechuanas
ever pay for a railway running through it, to place Cape Town and
Kimberley in communication with Mashonaland? Some say Yes;
others No. If the mineral riches of Mashonaland turn out as
satisfactory as it is believed they will, as satisfactory as its more
obvious features have been already found, we may imagine the
rush there will be of the sons who are now too many on the Cape
Colony farms, of the miners and others who may think themselves
too thick on the ground in the Transvaal, and of the many other
men who crowd the older countries of Europe. These are only
waiting to hear the truth, and for the country to be thrown open
and declared safe to travel and to live in. When this rush comes
there will be traffic by the Zoutpansberg and Tuli way from the
Transvaal, and by this Bechuanaland way from Cape Colony. For
a long time, moreover, supplies will be needed from the colony, the
Free Natal, the Transvaal, or wheresoever they may be obtainable.
But to carry a bag of mealies even from Kimberley to the
Macloutsie would make the price of the bag at Macloutsie 60s.
instead of 16s. The ox-wagon, with its sixteen miles a day, is a
slow business when your distance is many hundreds of miles. You

say there is to be a railway up the Pungwe from Sofala Bay, and
a sea-route by the Red Sea ; or there is the Zambesi ; or there is
that line across country from Walfish Bay or Mossamedes.   All
the same, I think the Americans would run the Cape Town-Mount
Hampden line right through had they the problem to deal with ;
even if they made it for part of the way one of those light railways for which the British Parliament voted money last session
in order to open up the remote parts of Ireland.   If there be a
railway, as well as a telegraph, then Mr. Rhodes's faintly-limned
vision of a Cape Colony extending to the Zambesi, and governed
as a homogeneous whole, may not be so utterly impracticable as
many now regard it.   If there be not a railway for more than
half the way, then, leaving the political problem out of the question, the thing to be done to cope with the rush before other

'STIFF BIT.'

routes are opened is to improve the roads.   Whether the future
capital of Charterland be called after the famous ancient town,
Rhodes, or whatever it may be called (I make Mr. Colquhoun a
present of the suggestion), no effort should be spared by the Cape
Colony to secure a road as straight and rapid as possible between
that town and Cape Town ; a railway as far as possible, and
beyond that a good straight well-kept road for stage-coaches and
ox-wagons.   The same remark applies to the Transvaal.   The road
we have travelled is not the most direct possible, allowing that water
has to be considered.   In some parts it is good, in others villainous.
The sections of it before and after Palapye are memorable, one for
the heavy sand, the other for the wilderness of stones.   Then there
are other sections where the idea seems to have been to make the road
as long as possible.   If the Government well-sinking promised in

the Southern Protectorate be also carried out on the more northerly portion of the route, the water difficulty will perhaps be solved, and the necessity of diverting the road in order to find water be thereby done away with. Then there is the state of the roads themselves—the big stones, tree stumps, yawning pits, which make the lot of driver and passenger anything but a happy one. Why not a road corps? One or two road-parties, equipped with axes, shears, picks, and hammers, and constantly engaged travelling over the roads from north to south, cutting trees here, smashing or removing stones or stumps there, shortening zigzags into straight lines, and making the crossing of the dangerous drifts as easy and safe as possible—such a body of men, or two or three such bodies, might work wonders in the direction of making travel from Vryburg to the north easier, safer, quicker, and less expensive than it now is.

Returning to the question of how to make the best of Bechuanaland, not simply as a kind of bowling alley for wagons bound beyond to roll over, but for itself as a vast expanse of land that might be usefully employed, it should be remembered that some gentlemen who have taken upon themselves to condemn the country in sweeping phrases, have either been innocent of travel in it, or having that qualification, have been innocent of the knowledge of soil. Some who have gone as far as Taungs have ridiculed the country; others who have gone as far as Mafeking have spoken better of it; others who have gone to Shoshong have spoken better still; and as for the country north of Shoshong, there lies there some of the very best of Bechuanaland. The richness of the Bechuanas in cattle is often spoken of. Heavy crops are frequently raised even by the natives. The country is well wooded, and in many parts well watered. The climate is beautiful and exceptionally healthy, nearly all the land being above the "immunity level" for fevers, until you begin to descend as you approach Macloutsie and the boundary of "disputed territory" between Khama's country and Matabeleland; while as regards heat, although September and October are very trying months for Europeans, the rest of the year is by no means too hot for them. A Cape Colonist might frequently complain of the cold. On the whole white residents of Bechuanaland ought to enjoy the climate. Then there is the sport. Not so much is seen of the big game hunters used to find in these solitudes, but there is still plenty, viz., the blue wildebeest, zwart wildebeest, rooi hartebeest, Zulu hartebeest (tssessibe), koodo, eland, gemsbok, zwart wittepansbok (sable antelope), rooibok (roan antelope), rietbok, kringbok, boschbok, steinbok, dyker, klipspringer, giraffe, zebra (or quagga), silver jackal, sepa, wolf, wild boar, hare, South African tiger, and lion; amongst birds, the wild ostrich, paauw, kohraan, guinea fowl, pheasant, partridge, Namaqua partridge, wild goose, wild duck; while in the rivers are not only crocodiles, but also edible fish, such as springers, barbel, and silver fish. In a land like this, with all its disadvantages, many a white man might make himself a home if he were but allowed to do so.

CHAPTER VII.

Lo Bengula's Mission and Letter to the Queen.—Her Majesty's
Reply.—How the Matabele Envoys were Received in
England.—The Impressions they Returned with.—The
Imperial Mission to Lo Bengula.—Their Reception at
the King's Kraal, and What they Saw.

HAVING familiarised my readers with Matabeleland as it was
under Mosilikatse, and as it is under Lo Bengula, it will be
convenient to pick up the thread of the history of the country,
with accounts of Lo Bengula's comparatively recent Mission to Her Majesty the Queen, and of the Imperial Government's
return Mission to Lo Bengula. I am glad to be able to supply
original narratives of both these Missions, containing a number
of hitherto unpublished particulars. For one I am largely indebted
to Mr. E. A. Maund, who came to England with the Matabele
Indunas, and for the other I owe acknowledgments to Surgeon-
Major Melladew, who has kindly placed all the information in his
power concerning the Mission, of which he was a member, at my
disposal.

To understand the *raison d'être* of the Matabele Mission to
England, it is necessary to go back to the time of Sir Charles
Warren's Expedition to Bechuanaland, when little gold-prospecting
or concession-hunting syndicates were formed, in conseque...
the reports which were brought down about Matabeleland. Mr.
Maund went up to Bulawayo in 1888, and found that no less
than eleven parties had been to the King to obtain concessions,
and that attempts were being made to arrange the disputed
territory. The Portuguese were harrassing the country in the
north (they afterwards came down as far as the Umfuli), whilst
the Boers threatened to come in from the Zoutpansberg district.
Lo Bengula was troubled, and talked with Mr. Maund about
all the rumours which reached him. Mr. Maund asked him for
the concession of the ground where the Portuguese were, and the
King was pleased with the idea of white men occupying the
territory. The King said, however, " But, Maundy, I want you
to do something for me first." Mr. Maund replied, " What is it ? "
and the King answered, " They tell me that the White Queen
no longer exists, and that is why the white men come up here and

bother me. I want you to take two of my men home to see whether the White Queen is living." Mr. Maund said, "No, I can't do it," to which Lo Bengula responded, "Ough, are you like all the rest, then?' Mr. Maund asked time to consider the question, and, in turning it over in his mind, came to the conclusion that it would be a good thing in the interests of the country if he consented to go. There was then no Imperial Government Representative in the country. Mr. Moffat having left, Mr. Maund was of opinion that it would be best to accept the situation as put before him. On the following morning he saw the King again, and he was much gratified to hear that Mr. Maund had decided to start with his Indunas "To-morrow morning." His Majesty directed that ink and paper should be brought, and, at his request, Mr. Maund wrote a letter. When the letter, which was to the Queen, was finished, the King sent off to the missionaries to bring it before them. This he did the next day, thus showing his respect and confidence in them. It was re-written, a clause about a protectorate being altered. In the first letter dictated to Mr. Maund, the King distinctly asked for a protectorate, but when the matter was further explained to him, he changed this to one to the effect that he wanted help against his enemies. The letter being written, the King sent to have it stamped with his official seal, and told Mr. Maund to come up and say "good-bye" to him next day, when he would show him the Indunas— Umshete and Babjaan, the former being about 60 and the latter about 75 years of age.

The following is the text of Lo Bengula's letter to Her Majesty :—

Lo Bengula desires to know that there is a Queen. Some of the people who come into this land tell him there is a Queen, some of them tell him there is not.

Lo Bengula can only find out the truth by sending eyes to see whether there is a Queen.

The Indunas are his eyes.

Lo Bengula desires, if there is a Queen, to ask her to advise and help him, as he is much troubled by white men who come into his country and ask to dig gold.

There is no one with him upon whom he can trust, and he asks that the Queen will send someone from herself.

The next day the King said to Mr. Maund, "These are the men who are to be my eyes, ears, and mouth. You carry the letter. Where you go they are to go and are to do what you tell them. I trust them absolutely to you." He made no distinction between them, though he told Mr. Maund afterwards he was very fond of Babjaan, who, he said, had the gift of a wonderful memory. Besides this he was a connection of his Majesty, and in the battle which secured the throne to Lo Bengula he saved the monarch's life, slaying the Induna who would have killed the King. Umshete, the King described as a good speaker, it transpiring afterwards that he was considered the best orator in Matabeleland.

The two men were willing to go—they had no option.   The party started, one of the Ambassadors being at first very sulky.   The King provided some cattle for the road and agreed to pay all expenses.   On asking how much the travelling expenses would be he was informed that their amount would be about £600. His Majesty thereupon got into his wagon and took down a handkerchief full of English sovereigns, some of which had been obtained by the Rudd concession.   He then counted out a sum for the expenses of his Embassy, though it was not quite sufficient.   "Albeit dirty, Babjaan was," according to Mr. Maund, and we shall allow that gentleman now to talk for himself for a bit, "a charming and dear old

Mr. DOYLE.   Mr. JOHN MOFFAT.   Dr. JAMESON.
(Interpreter.)   (British Resident at
                         Bulawayo.)

man, always ready to do anything he was bid, pleased with everything, and one of the most unselfish of men I have ever met.   He gave up all his presents.   I never had the least difficulty all the time with him.   The other man was about 65 years of age.   He was small and odious, was of a gouty temperament, had elephantiasis of one leg, and a weak heart.   He was the most vile-tempered man I ever met.   It was impossible to please him, do what one would, for he was ever trying to see how much difficulty he could put in the way.   He was enormously conceited, and gave me infinite trouble.   His abilities, for an untutored man, were of a good order. On the way down he stood up for being the first of the two.   He sometimes sulked for three days at a time under a tree and would not speak to any of us because we gave him the same food as the other. I treated him exactly like the other, though he considered he was of a better caste. We got to Shoshong, and finding the western road very dry chose the Transvaal one. I did this also with the idea of impressing them with the paucity in numbers of the Boers and their lack of power when compared subsequently with the English. I dressed them partly at Tati and partly at Shoshong. I halted the wagon several miles out of Pretoria, rode on, and rushed them into a store and clothed them in neat suits of blue serge. The inside of the Johannesburg and Kimberley coach was taken at a cost of £110. I had previously interviewed Oom Paul and Joubert, and found out they knew nothing about the Indunas, whom I thought would be stopped. At Johannesburg men who had booked their seats for the inside were furious at niggers being inside, but I stuck to my point, offering anybody, should it be rainy, to come inside and rest themselves if they liked. Two gentlemen accepted my offer and got into conversation with the Indunas. The health of the old men was very bad from the hard travelling, their legs and feet being swollen to an enormous size through sitting still. We got them down to Kimberley. On getting into the train for the first time at Kimberley a decided look of horror came into their eyes as they began to rush forward. I turned around to Babjaan and said, ' What, a King's soldier and afraid ! ' on which, to show that he was not, he put his head out of the window and kept it there for half an hour, much to my concern, for I was afraid it might come in contact with something. At Cape Town we found that many lies had preceded us, which I never troubled my head to answer or contradict, well knowing that ' though lies travel fast, truth catches them at last.' For instance, it was said I had picked up two negroes in the veld for my own purposes. I was delayed at Cape Town for a fortnight, there being some difficulty with Sir Hercules Robinson about being received there. When I accepted the mission there was no accredited Government agent with Lo Bengula, he being an independent king beyond English jurisdiction. He had chosen to send the men on his own account, specially instructing me not to halt by ' the gates by the sea,' but at once to go over the water where the white men came from, and that his Indunas must see with their own eyes before they return to him whether the White Queen was alive. "

Sir Hercules Robinson cabled as follows to Lord Knutsford on February 2, 1889, and a favourable reply was received :—

I have had long interviews with the two Matabele who are described as headmen in letter received from Lo Bengula ; they say Lo Bengula has been so often deceived by Europeans of different nations telling him there is no such person as the Queen, others saying that they come from the Queen, that they want to know whether England and the Queen exist; they have no other message. This, as far as they are concerned, is the sole object of their mission. They are to see with their own eyes and go back and report to King; they say they will be killed on their return if they do not cross the sea. I advise that they may be allowed to proceed. They have funds for such purpose. Mission is most anxious to proceed by next mail.

At last a start was made for England on board the *Moor*, and the Matabeles had further experience of the ocean which had interested them so much at Cape Town. They went into raptures over the incoming waves, likening the rollers dashing in to the shore to the columns of their impis rushing up to the King at a review. On board the steamer, which they called ' the great kraal that pushes through the water,' the Indunas were neither sick nor sorry. The officers and passengers were extremely kind to them, and Lady Frederick Cavendish, who was voyaging to England by the steamer, took a special interest in them. So much impression did this lady make on the natives that when they returned Babjaan desired specially to be remembered to the " Queen's woman Induna." We shall allow Lady Frederick to speak now as to the next experiences of the Matabele envoys :—

I had an interview with them, and took pains to convince them that there *was* a White Queen, assuring them that I had had the honour of serving Her Majesty and had kissed her hand. One of them thereupon touched his eyes and replied, " We believe it, as you say so, but we are taking our own eyes to see." When we got into rough weather in the Bay, they said, " The river is full to-day." Off Lisbon, when told it was Portuguese, they sat on deck with their backs turned to it, and said, " How is it the White Queen allows Portugal between her and Africa ? "
During the voyage I considered very much how I could advance the cause. I became very anxious indeed that it should be successful, and that we should contrive an interview, but I believe we should never have managed it if we had not fortunately touched at Madeira, and taken on board Lord Lothian. I knew very well that, even if Lord Knutsford approved of this deputation, there might still be some difficulty in obtaining Her Majesty's consent to an interview, as she is not in the habit of receiving stray black men, especially with no accredited person in attendance on them. However, when I saw Lord Lothian, I thought at once that he was the best person to interest in the matter, as a member of the Government, though not in the Cabinet. Fortunately I knew him slightly, and I thought if I could interest him he would probably influence the Cabinet, whilst his opinion would be one likely to weigh with Her Majesty. We had not much time, for we took him on board on Friday, and we landed at Southampton on Tuesday, but I at once introduced him to Lieut. Maund and to Mr. Selous (who was also with us, and who knew Matabeleland well, as he spends most of his time hunting there), and by the time we landed, Lord Lothian, after an interview with the two Chiefs, and after hearing the whole history, was quite as keenly interested as I was, and assured me he would do his utmost to bring about the interview. On the Tuesday when we arrived at Southampton a brother of Lieut. Maund came on board, and he caused us some dismay by saying that Her Majesty was going to Biarritz the very following Monday. So we had very little time to spare. Lieut. Maund gave up all for lost, but I assured him that the hurry was all for the best, as there would be so little time for pros and cons. On the Thursday afternoon I received a happy letter from him, saying

that consent had been given, and that the Chiefs were to be taken to Windsor Castle on Saturday, at 3 o'clock. I hoped all was now in good train, but on the following day—Friday afternoon—a terrible hitch occurred. Lieut. Maund wrote me word that, though the Chiefs were to be welcomed, he was not to be allowed to accompany them —the fact being, as Sir Hercules had foreseen, that it is not usual for a private gentleman to be received on such a mission at Court. He wrote to me therefore to say that he was in a great difficulty; he was not at all anxious to intrude on Her Majesty, but the Chiefs would not stir without him. They said, "The King told us that Maundy was to be our Father. We were not to be afraid of the great White Queen; we don't understand this at all, and if Maundy does not go with us, we shall go straight home to Matabeleland."

I immediately tried to find Lord Knutsford, and put the case before him, but I could not succeed in seeing him; I could merely send a note up to his room. However, late in the evening I ascertained that Lord Lothian had set to work afresh, and had overcome the difficulty, and that all was settled for the interview on the following day. It is amusing to notice how these two blacks had brought all the authorities round!

The scene on the arrival of the Indunas at Waterloo may be described. The night was a bitterly cold one, and the Matabeles needed the shelter of heavy overcoats to protect them from the "cauld blasts" which swept London. They had arrived during the day at Southampton, and little time was lost in conveying them to the capital. They left the port by the 5.15 train, and got to Waterloo Station "on time" at 7.40. As the train drew up to the platform one or two pressmen soon scented their presence. They had travelled in a first-class compartment, and were in custody— it almost seemed so—of a white gentleman whom ultimately I recognised as an old friend. A little natural eagerness was shown on the part of the small knot of Fourth Estate Scribes to come near the door of the compartment. Orders were quickly given by the gentleman in charge of the royal spokesmen to allow no one to approach the door. "Aye, aye, sir," was the ready response of two porters, who did not say they had any eye to the main chance in the shape of a possible lump of gold from one of the Matabele concessions. They were quickly joined by a stalwart commissionaire—not concessionaire—whose row of medals, hanging proudly on his manly bosom, glanced fitfully in the dismal lamplight. It was possible, just possible, to get a "keek" at the distinguished arrivals by watching a chance when the persons of the three conscientious guards unbent a very little. They—the distinguished arrivals—did not look happy, well, not so happy as they would have looked had they had no overcoats and no anything on, and had been dancing in a blazing sun a war fandango, preparatory to a look in on Khama or the Mashonas. They were huddled up in their respective corners, and from beneath their unaccustomed wideawakes there was to be seen no trace either of amusement or surprise at the bustling scene being enacted outside. Quite the reverse; they bore themselves, as far as the low temperature would allow them, with that impassive dignity familiar to all South Africans as a characteristic of the superior native. If they had voiced their emotions they would probably have asked for a fire. They were taken to Berner's Hotel, where they remained during their stay in London.

On the Saturday following, the Indunas travelled to Windsor by a train conveying the Cabinet Ministers, and royal carriages awaited

Mr. E. A. MAUND.

BABJAAN.   UMSHETE.   MR. COLENBRANDER.
(Interpreter.)

THE MATABELE EMBASSY.

them at the station. The Queen had considerately sent for picked men of the 2nd Life Guards, who lined the approaches to St. George's Hall, through which the party marched. The Indunas were so astonished at the immobility of the soldiers, that they concluded they were stuffed, until one of them saw their eyes moving. This speaks well for the steadiness of the troopers. On the conclusion of the business part of the interview, Her Majesty said to the Indunas, " You have come a very long way to see me ; I hope the journey has been made pleasant for you, and that you did not suffer from the cold." In acknowledgment, one of them stepped forward, bowing with truly courtier-like gesture, and replied, " How should we feel cold in the presence of the great White Queen ? " adding, with a shrug of his shoulders, " Is it not in the power of great kings and queens to make it either hot or cold ? " Having lunched and viewed the royal castle, the natives returned to London.

They were greatly delighted at their reception by the Queen, keeping on speaking about it. They said that their eyes had seen her and their ears had heard her voice. "It was easy," they declared, " to recognise among the assembly at Windsor which was the White Queen, from her manner and bearing."

Needless to say, the Envoys did a great deal of sight-seeing when in England, and some of their quaint impressions may be recorded. They consider (as of course they should) the Queen the greatest woman they ever saw, and Lady Randolph Churchill the most beautiful. Perhaps this latter impression will prove to be a useful passport to Lord Randolph, should he leave his card on Umshete and Babjaan at Bulawayo. The Envoys were taken to " see the lions "—among them the literal lions at the Zoological Gardens, which naturally attracted a good deal of their attention. Their excitement was intense. When they came to these animals Babjaan could scarcely be restrained from attacking one of the lords of his native forest with his umbrella, nor could he understand why he was prevented. It would interest Lo Bengula to learn that his representatives went to the Alhambra, and that they were undisguisedly satisfied with the ballet. For that occasion their eyes became twice their natural size. London, they said, was like the ocean ; a man might walk, and walk, and walk, and yet never get to the end of the houses. If Englishmen were killed, they reported, for every drop of blood in their bodies another would spring up to take their places ; but what most astonished them was the telephone. They were placed a mile apart, and talked together. Afterwards they declared that they could imagine such a machine might talk English, but how it could be taught to speak the Kafir language they could not understand. They visited Portsmouth, and were shown over the fort by the commander. A steam launch was placed at the disposal of the Envoys, and in this they steamed about, the places of interest being pointed out and described to them by one of the Flag-Captains. To these, however, they seemed to pay but lukewarm attention, and requested that a rocket, which produced such an effect in Zululand, might be sent up, and two were fired off for their benefit. The Nordenfelt guns were described to them, after which they were shown rifle practice at movable dummies. " Oh," said they, " is that the way you teach your men to shoot ? Capital practice too." As the grand finale to the sightseeing, the Indunas were taken to Aldershot, where a sham fight and inspection was held. It was the first big

field-day of the year, and it was whispered that the troops were
turned out earlier than they otherwise would have been, in order
to give the Envoys an idea of the capabilities of the English
soldiers. The elements were rather unkind, and the review was
opened under lowering skies and a drizzling rain. The programme
consisted of an inspection of cavalry and artillery, in the forenoon,
in the Long Valley, and subsequently a sham fight upon the Fox
Hills, to the west of the North Camp, in which about 10,000 men
of all arms were engaged, under the direction of the new commander
of the station, Lieut.-General Sir Evelyn Wood. The Envoys, who
were escorted by an aide-de-camp of the General, arrived from
Aldershot, where they slept overnight, in an open barouche, and
from this they witnessed the manœuvres. Needless to say, the
artillery and cavalry moved with that precision and dash, for which
the mounted portion, at least, of the British army have so long
been deservedly famed. After the charge of the cavalry upon the
artillery, the troops sweeping past like a tornado, the Lancers
spread out as if in pursuit of a discomfited force. Babjaan and
Umshete, who had never seen such a display before, were almost
mad with excitement. They fairly jumped with astonishment,
and, standing on their seats, eagerly watched every movement of
the troops. Babjaan was the first to speak. "Such mighty
horses—so big, so strong, and such discipline among the men,"
irresistibly exclaimed the old African warrior. "Come and teach
us how to drill and fight like that, and we will fear no nation
in Africa," remarked both. After the review, General Wood
expressed his pleasure at seeing the two visitors, and wished
them a pleasant journey back. He earnestly hoped that the
troops they had seen manœuvring that day would never be required to fight against the Matabele people. The Matabeles
replied that they had now seen the real strength of England, and
when it was explained to them that it was not a fair idea of
what England really could turn out in case of necessity, they
were greatly astonished, and remarked, "How can there be
more? this must surely be all!" It was explained to them that
General Wood was the General who turned Cetewayo out of his
stronghold, and brought the assegai to Queen Victoria. Prince
Albert Victor, who was with the General's staff, was introduced
to the two Chiefs, and they remarked, "We can see why the
Queen puts him with the big warrior—to teach him how to
manage the Army himself."

The Indunas were taken over the Bank of England. They were
first of all shown the room in which a machine automatically
weighs the sovereigns fresh from the Mint. On being allowed to
lift some bags of gold the Indunas remarked that it made their
hearts sick to see so much gold which they could not put into their
pockets. The mode of conveying an idea to them of a quantity of
gold was by saying how many bags containing about £1,000 each it
would take to give £1 to each of Lo Bengula's soldiers. The

Indunas were next conducted to the bullion room containing many
piles of ingots, some of which they tried to lift, Babjaan being
scarcely able to raise one of the ingots. To give them an idea of
the value of the ingots they were told that if these were made into
sovereigns they would give so many to each of Lo Bengula's
warriors, but at the same time it was impressed upon them that if
the same quantity was divided amongst the members of the Queen's
Army the individuals constituting the latter would receive a very
much smaller sum each. At this point one of the Indunas wished
it to be remembered that when any distinguished visitor was
received by their King he showed him his flocks and herds, generally
selecting the largest beast to present to the stranger. The hint
was not taken, I am sorry to say.

A South African native in the person of a dissolute Tonga may
be seen any day in the course of a walk through the London Docks.
But in London a South African native in the person of a barbarian
king or his embassy is *rara avis in terris, nigroque simillima cygno.*
So apparently thought the very large number of gentlemen who
met together one morning in Westminster Palace Hotel to greet the
Envoys from Lo Bengula, the paramount chief of Matabeleland, at
breakfast. The white swans crowded in large numbers round the
black pair, and it cannot truly be said that the dark ones showed
much evidence of an extraordinary appreciation of condescension
on the part of the white ones. The invitation of the Aborigines'
Protection Society asked the honour of the presence of the recipient
at the breakfast "to be given to the Envoys from the Chief
Lo Bengula, at Matabeleland." A note on the imposing card of
invitation ran thus :—" The Envoys who will take part in the
proceedings have visited England for the purpose of asking the
'Great White Queen' and the British Government to protect
Matabeleland from being 'eaten up' by intruders." It was a
pleasant morning as a harmonious company assembled in the hotel
to take their matutinal meal with Umshete and Babjaan. For the
moment the chief anxiety seemed to be that the chops would not
be " eaten up " before some of the guests got seated. We were
reminded later on by one of the speakers, that Lord Beaconsfield
once remarked that " those who breakfast out must be revolutionists."
The departed author of " Lothair " must have had the Latin Quarter
of Paris in his mind when he wrote such a sentiment. He certainly
never attended a breakfast given by the Aborigines' Protection Society,
or he could not have penned it. A milder-looking set of men could
hardly have been drawn together than those who gathered in the
reception-room with morning appetites to await the advent of the two
sable representatives of Mosilikatse's son. The Chairman, Sir T.
Fowell Buxton, was so gentle-looking that he might have been a lady
in a frock coat. Alderman Fowler, as he helped his nose from a
silver snuff box, looked like a fine old English gentleman very
averse to revolution. The well-known novelist, Rider Haggard,
certainly appeared as if he would prefer to wear a Lincoln

L

and Bennet rather than a red cap. Let us glance more closely
at the hosts of the Matabeles. It is altogether a very quiet, demure,
not to say slightly commonplace-looking crowd. The brothers
Haggard, a handsome trio, may be put down as the exception. But however the company may look, their hearts are in
the right place, and "humanity" is the word written on those hearts.
The conversation touches upon the debate in the House across
the way, on the previous night, and the letter which Sir Hercules
Robinson wrote to the Under-Secretary of State for the Colonies
comes in for a little weak chaff. The Envoys do not keep us
waiting long. .They enter, accompanied by Mr. Maund—dapper
and debonair—their escort from Matabeleland, and Mr. Johann
Colenbrander, their interpreter. The Matabeles are enveloped in
heavy hairy overcoats, of which they are relieved by an attendant
with gracious obeisance. The Envoys are dressed in costumes as
dark as their faces, so that the brilliant scarlet tie which each
wears in his gray flannel shirt shines out like a danger light in a
railway tunnel. Breakfast is announced, and we all file in, taking
our seats as we list. The repast is a substantial one, and all the
white folks tuck in with real British earnestness. Umshete and
Babjaan are at the head table with a waiter apiece behind them.
They evidently find the officious attention of the swallow-tailed
slaves oppressive ; indeed, they look as if they would much rather
be fingering a lump of beef. They take up the breakfast rolls, and
in a homely, stooping position, a yard away from the table, bite the
little loaves as they also chew the cud of reflection. They do not
seem to care for the made dishes, although they evidently relish
tea. When thanks are returned for the meal, the Chairman rises
well primed for a speech. He speaks volubly and does not seem
to require the notes he has in his hand. There are one or two
good touches in his address, as when he says that he hopes the
day is not far distant when Englishmen and Matabeles will meet
together in the valleys of the Limpopo as happily as they do that
day in Westminster. Mr. Maund, although saying that the
Envoys will thank them in their own poetical way for their
welcome, nevertheless delivers an incisive and dignified speech,
and tells us exactly why Lo Bengula sent his Envoys. By the way,
there is a little difference of opinion evidently as to the way to
pronounce Lo Bengula's name. One speaker has it Lo Ben Goola,
another has it Lo Ben Gyoola, another Lo Béngula, another has it
Lo Beng Waylo, while yet another, the Rev. John Mackenzie,
styles him Lo Pin Goola. Needless here to dwell upon the
speeches. Evelyn Ashley's is vigorous and eloquent, while
Commander Cameron speaks like an English curate reading off his
sermon at a high-pitched note. When they are asked if they will
speak, the Envoys look sheepish. Umshete twists in his seat and
says he has a cold, while Babjaan rises half up, and with an
unsuccessful endeavour to hide his head, sits down again. We are
left in doubt as to the meaning of this pantomime, but the

Chairman announces in loud tones, " The Envoys have replied." It is not so, however, as shortly afterwards, the spirit moves Babjaan to rise again. He crosses his arms and utters a few eloquent words in a quiet style, the following being the interpretation of them :—" We are very glad to see such a large gathering of those who have invited us here. You all know why we are here ; we have been treated kindly, and now we can go back to our homes, and say we have sat with people who have so much say in British rule, and can move it when they like. We can go back to our King, and say that we have had such a good breakfast and such a hearty welcome in England. We have been received by a number of elderly men here. We thank you for the welcome you have given us." Not the least interesting speech is that by Sir John Swinburne, a name well known in the epoch of exploration in Matabeleland 20 years ago. As Sir John tells us, he never experienced greater kindness in his life than in Matabeleland. We all believe that the same can be said to-day on behalf of the nation, and we think, as we leave, that the breakfast will do more and more to quicken the good feeling of the Matabeles towards Englishmen.

The Envoys took back the following letter from the Aborigines' Protection Society.

Aborigines' Protection Society,
3 Room, Broadway Chambers,
4, Broadway, Westminster, London, S.W.

To the Chief Lo Bengula.

Dear Friend,—We send you a greeting by your messengers, whom we have invited to meet us during their stay in London. The Society to which we belong has, for many years, striven to help distant races of men—races not well-known in England, and not knowing England well—to obtain justice at the hands of our fellow-countrymen. We wish you to know that there is such a Society, and that its great aim is to help the weak to live, as well as the strong, and to require that the strong shall also be just. We have to oppose the actions of our own fellow-countrymen when they do wrong, although those they are wronging may be strangers to us, and men of another race.

We are reminded by the presence of your messengers in our country, that our people have long been visitors to you, and to your father, Umsilikase, and that some of them have lived under your protection to the present time, as missionaries and traders.

We think you acted very wisely as a great chief when you despatched messengers to our Queen on the present occasion. The digging of gold is a new industry among your people. It is not new among white men. Hence your wisdom in sending to our Queen and her advisers on this matter. You already know the value of gold, and are aware that it buys cattle, and everything else that is for sale, and that some men set their hearts on it, and dispute about it as other tribes fight for cattle. As you are now being asked by many for permission to seek for gold, and to dig it up in your country, we would have you be wary and firm in resisting proposals that will not bring good to you and your people.

We trust your messengers will return to you accompanied by a messenger from our Queen who will tell you all her words, and who

L 2

will help you to understand matters on which you may need his assistance.

Wishing you and your people peace and prosperity, we sign ourselves, on behalf of the Aborigines' Protection Society,

YOUR FRIENDS.

Taken altogether, Umshete and Babjaan were thoroughly satisfied with their visit to England. They said that they could now go back and tell their King and people that they had found everything as it had been represented; indeed, it was far greater. The Chiefs had a final interview with Lord Knutsford, previous to their return to South Africa, when the reply to Lo Bengula was handed to them. Each was presented by Lord Knutsford with a ram's-horn snuff box mounted in silver, with which they were greatly pleased.

The following was Her Majesty's reply to Lo Bengula :—

The Queen has heard the words of Lo Bengula. She is glad to receive the messengers from Lo Bengula, and to learn the message which he has sent.

The Queen will send words in reply, through her Secretary of State, for the messengers to take to Lo Bengula.

A reply to the letter of Lo Bengula will be sent through the High Commissioner. Lo Bengula may trust in the advice and words of that officer, as he is specially appointed by the Queen to receive the words of all friendly chiefs in South Africa, and to send to them any reply which the Queen may be pleased to give.

The following was the fuller reply of Her Majesty to Lo Bengula through Lord Knutsford :—

(Entrusted to Umshete and Babjaan.)

I, Lord Knutsford, one of Her Majesty's Principal Secretaries of State, am commanded by the Queen to give the following reply to the message delivered by Umshete and Babjaan.

The Queen has heard the words of Lo Bengula. She was glad to receive these messengers and to learn the message which they have brought.

They say that Lo Bengula is much troubled by the white men, who come into his country and ask to dig gold, and that he begs for advice and help.

Lo Bengula is the ruler of his country, and the Queen does not interfere in the government of that country, but as Lo Bengula desires her advice, Her Majesty is ready to give it, and having therefore consulted Her Principal Secretary of State holding the Seals of the Colonial Department, now replies as follows :—

In the first place, the Queen wishes Lo Bengula to understand distinctly that Englishmen who have gone out to Matabeleland to ask leave to dig for stones, have not gone with the Queen's authority, and that he should not believe any statements made by them or any of them to that effect.

The Queen advises Lo Bengula not to grant hastily concessions of land, or leave to dig, but to consider all applications very carefully.

It is not wise to put too much power into the hands of the men who come first, and to exclude other deserving men. A King gives a stranger an ox, not his whole herd of cattle, otherwise what would other strangers arriving have to eat ?

Umshete and Babjaan say that Lo Bengula asks that the Queen will send him someone from herself. To this request the Queen is advised that Her Majesty may be pleased to accede. But they cannot say whether Lo Bengula wishes to have an Imperial officer to reside with him permanently, or only to have an officer sent out on a temporary mission, nor do Umshete and Babjaan state what provision Lo Bengula would be prepared to make for the expenses and maintenance of such an officer.

Upon this and any other matters Lo Bengula should write, and should send his letters to the High Commissioner at the Cape, who will send them direct to the Queen. The High Commissioner is the Queen's officer, and she places full trust in him, and Lo Bengula should also trust him. Those who advise Lo Bengula otherwise deceive him.

The Queen sends Lo Bengula a picture of herself to remind him of this message, and that he may be assured that the Queen wishes him peace and order in his country.

The Queen thanks Lo Bengula for the kindness which, following the example of his father, he has shown to many Englishmen visiting and living in Matabeleland.

This message has been interpreted to Umshete and Babjaan in my presence, and I have signed it in their presence, and affixed the seal of the Colonial Office.

(Signed)   KNUTSFORD.

Colonial Office, March 26, 1889.

Somewhat fagged from sightseeing, the Envoys left England in the *Grantully Castle* and waited at Madeira the coming on of Mr. Maund by another steamer. At Cape Town they spoke of the stairs and of the houses being built one over the other. They had rooms at the best hotel in Cape Town, the landlord assuring Mr. Maund that there were many visitors who could not feed themselves as well as the Indunas. I shall again allow Mr. Maund to speak in his own words :—" Directly the Indunas got back to the frontiers of their country on their return from Europe they began to be afraid of wearing the English clothes which they loved so well. First one garment disappeared and then another until I found them one day in trousers and jacket only. When we got absolutely to the frontier and were going to be doctored with the mystic rites, Umshete the odious appeared with nothing but his monkey tails around his loins, whereas the gentle Babjaan had on a waistcoat beside the national monkey tails. Every Induna in the country was given a complete set of corduroy clothes, a snuff-box, and a knife, and many of them wore the clothing during the cold weather. It was the dressing of the Matabele nation, for though they pretended to love their savage tail curios and despise the effeminate white man's dress they in reality liked the clothes and begged hard for them when the cold weather came on. For months after our return long palavers went on, and these old fellows gave the most minute descriptions of all they had seen, and very clever were many of their illustrations. Thus, describing the sea to the Indunas,

they said it was like the blue vault of heaven at noon, and the
floating kraal was as the sun in the centre; the water was mostly
thus calmly blue, the kraal being pushed through it by the steamer
(engine) from behind. The sapient remark of Lo Bengula was
—'How could such a vast iron kraal be sustained by the water,
unless it had supports from the bottom, by which it was pushed
along; truly these "Makeeweh" (white men) are the sons of the
sea.' Sometimes, the old men added, the sea was 'full,' *i.e.*,
like their boisterous rivers in the rainy season; then, the floors
and roofs of the kraal rocked till the white men danced. This
rough sea was seen after passing the Portuguese gate (Lisbon),
and refers to a gale in the Bay of Biscay; but they could not
understand how the Queen allowed the Portuguese to have a gate
on her water leading to Cape Town. London they described as the
place all white men must come from; people, people everywhere,
all in a hurry, serious of faces, and always busy like the white
ants. There was not room for anyone above ground in
this great kraal, for they could see men and horses moving
in a stage below, just as they live in houses built one above
the other (this referring to Holborn Viaduct). The fire-carriages,
too (locomotives), like those between Kimberley and Cape Town,
have to burrow in the earth under the streets for fear of being
stopped by the crowd. The sham-fight at Aldershot they described
very minutely, and, in my hearing, old Babjaan, turning round
to about 30 Indunas, said, 'Never talk of fighting the white
man again, aough! They rise up line after line, always firing.
Their little boys, the sons of headmen, all learn to fight like
men (referring to Eton boys). Their generals correct all faults;
they won't pass a man who is out of time as they dance by in
line coming from the fight (the march past).' Many was the
laugh we had over curious, but always reasonable, descriptions
of their recollections. Above all, the interview at Windsor most
impressed them, and the sight of Cetewayo's assegai in the
corridor of arms there. They told us that all the kings and
queens at Madame Tussaud's were those whom our present
Queen had conquered, because last, and downstairs, came Cetewayo—and was not his assegai at the end of the corridor?
This last idea we did not think it necessary to correct. Much
more could I tell you of their sayings; but the great result of
their visit is what we should appreciate. I have no hesitation in
saying that the recent peaceable occupation of Mashonaland by
our party of Pioneers is the direct outcome of the clever way in
which these two old men told their tale, and the King disseminated it among his people. The Queen did more good for the
empire by that kindly interview at Windsor than could have been
done by thousands of her soldiers. Had the same policy been
followed in Zululand, how much trouble, how many brave lives,
and what vast expenditure might have been saved! For
the Zulu is our natural ally in South Africa; he admires

us for our athletic tastes, manliness, and pluck. I remember well the description of the Bank of England, over which the Indunas were taken. They described every detail of the 'Queen's Storehouse' as they called it, to the King. When they told of the many ingots of gold they had seen on trucks in the vaults, the King immediately asked if it were in stone (quartz), and on being told no, that it was all ready to be cut up into money, he rejoined, 'Why, if the Queen has so great store of gold, do her people seek more?' 'That is the point,' said they; 'they go all over the world seeking it, not only in our own country, because they are all obliged to pay tribute to her in gold.' I believe this made a great impression on the King, and he certainly seems to have taken keenly to gold-mining since, for he has pegged in his own name, by means of authorised agents, forty reef claims and two alluvial gold claims, in accordance with the regulations of the British South Africa Company, which have been recognised as valid. How after this can the opponents of the Company deny that Lo Bengula does not recognise the jurisdiction he has bestowed on the Chartered Company? The papers were full of lies about the Indunas, it being stated that they were received with disfavour and not listened to by the King. Lo Bengula really was so interested in what they had to say, that week after week we used to go daily to his kraal, and the Indunas explained to him what they had seen. Any points they could not make properly clear, I did for them. I cannot say too much of the admirable way in which the interpreter, Mr. J. Colenbrander, conducted his work. The success of the mission was a good deal due to his clever tact and forbearance with the black men, and to the able manner in which he translated and described. The Indunas never left the King's presence for nearly two months, except one of them who had to go home because he was sick. They were always with the King. Sometimes as many as seventy Indunas listened to their accounts of the greatness of England. The Indunas were very minute in their description of the soldiers, and of the cannon (baiunbai), detailing how far the shots could be carried, and how they penetrated armour plate. The Indunas were most reserved, never showing surprise throughout. Their only exclamation of surprise was 'Ugh! Maundy,' under their breath. Their descriptions leavened among the Matabele, the story permeated throughout the land, and gradually we began to see its effect by the greater respect with which Englishmen were treated. Of course there were many reports of dangers that were really non-existent. Indabas were constantly held at which the question of the concession was discussed, but I believe the object was merely to educate the nation up to the idea, for the King had given his word. Lo Bengula was going to behave as he had behaved. I remained there seven months and took up presents to the King from those interested in the concession. I distributed the presents to every Induna in the country, and they all came to my camp to discuss the mission with me. My mornings, from shortly after sunrise until it got too hot, were engaged in doctoring. Among the patients was the King's son, who had broken his arm whilst out hunting ; for healing it the King presented me with oxen. The King was very grateful to me for having carried through his mission, and for having brought back the men alive. He said I must build a kraal, live among and be one of them."

Mr. Maund announced the return to Matabeleland to the Colonial Office as follows :—

The King's Kraal, Matabeleland,
August 7, 1889.

My Lord,—I have the honour to inform your lordship of the safe arrival in Matabeleland of the two Envoys, Umshete and Babjaan, recently sent to England under my charge by King Lo Bengula.

Your lordship's letter and the Queen's picture were duly delivered. The former was read by Mr. Moffat and translated to the King, who expressed himself greatly pleased with the contents and general tenor of the letter.

To-day the King called a meeting of all the white men in this part of the country, and the letter was read out to them.

The King was much struck with Her Majesty's picture, and made the minutest inquiries from the Envoys regarding their visit to Windsor, and ended by saying, "He could well see that it was written in her face—that she was the Great Queen."

After a very trying journey, owing to want of water and grass, the mission entered Matabeleland the 21st ult., and received the heartiest welcome. Every kraal passed turned out, and the headman brought presents in kind. Messengers and ceremonial halts delayed us to satisfy the national customs, and, ultimately, before arriving at the King's kraal, the witch doctors came, at the King's express command, and sprinkled us with some vile concoction according to their rites.

I mention this, as being the first time it has occurred in the country, o show how much importance the King attaches to the mission, and his evident desire that his people should look upon it in the same light.

It will probably be some weeks ere the King and his Indunas have sufficiently digested all his messengers have to tell him for any definite course of action to be decided on. But meanwhile the white men in the country will be more respected, and live in greater security than they have hitherto.

I have, &c.,
(Signed)   E. A. Maund.

Lo Bengula also wrote to Sir Sidney Shippard the following letter, " to be communicated to Her Majesty the Queen " :—

Matabeleland, August 10, 1889.

Sir,—I wish to tell you that Umshete and Babjaan have arrived with Maund. I am thankful for the Queen's word. I have heard Her Majesty's message. The messengers have spoken as my mouth. They have been very well treated.

The white people are troubling me much about gold. If the Queen hears that I have given away the whole country, it is not so. I have no one in my country who knows how to write. I do not understand where the dispute is, because I have no knowledge of writing.

The Portuguese say that Mashonaland is theirs, but it is not so. It is all Umziligazi's country. I hear now that it belongs to the Portuguese.

With regard to Her Majesty's offer to send me an envoy or resident, I thank Her Majesty, but I do not need an officer to be sent. I will ask for one when I am pressed for want of one.

I thank the Queen for the word which my messengers give me by mouth, that the Queen says I am not to let anyone dig for gold in my country, except to dig for me as my servants.

I greet Her Majesty cordially.

his

(Signed)   Lo Bengula ✕

mark.

Before me,   Present:

(Signed)   J. S. Moffat,   Umshete.

Assistant Commissioner.   Babjaan.

(Signed)   J. W. Fill,   Boyongwane.

Interpreter. (Signed)   J. S. M.

To this Lord Knutsford returned the following reply, by Sir Henry Loch :—

Downing Street, December 5, 1889.

Sir,—I have the honour to acknowledge the receipt of General Smyth's despatch of October 25 last, enclosing copies of despatches from Sir Sidney Shippard and Mr. Moffat, and of a letter from Lo Bengula, which he desired might be communicated to the Queen. Lo Bengula should be informed that this letter has been communicated to the Queen as he desired, and that before Her Majesty saw it she had already commanded me to write the message on parchment which has just been sent to him ; that the words about digging for gold in his country, which he says his messengers, Umshete and Babjaan, gave him from the Queen, were not exactly the Queen's words, but that he will see from the Queen's last message that she meant much the same thing, that is, that the men employed by the Company to manage the digging for gold will recognise him as King of the country, and will have such powers as he entrusts to them.

Lo Bengula should also be told that the Queen will not recognise as Portuguese any country that belongs to him.

I have, &c.,

(Signed)   Knutsford.

And as his name appears so frequently in these pages, I may state that Mr. J. S. Moffat, Assistant Commissioner in Bechuanaland, now represents the Imperial Government at Bulawayo. It was not possible to make a more suitable selection for this important post than Mr. Moffat. The Permanent Resident, however, did not take office except under a strong sense of duty. As he wrote in a letter to Sir Sidney Shippard :—" No man who knows anything about it could look forward to occupying such a post with feelings of satisfaction. It means a ghastly exile amongst unruly savages, from whom one has to tolerate daily rudeness and indignity, if not from the Chief and his Indunas, yet from any chartered libertine of a Metjaha. Things have not improved in this respect in Matabeleland. The laxer rule of Lo Bengula as compared with his father, and the greater familiarity with white men which has bred contempt, have changed the Matabele for the worse. I am at the same time perfectly at one with his Excellency as to the importance of having a representative of the Government always in the country." It is hardly necessary to add that Mr. Moffat is the son of the late Dr. Moffat frequently referred to in these pages, and that he is, therefore, peculiarly fitted for his present appointment. His reputation as a man of truth and tact stands clear as the noon-day sun, and he is held in great respect by Lo Bengula.

I shall now give some account of the mission from the Imperial Government to Lo Bengula sent to convey a message from Lord Knutsford, written by the Queen's direction, announcing the incorporation of the British South Africa Company by Royal Charter, and advising the King to give his confidence and support to the Company and to its representatives in Matabeleland. The message is printed in full in another chapter. After correspondence between the Colonial Office and the War Office two officers and one non-commissioned officer of the Royal Horse Guards were, at the

CAPT. VICTOR FERGUSON.
(Royal Horse Guards.)

SURGEON-MAJOR H. F. MELLADEW.
(Royal Horse Guards.)

request of the British South Africa Company, allowed to form a deputation to Matabeleland to deliver the message. Their names were Captain Victor Ferguson and Surgeon-Major Melladew, and Corporal-Major White, of whom Lord Knutsford wrote, "he is the senior non-commissioned officer of the regiment, and a gentleman of good education, and of much professional distinction." In a despatch from Sir Henry Loch to Sir Sidney Shippard, His Excellency wrote :—

By the officer or non-commissioned officer in charge of the police escort accompanying these officers you should address a communication to Mr. Moffat, instructing him as follows :—

(*a*) That a message from the Secretary of State will be handed to him

by a party of officers of Her Majesty's Royal Horse Guards, and that he
is to deliver this message to Lo Bengula.

(b) That he is to present these officers to the King, and in doing so to
impress upon Lo Bengula the friendly character of the communication.
He should also point out the importance attached by Her Majesty's
Government to the delivery of the letter, and the compliment conveyed
by Her Majesty in selecting officers of the high standing of these gentlemen as bearers of the message.

(c) Mr. Moffat should likewise avail himself of the opportunity to
inform Lo Bengula that Her Majesty has been pleased to appoint me as
Her representative as Governor of the Colony of the Cape of Good Hope
and Her Majesty's High Commissioner of South Africa.

He should also assure Lo Bengula of my friendly feelings towards
him.

The mission reached Cape Town comfortably in the *Hawarden
Castle*, and arrived at Kimberley without any adventure in
particular, being received most hospitably everywhere.

Two days later, writes one of the party, a four-wheeled coach,
specially set apart for the mission, and drawn by eight mules, stood
ready at our host's door, gorgeously painted in red and yellow, and
honoured by the royal " V.R." and Crown in gold. It was somewhat overloaded with baggage, which had been arranged round the
sides, on the roof, and behind, while a canteen dangled underneath, in happy ignorance of all the stumps and stones waiting to
make impressions upon it on the road. We started on our long
journey to Bulawayo, the Matabele capital, 850 miles away, with
the good wishes of our new friends, who all hoped that we should
soon shake down. This process commenced at once and continued
for many days. It was very pleasant travelling, and the climate
most beautiful. A cool breeze tempered the heat of the day, while
the nights were delightful, making sleep in the open most enjoyable.
Our road lay over the regular post-cart route to Palapye, Khama's
Mangwato capital, 650 miles from Kimberley. During the first
part of the journey we stopped for meals at the regular halting
places, generally traders' stores, afterwards in the veld, where we
prepared our own food and enjoyed it doubly, while the mules had
a roll and a feed on the then luxuriant grass. The post-cart takes,
according to the time-table, six and a half days, travelling with
relays day and night, and did really do so at that time under the
excellent management of Mr. Burnett. However, afterwards our
experience was very different. We passed through Vryburg, capital
of British Bechuanaland, the seat of the Administrator, Sir Sidney
Shippard, K.C.M.G., a wretched town of a few scattered houses,
but possessing a gold mine in the hotel bar. After some delay we
reached Mafeking, in the Protectorate, six miles from the Transvaal
border. Small at present—it was only created during Sir Charles
Warren's time—this town has certainly a great future before it
as a forwarding centre on the road north to the countries about to be
opened out, Matabeleland and Mashonaland. It will be a station on
the new railway now being constructed from Kimberley towards the

Zambesi, of which the first section is about to be opened. Already large godowns are springing up, and the Standard Bank of South Africa has lately opened a branch office; in fact, everybody is preparing for a very busy time. An excellently supplied market is held every morning, everything, however, being sent in from the adjacent Transvaal. The mission was delayed a fortnight at Palapye waiting for despatches.

KHAME AS HE APPEARED IN THE UNIFORM OF THE ROYAL HORSE GUARDS.

But I shall now allow Surgeon-Major Melladew to speak for himself. He has kindly described for me the following further experiences of the mission :—" On the 23rd January, 1890, we at last saw before us the huts and houses of the Tati Gold Fields, prettily situated on the slopes of low green hills beyond a narrow muddy river of the same name. It was a welcome sight, for now only about 100 miles remained to be done of our journey to Bulawayo, the Matabele capital. Our coach had experienced a very rough time since leaving Kimberley, and although never upset, its balance had often been most severely tried. Many a time it had obstinately refused to move from the soft bed of various mud holes until unloaded. The baggage piled on the rails outside had been swept off by trees and their branches on the narrow track, and it had had lucky escapes over rocky roads and steep river banks. Yet drawn by its ten mules, this—the pioneer coach of the upper country—had brought us safely and without mishap over the 850 miles which now lay between us and the Diamond City. After crossing the shallow river it dashed gaily up to the European enclosure at Tati, where we were most hospitably received by the manager and his staff. Tati is a small settlement on the border of the Matabele land, close to the ' disputed ' territory between the Shashi and Macloutsie Rivers, a country claimed by both Khama, Chief of the Bamangwato, and Lo Bengula, King of Matabeleland. A large enclosure contains the offices of the Tati Gold Fields and Exploration Company, the quarters of the officials, and a fortified house built as a means of defence against any possible Matabele raid. The settlement has a very pretty situation, though not by any means a healthy one; malarial fever is rife, owing to its position in a hollow, with marshy ground close to the river. Two messengers from Lo Bengula awaited us here, sent by the King to conduct us safely to the capital, 100 miles further north. These gentlemen were very glad to see us, partly no doubt in view of probable presents, for which all Matabeles have a hankering; much honoured with their mission they considered themselves, and were very important personages indeed. They were clad in kilts of fur, bangles, and high black felt hats. We added a coat and shirt, in which they soon appeared, greatly delighted with their new garments. A most unprepossessing individual came up soon after, a greasy, dirty, grizzly-haired little man in a fur waistcoat, old coat, and very shabby wide-awake hat, adorned with cotton band and waving ostrich feather. Through the pierced lobe of each ear was drawn a piece of scarlet rag. He had leather anklets and sandals, a jambok in his hand, a villainous countenance and very fiery eye. But his most curious possessions were hanging from his neck —a choice assortment of all the old leather straps and buckles with which it had ever been his good fortune to meet. Here were cocoons full of snuff, oval divining bones, greasy old pouches, and an ancient powder flask, while attached to his hair behind hung the dried inflated gall bladder of a sheep. A striking oddity, worth money to a showman, but a very important and dreaded person in his own country, for the little man was no less than Lo Bengula's spy and witch doctor. He had been sent here to report to his master on any suspicious occurrences on the frontier.

LOBENGULAS SPY & WITCHDOCTOR.

"Very little work was going on at the Tati Gold Fields; the Blue-jacket and New Zealand mines were almost at a standstill; but workmen were shortly expected to open up the Monarch Reef, supposed to be one of the richest in the world.

"In order to ease our heavily-loaded wagon over the rough country before us we had taken with us from Palapye, Khama's capital, a buggy and light cart, and very useful they proved, for the roads became rapidly worse, and from Tati we had additional passengers, the two King's messengers. Never having been on wheels before, these gentlemen did not seem at all happy when bumped over the rough road. It was a new experience to them, and the violent oscillations severely tried their equilibrium both of mind and body. Then, unfortunately, on the second day one of the front wheels suddenly broke against a stump, and our Matabele guardians were as suddenly thrown out on to the stony road. After this they decidedly objected to our mode of travel, and from that day, curiously enough, our friends preferred to walk.

"The country now greatly improved in appearance. Instead of the flat plains covered with grass and bush, over which we had journeyed for many a day, most picturesque hills made up of im-

ROYAL CHARTER HOUSE BULAWAYO.

mense boulders fantastically piled one upon the other, lay scattered around. The huge rocks, thickly covered with a bright red lichen, were in vivid contrast to the green trees and shrubs, and candelabra-like cacti, which grew among them. The high grass, at this season of the year in full bloom, the many wild flowers, and the deep blue sky formed a picture which made travelling delightful to the eye, though, thanks to the villainous road, trying to the body. A few small villages still exist among these rocky hills, but practically the people are in hiding from the dreaded Matabele warriors, who have already made the beautiful country a desert. Many a kraal has here been cleared out by order of the King, the men and women butchered, the boys and girls carried off, the former to become Matabele soldiers, the latter Matabele wives and slaves.

"After several mishaps we arrived at Bulawayo at the end of January, and finally outspanned at the enclosure of the British South Africa Company, distant about three-quarters of a mile from the Royal Kraal. The King's capital stands upon a ridge on the northern side of the Bulawayo River, in a most commanding position, overlooking as it does the entire country around. On this plain live the few European residents in huts surrounded by ring fences of thorny mimosa bush, the principal enclosure belonging to the above-named Company to which Lo Bengula has granted the right to open out and develop the resources of both Matabeleland and Mashonaland. It is occupied by the representative of the Company, the officer in charge, an interpreter, and store keeper, all of which officials live in huts and wagons round a larger central hut which has been christened the 'Royal Charter House.' During our stay the interior of this well-built house was decorated most tastefully by means of skins, shields, assegais, and curiosities

INTERIOR OF THE "CHARTER HOUSE."

(The first white dwelling under the ægis of the British South Africa Company at Bulawayo.)

from Mashonaland. It was the meeting-place of the European community at Bulawayo, and visited daily by most of the Matabele notabilities, while the natives generally hovered about all day long intent upon begging for all they saw. Queens, princes, and princesses of the blood royal, the regent, the rain and dance doctors, young and old ladies, old generals and young soldiers—all were anxious for presents from the white man, who is by them defined as the 'present-giving animal.' Close to the Royal Charter House

is the enclosure of the Assistant Commissioner, the Rev. Mr.
Moffat; another was inhabited by the representatives of the Exploring Company, now allied to the British South Africa Company,
and a fourth is tenanted by a trader and his stores.

"On our arrival at Bulawayo, his Majesty was living at
Enganine, a military kraal seven miles to the south, and there our
first interview took place with Lo Bengula, the dreaded ruler of
Matabeleland, who received us in native state, viz., clothed in
nothing but a narrow strip of monkey skin, and royal navy cap with
blue ostrich feather. With a most disagreeable face and immensely
stout body he was not at all prepossessing as we saw him seated
in a wheeled chair, for, suffering from gout, he was unable to stand
or walk. His power is absolute; there is no punishment but that
of death, and this is meted out with a most liberal hand, and no
consideration for persons. People of royal blood are strangled and
buried, the others killed by a blow from a knob-kerry, and left in
the veld for the hyenas, while the victim's property, wives,
children, and cattle are divided between the King and the men who
have just carried out the royal order. Lo Bengula has disposed of
nearly all his relatives, and any person whom he suspects or dis-
likes, or anyone who has become rich, is at once smelt out for
witchcraft, and sent into the other world. Two or three men are
ordered to call upon the doomed individual; they do so, and
probably have a friendly chat and a draught of beer which is un-
suspectingly offered. The executioners now suggest a walk outside, and the knob-kerry soon finishes the work.

"A cattle king, for all the cattle belong to him, Lo Bengula is
never so happy as when, seated in one of his kraals, he watches the
beasts, of each of which he knows the history.

"It was in a very dirty enclosure, surrounded by oxen, that he
received and welcomed us, and the presents we had brought, and
here he showed his hospitality by giving us beef to be eaten with
the aid of fingers and teeth, and native beer which was first
tasted by a plump slave girl to show that it contained no poison.
The beef was brought by the royal 'chef,' a greasy individual whom
we christened 'Francatelli,' by which name he was always known
afterwards. He certainly was an artist in the only *plât* he ever prepared—steamed beef. It was excellent, and cooked by being
allowed to simmer for many hours over a very slow fire in large earthenware pots. Boiled and softened maize is the main food of the
people. Beef the majority get rarely. No cattle are allowed to be
killed except by permission of the King, who is the food-giver of
his people. Beer made from fermented Kafir corn is the favourite
drink, and enormous quantities are consumed; it is very nourishing
and, no doubt, the cause of the rotundity of the people in general.
During our interviews with the King men were continually coming
up all the while shouting the royal titles, and gradually stooping
lower and lower as they approached nearer until at last they
crouched down before his Majesty. No arms are allowed to be

brought into his presence, nor is passing behind the King etiquette. Lo Bengula unfortunately would not allow his photograph to be taken. At first he gave permission, but finally refused on the plea of being unable to put on his war-dress—the only costume in which a Matabele warrior should appear. He never has been, and no doubt never intended to be photographed; it is against the Matabele creed. To take a man's picture is to take away his spirit, and his own spirit and those of his forefathers are the only things in which he believes. The photographs I took were taken without the knowledge of the individuals, for to ask permission to do so would have been useless.

"The country is divided into a number of military kraals, each kraal containing a regiment presided over by several head men; it is also the abode of a party of queens. Lo Bengula has 82 of the latter, so not unnaturally fearing dissensions among all these ladies, he has scattered them as much as possible about the country. His first ten wives had no children and accused his favourite sister of having bewitched them. Witchcraft is paramount, so her fate was sealed and rapid. Never more than ten days in one spot, the King, although over sixty years of age, travels about in his wagon from kraal to kraal, paying many of them a visit every year,—a tour of inspection of queens and cattle. Except when at the capital, Bulawayo, where he has a mud house, Lo Bengula always sleeps in his wagon. We paid him a visit in his 'Palace' afterwards and found his Majesty still in bed, the couch consisting simply of skins on the ground, an old blanket and dirty pillow on a gun case for the head.

"The male population may be divided into two classes, that which wears a ring and that which does not. The ring is oval, about the thickness of a finger, and made of grease and gum, and is fastened to the hair on top of the head. The scalp inside the ring is shaved by professional ring and hair dressers. A man thus adorned is responsible for his actions; for him who has no ring the father is responsible. It is the custom of the King when he thinks fit to grant permission to all the male members of a certain kraal to wear the ring, thereby bestowing a great honour, which, however, may possibly not be attained before the men have arrived at a mature age. The soldiers occupying a regimental kraal are generally more or less of one age. When sufficient young men have become fit to carry arms they are collected, made into a new regiment, and given a new location. A custom similar to the ring-giving appertains to matrimony. Lo Bengula gives his sanction to the marriage of the men of a certain kraal, that is, he recognises their already existing unions as marriages, for probably the men have for years lived with what virtually have been their wives. Thus the first regiment in the kingdom, the Imbizu, body guard of the King, received permission to marry only this year, though most of the men already had children and probably grandchildren; but even this corps had not yet received

M

the ring. When a man finds himself in love he asks the father of the object of his affections for the lady, giving, if he so pleases, nothing in exchange; or he may settle the bargain at once by payment. If no children appear the husband may return the wife to her parents and take one of her sisters instead, if there be one available. Should a child be born, however, and the man have given nothing to the father of his wife in the first instance, he will now have to pay double her former value and double it again for every other child. A widow and her children are generally taken by her late husband's brother, and probably become slaves.

"About a week after our arrival preparations began to be made for the great annual war dance, which it was our privilege to witness—a wonderful, never-to-be-forgotten sight. Every regiment ordered to be present sent in advance a certain number of men to Bulawayo to build temporary huts for their corps. Our enclosure became every day more crowded, and demands for presents, beads, knives, tinder boxes, &c., to be more constant. We received visits from the most distinguished persons of the realm, and were soon on the most friendly terms with all. The first callers were the Regent, Umthlaba, and the Commander-in-Chief, Xutwayo. They are tall, well-grown men with good-humoured faces and pleasant manner. The former has no hair on head or face, the other short grizzled whiskers and beard; both wore monkey-skin kilts only. Their offices are hereditary, and they are members of the Privy Council. To the Regent alone the King confides the secret about who is to be his successor on the Throne, and the name is not made public until after the decease of the last occupier. They are both old men, but well set up, and always glad to have a talk. A great friend of theirs, another elderly man, was the King's brother, a genial old gentleman clad in kilt, an old chlorodyne bottle full of snuff hanging from the neck. He was very fond of beef and came almost daily in search of it.

XUTWAYO.

(Commander-in-Chief of the Matabele Army, and noted for his cruelty.)

" But, *Place aux Dames*! make room, and a good deal too, for Loskay, head queen of the Capital, a very portly lady and ranking before all other queens. She used to sit for hours in the Royal

Charter House devouring sweets, biscuits, beef, anything and every-thing, and generally took away with her presents of beads and cloth; her appetite was difficult to appease and she was rarely satisfied. Her massive form was partly clothed in a coloured cotton sheet, while a black goat skin kilt with hair outside and fringed depended from her waist. The head was encircled with a coil of pink beads, her neck with tin, brass, and iron chains, captured probably in some Mashona raid, which people are skilled workers in those metals. Then with more beads round ankles and arms her visiting costume was complete. All the queens whom we had the honour to meet were similarly attired, but gorgeous creatures they became when in full state dress during the war dance; nothing could possibly have rivalled them in their startling and dazzling colouring. The Queens' dance was led by Loskay, who was followed in single file by about 20 royal ladies hopping about with a highly grotesque step, and resembling so many brilliant butterflies fluttering and spark-ling in the sunlight. The black fur kilt was now replaced by a heavy beauti-fully worked and parti-coloured bead apron; massive coils of beads encircled arms, legs, throat, and head; folds of bright cotton clothed the loins, while a bright orange handkerchief covered their shoulders, and dozens of blue jays' feathers were stuck singly into the hair. They danced slowly thus for hours almost, waving long

UMTHLABA.

(Hereditary Regent and Prime Minister of Matabeleland.)

wands; the high knee action and monotony of the measure must have been most tiring to the more portly ladies. These indeed were soon puffing and blowing from their exertions; still they went on with their gyrations in front of the whole Matabele army, which at that time was drawn up to the number of 11,000 to 12,000 men in an immense half-moon, the old Zulu war formation. Queens there were many about, and, though differing in age, they all resembled each other in portliness of form, due, no doubt, to sedentary lives and the large amount of beer consumed. Every queen carries on the top of her head a small circular button or plaited grass, coloured bright red and kept in its place by weaving the hair into it. These royal ladies have a truly marvellous appetite for sweets and desire for beads and limbo (cotton cloth), the favourite colour of the former being pink, of the latter blue bird's-eye. They are the beer makers of the kingdom, and have to supply his Majesty with that beverage, especially during the week of the big dance, when enormous quantities are consumed by the army.

MATABELE LADIES

Lo Bengula has, as already stated, 82 wives, and although over sixty, takes more every year. This honour is not much sought after, a fact not to be wondered at; many young ladies when threatened with this lot have preferred to commit suicide. There is no evasion, no wedded bliss in store for them, and if caught flirting afterwards they are at once killed.

"No man's or woman's life is safe; witchcraft reigns supreme and lies as a curse upon the country and everyone in it. The King is chief witch and rain doctor, but has assistance in each department. He makes the rain in the country in which he then resides, but sends his three deputies into other parts to make it there. Certain

LOSKAY. HEAD QUEEN OF BULAWAYO
WITH ANOTHER QUEEN & ATTENDANT.

rites are gone through, of course when the commencement of the rainy season has become assured by the appearance of

heavy clouds. The success of the crops certain, the rain doctors
are rewarded by the grateful villagers. During our stay at the
capital it rained almost constantly ; the King's command had been
too well obeyed by the elements—too well, indeed, for it poured too
hard for the crops, so we hinted at the desirability of stopping the
deluge for awhile, a hint smilingly put aside by the royal rain-
maker. It was quite delightful to watch one of the chief rain
doctors dripping wet almost daily wrapped in an old waterproof
coat which someone had given him ; he looked so thoroughly cross
and miserable, thanks to his own handiwork, that, had he been
anyone else, one might have pitied him.

MARRIED AND SINGLE.

" Besides rain and witch
doctors there are three
dance doctors who preside
over the big dance and,
indeed, rule the country
during that time, for the
King is busy with witch-
craft in the sacred buck
kraal, and transacts no
public business. The chief
dance doctor is a stout
old man clad in coat and
waistcoat and old hat. He
has a pleasant face and
came often to see us, have
a talk, drink beer, and
smoke. Number two is a
most disagreeable but
determined looking man
with a thin, pinched face.
He tries to talk fast and
stutters horribly. He has
presided over many a
murder, and Heaven pity
anyone who falls into his
clutches !

" Another doctor, and
then we have done with the
profession—the war doc-
tor. An old man in over-
coat and tall hat, very thin,
suffering with cataract of both eyes. He was a great personage in
Lo Bengula's father's time, and his particular trade is to sprinkle
the army with some witchcraft medicine which renders the men
invulnerable. We had many other visitors : sick people came in
the morning and were treated to castor oil, quinine, and eye lotions ;
hunger brought many, hunger for meat especially, for this was

scarce up at the kraals, and our enclosure was known to be a sure find. The chief Induna of Bulawayo, Magwegori, came very often, a portly chief who disposed of many a piece of beef or mutton with his friend Umthlaba, and others, the remains, if there were any, being handed to the hungry crowd outside. Swarms of young soldiers came and went from morning till night, dressed in monkey or leopard skin kilts, their heads adorned with large coloured

RAIN DOCTOR UMSHABATE.

rosettes made of grass or bright feathers, carried coquettishly above one ear, like the minute forage cap of a smart cavalry man. Others, especially those of the Imbizu regiment, wore in the same manner, high conical basket-work hats covered with jackal fur. As a rule, these guardsmen were well-grown and smart-looking, despising all other soldiers as far beneath them; theirs was the first regiment raised by the present King, and recruited from the best families, and it takes the post of honour in battle. Umjan, its commander, is a tall majestic man, wearing on ordinary occasions a European coat, long, very heavy monkey-skin kilt and busby of jackal fur. His son, whom we always saw in white man's clothing, was a great beggar; one day he brought a bridle to be repaired, asked for food, and suggested that we should mend a large rent in his trousers.

"Matabele soldiers never appeared in their war dress or with arms in our enclosure; it was strictly forbidden, but we saw them in full dress as they marched into their temporary camps round Bulawayo, and, of course, often afterwards during the dances. A more picturesquely magnificent type of the savage warrior than these men in full uniform it would be impossible to imagine. Well grown and tall, they looked immense in their black ostrich feather cape and hood, the latter again surmounted by a large upright feather of the blue crane. Heavy blue monkey or leopard skin kilts in many folds enveloped their hips and hung down to the knees; long white frills made of the bushy ends of ox tails encir-

SOLDIERS IN UNDRESS.

cled their arms above the elbow and legs above the knee, coils of coloured beads and cloth the loins, and heavy bracelets wrists and ankles. A large oval shield of ox hide, two assegais and a stout stick completed the outfit. When standing close together to the number of many thousands they looked a dangerous foe, and being well known for their savage cruelty, would, in a sudden, unexpected rush, prove very trying to any troops however well disciplined. The shields of the different divisions are of different colours, a black and white one being carried by the King and his body guard, while the others are made of brown, white, or brown and white hides.

"Lo Bengula's movements are very sudden. He starts off in his wagon at the shortest notice, and requires the various European residents at his court to be in attendance upon him during his peregrinations. His message to them when on the move is short but to the point : it is simply ' follow my wheels.' From Enganine Lo Bengula arrived at his capital in his wagon drawn by twelve black oxen, but he was on this occasion escorted by the regiment quartered at Bulawayo. The men wore full dress and walked alongside the wagon all the time shouting the King's praises and titles, ' Kumalo,' ' Majesty,' ' Eater of Men,' ' Mountain of Flesh,' ' Stabber of the Sun,' ' Owner of Everything,' &c., &c. He was on his way to preside over the great annual war dance which began a few days later and lasted a week. Regiments now marched in daily and took up their temporary quarters. Every morning and afternoon they were busily drilling, singing and dancing, and the crowd in our enclosure became very dense. Soon after his return to Bulawayo, Lo Bengula sent us a fat cow as a present for meat, and on the following day his messenger appeared to request our presence at the dance of one of the older regiments, the Mahlah-lenlele (Pioneers). The royal messenger was only a slave boy, but when on duty sent by the King the second man in the kingdom. He then almost burst with importance, swaggering about in the most ludicrous manner. When proceeding to the royal kraal he lbowed his way through the crowd, hitting right and left and shouting : ' The white men have not come to see you, but the King of kings ; make way you dogs.' He wore the usual dress with all his finery, the head adorned with the end of a box whereon was painted in large red letters, ' Fry & Co.'s Cocoa.' He was very proud of this, and only donned it on special occasions, a bale of coloured feathers taking its place on other days.

" The great dance has lately been well described in more than one paper, and having already sketched the full dress of the Matabele warrior, and the curious dance of the Queens, it will only be necessary now to give an outline of the week's festivities at Bulawayo. These commenced at full moon, but had been pre-ceded three weeks before by the little dance performed by the garrison of the capital, and the troops quartered in the vicinity. The big dance is the feast of thanksgiving and purification. thanks-giving for the harvest to the spirits of the Matabele forefathers, and purification because no one, man, woman, or child, is allowed to be present without previously having washed in the Bulawayo River. The first ceremony is that of the corn dance, and very pretty it proved to be. The regiments file past the King with a slow step and plaintive chant, waving sticks surmounted by a jackal's tail. When thousands of wands are moving in unison the result some-what resembles waving corn, which indeed it is intended to represent. The King has been busy preparing witch medicine of vegetable marrow, crocodile livers, &c., &c., to be used on the morrow to paint his own body. Cattle also are slaughtered, for no blood may be spilt on the day of the big dance. The following morning the regiments, having fallen in at their different camps, were marched into the immense enclosure adjoining the royal kraal, and with wonderful precision and little or no disorder, these 11,000 men took up their places to form the gigantic half-moon formation of the Matabele army. It was a grand impressive spectacle, and the men looked very imposing in their feathers; the Indunas especially, who stood in front and advanced now and then towards the King to shout his praises. A general charge was made by the whole army towards the sacred kraal while Lo Bengula was still in it, the men waving sticks and yelling for corn. Then the main body took up its former position, a few men being detached to drive the sacred black cattle into the veld, and to drive them back again, a custom symbolic of raiding the enemy's herds. Again the army recommenced its monotonous song accompanied by the stamping of feet, and beating of shields, to go on till dark. Men occasionally stepped out of the ranks and stabbed with assegai to show how they had killed their foes in battle. The King sat in his wheeled chair with assegai in hand, but he did not throw it this year as has hitherto been the custom, thereby to indicate the direction in which the army would have to march to raid and plunder. On the next day some 600 or 700 oxen were killed in an incredibly short time by men going among them stabbing right and left with assegais; the oxen, wounded in the heart or lungs, would stand for a moment and then fall on to their side. The carcases cut up, the flesh was piled into heaps and left for the night in order that the spirits of the people's forefathers might come and take what they desired. For the special benefit of Lo Bengula's ancestors 40 black oxen were slaughtered, and he himself was rubbed over with their gall, while his sons and daughters were given bracelets of intestines to wear during the day. Beer had been brought in calabashes from all the various kraals by strings of slave girls in readiness for the next two days, when the meat is cooked in 800 or 900 immense earthenware pots, and eaten by the whole army. The festivities ended with the burning of the various camps and all the bones, the King washed, and everybody departed.

"After a stay of three weeks in the Matabele capital the King 'gave us the road'—that is, permission to leave the country. He said good-bye to us with a friendly shake of the hand at the end of a long interview, during which the usual amount of beef and beer had been consumed, and herd after herd of picked cattle driven up for our inspection. Lo Bengula was then at the cattle station, Umguché, four miles from the capital, Bulawayo, to which, when all farewells were over, we returned as rapidly as possible in order to be in time for a very great event in the future history of South Central Africa, no less than the first meeting of the Zambesi Turf Club. The races had been got up by the few English residents at the capital, and all horses which the terrible sickness, then at its worst, had spared were entered. These, sad to say, were but few in number, although every care and supposed prophylactic measure had been taken for a long time before. Those which were left had therefore to do double duty, and were entered in all the five races, three of which were to be on the flat and two over hurdles. An oval course had been laid out on the plain south of the capital, and when we arrived from our farewell interview with his Majesty everything was ready to start the first race. Lo Bengula unfortunately, could not honour the meeting, his enemy, gout, keeping him away, but many of his subjects did, and his eldest son had entered a horse which, much to his regret, a broken arm prevented him from riding. The horse, however, won, ridden right well by a Matabele boy, who unable to pull up near the winning post disappeared in the far distance. In spite of pouring rain and the limited number of horses the races were well contested. One or two jockeys found the ground somewhat hard, but there was no real grief, and when all the difficulties

THE BRITISH AND MATABELE EMBASSIES.

which had to be surmounted are taken into consideration there can be no doubt but that the first meeting of the Zambesi Turf Club was a decided success."

"Captain Ferguson presented the Queen's letters to Mr. Moffat, and as he read them out Mr. Doyle carefully translated them to the King, who made a few remarks on one or two of the paragraphs. The presents, consisting of a very handsome revolver and case and field-glass from the Duke of Abercorn, as a Director of the

Company, and some good sporting knives and specially-selected blankets were then presented to the monarch and accepted with evident pleasure. Lo Bengula seemed much struck with the Blues' uniform, and asked several questions about it, remarking that he had been told that some of Her Majesty's soldiers were clad in iron, and that now he fully believed it. Here Babjaan, one of the Indunas who had been to England and who was standing close behind him, took the opportunity of asking him if 'he would not in future always believe the accounts he had given him of the wonders to be seen in England?'"

CHAPTER VIII.

BEFORE further describing Matabeleland it will be convenient to give some account of the main road to it through Bechuanaland. As the railway will soon be open as far as Mafeking, let us make a start from that thriving town. The country between Mafeking and Shoshong may be described as a slightly undulating table-land, broken by occasional ridges of rocks or ranges of rocky hills, and having an average height of 4,000 feet above the sea. As far as Kanya the drainage of the country runs south-west to the Molopo; the watershed appears to be midway between that place and Kanya, the drainage of the country south of the hills at Kanya running north-east and that of the country north of these hills east into the Notuani, so that the whole drainage of the country north of this watershed ultimately reaches the Crocodile River.

At Mafeking the underlying rock is old red sandstone conglomerate on the north side of the Molopo, but on the south side of the river this is overlaid by limestone which stretches to the east, at least as far as Rooi Grond, the junction being distinct in the bed of the river. The old red limestone (either in the form of conglomerate or stratified sandstone) stretches as far as Monogoe, generally at no great depth, and giving a marked red colour to the soil. There are, however, frequent "dykes" of igneous rock (porphyry or coarse granite), and the rocky hills (both ranges and isolated hills) are due to an upheaval of the same rock, the smaller hills being entirely composed of igneous rock, while the larger are composed of porphyry or granite below, and old red sandstone (generally conglomerate) above. These dykes cross the road in several places between Mafeking and Kanya, and are generally accompanied by a watercourse. At Kanya the range of hills on which the town is built is composed of conglomerate, but rests on a base of porphyry, and the rising ground at the foot of them is also composed of porphyry. The hilly country immediately to the north of Kanya is chiefly porphyry, but beyond that the sandstone reappears, crossed by occasional dykes of porphyry, which last forms a range of rocky hills at Mushupa. The hills at Molopololo are composed of old red sandstone, chiefly stratified, but the conglomerate appears again to the north, and is crossed by dykes of porphyry at Hottakana and Monocho. At Kopung the bed of the watercourse is composed of conglomerate, the only place where this occurs. At Machudi the hills are composed of conglomerate above and porphyry below, and along the course of the Notuani the underlying rock is conglomerate, except for about half a mile midway between Tchobula and Laloga Drifts, where it is covered by a layer of limestone (which rock has probably been removed by denudation over the rest of this tract of country). At Tchobula Drift there is a dyke of syenite (granite with horn-blende instead of mica—mica was nowhere observed throughout), and the range of rocky hills near Monogoe is also composed of syenite, which stretches to the rising ground on the north of the springs. From this place to the range of hills south of Shoshong the underlying rock is a coarse-grained light-coloured sandstone (buff, pink, or grey), which forms large flat tables round the water at Lotuala, Mamabula, and Kuunwa. At Lotlaka the ground round the water is so thickly encrusted with saline matter that it is difficult to ascertain the nature of the rock. The hills both to the north and south of Shoshong are composed of porphyry.

Over the old red sandstone the soil is a red sandy loam mixed with gravel near the dykes or hills of porphyry (which last is generally very coarse and weathers very rapidly). This soil is covered with good grass, but the bush chiefly consists of thorny acacia (A. Giraffia, Horrida, and Detuens) and buckthorn (a species of Prunus?), and is often so dense as to be almost impenetrable. Over the porphyry the soil is lighter in colour and mixed with gravel, and the grass is coarser and higher. The bush contains few thorny acacias, and afterwards becomes forest containing large trees, many of them valuable for timber, while the undergrowth consists largely of the Mahratta (the Falboss of the Dutch), an aromatic resinous shrub with grey foliage. Over the syenite and light-coloured sandstone the soil is composed of light sandy loam, often nearly pure sand, as on the rising ground between Mamabula and Lotlaka (which appears to be an offshoot of the Kalahari desert, the soil and vegetation being similar). This soil produces excellent grass, except when too sandy, when the grass is coarse and scattered, and the forest on it is rich and varied, including many valuable trees. There is also a rich alluvial soil in the valleys or hollows through which the larger streams run, and also between the two ranges of hills at Shoshong. This is generally used by the natives for cultivation, and produces rich crops of maize and millet. There appears to be no reason why other crops should not be produced, but the ordinary English cereals are precluded by the fact that the chief rainfall is in summer. Many parts of the country between

Molopololo and Shoshong greatly resemble the wilder parts of the North-west and Central Provinces of India, many of the trees, plants, and insects being of similar (sometimes of identical) species.

The water supply is very deficient for a great part of the year, although the rainfall is large during summer. This appears to be due to the porous nature of the soil, and could probably be remedied by engineering skill. Nearly all the watercourses occur when a dyke or a hard igneous rock breaks the contour of the surface and catches the surface drainage. It is extremely probable that this occurs also below the surface, and that the water, after sinking through the porous soil, runs along the surface of the impermeable rock below till it is arrested by a dyke or elevation of igneous rock, where it accumulates on the higher side. The water, where found, is of excellent quality, except in the stagnant surface pools, where it is contaminated by decaying vegetation.

The importance of Shoshong as a trade centre was till lately great, as all roads from and to the interior converge here. From here three roads leave for the interior, one to Matabeleland, one to Zambesia (the Victoria Falls), one to Lake 'Ngami, and so on to Damaraland, Walfish Bay, and Angra Pequina. The trade route from Cape Colony enters Shoshong by three routes from Sechele's; but Shoshong has now been deserted by Khama, and Palapye takes its place.

There is really plenty of water north and south of Shoshong. Hitherto it has been a safeguard to the Bamangwato to have a country with no waters between them and the Matabele, consequently the strongest water, i.e., about Palapye, has remained a secret. With a little trouble taken, there need be no fear of want of water along the trade route even in the driest season. Thus going from Sechele's, viâ the Notuani River, and then by what is misnamed the desert route, the following waters may be found: Moncho River, 10 miles; Solochama River, 17 miles; Kopon River, 24 miles; Mochudis (Linchwaye's), 39 miles; Monwanie, 43 miles (where you strike the Notuani River); Lokgalo, 102 miles, where you leave the Notuani River; Monokwe, 120 miles (strong spring); Lowalo, 133 miles, water in stone-paved vlei; Mamabula, 138 miles, permanent water in vlei (Lotlaka, 152 miles, salt vlei); Kunuwa, 171 miles, line of vleis, chief cattle station of Bamangwato; Shoshong, 189 miles.

The country through which the trade route runs to Matabeleland is a very rich one. The Chopon range is inhabited by the Machwapon, a tribe subject to the Bamangwato. They are famous for their skill in smelting iron, with which ore these hills abound, and out of which they make the hoes and axes used by the tribe. Beneath this range there is a very fertile valley and abundance of water, and large numbers of cattle are bred and kept here.

The trade road after winding round the Mangwato range

strikes in a north-east direction. The country is undulating with occasional small koppies scattered about. In the hollows and along the banks of the rivers the soil is deep and rich, and capable of growing the finest corn. The veld is sweet and well sheltered with bush. After passing the Mahalapsie River, 24 miles from Shoshong (or 16 by the bridle path through the hills), the country is well wooded with small mopani trees and mimosa.

The Mahalapsie has water in it at all seasons and is seldom known to dry up. So too with the Mitlie River, 5 miles further on, and the Tauani River, 8 miles beyond that. At all of these rivers the Bamangwato have cattle-posts, but there are no mealie fields as there might be. About the Mitlie River and Mahalapsie River there are rocky ledges of pink porphyry, which form beautiful falls when the river is full. The quartz here has evidently been worked in days gone by, as there have been found old Makalaka or Mashona smelting works, quartz, slag, and crucible pots, 4½ miles south of the Mahalapsie. For 10 miles after Tauani River the road crosses an extensive plain with detached granite koppies on one of which there are quartz and old smelting works. About the Chakanie Hills the

DON'T LET ME DROP?

soil is very good, being black peat-soil. There are several pans or vleis beyond the hills, but the water is not permanent. The road from Chopon comes in here, and thither the cattle are driven from this district during droughts. The road then runs over comparatively high ground for 16 miles, when you come to the basin of the Lotsani River, which runs down past the Palapye Hills and is joined by other streams from the Chopon range, ultimately finding its way into the Serule River. The veld is good, but the soil is, without irrigation, too sandy for cultivation. The sand makes the road very heavy in places, for traffic. The same trees are noticeable—mopani, mimosa, and other thorn bushes.

The country is undulating and well watered between Palapye and Chopon. It was formerly supposed there was no water when

the vlei near the road was dried up.   There is, however, a running
stream of excellent water flowing from the eastern extremity of the
two hills, and there are deep pools in the Lotsani, where this brook
joins it ; but this water being 5 miles off the road, traders believed
the bushmen, who live on its very banks, when they said " there
was no water," forgetting that their very presence made it
probable there was water of some kind there.   A footpath runs
south of the lesser of the two hills and leads over rocky hills to a
large boggy vlei under Chopon.   In this rocky defile the vegetation
is luxurious, wild oranges, amatungula, and figs growing in profusion on the east side of the valley, or west side of the hills.

The Palapye Hills are two remarkably bold features, the higher
rising as it does 1,000 feet above the landscape, clothed with mopani
woods at its base, and cactus, euphorbia, and aloes to its summit.
These hills and the downs south of them are composed of a
laminated kind of black slaty-looking rock.

For 22 miles the road runs over relatively high ground with good
veld, but without water until it descends to the Seruli River with
Seruli Hill just beyond.   There is no water in this river during
the winter, but it could be got by digging.   Seruli Hill is evidently
of volcanic origin, lava, ironstone, limestone, and copper quartz
forming its disordered mass.   Between Seruli drift and the hill
once stood the town of the Baseni.   The people were all massacred
by Lo Bengula, and the town destroyed.   From here the road runs
at a short distance from the western side of the Maore Hills, under
which, 7 miles from Seruli, water is found in three pits dug in the
quartzose sand.   There is water enough for two span of oxen at a
time, to be obtained from a pit dug in similar sand under Maretele
kopje, the nearer of two hills 2½ miles west of the road at this
point.   Near this water is a small kopje formed by a " blow " of
quartz.   These Maore Hills are granite and the soil at their foot is
very rich ; the veld is good, and water is doubtless to be found in
this same stratum a few feet beneath the surface all along this
valley.

Following this line of hills the road passes along under the
Mahibi Tchwanie range, which is nothing but a continuation of
the Maore ; it, however, is the source of the Gokwe River which
runs close to the left of the road for 7 miles, when the road crosses
it by an easy drift.   A few miles lower it is joined by the Lotlakana,
over which the road passes 5 miles further on.   On the eastern
side of these hills at this point is a very large reef of quartz.
These hills are also granite, and water is found in the same stratum
as below the Maore.   Fifteen years ago there was plenty of water
to be found in the Gokwe in the dry season, as also in the Seruli
River.

The land in the valley west of the Maore and Mahibi Tchwanie
hills is particularly well adapted for farming.   The soil is rich and
deep, the grass is good, it is well wooded with mopani and sheltering
bush ; there is plenty of permanent water if opened up, and the

River Gokwe runs through it during the rainy season. The baobab tree flourishes in this district, there being one 90 feet in circumference. There is quartz between the Gokwe and the Lotlakana.

Thirteen miles of open veld brings one to the Macloutsie River (21° 47' lat.), along which the Bamangwato used to have their most advanced line of cattle-posts. This river is recognised as the boundary line of the Disputed Territory between Khama and the Matabele.

There is plenty of water in this river, although at the dry season it is 6 inches below the sand. Splendid cattle farms could be made along this river, and when the thick bush is cleared the soil is so rich on the banks that almost anything could be grown.

After leaving the Macloutsie the road runs for 21 miles through a country covered with thick bush and belts of dense mopani woods. There are numerous granite koppies composed of huge blocks scattered about, and quartz crops in various places. The road is tortuous, winding to avoid a few heavy patches of sand. The Shashi River is 150 yards broad and there is plenty of water 1 foot under the surface of the sand in the dry season. The banks are sandy, with a fringe of large mimosa trees. Two miles below the drift beneath a rocky bank is a pool of water, 300 yards long by 30 yards wide, and seemingly deep; this is never dry; crocodiles live in it, and the Tati (cattle come here to drink when the Tati River fails. On the high ground above this pool is an old Mashona copper mine. There are five shafts, or holes, in the reef, and the quartz is very rich. When the old mines at Tati, both gold and iron, were being worked by the Mashonas the ore from this mine probably went up there to be smelted, as there are no traces of smelting on the spot.

After leaving the Shashi River the road goes into more hilly country as it approaches Tati ; quartz is seen on all sides, the sand on the road being principally crushed quartz.

In the hollows of the undulating country the soil is rich and the veld correspondingly good, while the country is covered with mopani woods on all sides, affording good fuel for the crushing works at the mines ; the bark of the mopani is being used by Mr. Vermaak in tanning leather at Tati, and seems to act as well as oak bark. The Shashi is 7 miles from Tati and is the southern limit of the concession granted by Lo Bengula, originally to Sir J. Swinburne, and later to the present Company. If Tati ever becomes what it should be, a thriving mining town, then its supplies might be drawn from farms on the Macloutsie and Shashi Rivers on the south, and the Ramaquaban River on the north.

Leaving Tati you pass over quartzose hills until you descend to the "Blue Jacket" spruit, which drains down from the Majuloju Hills, a series of high, well-wooded peaks, 6 miles north of Tati ; the road for 13 miles then crosses a plain well-wooded, with belts of mopani and intervening mimosa bush. The soil is rich, and grass good, well adapted, therefore, for cattle farming. At 12

N

miles from Tati there is a pan, which, however, is dry in the depth of winter. The scenery between this and Ramaquaban is described by Baines as " park-like," and well deserves the epithet. On the banks of the Ramaquaban, 19 miles from Tati, Mr. Tainton is cattle farming. There is plenty of water in the sand of this river during the dry season, and the soil is a rich loam on its banks. A more eligible situation for farming could not be chosen. The Ramaquaban is 90 yards broad here, and receives the Impakwe River, half a mile below the drift. There used to be plenty of game here, but it is well-nigh shot out. A few lions are shot between this and Tati, and sable antelope are found in the Majuloju Hills.

The road now runs for 9 miles close to the right bank of the Impakwe until it reaches a ford in that river. At this spot there is plenty of water in rocky pools, and the fish in these point to permanent water. The soil is not good here, the road passing over short undulations, granite cropping on the ridges and red sand filling the depressions. It is covered with mopani and thorn bush. Close by the drift, on a granite knoll, are the remains of old Mashona smelting works. There are the remains of several regularly-built chambers, with the ruins of a smelting furnace in the centre. The slag remaining looks as if they were old iron-works. For 9 miles further the road winds over similar country, passing several sluits and dongas, when it enters the region of granite hills at Manialala.

The Manialala Hills are rugged granite, and clothed with the same kind of tropical vegetation as at Palapye. Here the Batalouta tribe and Makalakas formerly lived, but silence, occasionally broken by the booming bark of a baboon, reigns where the Matabele assegai has been ; the only sign of life now being a few bushmen's paths. For 3 miles from here to the Umquesi River the soil and vegetation is conspicuously rich. Oranges (strichnia), tocolo (plum), cocholo (sort of bilberry), amatungula, and figs grow thickly along the roadside. The Umquesi River has plenty of water in rocky pools. The road now winds round Makhobi's Hills, named after the Batalouta, a vassal of Mosilikatse. Here there was once a thriving and populous town. The old road still remains leading up, but a curse seems to have fallen on this once fertile spot since the dastardly massacre of its inhabitants by the hell-hounds of Mosilikatse. Mr. Mackenzie has given a graphic account of this cruel slaughter, which he fitly calls an " African Glencoe." The ruins of the numerous huts still remain in this picturesque valley, where once a happy people gathered round a gigantic baobab tree in the centre of their town. Mahuka, the successor of Machobi, was treacherously massacred with the men, women, and children of his town, because he refused, although admitting his vassalship to Mosilikatse, to guide the Matabele to the cattle posts of the Bamangwato, with whom his people were closely con-nected. The valley north of these hills was once the garden ground of the Batalouta, and as late as 1864 a stream of water was running through it. This is now dried up, and the valley is a barren waste of bush; only the chopped tree stumps stand as monuments to the agricultural people who tilled it. The soil is very rich, and with water close by, in the Umquesi, and doubtless to be found by digging along this valley, it would be an excellent farming country.

Machobi's Hills are important as being claimed by Khama as a point on his north-east frontier. Both Machobi and Mahuku were undoubtedly vassals to Mosilikatse and Khama's people have done nothing either to occupy this fertile country or to avenge this slaughter of the Batalouta.

From Machobi's the road passes through a narrow poort in the granite hills, and for 10 miles runs across a plain covered with grass, and intersected by belts of mopani trees. The soil is good, and it would be a fine grazing country. The road again enters a region of granite koppies by a poort which leads down between water-worn granite hills to Mangwe spruit, passing through three spruits in as many miles, with water in all. On Mangwe spruit

LEE'S CASTLE, MATABELELAND.

stands Lee's Farm (59 miles from Tati, latitude 20° 44′ S., longitude 28° 14′ E., height 3,600 feet). The country here is a series of undulations with brooks watering the low ground, all draining into the Mangwe. The soil is very rich in the hollows. Grass is sweet and abundant, and the country is sheltered by trees.

John Lee, the son of a soldier by a Dutch woman, was permitted by Mosilikatse to live in Matabeleland, and received from him a hunting veld. He made money rapidly by cattle farming and trade. He built a substantial brick house, large timber-fenced kraals, and another house for his people; he also planted two gardens on the banks of the spruit, in which orange and lemon trees flourish. Lee made a fortune, and retired to Zeerust

N 2

where he is now living.   His farm is now unoccupied.   The house
could be purchased, or rather the materials, and Lo Bengula would
undoubtedly grant the farm to any one recommended by the right
persons.   A little capital for buying stock and starting trade is all
that is required to "lead on to fortune."

From Mangwe the northern road to the Zambesi branches off. The
name Lee's Castle is given to a huge monolith of granite on the top
of a koppie behind Lee's house.   Passing over several sharp undulations with watercourse running down to the Mangwe spruit, the
road runs through what is named the Tiger Poort.   This is a gateway through a bold range of granite koppies three miles beyond
Lee's.   Two miles further on is , the Samokwe River which
is usually running.   Quartz crops out both in this river and on
the road two miles from Lee's Farm.   From Tiger Poort the
view is very striking as you begin to enter the seething mass of
granite koppies ; it has been likened to a storm-tossed sea of
granite, a fitting introduction to the Matabele Highlands.   These
koppies are formed of immense blocks of granite piled up in every
conceivable form, sometimes looking like the ruins of old castles
perched on crags unassailable by aught but time.   Then others take
the fantastic shape of animals, or stand up like obelisk monuments
fashioned by nature out of one piece of granite of gigantic size,
often poised on the point of a steep koppie where none but the
Great Architect of the Universe could place it.   These hills are
covered with tropical shrubs, euphorbia and the tenacious mopa-
pama trees.   The country is one bristling mass of such koppies
from the Samokwe River to the Shashani River (75 miles from
Tati).   Thence they stretch away to the Matoppo Mountains, and
culminate near Old Gubulawayo in Tab Ingoko Mountain 5,030 feet
above the sea.   Quartz reefs show in the valleys, and there is
doubtless precious metal to be found in the numerous streams
draining these hills into the Shashani.   The Makalakas who have
submitted to the Matabele retain their kraals in these hills.   Their
cattle are small in breed, but numerous.   Their mealie gardens in
the rich soil of these valleys produce good crops.   Their method of
cultivation is to cut down the trees to within three feet of the
ground, or merely to strip the lower bark and so kill the tree.
They thus obtain the necessary light ; then with their mattocks
they raise the ground into ridge and furrow two feet high, and the
same apart.   On the ridges they plant the corn.   This method seems
universal with the Makalakas.

The Shashani River has water still running through rocky pools,
and the large mealie gardens on its banks testify to the richness
of the soil.   "Manyami's Outpost" is stationed at the entrance to
these hills, and in Mosilikatse's time no one could pass here into
Matabeleland without this janitor sending first for the King's
approval.   There is some attractive quartz on the banks of the
Maywi spruit, a torrent running down a narrow granite valley
(79 miles from Tati).

From here the road winds up a very stony and steep pass, and emerges on a plateau having an extensive view over the the valley running down to the Zambesi. Hitherto the rivers have been running down to the south and east into the Crocodile. We are now on the summit of the watershed between the Zambesi and Crocodile. The elevation is here 4,775 feet. The veld on this plateau is sour, and where the protea (or sugar) grows as it does here, it is noticeable cattle do not care for the grass. The Gwaii River rises here and flows northwards to the Zambesi; there are several water courses between this and the Mapui River (which also falls to the north-west) which run eastward through breaks in the Matoppo Range into the Crocodile. It was through these passes that the Boers came in 1853 against the Matabele. They were, however, repulsed, the cattle recovered which they had taken, and their native allies decimated. The extremes of climate are great on this high plateau. Mr. Maund registered, July 2nd and 3rd, 1885, 83° F. in shade during the day, and 25° F., or seven degrees of frost, during the night. The road continues along this high veld, and four miles from the Gwaii River you look eastward over a large valley shut in by the Matoppo Range, and extending in a north-east direction up to Old Gubulawayo. Here you see the first signs of the Matabele as a nation. A large military kraal, circular in shape, lies a few hundred yards north of the road, while smaller or family kraals lie scattered in the valley. The road rises from this valley and passes for 16 miles over less fertile undulating country, covered with thorn and studded with low koppies, until it reaches the kraal of the Mabukutwani regiment built in the poort of a ridge of seven low koppies above the Mapui River. This regiment is really the remnants of a tribe brought from the Zambesi and now incorporated into the Matabele nation; they seem numerous and prosperous, having very extensive cornfields. They were, however, very uncivil to Mr. Maund, and behaved in a most threatening manner because he had dared to photograph their picturesque kraal. Full of superstition, they said he was bewitching their town. "No other white man had ever shot their town with glass." Ten more miles bring you to the Kame River. On the banks of this river stands the Komalo Kraal, belonging to the Igokokwe regiment. A road here branches off on the right to Old Gubulawayo and Hope Fountain. The country round here is denuded of trees, which have been used as firewood. The depletion has served to lay bare mineral riches. A very large reef of quartz here crops through, running nearly north and south. Mr. Maund traced this reef some distance. It lies between the same slaty rocks as the quartz at Tati. Quartz crops all over this country. Mabukutwani may be called the western limit of a very rich quartz country. There is a very large reef crossing the road 4½ miles from Old Gubulawayo, and 17 miles further on a very large reef crosses the Umguza River close to Gubulawayo. Mr. Maund was informed this reef has been traced for nearly 40 miles, while quartz crops out, and there are large "blows," at several points between Mabukutwani and Umganene (9 miles further on), also along the hills on either side of the Umguza River.

The road rises and falls over frequent undulations for the next six miles up to the Umganene, the soil in the hollows being very rich, and produces splendid crops of mealies. On the Umganene River the King has one of his summer residences or cattle kraals. The nature of the soil here changes to a red sandy loam, and granite gives place to red sandstone. The scenery is pretty here, the banks of the brook being well wooded with acacias, mopani, and mogonono trees. Passing over a low range of sandstone hills you descend into the rich valley of the Umguza River. Large fields of Kafir corn wave in this valley. It is, however, denuded of trees round the large kraal of Gubulawayo, which stands on an eminence overlooking the river (118 miles from Tati). Gubulawayo, as we have seen, is Lo Bengula's head kraal. He has here two large houses, built for him by Europeans, behind which are the huts of his queens and wives. Lo Bengula has here a large quantity of goods stored—ivory, feathers, skins, and the numerous presents of all kinds he gets from those visiting Matabeleland. These buildings are surrounded with a high palisade of mopani poles 10 feet thick, and as many high. This also encloses his "buck-kraal," where, as has been detailed, he carries on the mysteries of "rain-making," and other rites of "doctoring." No one dare enter these sacred precincts without permission, death being the penalty. Beyond this is another palisade, 200 yards from the former. There are no huts within this 200 yards zone. It is kept for marshalling troops and celebrating the annual dance ; beyond this again, or, as it were, outside the walls, all the huts of the town are built, closely packed and palisaded with branches.

For the convenience of travellers I insert at the end of the book, as well as they can yet be compiled, some tables of distances on the way to, and throughout Zambesia. Vide Appendix C.

On the other side of the River Umguza Lo Bengula has another small kraal, Umvujene, where he lives with some of his wives for a month or so in the summer, spending his time in looking after his cattle. The country here is well wooded, but too sandy for much cultivation. Eight miles to the east is a very conspicuous table mountain, called Tab-Induna, to commemorate the massacre of some Indunas (or headmen) by Mosilikatse. Round this hill the road from Inyati to Old Gubulawayo runs. Eight miles again to the north rises another solitary conical hill, called Umfazimiti, a name which tells of the slaughter of women whose condition would have been sufficient to spare them, even had they been condemned to the extreme penalty of English law. A road, too, winds round this hill, leading from the Umguza drift to Shiloh, and thence on to Enhlangeni (Inyati). The most direct road lies between these two, going over a very heavy sand belt for seven miles. When leaving the sandy, wood-clad hills it descends to the Umgogeo

River, in which there is plenty of running water. On the banks of this river stands the kraal of the Imbezi regiment. This is a regiment of young men, 800 strong, and always attached to the King's person. The country here is all red sandstone; the corn land being a sandy loam. It is well wooded, except round the kraals. The native names of some of the most useful trees are umnonto, machabel, umchoosu, mankwe (a yellow wood), and impaca, which is the best and most useful wood of the country, though hard in grain.

For the next nine miles you pass over an extensive plain. Different belts of soil are noticeable by distinct belts of trees. Thus, after leaving the rocky vicinity of the river and passing Engwegani kraal, you pass through thick mopani woods, on clay soil. Further on you come to black, peaty soil, with open grass studded with mimosa bushes. The road now rises over comparatively high ground, a continuation of the Isi Pongweni range, from which you get an extensive view of the high veld-land on the east, with a table mountain, Amanexele, standing prominently up. Behind you Tab Induna and Umfazimiti are conspicuous objects, while on the horizon, in the north-east, you see the Emhlangeni hills. In the valley below these sandstone hills the soil is good, and there are many mealie gardens belonging to the Elibeni kraal, situate near the Old Gubulawayo road. Passing over another sandstone ridge you come in sight of the Induba kraal. Here the eastern and middle roads join. Reefs of quartz are now exposed again. Within a few miles after passing the Impembezi River the road crosses no less than five reefs, separated by slaty shale rocks in vertical layers. The country drained by the Inkwenwesi River, of which the Impembezi is a tributary, is a very rich one for farming. The soil is a deep rich loam, the grass is sweet and good, and there is plenty of shelter.

That the quartz was thought worth working by the old Mashona inhabitants is evident by an old shaft and workings to be found in the bush beyond the Impembesi River. From this river the road runs for 12 miles over a series of undulations, with water-course running down between a low, wooded range of hills, a little over a mile to the left of the road. This country is also very rich for farming purposes. It has all that can be desired in the shape of soil, grass, and water. Half a mile from the Imkwenkwesi River the western road from Shiloh comes in. On the left bank of the river is the house and store of Mr. Martin, an English trader. He has a grant of land here from Lo Bengula, and has already begun improvements by cutting a deep trench, 1000 yards long, to irrigate some of his land with water from the river. Three-quarters of a mile beyond the river are the houses of Mr. Sykes and Mr. Elliot, missionaries, this being the head-quarters of the London Missionary Society. There is a chapel, but no native kraal is within sight; in fact the nearest are at the Ingqobo kraal, 1½ mile distant. Emhlangeni is prettily situated beneath the Indumba

Hills, which are composed of rugged ironstone, and well wooded. The soil is rich here; oranges and bananas do well, and doubtless, corn would. The neighbourhood is healthy. When fever makes its appearance it is generally to be traced to want of care. This is the great camping ground for hunters and traders going into, and coming from the interior, and doubtless, when the riches of Mashonaland are opened up, and Matabele misrule has ceased to exist, Emhlangeni will become an important white settlement. The name it is known by on maps is Inyati, which was the name of the regiment statïoned here; the real name of the place, Emhalangeni, was lost in the name of the large military kraal. The regiment has now moved its kraal south-east of Old Gubulawayo, hence the name of that place is, for the time being, Inyati. The trade here is not great, most of it passing through to the south, but you come more into contact here with Mashona produce. Excellent rice is brought in in very neatly woven bags. You see blankets or shawls made from native cotton, and dyed with the indigo which grows here as a weed. Alluvial gold washed from the sands of rivers further north is brought down in quills; and gutta-percha is sometimes on barter, it being used by the natives to make a sort of rough candle with.

The regiments in this part of Matabeleland are not very loyal to Lo Bengula, who never comes into this part of his dominions. When Mosilikatse died, and his son Kuruman could not be found, Lo Bengula was made king by a section of the tribe. As I have described in a previous chapter, a pretender in the person of Kanda, a Zulu of Natal, arose, claiming to be Kuruman. The regiments about here refused to recognise Lo Bengula and a great civil war began. Lo Bengula attacked the supporters of Kanda near Sokindaba. This feud has never been forgotten, and may yet lead to the dismemberment of the country after the death of Lo Bengula.

The history of the Matabele nation is the career of Mosilikatse which I have traced. The actual country occupied by this strange people is very small, though the territory Lo Bengula claims to dominate is as large as Germany. Long lines of tribute-bearers may be seen bringing in tobacco, palm-leaves for baskets, ivory, and other goods as taxes to the great King; even from beyond the Zambesi these tributes are sent, evidencing the wide limits of the King's sway. The country actually occupied consists of the highlands mentioned, and is not more than 180 miles north to south, by 150 miles from east to west. Within this area the Matabele kraals are concentrated. As Mr. Mackenzie says, "This strange people can hardly with propriety be called a tribe." They are rather a military organization, occupying a rich country which they have depopulated. They live under a military despotism of the worst kind, presided over by a tyrant. They never can become a great nation, they have no industries, simply living by the assegai, and on the cattle they pillage. It is evident that the heterogeneous mass now forming the Matabele power must ere long break up. The original Zulu stock is fast being lost by the incorporation of the tribes which they conquer. From this cause they have much degenerated as a people since the exodus of the original tribe from Zululand under Mosilikatse. The reasons are not far to seek. On conquering a town or tribe, the men and old women are massacred, while the young women and children are carried away captive, and marked as Matabele and the King's property, by a hole made with an assegai in the lobe of the ear. The boys herd the cattle, and play at soldiering with small assegai and shield, until they grow up identified with their captors, having forgotten their mother-tongue, and even the whereabouts of their homes. The girls become the hewers of wood and drawers of water, and eventually are often taken as wives by their captors. Thus, there is a mixed people of Zulus, Bechuanas, Mashonas, and Makalakas with a large disproportion of women, simply held together under a military bondage. The population of Matabeleland proper has been estimated at 150,000, but it is probably nearer 200,000. Theoretically there is a distinction of caste made, and society is divided into three classes. This, without civilisation, is an element of weakness. In Matabeleland it keeps the different elements gradually being incorporated into the people at variance. This want of unity will prevent the Matabele ever becoming a nation, or even a powerful tribe. Their present power is simply the result of their military organization, founded by Mosilikatse; they are living upon the prestige gained by his warriors. Undermine that foundation, as is gradually being done, and the whole fabric will collapse like a house of cards.

The three classes among the Amandabele are—

1. Abezansi.—Consisting of the original tribe who came up with Mosilikatse, or their descendants.

2. Abemhla.—Original Bechuanas whom they took prisoners on their way up.

3. Maholi.—Gathered in from the tribes round about during their constant wars (or rather pillaging and massacring expeditions), Mashonas (Amaswina) and Makalakas (Makolanga).

The Abezansi are supposed not to marry out of their class; so with the Abemhla; while the Maholi are called slaves, but are practically their own masters. In war the loss of a few hundred soldiers who have been trained and incorporated into regiments from the Abemhla and Maholi is scarcely counted, while the loss of a few Abezansi is looked upon as a calamity; this was especially the case in the expedition some years back to Lake 'Ngami, when the Induba regiment, belonging to the first class, lost about fifty men.

It is principally owing to the practices of Nungu, the great war doctor, that so many expeditions are sent out, and it is owing to his influence that the missionaries can make no converts. No one is allowed to become rich, except Nungu, who is paid in cattle for doctoring an army before it leaves the country. In Matabeleland, if a man begins to acquire undue importance, either by property or through popularity, it is quickly reported at head-quarters by his enemies. Unlike Cassius, the lean and hungry man is viewed without suspicion, but should anyone dare to grow fat in this world's goods, he will quickly find it considered that "such men are dangerous." The cattle is the King's and is sent to different kraals to herd. Some of the Indunas have a few cattle, but it must be "a few," and if they wish to buy a horse they must have his sanction, or buy it through him. The result of all this is that till lately there was little or no trade to be done in the country. The people cannot raise cattle for fear of the consequences. The King's cattle is principally that obtained on the war path. The people have no industries, and consequently have nothing to offer traders. But all this, let us hope, will now change as the country merges into Zambesia.

The country is divided into four divisions, which really constitute the four great territorial divisions of their army. These divisions are presided over by the four chief "Indunas." Each division embraces a certain number of kraals. These kraals have one, two, and three Indunas, according to their size. A kraal which bears the name of a regiment is the head-quarters of that regiment. And the war shields and assegais are kept in a hut in the centre of a kraal; but, as a regiment becomes smaller by age or losses, the young men from other kraals are drafted into it, and, though living in a kraal in one division, they will tell you they belonged to the division in which their regimental kraal is situated. The Indunas of a kraal giving name to a regiment, *i.e.*, head-quarter kraal of a regiment, are Indunas, or officers of regiment in the field. Indunas of subsidiary kraals are inferior in rank to them. There are also National Indunas. The aristocracy of the country are of original Zulu blood, and they need not have charge of a kraal.

The men are divided up into regiments after the manner of the Zulus, according to age. Each regiment on formation receives a kraal named after it. This is the only kind of Matabele town existing. These kraals are posted near water, and when they have destroyed the wood for miles round, or there is not sufficient water or pasture for the cattle as it increases by pillage or breeding, then the kraal is burnt and the regiment builds another in a fresh bit of country. A large kraal or town can occupy a place for about ten years. This will account for Inyati having removed from the place marked as such on the older maps. Emhlangeni is the name of the place, and the Inyati regimental kraal is now 50 miles south-east of that; while Gubulawayo is 18 miles north of the position it occupied ten years ago. Soldiers are supposed to marry by regiments, and that only when they arrive at a certain age or have distinguished themselves in the field. The men then wear a ring on their heads similar to the Zulus, made by working up the hair with the gum of some tree, while the "moutcha," or long fringe apron, worn by the girls, gives place to the dressed hide petti-coat worn by the matrons. Things are becoming very lax now. You see very young men wearing the ring, when probably the only victims they can boast of having killed are some helpless old Mashona men or women. In the war dance on the return of an impi, or at the annual review, the old warriors only used to count the Zulus, Griquas, or Dutchmen they had killed, when showing with their assegais how they had killed them. Bechuanas or Maholi they murdered, but considered unworthy of their steel. The pre-sent crew now count old men, women, and children of the once despised Makalakas, Mashonas, and Tauani to their assegai when they go through the pantomime of recounting the incidents of their cowardly and brutal butchery. The present King not long ago permitted a military kraal to marry, because several hundred girls in it were reported to be in an interesting condition, and it was, therefore, considered inexpedient to put so many breeders of soldiers to death, the usual penalty for such frailty before marriage. In Mosilikatse's time they would certainly have been massacred.

The army is about 15,000 strong. Eight thousand men have been counted at the war dance. Some regiments were then known not to be present. Others had to leave men to look after their kraals and cattle. And no warrior can appear unless arrayed in the imposing dress of ostrich feathers, which numbers do not possess. This force is divided into four great divisions which give the names to the four divisions of the country :—1. Amabuto. 2. Amagapa (Egapa). 3. Amhlope. 4. Amakanda.

There are about 20 regiments which, putting the forces down at 15,000 men, would give 750 per regiment. Some few of these regiments are old Zulu ones, but few have any of Mosilikatse's warriors. Thus, of the old Ikwaikwe regiment there is only one veteran left, and he shows several slug wounds received from the Dutch under Maritz.

Some old regiments have been allowed to die out as not being loyal ; others constantly receive fresh drafts as men of their own class grow up. A new regiment is formed when there are sufficient young men of a class able to use the assegai. These are drafted from different kraals, and receive a regimental name and permis-sion to build a kraal to which they generally take their mothers and sisters. Thus 17 years ago was formed the Imbezu ("called") regiment which is posted 10 miles north of Gubula-wayo, the King's kraal. They are the King's favourites and act as his body guard. The Imbezu is 1,000 strong, the kraal turning out 800 men, 200 more young men from other kraals having joined its ranks.

When an impi goes out it is in two divisions under two Indunas acting under a selected general. They march in columns, and should the whole army go out it marches in five columns. One from each territorial division, and another consisting of the King's men, i.e.,

Imbezu and his own town. Their formation is similar to the Zulus; they deploy into a crescent, and try to outflank the enemy with the two horns. The crescent is about four deep at the two horns, and eight to ten deep in the centre. The tactics they pursue with people like the Mashonas is to surround the devoted kraal, and make an inrush at daybreak. Every man and old woman is mercilessly assegaied. The girls and children are taken as slaves, the cattle are driven off, and the kraal burnt. There are numbers of these slave children about the King's kraal, who are evidence of the yearly butchery of the peaceful industrious people who once lived in this country. These children are treated well, and soon forget their mother-tongue, and pride themselves on being Matabele.

Attack is entirely a matter of cunning and stalking. A Matabele impi (army) will approach as stealthily and as invisibly as snakes, crawling as closely on the ground, and concealed by the undergrowth, they watch the movements of their intended victims— the timid Mashona. Then, when a favourable opportunity occurs, up they rise, like a wild black cloud of destruction. Hissing and shrieking their fiercest battle-cry, they bound and leap like the klip-springer (a small but extremely agile antelope living in the rocky kopjes) from rock to rock, dealing with fearful precision the death-giving blow of the assegai; and ever anon shouting with thrilling ecstasy their terrible cry of triumph as they tear out the yet beating hearts of their victims. After a pursuit of the flying and panic-stricken horde, the savages herd in the straying cattle, and then the devastating cloud moves away, gathering in its circuitous route other nebulæ in the shape of slave girls and boys, as well as the cattle, from perhaps a hundred of hitherto quiet and smiling valleys. They return to their King with news of victory; dancing as they sing the story of their "daring" deeds, while in feasting they drink the beer made by the hands of the girls whose parents' lives and property were the fruits of the chase; their bones lying bleaching in the sun amid the weather-worn rocks of the deserted highland home.

With regard to arms, the Matabele put their trust in the large cowhide shields and assegais. A great number of them carry guns of old patterns and very large bore, but in the brunt of the fight these are relegated to bearers, and they try to get to close quarters with the assegai. Their confidence, however, was rudely shaken in the expedition to Lake 'Ngami, where the Tauani, a people whom the Matabele had hitherto despised, met them with a destructive fire from breechloaders, and drove them back with heavy loss, as will be seen a little further on.

A dozen years ago, when the Matabele feared an invasion by the Trek Boers, an impi of 5,000 men was hastily gathered armed with old guns of every conceivable pattern; the average amount of ammunition, however, did not exceed one and a half rounds per man. The King had some years ago collected between 600 and

800 breechloading rifles and carbines, and had six or seven thousand rounds of ammunition for them, but most of this was damaged by water during heavy rains. His Majesty has now as part of the purchase price of the great concession a thousand stand of Martini-Henrys and ammunition. But most probably these fine weapons will be allowed to become useless or rust, just as the rifles in the King's private armoury are allowed to—*i.e.*, the rifles he has received as presents. One of those mare's nests which Mr. Labouchere is always finding, when he goes looking for grievances in the tangled thickets of South African affairs, is the idea that Lo Bengula has not accepted these rifles from the British South Africa Company. The fact is he has specially requested that they be taken care of for him by the Company, and he has privately intimated that his notion is to arm his best behaved regiment with them if the time should ever come for his soldiers to take the field. Should any occasion arise whereby white men have to face the Matabele in the field I only hope that the latter *will* be armed with the Martini-Henry and not the assegai. With the former they would be absolutely harmless; with the latter they might be a little troublesome.

There can be little doubt that the army has much degenerated since the incorporation of the Maholi element. They have lost the dash of the old Zulu warriors, and there is not the same discipline. After witnessing the return of the impi from Lake 'Ngami, and hearing the reports concerning that campaign, Mr. Maund is of opinion that a force of 1,500 mounted men, well armed, could sweep the Matabele power out of the country. No trust could be placed on either Makalakas or Mashonas, to aid such a movement; they are cowards and totally devoid of any organization, but doubtless after the Matabele had met with one reverse the Maholi element would break up, and would aid by bringing in supplies. Let us hope it will not be necessary to put the question to the test. The Matabele know themselves that their time is well-nigh run out. Although they would not admit it, yet their headmen acknowledge that they cannot withstand the onward march of the white man. They know he covets the gold which lies rich and idle in their ground. For this reason doubtless they are sending out impis to spy out the land westward to Lake 'Ngami and northward beyond the Zambesi. Boats are now being built on that river in anticipation of a possible trek beyond that barrier. Two years ago they surprised the lake people, who are rather agriculturists than warriors. The Bartauani town was sacked, the people flying into the impenetrable marshes, north-west of the lake. The Matabele returned with 15,000 head of cattle, much loot, and many captive children and girls. The atrocities committed were frightful. The Matabele are said to have lost 600 men from thirst, fever, and other causes. The yearly raids are, however, becoming less and less successful. As we say, in 1885 another expedition went down to Lake 'Ngami, but the Bartauani were apprised of its coming. They prepared a warm reception for the Matabele. Armed with breechloaders they retired beyond the Okavango River, and kept up so well-directed a fire from the reeds and from boats on either flank of the Matabele as they attempted to cross, that the latter were compelled to retreat. About 1,000 emaciated men, without their shields and assegais, returned to report the disaster; and many of them said that if ordered on a similar expedition they would feign sickness. They have learnt that assegai and shield are no match for breechloaders; and acknowledge that by this defeat their former prestige is gone among the surrounding tribes. The Matabele have certainly chosen a fine country to dwell in. Compared with the country south of it, Matabeleland is like Canaan after the Wilderness. If it be not "flowing with milk and honey," its numerous rivers are either flowing, or have plenty of water in them; there is, too, abundance of cattle and corn and wood, and above all it is very rich in gold, copper, iron, and other minerals. The principal part of the country occupied by the Matabele comprises the highlands forming the watershed of numerous rivers running to the Zambesi on the north, and the Limpopo on the south. This country is from three to five thousand feet above sea level, and is an extensive high veld from which numerous spurs run off, forming rich, well-watered valleys. This high country is particularly healthy. Fever is unknown, and white children could be reared, which is a *sine quâ non* in a country if it is to be colonised by white men.

The soil is rich and admirably adapted for corn. Large masses of Kafir corn and mealies are grown here on the same ground year after year without manure and never ploughed, the earth being simply hoed up with mattocks. The valleys are less healthy, especially during the rainy season, when fever can be easily taken by the imprudent; but with care and abstinence from alcoholic drinks no white man need fear the climate. Lung sickness among cattle and horse sickness seem to decimate the live stock brought into the country by the Matabele from their frequent raids; but the cattle bred there appear to escape it. The Matoppo range forms a sort of rugged edge to this country on the south-east. They are composed of huge granite blocks, their jagged edges giving the country a picturesque aspect when contrasting these rocks with the fertile valleys below and the rich, well-wooded veld above. The Matabele build their kraals in the open, in contrast to the Mashonas and Makalakas who formerly occupied this country, but who are now exterminated, or driven beyond the immediate vicinity of their relentless enemies.

All this hill country is very rich in minerals. Like the Tati Hills, it is intersected by numerous reefs of quartz, while some of the hills are composed of ironstone, so rich that it requires very little smelting. One kopje near Maritele is formed entirely of one huge "blow" of quartz.

This high country slopes off towards the Zambesi, through what

is known as Mashonaland. The vegetation in the valley of the
Zambesi is so dense that wagon roads are almost impracticable.
The country towards the north-east of the watershed is studded
with solitary kopjes, often composed of one huge mass of granite,
on which the Mashonas dwell, getting up by means of ladders,
which they draw up after them; others are composed of ironstone,
Taba Incimba being almost pure iron, the natives wedging it out
and hammering it at once into assegai and arrow-heads. The
northern or alluvial gold fields are situated at the foot of the
northern slope of this high veld land. The natives wash the gold
from the sand of many rivers, and sell it in quills to the Portuguese. The richest district is about Moghunda. In this dense
country, the habitat of the elephant, the Mashonas, who are still
very numerous, live in comparative security, occasionally visited by
Matabele marauding parties in quest of cattle. They acknowledge
the Matabele sway, and their Chiefs or Indunas, as their masters
call them, are appointed by the King. But I shall devote
another chapter to Mashonaland.

The boundaries of Matabeleland, which, speaking roughly, lies
between the Limpopo and the Zambesi, will be seen from the maps
in this work. The direct road from Shoshong to the Victoria Falls
throughout is under Khama's jurisdiction; between this and the
Gwai River are to be found hunters belonging to both tribes, and
their respective stations seem to depend on their relative strength
at any time. There are Makalaka towns along the Nata River,
and towards the mouth of the river the Makalakas acknowledge
Khama as their chief; the Makalakas near the head waters of the
Nata must be considered subject to the Matabele, as they are
enclosed by the Impanden Regiment frontier kraals. Further
south there is as yet doubt as to the most equitable frontier.
Assuming that the Macloutsie River be taken as the boundary for a
certain distance, which Khama disputes, there is no natural feature to
carry the line up to the Zambesi. More exact knowledge of the country
between the Nata and head waters of the Macloutsie River is
wanted, but roughly speaking a line running through the junction
of the Tegwan and Nata Rivers, and up to the outlet of the Pandamatenka into the Zambesi River seems to meet the requirements of
the case. The country east of Matabeleland, i.e., between the
Sabi River and the coast, is called the Gaza country, which will be
found described in another chapter. The road from Gubulawayo
starts from the summit of the great watershed between the Zambesi and Limpopo Rivers. This watershed is about 5,000 feet above
sea level, and stretches from Mount Umtigesa in Northern Mashonaland to the Bakarikari Lake in Bechuanaland. It is healthy,
traversed by ever-running streams and gold-bearing reefs, and is
the leading feature of this part of South Africa. The chief strata
in this extensive formation are granitic, with occasional sand-
stones and shales. The northern slopes of the watershed fall
gently with broad undulations towards the Zambesi. On the

Limpopo side the ground falls suddenly from the edge of the watershed, forming a broad belt of rugged hills in which live the aboriginal tribes (Mashonas and Makalakas). Here the rapid denudation and desiccation of the granitic strata are most striking. The rains in summer are very violent, and have cut up the country into a mass of rugged hills that defy description. It has well been described as a "sea of granite."

Granite boulders of fantastic shape stand balanced on huge granite hills in bewildering confusion; it almost appears as if some violent convulsions of nature had suddenly been arrested midway. In the Sabi district the shapes of the hills are still more remarkable; many of them are of considerable height and might be called mountains, being formed of one gigantic block of granite. The valleys amongst these hills are well watered, very fertile, and covered with a higher class of vegetation than is found elsewhere. Amongst the trees may be noticed many wild fruit trees, euphorbias, and soft wooded trees, the chief of which are mopani. On the road this belt of hills is about 25 miles wide, and the ground falls 1,000 feet in that distance. Below the hills, with a sudden leap, the features of the country are marked by another geological stage. Here, except in a few districts, desiccation has almost finished its work and has covered the broad plains extending to the Limpopo with sheets of sand and alluvial soil. A few weather-beaten granite kopjes, scattered about in groups or apart, remain still defying time. Strange old trees belonging to the vegetation of the hills still cling to their sides, attesting to the relationship of the past. The rivers, winding through the forest-covered flats, are choked with sand brought down from the hills.

In the Economic Section of the British Association at its last meeting Mr. E. A. Maund made a contribution to a discussion on the "Lands of the Globe Still Available for Colonisation." It was as follows :—" I know there are many who hold the theory that no tropical countries are colonisable by Europeans, especially by the Saxon, as opposed to the Latin races. These theorists hold that this is more particularly applicable to Africa. The idea of lands available for colonisation I take to mean lands to which the poor and crowded out from England, or broadly, from Europe, can emigrate in the full sense of the word, i.e., to settle with his family, or to go out and bring up his family, unharmed by the climate—not, as on the West coast, to be obliged to return periodically to recruit his shattered health—not to be obliged to send his children home to be reared—in short, not to be dependent on Africa for his living and on England to live. This theory of incompatibility of climate is seemingly sound in theory, and as yet we have had little practice to definitely combat it. But as one who has visited the highlands of tropical Africa, I maintain that this theory is to be rebutted by stubborn facts. In Matabeleland Englishmen have lived for 20 years without needing homeward journeys for health. Missionaries have reared families, and their children have married other missionaries and settled in the country. True that these missionaries' children returned to England—not to be reared, be it understood, but to be educated, as used to be the case with Indian children at a very tender age, and when old enough for schooling to be beneficial. Traders and Dutchmen have reared families there, who have again married and reared children of the second generation, robust in health, but lacking, alas! education. This proved that white men can live there and colonise on sound principles. Then comes the question whether the country can support by food supply a white population. This, with regard to Matabeleland, I think I sufficiently proved in my paper, and Mr. J. Mackenzie will, I am sure, bear witness that the country is capable of great farming development. Wheat, maize, Kafir corn, and rice will doubtless be far more universally grown than it is now, when, as I expect, we shall shortly see a mining population to be supported. Having been in Matabeleland in all seasons, rainy and dry, I believe it to be thoroughly colonisable. This country, though within the tropics, has, perhaps, peculiar advantages not enjoyed by many tropical regions. A large portion of it lies at an elevation of from 3,000 feet to 5,000 feet above sea level. It has a good rainfall. The atmosphere during two-thirds of the year is exceptionally dry and salubrious, while the seasons are well marked. For these reasons I hope to see a large European population at no distant date supported there."

All accounts agree as to the great auriferous wealth of Matabeleland and Mashonaland. The question of gold in the latter and contiguous country will receive separate treatment. The original upheaval of the watershed is marked by numerous cracks running chiefly north-west and south-east now filled with quartz, rich in gold and other metals. The Tati Gold Field, to be further referred to, is the best known of the mineral districts; the gold reefs here are undoubtedly very rich and extensive. Insecurity has been the chief agent in the hitherto unsuccessful working of this district. A sum of £10,000 has been expended in machinery and plant which are now *in situ*. Security and fresh capital only are required to make this a payable gold field under good management. Farther north in Upper Mashonaland lie the northern gold fields, within easy reach of Tete, the limit of navigation on the Zambesi. Coal is said to have been discovered on this river.

Mr. Frank Mandy has lived twenty years in Matabeleland, and all he says regarding it is entitled to respectful consideration. He recently delivered at Johannesburg and Cape Town a lecture on the country, and this has been published in pamphlet form. The author declares that throughout its greatest extent the country is one vast and very rich gold field. He traces the history and describes the *locale* of the various concessions, and gives a mass of information from various sources as to the known and reputed gold fields. In one passage he says:—"It is not until climbing out of the

o

Limpopo basin, and surmounting the ridge, and descending into the Zambesi watershed, that you enter Matabeleland proper. Here outstretched before one is what will prove the largest and richest gold field that the world has ever seen ; extending from this great granite backbone in the south to within about sixty miles of the Zambesi in the north, and from the Sabi in the east to the Nata River in the west. This huge auriferous area ever improves and grows richer to the north, north-east, and east. The Matabele have never allowed any search for gold in the land actually inhabited by them; but the signs which greet the traveller's notice —the immense waves of promising quartz which seam the country, cutting through the soft soapy slate in a north-easterly direction ; the numberless old workings to be found in every direction, and the inability of some of the reefs to hide their gold from the prying though cautious gaze of the observant white man—all tend to prove the wonderful mineral wealth here locked up." One more passage may be given :—" Right through the Royal town of Bulawayo runs an immense reef carrying visible gold. Close along Umvotcha (the country residence of Lo Bengula) streams another great reef, also unable to hide the gold imprisoned within its bosom. Two miles to the north-east of the old capital is yet another grand quartz reef with 'visible.' All these reefs have been traced for some miles. But to the north of Gangane lie what I believe will eventually prove to be the alluvial gold fields of the world. The neighbourhood of the Amazoe River and its tributary streams is a veritable El Dorado. I have seen ignorant natives with the rudest appliances and practically no knowledge of gold-working wash large quantities of gold from the surface soil. Over an area of several hundred square miles gold is to be found in every stream. Mr. Selous and his party expressed their surprise to some of the Mashonas that no nuggets were found, and that their gold was not coarser than would easily pass into a quill. The natives informed them that in their gold-washing they did often come upon large nuggets; but they invariably threw these back, having a firmly-fixed belief that an awful curse will fall on those who remove them." A prospector in Matabeleland recently wrote:— " The richness of the country far surpasses anything I had previously imagined. You know how much I know about pro-specting,—well, out of 127 places I tried I found it in 124. These 127 places were at equal distances throughout a journey of about 240 miles, and include the beds and banks of rivers, roots of reeds and rushes (these are very rich always), small creeks and old dry water-courses and gullies—in fact every river, spruit, or hollow seemed auriferous. On an average I got from thirty to forty specks—some large—at every panning, and I am sure if only a thoroughly competent man were there he would soon follow up the 'spoor' of the gold and find the rich places."

A long-resident trader wrote not long ago to some of the South African papers a lengthy letter from which I make an extract:—

The mountain range of the Matabele takes somewhat the shape of an extended letter V, the extreme point being in the S.W., and on about the 21st parallel and 26th long. deg. E. of Greenwich, extended in a N.E. and N.W. direction, forming a huge basin extending to the Zambesi in the north and the Crocodile River in the south, forming the sources of numerous rivers, and leaving extensive and fertile valleys and numerous kopjes between them. It might be supposed that at some time of a grand upheaval of nature, an enormous wave of the earth's surface had rolled up this range of mountains travelling in a south-easterly direction, creating numerous black washes, which formed the broken ranges of mountains on the east of the Transvaal, and it may be surmised that the gold-bearing quartz was deposited in the mountains of Zoutpansberg, Lydenburg, and Barberton, and the conglomerate at the Rand, as the result of this enormous wave from the north, impregnating the molten quartz and wedging it between masses of rock, the ground wash of the wave sweeping bits of rock and pebbles and gold, depositing same in fissures of the earth, such as noticed in the banket of the Rand. One may go further to set forth the theory that if Matabeleland and Mashonaland are not actually the parent fields from which this gold has been washed, one may reasonably suppose that the parent field cannot be far to the north of these countries. There is a great similitude between the different sedimentary and crystalline rocks of Matabeleland and those of the Barberton district, and the consistent ingredients of the banket of the Rand have a striking resemblance to the bed surface rocks of this country. This is, however, a theory which I leave to wiser heads than mine to propound; it is one that may strike others as it struck me, on examination of this country after an intimate acquaintance with the Transvaal Gold Fields. The chance for finding alluvial gold amongst the rivers running into the Mashona mountains I should think would be good. There is one spot where the Shachani River leaves the granite formation; gold shows well in every panning from the river sand. The same refers to several places on the Ingwesi River, and near the source of the Tashangani River to the east of Inyati. In speaking of Matabeleland, one has to be very guarded when the matter refers to gold, and I think I have already said too much; but when once men can openly inspect the country without fear of molestation some surprising facts will come to light. The country has a grand future before it, if it can be opened up by Europeans.

About a hundred miles, as the crow flies, south-west from Bulawayo are situated the Tati Gold Fields. There is no doubt of the great possibilities inherent in these fields, but they have suffered much from bad management and lack of developing capital. The discovery of the Tati and of the northern or Mashonaland Gold Fields was so nearly simultaneous that it is hardly possible to separate them; yet as the Tati claims precedence by a month or two, it will be well for the sake of clearness to consider it first. "We had heard," says Baines, "for many years amongst the Dutch emigrants rumours of gold found beyond the Zoutpansberg, and about 1865, Mr. H. Hartley, while hunting in Matabeleland, observed groups of ancient diggings, and connecting these with the current stories, he invited Herr Carl Mauch to accompany him on his next trip; and in 1866, the then young and almost unknown traveller announced the discovery of a gold field eighty miles in length by two or three miles in breadth." Various companies, or, rather, exploring parties, were formed in South Africa, one of the first being headed by Captain Black, and another of ten men under Capt. McNeil, of Durban, Natal, besides many smaller ones. A party of thirty-four Australians was equipped in Natal in 1869, and sent up to test the richness of the reputed gold field. A party was also sent up from Port Elizabeth, but it is not on record that it discovered much at Tati. In 1868, the London and Limpopo Mining Company, headed by Sir John Swinburne, Bart., and Captain Arthur Lionel Levert, left England, taking with them an expensive equipment, including a traction engine, which, however, was left, and subsequently sold in Natal. They reached the Tati on the 27th of April, 1869, set up their steam engine and opened a store. Sir John and Mr. Levert proceeded to Inyati. The former obtained leave to proceed to the northern gold fields—the latter returned to Natal, and had a stamping machine constructed there by Mr. Gavin, of Durban. About this time quite a little village had arisen on the north bank of the Tati River, and nine companies were at work digging for gold. These were as follows :—(1) Dr. Coverly's party ; (2) Rocky, Dalton, and James ; (3) Burrill's party ; (4) King Williamstown party ; (5) Section of ditto ; (6) Old Charley's party ; (7) Pretoria party, Brown, and others ; (8) Two Carpenters ; (9) London and Limpopo Mining and Trading Company. A company of thirty-five Australians, sent up from Durban, went about thirty-two miles up the river and located themselves on "Todd's Creek." Several of the shafts were 50 feet deep ; but, though 150 tons of quartz, some of it apparently rich, had been got out, the crushing machines that had been extemporised did not succeed. Nevertheless, specimens had been sent home, and Messrs. Johnson, Matthey, and Co. assayers to the Bank of England, certified with others, that over 120 ounces were soon produced. Most of the working parties, being unprovided with funds sufficient for the long and laborious processes of mining till they reached the gold, and then requiring to provide machinery to crush it, had sold out or abandoned their claims, and yielded to the more brilliant attractions of the Diamond Fields.

The Tati Concession, which now belongs to Mr. Dan Francis, Mr. A. Beit, and a group headed by Baron Erlinger and Messrs. John Henry Schroeder and Co., is bounded at all points by the Shashi and Ramaquaban Rivers (the Tati being an intermediate river between), commencing in the south-east at the junctions of those two rivers, and terminating at their sources in the north-west. It has a length of about 85 miles, with an average width of 25 miles. The area of the Tati Concession is therefore more than 2000 square miles. The Blue Jacket is a good reef and in no case has it yielded less, I understand, than 3 ozs. to the ton recently. Within a radius of one mile of the Tati settlement there are no less than four large reefs (not including the Blue Jacket), all of which have been found payable by the crushing of parcels of stone varying from one hundred to three hundred tons. But it is not in the immediate vicinity of the Tati settlement that the wealth of the concession is most apparent. Apart from the above-mentioned reefs and within ten miles of the settlement, are many large gold-bearing reefs awaiting but the advent of labour and machinery, to yield up their hidden treasures, and beyond this again, right to Todd's Creek, a distance of 27

THE TATI RIVER.

miles from the settlement, is a succession of rich reefs. But it is even farther than this that one must go before any idea can be formed of the vast wealth of this concession. Ten miles above Todd's Creek is the Monarch, a reef 80 feet wide, and carrying gold from side to side. This reef would, one authority says, compare favourably with the Sheba of Barberton District. Beyond the Monarch, and right to the confines of the concession, is a continuation of gold-bearing reefs, which will some day be worked to advantage. The three principal rivers included in the Tati Concession, viz., the Shashi, the Ramaquaban, and the Tati, carry a permanence of water all the year round. In addition to those the concession is intersected by several smaller rivers, including the Little Tati, the Inswe, and the Umonkwa, and in no case are any of the gold-bearing reefs yet found more than four miles from permanent water, but by far the great majority of them are within one mile of that element.

Mr. U. P. Swinburne, who has lived in the country a considerable time, gives me the following notes :—

" Crossing the Shashi River about 8 miles further north, we come to the Tati River settlement, where gold has been worked more or less for the last twenty years. The Tati Concession, . through bad management and lack of interest, has never come to the fore as a mining success, but possesses within its boundaries gold reefs, which must, if properly worked, produce an enormous revenue. The formation here is the well-known quartz and blue slate, which is one of the best gold formations ; the reefs, as a rule, run almost east and west, and average from 1½ to 4 ozs. Close to the settlement the Blue Jacket and New Zealand Reefs are the most important ; the former was once worked by natives, who sunk 70 feet before water stopped their rude developing. Westward of the Tati River are the Todd's Creek, Golden Butterfly, and Monarch Reefs, all situated close to the river, and surrounded by forests of very fair timber. The Monarch Reef is a splendid body of rock 90 feet wide in places, and traceable for more than a mile on the surface ; some splendid specimens of ore have been taken from this reef, but there is no test like a trial crushing, and a few tons put through the mill would be worth a hundred Bank of England assays. All along the Tati River are traces of former inhabitants, and ruins of cut stone buildings and fenced cornfields show that an industrious race once lived and worked in this now deserted country. A very old Makalaka, who lived a long way westward of all the trade routes, once told me that he remembered long ago hearing of a people who used to live in the country round Tati, and who worked the gold stones, and smelted the copper and iron ore, and that if I searched the river bed I should find the large worn stones on which the natives used to crush and wash their gold. Kafirs, especially old ones, are not strictly truthful, and will tell you anything if they think it will please you ; but the large stones worn in the middle still exist in the bed of the Tati River, and there is every reason to believe that at one time a quiet and industrious race worked, in a rude way, all the metals which their country contained, and perhaps made the rich deposits pay better than ever registered Companies or ten-stamp batteries will. On the Impakwe River, 27 miles north-east of Tati, there are the remains of an old stone building, which at one time must have been used as a smelting furnace, for the ground round about is impregnated with slag, cinders, and burnt stone."

The author recently sent me a very interesting book, giving an account of the "First Gold Exploring Expedition into the Matabele Country." It is written by Mr. Duncan McIntosh, now of Greenock, N.B. He was one of a party who went into Matabeleland in 1868 for the Durban Gold Mining Company, and it may be interesting here to embalm the names of those who took part in the expedition:—Archibald McNiel, William Davies, Geo. Bottomley, Henry Duncan, David Guthrie, James Guthrie, William Rockey, Henry Ogden, Alexander Wills, and Duncan McIntosh. This party travelled from Durban to the Tati (over 1000 miles), accomplishing the distance in less than 80 days. A very few extracts from this book must suffice to show how the party fared.

Wherever we turned there was evidence, less or more, of the existence of gold. On the surface alluvial gold was scarce, but when coming in contact with the ancient workings, the auriferous character of the soil was beyond question. The magnitude of the ancient workings could only be ascertained by very extensive survey, and their character discovered after digging from five to ten feet below the surface of the earth. At these depths invariably were found stone flags covering up the mouths of the ancient workings, and beneath this the shaft was honey-combed on every side by the quartz reef being cleaned out in a manner altogether different from that pursued in modern times. It was generally in digging new shafts that we came across these old workings, and on removing the stone from the mouth of the shaft we were often repulsed for a time by the escape of obnoxious gases. The walls of these shafts also were perfectly dry, and on being touched crumbled away like powder. . . . As to how the ancient miners operated would seem a question not to be readily settled, although one thing appeared clear, that fire had been the principal agent employed, for at the bottom of all the workings ashes and sometimes charcoal were found; but as to how applied was not altogether apparent. Of course, it is well known that when rock or stone of any kind is subjected to any intense heat, then suddenly cooled, that it becomes brittle, and may be picked out in fragments, but it was difficult to conceive how this could be applied to the small surface leaders, or veins, near the top; yet there was the fact, the quartz only had been extracted, leaving behind the shell, or hard casing, undisturbed. Again who the miners were was no less a mystery which still remains unravelled, and likely to remain so, unless archæologists at work in various parts of the ancient world discover some hidden source of authentic information. That they were skilled workers in stone, iron, and gold, there can be no doubt. Stones were found hollowed out like mortars, wherein quartz may have been reduced to dust; crucibles of a concrete substance, not unlike that of the ant-hills now used as ovens in Africa; furnaces still surrounded by ashes and slag. . . . After procuring the required stores, and completing other arrangements, Dr. Bottomley, accompanied by Messrs. Guthrie, Duncan, and McIntosh, struck their tents and started to join their friends at Inyati on the 23rd March. The road for a distance of over twenty miles led through a dry sandy bush-land uninteresting country, which brought us to the Ramaquaban River, the bed of which was broad and deep but void of water. A few conical hills were seen by the way dotting the landscape. A river of water, however, was found some ten miles farther on, called the M'Pacwe The water was abundant and excellent, so near by it, on the south side, we squatted for a night. Shortly after encamping, we were agreeably surprised at meeting a couple of hunters from the north, with whom was no less a personage than the deservedly celebrated Herr Mauch, a Prussian mineralogist, who had distinguished himself not only in his profession but as a traveller, for pluck and perseverance stood eminent amongst gold-finders. It was this gentleman who first communicated the news to Natal of having found gold here, and discovered these ancient gold fields. Twice in his search had he been expelled from the Matabele country, and the third time they made him a prisoner. Yet, notwithstanding such obstacles, he had penetrated far into their country, and explored the northern gold fields, which he now declared to be richer than either of the other two auriferous belts. This gentleman conversed freely on the subject, and gave minute particulars as to localities where gold-bearing quartz would be found in the north. The warlike Matabele, however, in the meantime were somewhat unsettled on account of the recent decease of their Chief Mosilikatse, and to succeed in such an enterprise much circumspection would be necessary. . . . . At the present time the Matabele nation number from 300,000 to 400,000, and can turn out from 30,000 to 40,000 fighting men. Many of the old, and even some of the young warriors, bear marks about them of severe struggles through which they have passed during the last fifty years. . . . Much of the superstitious dread and suspicion enter- tained by natives regarding white men has been removed by the Durban Gold Mining Company, and a good opening made for future travellers; an assertion, not made by way of boasting, but simply stated as fact, and supported by results. It was the first expedition of that character which had penetrated into the Matabele country; and scarcely twelve months after its return the good people of Durban were no less sur- prised than pleased to find native traders and hunters, who previously had never ventured further south than Shoshong, coming down to do business by the sea-board of Natal. In this manner trade and friendly intercourse was promoted, much to the benefit of the Colony, and also to the advantage of the natives themselves.

Mr. John Dalton, an Australian who was attracted to South Africa by Carl Mauch's report, was at the Tati fields in the early days. He recently gave an interesting account of his experiences in the *Zoutpansberg Review*. It appears the diggers drew up a set of gold laws on the model of the laws of Australia and New Zealand, and that these were sanctioned by Mosilikatse. Mr. Dalton says the old workings in the Tati district number "literally thousands." "To give you an idea," he remarks, "of their great age, I may tell you that in the New Zealand shaft, the accumulations of time have filled it within four feet of the surface, and yet the work was as good as any we can do with all our modern appliances. When we had stripped the reef of *débris* for 12 feet, we came to flags of solid slate which we had some difficulty in removing. When we got them away, there was a tremendous rush of foul air, which would have killed us had we not been so near the surface. The fresh air rushing in through the opening caused a big falling of rock into the hole below. After the commotion had subsided, I went down

40 feet with a rope, and then I rolled a boulder down to the bottom, which I judge was at least 70 feet farther."

It may be asked, why have these fields not prospered then? The answer is, because they were badly managed. There has been the difficulty of obtaining labour, and the imperfection of the machinery to contend with. The men who in the early days tried their luck there were ultimately actually starved out. There was not the machinery to crush the quartz they raised, and when " stamps" were put up the tables were so badly constructed that it is calculated 90 per cent. of the gold was lost. Above all, the place did not grow to supply the miners' needs; there was no near market either to take the gold to or furnish necessaries. Business men in England would not risk their money in bogus companies situated in " No man's land," for though concessions were granted by Mosilikatse and Lo Bengula, of which Khama and Macheng were cognisant, yet it was disputed border territory, and it was impossible to say that the Transvaal Boers might not step in and seize the country and ruin the place by granting monopolies. For some little time the locality flourished and houses sprang up, the store of the " Limpopo Mining Company" doing good business. Sir John Swinburne, however, was so long in getting adequate crushing machinery up, that the miners, who had no capital, could not live, and the Diamond Fields being opened at this time, Tati was soon almost deserted. Five or six reefs had been opened and shafts sunk, but the means were exhausted in doing this, and there was no return, from the want of machinery to crush. It cannot be wondered at that the " Diamond Fever " should take off the disappointed miners. The " Limpopo Company " soon ceased to exist. Its payment of an annual rent to Lo Bengula was discontinued for seven years, when a new company was formed—" The Northern Light Company "—who obtained from Lo Bengula a new concession similar to Sir J. Swinburne's. This Company paid its rent yearly and sunk £30,000 in engines, pumps, stamps, and other machinery. A good deal of quartz has been got out, and some crushed, but not with good results, as the tables are so badly constructed that they act rather as a sieve to let the gold and quicksilver pass through than as an inclined plane which should put plenty of gold in the shareholders' pockets. The woodwork is only screwed or nailed together, instead of dove-tailed, and in this very dry atmosphere the interstices have opened wide enough to let a fortune through. The copper-plates are simply screwed on with iron screws without much attempt at any fit; in fact, the battery is of the most rustic and primitive construction, and as I say, is calculated to lose both gold and quicksilver. How can such management make a paying concern of any property? Mr. E. A. Maund copied a certificate of assay made in Coleman Street, London, January 6th, 1885, which gives a result of —gold 7 ozs. 5 dwts. 12 grs. per ton, and silver 2 ozs. 10 dwts. per ton, from the samples sent for examination. But what result do owners get from their own crushing machinery with identically the same quartz? Why, not enough to pay for the labour. Consequently Tati is again at a standstill for want of labour. The machinery is good if managed properly, and if it were supplied with a new set of tables. Labour is cheap enough. Native miners can be obtained for a cotton blanket per month, and five good English mechanics would make this property a paying one. The fields are no longer out of the world; and if farms are started on the Macloutsie and Shashi Rivers supplies will be obtainable. Tati is accessible, and, with energy, would yield well. It has now a desolate and forlorn look. The Jesuit Mission Station is deserted. There are four houses occupied by white men engaged in trade. The mining interest is at a standstill. There is water in the river sufficient for cattle and for crushing purposes if dug for and properly dammed. The soil is very rich, and cattle fatten and do well in the district. There are old Mashona ironworks on one of the hills, and very rich ironstone, which with the copper on the Shashi River might be worked on the Tati, as there is an unlimited supply of mopani wood for engine fuel and smelting purposes. The two essentials lacking are capital and labour.

CHAPTER IX.

ROMANCE AND REALITY.—MASHONALAND.—THE COUNTRY DESCRIBED.
—ITS BIG GAME.—MR. SELOUS' HUNTING EXPERIENCES.
—PORTUGAL'S ABSURD CLAIMS TO MASHONALAND.—MASHONA-
LAND'S AURIFEROUS WEALTH.—MORE EVIDENCE OF AUTHORITIES.

RECENT remarkable discoveries of gold in the Transvaal have
led to the active investigation of adjoining territories which
are still the undisputed home of the black man. Bordering on countries which have for many years enjoyed the
blessings of civilisation, there are vast regions possessing great natural
advantages and resources, but only just awakening the practical
interest of the enlightened world. The inhabitants of some of
these hitherto obscure regions are, as we have seen, barbarians,
steeped in ignorance and superstition. A few tribes are of warlike disposition ; but the majority are tractable, and susceptible
to the softening influences of truth and light. Until recently, the
few white men—intrepid hunters and adventurous traders—who
penetrated the depths of these unknown wilds, returned to civilisation
with glowing accounts of their beauty and wealth. Frequent dangers
were encountered and great hardships endured by the wanderers,
who were the only sources of information on the arcana of the
interior. Stretches of sandy desert—" thirst," as these arid tracts
are laconically called—where both themselves and their cattle
severely felt the want of water ; the tsetse fly, whose bite is as
fatal to cattle as that of the cobra is to human beings ; stony
plains, formidable hills, and malarious valleys were amongst the
difficulties they surmounted. Their toilsome journeys over, they
found lands of eternal spring, genial climes of such fertility that
the fruits of the earth were abundantly reaped without cultivation ;
flocks and herds roamed over the grassy undulations ; gigantic
forests ; rivers of clear water ; valuable wild beasts and birds ; and
game of all descriptions. They brought samples of virgin gold,
ornaments of rude workmanship, ivory, skins, and feathers, with
which to corroborate the stories of their adventures. Their
recitals of the wonders of the countries they had visited were
tinctured with archæology ; they gave graphic accounts of the
traces of mines, the gold diggings of past ages, old workings still

extant as examples of ancient engineering skill ; they told of mysterious caves where hidden treasures of gold, precious stones, and antique objects of vertu, were jealously guarded ; and they described magnificent ruins, the remains of departed civilisation and grandeur.   They depicted the natives in all the barbaric splendour of the skins of wild animals, gold and silver bangles, ear-rings and uncouth jewellery; fantastically carved clubs, assegais, and shields; their faces and forms painted and hideously disfigured ; their passions excited by war-dances, songs of triumph, and inordinate eating and drinking; and, in the pale clear light of the African moon, indulging in grisly orgies, attractive in their wild grotesqueness, but repulsive in their savage cruelty.   The existence of natural caves hollowed out with such precision as to look like the works of experienced engineers has suggested the theory of ancient mining operations.   Some of these caves, intricate and perplexing in their windings, the galleries opening into immense chambers, with beautiful stalactites and stalagmites, decorative pendants from the roofs studded with myriads of sparkling beads of water glittering in the fitful torchlight, and the statuesque figures of the native guides glancing silently from place to place, has supplied the excited fancy with material for speculation as to hidden stores of diamonds and gold.   The results of vast seismic disturbances, tumbled rock scenery, enormous piles of huge stones thrown into the fanciful shapes of broken walls, columns, and pinnacles, rugged reminiscences of geologic ages, which when viewed from a distance have the appearance of the wrecks of massive masonry, readily lend themselves to the supposition that they are the ruins of ancient architecture.   Greatly as the imagination assisted in these portrayals, they were, as a recent writer in *Chambers's Journal* points out, " founded on facts." Lo Bengula, King of the Matabeles; Umbandine, late King of the Swazies whom I visited and of whom I had much to say in " Golden South Africa " ; Khama, and many other paramount chiefs, have shown, in their receptions of white men, lavish hospitality, rude festivity, and displays of barbaric pomp and splendour, in which might be detected traces of Oriental magnificence.   Their war-dances, songs, incantations, and mystic ceremonies ; the savage paraphernalia of skins, feathers, horns, hair, and teeth ; the superstitions and cruelties manifested in their belief in witchcraft; and the supernatural powers attributed to certain animals, show that among the natives there is a fondness for pageantry, and a reverential fear of the weird and mysterious.   But we are now more concerned with the reality than the romance of Zambesia.   I have to deal with the grand territory which the British South Africa Company, by the terms of its Charter, is granted power to develop, administer, and govern. This vast addition to the British Empire includes some of the finest and fairest portions of the earth's surface. Matabeleland and Mashonaland, which are included within the scheme of the Company's operations, are eminently fitted for permanent occupation by Anglo-Saxon settlers. They are mostly high table-lands, 5000 feet above the sea level, which means in those latitudes a climate similar to that of the Transvaal high veld, almost ideal in its cool, clear, and invigorating character. The mere superficial exploration of British Zambesia reveals unlimited commercial and agricultural potentialities, numerous tribes of peaceful and industrious natives ready to ally themselves with those white nations who will treat them fairly and honestly, and protect them from slavery; wonderful fertility of soil, magnificent forests, plentiful streams, and abundance of useful minerals and precious metals. There are drawbacks, such as patches of waterless desert and swampy valleys productive of malaria; but they can detract very little from the advantages of a vast country on which Nature has bestowed her favours with such a lavish hand. In addition to Zambesia there were other portions of South-Eastern and South-Western Africa towards which, as lands of promise, European nations were till recently directing their attention. Exploration proves the existence, throughout the whole of the southern portion of the continent, of splendid natural resources of every kind. Scientific evidence points to further and further geological formations in which coal, iron, copper, gold, and diamonds may be looked for with certainty; and the belief that South-Eastern Africa is the Land of Ophir has every appearance of being founded on a rational basis. But I have now to describe Mashonaland.

Mashonaland may be said to encircle the country actually occupied by the Matabele on the north, and round to the south-east as far as the River Sabi. Some writers have held that formerly a great Mashona kingdom, with Zimbabye as its capital, existed where Matabeleland now is. The present condition of the Mashonas is one of complete disintegration. They live by families on separate hills, and though they intermarry they keep up perpetual blood feuds. It would be most difficult to fuse this mass into a united nation; their very division into units must ever prevent their holding their own against any organised power. The Makalakas on the west occupy a similar position to the Mashonas. They are an industrious people famous for working in metals, but gradually driven out from the hill country by the Matabele by repeated massacres. Some have acknowledged the sway of their persecutors, others have taken refuge with the Bamangwato tribe, and some have even trekked beyond the Zambesi. The western frontier line of Makalaka towns are said to serve two masters. When the Matabele are in their vicinity they are their very humble servants, while possibly they have some of Khama's hunters secreted in their huts, or are in communication with that Chief. The Matabeles away, they are said to acknowledge Khama. These are the industrious people hounded out of their country by Mosilikatse's "Dogs of War." Before giving further evidence as to the vast auriferous wealth of Mashonaland I shall devote space to a general description of The Promised Land. There is no more reliable

authority on the country than Mr. F. C. Selous, who has written
a good deal concerning it, and recently led the British South Africa
Company's Pioneer Force close to Mount Hampden. Here are
some extracts from an article he recently penned for the *Fortnightly Review* :—

The country stretching from the Limpopo to the Zambesi, which is
ruled over by Khama, the chief of the Bamangwato, is a territory which
has attracted much attention of late, and a part of which is embraced
within the British Protectorate.

Immediately to the east of Khama's country is Matabeleland, rich in
mineral wealth, and comprising the now famous gold fields of " Tati."

Far to the north-east, beyond the Matabele country, lies a land of
perennial streams where thirst is an unknown quantity. Here, on the
elevated plateau of what is known as Mashonaland, stretches the fairest
and perhaps also the richest country in all South Africa. This high
plateau, which is of very great extent, forms the watershed between the
Zambesi to the north and east, and the Limpopo and the Sabi to the
south, and is from 4,000 to 4,600 feet above the sea level. Nearly the
whole of it is magnificently watered by a perfect network of running
streams, the springs supplying which well out from the highest portions
of the downs, so that an enormous area of land could be put under
irrigation. The whole year round a cool wind blows almost continually
from the south-east, a wind which in the winter months becomes so cold
that it may well have its origin amongst the icebergs of the antarctic
seas. Owing to the elevation the nights are cool the entire year. From
September till March, the sun is hot during the day, though the excessive
heat is always tempered by the south-east breeze. During the winter
months the climate is perfection, a trifle bleak and cold perhaps during
June and July (midwinter in South Africa), but very healthy and bracing.
This is in fact a country where European children would grow up strong
and healthy, and our English fruits retain their flavour. The soil is very
rich and fertile, and owing to the facilities for irrigation enormous
quantities of wheat could be grown, and some day will be grown to
supply the large centres of population that will spring up in the gold-
producing districts to the north and east of the plateau. The highest
and healthiest portions of the country are very open, still one is never
out of sight of patches of forest trees, so that the luxury of a good fire
at night can always be enjoyed ; a luxury which will be appreciated by
South African travellers who have journeyed through the treeless wastes
of the Cape Colony, Orange Free State, and Transvaal Republic. There
is another point about the Mashona uplands well worthy of notice. In
all other portions of South Africa with which I am acquainted, whether
in the Transvaal, Bechuanaland, or the Matabele country, when the long
summer grass is burnt off, which usually happens in June or July, the
country remains a blackened, dreary, grassless waste until the following
rainy season commences. Or say that precautions are taken and the
grass is preserved ; well, then it becomes as dry as tinder, and all
nourishment being scorched out of it, cattle invariably get into very low
condition, and should the season be a late one, many die of starvation.
Now over a very large portion of the Mashona plateau, things are very
different. Say you burn off the long summer grass in June, there at
once springs up a short sweet herbage, which, after attaining about a
foot in height, seeds ; and on this grass cattle and horses thrive wonderfully. Thus, whereas in August, September, and October, all the
interior of South Africa, speaking generally, is a scorched and thirsty

land, well meriting the term of arid, and cattle look miserably gaunt and bony, the upland valleys of the Mashona plateau are covered with soft waving green grass, whilst small streams or little rills run brawling down every hollow, and all live-stock look fat and comfortable. The time to judge of the capabilities of a country in South Africa is not in May, at the end of the rainy season, when all the valleys and rivers still hold water, but in October and November, at the end of the dry season.

Some eighty years ago this fine country must have been thickly inhabited, as almost every valley has at one time or another been under cultivation. The sites of the villages are also very numerous, though now only marked by a few deep pits, from which the natives obtained the clay used by them in plastering their huts and making their cooking pots, and also by the presence of clusters of huge thorn-trees (*acacia giraffæ*), which grow to a larger size on the sites of old villages than anywhere else. The peaceful people inhabiting this part of Africa must then have been in the zenith of their prosperity. Their herds of cattle, of a small but singularly beautiful breed, must have fed in every valley; whilst the rich and fertile soil must have produced them an abundance of vegetable food.

Early in the present century, however, a Zulu horde (apparently the founders of the Angoni tribe now living to the west of Lake Nyaṣsa), known to the Matabele as the Ama Zwang Indaba, broke away from Zulu or Swazieland, and migrating northwards, spread death and desolation amongst the tribes inhabiting the Mashona plateau. These Zulus, however, simply passed through the country, and, crossing the Zambesi below Zumbo, established themselves on the high country to the north of that river; and the Mashonas once more dwelt in peace and prosperity throughout the land. About 1840, however, the Matabele, under their warlike chief Unziligazi, settled in the country which they now inhabit, and very soon bands of these ferocious savages overran Mashonaland in every direction. In a few years there were no more Mashonas left in the open country, the remnant that had escaped massacre having fled into the mountainous districts to the south and east of the high plateau, where they still live. Thus, in a short time, an immense extent of fertile country that had—perhaps for ages past—supported a large and thriving community, was again given back to nature; and so it remains to the present day, an utterly deserted country, roamed over at will by herds of elands and other antelopes.

Besides the high plateau of Mashonaland, the whole of which is over 4,000 feet above sea level, extending along the watershed for a distance of over 200 miles from the Matabele country to the sources of the Hanyane and Mazoe Rivers, with a breadth of 60 to 100 miles, and, though within the tropics, practically a temperate country, capable of producing all the fruits and vegetables of northern Europe,—there is a vast extent of country lying in the south, east, and north-east of the plateau well watered and fertile, having an altitude of from 3,000 to 4,000 feet, the greater part of which in time to come will probably be occupied by Europeans.

In 1882, 1883, 1885, and 1887 I travelled much amongst the various tribes of Mashonas, living in the hills to the north-east, east, and south-east of the high plateau of Mashonaland. I usually travelled with a very small following, and was always completely in the power of the natives, had they been evilly disposed towards me; but I never had any trouble with them at all, and personally I like them better than any other African tribe with which I have come in contact. They seem to have but little of the ferocity which usually forms so marked a feature in the character of uncivilised races, and in their inter-tribal quarrels blood is seldom shed. I have been assured over and over again, that even in cases where a man is believed to be guilty of witchcraft he is not killed, but merely banished from his tribe, his property of course being confiscated. Their religious beliefs are of the vaguest; and in this respect they may be considered fortunate, as on the one hand their minds are not oppressed by the fear in this world of the malice of devils and evil spirits, as is the case with many uncivilised races, and on the other they do not believe in a future of eternal punishment which, according to the popular teachings of dogmatic Christianity, is the cheerful doom that awaits the great bulk of mankind. It is worthy of remark that these people never call themselves Mashonas, and how the name has arisen which has now become the generic term for a great many different tribes speaking dialects of one language, but scattered over a large extent of country, I have not been able to discover. Amongst themselves, each community has its own tribal name, such as the Bambiri, Mabotcha, Barotse, &c., and the tattoo marks differ in each clan. The distinguishing mark of the Barotse living on the Upper Sabi is a broad open nick filed out between the two front teeth of the upper jaw, and it is a curious fact that this is also the tribal mark of the Barotse living on the Upper Zambesi. It is not at all impossible, or indeed improbable, that this latter tribe were originally an offshoot from the powerful Barotse nation that once occupied a large tract of country to the west of the River Sabi in southern Mashonaland. They themselves have a tradition that their ancestors originally came from a country far to the south, and, crossing the Zambesi, settled in the country they now inhabit. This must have been long ago, however, as the Makololo (when, under their warlike chief, Sebituane, they reached the Upper Zambesi some sixty years ago) found them the most powerful tribe in that region. The northern Barotse were then conquered and enslaved by the invaders and for two generations had no national existence, but were nothing more than one among many tribes subjugated by the Makololo. On the death of Sekeletu, the son of Sebituane, however, a civil war broke out among the Makololo so fierce and bloody, that the Barotse were encouraged to rise against their conquerors. They were well led by Sipopo, the lineal descendant of the old Barotse chiefs, a man of courage and ability, and after some hard fighting, the already exhausted forces of the Makololo were utterly destroyed.

The southern Barotse, from whom, as I have said above, it is probable that the people now dominant on the Upper Zambesi have sprung, were once the richest and most numerous of the tribes living to the south-east of the Mashona plateau. They occupied the rich and fertile country to the west of the River Sabi, and their headquarters were amongst a range of hills, two peaks amongst which are still known to the Mashonas as Mabangue and Mazeba. In the latter days of Umziligazi, these people were attacked by a strong force of Matabele and their country laid waste, their old chief Sebumbum being captured alive by the express order of the Zulu despot, and carried a prisoner to Matabeleland. In this raid great numbers of the Barotse were killed, many of the children taken for slaves, and their large herds of cattle, sheep, and goats driven off by their conquerors. The broken remnant of the tribe crossed the Sabi, and took up their abode in the fertile well-watered valleys amongst the hills along the course of the Ruzarwe and Masheke Rivers, where they are still living. There they have once more become a rich and prosperous people, possessing considerable herds of cattle and growing great quantities of rice, maize, " pogo," corn, sweet potatoes, ground nuts, &c., and it is amongst these people that the Mashonas may be seen and studied to the best advantage. As a race they are a strong able-bodied set of men, but lack the fighting qualities which distinguished the various branches of the Zulu tribes. The women and girls are particularly stout and sturdy-looking, and do not give one at all the idea of being worn out with overwork. Most of them have merry, cheerful faces, and seem very good-tempered.

The arms of these people are heavy assegais, with a good deal of iron worked round each end of the wooden shaft, or sometimes made entirely of iron, battle-axes, and bows and arrows. These arrows are feathered, the heads being made of iron, and are all barbed in such a way that they must be very difficult to extract from a wound. As far as I know they are never poisoned. The bows are from four to five feet long, the arrows being about two and a half feet in length. Altogether, compared to the old English longbow, with its cloth-yard shaft, the bow and arrow of the Mashonas is a very feeble weapon. Amongst the northern tribes of Mashonas bows and arrows have gone out of fashion, and are now seldom to be seen, but they are still in common use among the Barotse and other tribes on the Upper Sabi. One sees a good many guns, chiefly flint-lock muskets, that have been brought from the Portuguese trading stations on the Lower Zambesi, in the possession of the Mashonas, but they find it so difficult to procure powder, that these guns are not of much use to them. They make a very inferior sort of gunpowder themselves, but where they have learnt the art I cannot say. The grains of that which I have seen were perfectly spherical, and it had very much the appearance of dust shot. The natives said that it exploded properly in dry weather, but that in the rainy season it was very unreliable. They invariably use iron bullets, which they make themselves, and which are of no particular shape, and often as nearly square as round. Although always very eager for meat, the Mashonas do not seem to be very expert hunters, and what game they do manage to kill is almost invariably caught in pitfalls, which they construct in large numbers, at much expense of time and labour. At certain times of the year it may be said that wherever there are Mashonas there are elands.

And now it may be asked why I have written this article. Well, chiefly in the hope that it may call some attention to the condition of the Mashonas, a people amongst whom I have travelled extensively, and of whom I have very kindly recollections. Their country has now been proclaimed within the sphere of British influence. How is that influence to be used? Not, it is to be hoped, by assisting the Matabele king to close his country to British enterprise, and thus allowing him full scope to complete the annihilation of the independent Mashona tribes. It is only by the entry of Europeans and the occupation by them of the vast range of fertile country depopulated by the Matabele—a country, be it noted, that is now lying idle, and that may be re-peopled by Europeans without wronging any human being—and by the establishment of mining communities in Northern Mashonaland, that the Mashonas can be saved. And it is most necessary that the Mashonas should be saved, for they are the people who will supply the native labour that will be so necessary in the future development of Mashonaland.

The re-settlement of the high and healthy Mashona plateau by Europeans would be welcomed as the greatest of blessings by the broken tribes of Mashonas that still survive, as they would be freed not only from the disastrous consequences of their savage neighbours' raids, but also from the continual state of terror in which they live, in the ever-present expectation of attack. There is, I repeat, an immense extent of the finest country in South Africa lying idle, the occupation of which will wrong no man ; and until all this country is settled, the whites will not come into competition with the Mashonas. By that time there will be a settled form of government, which will be capable of controlling individual Europeans, and which ought to be capable of protecting the rights of the natives at least as well as they are protected in any other of our colonies.

One hears the gentlemen who have got concessions to exploit the Matabele and Mashona countries stigmatised as adventurers, and hopes expressed that our Government will assist Lo Bengula to repudiate his agreements. I think they ought to have every assistance the Government can give them in carrying out their ·schemes, for if they succeed, and mining operations are established in Mashonaland, English farmers will soon follow, and the richest country in South Africa will be, in fact as well as in name, within the sphere of British influence. "Adventurers!" yes, and not, after all, a term of reproach to an Englishman, for surely Clive and Warren Hastings were adventurers, and adventurers have made the British Empire what it is.

Mr. Mandy says :—

After reaching the table-land, by a rather stiff climb up from the River Ganyane, we shaped our course to the north-west and travelled on until we arrived on the edge of a vast basin. The table-land suddenly falls away to the north and south, and the huge basin in front is filled, as far as the eye can reach, with mountains, peak rising behind peak. From out of these mountains the Mashonas poured in crowds, and as soon as they understood that we required grain, mealies, corn, and rice were brought in abundance. In a very few days our wagons were loaded as heavily as it was prudent to load them with mealies, rice, and millet, all purchased with meat. The table-land swarmed with game, principally rhinoceros, elands, and tsesebe, and it was with the meat of these animals we bought our grain. The people are very timid, and build their towns on the tops of the hills in spots as difficult of access as they can find, and live in daily dread of the Matabele. In person they are moderately tall, but thin and of poor development, and very black. . . . . The time has arrived when, in the interests of humanity, the paramount power in Africa should either take upon itself the government of this magnificent country, or grant the Charter that is now being applied for by men able and willing to take upon themselves this vast responsibility. Then, in place of the deadly reign of terror, established by the merciless Matabele, there would succeed the peaceful and benign rule of an enlightened people. The industrious and intelligent, though timid, Mashonas would emerge from their rocky fastnesses and dwell once more secure in the open. Tens of thousands of busy, pushing white men would pour into the land, repeopling the territories laid desolate by the savages now devastating the country. And the problem, the solution of which has hitherto defied the great European powers, would be practically solved. The slave trade would be doomed. With its rivers spanned by bridges, and a railway from the Cape to the Zambesi, civilisation would light up the land, and our continent, no longer dark and silent, would throb with ceaseless industries. The fruitful plains and valleys of Matabeleland and Mashonaland would teem with well-to-do agriculturists, large towns and villages spring up at various centres, and Africa, the birthplace of a new and sturdy nation, would eventually take a prominent place in the councils of the world.

Those who wish to read all about Mr. Selous' wonderful and fascinating adventures in his own particular sphere—hunting—in

Mashonaland will get a copy of "A Hunter's Wanderings in Africa." Frederick Courteney Selous, at the age of 19 years, landed in South Africa in 1871, and has since built up for himself a great reputation as a sportsman of the first water, a very excellent shot, and a prince of good fellows. He has contributed many of his reminiscences to the *Field*, and I wish I could find space for some full extracts from these. A few must suffice, and even they will help to show what astonishing "bags" of big game Mr. Selous has had in his time. The recitals of some of his adventures might be pages from Mayne Reid or Fenimore Cooper, and they must be looked up in the book I have named by those who are desirous to learn all about the great game of the far interior of South Africa. Here are a few of Mr. Selous' diary jottings :—

The buffalo is known to be a very savage animal when wounded, though I cannot but think that he is generally credited with being a great deal more ferocious than he really is; nor can I understand how any man who has had a large personal experience of both buffaloes and lions can come to the conclusion that the former are more dangerous animals to deal with than the latter. However, a buffalo, whether wounded by a hunter's bullet or by the claws of a lion, is an animal to be dealt with cautiously, and in the interior of Africa probably quite as many men are killed by these powerful beasts as by lions, though it must always be remembered, in making this sort of comparison, that for every lion that is brought to bag, at least 100 buffaloes are killed. Considering the number of buffaloes that I have shot—now well over 200—I have met with but few vicious animals, and, therefore, have had but few adventures. There is no more exciting sport than following a wounded buffalo into thick covert, and it ought not to be undertaken by anyone unless he has very quick eyesight and good nerve. If the bush is dense, buffaloes will seldom run far in it when wounded, but after going a short distance will pull up and await the arrival of their pursuers. In doing this they seldom or never stand facing back on their own spoor, but always, in my experience, at right angles to it, and thus broadside on to anyone following on their tracks. In this position they stand quite motionless, evidently listening intently, and it is astonishing how difficult it is to see them in the gloom of thick bush. The experienced hunter will now advance, with his rifle at the ready and on full cock, treading cautiously to avoid breaking twigs, with every sense on the alert, and following the blood spoor step by step. If he sees the buffalo first, or exactly at the instant the animal sees him, he will get a very good shot, either before the brute moves or just as he is swinging round to charge; and if the bullet is well placed it will usually change his mind. Should the buffalo, however, be first seen when charging, it is a most difficult matter to stop him, and he is very likely to crumple up his pursuer. Should a wounded buffalo enter a bed of reeds or get into long grass, my advice is, leave him alone, unless you are anxious to solve certain psychological problems, about which one can do no more than theorise in this world. The great mass of the buffaloes that have fallen to my rifle were killed along the River Chobe, where these animals swarmed some years ago. They have now been driven far north along the western bank, but are still plentiful on the other side of the river from Linyanti north-wards. All shooting in this part of the country must be done on foot, as it swarms with tsetse fly. . . . . I did not know at this time that his right thigh was broken, but I knew that a wounded leopard is a very dangerous animal to deal with—as savage as a lion, and as agile as a cat—and so rode cautiously com-pletely round the bush beneath which he lay, to see if I could not get a sight of him. However, as he lay in the grass I could see absolutely nothing, although, being on horseback, my eyes were well above the ground. I now rode nearer, and began to think he was dead or dying, as he let me come within twenty-five yards before making a sign. When at about this distance, however, he suddenly raised his head, with a loud snarling grunt, and gave me a fine view of his open mouth, garnished with a very serviceable-looking set of teeth. Thinking he was coming, I instantly jerked my horse half round; but the apparition disappeared, and I could see nothing again. However, I had seen about where he was lying, and so determined to fire a shot or two, to make him show himself; but before I could do so he again raised his head, with another snarl, and immediately after came straight out at me, and at such a pace, that before I could turn my horse and get him started he was right under his tail. He chased me some sixty or seventy yards right into the open, keeping close up the whole time, when he stopped. I pulled in as quickly as I could, and before the plucky little beast regained the bush gave him a second shot, which quickly proved fatal. When charging and chasing me, this leopard growled, or grunted, or roared exactly like a lion under similar circumstances, and made just as much noise. Had it not been for his broken thigh, I believe he would have clawed the horse. He proved to be a fine male, and I was better pleased at shooting him than I should have been with killing a lioness, as he only made the third of these handsome animals that has fallen to my rifle during all my wanderings. . . . . I had ridden, perhaps, 100 yards in this way, when, suddenly, with the corner of my eye, as it were, I saw a something, and, turning my head, instantly became aware that it was the lion. He was lying exactly at right angles to the course I was riding, and was watching me intently. His hind legs were doubled in under him, and his head pressed flat upon his outstretched paws, just in front of which lay the fallen trunk of a small dead tree some eight or ten inches in diameter. As I first saw him lying at a distance of about forty yards, I had a perfectly clear view of him from my horse's back, and, pulling in instantly, tried to fire from the saddle. However, the horse would not stand, but moved on, bringing a tree in the line of fire; this I let him pass, and getting another good view beyond it, again pulled in, but, as the perverse animal would not keep still, I dismounted. All this time the lion had never moved, nor did he now, but lay watching me intently with his yellow eyes. Nothing stirred but his tail, the end of which he twitched slowly, so that the black bunch of hair at its extremity appeared first on one side of him, then on the other. As I raised my rifle to my shoulder I found that the fallen tree trunk interfered considerably with the fine view I had had of him from my horse's back, as it hid almost all his nose below the eyes. In the position in which he was now holding his head I ought to have hit him about half-way between the nostrils and the eyes, which was impossible; anywhere above the eyes would have been too high, as the bullet would have glanced from his skull, so that it required a very exact shot to kill him on the spot. However, there was no time to wait, and, trying to aim so that the bullet should just clear the fallen log and catch him between the eyes, I fired. With a loud roar he answered the shot, and I instantly became aware that he was coming straight at me with open mouth and flaming eyes, growling savagely. I knew it was hopeless to try and get another cartridge into my single-barrelled rifle, and utterly useless to try and mount, more especially as my horse, startled by the loud, hoarse grunts and sudden and disagreeable appearance of the charging lion, backed so vigorously that the bridle (to a running ring on which a strong thong was attached, the other end being fastened to my belt) came over his head. I had a strong feeling that I was about to have an opportunity of testing the accuracy of Dr. Livingstone's incredible statement, that, for certain reasons—explained by the doctor—a lion's bite gives no pain; but there was no time to think of anything in particular. The whole adventure was the affair of a moment. I just brought my rifle round in front of me, holding the small of the stock in my right hand and the barrel in my left, with a vague idea of getting it into the lion's mouth, and at the same time yelled as loud as I could "Loos de honden, loos de honden," which, being translated, means "Let loose the dogs." In an instant, as I say, the lion was close up to me. I had never moved my feet since firing, and, whether it was my standing still facing him that made him alter his mind, or whether he heard the noise made by my

people, who, hearing my shot immediately followed by the loud growling
of the lion, were all shouting and making a noise, to frighten the lion
from coming their way, I cannot take upon myself to say; but he came
straight on to within about six yards of me, looking, I must say, most
unpleasant, and then suddenly swerved off, and, passing me, galloped off.
(Mr. Selous goes on to describe how he shot the lion.)

It was within a mile of this spot (River Se-whoi-whoi) that two years
previously I shot two white rhinoceroses (R. simus), the last of their kind
that have been killed, and perhaps that ever will be killed, by an
Englishman. They were male and female, and I preserved the skin of
the head and the skull of the former for the South African Museum in
Cape Town, where they now are. I shall never cease to regret that I did
not preserve the entire skeleton for our own splendid Museum of Natural
History at South Kensington; but when I shot the animal I made sure
I should get finer specimens later on in the season. However, one thing
and another prevented my visiting the one spot of country where I knew
that a few were still to be found, and now those few have almost, if not
quite, all been killed; and, to the best of my belief, the great white, or
square-mouthed rhinoceros, the largest of modern terrestrial mammals
after the elephant, is on the very verge of extinction, and in the next
year or two will become absolutely extinct; and if in the near future
some student of natural history should wish to know what this extinct
beast really was like, he will find nothing in all the museums of Europe
and America to enlighten him upon the subject but some half-dozen
skulls and a goodly number of the anterior horns. In 1886 two Boer
hunters, Karl Weyand and Jan Engelbrecht, got into the little tract of
country where a few white rhinoceroses were still left, and between them
killed ten during the season; five more were killed during the same
time by some native hunters from the Matabele country. A few were
still left, as in the following year, 1887, myself and some English sportsmen saw the tracks of two or three in the same district, but could not
find the animals themselves. Some of these last remnants of their race
may still survive, but it is not too much to say that long before the close
of this century the white rhinoceros will have vanished from the face of
the earth. I hope your readers will pardon this long digression, but the
subject of the extinction of this huge quadruped has a melancholy interest
for me, who remember that less than twenty years ago it was a common
animal over an enormous extent of country in Central South Africa.
. . . . After breakfast I trekked on, and in the afternoon reached
the River Umgezi, where I slept. This little river is a favourite resort of
hippopotami, small herds of which animals are usually to be found in the
deep black pools (some over a mile in length) that lie on either side of the
Machabi Hills. Taking a ride along the course of the river late in the
afternoon, I came across much recent spoor, some of it not more than a
day or two old, but the animals themselves seemed to have moved northwards towards the deep pools which I knew lay beyond the hills. Whilst
riding down the river I saw a large herd of koodoos and a few water-
bucks, but, as they were all females, did not interfere with them. I also
saw several agile wiry-haired little klipspringers. It is worthy of remark
that in northern Mashonaland these compactly built, though active little
antelopes are to be found along the courses of all the larger rivers, such
as the Umgezi, Umniati, Umfule, and Hanyani, wherever they run (as
they often do) amongst boulders and masses of rock. Thus they may be
shot by walking along the banks of the river, and without ever climbing
a hill at all. . . . . The shooting of the lioness was a very tame
affair, and, owing to peculiar circumstances, was attended with as little

danger to myself as would be the shooting of a lion in a menagerie through the bars of a cage. It happened in this wise. I was riding one day in May, 1882 (without any attendants, as I had left all my Kafirs making camp), along the banks of a deep hippopotamus pool, nearly a hundred yards in breadth and half a mile or so in length, when I saw something move amongst the grass growing beneath a small bush on the opposite bank of the river, and some 120 yards away from where I sat on my horse. The next instant the head and shoulders of a lioness appeared, looking towards me; so, instantly dismounting, I fired at her across the river, and rolled her over. For some seconds I could see nothing of her, but I knew she was rolling about, as she kept the grass in continual motion, and, moreover, growled continuously. Suddenly she appeared again, evidently in a dying condition and half-falling, half-walking down the steep bank, lay all of a heap at the water's edge, holding her jaws, now all besmirched with blood, slightly open, and growling softly. I might have bombarded her in perfect safety; but, as I thought she was done for, and did not want to spoil her skin, I refrained from doing so, and, cantering up to the end of the pool, crossed the river, and rode down the bank to close to the spot where the lioness lay. She was not quite so dead as I thought, for as soon as she saw me she managed to raise her head and growl savagely, her eyes gleaming with all the fierce fury of her unutterable though futile rage. I may here say that anyone who has not seen at close quarters the fierce light that scintillates from the eyes of a wounded lion or any other of the large Felidæ can hardly imagine its wondrous brilliancy and furious concentration. Such eyes are more expressive than those of the heroine of a French novel, which I have known it to take a page and a half to describe. In the present instance the fury of the wounded lioness was impotent, as she had not the strength to raise herself from the ground, and, indeed, could do nothing more than lift her head and growl savagely. The small ·450-bore expanding bullet had done its murderous work, and the life that had so lately been strong within her was fast ebbing away. However, the sun was low, my wagons were some distance off, and I was alone, with no one to help me to skin the lioness; so I killed her with a shot through the brain, and at once set to work to remove her hide, which I then fastened to the saddle and carried back to camp—the first, but not the last, lion skin my good horse Nelson ever carried for me. . . . .

Whilst this hasty meal was preparing, I got everything ready. I determined to mount my Griqua lad Laer on the old horse Charley, and to take up the spoor with him alone, leaving all the Kafirs at the wagons, so that we could follow up the elephants at a canter. As I was still very weak, I was afraid that the weight of my 10-bore rifle would be too much for me, and finally decided to see what I could do with my little ·450-bore single Metford, by Gibbs, of Bristol. Of course I used the military cartridges, loaded with 75 grs. of powder, and long-pointed, toughened 540-grain bullets. I had already killed giraffes, buffaloes, hippopotami, and a few rhinoceros with one of these little rifles, and felt confident that I would be able to kill elephants, too. I fixed two strong leather pouches in front of my saddle, each containing twenty-five cartridges, and carried twenty more in my belt, being determined not to run out of ammunition whatever else might happen. I also tied a warm coat over the pommel of the saddle, thinking it more than probable that we should have to sleep out for a night; and put a few pieces of dried meat in the pockets. Laer carried a single 10-bore rifle and twenty cartridges, and tied a small kettle behind his saddle, together with a little tea and sugar in a handkerchief. As he was still quite a lad, and had had no experience at all with elephants, I told him to keep close to me, and not to fire except at animals which I had first disabled. It was still early when we took up the spoor, which there was no difficulty about following, as the herd was a very large one, and had trodden broad paths wherever they had crossed the open grassy glades, intersecting the belts of forest ; whilst in the forests themselves so many trees had been broken and stripped of their bark that one could ride straight ahead without looking at the ground at all. The elephants, I think, must have passed where I first saw their spoor in the early morning, not long before daylight, and had been moving very slowly, feeding quietly along, utterly unconscious of danger ; otherwise we should not have overtaken them as soon as we did. Cantering briskly along the spoor, we ere long crossed the Lundaza River, and upon emerging from a broad belt of forest, about a couple of miles beyond it, suddenly saw the elephants in front of us. The herd was one of the largest it has ever been my fate to look upon, and as, when the animals first came into view, they were crossing a broad open grassy valley between two patches of forest, I had an unusually good opportunity of observing them. They were moving in masses across the valley, walking at that slow majestic step natural to the wild elephant when entirely unsuspicious of the presence of man, that foe who, whilst immeasurably inferior in physical power to the elephant's giant strength, yet by the subtle power of intellect, which has enabled him to imagine and fashion weapons of deadly power, has ever been that animal's bane and curse, and bids fair to destroy ere long the last of his race in Africa, as in days gone by the savages of Central Europe utterly exterminated his mighty prototype, the mammoth, beneath the gloomy forests of Germany, Britain, and of Gaul.

As I reined in my horse on the border of the forest, and gazed over the valley across which stretched this great herd of mighty beasts, a thrill of excitement shot through my frame, and braced my fever-weakened nerves. Never can elephants be beheld by the South African hunter without feelings of intense excitement. There stand the possessors of that ivory, which, turned into money, will enable man to buy the salted horse, the span of oxen, the rifle, or what not that he covets ; the ivory for which he has perhaps toiled, oh! so wearily ; for which he has endured hunger, thirst, exposure to the fierce heat of the midday tropic sun, and the very uttermost fatigue. Yes! there they stand ; but the hunter knows, too, that before those gleaming tusks can be reft from their possessors there is a man's work to be done, possibly dangers to be met and overcome, and if he be on foot, that all his powers of wind and limb must be called to his aid before he can handle the ivory and estimate the value of the slain giants, the victims of his skill and perseverance. On the present occasion, however, I had come up with the elephants without having endured privation or hard ship of any kind. It was a pure stroke of luck, and in many ways never had I had such a chance of doing a good day's work with these animals before. There was an immense herd of them before me—numbering probably nearer 200 than 100—and for some miles all round me the forests were fairly open. I had also a good little rifle and 70 cartridges. My bodily weakness, the result of fever, was certainly much against me, but what militated more against my success that day than anything else, was the obstinacy of my horse, whose disposition I was soon to find out. Even to-day, as I think of this episode in my hunting career, I cannot but lament and rail at fate when I think of what I did and what I might have done that day had I but had my good horse Nelson between my knees. However, regret is vain ; the past is irrevocable, and I will now proceed to relate what happened to me.

But I cannot follow up that elephant hunt. Suffice it to say that five of these monsters fell to Mr. Selous' rifle that day. Let the sportsman look at the wonderful list of game shot by this Nimrod very modestly printed at the end of his book. A glance shows that in one period of four years he had shot 20 elephants, 100 buffaloes, 12 rhinoceroses, 4 hippos, 18 giraffes, 13 lions, 48 zebras, 548 antelopes, &c., &c. Sir John Willoughby, speaking to a representative of SOUTH AFRICA on Mashonaland, said :—" We are trying to preserve the game, of which there is any amount. We have had a meeting at which suggestions were made with the view of drawing up a code of game laws. We don't mean to allow animals to be killed for the sake of their hides. We want a six months' close season, and also to protect animals which may be useful for draught purposes. The quagga, for instance—if caught young, I don't see why it should not be broken to harness. The eland, too, would make a good post and draught animal ; in fact, I think it has already been used in some places for the latter purpose. Elephants, again, would be very serviceable. A troop of them was met near Umshabetsi beyond Tuli,—the latter is our first fort. It is a fine, strong, natural position, and it has been strengthened so as to render it impregnable. Leopards—there are no striped tigers as in India—have been seen occasionally at the post stations ; but our men don't kill them, because they are such useful scavengers, eating the carcases of dead horses, &c., which would otherwise have to be burnt. Mashonaland is the finest country in the world, having a splendid soil, a healthy climate, and magnificent scenery. had no idea, although I had been in Africa before, that it contained such a splendid country. It is far healthier than Kimberley, the elevation being between 4,000 and 5,000 feet above sea-level. A good many of the Pioneers will devote themselves to agriculture, but gold is the great attraction just now."

Such, then (and there is more yet to be said about its golden wealth), is the country which has fallen into the hands of the British South Africa Company, and which Portugal, with that amazing presumption which has characterised all her doings latterly in South-East Africa, recently set up a claim to. The hollowness of this claim was, of course, soon exposed ; but a reference to the matter may be made in this historical compendium. At the end of 1888 there was considerable astonishment in London on the receipt of news from South Africa that the Portuguese Consul at Cape Town had seen fit to issue the following notice in the press :—

NOTICE.

CONSULATE FOR PORTUGAL.

WHEREAS a notice signed by order of LO BENGULA, King of the Matabeles, has lately been published in the Newspapers giving notice that all Mining Rights in Matabeleland, Mashonaland, and adjacent territories, have already been disposed of, and soliciting the assistance of all neighbouring Chiefs and States in excluding all persons entering these territories hereafter, I, EDUARDO A. DE CARVALHO, Consul for Portugal, having received special instructions, do hereby make it known that His Most Faithful Majesty's Government does not recognise the pretended rights of LO BENGULA to Mashonaland and adjacent territories, over which the Crown of Portugal claims Sovereignty, and that, therefore, all Concessions of Land or Mining Rights granted, or that may be granted in future in the said territories of Mashonaland and adjacent, are null and void, as the Government of Portugal does not, and will not, acknowledge any such Concessions.

EDUARDO A. DE CARVALHO,
CONSUL FOR PORTUGAL.

Consulate for Portugal, Cape Town,
3rd December, 1888.

Of course the Portuguese claim, like most of her other claims in Africa, was a daringly preposterous one, and was only made with the view to increasing the chances of certain other claims nearer the coast being recognised. The political influence of the Portuguese in South-East Africa extends no further than the range of the cannon that moulder on the walls of their forts; as far as effective occupation of any part of the country is concerned they have at no time gone a further distance from their forts than they could speedily retraverse for protection from the natives they assume to lord it over. Mr. Selous, in a letter to the *Times* at this period, pointed out that the British and Dutch colonists of South Africa would laugh at the pretensions of Portugal to Mashonaland, even had they been "ratified by every Government in Europe;" and that gentleman concluded an interesting letter as follows:—

And should "the good old rule, the simple plan," have to be resorted to, "that those may take who have the power, and those may keep who can," it is not too much to assert that on the open plateau of Mashonaland 200 mounted South Africans would disperse all the native levies that the Portuguese could muster in South-Eastern Africa, and native levies are all that can be employed, for the military strength of Portugal in this part of the world consists of a few Portuguese and Goanese officers, a few black soldiers from Angola, and the native levies of Manoel Antonio, Ignacio de Jesus Xavier, Matakama, Kanyemba, and other native chiefs at present friendly to the Portuguese. Should white troops be sent from Portugal they would be decimated by fever on the coast or on the Lower Zambesi, as happened during the prosecution of the first Bonga War in 1868. Of late the Portuguese have talked much about British arrogance and presumption; but surely it can be retorted hat they themselves have shown over much pretension in the claims which they have lately put forward to Mashonaland. The South Africa Company claims the right to govern that country, to protect its people, and to develop its natural resources under the charter lately granted by the Queen. But before the charter was granted, the promoters of that great enterprise had gained an intimate knowledge of Mashonaland and its people, and that not from old Portuguese records, but from the writings, maps, and conversation of modern Englishmen, and they know that the native Mashonas would welcome the advent of British settlers in their country as a protection not alone against the bloodthirsty

Matabele, but also against the cruel and brutal slave-dealers from the Zambesi, such as Kanyemba, Matakama, Perizengi, Lobo, Chimbango, &c., all of whom have long Portuguese names, and all of whom hold the official position of "Capitas Mor" in their districts, and govern the countries they live in for the Portuguese, without the assistance or surveillance of a magistrate or any kind of Portuguese official. Or if it be asserted that they do not govern for the Portuguese, then I say that Portugal has no jurisdiction in any of the countries over which these men rule—a supposition which would reduce Portuguese territory in South-Eastern Africa to very small dimensions. For my part I always speak of countries governed by these native "Capitas Mors" as being indirectly under Portuguese rule. But give Portugal all the territory ruled over by these men (surely she cannot claim anything more) and not an acre of Mashonaland will come under her jurisdiction. The Chartered Company would be weak indeed should it recognise the validity of the annexations of the present year, said to have been made by Lieutenant Cordon and Colonel Paiva d'Andrada, to any part of the country which was long ago proclaimed within the sphere of British influence, and which has at any rate been travelled and hunted over by several British subjects, but never by a Portuguese before the present year. In the future, should trouble come between the servants of the British Company and the Portuguese, the latter will be responsible and must bear the blame. For British subjects have been the first to explore Mashonaland and to find out its value, and under the auspices of the Chartered Company let us hope that British subjects will develop it and make it the richest and most prosperous state in the South African Dominion of the future. This may be a dream that is never to be fulfilled; but, at any rate, I feel sure that it is not the Portuguese who will prevent its realisation.

But, fortunately, Lord Salisbury was not in any mood for diplomatic trifling, and the following documents appeared in the *London Gazette*:—

Foreign Office, Nov. 21, 1889.

The following despatch has been addressed by the Marquis of Salisbury, K.G., Her Majesty's Principal Secretary of State for Foreign Affairs, to John Glynn Petre, Esq., C.B., Her Majesty's Envoy Extraordinary and Minister Plenipotentiary to the Court of Lisbon, instructing him to protest against the Portuguese Royal Decree of November 9, 1889:—

Foreign Office, Nov. 21, 1889.

Sir,—In your despatch of the 16th inst. I received a copy of the following Royal Decree which was published in the official *Gazette* of the 9th inst. It purports to place a large territory under Portuguese administration in the interior of Africa to the north and south of the Zambesi River. The district, to which the name of Zumbo is given, appears to comprise a great part of Mashonaland and an immense tract to the northward, approaching the frontiers of the Congo Free State and the watershed of Lake Nyassa. I enclose a map indicating the frontiers set forth in that decree.

I have to request you to remind the Portuguese Government that Mashonaland is under British influence, and to state that Her Majesty's Government do not recognise a claim of Portugal to any portion of that territory. The agreement between Lo Bengula and Great Britain of the 11th of February, 1888, was duly notified to them in accordance with the instruction given by me to Sir George Bonham in my despatch of July of that year. It was also officially published in the Cape Colony. The

agreement recorded the fact that Lo Bengula is ruler of Mashonaland
and Makalakaland.

Her Majesty's Government are also unable to recognise the claims of
Portugal to the territory to the north of the Zambesi indicated in the
above-mentioned proclamation. So far as they are defined, they follow
the course of the Loangwa River, on whose banks there are tribes with
whom Her Majesty's Government have treaties; and they appear to be
inconsistent with British rights established by settlement upon the Shiré
River and the coast of Lake Nyassa.   Beyond this they assert the
jurisdiction of Portugal over vast tracts which are still unoccupied, but
the knowledge of which is principally due to British explorers. You will
refer Senhor Barros Gomes to the memorandum which you placed in his
hands, by my direction, on the 13th of August, 1887, in which it was
stated that Her Majesty's Government protested against any claims in
no degree founded on occupation, and that they could not recognise the
sovereignty of Portugal in territory of which she had not practically
taken possession, and in which she was represented by no authority
capable of exercising the ordinary rights of sovereignty.   You will
formally renew this protest.

You will inform his Excellency that Her Majesty's Government recognise on the Upper Zambesi the existence of Portuguese occupation at
Tete and Zumbo, but that they have no knowledge of the occupation of
any other place or district.

You will place a copy of this despatch at once in the hands of Senhor
Barros Gomes.

I am, &c.,

SALISBURY.

George Glynn Petre, Esq., C.B.

In March of 1889 an extra edition of the Cape *Government
Gazette* declared that Lo Bengula ruled Mashonaland under British
influence, and repudiated the sovereignty of Portugal over his
territory; and in the following month the Cape Town Consul for
Portugal was informed by the High Commissioner that " Mashonaland is unquestionably part of the territory ruled by Lo Bengula,
and, as such, is under British influence."

As I pointed out in " Golden South Africa," the auriferous
countries to the north of the Transvaal and Swazieland remain as
yet practically unexplored—certainly undeveloped. At some length
I have shown what old writers had to say about the auriferous
wealth of Mashonaland, known in their time and long anterior as
Monomotapa.   The re-discovery of the Mashonaland Gold Fields,
or, as they were called in Baines' day, the Northern Gold Fields (to
distinguish them from the Tati Fields), followed the discovery of
the Tati only by the interval of the few weeks necessarily occupied
in travelling 350 miles more to the north-east; but the difficulty of
exploring and ascertaining their value increased at every step.
Even during 1866 the suspicions of the Matabele were aroused, and
Mr. Hartley (Mr. Hartley, formerly of Bathurst, Lower Albany—a
well-known elephant hunter) dared not openly assist Herr Mauch
in searching for reefs because whenever they attempted to do so,
his native servants would ask, " What have you to do with seeking
stones ?   The King gave you leave to shoot elephants.   Why do

you not attend to your own business, and not meddle with things for which you have no liberty?" Nevertheless, by his own scientific skill and perseverance, by the guidance of a Mashona, a retainer of Mr. Hartley's head man, Inyoka, by such assistance as the hunters dare give, and chief of all by the immunity which almost all savages concede to men whom they believe "demented," Mauch was able to visit and make a hasty examination of several reefs in the vicinity of the Umvute and Sarua Rivers, as well as between the Quœ-quœ and Bembesi. "There," to use his own words, "the extent and beauty of the gold fields are such that I stood as it were transfixed, and for a few minutes was unable to use the hammer. . . . Thousands of persons might work on this extensive gold field without interfering with one another." A second visit in 1867 confirmed the impressions of the former year; but the fears of the Matabele had been excited to the highest pitch. They were aware that the knowledge of the richness of the country had already spread among the white men, and they expected that a rush of fierce and lawless desperadoes from all parts of a world more extensive than they had ever dreamed of, would set in at once and drive them from their land. Their anger was kindled against all who had helped to spread the gold news. Mr. Hartley himself, notwithstanding the personal favour and friendship extended to him by Mosilikatse, was at one time in danger of falling a sacrifice to the popular fury, but owed his life partly to the respect his honest manliness had earned among the people, and partly to the tact and knowledge of native character shown by the Rev. Mr. Lee, Missionary to the Matabele, in pleading for him. The news of these discoveries, backed by the exhibition of specimens of quartz more or less studded with gold, roused the public of Natal into action, as we have already seen. The further experiences of prospectors in Baines' time may be gathered from that able man's book, "The Gold Regions of South-East Africa." He freely asserted that he had reason to believe that in the direction of the Zimbabye ruins "alluvial fields as rich as and more extensive than those of Lydenburg, await the coming of the explorer who shall unite to skill in prospecting, patience, perseverance, and tact in dealing with the various native tribes, whose friendship must be cultivated, and assistance gained, before the richest of all the districts of South-Eastern Africa shall be ready to surrender its treasures to the enterprise and industry of Europe."

About the close of 1868 arrangements were made in London, by a small association of capitalists, to explore the region between the Limpopo and Zambesi Rivers which Carl Mauch had been exciting the world about, with a view to determine its gold-bearing character and value. Mr. Thomas Baines was selected as the leader of an exploring party consisting of himself, Nelson (an experienced mineralogist), Jewell, and Watson. The party spent some time in the very scenes in which the prospectors who went up with the

British South Africa Company are now busy. They made a careful examination of old workings for gold which Mr. Hartley had pointed out to them on the Simbo River, between it and the Sarua, two or three miles to the north of the Umfuli River. This district, on the whole, contained the most interesting specimen of the old native workings. The latitude of the spot was found to be 18° 10′ south, and the longitude about 30° 50′ east. The height above the sea-level was estimated at 3525 feet. The workings in this instance were on a somewhat elevated hill in two distinct ledges, or reefs, of quartz, 500 yards asunder, which cropped out to the surface of the ground for a direct extent of between 400 and 500 yards. For this entire length the veins had been more or less broken up and worked, the best and richest specimens of the quartz having been removed, and the poorer specimens left behind as refuse. The refuse fragments had been thrown back upon the reefs as the work advanced along them, so that they were entirely hidden by the débris. The discarded pieces were scattered in heaps of various sizes, sometimes from 15 to 20 feet across. The deepest pit was probably not more than 8 feet deep : but all the pits had an accumulation of the broken fragments at the bottom, so that the exact depth could not be ascertained unless the shafts were carefully cleared of the débris, an operation that is now proceeding in many cases to-day. It was perfectly manifest, in Mr. Baines's day, from the appearance of the surrounding heaps, that the pits were dug deeper in some places, where the richest specimens of rock were found, than they were in others. Trees had grown in several of the pits, but the largest observed was not more than 5 inches in diameter. Mr. Nelson felt confident, from all the facts which came under his notice, that these workings could not be more than from 150 to 200 years old. He concluded that they were made by the natives who occupied the spot before Mosilikatse came and drove them further towards the Zambesi River, and towards the East. One old Mashona told Mr. Baines that he could remember digging for gold having been carried on by his people on some of those very spots. It is certainly very wonderful that these Kafirs, so destitute of tools and mechanical aid, should have been able to extract gold from this adamantine rock. Mr. Nelson states that the work was effected by first breaking the quartz into small pieces, and picking out such scales of the bright metal as could be seen. The fragments were then placed in holes about 5 or 6 inches deep and broad, formed in granite or other hard rock, and round, hard boulders, of suitable size, were then rubbed round and round upon them ; and the silica and lighter particles were afterwards washed away from the gold, either in clay bowls or in cavities hollowed out in wood. How they contrived to break the quartz away from the solid hard reef still remains a mystery, though a writer in a previous page throws some light on it. There is no doubt, however, that the want of effective tools always pre-vented them from penetrating into the quartz veins to any material depth. Mr. Nelson, after mature consideration, came to the conclusion that this particular sett was the most promising that he had examined. It was therefore determined to endeavour to arrange with Um-Numbata for a grant of the right to crush for gold. Certain boundaries of ground were agreed upon, indicated in the north and east by the line of the River Simbo and by a chain of small hills, and in other directions by large ant-heaps with trees growing out of them, which were marked. A Matabele guide was then called, and these beacons and boundaries were pointed out to him as defining the ground which it was intended to ask from the chief; but as I show later on, poor Baines made nothing out of these researches. It was considered a very important point that there was an unlimited abundance both of wood and running water contained upon the actual ground. The rock enclosing the quartz veins was found to be gneiss, and a mixture of talcose and chloritic slates striking about north-east and south-west, and dipping at an angle of from 70° to 80°. What stratified rocks could be examined throughout the entire district were so hardened and metamorphosed that it was exceedingly difficult to arrive at any satisfactory conclusion regarding their geological age. Mr. Nelson, however, inclined to refer them to the Lower Palæozoic epoch. The quartz veins were so buried in the débris produced by the workings, that it was altogether impossible to ascertain their breadth below the surface of the ground but this we were told a score of years ago was certainly very considerable. Mr. Nelson found silver-bearing galena disseminated through the auriferous quartz; and this was the only spot in which this was the case in any of the extensive explorations made. Suitable bits of quartz rock were taken indiscriminately from the refuse of the workings at various places, and six of these were submitted to careful assay in England. Two specimens taken from one of the veins yielded at the rate of 0.825 and 1.950 ounces of gold per ton. Four specimens taken from another vein yielded 0·975, 3·125, 3·500, and 8·150 ounces per ton. From one choice piece of quartz, belonging to this second vein, Mr. Nelson procured gold at the rate of 60·75 ounces, and silver at the rate of 17·1 ounces per ton. Of course we are all very wise now, and are not carried away by assays. Under the circumstances in which this exploration had to be made, it was found to be quite impracticable to do more than take fragments of the rock lying ready to hand on the surface; and it should thus be remembered that these were all of the character of refuse which had been cast aside as valueless by the native workmen. There was no doubt in the mind of Mr. Baines that the pieces selected by the old natives for the extraction of gold, were of a much richer nature than the average range of these specimens, and that the substance of the quartz reefs, if they could have been got at, would have yielded rock of a similarly high value. Through the entire extent of this high region, granite seems to form the backbone, or foundation, of

the ridge of the watershed. It is, in many places, intersected with felspathic greenstone, and is associated with gneis-
and hornblende schist in various forms of diversity, and with
a hard rock containing comminglings of talc and quartz.
There is also connected with the escarpment of the granite,
a dark-coloured slate formation, about a mile across, in
many places standing almost perpendicularly, and forming high
bluffs on both sides of river channels. The slate band also forms
regular high mountain ridges that can be seen for a long distance.
It is this slate formation that is the principal seat of the quartz
veins, which run in all directions, and are sometimes as much as
75 feet wide. Mr. Nelson remarked that here, exactly as in
California, no gold was found along the main central line of the
granite ; the gold occurred where the stratified rocks trenched upon
the great granitic axis. This explains the presence of gold among
the affluents of the Limpopo on one side, and among the affluents
of the Zambesi on the other side, of the leading crest of the watershed. The river courses are commonly paved with greenstone
boulders, black iron sand, cornelians, agates, jasper, chalcedony,
hornstone, and flint ; and amidst these deposits there are many
traces of alluvial gold. In most of the trials which Mr. Nelson
made, the quantity was small ; but he was of opinion that it was
very likely to be found in larger quantities in deeper parts of the
river-bed. The River Changani seemed to him to be one of the
most promising rivers for the extraction of gold from alluvial
deposit by washing.

Mr. A. A. Anderson, in his " Twenty-five Years in a Wagon in
South Africa," says :—

Finally, we may conclude, in leaving this region, that the knowledge
already obtained of the richness of the Matabele and Mashona country
by exploring parties that have been allowed to prospect, only in
certain districts, and by others who have travelled through it in
other parts, and from my own observations, there is not a shadow of
a doubt that eventually this part of the continent will surpass all
others in Southern Africa as a gold-producing district, in the
cultivation of cotton, and other valuable products, that cannot but
prove most beneficial to the power who may obtain it ; and to the
benefit of its people, instead of its remaining in its present barbarous
state, where the slaughter of its inhabitants depends on the present
whims of its despotic monarch. From what has already been discovered of its richness, we see plainly the ancients, who extracted
the gold, have only done so to a limited extent—what may be termed
surface workings ; for their numerous pits, after all, are mere scratches
in the ground at places, but when they are properly worked and
greater depth attained, the mines may be found almost inexhaustible.
And if the gold dust, found in the sand of the rivers, can be procured
by a few single washings from a small dish, what may be expected
when the whole of these rivers have been properly worked ?

Mr. John Dalton, the Australian whom we quoted on the Tati
Fields, says of Mashonaland :—

It is impossible for a man who knows how to use his eyes to travel over a country for a year and a half without seeing a good deal, and I dare say that my opportunities were as good, and my authority to speak on the subject as great as anyone else who has been there. From what I saw, I am satisfied that payable gold exists in Mashonaland, and there is a good prospect of both alluvial and quartz.

With regard to the auriferous nature of Matabeleland and Mashonaland, in 1884 Sir H. Robinson wrote to the Secretary of State for the Colonies as follows :—

Gold is found there, not only in quartz, but in extensive alluvial deposits. Mashonaland possesses a soil of unsurpassed fertility, and is capable of yielding tropical products in great variety. The development of the natural resources of this country is, I believe, merely a question of time, and a valuable new market will then be opened to British commerce, if the trade be not diverted into other channels by a prohibitory tariff or vexatious restrictions.

The Rev. John Mackenzie, in his " Austral Africa ; Losing It or Ruling It," writes :—

Although discovered twenty years ago, the gold of Mashonaland and Bechuanaland still lies waiting the hand of enterprise and industry—preceded, let us hope, by friendly engagements with Lo Bengula and other native chiefs, on the part of the British Government. The discovery at the same time of the diamonds, and afterwards of the gold mines of the Transvaal— some of which are proving so valuable—combined to direct men's attention away from this part of the country. Nature, however, keeps securely her own treasures for centuries and ages. There are many reefs in the country I am describing which have never been worked. In other cases the modern digger and miner, when he appears on the scene, will clear out the workings of the Phœnicians, and the gold of Ophir will once more circulate in the commerce of the world.

Lieut. Haynes, who visited the country with Mr. Maund on behalf of the British Government, says :—

Upper Mashonaland has never properly been explored, and fabulous tales of its wealth are current. There appears to be no wagon road beyond Hartley Hill, and journeys through the country are mostly undertaken on foot ; tsetse fly is also said to be found beyond Hartley Hill. It is now the best hunting ground in Matabeleland, and elephants are still to be found there. The gold fields are very rich in reefs and alluvial gold, but native enterprise has long been dying out, and the export of gold from Portuguese ports has fallen to a very low degree. It is a first-class country. The natives work in iron, copper, wild cotton, which they dye in wild indigo.

Viscount E. de la Panout (surely an appropriate name for a prospector), describing his explorations in Mashonaland, writes :—

After crossing the Umvuli River, I went north-east in the mountains, and in the basin of the Mazoe River. I saw there the most beautiful country, as regards the salubrity, the agriculture, and the mineral richness. I found gold in payable quantity in all the rivers, principally on the north side of the Mazoe, all of whose affluents contain it. According to the opinion of several diggers, the specimens I brought showed that the reef must be very rich, and that they

Q

must have been washed close by the mine, the dust being very coarse. This opinion is in agreement with my own according to the conformation of the ground, the mountains being very near and the rivers very short on this side of the Mazoe. Besides, I found several reefs, and in each one I saw some gold. Unfortunately, I was not allowed to look for gold, and the King being very suspicious about it, I had to be careful to send my boys away when I wanted to prospect. . . . I saw a few days ago a map, lately printed in Germany, where the gold fields I am speaking of are indicated as King William's Gold Fields.

Mr. Mandy, whom I have quoted on Matabeleland, describes Mashonaland as rich in mineral wealth :—

The whole of Mashonaland is rich in mineral wealth. During the time spent by us on the edge of the mountain-filled basin I described just now, we were visited by several thousand people, and almost all the men carried gold for sale, alluvial gold, in small, rough, irregular-shaped nuggets, stored in quills. We were shown one working not far from where our wagons stood ; and from here the red soil was scraped up and carried in calabashes to a stream some distance away and washed. Often when hunting I have come across abandoned quartz workings and smelting places . . . . Gold has been brought to me for sale from Chillimanzi's, not in quills, but the full of a snuff-box at a time. North and north-eastern Mashonaland is very healthy, and there is not much danger from fever, if only low-lying ground is avoided in summer. Eastern Mashonaland is not so healthy ; but I believe the proper settlement of the country would have a great effect in reducing the danger from fevers ; that is, good houses, regular living, and proper cultivation, would have the effect of making the country more habitable. I saw some old diggings in several places, and I always found some good quartz in them. Why they were abandoned, and by whom explored, I cannot say. I never found any indications. That must have been many, many years ago,' because there are no remains of habitations or walls near them. The inhabitants affirm that it is not the Portuguese, that they know well ; and that it was done long before they came in the country by white men with long black hair—that is the translation of the name they give them—and that those men went in the direction of the north when they left the country. The rivers where I found the best prospects are the Watakai, the Umvosi, and the Culumaputsi. Those names are the ones used by the Mashonas. Only one of them is indicated on the map of Mr. Baines ; it is the last one, which is called by him the Lina. There is gold also on the other side of the Mazoe, because I saw some specimens which were washed by the wives of a Chief called Leanda, who is a sort of god in the country.

Mr. Selous says of Mashonaland that it is :—" A country which is bound to be of great importance in the near future, for there is an alluvial gold field of large extent and wonderful richness. I speak with some authority, as it has this year, 1888, been roughly tested with really extraordinary results." In the latter part of 1889 Mr. Selous went up the Zambesi to Tete. From there he struck to the west, and succeeded in getting to Mashonaland ; but he had great difficulties, owing to the porters hired at Tete deserting him. His opinion now is that the road to Mashonaland is impracticable from the Zambesi. Although the distance is very short compared with the distance to be travelled through the British colonies in South Africa, yet between Zambesi and Mashonaland there is a strip of very difficult country. It is rough and mountainous, is infested with the tsetse fly, water is very scarce, and the native inhabitants so few and poverty-stricken that it is impossible to obtain provisions for any but the smallest expedition. "I have no doubt," added Mr. Selous, "of the whole country being auriferous, and I found traces of old workings, which we attributed to people who worked gold in South-Eastern Africa long before the Portuguese came to the country at all."

Mr. U. P. Swinburne tells me in the course of some notes :—

Thirty miles north-east of Tati the formation changes, and the country is covered with blocks and koppies of coarse granite, while the river beds are chalky instead of sandy. Twenty miles further north the gold formation commences again, and stretches across the Mangove and Shashani Rivers through the heart of Matabeleland and Mashonaland. The whole of the country stretching north is probably gold bearing, but the next 200 miles is so jealously guarded by the natives, that prospectors have little or no opportunity to examine the many reefs which crop out on all sides. It has been ascertained, however, that many of the reefs are gold-bearing, and could be easily worked . . . . This Mashonaland is truly a wonderful country, covered with splendid pasture, full of rivers, and studded with forests of excellent timber, all necessary adjuncts for the successful working of the gold and other minerals with which this country teems. On the Umfuli River, especially, there are some splendid gold reefs, and further north both alluvial and quartz gold is very abundant. To sum up—the whole of Matabeleland and Mashonaland is a well-watered and well-timbered country, rich in gold, copper, and iron ; the climate, with care, can be generally withstood by most Europeans, for fever can be reduced to a minimum with care and attention. These thousands of miles of country are now going to be opened up by Englishmen and English money.

At Gresham College, London, recently, Professor E. Symes Thompson, M.D., Gresham Professor of Medicine, delivered the third of a series of four lectures on sea voyages and climate in the southern hemisphere. Leaving the question of climate for a time, Professor Thompson spoke of the new gold discoveries :—

There was reason to believe that even more rich than the Transvaal in gold was the little-known portion of South Africa called Mashonaland. Recent investigation had shown that the land, which was just at the eastward of Bechuanaland, was rich in gold above all the regions of South Africa, and, moreover, in alluvial gold, the easiest to work. Where gold had to be extracted from quartz and rock, as in other parts of Africa, it only offered scope for large and rich companies, who could afford to bring expensive machinery there for crushing purposes. But in this region gold was found in the sand by the sides of the river, and he had been told by a resident there that some explorers who had tested the river bank a distance of ten miles on 148 occasions, had, in 144 instances, found visible gold, even

Q 2

with the rough washing of the river sand which they were able to give it, and this was pretty fair evidence that on the river workable and profitable gold was to be found ; and if that was the case, it was safe to predict that a large number of gold-seekers would settle down in that region. Mashonaland had hitherto been attractive only to sportsmen and farmers, and even the number of those was very limited ; but when it was found that gold was there, at once it would become a largely-populated region. It was a curious fact that, though the production of gold was very large, it did not satisfy the demand at the present time, so that it was a peculiarly convenient time for great gold discoveries, such as they anticipated in this region ; and he spoke with more interest about it because it was an extremely healthy part of Africa, the general elevation being between four and five thousand feet, which secured a great degree of healthiness.

Mr. H. C. Moore, an American of large gold-field experience, who lived two years in Matabeleland, describes " South Africa, from the Zambesi southwards, as likely to turn out a trump card in the gold and other mineral-bearing countries of the universe." Speaking of Mashonaland, he says :—

I know that reefs exist, and, with the advantages of rapid streams, lots of growing large wood for timbering the future mines, native labour abundant, and a country largely provided by Nature for raising immense crops of rice and maize (mealies), and with the introduction of the white man, no doubt any amount of produce can be grown eventually by an influx of population to make Mashonaland a really good country to dwell in.

Mr. E. A. Maund writes :—

The' northern gold fields are said to be far richer than those at Tati. Fabulous stories are told of their wealth in alluvial deposits as well as quartz. They have never been properly explored. Between these two districts along the watershed lie several extensive gold reefs, while iron and copper may be found in Mashonaland and near Tati in large quantities. . . . We know that Mashonaland's rich alluvial soil, of which a few patches only are scratched by native unskilled labour, and yet yield abundant supplies for their own wants and to spare, has only to be taken in hand to supply all kinds of agricultural wealth. Already upwards of 180 squatters' farms have been applied for in the rich unoccupied district about the head-waters of the Hunyane, Umfuli, Sabi, and Rusarive Rivers. The terms at present are nominal, but include a liability to be called upon by the Company to assist in the defence of law and order. But the main object of the British South Africa Company is to develop its reputed vast mineral resources. The gold in Mashonaland will, I believe, create a rush next summer only to be paralleled in the development of California and Australia. The pioneers are already within the region of a gold belt of an enormous extent, and upwards of 1000 claims have already been pegged off. The latest news is that reports of the most promising and encouraging nature come in of reefs being struck and shafts being sunk, and applications are made daily for the due registration of claims under the terms of the Company's mining laws. And some of these reefs must be of extraordinary richness, judging by the specimens brought in. The Company's mining laws reajust and liberal. The size of claims are : alluvial, 150 ft. by 150 ft. ; quartz reef, 150 ft. in the direction of the reef and 400 ft. broad. But the claim-holders may follow this reef in all its dips, spur, angles, and variations. Every licensed prospector has the right to peg off one alluvial claim and ten quartz reef claims in block. On flotation the Chartered Company receives half the vendor's scrip, whether the Company float the block themselves or the claim-holder obtains better terms than those proposed by the Company. Numerous ancient workings of this valuable commodity have been found all over the country, and the many and vast remains of ancient buildings all point from their propinquity to old workings to an extensive gold industry, when the means of extraction were crude when compared with modern appliances.

Sir John Willoughby (who was with the Pioneer Force in Mashonaland, and who recently set out again for that country), in reply to questions from a press interviewer respecting Mashonaland, said that gold is found alluvially in the country and in reef :—

According to the scientific report the Hartley Hill reef, which is 4 ft. in thickness, produces 3 ozs. or 4 ozs. to the ton. Nearly every river has traces of gold. At the Mazoe there is plenty of alluvial. In twenty-four hours by the use of a rough sluice-box one man obtained a tablespoonful of gold, and a nugget. The police at Fort Victoria have discovered alluvial gold to the west of the fort. They report that it would pay men £1 a day to prospect it. The alluvial, however, is a poor man's claim, and most of our men devote their attention to the reef. The opinion of practical men on the spot is that the country is very rich. A reef has also been discovered north of Mount Hampden. There is no water near Mount Hampden suitable for a town, so Colonel Pennefather chose a spot for a township about eight miles from it. The Mount is 920 miles from Mafeking. There is any amount of water in the country. In one way we had a surplus of it, there being too many rivers. All things considered, I should suppose that our effective occupation of all that country will be phenomenally rapid. As I rode south from Mount Hampden in October, at every point on the road I met prospecting parties journeying north—men who had been through the gold fever in America and Australia ; the kind of settlers who will settle other things besides the soil, without waiting over long for politicians ! And why should not progress be rapid ; the very pick of that region is within 250 miles of the navigable waters of the Pungwe River ; how long would it take under similar conditions to settle Manitoba, if Manitoba also enjoyed the same delightful winters as the African highlands, and the settlers' farmsteads were 250 miles from a waterway, and 400 from an ocean port, instead of, as west of Winnipeg, being nearly as many thousands ? Moreover, although it is a large claim to make, probably the soil of the Mashonaland veld is not less fertile than that of the valleys of the Red River. You may recall in this connection the remarkable growth of Johannesburg ; in four years a desert area was converted into a town of nearly forty thousand people, and this, too, at a distance of more than a thousand miles from a seaport, and five hundred miles from a railway. Of course it was the Rand Gold Field which effected this transformation, but the expert miners who accompanied our force to Mashonaland declare that the reef at Hartley Hill is much richer, and the entire gold field is on a larger scale, than is the case at Johannesburg. And then, also, in considering the development of Africa, you must remember that the African quartz formation with few exceptions is the least refractory known to geologists : the ores are easily worked, and yield their gold without the necessity of any costly chemical treatment, as in Australia and elsewhere. Speaking of the chances for young men in Mashonaland, Sir John proceeded : They must take their chance, of course, shoulder to shoulder with the rough element that always appears in mining camps. But the country will be well administered by Mr. Colquhoun and his staff, and roughing it in such a climate, and where the chances of big prizes are so favourable, will do no one any harm. That there is a great gold field in that region, perhaps the greatest the world has ever known, I have no doubt whatever ; nearly every stream we crossed after entering Mashonaland showed either alluvial gold or traces of it ; and now is the time to get in, before, not after, the inevitable rush, which can but increase the cost of labour, and bring with it excessive competition in its search for the rich reefs.

Mr. Dixon, who went up with the Pioneer Force to Mashonaland, returned to Cape Colony, where he had intended to settle ; but he made arrangements to return to Mashonaland. A pressman who saw him writes :—

I learnt from him that the alluvial prospects are good, while there are a number of reefs showing visible. There are four fine reefs by the Umfuli River, Fort Salisbury being about the middle. There are many prospectors working at these reefs, and they are still working with a secret enthusiasm which leads Mr. Dixon to infer that they have got hold of something really good. The prospectors engaged in the old workings recently brought back some wonderful samples of quartz. Mr. Dixon had heard consistently good accounts of the alluvial diggings, but had not seen for himself ; but the reefs paid prospectors well to work, even with their primitive appliances.

The British South Africa Company not long ago received a telegram from their Kimberley office stating that reef and alluvial gold claims were being pegged out on the Umfuli River in Mashonaland ; that without doubt a rich reef had been struck in many places ; that more than 800 claims had been registered on tested reefs, some of which were very valuable and proved to a depth of 58 ft. Samples from these and from croppings average from 4 to 5 ozs. per ton. A large number of men had left Cape Colony to commence prospecting, as had also the representatives of scores of powerful syndicates. I am favoured by the British South Africa Company with the following copy of a private letter, which has been received by that Company with regard to reefs lately discovered :—

One reef, the Cecil reef, is particularly good ; several other good things have been found south of the river, the Monarch, a most important and rich lode, being about the best of them. Williams, who has been working many years upon the Tati Monarch, considers its namesake here by far the better of the two. Three or four ounce prospects are very common, and yielded by the greater number of the reefs showing old workings. Our own people are the only ones carrying on prospecting with much system. I fancy the place will prove healthy, but to make doubly sure I have taken the precaution to place our standing camp upon the flat top of one of old Hartley's Hills. After two days at the Umfuli Zumbo fields we rode on to the Upper Umfuli. Very extensive old workings exist here; I should say the largest in the country. On one of the reefs here we have our work done by a thirty-foot, well-timbered shaft, which we have put down, without help, from the old workings, and have struck the reef at that depth, going down between slate walls. It is about 2 ft. thick, dips at a sharp angle, and the beauty of the vein stuff is that it carries gold through and through, being beautifully consistent throughout, any and every piece yielding the same fine prospects. Even old Harman, with all his caution, could not say it is less than a three-ounce reef, and I believe that it will mill above that. We have seen some very good specimens from the country between Forts Charter and Victoria, and are shortly going down that way. There is no manner of doubt that when well prospected the Mazoe district will prove fully as rich as the Umfuli. In addition to these places we are going to mark off on the Sebakwe-Bembesi gold area mentioned by Baines, and also as soon as everything is settled we will turn up at Manica with a Company's licence, and see what can be done there. The gold is the backbone of the country, and it is well that you should know the important dimensions it is assuming. I have not met a man who is not over well pleased with his gold prospects, and the sooner the Company realise the fact that they now have in their control one of the three chief gold areas of the world, and all that that means indirectly, the better; 845 claims have already been pegged out and registered.

Referring to the most recent reports from Mashonaland, a well-known London weekly paper of position had the following:—

The manner in which the British South Africa Company proposes to enrich itself from these vast deposits of gold is characteristic of Mr. Rhodes's prudence and moderation. The Company will share equally with the digger. If he makes nothing, neither will they. If, however, he is successful, they will benefit by his success. The result of this policy will be to encourage the influx of the digger, who, not being a man of capital, would be unable to put down money to pay for a claim which might turn out valueless, but will not trouble about a 50 per cent. royalty. If then, as we have said above, a rush takes place, it will be one of the biggest of modern times. At this moment there are thousands of men in the Transvaal hungering for a fresh field of enterprise—smitten, as the gold-seeker always is, with the notion that Fate will smile on him if he only presses on. These, at the first word from the Company, will pour into Mashonaland; and since the gold of the land of Sheba needs no advertisement, they will be followed by swarms upon swarms of adventurers from America and Australia, as well as from England. When once the Anglo-Saxon public learns that it can go and try for gold under the English flag, and with every prospect of success, we shall see a gold-fever as violent as that of the "fifties" overtake the English-speaking race. Though gold-rushes have a bad name, and rightly so, the result of one in the centre of Africa would in many ways be beneficial. It would open up Zambesia, and teach the world its capabilities in a way that nothing else ever will. To begin with, it would show Colonists the road, a matter of no small importance. The digger does not, of course, establish a permanent civilisation, or, indeed, any civilisation at all; but at least he tears aside the veil that shrouds unexplored and unpeopled lands, and lets in the light. But for the discovery of gold, the Pacific slope of America would have taken twenty years longer to become known and peopled by white men. The diggers, determined as they are to reach a particular destination, and following thick upon each other, will force a road through any impediments. Again, the necessity for sending back their earnings, and for supplying them with the luxuries which they will have at any cost, obliges the organisation of rapid modes of communication. Depend upon it, ix months after a big rush, if a big rush comes, we shall all be looking upon Mashonaland as one of the best-known places in the world, and the Post Office will be organising a parcel-post in order that the diggers may have the finest Havannahs and the best champagne sent direct from the Army and Navy Stores. Fortunately for those who intend to try their fortunes in Mashonaland, as soon as the promises of vast mineral wealth have been verified, the means of reaching that part of Lo Bengula's territories are not difficult. Even if the Portuguese delay the making of the railway between the possessions of the British South Africa Company and the coast at Pungwé Bay, there will be other ways of reaching the auriferous districts. By steamer up the Zambesi to Zumbo, and thence across country, would be one method of access; but a still better, though somewhat longer route, will be afforded by the great trunk railway, which is being steadily pressed up from Cape Colony. Already the line is complete to Vryburg, the capital of British Bechuanaland; and by next May it will have reached the frontier of the Crown Colony at Mafeking, the most northerly of its settlements. Meanwhile the telegraph will very shortly reach Palapye, the capital of Khama's country. From these points of vantage fresh developments could easily be made, and the great demand that would be created by a gold-rush would soon cause railway extensions to the northward at a rate which in cold blood sounds fabulous. In this way, then, the discovery of a rich gold field in Mashonaland would do an immense deal to quicken the completion of that great Central African highway under British control, which is destined to begin at Cape Town and end at Alexandria.

I refer in another chapter to the latest news to hand concerning the gold fields of Mashonaland. It need only be stated here that all the accounts agree with those I have quoted. Shafts have now been sunk a hundred feet in districts a hundred miles apart and the results justify all that has been said and written about the golden wealth of Mashonaland.

CHAPTER X.

The Zambesi River.—The Course of the Mighty Stream Described.—The Victoria Falls.—An Earthly Paradise.—Livingstone's Description of one of the Sights of the World.—Sketches of Livingstone and Baines.

"LIKE some grave, mighty thought threading a dream " flows the mighty Zambesi to the sea. But the dream of long ages is passing away, and what was vague and shadowy about this great river is now becoming more and more a reality. Whatever pother there may be with the Portuguese about territory, the Zambesi—Vasco da Gama's " River of Good Signs "— is a highway for the nations of the world. No Lusitanian dogs in the manger can prevent vessels of any nation from navigating its waters ; to prove this, a British warship now puffs its way along the silent bosom of the river. The Zambesi is the great river of Eastern Africa, and, after the Congo, the Nile, and the Niger, the most important on the Continent. Rising in the far interior, among the marshes of Lake Dilolo, and gathering volume from the streams which flow from the high lands connecting the no th of Lake Nyassa with Suner Angola, it curves across the country for over a thousand miles, like an attenuated letter S, and before its four great mouths empty the far-travelled waters into the Indian Ocean, drains an area of more than half a million square miles. As it cuts its way down the successive steps of the central plateaux, its usually placid current is interrupted by rapids, narrows, cascades, and cataracts, corresponding to the plateau edges, so that like all the rivers of Africa, it is only navigable in stretches of one or two hundred miles at a time. From the coast the Zambesi might be stemmed by steam power to the rapids of Kebrabasa, and from above that point intermittently as far as the impassable barrier of the Victoria Falls. Above this, for some distance, again follow rapids and waterfalls ; but these are at length succeeded by an unbroken chain of tributaries, which together form an inland waterway of a

thousand miles in length. The broad lands along the banks of
this noble river are subject to annual inundations like the region
of the Nile, and hence their agricultural possibilities are unlimited.
On the lower Zambesi, indigo, the orchilla weed, and calumba-
root abound, and oil-seeds and sugar-cane could be produced in
quantity to supply the whole of Europe. The course of the
Zambesi may be traced on the maps I publish. Shortly before
entering the low-lying country, in which ninety miles from the coast
it begins to form a delta, the Zambesi receives through its left bank
the tributary waters of the Shiré, itself navigable for a considerable

THE STEAMER "GOOD NEWS" ON LAKE TANGANYIKA.

This auxiliary steam-yacht belongs to the London Missionary Society. It is 54 ft.
long by 12 ft. beam, and is constructed of steel, and fitted up in modern fashion.
By its means the 1,000 miles of coast round Lake Tanganyika, the longest lake
in the world, can be visited by the missionaries.

distance. The entire delta of the Zambesi, comprising an area of
25,000 square miles, is only slightly elevated above the level of
the sea, into which it imperceptibly merges. Of the innumerable
channels, only seven may be regarded as the actual mouths of
the river, and of these the Madredane is the channel most used for
navigation. Unfortunately, all the mouths of the Zambesi are

barred, as they are constantly silting up, and the river-beds consequently undergo changes of level, which present serious obstacles to navigation. The Madredane itself is frequently choked with vegetation. Mr. Daniel J. Rankin claims to have discovered in the Chindé (Shindé) mouth an alternative passage from the sea into the Zambesi, which ultimately may prove to be of value. Mr. Rankin says :—

There are at present two mouths open to navigation, the Kongoni and the Chindé, of both of which I have made recent surveys. The latter will permit of an ocean-going steamer entering the Zambesi and trans-shipping immediately from and into the river craft. Hulks to meet the exigencies of trade should, without delay, be placed in the Chindé entrance. These being used as floating wharves, would afford very considerable facilities to trade development. By this means those crushing and paralysing

Zambesi Sketches

conditions that are now killing all commercial enterprise in these re
gions would be altogether avoided. Compared with the other outlets
of the Zambesi, the Chindé presents peculiar characteristics. The
formation of its confluence with the main stream is of such a nature
that the vast volume of suspended alluvial matter brought down from
the interior is swept past, and even in its greatest floods only an insignificant portion finds its way into this channel. As a result of its extremely tortuous course, and the fact that its whole length is subject to
tidal influence, whatever fluvial *débris* finds its way into the Chindé is
invariably precipitated before the bar is reached, much of it, indeed,
being carried back into the main stream. This is naturally of
primary importance in estimating the probabilities of the permanency
of this outlet for navigation. On the Chindé Bar, there is scarcely
a trace of alluvial deposit, and it possesses all the characteristics of
an estuary of the sea.

As I have been saying, the veil which (notwithstanding all
Livingstone told us) has hitherto enshrouded the mysteries of
the great Zambesi is rising slowly. England's navy is assisting in
solving the secrets of the vast river which flows through a land to
be heard of in song and story long after the present generation has
passed away. An Anglo-Saxon nation will yet rear its towns by
the banks of these wide waters, and, peradventure, Macaulay's New
Zealander may here revive his drooping spirits when he has
mourned over a ruined London. But much has yet to be done in
the way of exploring the Zambesi, and for the adventurous traveller
I know no more fascinating field open than tracing the mighty
stream from its mouth to its source, in a flotilla of canoe house-
boats. The length is 1550 miles, and if the traveller did not
care to go the full distance he would have done a great public
service if he had taken soundings and notes for the navigation
of the river as far as the Victoria Falls, 900 miles from the sea.
In connection with this important subject it will be well to reprint
here the remarks of Lord Salisbury when in May, 1889 he
received a deputation of the representatives of the joint Committee
of the Presbyterian churches of Scotland. It is to be borne in
mind, however, in reading these remarks that Britain is now
represented in these regions by Mr. H. H. Johnston, and that
Nyassaland, none too soon, has been taken under the protection of England. Lord Salisbury after some preliminary
observations, proceeded to say to the deputation referred to:
—First, let me say a word, and separate the subject
from all the rest, about the River Zambesi—you must keep that
far apart from the rest as a question of international law. The
Zambesi is a great river, traversing the dominions of one State and
going into what is practically now the dominions, or rather the
protectorate, of another state—that is, of England. Matabeleland
is under the protectorate of England, and the Zambesi runs
through it and then through Portuguese territory to the sea.
Although the current of authorities is not entirely unbroken, it is
right to say that the general and received tendency of international
law is that these great rivers, which pass through more than one

dominion, are the property of no special country, but are the high-way of nations. Two qualifications must be carefully borne in mind. The one is that those who use a road must pay for it, and that all such tolls as may be necessary for the mere purpose of keeping a river of that kind in order are legitimately levied and always have been levied. The other qualification is imposed, not by political considerations, but by nature. It is not yet certain whether the Zambesi will be an international highway or not. It is a splendid water way when you once get inside it; and there appears to be good access from the sea; but it is an access so frequently changing that at present it is not of much use to navigators. Whether a better or more enduring access will be found, whether a means of keeping a steady channel will be dis-covered, of course it is impossible to say. Let us hope that in the course of time, as the country gets settled up, that difficulty will be overcome. But the point is this—that what is ordinarily called now the passage by the Zambesi is not a passage by the Zambesi. What the traffic does is to go on a Portuguese river, and to be carried over the Portuguese land, and then to get into the Zambesi. That cannot be called a great international high-way. Leaving the Zambesi altogether, we come to the Nyassaland, and the Shiro Highlands. The actual state of facts there is that these gallant missionaries and the Company are maintaining them-selves against a great attack of Arab slavers, who recognize in them their natural and greatest enemy. This is a desperate struggle, but it is a struggle which does not at present apparently involve any direct co-operation of the Portuguese. The fight is at present entirely between the missions and the Company on the one hand, and the Arabs on the other. But the Europeans depend for their defence upon the possession of arms. Those arms can at present only be introduced through Portuguese territory, and Portugal, from motives which I will not scrutinize, has thrown the utmost possible impediment in the way of furnish-ing those arms. Now that was an inconvenience to which, unless the mind of the Portuguese authorities changes, I do not at the present moment see a remedy. I do not mean to say that I think that it is a difficulty that will permanently continue. I think that it is very possible that other ways of supplying arms and necessaries to that country will be discovered. But, undoubtedly, holding the coast through which communication is made to the sea, the Portuguese authorities have had the opportunity of very seriously imped-ing the Europeans in their conflict with the Arab slavers, and I regret to say that the conduct of the Portuguese authorities has not been such as to show that they have very much sympathy with this conflict in which all civilized nations are concerned. But you have come here for something more than this. You say that you are afraid that Portugal will make herself the mistress of those stations where your missionaries and traders are stationed, which you have occupied, and where you have been labouring for so long.

Though I am aware that Portugal claims the whole territory from the Atlantic to the Indian Ocean, it is a claim which this country has never admitted; and we do not consider that Portugal has any claim either to the Shiré Highlands or to the banks of the Zambesi. I regard that as an interesting and important but not immediately urgent question. I think you are attaching to it more importance as a practical matter than it really deserves. The suggestion that the Portuguese authorities will lay violent hands upon any of your mission stations seems to me an entirely groundless and impossible hypothesis. I should as soon expect to be told that there was a danger that Portugal would go into Table Bay and annex Cape

A PORTUGUESE GUNBOAT ON THE RIVER ZAMBESI.

These gunboats, which are stern-wheelers, carrying three quick-firing or machine guns, were employed to back up a force of 2,000 men to carry out "a scientific and civilising mission to the interior"—really a war of conquest against the Makololo.

Town. There is no danger of any such thing. What there is a danger of, and it is one which will be constant for some time to come, with the sea coast in the hands of the Portuguese authorities as long as they are in their present mood, is that a very considerable impediment will be added to the many difficulties with which you have now to struggle. Not only is there this difficulty about the furnishing of arms, but of course the tariff is to a great extent in their hands, and as long as the supplies come through Portuguese territory you must necessarily submit to whatever tariff they are pleased to impose. Your position is a peculiar one, and I wish you not to expect more of the Government than the Government can do. We have not raised the British flag in Nyassaland; it is not British territory. We are not bound to send an armed expedition there. Consequently, to a great extent, as I had the honour of saying in Parliament, this great enterprise is left to the action, ability, zeal, and courage of Englishmen, not in their corporate, but in their individual capacity. We treat as an impossible hypothesis that any foreign power should furtively interfere with you; but we cannot protect you from the powers which the possession of the coast gives to a foreign Power. That is precisely the position in which you stand. I can assure you that so far as any diplomatic action of ours can go, you may command our most earnest sympathy and every effort we can make, but it must be within the limits that I have traced out to you. I think you may dismiss as idle any danger of actual Portuguese annexation. But against all the troubles which we naturally would spare you, all the troubles which come from the Arabs, all the troubles which come from the difficulty of importation—against those troubles you must oppose that resource and that courage which in the face of such difficulties up to this time you have shown. As civilisation extends from the south perhaps, and perhaps from the north, the features of the problem will be changed. I have only laid it before you exactly as it exists to this day. I can assure you that to the utmost of our power you may count upon the sympathy of Her Majesty's Government."

In the two years since these words were spoken the features of the problem have very much changed.

A good deal has been heard of the Limpopo or Crocodile River of late, and as more will yet be heard of it, a description of the important stream may be given. The entrance, as nearly as I can gather, is in 25° 15' to 17' S. Lat., and 33° 30' to 40' E. Long. A glance at the map will show that the river, which forms the northern boundary of the South African Republic, describes with its course (about 850 miles) something like three quarters of a circle. The Limpopo, along the banks of which there is a limitless supply of game, rises between Potchefstroom and Pretoria, and after it leaves its easterly direction, as the Transvaal northern border, it flows through the flat, unhealthy country of Southern Gazaland for 250 miles S.S.E. to the sea. The Portuguese claim the estuary, but, if the natives wished to test the question, the King of Gazaland would counterclaim in a sufficiently emphatic manner to preserve the dominion his father had before him. Mr. St. Vincent W. Erskine performed in 1868 a journey (for the first portion in the company of Carl Mauch) from Natal to the mouth of the Limpopo, and he has written a very interesting record of his experiences. He was not greatly impressed with the Limpopo mouth. He says: "A few moments after I stood gazing at the long-sought mouth of the Limpopo or Bembe River. The thought crossed me 'Is it worth while to have gone through so much to get so little?' A stream of about 300 yards wide (at full tide) flowed into the ocean, and although it was not rough in shore, I noticed the sea breaking some three miles out, not in one roller as

GAME ON THE LIMPOPO RIVER.

on a bar, but in a succession of small breakers, until it reached the shore, thereby, I think, demonstrating, that though no marked sand bar existed, there was great shallowness of water outwards for about three miles. . . . . I bathed in the mouth of the river, but on account of the crocodiles, and the feeling that if I was lost, no account could be given of my expedition, as I was alone, I refrained from going further than where the water reached my chin. This was about 20 yards from the shore, and at that point there was evidently a deep channel, as the bottom shelved so sharply that I could hardly stand. This was at low tide." Since this was written it has been proved that the Limpopo is navigable for sixty miles from its mouth for vessels of 200 tons. The valley of the Limpopo, which swarms with crocodiles and hippopotami, is, it is evident, of some consequence as a means of communication. The Portuguese talk of getting up a company to navigate the Limpopo, run a railway alongside it, &c. They forget, evidently, that one thing is lacking to make their enterprise successful, viz., the consent of the paramount chief of the country through which the river flows for a considerable distance from the ocean. North of the Limpopo the coastal zone begins to broaden out, until it merges in the valley of the Zambesi. The watershed between these rivers and the Sofala coast is considerably cut up, and sends no important streams to the sea, although the Pungwe and Busi rivers may serve as temporary partial means of communication with the interior.

And now I must give my readers some letter-press description of the great Victoria Falls, which I sketch pictorially. Those who have been fortunate enough to see both the Niagara and the Victoria Falls yield the palm for majestic grandeur and impressiveness to the latter. There are not many authorities to appeal to for information about these stupendous works of nature. Selous has seen them, and his " Hunter's Wanderings " gives a fine stirring word picture of them, telling us they are " the most transcendently beautiful natural phenomena on this side of Paradise." Frank Oates enters in his useful diary on New Yeay's Day, 1875, " I visited the Falls—a day never to be forgotten." Poor wanderer ! He did not live long to remember. The great explorer, Thomas Baines, visited the Falls, and both with pen and pencil left behind him a lucid conception of them. In his vivid description he likens them to "The Peri's glimpse of Paradise," and says :—" Now stand and look through the dim and misty perspective till it loses itself in the cloud of spray to the east. How shall words convey ideas which even the pencil of Turner must fail to present ? Stiff and formal columns of smoke there are none—the eastern breeze has blended all in one. Think nothing of the drizzling mist, but tell me if heart of man ever conceived anything more gorgeous than those two lovely rainbows, so brilliant that the eye shrinks from looking on them, segments of which, rising from the abyss, deep as the solar rays can penetrate it, over arch, spray, rock, and forest,

R

THE VICTORIA FALLS ON THE ZAMBESI RIVER.

till rising to the highest point they fail to find refractory moisture to complete the arch."

But I shall turn to the one who discovered and christened the

THE VICTORIA FALLS.   BIRD'S EYE VIEW FROM THE WEST.

Victoria Falls—David Livingstone—for the best detailed description of them.

As this was the point from which we intended to strike off to the

R 2

north-east, I resolved on the following day to visit the Falls of
Victoria, called by the natives Mosioatunya, or more anciently
Shongwe.   Of these we had often heard since we came into the
country; indeed, one of the questions asked by Sebituane was,
"Have you smoke that sounds in your country?" They did not go
near enough to examine them, but, viewing them with awe at a
distance, said, in reference to the vapour and noise, "Mosi oa tunya"
(smoke does not sound there). It was previously called Shongwe,
the meaning of which I could not ascertain. The word for a "pot"
resembles this, and it may mean a seething cauldron; but I am not
certain of it. Being persuaded that Mr. Oswell and myself were the
very first Europeans who ever visited the Zambesi in the centre of
the country, and that this is the connecting link between the known
and the unknown portions of that river, I decided to use the same
liberty as the Makololo did, and gave the only English name I have
affixed to any part of the country. No better proof of previous
ignorance of this river could be desired, than that an untravelled
gentleman, who had spent a great part of his life in the study of the
geography of Africa, and knew everything written on the subject
from the time of Ptolemy downwards, actually asserted in the
Athenæum, while I was coming up the Red Sea, that this magnificent river, the Leeambye, had "no connection with the Zambesi,
but flowed under the Kalahari Desert, and became lost;" and "that,
as all the old maps asserted, the Zambesi took its rise in the very
hills to which we have now come." This modest assertion smacks
exactly as if a native of Timbuctu should declare that the "Thames"
and the "Pool" were different rivers, he having seen neither the one
nor the other. Leeambye and Zambesi mean the very same thing,
viz., the RIVER.

Sekeletu intended to accompany me, but, one canoe only having
come instead of the two he had ordered, he resigned it to me.
After twenty minutes' sail from Kalai, we came in sight, for the first
time, of the columns of vapour, appropriately called "smoke," rising
at a distance of five or six miles, exactly as when large tracts of
grass are burned in Africa. Five columns now arose, and bending in
the direction of the wind, they seemed placed against a low ridge
covered with trees; the tops of the columns at this distance appeared
to mingle with the clouds. They were white below, and higher up
became dark, so as to simulate smoke very closely. The whole scene
was extremely beautiful; the banks and islands dotted over the river
are adorned with sylvan vegetation of great variety of colour and
form. At the period of our visit several trees were spangled over with
blossoms. Trees have each their own physiognomy. There, towering
over all, stands the great burly baobab, each of whose enormous
arms would form the trunk of a large tree, beside groups of graceful
palms, which, with their feathery-shaped leaves depicted on the sky,
lend their beauty to the scene. As a hieroglyphic they always mean
"far from home," for no one can ever get over their foreign air in a
picture or landscape. The silvery mohonono, which in the tropics is
in form like the cedar of Lebanon, stands in pleasing contrast with
the dark colour of the motsouri, whose cypress-form is dotted over
at present with its pleasant scarlet fruit. Some trees resemble the
great spreading oak, others assume the character of our own elms
and chestnuts; but no one can imagine the beauty of the view from
anything witnessed in England. It had never been seen before by
European eyes; but scenes so lovely must have been gazed upon by

angels in their flight. The only want felt, is that of mountains in the back-ground. The falls are bounded on three sides by ridges 300 or 400 feet in height, which are covered with forest, with the red soil appearing among the trees. When about half-a-mile from the falls, I left the canoe by which we had come down thus far, and embarked in a lighter one, with men well acquainted with the rapids, who, by passing down the centre of the stream in the eddies and still

THE VICTORIA FALLS.   A LITTLE CORNER.

places caused by many jutting rocks, brought me to a island situated in the middle of the river, and on edge of the lip over which the water rolls. In coming hither, there was danger of being swept down by the streams which rushed along on each side of the island ; but the river was now low, and we sailed where it is totally impossible to go when the water is high. But though we had reached the island, and were within a few yards of the spot, a view from which would solve the whole problem, I believe no one could perceive where the vast

body of water went ; it seemed to lose itself in the earth, the opposite
lip of the fissure into which it disappeared, being only 80 feet
distant. At least I did not comprehend it until, creeping with awe
to the verge, I peered down into a large rent which had been made
from bank to bank of the broad Zambesi, and saw that a stream of a
thousand yards broad, leaped down a hundred feet, and then became
suddenly compressed into a space of fifteen or twenty yards. The
entire falls are simply a crack made in a hard basaltic rock from the
right to the left bank of the Zambesi, and then prolonged from the
left bank away through thirty or forty miles of hills. If one imagines
the Thames filled with low tree-covered hills immediately beyond the
tunnel, extending as far as Gravesend ; the bed of black basaltic
rock instead of London mud ; and a fissure made therein from one
end of the tunnel to the other, down through the keystones of the
arch, and prolonged from the left end of the tunnel through thirty
miles of hills ; the pathway being a hundred feet down from the bed
of the river instead of what it is, with the lips of the fissure from
eighty to one hundred feet apart ; then fancy the Thames leaping
bodily into the gulf ; and forced there to change its direction, and
flow from the right to the left bank ; and then rush boiling and
roaring through the hills,—he may have some idea of what takes
place at this, the most wonderful sight I had witnessed in Africa.
In looking down into the fissure on the right of the island, one sees
nothing but a dense white cloud, which, at the time we visited the
spot, had two bright rainbows on it. (The sun was on the meridian,
and the declination about equal to the latitude of the place.) From
this cloud rushed up a great jet of vapour exactly like steam, and it
mounted two hundred or three hundred feet high ; there condensing,
it changed its hue to that of dark smoke, and came back into a
constant shower which soon wetted us to the skin. This shower falls
chiefly on the opposite side of the fissure, and a few yards back from
the lip there stands a straight edge of evergreen trees, whose leaves
are always wet. From their roots a number of little rills run back
into the gulf ; but as they flow down the steep wall there, the
column of vapour, in its ascent, licks them up clean off the rock, and
away they mount again. They are constantly running down, but
never reach the bottom.

On the left of the island we see the water at the bottom, a white
rolling mass moving away to the prolongation of the fissure, which
branches off near the left bank of the river. A piece of the rock has
fallen off a spot on the left of the island, and juts out from the water
below, and from it, I judged the distance which the water falls to be
about one hundred feet. The walls of this gigantic crack are
perpendicular, and composed of one homogeneous mass of rock. The
edge of that side over which the water falls, is worn off two or
three feet, and pieces have fallen away, so as to give it somewhat of
a serrated appearance. That over which the water does not fall, is
quite straight, except at the left corner, where a rent appears, and a
piece seems inclined to fall off. Upon the whole, it is nearly in the
state in which it was left at the period of its formation. The rock
is dark brown in colour, except about ten feet from the bottom,
which is discoloured by the annual rise of the water to that or a
greater height. On the left side of the island we have a good view
of the mass of water which causes one of the columns of vapour to
ascend, as it leaps quite clear of the rock, and forms a thick unbroken
fleece all the way to the bottom. Its whiteness gave the idea of

snow, a sight I had not seen for many a day. As it broke into (if I may use the term) pieces of water all rushing on in the same direction, each gave off several rays of foam, exactly as bits of steel, when burnt in oxygen gas, give off rays of sparks. The snow-white sheet seemed like myriads of small comets rushing on in one direction, each of which left behind its nucleus rays of foam. I never saw the appearance referred to noticed elsewhere. It seemed to be the effect of the mass of water leaping at once clear of the rock, and but slowly breaking up into spray.

I have mentioned that we saw five columns of vapour ascending from this strange abyss. They are evidently formed by the compression suffered by the force of the water's own fall, into an unyielding wedge-shaped space. Of the five columns, two on the right, and one on the left of the island were the largest, and the streams which formed them seemed each to exceed in size the falls of the Clyde at Stonebyres, when that river is in flood. This was the period of low water in the Leeambye, but, as far as I could guess, there was a flow of five or six hundred yards of water, which, at the edge of the fall, seemed at least three feet deep. I write in the hope that others more capable of judging distances than myself will visit this scene, and I state simply the impressions made on my mind at the time. I thought, and do still think, the river above the falls to be one thousand yards broad; but I am a poor judge of distances on water, for I showed a naval friend what I supposed to be four hundred yards in the bay of Loanda, and, to my surprise, he pronounced it to be nine hundred. I tried to measure the Leeambye with a strong thread, the only line I had in my possession, but when the men had gone two or three hundred yards, they got into conversation, and did not hear us shouting that the line had become entangled. By still going on they broke it, and, being carried away down the stream, it was lost on a snag. In vain I tried to bring to my recollection the way I had been taught to measure a river, by taking an angle with the sextant. That I once knew it, and that it was easy, were all the lost ideas I could recall, and they only increased my vexation. However, I measured the river farther down by another plan, and then I discovered that the Portuguese had measured it at Tete, and found it a little over one thousand yards. At the falls it is as broad as at Tete, if not more so. Whoever may come after me will not, I trust, find reason to say I have indulged in exaggeration. With respect to the drawing, it must be borne in mind that it was composed from a rude sketch as viewed from the island, which exhibited the columns of vapour only, and a ground plan. The artist has given a good idea of the scene, but, by way of explanation, he has shown more of the depth of the fissure than is visible, except by going close to the edge. The left-hand column, and that farthest off, are the smallest, and all ought to have been a little more tapering at the tops.

The fissure is said by the Makololo to be very much deeper further to the eastward; there is one part at which the walls are so sloping, that people accustomed to it can go down by descending in a sitting position. The Makololo on one occasion, pursuing some fugitive Batoka, saw them, unable to stop the impetus of their flight at the edge, literally dashed to pieces at the bottom. They beheld the stream like a "white cord" at the bottom, and so far down (probably 300 feet) that they became giddy, and were fain to go away, holding on to the ground.

Now, though the edge of the rock over which the river falls, does not show wearing more than three feet, and there is no appearance of the opposite wall being worn out at the bottom in the parts exposed to view, yet it is probable that, where it has flowed beyond the falls, the sides of the fissure may have given way, and the

VICTORIA FALLS——WESTERN EXTREMITY.

parts out of sight may be broader than the "white cord" on the sur-face. There may even be some ramifications of the fissure, which take a portion of the stream quite beneath the rocks ; but this I did not learn.

If we take the want of much wear on the lip of hard basaltic rock as of any value, the period when this rock was riven is not geologically very remote. I regretted the want of proper means of measuring and marking its width at the falls, in order that, at some future time, the question whether it is progressive or not, might be tested. It seemed as if a palm-tree could be laid across it from the island. And if it is progressive, as it would mark a great natural drainage being affected, it might furnish a hope that Africa will one day become a healthy continent. It is, at any rate, very much changed in respect to its lakes within a comparatively recent period.

At three spots near these falls, one of them, the island in the middle, on which we were, three Batoka chiefs offered up prayers and sacrifices to the Barimo. They chose their places of prayer within the sound of the roar of the cataract, and in sight of the bright bows in the cloud. They must have looked upon the scene with awe. Fear may have induced the selection. The river itself, is, to them, mysterious. The words of the canoe-song are :—

> The Leeambye! Nobody knows
> Whence it comes and whither it goes.

The play of colours of the double iris on the cloud, seen by them elsewhere only as the rainbow, may have led them to the idea that this was the abode of Deity. Some of the Makololo who went with me near to Gonye, looked upon the same sign with awe. When seen in the heavens it is named "motzé oa barimo"—the pestle of the gods. Here they could approach the emblem, and see it stand steadily above the blustering uproar below—a type of Him who sits supreme —alone unchangeable, though ruling over all changing things

David Livingstone, born at Blantyre, near Glasgow, in 1817, went to South Africa in 1840, and soon went inland to spend many useful years in medical, missionary, and geographical labours. He proceeded at once to Kuruman, Moffat's station, seven hundred miles north of the Cape, and began those wanderings which ultimately carried him all over Central Africa, and rendered his name immortal as one of the greatest of all explorers. In two years after his arrival he had succeeded in reaching to within ten days' journey of Lake 'Ngami, and ultimately settled at Kolobeng, some two hundred and fifty miles north of the station of Moffat, whose daughter he had meantime married. Here Livingstone found himself among the Bechuanas whose country has so recently become a part of the British empire. But he could not rest. In 1849 he undertook his first extensive journey, during which he discovered Lake 'Ngami and the Kalahari desert, bringing back with him a rich harvest for geography and natural history. Again on the move, in 1851 he made his way northward, winning the favour of chiefs and people by his gentle and gentlemanly treatment, until, to his surprise, he came on the great Zambesi, which no one had dreamt penetrated so far into the continent. There was no more rest for his eager spirit and restless feet until he had solved the mystery of this remarkable river. Sending his family home to England, and returning once more to the Zambesi, in 1853 he gathered a band of loyal natives and patiently traced the river

THE PROFILE CLIFF. NARROW GORGE AND TORRENT OF THE ZAMBESI BELOW THE VICTORIA FALLS.

and its tributary, the Leeba, up to Lake Dilolo. Passing westward and crossing the Kwango and other streams, Livingstone and his men, himself a "ruckle of bones," and nearly dead from dysentery and fever, suddenly—May, 1854—entered the city of Loango, much to the surprise of the Portuguese, who gave him a hospitable reception. The narrative of this journey, which he sent home to the Royal Geographical Society, at once made him famous, and gained

THE LATE DR. LIVINGSTONE.

(By permission of Messrs. Mayall and Co., Ltd.)

for him the gold medal of that society. The return journey was begun in September. Livingstone spent some time in the Lake Dilolo region, studying the wonderful watershed of the country, which threw so much light on the river systems of the continent. A year later he reached his starting-point, but was not content to rest there. A few weeks later he started once more to trace the Zambesi down to its mouth in the Indian Ocean, and by the end of November made the great discovery with which, in popular imagination, his name is so intimately associated, the famous Victoria Falls, of which we have just given his description. Pursuing what proved a weary journey down the great river, rendered more difficult in the region to which the Portuguese slaves had penetrated by the suspicion of the natives, he reached Quilimane, at the mouth of the river of that name, in May, 1856, completing, in two years and a half, one of the most fruitful

THE LATE MR. THOMAS BAINES.

journeys on record. His observations necessitated the reconstruction of the map of Central Africa. He diagnosed, with his keen geographical instinct, the true configuration of the continent as a great hollow or basin-shaped plateau, whose outer edge dropped down in terraced escarpments to the low-lying land on the coast. Little more than a year after his arrival home, he was again on his way to the mouth of the Zambesi, in command of a great expedition fitted out at Government expense. For six years did Livingstone and the able men of his staff, among whom was Sir John

Kirk, explore the region to the north of the Zambesi, re-discovered Lake Nyassa (for it will be found in old maps), laying down the course of the Rovuma, revisiting the Victoria Falls and his old friends at Seshekke, and penetrating many miles to the north-west of Nyassa. These twenty years' almost incessant work of Livingstone made a very solid inroad in the blank space of Central Africa, and gave a stimulus to African exploration which has been gathering in strength ever since. Livingstone first, of all white men, explained the whole course of the Zambesi; Livingstone first mapped out the Shiré districts, Lake Shirwa and the west coast of Lake Nyassa, the eastern limits, in short, of our Central African Protectorate. Livingstone first discovered the south end of Lake Tanganyika, Lake Moero, and the Lualaba, which roughly bound our sphere of influence on the north; and lastly, Livingstone died on the southern shores of Lake Bangweolo, right in the centre of what is now to become British Central Africa. Livingstone's work in this district has been ably seconded, and continued by men like Mr. (now Sir John) Kirk, Westbeach, Selous, Lieutenant Young, Dr. Stewart, Dr. Laws, Joseph Thomson, the two Moirs, H. H. Johnston, Consuls Hawes and O'Neil, F. Arnot, Captain Hore, and Alfred Sharpe. And these among them have mapped out much of the Zambesi basin, and the shores of Tanganyika and Nyassa. Their work, too, superadded to that of Livingstone, has prepared the way for the taking over of these fine territories by the British Crown.

Yet another name deserves prominent mention here, that of Thomas Baines, whose achievements in the field of South African exploration will long be remembered. Baines was born at King's Lynn, in 1822, and arrived in the Cape Colony in 1842. He made a trip to the north of the Orange River, using his gifted pencil to some purpose. Sketch-book always in hand, he was in the thick of the Kafir wars of 1848 and 1851. In 1854 he returned to England and became attached to an exploring expedition to Northern Australia as artist, and as usual took his full share of the dangers and fatigues. On his return to his native town in 1856-7 he was presented with the freedom of the borough, and in 1858, on the recommendation of the Royal Geographical Society, he was appointed as artist to the Livingstone Zambesi Expedition. This was an unfortunate connection for him for reasons which we need not follow here. He joined Chapman's expedition to the Zambesi in 1861, and at this time visited the Victoria Falls, when he made the vigorous sketches of these grand phases of nature, some of which are reproduced here on a small scale. His pictures of these, and of scenes on the Zambesi and other parts of South Africa, were much admired in London on his return. About this time Carl Mauch had called attention to the great gold regions of the Transvaal and Matabeleland, and Baines, as we have seen, was selected by a limited liability company to represent them in South Africa. He went to South Africa, and his book, "The Gold Regions of South-East Africa," to which I have called attention, testifies to the value of his labours as an explorer. Like too many other pioneers poor Baines never reaped the harvest he had sown. As shown elsewhere, he obtained a valuable concession from Lo Bengula, who had a great liking for him, but he died at Durban of dysentery on the 8th of May, 1875, without having gained any benefit from it. In 1873 the Royal Geographical Society recognised the value of Baines's geographical services by presenting him with a gold watch. Baines also wrote " Explorations in South-west Africa, being an Account of a Journey in the Years 1861 and 1862 from Walfisch Bay on the western coast to Lake Ngami and Victoria Falls," a peculiarly interesting work with characteristically vivid illustrations. Baines's name deserves an honoured place in the bead roll of South African Explorers.

CHAPTER XI.

Early Matabeleland Concessions.—How the Chartered Company's Concessions were Obtained and United.

IN dealing with this portion of my subject, it is not necessary to again dilate on the fact that for many years past Matabeleland and Mashonaland had been reputed to possess enormous mineral wealth, nor to again describe how travellers and hunters had for at least thirty years known of the existence there of gold in large quantities, a fact which had been brought prominently to their notice by the numerous old " workings " they had observed throughout the country. We have seen that Baines in 1870, and Sir John Swinburne in 1872, obtained concessions from Lo Bengula to carry on gold mining operations in certain districts. Again in 1885 more tangible proof of the reported auriferous wealth of Matabeleland was forthcoming. In that year Mr. E. A. Maund, who was a member of Sir Charles Warren's staff in the Bechuanaland Expedition, visited Lo Bengula and brought back with him a number of specimens of gold quartz which satisfied the most critical experts as to its richness. At this time Sir Hercules Robinson, as High Commissioner for South Africa, received information that the Boers intended to make a rush for Matabeleland, and in order to prevent this he secured the treaty with Lo Bengula which I set out in the next chapter, by which Matabeleland was brought within the sphere of British influence. After the negotiations between Mr. Cawston and the Colonial Office referred to also in the next chapter, Mr. E. A. Maund was despatched to Matabeleland by the Exploring Company, Limited, for the purpose of endeavouring to secure a concession from Lo Bengula. This idea had also occurred to other persons, of whom the most powerful group was one under the direction of Mr. C. D. Rudd, acting for the Gold Fields of South Africa, Limited, and a Syndicate including Mr. C. J. Rhodes and Mr. Alfred Beit. Previous to this, however, a number of speculators and traders had interviewed Lo Bengula, and, as they alleged, had obtained from him various concessions over the minerals of the country. The King, indeed, was pestered with applications of this kind, but he appears to have dealt with them after the manner of Zulu lawyers, who delight in playing off one white man against another. Some of these obtained con-

cessions, others conditional promises, but most had evasive answers
returned to them.

The first grant in point of time was that made to Mr. Baines, on
behalf of the South African Gold Fields Exploration Company,
Limited. We have seen that Baines visited Matabeleland on
several occasions, and acquired very considerable influence over
Lo Bengula. The King had a great belief in Mr. Baines's sincerity
and honesty, and always treated him with respect. On April 9th,
1870, Lo Bengula verbally promised a concession to Baines, who
represented the Company named. This Company was, not unnaturally, anxious to possess something less shadowy than the
mere verbal promise of the King, and notwithstanding remon-
strances and assurances on the part of Baines, they induced the
latter to return to Matabeleland with the object of obtaining a
written ratification of the concession. He left Pietermaritzburg on
May 16th, 1871, and on August 11th reached Bulawayo. Courteously
received by Lo Bengula, the diplomatic part of the work of getting
the concession confirmed was undertaken by Mr. John Lee, who
succeeded after a short time in gaining the King's consent. In
preparing the document care was taken to reproduce, as far as
possible, the words which Lo Bengula had used in making the
grant originally, and on August 29th, 1871, the ratification was
signed and sealed by the King (with a seal Baines had made for
him) in the presence of witnesses. The following is a copy of this
interesting document :—

I, Lo Bengula, King of the Matabele nation, do hereby certify that
on the 9th day of April, 1870, in the presence of Mr. John Lee, acting
as agent between myself and Mr. Thomas Baines, then and now commanding the expedition of the South African Gold Fields Exploration
Company, Limited, I do freely grant Mr. Thomas Baines, on behalf
of the above-named Company, full permission to explore, prospect,
and dig or mine for GOLD in all that country lying between the
Gwailo River on the south-west, and the Ganyana on the north-east,
and that this, my permission, includes liberty to build dwellings or
storehouses, to erect machinery for crushing rocks or other purposes,
to use the roads through my country freely for the purpose of introducing and conveying to the mines such machinery, tools, provisions, materials, and other necessaries, and for the removal of gold
so obtained ; and it also includes all lesser details connected with
Gold Mining.

In making this grant I do not alienate from my kingdom this or
any other portion of it ; but reserve intact the sovereignty of my
dominion, and Mr. Baines engaged on behalf of said Company, not
to make any claim contrary or injurious to my right as sovereign of
the country, but to recognise my authority as King, and to apply to
me for such protection as he might require, and I engaged to grant
such protection to Mr. Baines as should enable him to enjoy all lawful and proper use of the privileges granted him by me ; and I also
certify that when in November of the same year, 1870, Mr. Baines
asked me what tribute or payment he should make me in return for
said privileges, I declined to name any sum, but left it to the judgment of Mr. Baines to make me annually, on behalf of the said Com-

pany, such present as might seem proper to him and acceptable to me.

Among the Matabele the verbal promise of the King has always been regarded as a sufficient guarantee, and many white men now enjoy privileges in virtue of grants made by my father, Umzelegazi, which I regard as binding on me.

I also regard my verbal permission given to Mr. Baines as valid and binding on me and my successors; but finding that the customs of white men require that such grants or promises should be made in writing, I now hereby solemnly and fully confirm the grant verbally made to Mr. Baines on behalf of his Company. In witness of which I hereto append my sign manual.

his
Lo Bengula X
mark.

(Here his seal was affixed.)

Signed the 29th day of August, 1871.

Signed the same in witness hereof :—

G. A. Phillips.
F. Betts.
Robert J. Jewell.
John Lee.

This concession, after being in the possession of the South African Gold Fields Company, Limited, was sold by Mr. J. Berg-theil, acting on behalf of the two companies, to Mr. A. L. Ochs, Mr. F. A. Gillam, and others, by whom it was subsequently transferred to the Matabeleland Company, and sold by it to the British South Africa Company.

The next concession was that of the Tati district, made to Sir John Swinburne in 1872. It is unnecessary to go into its details, as it was expressly excepted from the operation of the subsequent Rudd concession, and forms no part of the Chartered Company's property.

We come now to the so-called concession to Messrs. Wood, Frances, and Chapman. This had been made over what is known as the "Disputed Territory," but was conditional upon the payment of a consideration of £100. The bargain was subsequently repudiated by Lo Bengula, who declined to receive the money, as it had come to his ears that before asking him for the concession, Messrs. Wood, Francis, and Chapman had attempted to obtain one over the same district from Khama. The latter turned them out of his country, saying to Mr. Chapman, "You had better leave my country at once; do not return again to my place. Never let me see you again." They were sent down country under the escort of the Deputy Commissioner's body-guard.

As regards the Moore "concession," it was simply verbal, and was never formally completed.

Mention may be made, at this point, of Mr. Alfred Haggard, who got up as far as Tati in quest of such concessions as good luck might have in store for him. He was turned back, however, by Mr. Maguire and a party of natives commanded by an Induna, and afterwards complained to the Colonial Office of the treatment he had received in the matter. It may, however, be stated that he and the other holders of concessions, or supposed concessions, were liberally dealt with by the Chartered Company, by which their claims were absorbed.

A Mr. F. Johnson and Lieutenant Bates also went into Matabeleland with the object of getting a concession from the King, but failed, and we believe actually got into trouble with Lo Bengula owing to their having gone gold-seeking instead of buck-hunting. As soon as they could conveniently get away they left Matabeleland for the more genial territory of Khama, where they obtained a concession which is at the present time held by the Bechuanaland Exploration Company.

We must now revert to Mr. Maund's journey to Matabeleland on behalf of the Exploring Company. On his way up through Bechuanaland, that gentleman was detained for some days in connection with the Grobler "incident," and on his arrival at the King's kraal found Mr. Rudd and his party (Messrs. Maguire, M.P., F. R. Thompson, and Burnett) already encamped within a mile and a half of Bulawayo. Mr. Rudd had been in active negotiation with Lo Bengula, and in the former's own words, "stuck to him with bull-dog tenacity." The methods of diplomacy adopted by the party were those in common use. The process may be briefly described as follows:—The white men go up and sit before the King, not always on the cleanest ground, nor in the most comfortable of positions. The usual "palavering" goes on, agreeably interspersed—such is that touch of nature which makes the whole world kin—by drinking large quantities of native beer and eating beef cooked à la mode Matabele. If one has not a pocket-knife, one has to eat with one's fingers; but that is a detail. Each rival party present tries to sit out the others, and when the opposing elements have taken their departure, opportunity is seized to mention the subject that lies nearest to the hearts of the applicants. Lo Bengula, who is very shrewd, and knows exactly "how many beans make five," generally has an Induna near him, to whom he confides his ideas upon the subjects mentioned. The Induna acts as a go-between, and does his best for the King's hand. The advantages to Lo Bengula of a given course are put before the Induna, who duly weighs them and communicates his opinion to his master. When Mr. Rudd was conducting his negotiations, a large number of Indunas were, we believe, summoned to hold council with the King. It may be here mentioned that Mr. Thomas Rochfort Maguire, who was of Mr. Rudd's party, is now M.P. for North Donegal, is a native of County Fermanagh, and was born about the year 1856. He was educated at Merton College, Oxford, where he was well known as an athlete, and took his bachelor's degree in 1877, and a double first-class. He was shortly afterwards elected to a fellowship in All Soul's College, and graduated Master of Arts. Here are some lines expressive of the many-sided accomplishments of Mr. Maguire, written in imitation of Mr. W. S. Gilbert's style, by a contemporary in his undergrad. days :—

> Versatile Mister Maguire
> 'Tis you are the bhoy I admire,
>> For you come from the west,
>> The land I love best,
> The land of the Emerald Isle.
> Affable Mister Maguire,
> With your languidly amiable smile,
>> With your smile and your sigh
>> And the droop in your eye,
> Versatile Mister Maguire.

> Affable Mister Maguire
> To a peerage one day might aspire
>> He'd do equally well
>> For a cavalry swell,
> A parson, a don, or a squire ;
> Or perhaps he will brew an " entire,"
> Or apply for the post of town crier,
> Or fashion the roots of the briar
> Into pipes, or perform on the lyre,
> Or conduct the Leeds Festival Choir !

On October 29th, 1888, Lo Bengula granted the concession asked for by Mr. Rudd, and Mr. Maund's application for a mineral concession was received very favourably, the King making him definite promises, subject, however, as we have seen, to the obligation that two of his Indunas should accompany Mr. Maund to England to report to the King as to the existence of that country and of the Great White Queen, doubts of those facts having been raised in his mind by the statements of the Boers. Mr. Maund played his part with admirable skill and tact, and that cool calculation characteristic of a man educated at Cambridge University. There is reason to believe that when the King made the Rudd grant he considered there was no impediment of any kind in the way of his doing so, save the Tati concession, which was expressly excepted. The Rudd concession superseded all others (with the exception of the Tati), the consideration being 1000 rifles and a payment of £100 per month.

As to Lo Bengula's "denial" of the grant, advertised in a Colonial newspaper, that step was taken with an ulterior object. He was much pestered at this time by a host of applicants for concessions, and he was worked upon by the opponents of the Rudd-Rhodes party, who, having nothing to lose and possibly something to gain, tried to get the King to repudiate the grant. His people, also, were hardly prepared for his new departure, and he, no doubt, had difficulties to contend with in reconciling his Indunas to his policy in the matter. It is probable that Lo Bengula was endeavouring, by the course he took, to educate his people up to the idea that he was receiving value for that which he had given away; and finding, from the Indunas who visited England, that

Mr. Rhodes was a man held in high consideration by the "white men's" authorities, he adopted every means in his power to make his people see : firstly, that he had the right to give mineral concessions ; and secondly, that their interest lay in his granting such to men like Mr. Rhodes, who, in gaining the minerals, would respect native institutions and would not disturb their country. Mr. Rhodes arrived at England during the visit of the Indunas and after consultation with Mr. Maund, the Directors of the Exploring Company made an agreement with Mr. Rhodes, under which they agreed to support the Rudd concession with all Mr. Maund's influence with Lo Bengula, on condition of receiving a share in the profits of that concession. Under the arrangement made it was settled that the Exploring Company was to have one-fourth interest in the concession, and one half of the special concession in the Mazoe district. That Company had a capital of £12,000, which was increased to £35,000 and subsequently to £70,000 ; whilst the Gold Fields of South Africa, Limited, had a capital of £250,000, since increased by fresh issues of shares to do what may be requisite to uphold the concession and for other purposes. The amalgamation of the

FLAG OF THE BRITISH SOUTH AFRICA COMPANY.

various interests was effected by the formation of the Central Search Association, Limited, with a capital of £120,000, subsequently increased by £1000, the special rights of the Exploring Company in the excepted portions being protected by independent agreements. A portion of the capital of the Association was allotted in fully paid shares in accordance with the agreements entered into, and the balance subscribed in cash, in the same proportions by the allottees of the fully paid shares. The capital was merely a figure, and was not intended to, and did not in fact, represent the real value of the concession, being only taken as a multiple, by which the interests of the parties concerned could be adjusted. The Central Search Association, having served its purpose, went into liquidation, and another Company, called the United Concessions Company, Limited, was formed in July, 1890. This Company having absorbed all the interests in the Rudd-Rhodes Concession, made over its rights to the Chartered Company (which had just then been established) for development, on the basis of an equal division of profits—the Chartered Company to pay 50 per cent. of the net profits among the various owners of rights, and itself retaining the other 50 per cent. for its own shareholders. The capital of the United Concessions Company (£1,000,000) was merely intended to represent the supposed value of the concession for the purpose of satisfying certain liabilities, and allotting the proportionate interest of each party concerned.

The capital of the Chartered Company is £1,000,000 in shares of £1 each, and in this Company the De Beers Diamond Mining Company (who provided £210,000 towards the amount required before the Government would grant the Charter) and the Matabeleland Company are large shareholders. Arrangements have also been made between the British South Africa Company and the  African Lakes Company by which the latter agree to amalgamate with the former. The other companies owning Shares are described in Appendix A.

CHAPTER XII.

The Origin of the British South Africa Company.—Sketch of the Events which led to its Formation.—Lo Bengula's Treaty with England.—Mr. Cawston and the Colonial Office.—Interviews and Correspondence.—The Rudd Concession.—Amalgamation of Interests.—Applying for the Charter.—Favourable Answer to the Petition.—Full Text of the Charter.—Lord Knutsford Explains its Provisions.

I SHALL now proceed to give a brief and succinct account of the origin of the Chartered Company, or, rather, strictly speaking, of the events which led up to its development from a number of other Companies. Readers of Blue Books and similar literature will remember that in the month of February, 1888, a treaty was signed between Lo Bengula, King of the Matabele, and Great Britain. This treaty was a very important one for several reasons, but chiefly because it secured Matabeleland and Mashonaland to British influence, as against that of the Boers. In a letter from Sir Hercules Robinson, G.C.M.G., the then High Commissioner for South Africa, to the Colonial Office, the text of the treaty is set forth as follows :—

"The Chief Lo Bengula, ruler of the tribe known as the Amandebele, together with the Mashuna and Makakalaka tributaries of the same, hereby agrees to the following articles and conditions :—

" 'That peace and amity shall continue for ever between Her Britannic Majesty, Her subjects, and the Amandebele people ; and the contracting Chief Lo Bengula engages to use his utmost endeavours to prevent any rupture of the same, to cause the strict observance of his treaty, and so to carry out the spirit of the treaty of friendship which was entered into between his late father, the Chief Umsiligaas, with the then Governor of the Cape of Good Hope in the year of our Lord 1836.

" 'It is hereby further agreed by Lo Bengula, Chief in and over the Amandebele country with its dependencies as aforesaid, on behalf of himself and people, that he will refrain from entering into any correspondence or treaty with any foreign State or Power to sell, alienate, or cede, or permit, or countenance any sale, alienation, or cession of the whole or any part of the said Amandebele country under his chieftainship, or upon any other subject, without the previous knowledge and sanction of Her Majesty's High Commissioner for South Africa.'

"In faith of which I, Lo Bengula, on my part have hereunto set my hand at Gubulawayo, Amandebeleland, this 11th day of February, and of Her Majesty's reign the 51st.

"(Signed)   Lo Bengula   ^{his} X _{mark.}

" Witnesses (Signed)   W. Graham.
G. B. Van Wyk.

" Before me,
"(Signed)   J. S. Moffat,
" Assistant Commissioner.

" February 11th, 1888.
" I certify the above a true copy,
"(Signed)   J. S. Moffat,
" Assistant Commissioner.

" February 11th, 1888."

On April 24th Lord Knutsford cabled to Sir Hercules Robinson, " You have authority to ratify agreement signed with Lo Bengula." On May 4th Mr. George Cawston, of the firm of Messrs. George Cawston and Co., wrote to the Colonial Office calling attention to this treaty, and announcing the intention of himself and other gentlemen to send a representative to Matabeleland " to negotiate with Lo Bengula a treaty for trading, mining, and general purposes." That gentleman's letter was as follows :—

" Hatton Court, Threadneedle Street,
" May 4, 1888.

" My Lord,
" I have the honour to request you to permit me to draw your attention to the treaty of Peace and Amity which has been signed between the High Commissioner of the British Government in South Africa and Lo Bengula, Chief of the Matabeles.

" It is the intention of myself, in conjunction with others, to send a representative to Matabeleland to negotiate with Lo Bengula for a treaty for trading, mining, and general purposes.

" Before doing so we are desirous of ascertaining whether we shall have the support of the British Government. For, of course, capital will not be expended in the development of the country unless encouraged, as we trust it will be.

" In the event of such encouragement being obtained, would the High Commissioner at the Cape be requested to render such assistance as will be compatible with the wishes of Lo Bengula and with the best interests of his country?

"(Signed)   GEORGE CAWSTON.

"The Right Hon. Lord Knutsford, &c."

Lord Knutsford replied, under date, May 14, 1888, that it was "the province of the High Commissioner to decide what advice he should give to a Native Chief entitled to his advice; that Her Majesty's Government would give no countenance to any concession or agreement unless it were concluded with the knowledge of, and approved by the High Commissioner; and that if you decide to proceed with the undertaking which you contemplate, you will do well to be prepared to satisfy Sir Hercules Robinson of your strong financial position." Lord Knutsford also expressed his willingness to transmit to Sir Hercules any evidence with which he might be furnished as to the personal standing of the leading promoters of the scheme, and of those whom they might select to act for them in South Africa. Further letters passed, followed by an interview between Mr. Cawston and his colleagues and the Secretary of State, as a result of which the latter expressed himself satisfied, and, as we have seen, a company was formed called the "The Exploring Company, Limited" (*see* Appendix A), Mr. E. A. Maund being selected to proceed to South Africa on its behalf.

Simultaneously with these events other persons appear to have hit upon the same idea, and accordingly on December 17 Lord Knutsford telegraphed to Sir Hercules Robinson in these terms:

Is there any truth in report grant of mining concession over the whole of Matabeleland to Rudd in consideration of monthly payment of £100, and 1000 Martini-Henry rifles? If rifles part of consideration, as reported, do you think there is danger of complications arising from this?

To this telegram Sir Hercules replied affirming the truth of the report, and stating that a copy of the concession had been sent on to the Colonial Office. Lord Knutsford's alarm about the rifles was shared by a good many people, including the Bishop of Bloemfontein, but Dr. Knight Bruce subsequently withdrew his strictures on obtaining further information. "Having heard" (wrote the Bishop) "that rifles were about to be sent to the Matabele, I expressed myself strongly as to what I considered the consequences of such action would be. When I afterwards learnt that these rifles were a necessary factor in an agreement by which it was hoped that the Mashona would be benefited, I thought it but just to give others credit for wishing as well to the Mashona as myself, and withdrew any reflections that I had made on the transaction."

The following is a copy of Lo Bengula's concession to Mr. C. D. Rudd:—

Know all men by these presents that whereas Charles Dunnell Rudd of Kimberley, Rochfort Maguire of London, and Francis

Robert Thompson of Kimberley, hereinafter called the grantees, have covenanted and agreed, and do hereby covenant and agree, to pay to me, my heirs and successors, the sum of one hundred pounds sterling British currency, on the first day of every lunar month, and further to deliver at my Royal Kraal, one thousand Martini-Henry breech-loading rifles, together with one hundred thousand rounds of suitable ball cartridge, five hundred of the said rifles, and fifty thousand of the said cartridges to be ordered from England forthwith, and delivered with reasonable despatch, and the remainder of the said rifles and cartridges to be delivered so soon as the said grantees shall have commenced to work mining machinery within my territory, and further to deliver on the Zambesi River a steamboat with guns suitable for defensive purposes upon the said river, or in lieu of the said steamboat, should I so elect, to pay to me the sum of five hundred pounds sterling British currency, on the execution of these presents, I, Lo Bengula, King of Matabeleland, Mashonaland, and other adjoining territories, in the exercise of my sovereign powers, and in the presence and with the consent of my Council of Indunas, do hereby grant and assign unto the said grantees, their heirs, representatives, and assigns, jointly and severally, the complete and exclusive charge over all metals and minerals situated and contained in my kingdoms, principalities, and dominions, together with full power to do all things that they may deem necessary to win and procure the same, and to hold, collect, and enjoy the profits and revenues, if any, derivable from the said metals and minerals subject to the aforesaid payment, and whereas I have been much molested of late by divers persons seeking and desiring to obtain grants and concessions of land and mining rights in my territories, I do hereby authorise the said grantees, their heirs, representatives, and assigns, to take all necessary and lawful steps to exclude from my kingdoms, principalities, and dominions all persons seeking land, metals, minerals, or mining rights therein, and I do hereby undertake to render them such needful assistance as they may from time to time require for the exclusion of such persons and to grant no concessions of land or mining rights from and after this date without their consent and concurrence, provided that if at any time the said monthly payment of one hundred pounds shall be in arrear for a period of three months then this grant shall cease and determine from the date of the last made payment, and further provided that nothing contained in these presents shall extend to or affect a grant made by me of certain mining rights in a portion of my territory south of the Ramakoban River, which grant is commonly known as the Tati Concession.

This given under my hand this thirtieth day of October in the year of our Lord eighteen hundred and eighty-eight at my Royal Kraal.

his
(Signed)   Lo BENGULA X
mark.
C. D. RUDD,
ROCHFORT MAGUIRE,
F. R. THOMPSON.

Witnesses,
(Signed)   CHAS. D. HELM,
    J. D. DREYER.

Copy of indorsement on the original agreement.

I hereby certify that the accompanying document has been fully interpreted and explained by me to the Chief Lo Bengula and his full Council of Indunas, and that all the constitutional usages of the Matabele nation had been complied with prior to his executing the same.

Dated at Umgusa River this thirtieth day of October, 1888.

(Signed) ' CHAS. D. HELM.

Mr. Rudd, as I have informed my readers, was acting on behalf of a Company known as " The Gold Fields of South Africa, Limited," and a syndicate including Mr. Cecil Rhodes and Mr. Alfred Beit. Upon the above concession, Sir Sidney Shippard, the Administrator of the Bechuanaland Protectorate, issued the following important " Minute ":—

1. The " Indaba " or Council of Matabele Indunas at which Mr. Rudd's concession was discussed at Umvootja and the actual signing of the concession by the Chief Lo Bengula took place, as I understand, three days after the departure of Mr. J. S. Moffat, the Assistant Commissioner, and more than a week after I had left Umgusa River on my return from Matabeleland. I had carefully impressed upon Lo Bengula's mind that Her Majesty's Government was not in any way concerned with either mining schemes or trading ventures, and that he might be quite certain that any private concession seeker who professed to represent the British Government was trying to deceive him by false representations.

No Government officer or representative had anything to do with the concession in question, and my knowledge of what took place is limited to hearsay and to the contents of the document itself, which was shown to me by Mr. C. D. Rudd, when his mule cart overtook my ox wagons near Palochwe, on the road between the Tati and Shoshong.

2. The Rev. C. D. Helm, of the London Missionary Society, attested the document, and, as Mr. Rudd informed me, interpreted throughout for him, and was strongly in favour of the concession on two grounds : (*a*) because the substitution of long-range rifles for the stabbing assegai would tend to diminish the loss of life in the Matabele raids, and thus prove a distinct gain to the cause of humanity ; and (*b*) because the great increase of trade promised by Mr. Rudd would tend to introduce civilisation among the Matabele.

3. On the other hand, the Right Rev. the Bishop of Bloemfontein and the Rev. J. D. Hepburn, London Missionary at Shoshong, are strongly opposed to the supply of firearms and ammunition to the Matabele on account of the increased facilities likely to be thus afforded for their cruel raids, the atrocity of which appears to be beyond question.

4. I felt it to be my duty to explain fully to Khama the conditions of Mr. Rudd's concession especially as related to the promised supply of arms and ammunition to the Matabele. Khama appeared very apprehensive that such a supply of arms and ammunition to the Matabele might be followed by a raid by them on the Bamangwato, though I did not gather that he would attempt to prevent the conveyance of such arms and ammunition through his territory. Mr. Rudd would, I understand, be prepared to give arms and ammunition to Khama also, for defensive purposes, and the relative position of the Chiefs would thus remain unchanged.

5. As regards the arguments based solely on the humanitarian point of view, I am inclined to agree with the Rev. C. D. Helm in thinking that the gradual substitution of the rifle for the stabbing assegai will directly tend to diminish instead of increasing bloodshed and loss of life. A Matabele Matjaha unaccustomed to the use of firearms, with only a rifle in his hands, would, in my opinion, be far less formidable than when, assegai in hand, he stalks his victims as at present. The experience of all those who have fought in Native wars in South Africa proves that bloodshed is decreased in proportion as the Native discards the stabbing assegai and takes to missiles or fire-arms; and experience elsewhere, to say nothing of the teachings of history, appears to confirm this view. Mr. Hepburn contends that in this case it will be the stabbing assegai plus the rifle, and that the combination will render the Matabele invincible by any other native race; but this may, I think, fairly be doubted. At any rate, I have noticed that other natives who have once acquired familiarity with the use of fire-arms discard all other weapons in favour of the rifle. The use of fire-arms in modern warfare has notoriously diminished loss of life in action.

6. In a political point of view it would in my opinion be inexpedient to place any restriction on the supply of fire-arms and ammunition to Lo Bengula, while, as he is quite aware, we allow an unlimited supply to be furnished to the Bechuana and other chiefs in and beyond our Protectorate. Any such attempted restriction on our part as regards Lo Bengula would be wholly inoperative, as he can always obtain large supplies through the Transvaal, and our refusal would merely have the effect of throwing him, so to speak, into the arms of the Transvaal Boers.

Lo Bengula is desirous of defending himself against filibusters from the Transvaal, against marauders claiming to act under Portuguese authority, and against certain regiments of unruly and virtually mutinous Matjaha consisting mainly of Maghole or captives who have grown up to be a source of perpetual danger to him. Bad as Lo Bengula's government may be from our point of view, it is the only means of maintaining order and preserving any vestige of respect for life and property among his ferocious subjects; and until, in the fulness of time, some salutary changes can be introduced, it will, in my opinion, be sound policy for us to furnish Lo Bengula with the means of maintaining his authority.

(Signed) SIDNEY SHIPPARD.

December 20, 1888.

In support of the attitude assumed by Sir Sidney Shippard, it is instructive to read the following passages from a despatch of Sir Hercules Robinson to Lord Knutsford, dated March 18, 1889 :—

The alternative before us as regards Matabeleland is to recognise a monopoly, which may possibly develop into a Royal Charter, or to follow the Swazieland course of allowing a number of competing concession-seekers of different nationalities to establish themselves in the country. Lo Bengula would be unable to govern or control such incomers except by a massacre. They would be unable to govern themselves; a British Protectorate would be ineffectual, as we should have no jurisdiction except by annexation; and Her Majesty's Government, as in Swazieland, would have before them the choice of letting the country fall into the hands of the South

African Republic or of annexing it to the Empire. The latter course would assuredly entail on British taxpayers for some time, at all events, an annual expenditure of not less than a quarter of a million sterling.

I am far from contending that, apart from money considerations, the annexation of Matabeleland would not be the best and most effectual mode of widening the base of British prosperity in that part of South Africa. I wouldonly suggest that before advising Lo Bengula to reject a monopoly in favour of a more general admission of foreigners, Her Majesty's Government should count the cost of such a policy, and if they adopt it, should not endeavour subsequently to escape from its inevitable consequences. Hitherto annexations and protectorates seem to have been decided on only to be followed later on by a perpetual wrangle with the Treasury for the means of maintaining a decent administration.

But Sir Hercules Robinson's was not the first reference in print to the scheme of a Royal Charter being granted to a company to govern and develop the territories north of the Limpopo. Before these pages pass into permanent form as the standard record on this subject I must in fairness to the writers refer to an able and prophetic article which appeared in the *Fortnightly Review* of March, 1889 under the joint authorship of Major F. J. Ricarde-Seaver and Sir Charles Metcalfe. The article was entitled "The British Sphere of Influence in South Africa," and its conclusion should be inserted here :—

A word as to the way in which the countries within the British sphere of influence in South Africa should be civilised and developed. The chief means plainly is the iron way : this is the great civiliser, the great developing force of the nineteenth century. But what as to government? England has undertaken duties which she must perform, responsibilities which she cannot shirk, and unquestionably there appears to be a sort of feeling in the minds of the chief officials of the Imperial Government that in the present state of things grave difficulties may arise. The dual commissionership has been a subject of attack, and any active advance on the part of England in developing the grand regions which extend up to the Zambesi will doubtless necessitate the division of the office; it is impossible for the government to be carried on with due efficiency under such conditions and from such a distance. Again, the fact that any such advance is a political movement on the part of England no doubt tends to excite the suspicion of the Boer. What then remains for us to do? Perhaps the best way of effecting what we are bound to do, would be by granting a charter to some powerful company or corporation, which might include the countries shown within the sphere of British influence as marked on the map already referred to. This has been our practice in the past. We owe our Indian Empire to the East India Company. This is our practice in the present. Witness the North Borneo Company. Witness the East African Company, whose territory was so ably described by Mr. H. H. Johnston in a recent number of this Review. This will be found to be the best available solution of the difficulties of the situation in Southern Africa. Such a corporation should be bound to extend the same safeguards against the liquor traffic that the

Imperial Government now affords, should be strong enough to take up the responsibilities that England has incurred, and to develop the country on commercial principles. All the leading Europeans in South Africa would gladly join hands with such a company. And thus, without expense or outlay on the part of the Imperial Government, without exciting angry suspicions on the part of the Boers, there might be formed a federation that by its personal relations in Southern Africa would secure peace and prosperity, would protect the natives and restrain the freebooting Boers, would effect without an army a peaceful conquest fraught with the most advantageous results alike for the natives and for England and her people; the sphere of British influence would then be, as it ought to be, the sphere of British commerce. The time is ripe for such an enterprise.

One of the authors of this article—Major Ricarde-Seaver—not only held these views but expressed them repeatedly before they appeared in this form. A close confidant of Mr. Rhodes this gentleman would doubtless have been on the directorate of the British South Africa Company had his private and business concerns not called him to permanent residence in Paris.

Coming back now to the subject of the concessions, when Mr. Maund arrived in Matabeleland and found that Mr. Rudd had anticipated him in obtaining a concession from Lo Bengula, negotiations were entered into between the rival parties which, as I have already shown, resulted in a union of interests. Under the arrangements made, the Exploring Company acquired one-fourth share of the greater part of the concession, and a larger interest in certain excepted parts. Accordingly on April 30, 1889, the following two important letters were addressed to the Colonial Office—the first by Lord Gifford, the Chairman of the Exploring Company, and the second by Messrs. Rhodes, Beit, and Rudd.

LORD GIFFORD, V.C., to COLONIAL OFFICE.
The Exploring Company, Limited,
14, George Street, Mansion House, E.C.,
London, April 30, 1889.

MY LORD,—

With reference to our conversation at the interview kindly accorded by you to the Directors of the Exploring Company on the 17th instant, I beg herewith to submit the outlines of the scheme for the formation of a Company having for its object the development of the Bechuanaland Protectorate and the countries lying to the north.

The objects of this Company will be fourfold :—

1. To extend northwards the railway and telegraph systems in the direction of the Zambesi.

2. To encourage emigration and colonisation.

3. To promote trade and commerce.

4. To develop and work mineral and other concessions under the management of one powerful organisation, thereby obviating conflicts and complications between the various interests that have been acquired within those regions and securing to the Native Chiefs and their subjects the rights reserved to them under the several concessions.

I am authorised by the gentlemen who are willing to form this association to state that they are prepared to proceed at once with the construction of the first section of the railway and the extension of the telegraph system from Mafeking, its present terminus, to Shoshong, and that for this purpose a sum of £700,000 has already been privately subscribed.

Having regard to the heavy responsibilities which are proposed to be undertaken by the association, and which cannot be considered as likely to be remunerative for some time; and whereas a proper recognition by Her Majesty's Government is necessary to the due fulfilment of the objects above-mentioned, we propose to petition for a charter on the above lines, and we ask for an assurance that such rights and interests as have been legally acquired in these territories by those who have joined in this association shall be recognised by and receive the sanction and moral support of Her Majesty's Government.

By this amalgamation of all interests under one common control, this association as a Chartered Company with a representative Board of Directors of the highest possible standing in London, with a local board in South Africa of the most influential character, having the support of Her Majesty's Government and of public opinion at home, and the confidence and sympathy of the inhabitants of South Africa, will be able peacefully and with the consent of the native races to open up, develop, and colonise the territories to the north of British Bechuanaland with the best results both for British trade and commerce and for the interests of the native races.

THE GOLD FIELDS OF SOUTH AFRICA, LIMITED, to COLONIAL OFFICE.
The Gold Fields of South Africa, Limited,
2, Gresham Buildings, Basinghall Street,
London, E.C., April 30, 1889.
MY LORD,—

Having perused the letter of this date addressed to your Lordship by the Chairman of the Exploring Company, Limited, with regard to the development of the territories to the north of the Cape Colony, we beg to state that we are prepared, as representing the Matabele Concession, and having a very important stake in South Africa, to co-operate cordially, with the approval of Her Majesty's Government, in carrying out the scheme proposed. Arrangements have already been made to that effect between the Exploring Company and ourselves.

We have, &c.,
(Signed)   C. J. RHODES,
                  A. BEIT,
                  THOMAS RUDD,
Chairman of the Gold Fields of South Africa, Limited.

Lord Knutsford replied thereto asking for a draft of the proposed Charter, and enquiring whether the course suggested would have the approval of Lo Bengula. That his lordship was inclined to favour the scheme may be gathered from a passage in a letter which he addressed the same day to the Foreign Office:—

. . . In consenting to consider this scheme in more detail, Lord Knutsford has been influenced by the consideration that if such a Company is incorporated by Royal Charter its constitution, objects and operations will become more directly subject to control by Her Majesty's Government than if it were left to these gentlemen to incorporate themselves under the Joint Stock Companies Acts, as they are entitled to do. In the latter case, Her Majesty's Government would not be able effectually to prevent the Company from taking its own line of policy, which might possibly result in complications with Native Chiefs and others, necessitating military expenditure, and, perhaps, even military operations. The example of the Imperial East African Company shows that such a body may to some considerable extent relieve Her Majesty's Government from diplomatic difficulties and heavy expenditure. In Lord Knutsford's judgment such a Company as that proposed for the Bechuanaland Protectorate, if well conducted, would render still more valuable assistance to Her Majesty's Government in South Africa. At present nothing could be more unsatisfactory than the condition of things existing in that quarter.

A doubt having been raised in certain quarters as to the genuineness of the concession, the original was sent out to Lo Bengula's kraal for the purpose of comparison with the King's copy, Lo Bengula having written to Her Majesty the Queen, upon the subject, as follows :—

To Her Majesty QUEEN VICTORIA from Lo BENGULA, King of the Amandebele.

King's Kraal, Ungusa River,

Greeting : April 23, 1889.

SOME time ago a party of men came into my country, the principal one appearing to be a man named Rudd. They asked me for a place to dig for gold, and said they would give me certain things for the right to do so. I told them to bring what they would give and I would then show them what I would give.

A document was written and presented to me for signature. I asked what it contained and was told that in it were my words and the words of those men.

I put my hand to it.

About three months afterwards I heard from other sources that I had given by that document the right to all the minerals in my country.

I called a meeting of my Indunas and also of the white men, and demanded a copy of the document. It was proved to me that I *had* signed away the mineral rights of my whole country to Rudd and his friends.

I have since had a meeting of my Indunas, and they will not recognise the paper as it contains neither my words nor the words of those who got it.

After the meeting I demanded that the original document be returned to me. It has not come yet, although it is two months since, and they promised to bring it back soon.

The men of the party who were in my country at the time were told to remain until the document was brought back. One of them, Maguire, has now left without my knowledge and against my orders.

I write to you that you may know the truth about this thing, and may not be deceived. With renewed and cordial greetings:

I am your friend,   his

(Signed),   Lo BENGULA   ×

As Witnesses :   mark.

G. A. Phillips,
Moss Cohen,
James Fairbairn.

> Elephant
> Seal of
> Lobengula.

W. F. Usher, Interpreter.

This letter having been brought to the knowledge of Mr. Rhodes, that gentleman consulted with Mr. Maguire, who made the following important written statement thereon, which was forwarded to Lord Knutsford :—

London, June 21, 1889.

I have read the letter dated April 25 purporting to be written by Lo Bengula respecting our concession.

It appears to be a portion of the organised opposition offered by a certain section of the white inhabitants of Matabeleland to all attempts to promote the development of that country, of which opposition we have already had some experience.

With reference to the specific allegations contained in the letter I wish to observe :—

1. That from the date of the signing of the concession Lo Bengula has never varied in his assurances to us that he intended to fulfil the obligations which he had undertaken towards us, nor do I gather that by this letter, even if genuine, he expresses the intention of repudiating these obligations.

2. Statements have from time to time been made to Lo Bengula that the concession signed by him was in substance different from the copy left in his custody. This is what would be meant by the statement in the letter on page 3 that neither the Chief nor Indunas would recognise the copy of the concession then in the country. In order to prove that the copy and original are identical the original was sent for by us, but Lo Bengula has assured Mr. Thompson, one of the concessionaires, that if the documents are identical he will be perfectly satisfied.

3. The Chief never ordered me to remain in the country until this document was brought back.

4. When I resolved to come down country, on the day before my departure I obtained permission from Lo Bengula, in the usual course, to leave his kraal. The statements therefore contained in the letter respecting myself are untrue, which fact to my mind throws grave doubt upon the credence to be attached to the document.

5. The elephant seal referred to is in the custody of Mr. Fairbairn, a local store-keeper, and is practically at his disposal.

6. Those acquainted with Matabeleland, as a rule, attach little importance to any document stated to be signed by Lo Bengula which is not witnessed by one of the missionaries, whom the Chief regards as his most independent advisers.

7. Previous statements, detrimental to our concession, have been published purporting to bear the chief's signature, which have subsequently been proved not to have been signed by him.

8. The practical, and to my mind conclusive, answer to the statements contained in this letter consists in the facts that, although the

discussions based upon the representations of disappointed concession-seekers have been going on almost from the date of the signature of our concession, still the Chief has throughout regularly continued to receive his payment of £100 per month, and that we have received a cable bringing news from Matabeleland a fortnight later than April 25, stating that the rifles, the principal remaining portion of our payments due to him, had been by his orders brought to one of his royal kraals, this being done, it must be remembered, after a prolonged and exhaustive series of explanations and discussions which render it impossible for Lo Bengula to say that he is now unaware of the precise nature of the concession which he acknowledges he has granted. These facts appear to afford the best proof possible that he intends to carry out his engagements to us, as indeed he has always stated his intention of doing.

Yours, &c.,

(Signed) ROCHFORT MAGUIRE.

Mr. Moffat, the Assistant Commissioner to Sir Sidney Shippard, in a letter dated August 28th, 1889, to the latter, reported that he had had an interview with Lo Bengula, and with Messrs. Cohen, Fairbairn, and Usher (Phillips being absent), in which he pointed out to them " that though in an ordinary way a man may sign as witness to another man's signature, without reference to the tenor or contents of the document, yet in the case of a letter written for an illiterate native, those who append their names can hardly escape a certain measure of responsibility for what is written, especially where interpretation comes into the case."

"And that as to this particular matter, without attempting to fix upon them any specific charge, and without entering into any discussion of the questions raised in this letter, his advice to them would be in future to abstain from any controversy which might hereafter cause a stumbling-block in the way of a fair and peaceful adjustment of relations between the Matabele and the powerful interests desirous of working minerals in that country. . . . There is quite enough strong and respectable evidence that the Chief knew perfectly well what he was about when he signed that concession to Mr. Rudd, that this repudiation of it is an afterthought, and that the assertions about Mr. Maguire having clandestinely left the country are untrue."

It may be also stated here that the following letter appeared in the Cape press :—

SIR,—In reference to certain reports which have recently appeared in the newspapers of events connected with gold concessions in Matabeleland, we wish to say that in any help which the Rev. C. D. Helm has given to strangers and others, by way of interpretation, he has in no wise forfeited our esteem and confidence.

Of his abilities to interpret, we believe no reasonable person competent to judge can entertain a doubt. Difference of opinion may exist between closest friends without any loss of mutual respect, and this is no doubt difficult for the native mind (and other minds akin) to understand, but it is, nevertheless, a mere truism. Mr. Helm has ever been ready to help anyone in need of an interpreter in anything reasonable, though not at all anxious to undertake an office not

T

always pleasant. He has never sought or accepted remuneration for any assistance which he has thus been able to render.

We ask you to be good enough to give this note space in your paper, inasmuch as you have already inserted reports, to a greater or less extent false, calculated to injure Mr. Helm in the eyes of those who do not know him, and of those who are ever ready to believe anything to the discredit of a missionary.

We are, &c.,

W. A. ELLIOTT, } London
BOWEN REES, } Missionary
D. CARNEGIE, } Society.

Matabeleland, July 4, 1889.

Leaving this matter at this point for the present, I may return to the negotiations with the Colonial Office for the Charter. Lord Salisbury had expressed his concurrence with the view of Lord Knutsford that Lord Gifford's proposal deserved consideration, and on June 1st, 1889, Mr. Rhodes, who was then about to return to South Africa, addressed another letter to the Colonial Office in these terms :—

It is within your knowledge that the holders of the concession obtained by Messrs. Rudd, Maguire, and Thompson, have arranged with the majority of the other persons claiming interests in Matabeleland, and that the amalgamated Company intends to proceed forthwith with the opening up of that country, having due regard to the sensibilities of the Matabele nation, and the necessity of extreme caution in the gradual development of their enterprise. I would suggest, for the consideration of Her Majesty's Government, that an officer should be appointed at an early date to reside in that country. This officer should be under the Deputy Commissioner at Vryburg and the High Commissioner at Cape Town, and should be instructed to advise Lo Bengula, and give to the Company moral support so far as this can be done without entailing on Her Majesty's Government any responsibility or expense. In return for this I would offer, on behalf of the Company, to pay for the immediate construction of a telegraph from Mafeking through the Protectorate *viâ* the new Police Camp at Palachwe to Tati, and also to give a contribution to Her Majesty's Government which would be sufficient to cover all expenses of the supervision of Matabeleland. The construction of the telegraph would certainly cost between £35,000 and £50,000, and the expense of supervision would probably amount to £4000 a year, as follows :—

Resident	..	..	..	£1000
Contingencies ..	..	..	..	500
Escort and travelling expenses		..		2000
Telegraph clerks at Palachwe and Tati				500
				£4000

I do not think that it would be desirable that the Resident or his establishment should be in any way connected with the Company, as it would be better that they should be appointed and paid by Her Majesty's Government, and that the telegraph should in like manner be constructed and worked by the officers of the British Bechuanaland Government. With a view, therefore, of carrying out these proposals, and pending the decision of Her Majesty's Government as to the granting of a charter, I offer, on behalf of the Company, to pay to Her Majesty's Government a capital sum of £30,000 for the construction of the line of telegraph, and a contribution of £4000 per annum to be paid quarterly in advance for the maintenance of an officer in that country.

Lord Knutsford forwarded this letter to Lord Salisbury, intimating at the same time Sir Hercules Robinson's approval of the proposals " as affording a safe and efficient means of providing for the more pressing requirements of the case pending the consideration of the application for a Charter." In this opinion Lord Salisbury agreed, and on Mr. Rhodes being so informed he expressed his readiness, on behalf of the Company, to hand over to the Government the sum of £30,000, as well as £1000, and to cause the future payments of £1000 to be made at the commencement of each quarter as they became due. Further correspondence ensued between the Colonial and Foreign Offices, of which it is, perhaps, only necessary to notice one letter containing a fuller expression of Lord Knutsford's opinion regarding the Charter. His Lordship asks the Foreign Office (June 28, 1889) " whether, subject to such alterations in detail as may be required, Lord Salisbury concurs with Lord Knutsford in thinking that the Company may be informed that Her Majesty will be advised to grant a Charter." He goes on to say :—

Lord Salisbury will observe that the Charter, as drafted, will incorporate the Company for the purpose, in the first instance, of trading, and working the various concessions which have been or may be obtained, and will empower the Company, if and when it acquires from the Native Chiefs grants of territory or powers of government, to assume such functions of Government as Her Majesty may think desirable for it to undertake. Lord Knutsford presumes that it will be thought advisable eventually to consult Mr. R. S. Wright as to the details of the draft, if it is decided to proceed with it, but as Mr. C. J. Rhodes, who is principally responsible for the proposals and proceedings of the suggested Company, is obliged to leave for South Africa in a few days, it is desirable, if possible, to inform him at an early date whether Her Majesty's Government are prepared to advise Her Majesty to grant a Charter, if satisfied of the stability of the Company, and if the conditions upon which it is to be granted are agreed to.

A week later (July 5) Lord Salisbury signified his assent to the course proposed, and Lord Gifford, as Chairman of the Exploring Company, was requested to forward the petition praying for the Charter. The body of the petition, " To the Queen's Most Excellent Majesty in Council," will be found in the first clauses of the Charter. It concluded :

Your Majesty's Petitioners therefore most humbly pray that Your Majesty will be graciously pleased to grant them Your Majesty's Royal Charter of Incorporation, by the name or title of the " British South Africa Company," or such other name or title as to Your Majesty may seem fit, with limited liability, and with such other powers and privileges as to Your Majesty may seem fit, and as may enable Your Majesty's Petitioners to accept the full benefit of such concessions, agreements, grants and treaties as in this Petition mentioned, and of such further concessions, agreements, grants, and treaties as they may be enabled to obtain, and all rights and interests, authorities and powers necessary for the purposes of government, administration, preservation of public order and commerce in the said territories and regions, and all such other powers, privileges and authorities in relation to the premises as to Your Majesty may seem meet, subject nevertheless to such conditions as Your Majesty may think fit to impose.

And your Majesty's Petitioners will ever pray, &c.

The following is the

FULL TEXT OF THE CHARTER,

granted on October 15, 1889 :—

VICTORIA by the Grace of God, of the United Kingdom of Great Britain and Ireland, Queen, Defender of the Faith.

To all of whom these presents shall come, Greeting :

WHEREAS a Humble Petition has been presented to Us in Our Council by THE MOST NOBLE JAMES DUKE OF ABERCORN Companion of the Most Honourable Order of the Bath ; THE MOST NOBLE ALEXANDER WILLIAM GEORGE DUKE OF FIFE Knight of the Most Ancient and Most Noble Order of the Thistle, Privy Councillor ; THE RIGHT HONOURABLE EDRIC FREDERICK LORD GIFFORD, V.C. ; CECIL JOHN RHODES, of Kimberley, in the Cape Colony, Member of the Executive Council and of the House of Assembly of the Colony of the Cape of Good Hope ; ALFRED BEIT, of 29, Holborn Viaduct, London, Merchant ; ALBERT HENRY GEORGE GREY, of Howick, Northumberland, ESQUIRE ; and GEORGE CAWSTON, of 18, Lennox Gardens, London, ESQUIRE, Barrister-at-Law.

AND WHEREAS the said Petition states amongst other things :—

That the Petitioners and others are associated for the purpose of forming a Company or Association, to be incorporated, if to Us should seem fit, for the objects in the said Petition set forth, under the corporate name of the British South Africa Company.

That the existence of a powerful British Company, controlled by those of Our subjects in whom we have confidence, and having its principal field of operations in that region of South Africa lying to the north of Bechuanaland and to the west of Portuguese East Africa, would be advantageous to the commercial and other interests of Our subjects in the United Kingdom and in Our Colonies.

That the Petitioners desire to carry into effect divers concessions and agreements which have been made by certain of the chiefs and tribes inhabiting the said region, and such other concessions agreements grants and treaties as the Petitioners may hereafter obtain within the said region or elsewhere in Africa, with the view of promoting trade commerce civilisation and good government (including the regulation of liquor traffic with the natives) in the territories which are or may be comprised or referred to in such concessions agreements grants and treaties as aforesaid.

That the Petitioners believe that if the said concessions agreements grants and treaties can be carried into effect, the condition of the natives inhabiting the said territories will be materially improved and their civilisation advanced, and an organization established which will tend to the suppression of the slave trade in the said territories, and to the opening up of the said territories to the immigration of Europeans, and to the lawful trade and commerce of Our subjects and of other nations.

That the success of the enterprise in which the Petitioners are engaged would be greatly advanced if it should seem fit to Us to grant them Our Royal Charter of incorporation as a British Company under the said name or title, or such other name or title, and with such powers, as to Us may seem fit for the purpose of more effectually carrying into effect the objects aforesaid.

That large sums of money have been subscribed for the purposes of the intended Company by the Petitioners and others, who are prepared also to subscribe or to procure such further sums as may hereafter be found requisite for the development of the said enterprise, in the event of Our being pleased to grant to them Our Royal Charter of incorporation as aforesaid.

NOW, THEREFORE, We having taken the said Petition into Our Royal consideration in Our Council, and being satisfied that the intentions of the Petitioners are praiseworthy and deserve encouragement, and that the enterprise in the Petition described may be productive of the benefits set forth therein, by Our Prerogative Royal and of Our especial grace, certain knowledge and mere motion, have constituted erected and incorporated, and by this Our Charter for Us and Our Heirs and Royal successors do constitute erect and incorporate into one body politic and corporate by the name of The British South Africa Company the said James Duke of Abercorn, Alexander William George Duke of Fife, |Edric Frederick Lord Gifford, Cecil John Rhodes, Alfred Beit, Albert Henry George Grey and George Cawston, and such other persons and such bodies as from time to time become and are members of the body politic and corporate by these present constituted, erected and incorporated with perpetual succession and a common seal, with power to break alter or renew the same at discretion, and with the further authorities powers and privileges conferred, and subject to the conditions imposed by this Our Charter: And We do hereby accordingly will ordain, give, grant, constitute, appoint and declare as follows (that is to say) :—

1. The principal field of the operations of The British South Africa Company (in this Our Charter referred to as "the Company") shall be the region of South Africa lying immediately to the north of British Bechuanaland, and to the north and west of the South African Republic, and to the west of the Portuguese Dominions.

2. The Company is hereby authorised and empowered to hold, use and retain for the purposes of the Company and on the terms of this Our Charter, the full benefit of the concessions and agreements made as aforesaid, so far as they are valid, or any of them, and all interests, authorities and powers comprised or referred to in the said concessions and agreements. Provided always that nothing herein contained shall prejudice or affect any other valid and subsisting concessions or agreements which may have been made by any of the chiefs or tribes aforesaid. And in particular nothing herein contained

shall prejudice or affect certain concessions granted in and subsequent to the year 1880, relating to the territory usually known as the District of the Tati, nor shall anything herein contained be construed as giving any jurisdiction, administrative or otherwise, within the said District of the Tati, the limits of which District area as follows, viz.: from the place where the Shasi River rises to its junction with the Tati and Ramaquaban Rivers, thence along the Ramaquaban River to where it rises, and thence along the watershed of those rivers.

3. The Company is hereby further authorised and empowered, subject to the approval of one of Our Principal Secretaries of State (herein referred to as " Our Secretary of State "), from time to time, to acquire by any concession agreement grant or treaty, all or any rights interests authorities jurisdictions and powers of any kind or nature whatever, including powers necessary for the purposes of government, and the preservation of public order in or for the protection of territories, lands, or property, comprised or referred to in the concessions and agreements made as aforesaid or affecting other territories, lands, or property in Africa, or the inhabitants thereof, and to hold, use and exercise such territories, lands, property, rights, interests, authorities, jurisdictions and powers respectively for the purposes of the Company and on the terms of this Our Charter.

4. Provided that no powers of government or administration shall be exercised under or in relation to any such last-mentioned concession agreement grant or treaty, until a copy of such concession agreement grant or treaty in such form and with such maps or particulars as Our Secretary of State approves verified as he requires, has been transmitted to him, and he has signified his approval thereof either absolutely or subject to any conditions or reservations. And provided also that no rights, interests, authorities, jurisdictions or powers of any description shall be acquired by Company within the said District of the Tati as hereinbefore described without the previous consent in writing of the owners for the time being of the Concessions above referred to relating to the said District, and the approval of our Secretary of State.

5. The Company shall be bound by and shall fulfil all and singular the stipulations on its part contained in any such concession agreement grant or treaty as aforesaid, subject to any subsequent agreement affecting those stipulations approved by Our Secretary of State.

6. The Company shall always be and remain British in character and domicile, and shall have its principal office in Great Britain, and the Company's principal representative in South Africa, and the Directors shall always be natural born British subjects or persons who have been naturalised as British subjects by or under an Act of Parliament of our United Kingdom ; but this Article shall not disqualify any person nominated a Director by this Our Charter, or any person whose election as a Director shall have been approved by Our Secretary of State, from acting in that capacity.

7. In case at any time any difference arises between any chief or tribe inhabiting any of the territories aforesaid and the Company, that difference shall, if Our Secretary of State so require, be submitted by the Company to him for his decision, and the Company shall act in accordance with such decision.

8. If at any time Our Secretary of State thinks fit to dissent from or object to any of the dealings of the Company with any

foreign power and to make known to the Company any suggestion founded on that dissent or objection, the Company shall act in accordance with such suggestion.

9. If at any time Our Secretary of State thinks fit to object to the exercise by the Company of any authority power or right within any part of the territories aforesaid, on the ground of there being an adverse claim to or in respect of that part, the Company shall defer to that objection until such time as any such claim has been withdrawn or finally dealt with or settled by Our Secretary of State.

10. The Company shall to the best of its ability preserve peace and order in such ways and manners as it shall consider necessary, and may with that object make ordinances (to be approved by Our Secretary of State) and may establish and maintain a force of police.

11. The Company shall to the best of its ability discourage and, so far as may be practicable, abolish by degrees, any system of slave trade or domestic servitude in the territories aforesaid.

12. The Company shall regulate the traffic in spirits and other intoxicating liquors within the territories aforesaid, so as, as far as practicable, to prevent the sale of any spirits or other intoxicating liquor to any natives.

13. The Company as such, or its officers as such, shall not in any way interfere with the religion of any class or tribe of the peoples of the territories aforesaid or of any of the inhabitants thereof, except so far as may be necessary in the interests of humanity and all forms of religious worship or religious ordinances may be exercised within the said territories and no hindrance shall be offered thereto except as aforesaid.

14. In the administration of justice to the said peoples or inhabitants, careful regard shall always be had to the customs and laws of the class or tribe or nation to which the parties respectively belong, especially with respect to the holding, possession, transfer and disposition of lands and goods and testate or intestate succession thereto, and marriage divorce and legitimacy and other rights of property and personal rights, but subject to any British laws which may be in force in any of the territories aforesaid, and applicable to the peoples or inhabitants thereof.

15. If at any time Our Secretary of State thinks fit to dissent from or object to any part of the proceedings or system of the Company relative to the peoples of the territories aforesaid or to any of the inhabitants thereof, in respect of slavery or religion or the administration of justice, or any other matter, he shall make known to the Company his dissent or objection, and the Company shall act in accordance with his directions duly signified.

16. In the event of the Company acquiring any harbour or harbours, the Company shall freely afford all facilities for or to Our ships therein without payment except reasonable charges for work done or services rendered or materials or things supplied.

17. The Company shall furnish annually to Our Secretary of State, as soon as conveniently may be after the close of the financial year, accounts of its expenditure for administrative purposes and of all sums received by it by way of public revenue, as distinguished from its commercial profits during the financial year, together with a report as to its public proceedings and the condition of the territories within the sphere of its operations. The Company shall also

on or before the commencement of each financial year furnish to Our
Secretary of State an estimate of its expenditure for administrative
purposes, and of its public revenue (as above defined) for the ensuing
year.   The Company shall in addition from time to time furnish to
Our Secretary of State any reports, accounts or information with
which he may require to be furnished.

18.   The several officers of the Company shall, subject to the rules
of official subordination and to any regulations that may be agreed
upon, communicate freely with Our High Commissioner in South
Africa and any others Our officers, who may be stationed within any
of the territories aforesaid, and shall pay due regard to any requirements suggestions or requests which the said High Commissioner or
other officers shall make to them or any of them and the Company
shall be bound to enforce the observance of this Article.

19.   The Company may hoist and use on its buildings and elsewhere in the territories aforesaid, and on its vessels, such distinctive
flag indicating the British character of the Company as Our Secretary of State and the Lords Commissioners of the Admiralty shall
from time to time approve.

20.   Nothing in this Our Charter shall be deemed to authorise the
Company to set up or grant any monopoly of trade ; provided that
the establishment of or the grant of concessions for banks, railways,
tramways, docks, telegraphs, waterworks, or any other similar undertakings or the establishment of any system of patent or copyright
approved by Our Secretary of State, shall not be deemed monopolies
for this purpose.   The Company shall not, either directly or indirectly, hinder any Company or persons who now are or hereafter
may be lawfully and peaceably carrying on any business concern or
venture within the said District of the Tati hereinbefore described,
but shall by permitting and facilitating transit by every lawful
means to and from the District of the Tati across its own territories
or where it has jurisdiction in that behalf and by all other reasonable and lawful means encourage assist and protect all British subjects who now are or hereafter may be lawfully and peaceably engaged in the prosecution of a lawful enterprise within the said
District of the Tati.

21.   For the preservation of elephants and other game, the Company may make such other regulations and (notwithstanding
anything hereinbefore contained) may impose such licence duties on
the killing or taking of elephants or other game as they may think
fit : Provided that nothing in such regulations shall extend to
diminish or interfere with any hunting rights which may have been
or may hereafter be reserved to any native chiefs or tribes by treaty,
save so far as any such regulations may relate to the establishment
and enforcement of a close season.

22.   The Company shall be subject to and shall perform and
undertake all the obligations contained in or undertaken by Ourselves
under any treaty agreement or arrangement between Ourselves and
any other State or Power whether already made or hereafter to be
made.   In all matters relating to the observance of this Article, or
to the exercise within the Company's territories for the time being,
of any jurisdiction exercisable by Us under the Foreign Jurisdiction
Acts, the Company shall conform to and observe and carry out all
such directions as may from time to time be given in that behalf by
Our Secretary of State, and the Company shall appoint all necessary
officers to perform such duties, and shall provide such Courts and

other requisites as may from time to time be necessary for the administration of justice.

23. The original share capital of the Company shall be £1,000,000 divided into 1,000,000 shares of £1 each.

24. The Company is hereby further specially authorized and empowered for the purposes of this Our Charter from time to time—

(I) To issue shares of different classes or descriptions, to increase the share capital of the Company, and to borrow moneys by debentures or other obligations.

(II) To acquire and hold, and to charter or otherwise deal with, steam vessels and other vessels.

(III) To establish or authorize banking companies and other companies, and undertakings or associations of every description, for purposes consistent with the provisions of this Our Charter.

(IV) To make and maintain roads railways telegraphs harbours and any other works which may tend to the development or improvement of the territories of the Company.

(V) To carry on mining and other industries, and to make concessions of mining forestal or other rights.

(VI) To improve develop clear plant and irrigate and cultivate any lands included within the territories of the Company.

(VII) To settle any such territories lands and as aforesaid, and to aid and promote immigration.

(VIII) To grant lands for terms of years or in perpetuity, and either absolutely, or by way of mortgage or otherwise.

(IX) To make loans or contributions of money or money's worth, for promoting any of the objects of the Company.

(X) To acquire and hold personal property.

(XI) To acquire and hold (without license in mortmain or other authority than this Our Charter) lands in the United Kingdom, not exceeding five acres in all, at any one time for the purposes of the offices and business of the Company, and (subject to any local law) lands in any of Our Colonies or Possessions and elsewhere, convenient for carrying on the management of the affairs of the Company, and to dispose from time to time of any such lands when not required for that purpose.

(XII) To carry on any lawful commerce, trade, pursuit, business, operations, or dealing whatsoever in connection with the objects of the Company.

(XIII) To establish and maintain agencies in Our Colonies and Possessions, and elsewhere.

(XIV) To sue and be sued by the Company's name of incorporation, as well in Our Courts in Our United Kingdom, or in Our Courts in Our Colonies or Possessions, or in Our Courts in Foreign countries or elsewhere.

(XV) To do all lawful things incidental or conducive to the exercise or enjoyment of the rights interests, authorities and powers of the Company in this Our Charter expressed or referred to, or any of them.

25. Within one year after the date of this Our Charter, or such extended period as may be certified by Our Secretary of State, there shall be executed by the Members of the Company for the time being a Deed of Settlement, providing so far as necessary for—

(I) The further definition of the objects and purposes of the Company.

(II) The classes or descriptions of shares into which the capital of the Company is divided, and the calls to be made in respect thereof, and the terms and conditions of Membership of the Company.

(III) The division and distribution of profits.

(IV) General Meetings of the Company; the appointment by Our Secretary of State (if so required by him) of an Official Director, and the number qualification appointment remuneration rotation removal and powers of Directors of the Company, and of other officers of the Company.

(V) The registration of Members of the Company, and the transfer of shares in the capital of the Company.

(VI) The preparation of annual accounts to be submitted to the Members at a General Meeting.

(VII) The audit of those accounts by independent auditors.

(VIII) The making of bye-laws.

(IX) The making and using of official seals of the Company.

(X) The constitution and regulation of Committees or Local Boards of Management.

(XI) The making and execution of supplementary deeds of settlement.

(XII) The winding up (in case of need) of the Company's affairs.

(XIII) The government and regulation of the Company and of its affairs.

(XIV) Any other matters usual or proper to be provided for in respect of a chartered company.

26. The Deed of Settlement shall, before the execution thereof, be submitted to and approved by the Lords of Our Council, and a certificate of their approval thereof, signed by the Clerk of Our Council, shall be endorsed on this Our Charter, and be conclusive evidence of such approval, and on the Deed of Settlement, and such Deed of Settlement shall take effect from the date of such approval, and shall be binding upon the Company, its Members, Officers and Servants, and for all other purposes whatsoever.

27. The provisions of the Deed of Settlement or of any supplementary Deed for the time being in force, may be from time to time repealed, varied or added to by a supplementary Deed, made and executed in such manner as the Deed of Settlement prescribes. Provided that the provisions of any such Deed relative to the Official Director shall not be repealed, varied or added to without the express approval of Our Secretary of State.

28. The Members of the Company shall be individually liable for the debts contracts engagements and liabilities of the Company to the extent only of the amount, if any, for the time being unpaid on the shares held by them respectively.

29. Until such Deed of Settlement as aforesaid takes effect the said James Duke of Abercorn shall be the President; the said Alexander William George Duke of Fife, shall be Vice-President; and the said Edric Frederick Lord Gifford, Cecil John Rhodes, Alfred Beit, Albert Henry George Grey, and George Cawston, shall be the Directors of the Company; and may on behalf of the Company do all things necessary or proper to be done under this Our Charter by or on behalf of the Company: Provided always that, notwithstanding anything contained in the Deed of Settlement of the Company, the said James Duke of Abercorn, Alexander William George Duke of Fife, and Albert Henry George Grey, shall not be

subject to retire from office in accordance with its provisions but shall be and remain Directors of the Company until death, incapacity to act, or resignation, as the case may be.

30. And We do further will ordain and declare that this Our Charter shall be acknowledged by Our Governors and Our naval and military officers and Our consuls, and Our other officers in Our colonies and possessions, and on the high seas, and elsewhere, and they shall severally give full force and effect to this Our Charter, and shall recognise and be in all things aiding to the Company and its Officers.

31. And We do further will, ordain and declare that this Our Charter shall be taken construed and adjudged in the most favourable and beneficial sense for, and to the best advantage of the Company as well in Our Courts in Our United Kingdom, and in Our Courts in Our colonies or possessions, and in Our courts in foreign countries or elsewhere, notwithstanding that there may appear to be in this Our Charter any non-recital, mis-recital, uncertainty or imperfection.

32. And We do further will ordain and declare that this Our Charter shall subsist and continue valid, notwithstanding any lawful change in the name of the Company or in the Deed of Settlement thereof, such change being made with the previous approval of Our Secretary of State signified under his hand.

33. And we do further will, ordain and declare that it shall be lawful for Us Our heirs and successors and We do hereby expressly reserve to Ourselves Our heirs and successors the right and power by writing under the Great Seal of the United Kingdom at the end of 25 years from the date of this Our Charter, and at the end of every succeeding period of ten years, to add to alter or repeal any of the provisions of this Our Charter or to enact other provisions in substitution for or in addition to any of its existing provisions. Provided that the right and power thus reserved shall be exercised only in relation to so much of this Our Charter as relates to administrative and public matters. And We do further expressly reserve to Ourselves, Our heirs and successors the right to take over any buildings or works belonging to the Company, and used exclusively or mainly for administrative or public purposes on payment to the Company of such reasonable compensation as may be agreed, or as failing agreement may be settled by the Commissioners of Our Treasury. And We do further appoint direct and declare that any such writing under the said Great Seal shall have full effect, and be binding upon the Company, its members, officers and servants, and all other persons, and shall be of the same force, effect, and validity as if its provisions had been part of and contained in these presents.

34. Provided always and we do further declare that nothing in this Our Charter shall be deemed or taken in any wise to limit or restrict the exercise of any of Our rights or powers with reference to the protection of any territories or with reference to the government thereof should we see fit to include the same within Our dominions.

35. And we do lastly will, ordain and declare, without prejudice to any power to repeal this Our Charter by law belonging to Us Our heirs and successors, or to any of Our court, ministers or officers independently of this present declaration and reservation, that in case at any time it is made to appear to Us in Our Council that the Company has substantially failed to observe and conform to the provisions of this Our Charter, or that the Company is not exercising its

powers under the concessions agreements grants and treaties aforesaid, so as to advance the interests which the Petitioners have represented to Us to be likely to be advanced by the grant of this Our Charter, it shall be lawful for Us Our heirs and successors, and we do hereby expressly reserve and take to Ourselves Our heirs and successors the right and power by writing under the Great Seal of Our United Kingdom to revoke this Our Charter, and to revoke and annul the privileges powers and rights hereby granted to the Company.

In Witness whereof We have caused these Our Letters to be made Patent.

Witness Ourself at Westminster, the 29th day of October, in the fifty-third year of Our reign.

By warrant under the Queen's Sign Manual.

MUIR MACKENZIE.

On 22nd October a communication was sent from the Colonial Office to Lord Gifford, stating that Lord Knutsford " understands you have authority to pay over the sum of £30,000, offered by Mr. Cecil Rhodes, on behalf of the British South Africa Company, to the Government of British Bechuanaland for the extension of the telegraph through the Protectorate," and also that the Crown Agents had been " instructed to take immediate steps for obtaining the materials for the telegraphs." Lord Gifford replied on the 25th October, stating that that day a cheque for £30,000 had been forwarded to the Crown Agents for the construction of the telegraph line. As setting forth the manner in which the Charter was viewed by the Imperial Government, I reproduce a despatch from Lord Knutsford to Sir Henry Loch (who had become Governor of the Cape Colony and High Commissioner for South Africa, during the progress of the negotiations) :—

Downing Street, November 14, 1889.

SIR,—As you are already aware, the petition some time ago presented to Her Majesty by the Duke of Abercorn, the Duke of Fife, Lord Gifford, Mr. C. J. Rhodes, Mr. Albert Grey, Mr. Alfred Beit, and Mr. George Cawston, praying for the grant to them of a Charter, has been complied with, and the Queen has given direction for the incorporation of their Company by Her Majesty's Letters Patent under the name of the " British South Africa Company," of which the principal field of operation will be in the territories north of Bechuanaland, and west of Portuguese East Africa. . . . .

3. The Charter is framed in accordance with the precedents, so far as they are applicable, of the British North Borneo Company's, the Royal Niger Company's and the British Imperial East African Company's charters, and in the first clause the principal field of the Company's

operations has been defined somewhat more precisely than in the petition, and is declared to include the region of South Africa lying immediately to the north of British Bechuanaland, and to the north and west of the South African Republic, and to the west of the Portuguese Dominions.

4. It is to be observed that this definition does not supersede or affect the Protectorate of Her Majesty over the country north of British Bechuanaland, and south of the 22nd parallel of south latitude; although the Company is empowered to acquire (subject to the approval of the Secretary of State) from the lawful rulers, either within or beyond that Protectorate, certain powers of government or administration whereby it is anticipated that hereafter Her Majesty's Government may be much assisted in the control and protection of the territories lying within the present British Protectorate.

5. The Company is further authorised to have the benefit of, and to carry out, such valid concessions as it has already acquired, or may acquire ; and you will perceive that in the second clause besides a general recognition of any other valid and subsisting concessions or agreements, a special restriction has been inserted as to the Tati district, the holders of what is called the Tati concession having made a request, which appeared to Her Majesty's Government to be well founded, and in accordance with the concession granted by Lo Bengula to Mr. Rudd and others, for the insertion of words saving their claims, and excluding them from the operations of the Chartered Company. In the 20th clause further provisions will be found safeguarding the interests of persons lawfully and peacefully carrying on business in the Tati district.

6. Clauses 3 and 4 are those to which I referred in paragraph 4 of this despatch as empowering the Company, subject to the approval of the Secretary of State, to acquire further authorities and powers, including powers of government and administration either within or beyond the territories affected by the concessions or agreements recognised by the Charter, and clause 6 following the precedents of previous chartered companies, provides that the Company shall be British in character, and that its Directors and principal representative shall be natural-born British subjects, but an exception is made in favour of any Director nominated in the Charter itself (Mr. Alfred Beit not being a British subject), and of any alien Director whose future election may be approved by the Secretary of State.

7. Clauses 8, 9, and 15 secure to the Secretary of State the power of restraining the acts of the Company if they should appear to him inimical to public interests, and clause 10 enables the Company to enact ordinances, and to maintain a police force by the Company. Provision is made in clause 11 for the discouragement and, so far as practicable, the abolition of slave trade or domestic servitude, and in clause 12 for the regulation of the liquor traffic, and, as far as practicable, for the prevention of the sale of liquor to natives within the Company's territories. Under clause 13 the Company is bound not to interfere with the religions of the natives, except so far as may be necessary in the interests of humanity, and under clause 14 it is required in the administration of justice to have regard to native customs and laws.

8. You will observe in clause 18 of the draft Charter that the Company's officers are to communicate freely with the High Commissioner and with Her Majesty's officers stationed in their territories, and it will be desirable that you should consider, in conjunction with Mr. Rhodes, what rules should be framed in accordance with this clause of the Charter for the conduct of the correspondence in question. These rules,

when drafted, should be sent home for my consideration, and will be communicated by me, with such modifications, if any, as may seem desirable, to the Company for its guidance. In the meantime I request that you will give such instructions as may ensure that the representatives of the Company shall receive all proper support and assistance from Her Majesty's officers in British Bechuanaland and the Protectorate.

9. I desire to call your special attention to clauses 33, 34, and 35, relating to the powers reserved by the Crown in the future over the rights of the Company and the Charter itself.

Clause 33 provides that at the end of the first 25 years, and at the end of every subsequent period of 10 years, the Crown shall have the right of repealing or varying any of those provisions of the Charter which relate to administrative and public matters. Clause 34 saves in terms the rights of the Crown to declare protectorates over or to annex any territory, and clause 35 reserves the right to revoke the Charter at any time in case it shall appear to the Crown that the Company is not acting in conformity with the Charter, or it is not promoting the objects which its promoters profess to have in view.

The last of these clauses is taken from previous Charters, but the principle of the 33rd clause, which is obviously of much importance, has not, I believe, been adopted in previous cases. It precludes any objection which might otherwise be made that the grant of a Charter locks up indefinitely a large portion of South Africa in the hands of a commercial association.

The Queen can, of course, at any time annex or declare a protectorate over any part of the territory within which the Company operates, and in the absence of any paramount necessity for such annexation or protectorate, or of the failure, or misconduct of the Company, security of tenure is granted to the Company for the limited time of 25 years, which is deemed by Her Majesty's Government the shortest period within which the Company can be expected to develop and perfect the public part of its enterprise; whilst there is reserved to the Government of the day at the end of that time, and at every succeeding period of ten years, the right of considering, in the interests of the Empire generally, and of South Africa in particular, how far the administrative and public powers of the Company should be continued.

10. I request that you will communicate Her Majesty's Order in Council and this despatch to your Ministers, expressing to them the hope of Her Majesty's Government that the experiment which is now being tried is one the success of which they will be disposed to advance by all proper means, as affording, perhaps, the best prospects of developing the interior of South Africa in a manner advantageous to all interests.

It is desirable that the Charter should be published in the Cape Government *Gazette*, and you will give instructions for its publication, at such time as you may see fit, in the Bechuanaland Government *Gazette*. I shall be obliged by your considering also the propriety of communicating the Charter at an early date to the Governments of the two Republics.

I have, &c.,
(Signed)   KNUTSFORD.

———

The following was the Order in Council referred to in Clause 9 of the foregoing dispatch :—

At the Court at Balmoral, the 15th day of October, 1889.
Present :
The Queen's Most Excellent Majesty in Council.

Whereas there was this day read at the Board a Report of a Committee of the Lords of Her Majesty's Most Honourable Privy Council, dated the 14th day of October, 1889, in the words following, viz. :—

" Your Majesty having been pleased by Your Order of the 23rd of July, 1889, to refer unto this Committee a Petition of the Most Noble the Duke of Abercorn and others, praying for the grant of a Charter of Incorporation by the name or title of the ' British South Africa Company ' : The Lords of the Committee, in obedience to Your Majesty's said Order of Reference, have this day taken the said Petition into consideration, and do agree humbly to report, as their opinion, to Your Majesty that a Charter may be granted by Your Majesty in terms of the Draft hitherto annexed."

Her Majesty, having taken into consideration the said Report, and the Draft Charter accompanying it, was pleased, by and with the advice of Her Privy Council, to approve thereof, and to order, as it is hereby ordered, that the Right Honourable Henry Matthews, one of Her Majesty's Principal Secretaries of State, do cause a Warrant to be prepared for Her Majesty's Royal Signature for passing under the Great Seal of the United Kingdom a Charter in conformity with the said Draft which is hereunto annexed.

C. L. PEEL.

On November 15, 1889, the grant of the Charter was announced to Lo Bengula by a further message from Lord Knutsford, sent by the special embassy previously referred to, and conveyed through Mr. Moffat, who was enjoined by his lordship to advise Lo Bengula " to give his confidence and support to the Company and to its representatives in Matabeleland."

The text of the message itself was as follows :—

I, LORD KNUTSFORD, one of the Queen's Principal Secretaries of State, am commanded by Her Majesty to send this further message to Lo Bengula. The Queen has kept in her mind the letter sent by Lo Bengula, and the message brought by Umshete and Babjaan in the beginning of this year, and she has now desired Mr. Moffat, whom she trusts, and whom Lo Bengula knows to be his true friend, to tell him what she has done for him and what she advises him to do.

2. Since the visit of Lo Bengula's envoys, the Queen has made the fullest inquiries into the particular circumstances of Matabeleland, and understands the trouble caused to Lo Bengula by different parties of white men coming to his country to look for gold ; but wherever gold is, or wherever it is reported to be, there it is impossible for him to exclude white men, and, therefore, the wisest and safest course for him to adopt, and that which will give least trouble to himself and his tribe is to agree, not with one or two white men separately, but with one approved body of white men, who will consult Lo Bengula's wishes and arrange where white people are to dig, and who will be responsible to the Chief for any annoyance or trouble caused to himself or his people. If he does not agree with one set of men there will be endless disputes among the white men, and he will have all his time taken up in deciding their quarrels.

3. The Queen, therefore, approves of the concessions made by Lo Bengula to some white men who were represented in his country by Messrs.

Rudd, Maguire, and Thompson. The Queen has caused inquiry to be made respecting these persons, and is satisfied that they are men who will fulfil their undertakings, and who may be trusted to carry out the working for gold in the Chief's country without molesting his people, or in any way interfering with their kraals, gardens, or cattle. And, as some of the Queen's highest and most trusted subjects have joined themselves with those to whom Lo Bengula gave his concessions, the Queen now thinks Lo Bengula is acting wisely in carrying out his agreement with these persons, and hopes that he will allow them to conduct their mining operations without interference or molestation from his subjects.

4. The Queen understands that Lo Bengula does not like deciding disputes among white men or assuming jurisdiction over them. This is very wise, as these disputes would take up much time, and Lo Bengula cannot understand the laws and customs of white people; but it is not well to have people in his country who are subject to no law, therefore the Queen thinks Lo Bengula would be wise to intrust to that body of white men, of whom Mr. Jamieson is now the principal representative in Matabeleland, the duty of deciding disputes and keeping the peace among white persons in his country.

5. In order to enable them to act lawfully and with full authority, the Queen has, by her Royal Charter, given to that body of men leave to undertake this duty, and will hold them responsible for their proper performances of such duty. Of course this must be as Lo Bengula likes, as he is King of the country, and no one can exercise jurisdiction in it without his permission; but it is believed that this will be very convenient for the Chief, and the Queen is informed that he has already made such an arrangement in the Tati district, by which he is there saved all trouble.

6. The Queen understands that Lo Bengula wishes to have some one from her residing with him. The Queen, therefore, has directed her trusted servant, Mr. Moffat, to stay with the Chief as long as he wishes. Mr. Moffat is, as Lo Bengula knows, a true friend to himself and the Matabele tribe, while he is also in the confidence of the Queen and will from time to time convey the Queen's words to the Chief, and the Chief should always listen to and believe Mr. Moffat's words.

(Signed) KNUTSFORD,
Her Majesty's Secretary of State for the Colonies.

Downing Street, November 15, 1889.

I have now traced the history of the inception of the British South Africa Company down to the point of the granting of the Charter. In a final letter from the Colonial Office to the Chartered Company, dated January 24, 1890, the progress of the negotiations is so admirably reviewed that I may be excused for quoting it at some length :—

. . . 2. It may be convenient to take this opportunity of recapitulating the steps by which the arrangement has reached its present stage. In the summer of 1888 negotiations were opened by "The Exploring Company, Limited," with this Department, and progressed so far that in April last that Company was requested by this Department to prepare for the consideration of Her Majesty's Government the draft of a concession upon a basis approved by the Secretary of State after considering the proposals of the Company proposed that it should be bound to construct a railway from Kimberley to Mafeking, in return for certain land grants, mining rights, and fiscal privileges.

3. In the meantime the formation of a Chartered Company which

should take over much of the work lying before the Exploring and other companies, was proposed by the Exploring Company and approved; and, in accordance with that Company's suggestions, contained in a letter dated April 30, 1889, the British South Africa Company was, when constituted, substituted for the Exploring Company, as the association with which the Government of British Bechuanaland would thenceforth deal in respect of this railway. In the course of the renewed negotiations the British South Africa Company expressed its willingness to accept, in substitution for some of the fiscal and mining privileges which the Exploring Company had previously desired to receive, a grant of 6000 square miles of vacant Crown land, with the mineral rights thereon, in the respect of the construction of the line to Vryburg, and a similar grant in respect of the extension to Mafeking, if such extension should be proceeded with. Lord Knutsford intimated his readiness to agree, as far as this Department can do so, to the proposed grant of 6000 square miles in respect of each section of the line; but explained to the Company that only a portion of the revenue resulting from the discovery of gold on any portion of the lands so granted could be surrendered to it.

4. The reason of this restriction is that the opening of a gold field involves new expenditure on the part of the Colonial Government for police, administration of justice, and sanitation. Under the existing law of British Bechuanaland, when gold is discovered on land held from the Crown by private parties, and a gold field or diggings opened, the proprietor of the farm is entitled to select 20 claims, and to receive a half share of the "licence moneys, rents, or royalties collected by the Government." Lord Knutsford is willing to recommend to the Treasury that the Company should enjoy these rights in respect of land in its own hands, or in respect of which it has reserved its gold rights as proprietor.

5. On October 29, 1889, Mr. Rhodes, on behalf of the British South Africa Company, entered into a provisional agreement with the Cape Government, by which the latter undertook to give the British South Africa Company all facilities for making the line up to the Colonial border, and undertook to work the whole line at the rates in force in the Colony, if so required by the Company; Mr. Rhodes on his side undertaking that the Company should continue the line to Vryburg, with a condition that the Colonial Government should have the right to acquire the line, or any portion thereof, at any time on terms defined in the agreement.

6. This agreement was, it is understood, ratified by the Chartered Company in December last; and the recent telegraphic correspondence shows that Mr. Rhodes and the Colonial Government have considerably advanced their negotiations. By the agreement of October 29 the Colonial Government was not bound to exercise the option of purchase, but it has now expressed itself as willing to purchase the Vryburg section in 1891; and in consideration of this undertaking on the part of the Cape Ministers, which would obviously set free a large amount of capital, Mr. Rhodes has consented that the Company should construct the second section of the line to Mafeking, receiving from the British Bechuanaland Government the further grant of 6000 square miles. Lord Knutsford has authorised Sir H. B. Loch to express his approval of these proposed arrangements.

7. There is a further arrangement between Mr. Rhodes and the Cape Government, by which the latter is to receive a share in the profits accruing from the first grant of 6000 square miles. Lord Knutsford does not think that this arrangement directly concerns Her Majesty's

U

Government, but he sees no objection to it. The railway conventions recently concluded with the Orange Free State by the Cape Colony and Natal have established the principle in South Africa of the government of a maritime colony undertaking the construction and working of a railway in territory beyond its political jurisdiction. The proposed arrangements in respect of the Bechuanaland Railway are merely an extension of this principle, and it is for the Colonial Government and the Company to settle the terms on which the work can be done to their mutual profit and satisfaction.

8. Her Majesty's Government necessarily reserve to themselves on behalf of British Bechuanaland, the right of approving the details of the arrangements between the Cape Government and the Company as far as they affect local rates in Bechuanaland, through rates, passenger fares, number of trains, and rate of speed ; but Lord Knutsford does not anticipate that the proposals which will in due course be submitted to him will be found on examination to be otherwise than fair and satisfactory.

9. With regard to the land grants, I am to observe that although their extent is large, they are justified by the advantages which must accrue to the province from the construction of the railway, and having regard to the cost of the line, the probable situation of the blocks, and the general price of land in the territory, Lord Knutsford will in due time be prepared to recommend the Treasury to assent to parting with this portion of the public domain, as a reasonable inducement to the Chartered Company to undertake the responsibility of this important work.

In the foregoing narrative I have purposely refrained from again touching on the financial details of the scheme of the British South Africa Company ; nor have I mentioned the various Companies (other than the Exploring Company and the Gold Fields of South Africa, Limited) which were called into existence for the purpose of carrying it out. These have been fully set forth in the previous Chapter, and will also be found referred to in Appendix A. It will be observed that, avoiding all controversial matter, I have confined my summary strictly to the letters and documents published in the Blue Books relating to the subject ; and I hope that the result is an interesting  résumé—reliable I claim that it undoubtedly is—of the origin of a Company which is destined to play a highly important part in the future of that grand united Empire upon which the sun never sets.

CHAPTER XIII.

THE CHARTERED COMPANY'S DIRECTORS.—BRIEF BIOGRAPHICAL SKETCHES.

BELIEVING that The British South Africa Company is destined to play a great part in the development of Africa, I have been at some pains to give in this work personally approved portraits of the first Directors of the Company.

HIS GRACE THE DUKE OF ABERCORN, C.B.

(President of The British South Africa Company)

U 2

I shall now supplement these counterfeit presentments with a few personal details of the various members of the Chartered Company's Directorate.

THE DUKE OF ABERCORN, C.B.

(*The President*).

His Grace James Hamilton, 2nd Duke of Abercorn, is one of the only two Irish Dukes in our peerage, and he is as popular in Ireland as he is out of it—which is saying a good deal for an Irish landlord in these times. Born in 1838, he succeeded in 1885 his father, the 1st Duke—a Viceroy of Ireland whose all-too-short rule is still looked back to with pleasure and pride by all shades of Irishmen. Educated at Harrow and Christ Church, Oxford, His Grace has been, and is, a *personâ gratâ* at Court, at which he filled the office of a Lord of the Bedchamber to the Prince of Wales for twenty years, becoming in 1886 Groom of the Stole. From 1860 to 1880 he (as Marquess of Hamilton) represented Donegal as a Conservative in the House of Commons, and he is now Lord Lieutenant of that county. By way of variety in his sixteen titles, he was created a C.B. in 1885, and a Privy Councillor in 1887, and it is generally believed that Lord Salisbury wished him to become Lord Lieutenant of Ireland in 1886. He is President of the Board of Directors of the British South Africa Company, and is a very regular attendant at its meetings. His Grace married in 1869 Lady Mary Anna Curzon, daughter of Earl Howe, and has five children.

THE DUKE OF FIFE, K.T.

(*The Vice-President*).

Alexander William George Duff, K.T., P.C., 1st Duke of Fife, is probably one of the happiest; as he certainly is one of the most fortunate, men in the kingdom. Born in 1849, he succeeded to his ancestral titles at the age of thirty, and ten years later married the charming daughter of a charming mother—H.R.H. Princess Louise of Wales, the eldest daughter of the Prince of Wales. His Grace is very wealthy, being a partner in the London banking firm of Sir Samuel Scott and Co., and needless to say he fills all the usual offices in the counties where he has estates—Lord Lieutenant of Elginshire; Deputy Lieutenant of Banff and Aberdeen; Hon. Colonel of the Banffshire Artillery Volunteers, Member of the Council of the Royal Duchy of Lancaster and Trustee of the Imperial Institute. The House of Commons knew him for five years as the Liberal Member for Elgin and Nairn, and at Court he has figured as Captain and Gold Stick of the Corps of Gentlemen-at-Arms, during which time His Grace represented the Home Office in the House of Lords.

HIS GRACE THE DUKE OF FIFE, K.T.

(*Vice-President of The British South Africa Company.*)

LORD GIFFORD, V.C.

The Right Hon. Edric Frederick Gifford, V.C., is a man of many parts. His prowess as a soldier is attested by the fact that he holds the " Blue Riband " of the Army—the Victoria Cross, gained during the Ashantee Expedition. He was formerly a Major in the " Duke of Cambridge's Own" (Middlesex Regt.), and was on the staff of Lord Wolseley (then Sir Garnet), Governor of Natal, 1874. Lord Gifford also took part in the Zulu war of 1879, for which he has the medal and clasp. From 1879 to 1880 his lordship was Colonial Secretary of Western Australia ; was a member of the Legislative Council of that Colony from 1880 to 1883, and was Colonial Secretary at Gibraltar from 1883 to 1888. Born in 1849, Lord Gifford, who succeeded his father, the 2nd Baron, in 1872, married in 1880

Miss Sophie Catherine Street, daughter of General John Alfred Street, C.B.

THE RIGHT HON. LORD GIFFORD, V.C.
(*Director of The British South Africa Company.*)

THE HON. CECIL RHODES.

Unnecessary it is, here of all places, to say who and what Mr. Rhodes is. Everybody who is anybody knows who Mr. Rhodes is, what he has done, and what he has become. Amalgamator of the great Kimberley diamond mines, the head and front of the great South African Chartered Company, Prime Minister of the great Cape Colony, and possessor of a great fortune, surely this Director of the British South Africa Company is the happiest of mortals! But what my readers may not know, at least what they may have forgotten in the blaze of his fast-crowding triumphs, is the fact that Mr. Rhodes is but thirty-seven years of age. When most men are only thinking of settling down to the serious business of life, Mr. Rhodes has achieved more than one man in a million can accomplish in the span allotted by the Psalmist. But I shall have more to say about Mr. Rhodes. Meantime I devote a few lines to the leading particulars of his career. The Premier of Cape Colony is the fourth son of the late Rev. Francis William Rhodes, twenty-seven years vicar of Bishop Stortford, Herts, who resigned

THE HON. CECIL J. RHODES.

(*Managing Director of The British South Africa Company.*)

the living in 1876, and died in 1878, at the age of seventy-two. The Vicar's family consisted of seven sons and two daughters. Misses Louisa and Edith. The latter is the authoress of an interesting book on "The Adventures of Five Spinsters in Norway." The eldest son, Herbert, who was educated at Winchester, died whilst elephant hunting in the Shiré district in 1877. The second son, Francis William, who was educated at Eton, is Colonel of the 1st (Royal) Dragoons, and is now Military Secretary to the Governor of Bombay. The third son, Ernest Frederick, is a

Captain of the Royal Engineers. The fourth son is the subject of the present sketch, and the fifth son, Elmhirst, is a Captain of the Princess Charlotte of Wales's (Royal Berkshire Regiment), the old 49th and 66th. The sixth son, Arthur M., is ostrich farming near Port Elizabeth, and the youngest, Bernard M., who was educated at Woolwich, is a Captain of the Royal Artillery. Mr. Cecil Rhodes was born at Bishop Stortford on July 5th, 1853, and is therefore in his thirty-eighth year. At the age of eight he was sent to the Bishop Stortford Grammar School, where he remained a scholar from 1861 to 1869, winning scholarships and prizes. His master was the late Rev. Godfrey Goodman, D.D., afterwards rector of Fairstead. Mr. Rhodes went from the Grammar School to the Cape on account of his health, settling with his eldest brother in the south of Natal as a planter. It was this eldest brother who was one of the first pioneers with Major Dartwich at the River Diggings, and who afterwards summoned his brother, Mr. Cecil, from the Natal farm, with all his Kafirs, to work at the New Rush at Kimberley, where Mr. Cecil Rhodes was destined to make a great name for himself. He came home to Oxford, to Oriel College, but the English climate was again too much for him, and he returned to Kimberley. However, in the busy intervals of his South African work, it came into his head that he would like to take his degree. Accordingly, he worked up for a pass, came back, and took his degree. General Gordon, who was on a special mission with Mr. Rhodes in Basutoland—a mission which led to the Imperial Government taking over the country—took a fancy to our subject, and when he was going to Khartoum he wrote to the young colonist asking him to join him as his private Secretary. Mr. Rhodes, however, had just taken office in the Ministry of Sir Thomas Scanlen, and (happily for his present undertakings) could not go. In some ways, Mr. Rhodes, with his robust faith in the part to be played in the world by " God's Englishmen," was a man after Gordon's own heart. However, they had some battles of opinion, and Gordon once exclaimed, in characteristic fashion, " You are one of those men who will never approve of anything you don't organise yourself." In 1884, Mr. Rhodes saved the trade route to the interior by his preliminary settlement of Stellaland before Sir Charles Warren arrived in force. Mr. Rhodes has sat in the Cape House of Assembly for over ten years as one of the members for Barkly, and he assumed office as Premier of the Colony last year on the resignation of Sir Gordon Sprigg's Ministry.

ALBERT H. G. GREY, ESQ.

Mr. Albert Grey is a son of the late General the Hon. Charles Grey, M.P., and is nephew and heir-presumptive to the veteran Earl Grey, a former Secretary of State for the Colonies. Mr. Grey, who is in his fortieth year, was educated at Harrow, and

Trinity College, Cambridge, of which latter he is a B.A. He was elected in 1878 as one of the Members of Parliament for South Northumberland, but was unseated as he objected to a scrutiny. Two years later, however, he successfully wooed the same constituency, which he continued to represent until 1885, when he

ALBERT GREY, ESQ.

(*Director of The British South Africa Company*)

became member for the Tyneside division of the same county; but in 1886 he failed to secure re-election. He is a J.P. and County Councillor for Northumberland. In 1877 he married Miss Alice Holford, by whom he has a family of four children.

GEORGE CAWSTON, ESQ.

Mr. George Cawston was born in 1851. He is a member of the Inner Temple, was called to the Bar in 1882, and is senior partner in the firm of Messrs. George Cawston & Co., of Hatton Court, Threadneedle Street. Mr. Cawston is the second son of the late

GEORGE CAWSTON, ESQ.

(*Director of The British South Africa Company*.)

S. W. Cawston, Esq., of Balham, Surrey, and married Mary Ellen, younger daughter of the late Richard Haworth, Esq., of The Argoed, near Shrewsbury.

ALFRED BEIT, ESQ.

This gentleman was born at Hamburg on February 15th, 1853. In 1875 he went to Kimberley and became a successful diamond merchant. He also took much interest in mining concerns there, having several claims in De Beers, which he eventually amalgamated with the property of the Company of that name. In 1882 he joined the firm of Messrs. Jules, Porges, and Co., now Messrs. Wernher, Beit, and Co., of Holborn Viaduct, E.C. In 1887, Mr.

Beit was instrumental in bringing about the fusion of the Victoria Company with the De Beers Company (of which he is a Life Governor), and thus enabled the general amalgamation of the mines to become a practicable step. Since then he has been closely associated with Mr. Rhodes in financial matters. After the latest discoveries of the precious metal in the South African

ALFRED BEIT, ESQ.
(*Director of The British South Africa Company.*)

Republic Mr. Beit became much identified with the great gold industry, his firm at Johannesburg—Messrs. Eckstein and Co.—being a very prominent and popular one. The services of Mr. Beit to the cause of South African mining progress are well nigh incalculable. His has ever been the ready, resourceful help in times of trouble and doubt. If Mr. Rhodes was able to amalgamate the Kimberley diamond mines and bring a great industry to the pitch of prosperity it has reached, he would himself be the first to acknowledge the great assistance which Mr. Beit has been to him in his schemes. Even in the still more colossal project of the Chartered Company it is fair to say that Mr. Beit's share of the financial launching of this huge concern has been as great as any other's, and none the less so because it has been of a silent and less prominent character. In short, what Mr. Rhodes is in financial circles in South Africa, Mr. Beit is in South African financial circles in London. He is the Cape Pr mier's *alter ego* in England, and no more capable and trustworthy other self could Mr. Rhodes have. In April last Mr. Beit went on a visit to South Africa, to establish branches of his firm in Mashonaland.

HORACE BRAND FARQUHAR, ESQ.

Mr. Horace Farquhar is the brother and heir-presumptive of Sir Robert Townsend-Farquhar, Baronet. He was born in 1844, is

HORACE FARQUHAR, ESQ.

(Director of The British South Africa Company.)

a J.P. for the County of Middlesex, and is a member of the London County Council. The first Baronet was the first British Governor and Commander - in - Chief of the Mauritius, and distinguished himself by his able government of that Colony from its conquest. He was also for some years Governor of the East India Company, and successively M.P. for Hythe and Canterbury. Mr. Farquhar occupies an eminent position in connection with business in the City of London. For the last quarter of a century he has been a banker and merchant, being now a partner of the London banking firm of Sir Samuel Scott & Co.

CHAPTER XIV.

How The Royal Charter Was Received.—The British South Africa Company Gets a Warm Welcome From The Press.

OF course it was some time before the English public—at any rate the public represented by Parliament—could understand why a Royal Charter was granted to the British South Africa Company. It took them a good while to realise, firstly, that the Chartered Company would much have preferred that the Imperial Government had assumed the direct control of the regions to the north of the Transvaal, and secondly, that they but consented through a not extraordinary admixture of patriotic and financial motives to pull the chestnuts out of the fire for John Bull. So it was hardly to be expected that the progress of the negotiations I have described should be exempt from that criticism, sometimes inconveniently exercised, of the House of Commons. At first it was of a serious and very proper character, and the explanations of the Government were accepted by the members generally as clear and sufficient. In regard, however, to all matters before the House, though these may have been, in the eyes of the great majority, satisfactorily disposed of, there is always a small, and usually very insignificant opposition coterie, sometimes led by those who elect to play the dual part of parliamentary profligate and journalistic Jeremiah. It is not necessary to reproduce any of the criticism of this coterie. It has been forgotten, and no public gain would result from resurrecting it from the pages of Hansard. It is sufficient to say that it has become thinner and thinner with time, that the reasoning of it is equally impalpable, and that it is less harmful than the cigarettes over which it is jokingly concocted in the smoking-room of the House.

The English public, as represented by the press of the country, appreciated the objects of the British South Africa Company and gave a hearty welcome to it and the Royal Charter. I propose now to give some indication of the opinions expressed by the press. They have been faithfully collated, and if views adverse to the company are conspicuous by their almost total absence, it is because I could find but very few after very diligent search. I may mention here that the leading newspapers in South Africa received the intelligence of the granting of the Royal Charter very cordially.

The Times from the earliest hint of the scheme of the Chartered Company has been noticeably favourable to it and its objects. But it has not given an unreasoning support to these; it has consistently explained why it thought it a righteous and proper thing that the British South Africa Company should be called into being. It will not be possible to give more than the briefest extracts from the British journals, but it will be well to place on permanent record some outline of the views expressed on the appearance of the Royal Charter.

(*The Times.*)

Great Britain has at last stretched out both her hands to the banks of the Zambesi, the great river whose chequered course was first made known to Europe by our countryman, Livingstone. It was announced as long ago as May last that steps were being taken to obtain a Charter for a Company which would embrace in its operations the immense area lying between the Lower and Central Zambesi on the north and the Transvaal border on the south. The Charter has now been granted, it having been passed by the Privy Council at its meeting on Wednesday, and in a week or two receives the Royal signature and the impress of the Great Seal. The new

BRITISH SOUTH AFRICA COMPANY,

as it is called, will begin immediately to work on much the same lines as those along which the Imperial British East Africa Company has been so far wonderfully successful. The long delay in finally passing the Charter is proof of the care which has been taken in arranging its details; but it has also been partly due to opposition in certain quarters from considerations which could not bear examination. It is right and proper, however, that before so stupendous an implement as a Royal Charter is put in the hands of any Company the ground should be perfectly clear, all the more when the highest Imperial interests are involved, as well as many thousands of square miles, millions of money, and the welfare of a large population.

The names at the head of the Company to which the Charter is to be granted ought to command public confidence that its terms will be honestly adhered to. The "body politic and corporate" in whose names the Charter has been drawn are the Duke of Abercorn, the Duke of Fife, Lord Gifford, Cecil John Rhodes, Albert Beit, Albert Henry George Grey, and George Cawston. Here, then, we have social position—even a flavour of Royalty—business capacity, broadminded enterprise, and ample means. It is no secret that

THE LEADING SPIRIT

in this new and somewhat gigantic enterprise is Mr. Rhodes, whose life in South Africa has been as adventurous as it has been successful. An old Eton boy and Oxford graduate, who went out primarily to South Africa for the sake of his health, he has taken advantage of exceptional opportunities which legitimately presented themselves to accumulate wealth, but also, it is to be hoped, to initiate and carry out enterprises which will satisfy a nobler ambition than that of "making a pile," and which will connect his name with the expansion of the British Empire. Before deciding to recommend the grant of a Charter Her Majesty's advisers must have satisfied themselves that of the new powers granted to him he will make the best use, not only for the Company, but for the interests of the Empire.

What, then, is

THE SPHERE OF OPERATIONS

of the British South Africa Company? Its boundaries are left happily vague. The principal field of operations, according to the Charter, shall be the region of South Africa lying immediately to the north of British Bechuanaland, and to the north and west of the South African Republic (the Transvaal) and to the west to the Portuguese dominions. No western limit, it is seen, is stated; that was, perhaps, unnecessary, as of course it is settled that the 20th degree of east longitude marks off the widest German claims. Ample room is thus left to the Company for the

EXPANSION

of its territory, and the Charter expressly stipulates that it is at perfect liberty to do so by every legitimate means, east and west and north. Meantime, with the territory thus vaguely defined, they will have their hands full. There will be many interests to consider, native and white, many concessionaires to satisfy, much to do to discover and exploit the resources of the country, and to establish suitable routes to the outside world. The Company is not only authorised to take full advantage of all its own concessions, and they are large enough, including the whole of Matabeleland, but it is bound to show every consideration for the concessions of others. The Company is authorised to acquire whatever other concessions it can, including "all or any rights, interests, authorities, and powers of any kind or nature whatever, including powers necessary for the purpose of government and the preservation of public order in and for the protection of territories, lands, or property comprised or referred to in the concessions and agreements made as aforesaid, or affecting other territories, lands, or property in Africa or the inhabitants thereof." In short, the Company is empowered to govern the territories embraced in its Charter in the name and in behalf of the interests of

THE BRITISH EMPIRE.

Thus, therefore, it is stipulated that the Company must always remain British in its directorate, composition, and domicile, and that no Director shall be appointed without the approval of "our Secretary of State." Indeed, no important step can be taken without such approval. Naturally, therefore, the Company is empowered, to the best of its ability, to preserve peace and order "in such ways and manners as it shall consider necessary, and may with that object make ordinances (to be approved by the Secretary of State), and may establish and maintain a force of police." It must be especially gratifying to philanthropists to find that the Company is empowered to abolish by degrees "any system of slave trade or domestic servitude in the territories aforesaid;" and what will be deemed by many of equal importance, to regulate the traffic in intoxicating liquors in such a way as to prevent their sale to the natives. That the injunction will be carried out as far as practicable we may be assured from the fact that, mainly through Mr. Rhodes's exertions, 700 native workers at the famous De Beers mine are practically teetotalers. Another laudable clause in the Charter is the injunction to have careful regard to native customs and law, to the administration of justice, and in all dealings with the natives.

With regard to

FINANCE,

the British South Africa Company, like the British East African Company, is enjoined to furnish annually to the Government accounts of its expenditure for administrative purposes, and all sums received by it by way of public revenue, as distinguished from its commercial profits, together with a report as to its public proceedings and the condition of the territories within its sphere of operations. Moreover, the Company is bound at any time to furnish the Government with whatever information it may require. Again, the Company must pay due respect to any requirements or suggestions of Her Majesty's High Commissioner and other Imperial officers in South Africa. It may have its own flag, but that flag must indicate the distinctively British character of the Company. No monopoly of trade will be allowed, though of course concessions may be granted for public works, and precautions may be taken, and rightly so, for the preservation of elephants and other game. All due observance must be had to Imperial obligations to other states; the Company must appoint all necessary officers, and establish courts for the administration of justice.

As to the

SHARE CAPITAL

of the Company, that is set down at a million sterling, in one pound shares, though, as a matter of fact, the paid-up capital does not amount to anything like this. This capital the Company is authorized to increase as it may deem necessary, to borrow money by debenture or otherwise, and to establish banks and associations. One point is worth mentioning—the Company has decided not to pay its members a farthing of dividend for two years. It goes without saying that the Company has power to make and maintain railways, telegraphs, and all other works required for the development of its territories; to carry on mining, agricultural, and other industries and enterprises of all kinds; to promote immigration and settlement; to grant lands on lease or in perpetuity; in short, to do everything legitimate for making the most of the extensive territories thus entrusted to its keeping by Royal Charter.

Within a year the Company is bound to execute

A DEED OF SETTLEMENT

for the more effective carrying out of the various purposes mentioned in the Charter, for the division and distribution of profits, the audit of accounts, and others matters of detail. Meantime the persons already named will act as Directors of the Company; while, under any circumstances, the Duke of Fife, the Duke of Abercorn, and Mr. Albert Grey will remain permanent Directors. The present Charter is to subsist for 25 years, at the end of which, and at the end of every succeeding 10 years, the Crown may revise or repeal so much of the Charter as relates to administrative and public affairs; that is, the Crown reserves the right to take over these territories and administer them directly as colonial possessions of the United Kingdom. Of course, also, if the Company does not behave itself, its Charter may be revoked.

Such, then, are the leading provisions of this new implement for the extension of British influence over South Africa. They suggest many

X

CONSIDERATIONS.

So far as England is concerned, the old days of territorial aggrandisement by ruthless seizure are over ; the same end is accomplished by concession and charter. What about the natives ?—the "poor" natives, some may be inclined to say, but in this case the term would be misapplied. Any one who takes the trouble to read the graphic reports buried in Blue Books of Sir Charles Warren's interviews with Sechele, Khama, and other chiefs of Bechuanaland and neighbouring territories must be convinced that in placing themselves under British protection not only did they know well what they were about, but they saw it was absolutely necessary to protect themselves from the land-grabbing raids of white freebooters and the merciless invasions of the unscrupulous and cruel Lo Bengula, Chief of Matabeleland. They are now maintained in peaceful possession of their lands ; they have been assured of all the rights as to planting and hunting which they asked for ; they contribute voluntarily a moderate tax for administration ; and they may now go on increasing their flocks and herds, and acquiring all the civilisation of which they are capable, without fear of hostile attack or of being ousted from their lands without their consent. What will be their ultimate fate, who can say ? Will they meet the fate of other black peoples with whom the white man has come into contact, or will they acquire habits of steady industry and co-operate with their British protectors in the development of their country ? To discuss these questions would be premature. The native African has not shown himself ready to sink before a higher civilisation ; and either their labour or that of natives imported from other countries will be absolutely necessary over a considerable area of the conceded territories. But chiefs like

KHAMA AND SECHELE

and their people have shown themselves so capable of progress, and of assimilating civilised ideas and habits, that there is every reason to hope that, under good guidance, they may become creditable British citizens. As to Lo Bengula, he also has seen the advisability of claiming British protection ; and, as a first step, he made over to Mr. Rhodes some time ago all the mining concessions in his country. As a matter of fact, he made them over to Messrs. Rudd, Maguire, and Thompson, who on the same day parted with them to Messrs. Rhodes and Rudd. The deed by which Lo Bengula parted with the richest territory in South Africa is drawn up in due form, having been clearly explained and witnessed to by the Rev. C. D. Helm, an old and well-known missionary in Matabeleland, and by Mr J. F. Dreyer. Evidently Lo Bengula was quite satisfied with the £100 per annum and the 1000 rifles and supply of cartridges which he received as an equivalent. Lo Bengula apparently realised that, without some stronger barrier than he can provide, his territory would be overrun by unscrupulous adventurers, just as his father overran the country of the poor Mashonas and all but extinguished them. Should he and his savage warriors be in the end compelled by the advance of civilisation to migrate beyond the Zambesi, no one need regret it ; the real aborigines, the industrious Mashonas, will once more have a chance. Meantime, these questions need not be discussed in detail. Nor, now that British power encircles the Transvaal and the Orange Free State, and extends to the Zambesi, need we enter on the question of the future of South Africa. The new Company, to which Imperial interests have been intrusted, has

MANY YEARS OF WORK

to look forward to before it can place its territory on a footing of equality with the older colonies and states. In the interests of the natives, the step which has just been taken was really necessary. The Charter will unite a variety of mining concessions granted by Khama and Lo Bengula, and so secure to the natives the royalties agreed upon. Otherwise there would be a danger of quarrels arising between the different concessionaires and the interests of the natives would have little chance of consideration. Now, with this Company, headed by responsible men, the terms of all agreements will be insisted on and carried out; so that so far as the natives are concerned, they are much better off under the Charter than they could have been had matters been allowed to drift. As to the character and resources of the territories which have been added to those other appendages to the Empire governed by Royal Charter, they have certainly considerable advantages to start with, over those for which Sir William Mackinnon and his partners received a Charter a year ago. According to the terms of the Charter,

THE SPHERE OF THE COMPANY

includes the British protectorate of Bechuanaland, the whole of Khama's country, and north to the Zambesi, and west to 20 deg. east longitude, and the whole of Matabeleland, or Lo Bengula's country, the limits of which to the east are undefined. The total area cannot be less than between 360,000 and 400,000 square miles, three times the size of the United Kingdom, and one-third greater than the area of Germany. But the population is not at all commensurate with the area. Even the rich country of the Matabeles and Mashonas is but sparsely inhabited. From an economical standpoint this region is of very unequal value. After the best has been said about Bechuanaland and the country immediately to the north, it is, on the whole, a poor region so far as colonisation and capacity for industrial development are concerned. Much of it is quite waterless, though with proper appliances the underground supply might be tapped and irrigation established. As the Zambesi is approached, the country becomes more fertile, but there, again, the tsetse kills off the cattle, and malaria attacks humanity. Here and there the natives cultivate their fields and gardens, and where the tsetse is absent some cattle-rearing is possible. North and south of Shoshong in Khama's country water is more plentiful, and the country greatly improves as Matabeleland is approached. But here and there over the whole of what may be called the Bechuana country water is found at intervals, and in time, when the more southern districts become filled up, something may be made of it, even for agriculture and stock-rearing, under skilled manipulation. Even the dreaded Kalahari desert itself, included in the concession, has been whitewashed. There is no doubt that this desert region is not nearly so extensive as it was at one time believed to be. Large areas are known to be covered with bush and other vegetation. Attempts, more or less successful, have been made to establish farming and cattle-rearing, and in time this so-called desert may sustain a fair population. Great sand-belts, some of them more than 50 miles wide, are scattered through the centre of the country, and altogether it can never support a

population commensurate with its area.   The total native population
probably does not exceed half a million.
    It is very different with

MATABELELAND,

to the development of which the energies of the Company will, no
doubt, be mainly directed.   As that country is approached from the
west, and the Tati River is reached, signs of gold begin to appear ;
and in the Matabeleland country itself there seems little doubt that
great areas of gold-bearing reefs exist, while north in Mashonaland
there is reason to believe that alluvial gold abounds.   Twenty-five
years ago there was a gold rush on Tati, but nothing came of it ;
the settlement was ruined from bad management.   All the reports
about Matabeleland speak of it in glowing terms.   The Matabeles,
one report states, have certainly chosen a fine country to dwell in.
Compared with the country south of it, Matabeleland is like Canaan
after the Wilderness.   If it be not "flowing with milk and honey,"
its numerous rivers are either flowing, or have plenty of water in
them ; there is, too, abundance of cattle and corn and wood, and
above all, it is very rich in gold, copper, iron, and other minerals.
The principal part of the country occupied by the Matabele comprises the highlands forming the watershed of numerous rivers
running to the Zambesi in the north and the Limpopo in the south.
This country is from 3000 to 5000 feet above sea level, and is an
extensive high veld, from which numerous spurs run off, forming
rich, well-watered valleys.   The high country is particularly healthy.
Fever is unknown, and white children could be reared, which is a
sine quâ non in a country if it is to be colonised by white men.   The
soil is rich and admirably adapted for corn, Lieutenant Maund,
from whose careful report we take our information, assures us.
Large masses of Kafir corn and mealies are grown in the same
ground year after year, without manure, and never ploughed, the
earth being simply hoed up with mattocks.   The valleys, as elsewhere in this part of Africa, are less healthy, especially during the
rainy season, but with care and abstinence from alcohol no white
man need fear the climate.   The cattle reared in the country
thrive, though those taken from the outside in raids suffer from
disease.   All the hill country is rich in minerals.   Like the Tati
Hills, they are intersected by numerous reefs of quartz, while some
of the hills are composed of ironstone, so rich that it requires very
little smelting.   Another report, by Lieutenant Haynes, divides
Matabeleland into three sections—first, the high slopes of the watershed, well watered, fertile, abounding in minerals, a good cattle
country, capable of growing wheat, healthy for Europeans, and
probably the best land in South Africa ; secondly, the fringe of
mountainous country encircling it to the south, south-east, south-
west, and north-east, including Mashonaland and the hills occupied
by the Makalakas.   This is well-watered and intersected by very
fertile valleys, in which grow rice, sugar, and cotton.   The hills
abound in minerals.   Thirdly, the low veld in the Zambesi and Limpopo
valleys, covered with dense bush, and not well supplied with water.
The Limpopo valley is known to be excellent veld for cattle.   The
Zambesi valley is chiefly hunting veld, and the tsetse fly is known to
infest districts, especially in the neighbourhood of the river.
    These glowing accounts by British officers are confirmed by the
observations of one who probably knows the whole country more

intimately than any other individual—Mr. Selous, the mightiest of South African hunters. Of

THE MASHONA COUNTRY

especially, to the north and north-east of the district inhabited by the Matabele, Mr. Selous finds it difficult to express the high opinion he has formed. A tableland of an average of 5000 ft., clad with forests, the greatest elephant-hunting ground in South Africa, watered by a network of perennial streams, covered with the richest soil, abounding in gold in reefs and in rivers, as well as other minerals, and capable of growing almost every class of agricultural product from tropical to temperate, he predicts that it will in the future be the great centre of white colonisation in South Africa. For he, like those who have gone before him, maintains that it is perfectly adapted for European settlement and for the labour of white men. It now forms the retreat of the remnant of the Mashonas driven from their homes by the Matabele, who even now make occasional raids, though the Mashonas keep out of their way in inaccessible retreats. These poor broken-spirited people work in iron, copper, and wild cotton, and sometimes collect gold from the rivers, which they sell to the half-caste Portuguese traders in quills. They throw back the nuggets because they think it is unlucky to take them. Moreover, some parts of the country are very highly cultivated. Traditions abound as to the former greatness of these people.

Altogether, then, this new Chartered Company has obtained virtual possession of a country of the richest resources, a country which in time, under reasonable management,

MUST BECOME ONE OF THE MOST FLOURISHING CENTRES OF WHITE

COLONISATION IN AFRICA, IF NOT IN THE WORLD.

It is not only its gold. When the gold fever exhausts itself, and the metal becomes scarcer and more difficult to find, the treasures which its soil will yield should enable it to flourish perennially. Meantime the gold will prove of real service if it enables the Company to develop the other resources not only of Matabeleland, but of the less-favoured regions to the west, and of the other regions which no doubt in time will come under its sway. There is ample scope for extending the Company's sphere of action as well as British influence in more directions than one ; there are lands to occupy and develop which must fall to those who have the courage and the capital to go in and occupy them, and we may be sure that in this respect the Company will not let the grass grow under its feet. It may be taken for granted that any shadowy claims of the Portuguese over Mashonaland have been settled before this Charter has reached its present stage, and that in the future our Government will show no weakness as to frontier. . . . And no doubt the Company will exercise judgment and a wise discrimination in the selection of its officials, appointing only men whose training and habits will give assurance that they will loyally carry out the great object for which the Charter has been granted ; and that object, it should be remembered, is not simply to enable the Company to fill its coffers. As to natives, let us hope that the opinion expressed in one report will turn out to be justified : "There appears to be no reason to suppose that under a civilised form of government the Matabele would not become as useful a member of society as the Natal Zulu." No doubt Mr. Rhodes will give him a fair chance.

As to the means by which all the fine country described above is to be developed, one of them, the Company has expressly stated, is the extension northwards of the

RAILWAY AND TELEGRAPH SYSTEMS

of the Cape in the direction of the Zambesi, which will be the goal, not, it is to be hoped, the ultimate one, of both means of communication. A sum of £700,000 has been already subscribed for the purpose of proceeding at once with the construction of the first section of the railway, and the extension of the telegraph system from Mafeking, its present terminus, to Shoshong. The railway again must be brought from Kimberley, a distance of 400 miles. The railway must ultimately be carried to the Zambesi, and throw out branches right and left, and the sooner the better, for then British South Africa will be independent of obstructive neighbours. On the other side, the Zambesi itself is an international highway, and, so far as it can be used for navigation, the Company has a right to do so, without paying blackmail so long as its vessels do not touch Portuguese territory; and in taking advantage of this right it will no doubt be supported by the British Government. Of course the concessionaires, who form an important section of the Company to whom the Charter has been granted, have mainly their own interests in view, and naturally so. There are several Companies, whose separate interests must be adjusted, and their interests may not always coincide with the great reasons for which the Charter is granted. In this respect the new Company differs from the British East African Company. But it may be taken that the other element in the Company—that mainly represented by the Duke of Fife and the Duke of Abercorn—will see that sordid motives are not allowed to have unreasonable sway, and that the provisions of the Charter are carried out in a way that will be creditable to the Empire.

Thus it will be seen this new Chartered Company has intrusted to its keeping on behalf of the Empire

AN AREA OF IMMENSE EXTENT, OF VERY VARIED ECONOMICAL VALUE, WITH A COMPARATIVELY SCANTY NATIVE POPULATION; BOTH LAND AND PEOPLE, HOWEVER, HAVING THE POSSIBILITY OF A GREAT FUTURE BEFORE THEM.

This is the fourth Royal Charter granted within the last few years. The British North Borneo Company has faithfully adhered to the terms of its Charter, and has proceeded energetically and steadily to make itself acquainted with its territories and to develop their resources. Mistakes may have been made, but on the whole we have every reason to be satisfied with the conduct of the Company and with the prospects of British interests in that exceedingly important part of the earth. The other three recent Charters embrace a very considerable area of Central and Southern Africa. This is not the place to discuss the manner in which the Royal Niger Company has carried out the task laid upon it by its Charter. Things may have been done which require a somewhat charitable construction; but there cannot be a doubt that under the operations of the Company the whole lower Niger and Binué region is being steadily developed, British connections pushed into the far interior, and a prospect held out that under judicious management much of the great trade of the Central Soudan States will be drawn within the British sphere.

Considering the way in which British interests have been trifled
with in other parts of West Africa, it is a comfort that in one region
at least these are sharply looked after. With the share England has
obtained in this part of Africa we have no reason to be dissatisfied.
It is just a year since the British East African Company began
operations under its Charter. Quite recently it was shown in the
Times how diligently and with what good results this Company has
been working to explore its territory, to ascertain its capabilities, to
extend British interests, not only along the coast, but into the highly
important region around the great lakes. There is no reason why,
by keenness and tact, these East and West African Companies
should not

JOIN HANDS IN THE HEART OF AFRICA.

Nor is there any reason why the new Company that has just obtained
its Charter might not make British influence supreme over a great
portion of the Zambesi region. Whatever the commercial and
economical value of Central Africa may be, there are other reasons
why England should keep herself well to the front in its partition.
We cannot, with so many eager competitors in the field, afford to
neglect any country likely to yield new fields for commercial enterprise; nor can we afford to allow any section even of the Dark
Continent to believe that our Imperial prestige is on the wane.
Among them these three great Chartered Companies, without
infringing on the legitimate claims and aspirations of other
enterprising European nations, ought to be able to draw into
their nets most that is worth having in Central Africa. . . . .
It will be observed that the sphere of the Company is not expressly
confined to the south of the Zambesi or to the east of the 20th degree
of longitude which marks the beginning of German Damaraland.
There is nothing in the Charter to prevent the Company crossing the
Zambesi, and nothing to hinder it from entering Damaraland if the
Germans, tired of the losing game they are playing there, decide to
leave it to people with a greater genius for colonisation. But the
Company has enough, and more than enough, to occupy its energies
in the Bechuanaland Protectorate and in the country at present
occupied by Khama, Lo Bengula, and the Mashonas. The total area
of this territory is three times as large as the United Kingdon. It
may be assumed that the Bechuanaland Protectorate will be comparatively neglected for the present, as the poorer corner of the
Company's sphere. In Matabeleland and Mashonaland the Company
has a domain which the few white men who have traversed it vie
with one another in extolling. It is rich, fabulously rich, we are
told, in the precious metals, and half a dozen others besides. In the
uplands, where all this mineral wealth is situate, forests full of
elephants and big game, alternate with cultivable land, which only
needs scratching to smile with corn and all kinds of agricultural
wealth ; the whole is intersected by a network of unfailing streams ;
cattle fatten in peace, unplagued by their enemy, the tsetse fly ; and,
last, but most important of all, the climate is an ideal one for
Europeans. . . . . We earnestly hope, however, that the
relations between the Company and the native inhabitants of its
territory may be uniformly peaceful. The British South Africa
Company now has its Charter. It remains for it to go forward and
prosper. Whether it finds the wealth of Ophir in the mountains and
rivers of Mashonaland or not, we cannot doubt that it will lay the

basis of a great English-speaking colony in what appears to be the fairest region of Africa.

(*The Standard.*)

The extension of what is virtually the Sovereignty of Great Britain northwards and westwards from the present northern confines of our Bechuanaland Protectorate, and the Boer filibusters and the utterly irresponsible white intriguer effectually shut out. That is, in short, from the political point of view, the salient feature of the settlement. An impassable barrier has been put to the march of the Dutch Republic. There is to be an end of the "trekking" and the freebooting which have hitherto made up the sum of Boer progress. . . . The young Company, in short, is deliberately authorised and instructed at its birth to address itself to the functions which the old East India Company blundered and stumbled into performing, before it passed away. We can only hope that the history of the merchant adventurers in the barbarous wilds of Mid Africa will be as glorious as that of their forerunners in the ancient and teeming States of Hindostan.

(*The Daily News.*)

Opportunity there is in plenty, and only time is needed for the systematic development of what appears to be potentially one of the richest virgin districts of the whole bounteous earth.

(*The Daily Chronicle.*)

It is at best humiliating that we should, in the nineteenth century, fall back on the crude ideas of the Stuarts for the means of fulfilling an imperial mission in any part of the world. Still when the Colonial Office refuses to guide the expansion of the empire in any region into which our settlers press, we have nothing to resort to but the antiquated and semi-barbarous administrative machinery of Chartered Companies and State Monopolies.

(*Financial News.*)

The terms of the Charter, as explained by Baron Henry de Worms, seem as unexceptionable as the character of the enterprise and the men who have it in hand.

(*The Globe.*)

The private "landgrabber"—to borrow an entirely appropriate term from the Parnellite vocabulary—does not do his spiriting gently in Africa, whether he be of English or Dutch descent. As soon as he has secured a territorial concession by a combination of intimidation and backsheesh. he proceeds to let the natives understand that he considers himself monarch of all he surveys. The consequence is that the tribes come to regard all white men as unscrupulous plunderers, who are every whit as bad as the Arab slave dealers. Sir John Swinburne is, of course, quite guiltless of such doings ; but for all that, we prefer a Chartered Company under Government control to any sort of private landgrabbing.

(*St. James's Gazette.*)

It is a fascinating prospect, and we do not wonder that it stirs the imagination of an age which is not yet quite dead to the traditions and the aspirations of the past. It should be for the central Government—which has reserved exceedingly ample powers over the operations of the Company, to see that it so manages its affairs as to make its activity useful instead of dangerous to the Empire as a whole. There will be, in fact, less room than ever for the policy of shirk in South Africa.

(Pall Mall Gazette.)

The precise future of South Africa is still uncertain; but in one form or another the new Charter will in the end add another stone —how precious a one those who know the mineral wealth of Zambesia can tell—to the golden circlet of the Crown. It is a fresh expansion, not merely of the Anglo-Saxon race, but also of the British Empire.

(The Echo.)

If the injunctions of the Charter are carried out in the spirit which pervades them, the advent of the South Africa Company ought, indeed, to be a blessing to the Dark Continent.

(The Saturday Review.)

The real justification is that modern politics, at least in England, makes it sometimes difficult for the State itself to annex openly, and that the recent awakening of European nations to the fact that they need swarming-grounds threatens a somewhat rapid exhaustion of the swarming-grounds available. The world is just now being "claimed" with remarkable rapidity; and, though long heads and strong hands will undoubtedly in the long run profit by the claims of incompetent and hasty speculators, it hardly does to trust to this only. The Chartered Company is a most convenient warming-pan for the State, as well as a useful method of regimenting and directing private enterprise, and we do not care how many examples we see of it. Only let the promoters of such companies remember certain dismal examples which, to avoid ill omens, shall be nameless, and they can hardly fail to do well.

(Spectator.)

Even if the Company had not been formed, we should have been bound in some form or other to have assumed a position of sovereignty. The Company has all the powers of the old East India Company, and will, we trust, like its prototype, solve the problem of creating an efficient native army. That is what is now wanted for our South African and East African dominions; and until it is secured, our position in the immense provinces we have recently acquired must remain a little uncertain.

(South Africa, May 11, 1889.)

They would, no doubt, we can well believe, have preferred that the British Government should undertake these important works, but, as several millions of money are involved, there does not seem much hope of the expenditure coming from the Imperial Exchequer. The Imperial Government, however, can do the next best thing. They can lend encouraging concurrence to a huge and universally beneficial enterprise. They can grant, subject to special guarantees, a Charter to protect the rights of a Company who should undertake these great progressive works. We sincerely hope that they will either carry out this colossal scheme under the ægis of the Crown, or will grant the Charter we speak of. The peaceful and industriously progressive development of a great territory, and other far extending regions, and by consequence also of South Africa as a whole, depends upon the result of the negotiations at present being carried on, we are glad to learn harmoniously, between the combination of capitalists concerned and the Imperial Government.

(Ditto, June 8.)

It may fairly be hoped that the means of upholding British influence in Africa will be found in some such scheme as that which has been put forward ; and it is safe to say that no other solution of the difficulty can be found. The British nation has to decide whether it will advance in this way or retire altogether from one of the grandest fields of enterprise that has ever been laid open to it.

(Ditto, August 31.)

Chartered Companies, it has been found by experience, are the best instruments for furthering civilisation in distant parts. They are, in fact, the only means for preserving subordination, within certain limits, to the Imperial Government, with the freedom and readiness of action by which alone any material advance can be made. We look with great interest for the full details of this measure, which we hail as a new era of advance in South Africa, and the inauguration of a system which is certain to be productive of the very best results.

(Ditto, October 19.)

It is a subject of sincere congratulation that this important measure has been brought to a satisfactory issue, and that it comes before the public under such favourable auspices. It is a new era for British interests in South Africa.

(Ditto, November 9.)

No one who studies carefully the Charter of the Company and the Order in Council, can fail to appreciate the care and skill which have been devoted to them both. They form, in fact, the commencement of an entirely new era in our relations with South Africa ; and if handled only with ordinary care and skill, cannot fail to be the means of gradually colonising and civilising one of the most important parts of the world with which Great Britain has been called upon to deal.

(The Sunday Times.)

First the Borneo, then the Niger, then the Imperial British East African Company was founded, and now last and mightiest of them all, the British South Africa Company has been launched upon its course with the approval of men of all classes and of all shades of politics. The leading strings of the young giant as defined in the Charter of incorporation are strong enough in all conscience ; but what we know both publicly and privately of those to whom the grant has been made, of those with whom they are associated, and of those to whom the executive work is to be entrusted, enables us to state our positive assurance that, if they had been light as the threads of a gossamer, they would never be strained.

(The Observer.)

To us the organisation of chartered companies is merely a sign that English public opinion is sick of the apathy of the Colonial Office, and that rather than let the opportunity slip by for extending British influence in newly-opened regions, Englishmen will fall back on the comparatively clumsy machinery of their ancestors—even to the extent of organising trading companies to take over the work of civil and military administration in half a continent as a mere incident to their primary business.

(*The Economist.*)

The British Government in granting these charters, accepts for great and growing territorial governments full responsibility without assuring to itself at the same time full practical control. It is perhaps useless to argue, for Parliament understands little of such matters, and the trading community is growing intoxicated with its new hopes of gain—hopes sometimes disappointed, but often realised on a large scale—and the consequences seem to be far off. The Colonial Office, however, understands, and we doubt if it wholly performs its duty in sanctioning projects so gigantic while the people, who must in the end ensure their success, remain practically ignorant of what is being done.

(*Home News.*)

All things considered, the British South Africa Company holds in its hands the destinies of a region of the fullest resources, capable, too, of white colonisation and of expanding under its fostering care and guidance into an important and flourishing appendage of the British Empire.

(*Vanity Fair.*)

The Government have delegated it to certain fit and proper persons to see that Zambesia be properly opened up and be properly brought within the lines of an established Government; with the provision that, when these delegates have done their work, and when the country has been made ripe for inclusion within the British dominions proper, it shall be handed over to the Crown on equitable terms. It is an excellent method of colonising, when properly safeguarded from abuse, as we have shown that this grant is; and no real objection can be taken to it as compared with any other form of annexation. If Zambesia is to be annexed at all, this is the best method of annexing it. The country is very thinly populated; it is fabulously rich; it abounds in big game; it is well watered; and its climate is magnificent.

(*The News of the World.*)

It is a grand idea, worthy of England's private enterprise, and still more worthy of the support of the English Government. There never was a period in our history when it was more desirable to seek "fresh fields and pastures new" for the ever-increasing population, and it has been proved that no quarter of the world offers us such ready-made facilities for extending colonisation.

(*Birmingham Post.*)

The foundation of the British South Africa Society is regarded as a mortal blow to the pretensions of any other Power, and Africa is destined to become a far more important possession than India, or, indeed, the whole of the other British Colonies put together. The suppression of slavery and the regulation of commerce in the lawless countries over which will be extended British domination is regarded of small significance compared to the stupendous political advantages the English traders had in view from the very first.

(*Birmingham Gazette.*)

The short-sighted fools who used to cry " Perish India," may in like spirit raise their voices in a weak protest against handing over to a Company of English noblemen and merchants the almost absolute control of a territory more extensive than that of France, and which is capable of almost indefinite expansion. But the practical common sense of our countrymen cannot be misled. They see that Africa is to be one of the greatest fields of commercial and industrial activity in the future, that if we do not step in promptly others will, and that the chance once lost can never be obtained again.

(*Manchester Guardian.*)

It is a great and even admirable venture, such as none but Englishmen have hitherto been found to carry out. We trust and may believe that in all their work they will be sensible of the deep responsibility which lies upon them to their countrymen and to the inhabitants of the vast and wealthy region of which they are about to become the virtual governors.

(*Manchester Examiner.*)

What is really wanted in these unsettled South African territories is that the native chiefs shall be protected from land freebooters and speculators ; although the Government would have acted more wisely in accepting the policy long advocated by the Rev. John Mackenzie, they cannot be charged with neglecting British interests. They have at least secured—and this partly through the efforts of Mr. Cecil Rhodes—that the immense territory north of the Molopo River shall not be removed from the control of the Imperial Government.

(*Manchester Courier.*)

It was high time for the English Government to intervene, and the grant of a Charter to a powerful company will afford the best means of protecting the native chiefs against making lavish grants of land on ruinous terms, as well as of preventing any extension of territory or influence on the part of the Transvaal or the Portuguese.

(*Liverpool Courier.*)

The British South Africa Company will probably act on identical lines with the British East African Company—purchasing instead of plundering, making roads and bridges, employing animals to do what was formerly done by men, acting justly among those under its administration, and with conciliation towards neighbours. If so it will do well.

(*Liverpool Mercury.*)

Meanwhile, against the various anxieties which the mere mention of so immense an undertaking suggests—anxieties as to the natives and as to our relations with other European Powers—we may reasonably set the consideration that it has been taken up not rashly nor in a spirit of speculation, but after long thinking and full information, by men who have unlimited command of means as well as characters to lose.

(*Leeds Mercury.*)

The character and credit of this nation are not to be maintained by the delegation to trading companies, but by the direct discharge of such responsibilities as in the interests of Imperial security and development the present or previous Governments have thought it right to undertake.

(Later.)

The Company and its officials are certainly to be congratulated on the fact that the occupation of this important territory has been accomplished without any collision with the native tribes, and without the necessity of firing a single shot in self-defence in the course of the long march into the interior. It forms, perhaps, the most important practical result of that partition of African territory among its European claimants which will render the year just closed conspicuous in our history as a great Colonial Power.

(Yorkshire Post.)

The Company's operations are subject to the perpetual supervision of the British Government, which has reserved the right of stepping in at any time justice and expediency may decree it to be necessary. Practically the Company only exists for the purpose of working the country, of developing its resources, and of regulating its internal economy according to British ideas and as the delegate of the British Government. Everything points to a splendid future for the undertaking.

(Sheffield Telegraph.)

The new enterprise is, however, just in time. If British pluck had not taken charge of the great region offered to their hand, some other nation would probably soon have stepped in, and a golden opportunity been lost for ever.

(Newcastle Journal.)

If not under the British flag the whole of South Africa is at least dominated by British influence, owes its prosperity chiefly to British trade and enterprise, and is most largely populated by the British race. It is a further, and a wise and sagacious step, therefore, to establish a British South African Company, able to repeat in another direction the philanthropic and commercial achievements of the British East African Company, with its own flag, and that flag indicating the distinctively British character of the Company, with full powers to extirpate slavery, and also to regulate the traffic in intoxicating liquors in such a way as to prevent their sale to the natives.

(Leicester Post.)

Though a perilous, it is, however, an interesting experiment; and there is no reason why the new South African Company should not make as great a name for itself in the annals of the Empire as did the old "John Bull Company" before the days when corruption ate away its vitality and its strength.

(The Scotsman.)

It will probably be met by loud outcries at Lisbon and at Pretoria; possibly also at Cape Town, in London, and even in Berlin. But all that is a thing to be reckoned with; it will not daunt the projectors, among whom are men of such standing as the Dukes of Fife and Abercorn; nor abate the hope that by this New Departure not only the British flag, but legitimate British influence and European civilisation are about to be definitely and successfully introduced into Matabeleland, the country of the Makalaka and Mashona, and the region lying beside and beyond the Zambesi.

Mr. Grant.   Mr. J. W. Moir.   Mr. Jos. Thompson.

Mr. R. Maguire, M.P.   Mr. H. H. Johnston.   The Hon. C. J. Rhodes.   Mr. A. R. Colquhoun.

From a Photograph by   *J. E. Middlebrook, Kimberley.*

SOME WELL-KNOWN FACES.

(*The Glasgow Herald.*)

It is impossible not to heartily wish well to the British South Africa Company as to its predecessor which is seeking to open up East Africa to the world.

(*Aberdeen Free Press.*)

It is a great and laudable work in the line of the best traditions of British enterprise in the reclamation of the wastes in which barbarism had hitherto stalked at large.

(*The Irish Times.*)

The gigantic character of the undertaking renews the days when "John Company" laid the foundations of the Indian Empire, and the association of free traders who "prospected" the Hudson's Bay territory "played so large a part in developing the mighty States of the new world." To business folk among us it seems a happy thought which inspired the Duke of Abercorn and his brethren of the syndicate to turn from the precarious venture of investing in American land to the Dark Continent with its magnificent posisbilities.

(*Belfast News Letter.*)

Such restrictions are, of course, inevitable, but they will not interfere with the legitimate operation of the enterprise in which the Duke of Abercorn, the Duke of Fife, and other noblemen are interested. We are glad to know that the Charter will be granted without delay, and we cannot doubt that it will be found to operate for the great benefit of the natives of the territory to which it refers.

CHAPTER XV.

HAVING ascertained how the Royal Charter was obtained and the nature of its reception by Parliament and the press, let us now see how the Company proceeded to honour the great Trust imposed on them by Her Majesty and her advisers. Immediately on the granting of the Charter all sorts of alarmist rumours were spread about both in South Africa and England, either by those who conceived they had a grudge against the British South Africa Company (possibly because their friendship had not been rated at the cash value which they themselves placed on it), or by sentimentalists whose head-shaking did less credit to what was shaken than to their hearts, or by the member for the shoemakers and his satellites. It was freely asserted that Lo Bengula would massacre any one attempting to enter his country to carry out the terms of the contract he entered into with Mr. Rudd, and numbers of stories were put about that in his wrath he had murdered all missionaries and traders at and near his kraal. It was declared also that the Boers viewed the Chartered Company with angry eyes, and that the South African Republic would themselves destroy the Company's forces either by sending in a commando to annihilate them or by encouraging the Matabele to do this for them. It is needless now to say that all these rumours were not only groundless, but mostly pure inventions of mendacious or silly people. The British South Africa Company went quietly on their way. They knew that if they had to pull the chestnuts out of the fire for John Bull they must be circumspect. They never affected to despise the real danger, but they did not think they would minimise it by speaking about it. They grasped the nettle and it is a great relief to all well-wishers of a great and glorious enterprise that they have almost succeeded in plucking from it the flower of safety. All the circumstances were fully recognised by the founders of the Company who went noiselessly and peacefully, but none the less judiciously and effectively to work. If they were to have a collision with the Matabeles—well, let it be on fair terms. They took all possible precautions against such a collision, as, for instance, by consulting Lo Bengula about the route their representatives were to take to Mashonaland; but at the same time they prepared themselves against an attack in such a way that had it unfortunately come about the issue could scarcely have been in doubt. However, there has been no unseemly "crowing" over what has been so far accomplished; no halloaing as if the Company were necessarily yet out of the wood. Practically they have but started on their enterprise; so far it has been more successful than the most sanguine anticipated, and all will wish that the same tale of harmonious co-operation with the aborigines may continue to the end. *Apropos*, on the day the Charter was signed the Duke of Fife made a neat and telling speech about the objects of the Company at the Mansion House. He showed that the Company was not only willing, but bound by its charter to aid in the great work of spreading civilisation and Christianity in the sphere of its operations. Those who had doubted the effect of the Chartered Company's operations on the high work which Great Britain is destined to perform in South Africa, were reassured by the straightforward utterances of the Duke. He also intimated that steam locomotion was to be established on the Zambesi and Shiré Rivers, which would be a powerful means at once of checking the raids of slave dealers and of putting a stop to the introduction of liquor and other "objectionable commodities" into the country.

It is but a year and a half since the Charter was signed; and what has the British South Africa Company already accomplished? In this short time the Cape Railway system has been extended from Kimberley to Vryburg, a distance of 148 miles, being constructed at the rate of three miles a week. The telegraph system, which terminated at Mafeking, has been carried to the Macloutsie River. Khama's Town, Palapye, the camp of the Bechuanaland Border Police, and the headquarters camp of the British South Africa Company's police, are now in telegraphic communication with London. A force of police, numbering 500 men, has been enrolled and despatched to the various forts, viz., Fort Tuli, Fort Victoria, Fort Charter, and Fort Salisbury, which have been established between the British Protectorate and Mount Hampden. The expedition, which numbered in all about 700, was placed under the command of Colonel Pennefather, the Commandant of the Company's police, Mr. Selous, the celebrated African traveller, preparing in advance of the column a broad wagon road from Tuli to Mount Hampden, a distance of over 400 miles.

Nor must I omit to give Major Johnson and Mr. H. J. Borrow their full share of credit for the successful result of this part of a difficult and hazardous enterprise. By this expedition the British South Africa Company may claim to have occupied a country described as the richest gold field in the

MAJOR F. JOHNSON.

world, without firing a single shot, and with the fullest consent of the natives. Moreover, a picked number of colonists, comprising farmers, mechanics, and artisans, have been introduced into Mashonaland, with ample supplies of food. "It would," triumphantly and with just pride, exclaims Mr. Geo. Cawston, "be impossible for any company in this short space of time more thoroughly to justify its existence, or to give more solid and substantial evidence of *bonâ fide* occupation of the territories within the field of its operations. I believe the success that has invariably attended the work of the British South Africa Company is entirely unprecedented in the annals of English commercial enterprise. It is thoroughly characteristic of British pluck, and will result, I firmly believe, in the foundation of a vast and valuable addition to the English Crown not unworthily competing with the career of the old East India Company."

But to go more into detail. The Charter was signed on October 29, 1889, and Mr. Rhodes arrived in South Africa from England in the previous month. At that time the Rudd concessionaires were represented in the interior by two gentlemen resident at Bulawayo, the capital of Matabeleland. The terminus of the colonial railway system was Kimberley, and of the telegraph system Mafeking. During the period under review the line of railway has been extended, as we have seen, a distance of 148 miles, and the telegraph line has been continued to beyond Palapye, some 360 miles distant from Kimberley. By virtue of the agreement made by Mr. Rhodes with Sir Gordon Sprigg and his colleagues in the early part of the year, the work of the construction of the line of railway to Vryburg was carried out entirely at the cost of the Colonial Government, and the Company have consequently now the great advantage of these additional miles of railway, without having incurred any expense in

MATLAPUTLA FORT.

their construction. Conjointly with the extension of the railway from Kimberley, the Company proceeded with the making of the telegraph system from Mafeking, and authorised the construction of a line to Matlaputla Camp, near the Macloutsie River, which is some 465 miles north of Mafeking, and the boundary between British Bechuanaland and the Disputed Territory. The Matlaputla Camp is for the present the base of the Company's operations. Here are encamped two troops of the British Bechuanaland Police and one troop of the Company's police. The extension of the telegraph line was carried out under the immediate supervision of Mr. James Sivewright, who was for many years General Manager of the Colonial Telegraphs, and who is now Commissioner for Public Works in the Cape Ministry. The actual work of construction northwards from Mafeking was commenced on May 12. It was decided to establish offices for the receipt and despatch of telegrams at Ramotsa (Ikaning's chief town), Palla (at the junction of the Notuani and Limpopo Rivers), Palapye (Khama's chief town), and at Matlaputla Camp near the Macloutsie. The work, the cost of which was entirely borne by the British South Africa Company, was found to be more arduous than anticipated as the country traversed was covered with dense bush, and anxiety was caused by the hostile attitude of the tribe who acknowledge as their chief Linchwe, who resides at Moschudi. Transport, moreover, always a controlling factor in South Africa, at one time, threatened to seriously hamper, if not entirely stop the construction; but in spite of all those difficulties the work was performed with great despatch, as will be gathered from the fact that the office at Ramotsa was opened on June 13, that at Palla on August 16, and at

A KIMBERLEY GROUP.

Palapye on October 12. The extension to Macloutsie is now being carried on with all expedition.

Some correspondence took place between the Chartered Company and the Imperial Government on the question of raising the necessary police force in connection with the enterprise of the former. The Company offered to provide the funds for an increase of the Bechuanaland Police, to enable that corps to operate in the Bechuanaland protectorate and in Matabeleland; but this suggestion was found not to be feasible. The Government, however, gave their consent (a right they had granted under the charter) to the raising of a special force of police by the

Company, and this was speedily recruited in South Africa, a very fine body of 500 men being the result. In raising and equipping the force the Company had the cordial co-operation and assistance of the High Commissioner and Bechuanaland authorities. Mr. Rhodes, being fully aware of the necessity of occupying, at as early a date as possible, the territory within the sphere of the Company's operations, turned his attention to what has been shown to be the rich region of Mashonaland, and, in order to avoid any possible conflict with the Matabeleland regiments or interference with their kraals and gardens, deemed it advisable to advance northward into the country by an easterly route. Dr. Jameson was selected by Mr. Rhodes for the difficult and responsible task of securing the King's approval of the proposed operations of the Company in Mashonaland. In this undertaking Dr. Jameson was eminently successful, and in May active operations for the advance

were commenced. The following telegram from the High Commissioner was received by the Secretary of the Chartered Company at Kimberley :—

June 6, 1890.

Having carefully considered the political position, the Governor and High Commissioner considers the time has arrived to give his consent to the entry of the Company's forces into Mashonaland by the route already agreed upon—that is to say, by a route which will skirt Matabeleland proper and leave all Matabeleland kraals to the north and west of the expeditionary force.

You are therefore at liberty to instruct Colonel Pennefather that as soon as he receives from Major-General Methuen a certificate in writing that he is satisfied with the general efficiency of the Company's forces, the pioneer force may advance on the authorised route, supported by such portion of the Company's police as may be deemed necessary by Colonel Pennefather.

Should the preparations of the Company's police force be in advance of the pioneer forces, and should circumstances render the earliest possible advance expedient, Colonel Pennefather may then use his discretion as to crossing the Macloutsie in advance of the pioneer force, but he should not proceed far ahead ; the object to be attained is the peaceful occupation of Mashonaland, and it is desirable that all officers should be instructed to be most careful and prudent in the treatment of the natives with whom they may be brought in contact, and to respect their prejudices and susceptibilities.

With regard to the men at the Macloutsie camp I may here reproduce some remarks made to them by Sir Henry Loch on the occasion of His Excellency's visit last year to the camp :—

Captain Leonard and Men,—I am very glad to have the pleasure of seeing you here to-day and to hear how well you hold with your fellow-men of the Bechuanaland Border Police. Although you are not at the front, you cannot be in a more important post than this, where you are at present stationed. Everybody cannot be in front ; but I understand from Mr. Rhodes that you will be in an equally good position as your comrades are up at Mount Hampden, or Fort Victoria, or Fort Tuli. Therefore you have no reason to complain, and you may, I think, feel satisfied that in being here you are assisting in holding one of the most important positions in the country. Fortunately, your comrades have got up to Mashonaland without having to fire a shot. I trust that state of things may continue, but it is impossible to say whether it will be so or not. You may in the meantime rest assured that if there is any difficulty up in Mashonaland there is no part of the country where there will be greater difficulties than where you are now stationed. Therefore it is with the greatest satisfaction that I see before me now one of the finest bodies of men it has ever been my good fortune to see. I understand from the officer commanding that your conduct has been exceptionally good while in camp, and I think the amount of work that has been done at Macloutsie within so comparatively short a time reflects great credit upon the men of both forces who have been quartered here. I look upon you and the British Bechuanaland Police as one body, as comrades who will work together in the future as you have worked together in the past.

The following is a complete list of the officers who were recently serving with the expedition to Mashonaland. All hold commissions under the Chartered Company :—

Lieutenant-Colonel E. G. Pennefather, 6th Dragoons (Commandant); Captain Sir John Willoughby, Royal Horse Guards (staff officer); Brevet-Major Arthur G. Leonard, late 2nd battalion East Lancashire Regiment ; Captain Patrick W. Forbes, 6th Dragoons ; Captain C. F. Lendy, Royal Artillery (commanding the artillery); Captain H. M. Hayman, late Cape Mounted Rifles ; Captain W. Molyneux, Natal Mounted Police (paymaster); Captain E. C. Chamley-Turner, Lieutenant Royal Scots Regiment ; Lieutenant W. Hicks-Beach, captain 4th battalion Gloucestershire Regiment ; Lieutenant C. W. P. Slade, captain 3rd battalion Wiltshire Regiment ; Lieutenant H. V. Brackenbury, captain 3rd battalion Lincolnshire Regiment ; Lieutenant F. W. Bruce, Bechuanaland Police ; Lieutenant R. H. O. Capper, 1st battalion North Staffordshire Regiment (signalling officer); Lieutenant R. P. J. Codrington, 8th Royal Irish Hussars ; Lieutenant M. D. Graham, 2nd battalion Northamptonshire Regiment ; Lieutenant C. E. Keith-Falconer, 1st battalion Northumberland Fusiliers ; Lieutenant E. Dunne, Colonial Forces (transport officer); Lieutenant A. E. C. Grey, 3rd battalion North-umberland Fusiliers; Lieutenant Hon. Eustace Edward T. Fiennes, late Canadian Police; Lieutenant G. Chaplin, captain Forfar and Kincardine Artillery Militia; Lieutenant Harford; Lieutenant Shep-stone; Surgeons R. S. Rand and E. Goody.

In addition to the foregoing, Captain C. H. Tye, late adjutant 6th Dragoons, is also holding a commission under the British South Africa Company, and is on service as commandant of the fort at Tuli. Several of the officers whose names figure in the fore-going list are well known in the service, Lieut.-Colonel Pennefather,

LT.-COL. E. G. PENNEFATHER.

the Commandant, having gained brevet promotion in the Innis-killing Dragoons for service in the Boer campaign and in Zululand, while Sir John Willoughby was with the Blues in the cavalry charge at Kassassin and at Tel-el-Kebir, and has made a name for himself in various fields of sport, after gaining Derby honours with Harvester, whose dead heat with St. Gatien will always remain famous in turf history. Major Leonard was with the 59th in the last Afghan War, and as a transport officer served in the Egyptian campaign of 1882, and in the Soudan under General Graham, gaining a brevet majority for services at El Teb and Tamai. In the list will be noticed the names of Captain Slade, son of the late Colonel Slade, of the 5th Lancers; Mr. Keith-Falconer, son of the late Major the Hon. Charles Keith-Falconer, and cousin of Lord Kintore; the Hon. Eustace Fiennes, second son of Lord Saye and Sele; Lieutenant Shepstone, a son of Sir Theophilus; and Lieutenant Codrington, who gained a commission from the 11th Hussars. To return to Sir John Willoughby, the name of that popular officer has been much before the public of late in connection with the wanton attack by the Portuguese upon him and his escort at the mouth of the Pungwe River. Sir John has taken a very active interest in the great enterprise of the Chartered Company, and has contributed to the *Fortnightly* a highly interesting and valuable article, entitled "How We Occupied Mashonaland." As Sir John points out, the Company had, in coming to a decision as to how to enter Mashonaland, four courses open to them: (1) To send in small parties consisting each of two or three wagons in charge of five or six white men. (2) To equip a small armed road-making party. (3) To arm a force not too large to arouse the jealous suspicion or fears of the neighbouring monarch, but sufficiently strong to keep up communications along the road, and protect itself from treachery or any possible attack unauthorised by the King. (4) To send a force large enough to ensure success in the face of any eventuality or opposition. The first of these courses was abandoned at once, as apart from the almost certainty of small parties meeting with considerable delay and probable annoyance from roving bands of Matabele, such an entry into Mashonaland would not have been recognised as occupation. It would certainly have been followed by numerous small parties of Portuguese and Boer adventurers, who would have caused endless complications and disputes as to rights of occupation, and there were already rumours of a large Boer expedition, 1,500 strong, being about to start for the Promised Land. The third course, in a modified form, was decided on. It will have been observed by the dispatch of June 6th, that Sir Henry Loch, the Governor of the Cape Colony, concluded at the eleventh hour that the expedition must not be such as to provoke suspicion and opposition on account of its strength, while being too weak to overcome such opposition. His Excellency decided that a military officer of tried experience should take with him such a force as would be able to guard against a treacherous surprise and enable him to keep open his lines of communication. Consequently, towards the end of April, Brevet Lieut.-Col. Pennefather was appointed to the supreme command, with Sir John Willoughby as his staff officer.

The police force, numbering, as I say, some 500 men, was, at a

WITH THE PIONEERS.—A COMMON OCCURRENCE ON THE ROAD.

cost of about £100,000, raised, organised, and admirably equipped. A better commander could not have been found than Lieutenant-Colonel Pennefather, of the Inniskilling Dragoons, whose experience of native warfare in Zululand would be invaluable, and would inspire confidence, both amongst officers and men, should any occasion arise to prove it. This police force, apart from the general protection it afforded to the expedition on the march, is being used for maintaining the administration of the Company in Mashonaland, as well as for keeping up communications with the Imperial police in Bechuanaland. Further, together with the police, and on the same lines, a so-called Pioneer Corps was raised under contract with Messrs. Johnson, Heany, and Borrow. It numbered about 200 men, and was placed under the immediate command of Major Johnson, whose vigorous mind and indefatigable energy were a sufficient guarantee for the efficiency of the work done by this section of the expeditionary force. As the name denotes, the Pioneer Corps was to be primarily employed in making a road, 400 miles long, from the Macloutsie River, in the disputed territory, to Mount Hampden, in Mashonaland. Upon its arrival there, and upon the due occupation of the country, it was arranged that, as soon as practicable, the members would be released for the purposes of prospecting, settling, and filling other civil employments. In this connection, it should be remembered that both the Pioneer Corps and police force were composed of carefully-picked men—farmers, miners, prospectors, crack shots, good riders—in a word, the flower of South African manhood. I have heard there are some baronets and members of the Pelican Club among them, but cannot vouch for the accuracy of the statement. Recreation and its means were not forgotten, the wagons (numbering 65) carrying the paraphernalia of a cricket club, a football club, a lawn-tennis club, and a theatre and scenery. It will also interest all to hear that both the spiritual as well as the medical necessities of the expedition were amply provided for.

The plan of action being now definitely settled, there was no time to be lost if the expedition was to get off in time to enter Mashonaland before the heavy rains set in. On the 12th of May, Sir John Willoughby started by post-cart, *via* Vryburg, Mafeking, and Palapye, for the Police base camp, situated on the Macloutsie River, a distance of 720 miles from Kimberley, and Lieut.-Colonel Pennefather followed a week later. Here they found the Company's police, respecting which corps Sir John is very enthusiastic. A finer body of men one could not wish to see, he says, but they were practically untrained to the work of mounted infantry, and, though well equipped for stationary duty on the banks of the Macloutsie, for which the force had originally been raised, were naturally incomplete as regards transport and supplies, and the general organisation necessary for the arduous undertaking now in view. They were intended to be a mounted corps, but the horses had not yet arrived, as it was considered advisable not to start them from

WITH THE PIONEERS.—A LAAGER SHOWING THE PORTABLE ENGINE FOR THE ELECTRIC LIGHT.

Kimberley until the " horse-sickness," that terrible scourge of South Africa, became less prevalent than it is during the early months of the year. Sir John Willoughby says he cannot speak too highly of the intelligence and aptitude of the men. They were all eager to be taught, and the more drills they had the better they seemed to like it. In three weeks' time they had thoroughly mastered nearly everything it was necessary to teach them in the way of skirmishing, dismounted duty, advance guards, outpost duty, bayonet exercise, and general mounted infantry drill, and on the arrival, in the middle of June, of Major-General the Hon. P. Methuen, Adjutant General of the Forces in South Africa, who had been specially deputed to inspect and report on the general efficiency of the pioneers and police, Sir John considered that, as far as training went, the force was fit to start at once. Three troops of the B.B.P., under the command of Major Grey, Staff Officer, were also encamped on the Macloutsie, and a strong pentagonal fort had been constructed for the defence of the camp. It is very satisfactory to note that Sir John speaks in unqualified appreciation of the great assistance rendered him on all occasions by Major Grey and the officers of the B.B.P., while that force and the Company's police were together. The site of the Macloutsie camp had been carefully chosen on the highest ground near a small tributary stream called the Matlaputla, which supplied excellent drinking water. A great deal of work has been done in this camp; the thick mopani bush having been cleared for a distance of 1,000 yards, huts of poles and daaga built for officers and men, and substantial stables of the same materials for the horses. The elevation is 2,270 feet above the sea level, and the situation, up to the present, has proved most healthy for the men, but the reverse for the horses, as the mortality from " horse-sickness " during the past year has been considerable, even during those months when most other places appeared to be free from the disease. In six months the police lost 160 horses out of 500, from the scourge, only five out of those attacked recovering.

The force having been inspected by General the Hon. Paul Methuen, that officer signified his entire approval of its condition and efficiency, and thereupon authorised the northward movement to commence. And so, notwithstanding a certain amount of petty intrigue and opposition from interested and unscrupulous white men, the expedition started under the best of auspices, hopeful of a successful and friendly occupation of Mashonaland. The men were eager, the natives friendly, and no less an authority than Mr. Moffat (recently made a C.M.G., and now officially representing English interests at Bulawayo) was, as I always had been, most sanguine about the result. There is also no doubt now that Lo Bengula himself and his leading men were disposed to regard favourably the operations of the Company, which, wild savage though he is, he clearly sees must in the end prove of immense benefit both to himself and his country. The latest news is that Lo Bengula has undertaken to supply the Company with cattle and has delivered his first instalment of 250 head at the Company's station. Apparently the only possible element of danger to the expedition lay in the chance that the King might be unable to control the more turbulent spirits among his younger warriors, who might clamour against the King's policy in favour of the white man. However, everything pointed to a peaceful and successful issue. Notwithstanding, the utmost precautions were taken on the line of march, and all reasonable measures adopted to prevent the occurrence of one of those disasters for which in the past South Africa has been so unhappily notorious.

Many persons in England and throughout South Africa read the news from the gallant forces with keen personal interest, and learnt with relief that an arduous and difficult task was being prosecuted under conditions as favourable to those engaged in it as could reasonably be expected. A much wider circle followed with interest and pride the operations of the small body of Englishmen who were maintaining in the heart of Africa the courageous and adventurous traditions of the race. That little band of Pioneers was laying the foundations of an Empire, and its members were opening up new outlets of incalculable magnitude for their countrymen. It was more than gratifying to learn that various sinister predictions had been falsified and that the Pioneers had met with no obstacles, except such as were offered by the physical conditions of a new country. Every care had, indeed, been taken to reduce as far as possible the risks of conflict with the natives. The route chosen for the new road, by which the South African Colonies will eventually join hands with British settlements north of the Zambesi, skirts the south-eastern boundary of Matabeleland, leaving the capital and kraals of Matabele warriors well on the left. Lo Bengula was friendly, and possessed as much statesmanship as to understand the advantages his people may derive from intercourse with white men. But, as all his people are not equally enlightened, it was wise not to push on their education at too great a pace. It showed sound discretion to let them become accustomed to the proximity of strangers before actually entering into close relations. The British South Africa Company's plan of operations was at once simple and comprehensive. It was simultaneously consolidating its base, completing its communications, and pushing forward its explorations.

It was decided to make Mount Hampden the objective point of the expedition, and arrangements were made to construct a rough road from a point below the junction of the Tuli and Shashi Rivers to the Lunde River, thence north-east to Mount Wedza, and thence somewhat north to Mount Hampden. On June 25 Major Johnson and Mr. Selous crossed the Macloutsie River with the Pioneers, who were accompanied by several prospecting parties and the police force, the whole expedition being under the command of Colonel Pennefather. Mount Hampden was reached early on the morning of September 12, without a single shot being fired, and without the loss

THE PIONEER EXPEDITION PASSING A KOPJE.

of a single life.   The road made by the expedition is known as the
Selous Road, and from the Shashi to Mount Hampden is a distance
of about 400 miles.   The country through which the expedition
passed was reported as being very well watered and plentifully
timbered, and the high plateau extending from the Umzingwane
River, some 3,000 feet above the sea level, to Mount Hampden, the
altitude of which is 5,000 feet, was reported by all to be an exceptionally fine stretch of country, offering, in addition to its mineral
wealth, exceptional facilities to both stock farmers and agriculturists.
The road made by the expedition was constructed at a cost of less than
£90,000.   Forts were erected at various points along the line of
march, and these will serve for the time being as headquarters of
the police detachments, and hereafter as centres for the purposes
of the civil administration of the country.

Let us follow the Pioneers as they established themselves
in the country at these forts.   Up to Macloutsie Camp the
force had been carried by rail and wagon and had marched on
foot.   There was the usual number of false alarms and the usual
rushes to the forts for protection from an enemy that never came ;
but these all served to show the admirable discipline which so soon
characterised this peaceful force.   The members of it, of course,
had many adventures, some of an exciting kind, and all these
formed material for very interesting letters written to the papers
or to friends.   A good road was made all the way to Mount
Hampden ; trees were cut down by the Pioneers, and bad bits filled
with sand in an incredibly short time.

The force was under the strictest military discipline, and every
precaution was taken for the safety of the camp, which after every
trek was formed into laager, guarded at each corner by the machine
guns and seven-pounders.   An engine kept up full steam all
through the night, so that the search-light could be thrown into
the bush at any moment.   Every preparation was made against a
surprise in the way of advance and rear patrols, advance guard,
rear guard, and flanking parties.   Every night the wagons were
laagered, and the men had orders to sleep in their clothes with their
arms beside them.   The horses were either "linked" across the
laager or else "rung" in their respective divisions.   Every morning
the men stood to arms from reveillé to daybreak (one hour), and
then, before the laager was broken up, the country was carefully
surveyed, and the native scouts sent out.   About every thirty-
five or forty miles a post station was formed, four men being
left at each.   At the Matlaputla Camp the men were agreeably
surprised at the arrival in their midst of six Sisters of Mercy
to tend the sick and wounded should there unfortunately be any.
On alighting from their wagon they passed in procession through the
camp to the hospital, the men forming line on each side for them to
walk between, while the hearty cheering and welcome they got
were unrestrained.

As already stated, it was on the 25th of June that the actual first

WITH THE PIONEERS.—AN INTERVIEW WITH THE MATABELE.

start was made by one troop of the police (100 strong), who escorted the pioneers to the Tuli River. On the 5th of July, Colonel Pennefather went forward with two more troops of the police and 130 horses and two months' supplies, he having decided not to wait for the remainder of the horses. Sir John Willoughby remained at the Macloutsie to bring on the balance of the horses and supplies.

Between Macloutsie Camp and Fort Tuli the march was a forced one, no time being unnecessarily wasted in such a luxury as sleep. A halt was called every now and then to allow the wagons with the baggage and the commissariat to overtake those on foot or horseback. After six days' march the site of Fort Tuli was reached. The Fort is an almost natural one, situate on the top of a small, nearly circular kopje,

THE " WAIT A BIT " THORN—A COMMON VELD INCIDENT.

and forming a very strong position. The River Tuli, from which the name of the fort is taken, is a remarkably fine one, in breadth about 500 yards. The banks are covered with reeds reaching to the height of some 12 to 15 feet. The country all along the line of march, so far, was densely wooded with " vachte-en-beitje " (wait a bit), " cameeldoorn " (cat thorn), and thorn trees of various other kinds, and it was well watered. At night, from the tents, the men could hear the lions roaring down among the river reeds, the jackals barking, hyenas laughing, and wolves howling and quarrelling over their prey. One night a lion visited the sentry on horse guard, and walked up and down in front of him at a distance of some twelve yards—not a very pleasant visitor. About 150 of Khama's men at Tuli Fort helped greatly

CROSSING A RIVER.—A TOUGH JOB.

with the work of strengthening the position in the way of making a
zereba round the base of the kopje, clearing the immediate
locality of bush,
&c. The country in
the neighbourhood
of the Tuli River
is a veritable Eden.
All kinds of wild
fruit grow in abun-
dance, and there
are some enormous
cream of tartar
trees measuring
from 55 to 65 feet
in circumference.
The pulp of the
tree is manufactured
into a beer, which
is more freely used
as a medicine than
as a beverage. The
soil is remarkably
rich, but there is
almost no popula-
tion.

On July 11th the
advanced column,
consisting of 180
pioneers, 200 police, and small prospecting parties, with 62 wagons and

THE ARTILLERY TROOP PIONEERS.

two months' supplies for the whole force, started to cross the Tuli
River, accompanied by Mr. Colquhoun, who had been appointed Administrator of Mashonaland. A drift of corduroy, consisting of poles

and reeds, had been made at the Tuli, but the column took a day to
cross. Owing to many other rivers having to be negotiated and the
road having in many places to be cut through thick bush, it was
not till the 2nd of August that the Lunde, another big river, 141
miles beyond the Tuli, was reached. Meanwhile Sir John
Willoughby was occupied in getting together the remainder of the
supplies, his operations being much facilitated by the cordial co-

WITH THE PIONEERS.—OBJECTING TO BE INSPANNED.

operation of the Chief Khama. In due course he got to Fort Tuli,
where he left a troop as garrison. On July 29th he crossed the
Tuli with 16 wagons, 110 men, 30 of Khama's natives to drive
loose cattle and act as scouts, 130 horses, and about 250 slaughter
cattle and goats. On the following day, Sir John and his force

began their stern chase after the advance column, which they expected to overtake at the Lunde River.

Between the Tuli and Bubye Rivers, a distance of 74 miles, lies a belt of wholly uninhabited country, consisting mainly of monotonous tracts of open bush, diversified at intervals with bold, rocky kopjes and streams. Here many species of the magnificent fauna of South Africa still find an asylum. In the dense forest between the Umzingwane and Umshabetzi Rivers, elephants, giraffe, and sometimes buffalo are to be found. All along the rivers, koodoos, water-buck, and bush-buck are numerous, whilst sable and roan antelopes are common among the picturesque granite hills, which are so conspicuous a feature in the scenery of this part of South Africa. Other game to be enumerated are the beautiful striped Burchell's zebra, duikers, and stein-buck. To the country between the Tuli and Lunde Rivers the name of Banyailand may very properly be given, as it is inhabited by a number of petty so-called Banyai chiefs, who, by some accounts are tributary to Lo Bengula, but who by others refuse to recognise the Matabele monarch as their King. Three of these chiefs visited the camp—Sitoutski, Matipi, and Chibi— and were duly interviewed by Lieut.-Colonel Pennefather—the great White Queen's Induna, as he is termed by them. Their attitude and demeanour were invariably most friendly; mutual exchanges of presents took place, and the most amicable relations were at once established. In exchange for a goat or a cow they would receive a gaudy blanket, a Martini-Henry rifle, with bandolier, containing a few rounds of ammunition, and other trifles, and would leave in a high state of satisfaction and with certainly not the worst of the bargain on their side. As with the chiefs, so with their people. All along the line of march the natives met with were most friendly, and visited the camp fearlessly and freely. They were willing and eager to trade, bringing in (in small quantities, it is true) supplies of mealies, beans, tobacco, &c., in exchange for limbo, "white-eyed" beads, and coloured handkerchiefs. Others, too, offered to act as guides or accept service in the camp in any small menial capacity. When requested, they readily gave any information asked of them as to the nature and character of the country ahead, the presence or absence of any bodies of Matabele, and the information given uniformly proved to be reliable and correct. The lot of these Banyai natives can hardly be regarded as a happy one. These unfortunate people live in constant dread of ever-recurring raids from the Matabele, who, apparently, when they have nothing better to do, and out of sheer wantonness, raid down and kill them indiscriminately, carrying off their wives, children, cattle, and corn, just leaving them enough of the latter to grow another year's crop and keep them from starvation. In consequence, their villages are perched upon high declivitous and almost inaccessible granite rocks, every available point being used on which to erect their huts. But let us hope this will all be altered now.

At the Lunde River lions were seen playing in the sandy bed of the river. The natives in the villages round about are very friendly, and have helped considerably by cutting grass for thatching the huts, bringing in poles and bamboo for roofing, and in many other

NATIVE HUTS IN THE HILLS OF MASHONALAND.

ways. But if the men had occasion to patrol through their villages they hid all their young intombis (unmarried girls) and imfasis (married women), as no doubt they thought they would do as the Matabeles have been in the habit of doing, *i.e.*, make periodical raids and carry their young women off.

Since the memorable march I am writing of was made, this particular territory has assumed an extra importance as the country on which a party of Boers are said to have cast covetous eyes. Recent intelligence from Cape Town stated that it had been found necessary to issue an Imperial Proclamation announcing to filibusters that any attempt to occupy Banyailand (the territory

being thus described, though Banyailand proper is somewhat further
north) would be resisted as an infringement of the rights of the
British South Africa Company. This was a stern and politic warning, and no doubt it quickly had good effect. Various statements
have been lately afloat respecting the proposed trek of a certain
number of Boers from the Transvaal to the north. It has been
put forward that the intention was to establish, with the connivance
and consent of Portugal, a "new Republic," having for its borders
the Zambesi on the north, Matabeleland on the west, Portuguese
territory on the east, and the Limpopo on the south. The audacity
of the proposal would be amazing if South Africans did not know
that the more ardent spirits among the young Boers are ever ready
to take full advantage of masterly inactivity on the part of the
Imperial Government. They got the fairest moiety of Zululand
by sheer bounce. But England did not allow them to repeat the
experiment either in Mashonaland or Gazaland. Some people
took into account the possibility that the Portuguese (their South
African representatives rather) and the Boers (the ardent spirits I
refer to) had come to an understanding that Portugal's monstrous
claim to Gazaland not having been allowed by England, they might
conspire in a joint juggle to secure that country under some kind
of dual control. If the South African Portuguese had any such
notion they did not know the men that they had to deal with. It
might suit the temporary convenience of certain Boers to act as
Portuguese cat's-paws; but the monkey would very soon get the
worst of it. Sir Henry Loch followed up his proclamation respecting Banyailand with a prompt despatch to President Kruger, who
met it in a spirit which augurs well for the determination of the
Transvaal Government to abide loyally by their agreements with
England. He laconically but expressively wired that he had
"damped" the trek, and issued a sharp proclamation prohibiting
any subjects of the Republic from taking any part in it. News
also arrived from Cape Town stating that a meeting of the
Africander Bond had approved of a proposal put forward by Mr.
Rhodes to prevent a collision between the Boers and the Chartered
Company. It was founded on a scheme for the pacific occupation
of Mashonaland by anybody, be he Boer or British, under the
ægis of its British-countenanced governing body. The Banyailand
Chiefs are said to have years ago granted concessions of their
country to certain Boers, concessions which were hawked about
Europe. Mr. Rhodes openly showed in a speech at the Paarl,
that the possessors of these concessions had endeavoured to levy
blackmail on him, threatening him with "trouble" if he did not
pay a long price for the documents. Apart from these concessions
becoming the property of the Chartered Company, if a
large trek of Boers takes place under the terms I have mentioned,
all will not only be well in that quarter, but another definite and
satisfactory step towards opening up Mashonaland will be taken. .
But to return to the march of the Chartered Company's gallant

forces. One wonderful feature of the country has been named "Providential Pass." This pass or "gorge" was struck quite unexpectedly by the Pioneer Force, and Sir John Willoughby inclines to the opinion that it was never traversed by white men until the expedition made the road through it. It is about seven miles long, and the road which has been made forms a gradual easy ascent to the top, the altitude when the head of the pass is reached being 3600 ft., as compared with 2600 ft. at the bottom. There is no difficulty for a wagon or wagons to encounter in any part of this pass, which has been almost designed by nature as a highway for civilised man to the magnificent high veld beyond. "The scenery in the pass," said Sir John in South Africa, "is grand and impressive, the mountains rising rugged and commanding on either side,

AFTER THE DAY'S MARCH.—AT THE LUNDE RIVER.

the lower slopes and ' bed ' of the gorge being covered with thick bush. Our thoughts, as we made our way slowly and tediously for the first time through this remarkable cleft of nature's formation, centred in the one idea—what a horribly suitable place for an ambuscade! The narrow roadway, the thick bush, the stony ridges to the right and left, all would favour an attack from barbarians against even a powerful force provided with the most modern equipments of war. But we were in a land of peace, and but for the presence of our own column, with its medley of sounds, a land of silence and solitude, and ere the seven miles were accomplished we were mostly engrossed in speculations as to the nature of the country which lay beyond the pass. And the contrast was not more wonderful than welcome, for we emerged from the some-

what dispiriting gloom of dense bush and overhanging rocks into a
vast open country, smiling in the sunshine and fair to look upon."
It is about a mile and a half beyond the pass that Fort Victoria,
named presumably after the Queen, has been erected, and some
12 miles to the eastward are situated the remarkable ruins of
Zimbabye, fully described in an early chapter. The country here is
perfectly open as far as the eye can see, and the elevation is
stated to be much higher than was estimated in the previous
rough surveys, the altitude averaging about 4700 ft., and being in
one place, indeed, not less than 5200 ft. In regard to those Boers
who intended to make a rush for Matabeleland, when they
were checkmated by the treaty concluded with Lo Bengula

MASHONA MOUNTAIN SHELTER.

declaring his country to be within the British sphere of influence,
it is interesting to note that at several stages of the route northwards the Pioneer Force were confronted with proofs that the
Boers, many of whom professed to know so much about Mashonaland, had never been seen in the country, and were totally unac-
quainted with the natives and their natural surroundings.
Many of the natives, indeed, had never before seen a white

man, and, more curious still, it is observed, had never seen a horse. They were much interested in the horses of the Pioneers, and were greatly puzzled at the sight of the horses trotting.

A brief extract or two from Sir John Willoughby's article will be acceptable.

Our progress, though nearly double as quick as that of the force ahead, was very slow and tedious, for, owing to the military precautions necessary and the careful scouting required, we could not trek by night, the time best suited for oxen, and at the best of times ox-wagons are the slowest of all modes of transport. I will try to give a short description of the road through the Banyai country from the Tuli to Fort Victoria, our first fortified post in Mashonaland. After crossing the Tuli the road leads, for the first thirty miles, through most uninteresting bush country, chiefly covered with mopani trees interspersed with mimosa, and only broken here and there by an occasional kopje ; but there were no obstacles to be overcome except two unimportant streams and a few patches of stony ground. Then comes the first serious obstacle in the shape of a sandy river, some two hundred yards wide, called the Umzingwane ; but as a good corduroy drift had here been made, we crossed in about three hours and with little difficulty. From Umzingwane to the next big river, the Umshabetsi, is a distance of eighteen miles ; there is no water, and the road continues through uninteresting bush country, similar to that just mentioned. Fresh tracks of elephants were here seen, and lions are numerous in the neighbourhood. From this point the scenery improves in character, for though the dense bush continues along the whole line of march taken by the expedition right up to Fort Victoria, the long rolling country becomes broken by granite kopjes, and even mountains of the most grotesque shapes ; and these become more frequent the farther north the traveller proceeds. Soon after leaving the Umshabetsi we came to the Nambandi hills, inhabited by a tribe of Makalaka, or Banyai people, a mild and inoffensive race living in daily and hourly terror of the Matabele. They occupy round huts, built of clay and thatch, among the rocky boulders, in almost inaccessible places on the summits of the hills or kopjes. Our arrival was naturally a great event in their lives, and the surrounding heights were black with crowds of these poor people, who watched our approach with fear and trembling, as we encamped for the day on a circular space shut in on all sides by these granite hills.

Although friendly enough, we found all the Makalaka we met on the road disposed to hold aloof from us ; the reason being that they regarded us as doomed to be destroyed by the Matabele, and feared they would suffer for it, later on, if they appeared too friendly or rendered us any assistance. . . . At this place we had our first scare. Mr. Colenbrander, one of the British South Africa Company's agents at Bulawayo, the capital of Matabeleland, arrived, as a special envoy from Lo Bengula, with an order from the King (in the form of an ultimatum) requiring the expedition "to turn back or take the consequences." Subsequent events proved that Mr. Colenbrander had formed a misconception of the state of affairs in Matabeleland, and that the King was merely indulging in "bounce," or, more probably, only temporising with his young warriors, who were doubtless in a most excited state and clamouring to be let loose at us. At the time, however, one could not possibly know this, and it was discomforting to be told we should probably have the Matabele army on the top of us within the next week, when another 150 miles of broken bush country had still to be traversed before we could reach the high veld, or the main column ahead, or any open country where we could reasonably hope to defend ourselves against heavy odds.

Mr. Colenbrander, after informing me of the contents of his *billet-doux*, pushed on to deliver it to Colonel Pennefather, leaving us to continue our weary journey towards the Lunde River, now rendered doubly tedious by the extra precautions I deemed it necessary to take. From Nambandi to the Lunde there is not much variation in the physical features of the country, but the numerous kopjes to be met with on either side of the road are more thickly populated, and here and there extensive clearings have been made for the purpose of cultivation. The soil is wonderfully fertile, and after being cleared yields Indian corn, mealies, sweet potatoes, beans, and tobacco in abundance, and this under the merest scratching with the primitive hoes in use amongst the natives. Water is everywhere plentiful, and may be drawn from the pools of the numerous sandy rivers intersecting the road, or from the springs which abound amongst the granite kopjes.

The above-mentioned rivers, on account of their steep banks and sandy beds, were great natural obstacles to the advance of the main column, and also to us, though to a somewhat lesser degree. Drifts had to be made over each, the banks being cut away and the sandy beds corduroyed; but even then, with new drifts, until they have settled down and become hard by the frequent passage of many wagons, it takes hours of hard labour, with double spans of oxen, hauling of ropes, breaking of trek gear, shouting and swearing, and general trial of temper, to get a convoy of wagons across one river, and sometimes as many as three such obstacles would have to be negotiated within as many miles. The character of the bush after leaving Nambandi presents an agreeable change as the monotonous mopani is almost replaced by the brighter-coloured machabel, interspersed with vegetation of larger growth; wild orange trees, giant fig trees, and cacti are common, and an occasional mahogany tree is seen at long intervals, while to the left of the road, in the far distance, a long range of broken mountainous country, where the numerous rivers take their rise, extends to the south-west border of Matabeleland.

On August 8th, our ninth day out, we reached the Wanetsi, or Nuanetsi River, 112 miles from Tuli. The crossing of this river gave us as much trouble as others of much greater width, for its banks are very steep, and its bed, unlike that of the others, rocky, and therefore difficult for oxen; there was also a running stream of considerable depth with a strong current, but this had already been well filled in with stones, and thus made practicable for the wagons. Thirty miles further on we came to the Lunde, the widest river next to the Tuli, and one which had previously been reported, by natives and Boers, to be impassable for wagons under any circumstances. This report, luckily, proved erroneous, as, though the bed of this river is three hundred yards across and traversed by a considerable stream of water, it presented no greater obstacle than any of the other rivers after we had made a good corduroy drift and partially filled up the stream with bags of sand and stones. Three hippopotami were here shot by members of the main column.

Slow as our progress had been hitherto (an average of twelve miles

THE BRITISH SOUTH AFRICA COMPANY'S PIONEERS CROSSING A STREAM.

a day), it was now still slower, as many of the oxen, overstrained by the work between Mafeking and Macloutsie and Macloutsie and Tuli, began to knock up. As it was most necessary to give them a rest, they had to be replaced with untrained slaughter oxen, and these gave us no end of trouble. Some declined to be inspanned at any price, and were constantly breaking away and careering wildly through the bush; others either refused to pull at all or pulled in the wrong direction, while others again would lie down, out of sheer perversity, and stubbornly refuse to get up, though they might be half choking themselves with the yokes. Thus it would sometimes take a couple of hours to get under weigh.

A toilsome time the rear column had as it moved along, and then up through "Providential Pass," with its steep and densely-wooded slopes, with ravines and valleys big enough to conceal countless impis. At last, on the eighteenth day after leaving the Tuli River, they emerged on the high veld and sighted, with a sense of great relief, the laager of the main column, feeling fully rewarded for their anxious time in the two-hundred-mile wilderness of dense bush.

They now saw a glorious expanse of open grass country stretching for miles in every direction, with its bright and fresh plains smiling in the morning sunlight, and only diversified here and there by a kopje or a small clump of bush just sufficient to break the sameness of its undulating surface.

A feeling, too, of security, to which we had all been strangers for some time, no doubt added to the general charm of the surroundings. for here we were at last inside the promised land, and what matter now if the Matabele did come down on us? They had missed their opportunity, if they ever meant to oppose us, for they would stand no chance against our well-armed little force in the open, however great their numbers might be; in fact, one felt as if Mount Hampden, the goal of our endeavours, had been practically reached, and the object of the expedition already attained.

About one and a half miles from the head of the gorge was the laager of the main column, presenting a most animated appearance, and reminding me very much of a village fair at home. Football and cricket were in full swing on one side, and a rifle match between the pioneers and police on another; _tentes d'abri_ and tents of all shapes and sizes, many-coloured rugs hung out to air, and here and there a flag or two, added to the general gaiety of the scene, while the black funnel of the electric light engine, rising above the tops of the wagons, made one almost expect every minute to catch sight of a steam merry-go-round, or the ordinary swings to be seen at a village fair.

The column, after our arrival, halted for two more days to rest the oxen, and during this time the construction of a lunette fort, since called Fort Victoria, was completed.

Horse-sickness disappeared on the plateau, but four horses were taken by lions on the march. The forward march from Fort Victoria was uneventful and needs little description. The troop and the Gatling gun Sir John Willoughby had brought up with him being left to garrison this fort, the rest of the column, consisting of two troops of police and the pioneer force with one Maxim, one

Gatling, and two seven-pounders, broke up laager on the 19th of August.

It will be sufficient to describe one day's routine to give a general idea of how the march was conducted. "Reveille" sounded at 4.30 A.M., when the whole force had to stand to arms till daylight appeared and the "dismiss" sounded. Patrols were sent out at "reveille," and after the "dismiss" had sounded and the pickets for the day had been posted, the night pickets were called in. Scouts in parties of two were always sent out at daybreak to reconnoitre the country fifteen miles to the front, to the rear, and to the left or threatened flank; these would return during the evening of the next day. On occasions when the column did not trek till the afternoon the horses and oxen were turned out to graze till an hour before the time of trekking, and patrols were again sent out at midday. A troop of pioneers, with Mr. Selous and the native guides, were always one day ahead, selecting the line of march and making the road. The order of march was as follows: One troop as advanced guard, and with it the Maxim gun, drawn by horses; at the head of the column the two seven-pounders, drawn by oxen, and an escort of surplus mounted men of the pioneer artillery troop and all the dismounted men of the police; then the convoy of wagons marching in two parallel lines, for after crossing the Umzingwane it was found advisable to make two roads, and thus decrease by half the original length of train, with the view to quick formation of laager in the event of attack. In rear of the convoy followed a third troop as rearguard with the Gatling gun, also drawn by oxen, while the fourth troop was employed on either flank, in small flanking parties with supports. In this manner, by means of the detached scouts, the troop one day in advance, patrols, advanced and rear guards and flanking parties, the country was most efficiently scouted for a radius of fifteen miles all round, and in the event of an intended attack the force would have had ample notice given in time to form laager. Of course the hours for trekking varied according to the nature of the country; in the open country it was possible to trek at the time best suited for the oxen, which is during the early morning or the moonlit night; otherwise the usual hours of trekking were from 2 till 7 P.M. When a suitable site was selected, the laager was formed without delay, each wagon proceeding to the place it should occupy, with little noise and no confusion, picket lines, in the meantime, being put down inside for the horses and the mess fires lighted. The grass was burned for a radius of fifty yards when necessary to avoid the risk of a grass fire. At 8.30 P.M. "first post" was sounded and all the force stood to arms and was told off by sections to the wagons. By 10 o'clock each man would be sleeping under the wagon he had been appointed to defend in case of attack. The electric light engine was kept under steam all night and the light turned on at regular intervals, at 8 P.M., midnight, and one hour before daylight, and by its rays the surrounding country to a radius of a thousand yards carefully searched. In the daytime when the halts were made the natives came to trade mealies,

Kafir corn, pumpkins, rice, sweet potatoes, beans, Kafir beer, and tobacco. They exchanged these for pieces of limbo (blue or white calico), beads, or even empty cartridge cases, which, as snuff-boxes possess no mean value in the eyes of the natives of both sexes.

It was intended to proceed to Mount Wedza, some 70 miles N.E., and there construct a fort; but the idea was abandoned on account of the marshy nature of the ground it would be necessary to traverse. It was decided to erect a fort at the head waters of the Umgezi and Sabi Rivers. About 50 miles south of Mount Hampden, and 30 miles west of Mount Wedza, Fort Charter (the outlines of a square fort) was built and manned like all the others by a garrison of mounted police. Huts have been erected as at the other forts, and the men made as comfortable as the circumstances will allow. The site of the fort is well chosen, commanding a fine view from a very elevated position. There is good bathing in a river close by. After leaving one troop of the Company's police, under Captain Heyman, at Fort

SIR JOHN WILLOUGHBY, BART.

COL. FENNEFATHER POINTING OUT MOUNT HAMDEN.—AN INCIDENT ON THE MARCH.

A A

Charter (so named to commemorate the fact of the Royal
charter that had been granted to the Company the previous year),
the expeditionary force pushed its way rapidly forward along
the open high veld for 68 miles across the head-waters of the
Umfuli and Hanyani Rivers. When the Pioneers camped
for the night, Captain Heany announced that the expedition had almost reached its destination. So it had! On
the next dawn they moved on under a hill to their right, from the
top of which Colonel Pennefather saw Mount Hampden, 15 miles
to the north. The original intention had been to halt the expedition at Mount Hampden, some 10 miles north; but it having been
ascertained that there were water difficulties connected with that
site, the present station was selected and occupied. The Colonel
pointed out the camping ground, now called Fort Salisbury. The
Pioneers sauntered on, some in shirts, some in football jerseys, and
in the most nondescript articles of apparel. A barrister was
carrying a pick, an ex-sculptor an axe, and so on. Presently the

HOISTING THE BRITISH FLAG AT FORT SALISBURY.   SALUTE OF GUNS.

column was seen about four miles off to the south, rounding the
end of a wood. It was the 12th of September, and a fresh, glorious
morning. Occasionally a stray buck ran across the line of march,
and away would go the camp dogs. By 10 a.m. the column had
caught up with the Pioneers, and laager was formed. The expedition of the British South Africa Company to take possession of
Mashonaland had happily reached its destination. Not a shot had
been fired, not one per cent. of the expedition was sick, and all the
others were in robust health after 850 miles of weary marching from
Mafeking. All were in perfect health and in most exuberant
spirits. Colonel Pennefather paraded the men the next day. The
British flag was hoisted, after a short ceremony, by Lieutenant
Briscoe, late R.N., Canon Balfour saying a short prayer. Three
cheers were given for our gracious Queen, and a salute of 21 guns

echoed the "Amen" to a memorable event in South African annals.

Fort Salisbury, which is called after England's premier, is situated on an open, breezy upland, has been fixed as being in S. latitude 17° 54' and E. longitude 31° 20' and at an altitude of 4900 ft. above the general sea level. Twelve miles further north the great tableland terminates abruptly; one is there confronted by bold mountain ranges, amongst which meander the head waters of the Mazoe River, and sometimes the mind will wander to the wide reaches of the Zambesi, now within easy distance. One will occasionally feel a strong impulse to thread one's way through

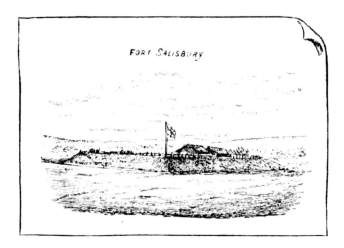

the forest-clad hills to its swampy shores, and float lazily down to the Indian Ocean, just to get a glimpse of the sea once more. The surrounding heights are dotted with kraals, and away down in the hot valley lies Wahta's Town, whence the natives come streaming in laden with mealies, mealie meal, pumpkins, lemons, ground-nuts, tobacco, beer, poultry, eggs, and milk, all of which they gladly barter for small quantities of beads or limbo.

It was a grand performance that the Pioneers could congratulate themselves upon when they drew breath at Fort Salisbury. Not only had they completed what was regarded as a journey with no little personal peril attached to it, but into this new country they had made a good serviceable road over 400 miles in length, a task frequently necessitating much heavy labour in felling the thick bush, which at times rose to the proportions of forest timber. Substantial "drifts" had been formed across big rivers, such as the Tuli, Nuanetsi, and Lunde (the last-named running at a depth of 40 ft. during the rains). "Corduroy" bridges had been constructed across smaller streams and boggy places, and the whole work had been completed without the loss of one single life

A A 2

either in the hospital or in the field. These are feats of which all Englishmen—be they colonial or home born—must feel justly proud, and prove to the cynic and pessimist that the age of British energy and enterprise has not yet gone by. Again, the daily distance or "trek" compassed by the heavily-laden 65 or more ox-wagons averaged 10¾ miles, an excellent performance those versed in such matters will at once admit, and proving as well that the first English "trek" ever made on a large scale has, in the matter of distance, at any rate, covered each day, managed more than to hold its own. As I have shown, along the line from the north of Bechuanaland to Mount Hampden five forts had been erected—namely, at Macloutsie, then at Tuli, and beyond that Fort Victoria, Fort Charter, and finally Fort Salisbury. There is a garrison at each fort, and men sent out on patrol were expected to learn all they could of the topography of the district, and the habits and character of the natives, whom they were instructed to treat with every possible friendliness. Between the forts are numerous intermediate stations, manned by 40 or 50 men, and made fairly defensible with a zereba. The huts for the men are strongly constructed, and there is a block-house at each, built in the centre, capable of containing many months' supplies of food, water, and munitions of war. The walls are loopholed, and these stations could be successfully held against almost any force of natives. Though Lo Bengula has been so far friendly to the operations of the Chartered Company, yet it will be seen that every precaution has been taken against any change of attitude on the part of the Matabele. The forts and stations are useful for the maintenance of communications with Mount Hampden, and the Company has established a regular weekly mail service letters taking 18 days between Kimberley and Mount Hampden.

Again to quote Sir John Willoughby :—

The expeditionary force arrived at this point on September 12th, just two months after the start of the advance column from the Tuli. It had then traversed a distance of 438 miles from the Macloutsie to Mount Hampden, over a completely unknown country, half of which led through thick bush, and had successfully crossed thirteen big rivers, besides a host of lesser ones, necessitating the utmost trial of patience and endurance on the part of all concerned. All this had been accomplished without the loss of a single human life, notwithstanding the prophecies of the Boers and all who professed to know anything about the country, that we should never gain the promised land, as we should either be decimated by fever, drowned in impassable rivers, stopped by the swamps, or annihilated by the Matabele, before reaching that impenetrable chain of mountains which would effectually bar our way to the high veld, if everything else failed to do so. One of the highest military authorities on native warfare in South Africa, when asked his opinion, stated that he would not undertake the enterprise with less than seven thousand men. But what cannot be accomplished with patience and perseverance when all are of the same mind, determined to succeed in the face of every difficulty, and prepared to face cheerfully whatever obstacles or dangers fortune may have in store for them? I do not think I am guilty of exaggeration in declaring that this has been one of the most successful expeditions of its kind ever undertaken, and a worthy introduction to the history of a Company with a grand future before it, whose great enterprises and achievements bid fair to rival those of its far-famed predecessor, the old East India Company.

On the day following our arrival the Company's flag was hoisted in the presence of the whole force with all the honours of a royal salute from the "seven-pounders," and by the end of the month a strong fort had been constructed, and christened Fort Salisbury, in honour of him to whose kind aid and patriotic sympathy the young Company owes so much. On October 1st, the laager was finally broken up and the pioneers disbanded, the remaining troop of police occupying the fort near which they had almost completed the construction of the huts. The pioneers though scattered in various directions, prospecting for gold, still constitute a burgher force, ready to be re-united should hostilities at any time become imminent.

In all we have ten block-houses as postal and despatch riding stations and the four forts already mentioned. Our signalling communication and our postal service by ox-cart already extends from the Macloutsie to the Tuli, and every preparation is being made for its rapid extension to Fort Victoria, a further distance of 189 miles. . . . . Although it was supposed the road would not be thoroughly opened up till next year, over 150 wagons have already gone into the country, and many more are on their way, and though we thought the road would be closed by the rainy season as early as September, it was still open up to December 12th, and on account of the general lie of the country I doubt whether the rivers will ever become impassable for more than a very short time. They will, of course, be in flood after heavy rains, but from their conformation they should run down almost as rapidly as they rise.

As for the general security of the road, I may mention that I travelled from a place thirty miles north-west of Mount Hampden to Kimberley in twenty-three days, stopping two days at intermediate stations and being further delayed by break-downs of the mail-cart between Palapye and Mafeking. From my starting-point to Tuli, a distance of 400 miles, I rode by myself in nine days, sleeping sometimes at intermediate stations and at other times in the bush or open veld, a sufficient proof, I think, of the safety of the road.

In addition to the work done by the expedition we have the railway from Kimberley now open to Vryburg, a distance of 140 miles, and the telegraph from Mafeking to Palapye, which by now should have reached the Macloutsie, a total distance of 480 miles. In the meanwhile a small expedition under Mr. Lockner has penetrated to the Barotse country, north of the Zambesi, and obtained a concession over another splendid tract of upland country 200,000 square miles in extent, and, if report be true, this is in every way as fine a country as Mashonaland.

Thus we have as the result of one year's work, a magnificent country occupied, forts built, and excellent communication by a good wagon road 440 miles in extent established ; 140 miles of railway, and 480 miles of telegraph laid down, and the right to a further 200,000 square miles of fine territory conceded. This is no bad record for a twelvemonth's work, and one that augurs well, I think, for the future prospects of all concerned in the welfare of the Company, especially as a good and cheap coast route from Mashonaland has now been discovered.

Finally, I would point out that the effects of the Government policy in granting the Charter have been twofold :—

(1) To secure " Fairest Africa " to England : for had it not been for the prompt action of Mr. Rhodes these lands would have been annexed by the Boers, the Portuguese, or the Germans.

(2) To bring the blessings of hope, peace, and security to the natives, who, up to the time of the arrival of our pioneer force, were compelled by fear of the Matabele on the one side and of Gouveia, the half-caste Portuguese slave-owner, on the other, to live like crows in the most inaccessible fastnesses of the mountains and kopjes.

One gentleman deserves special prominence at this point again, and that is Mr. F. C. Selous, who led the pioneers so safely to the Promised Land. He is a son of Mr. Fredk. Lokes Selous, of Regent's Park, London. He was educated at Rugby (where he had a distinguished school career) and Neuchatel, Switzerland. From a very early age he manifested a great interest in books relating to African travel and adventure. After leaving school he studied medicine for a short time; but in 1871, when between 18 and 19 years of age, he resolved to go out to South Africa, where he has since gained great renown as a hunter. A title to more enduring fame in that country is his, however, by virtue of the part he took in making the road to Fort Salisbury—a highway which, as we have seen, was constructed under extraordinary difficulties, and which has been named after him. Mr. Frederick Courteney Selous may claim one additional link with South Africa, in that he is of French-Huguenot descent on his father's side. When he went to South Africa he made a trip to Kimberley, and thence to the Orange River. Ultimately he went up to the interior, and spent several years in elephant hunting in the countries to the north, north-east, and north-west of Matabeleland. He returned to England in 1875 ; but his heart soon turned to South Africa, for in 1876 we find him again there. He at once went up-country and resumed the wandering and adventurous life of an elephant hunter until the beginning of 1881, when he paid a second visit to England. Towards the end of that year he again went to South Africa, and from that time until the end of 1888 he has been constantly travelling in the interior, no longer as an elephant hunter, but as a collector of specimens of natural history for museums. Mr. Selous has shot wisely and well, and has enriched the British Museum with its finest specimens of the big game of South Africa. The Cape Town Museum is also indebted for its finest specimens of South African mammalia—the best half of which, owing to want of space, are unfortunately not yet on view—to Mr. Selous, whilst many of his specimens, through the medium of a London dealer, have been sent to Edinburgh and to Melbourne, and others to various museums on the continent of Europe and in America. In the course of his travels, Mr. Selous has penetrated into regions hitherto unvisited by Europeans, and in such cases has always made careful sketch maps of the countries through which he passed. Six of these maps, with descriptive accounts of his journeys, have been contributed by Mr. Selous to the Royal Geographical Society of London, and published by them in their "Proceedings." All these explorations have been undertaken at Mr. Selous' own cost. and carried out in a very inexpensive way. In recognition of his

MR. F. C. SELOUS.

services as an explorer, Mr. Selous has twice received awards from the Royal Geographical Society, having obtained the "Cuthbert Peek Grant" in 1883, and the "Back Premium" in 1889.

The natives received the new-comers with open arms. They are peaceful to the point of timidity, and have till now lived in dread of the Matabele. Hitherto they have not been accustomed to hard work; there has been no necessity for it in their simple lives, broken only by an occasional Matabele raid. If they merely scratch the ground they get anything to grow—

mealies, sweet potatoes, tobacco, rice, and all kinds of produce—
the country is so wonderfully fertile and so abundantly watered.
There were no signs of hostility anywhere. In some parts the
natives were rather afraid to be over-demonstrative in their welcome,
fearing perhaps that the tidings of their friendly attitude would
reach Lo Bengula, and make him angry, or, having an idea that
the Pioneer force would be "wiped out" by the Matabele, that
they would gain nothing by showing a lively interest in their
proceedings. But, as a rule, the people were very friendly,
and openly told the men that they were glad they
had come, as they would be able to protect them from
the much-dreaded Matabele. Very shortly the Makalakas and
other peaceful tribes will take to a more effective system of
husbandry. They will have a good market, or rather markets,
for their produce, and they will also have before them the example
of the white settlers, who are to receive every encouragement to
cultivate the ground and make it yield its fulness of fruits. A
great many of the natives have already shown an aptitude for work
to which they had never been accustomed. Besides making very
good servants (nearly every member of the Police force has a "boy")
they are proving useful labourers in fort and hut building, and
for work connected with prospecting operations. Their manual
skill in the manufacture of various iron implements, such as
assegai-blades, axes, &c., will no doubt be turned to very good
account. All the specimens of their work are surprisingly excellent, taking into account the rude appliances they have had to put up
with. It is curious that the implements they make are always
ornamented with the figures and designs, rudely engraved, which are
so plentiful on the masonry at the ancient ruins in the country. At a
picturesque village the force passed the natives were busily engaged
in forging assegai blades, using sewn-up bags of ox hide as bellows and
stones for hammers. The women were sewing reed mats with long
iron needles and string made of fibre. They wore woven kilts of their
own manufacture. The Makalakas do not consider thieving an offence
against whatever moral code they are possessed of, and the Company's
men, until a process of teaching becomes effectual, have to look well
after their belongings, as the "boys" engaged in the different
camps are not slow to appropriate anything that takes their fancy.
No doubt they think it is a right thing to copy the example
of that superior people—the Matabele! One day a native was
detected running off with a packet of salt, and a couple of shots
were fired over his head to frighten him, and for the encouragement of the others. This proved a salutary lesson, for not only
did the peculating savage return with the salt, but he also brought
back a couple of blankets and some other articles which he or
some of his brethren had stolen. Their peaceful disposition
amounts to cowardice most pitiful, and their self-confidence
strength, and courage require development very badly. They are
so impressed with the conviction that the Matabele are an all-

powerful race, having a kind of prescriptive right to perpetrate
any barbarous outrage upon them, that resistance never occurs to
their minds. Yet they build their settlements on hill-tops and
sides—fastnesses almost impregnable, and which could be rendered
wholly so if the chicken-hearted Makalakas only knew and had the
courage to use their own strength. At one place where the force
laagered for a little while, Sir John Willoughby was informed that
two Matabele men had suddenly made their appearance at the
Makalaka settlement close at hand. Although the huts were built
amongst the rocks, in a position which the people could have
successfully defended against all odds, they tamely allowed this
pair of Matabele rascals to enter their village and take away the
wives of some of the men without saying why or wherefore. Sir

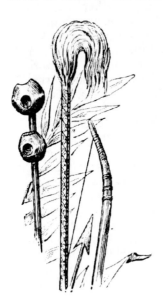

John asked, " Why do you allow these
men to commit such an act? Some of
you have guns, and you could easily have
sent them about their business." But
they only shook their heads and remarked, " We are only women ; we can't
fight against the King's warriors."

A correspondent with the column had
the following interesting references :—

Unlike Matabeleland, where the women
do most of the marketing, and the slaves,
both male and female, do the work of the
fields, these are all men and boys, the women, who have probably never set eyes
upon white men, and have not yet discovered how gallant they are, and to what
greater advantage the trading could be
done by the fair sex, studiously avoiding
our camps. Strange-looking creatures
some of the men are. Every possible
variety of fantastic method in dressing their woolly locks has been adopted
by them. Some are shaved close, with
the exception of a small tuft on the crown of the head, inter-
twined with grasses, until it assumes the form of a miniature
Eiffel Tower. Others have cultivated a luxuriant growth, and
worked their wiry hair into long thin ringlets, which are kept in
shape by some resinous or saccharine matter, and, being cut in a
straight line across the nape of the neck, and shaved well back from
the forehead, give the wearers a remarkably sphinx-like appearance.
The chignons, side tufts, top tufts, diadems, rolls, all ingeniously
worked in with beads, shells, or grasses, and all of a permanent
nature, must be sources of great discomfort. The little wooden stools
made to fit the neck, which are used by the natives as pillows and
as a means of preserving their head gear intact, appear to be simply
instruments of torture. *Mais il faut souffrir pour être beau.*

The men have taken a great fancy to empty cartridge cases, and
wear them partly for ornament, partly for use as snuff-boxes. The
tobacco from which their snuff is made is, by the way, of excellent
smoking quality, possessing a peculiarly mild, nut-like flavour.

The Mashona are of a different type from the Matabele; they are blacker, and have a patient, subdued look, entirely foreign to their swaggering neighbours, the constant dread of whom has certainly left its mark on their character, and destroyed that manly bearing which should be common to all human beings, of whatever type or colour. But they are honest, eager to please, and willing to work for small wage. Should this country ever become a great mining centre, the natives, although limited in numbers, will prove an invaluable aid, and in course of time these will be reinforced by low-grade Matabele who will leave their regiments to work for the white man at a distance from their masters or owners, to live under a milder rule, and accumulate sufficient money for the purchase of wives and cattle.

I was much struck during a recent visit to a small kraal at the variety of useful articles of native manufacture procurable in exchange for a few beads—nets, rugs, and bags, all made of strong durable fibre string, baskets of many shapes and sizes, cane mats, and a variety of agricultural implements in well-wrought iron. I have not yet had an opportunity to gratify my curiosity as to the methods employed in smelting the ore. It is, I believe, a lengthy and laborious process, effected by means of crucibles; but I have watched the smiths working their forges with primitive bellows, and have been astonished at the dexterity with which they weld and shape the metal, using a round stone as a hammer. Iron of a fine quality and close texture is very widely spread over this country; there is a mountain not a dozen miles from here the greater part of which is said to be composed entirely of the metal.

The Matabele raids have almost emptied the kraals of their small breed of cattle; those left are pretty as paint and fat as butter. Very shy they are of the white man; at my approach some cows which were being milked jumped away and snorted. The Kafir dogs also showed symptoms of fear. I have observed the same aversion to a strange race in the wilds of Texas, where the Indian horse is scared at the cow-boy, and the latter in return experiences difficulty in persuading his animal to approach the red man.

Of course the days were full of incident to those on the march; the new country and the shrinking Mashonas interested them. Then oxen would be taken by lions as they were drinking at the river, and storms would blow down tents, surprising the inmates. At one of the rivers "The Baby"—the wagon carrying the engine —capsized. It was eventually got up again with but little damage done. This engine was used for a 10,000 candle-power searchlight. As we have seen, every night steam was got up, and every few hours for ten minutes the light swept all round the laager. This was done to prevent the Matabele creeping up without being seen. The moral effect of the light cannot be overrated. The natives said that the "white man carried thunder and lightning about with him." There were social gatherings, when there would be smoking concerts in the wilds, and songs more or less appropriate to the occasion would be sung. As time wore on life at the various forts began to have attractions all its own, and the arrival of the weekly mail was a great event. Sometimes shooting expeditions are organised, and though ostriches manage to get out of the way of tired horses, good game falls to the guns of the strange white man who now possesses the land. Now and then greenhorns—"Jimmies" they are called in South Africa—have come near to making a mistake. One day a small party out for a shoot thought they

CHARTERED COMPANY'S BOAT ON THE UMFULI RIVER.

saw a herd of sable antelopes. They prepared to fire among them, when arms were held aloft and Mashona cries for "Mercy" rent the air. Fortunately the cries came before the crack of the rifles. Of course there were the usual "scares" at the forts. Messages would come in that an impi was in sight, and then every man would set to work clearing the bush round the fort in a manner that would have surprised his mother.

We have the authority of Mr. Gilbert for saying that "The policeman's life is not a happy one." However true this may be of the blue-coated officer so useful in the streets at home, I cannot say that it altogether applies to the members of the Chartered Company's Police in Mashonaland. There are times, of course, when it does, as when during the recent heavy rains the lines of communication were stopped. The rivers were so swollen that it was impossible for even the most daring to cross with any degree of safety. The current in most of the streams was so strong that horse and rider would be borne down many hundred yards ere a landing on the opposite bank could be effected. In the case of some rivers it was impossible to cross under any circumstances. Take the least dangerous risk first. Your horse, whilst swimming, strikes his hoof against a rock, " turns turtle," and you (his rider) are left floundering in the current, encumbered with rifle, clothes, and boots. What under the circumstances is your chance of reaching the bank again? Very little when you consider that the rivers swarm with crocodiles. Now the crocodile is a very selfish animal, never thinking, probably, that in snapping up a post-rider he is causing pain not only to his victim, but also to that victim's people, to say nothing of the anxiety of hundreds who receive no letters by such a mail. Not long ago a prospector crossing one of the rivers, and that river at the time easily fordable, had his foot taken off by a crocodile, and was for several hours in the water ere he was found by his friends in a very exhausted state. His leg was amputated, but the shock to his system was so severe that the poor fellow died a few days later. One of the Company's troopers had also a very narrow squeak a short time before. His horse, while crossing a shallow drift, had its flank sadly torn and its belly laid open by a crocodile's claws. Neither is colour a matter of consideration to this voracious reptile, for a Kafir whilst washing was visited by one which tore the poor man's leg badly and left him minus a thumb. So much for the dangers of the waters ; now for those encountered on land. Not long ago a lion met two postriders, and so persistent was he in his attentions that they thought it safest to climb a tree, whereupon their horses bolted, mail and all. This proceeding did not satisfy the lion, who promptly seated himself below the tree, licking his chops, and doubtless thinking to himself that he could hold out longer against hunger than a policeman. Luckily the " up postriders " appeared upon the scene five hours later, and the odds being thus in favour of the police once more, and not having any wish to become acquainted with the penetrating power of a Martini-Henry bullet, the lion discovered that he had a pressing engagement elsewhere. Later two troopers taking some oxen from one station to another shot a large lion. A couple of postriders, being unable to cross a flooded river whilst returning to camp, were followed for a considerable distance by a lioness, but would not fire till they came to a tree, up which they would be enabled to take refuge in case of only wounding her ladyship. Another danger against which man is powerless to contend is lightning, through which there have recently been several accidents, happily none of them fatal.

But, as the correspondent who sends these yarns reminds one, every cloud is said to have a silver lining, and such is certainly the case with the Mashonaland police. Almost every week there is a shooting competition. Now the prize is a watch, next week a donkey, then a shotgun, and so on. These competitions naturally bring some excitement into what would otherwise prove a somewhat dull life. Betting books are opened, and a good deal of betting takes place on a small scale. Leave of absence from camp, either with or without one's horse, is always obtainable; and many and pleasant are the shooting parties and excursions in consequence. Game of all sorts is very plentiful, and at no great distance from camp. For those who prefer the rifle there are hippopotami in the rivers, while antelope, koodoo, waterbuck, and reedbuck are amongst the most common of the large game. For the sportsman in whose hand the shot-gun is a deadly weapon there are the pretty little buck-duiker and klipspringer. Amongst the feathered tribe are guinea-fowl, partridge, and quail. To the angler the rivers offer plentiful sport, abounding as they do in fish of various kinds, and weighing from 1 oz. or 2 oz. to 20 lb. and 30 lb. Botanists and naturalists have here ample scope for the pursuit of their studies. Orchids and lilies grow wild, which would do credit to any orchid-house or conservatory; while an artist, could he but faithfully represent in colour some bits of nature which one almost daily drops across in one's rambles, would make a fortune. One has only to follow the call of the honey bird to discover the whereabouts of a bee-hive, thousands of which there must be in the bush. So plentiful, indeed, is honey, that in many a mess it is passed round in a bucket. The natives have a rather remarkable way of making their bee-hives. It is as ingenious as it is simple, and a description may interest bee-keepers. A tree is selected, the trunk of which measures some three feet in circumference. Two incisions are first made through the bark completely round the trunk, and about three to three and a half feet apart. Another incision joins the two before mentioned, and then the bark between the two parallels is carefully taken off. The bark so taken off is now cylindrical but open the whole length. This opening is carefully closed with wooden pegs, and grass plaited into thick mats is next placed in the ends. In the centre of one of these mats a small hole is left, which is to serve as a door for the future inmates. The hive is now complete, and all that remains is to place it in a suitable tree and wait for a swarm to take possession. Truly, Mashonaland may be termed a land "flowing with milk and honey," for, besides the latter article, milk is brought into camp by the natives in large calabashes, and can be purchased for a single "mashloshla," or empty brass M.H. cartridge case. Vegetables and fruits are also procurable for cartridge cases. Green mealies were recently becoming plentiful, and they make a very pleasant change from the ration vegetable, which is either the compressed article or else rice.

There were many colonial farmers in the expedition, and these declared the country to be fertile and well-watered beyond their fondest hopes, and already saw themselves in imagination comfortably housed with wife and chubby children, surrounded by countless herds, and growing tobacco, rice, mealies, potatoes—in short, all the produce both of the tropical and temperate zones. When a settlement of the land question has been come to with Lo Bengula, the Pioneers will have farms given them, and the Company will doubtless let the land in plots on reasonable terms. Col. Pennefather was on a trip to the south recently, when he said :—"The disbanded Pioneer force, the bulk of whom are now farming and digging under the Company's rules,

SYLVAN SCENE, MASHONALAND.

have provisions enough to last for twelve months, and before I left, a three months' supply of rations had been dealt out to them. They are living in well-built huts, formed of poles placed close together and plastered over with mud, which we find to stand the weather better than the ordinary wattle and daub huts. These are thatched over. A quantity of garden seeds have arrived, and most of the Pioneer force have gardens in which vegetables are growing. The police also have gardens. The health of our people has been exceedingly good ever since our departure from Bechuanaland, and the few deaths recorded, I, as a military man, consider a wonderfully small percentage."

The Chartered Company, ever ready to improve the condition or strength of their forces, have recently furnished two companies of their police with lancer equipment for service as light cavalry. The lances are strong formidable-looking weapons, which one would prefer should make holes between anybody else's ribs but one's own. Surmounted by the pennons bearing the Company's colours they look decidedly ornamental as well as useful, and when supplemented, as they will be, with the new carbines, the equipment of the force will be of such an effective character that most people will be seized with an extraordinary desire to be perfectly civil, not to say prodigiously polite to the Company's lancers.

The question of introducing camels into the country is also occupying attention. The ravages of horse sickness in some parts are so serious that it would be well if these useful desert animals could be brought into use in South Africa. If imported to districts not supplied with railways, they would become a formidable rival to oxen, that is, if they would bear transplanting. It might be worth the while of the Chartered Company, or other company, to test the question.

In terms of their contract the Pioneers were disbanded on September 30, and Mr. A. R. Colquhoun assumed the duties of Administrator of Mashonaland, including the government of some thousand whites who have entered the country either as pioneers, prospectors, or police. The administrative experience of Mr. Colquhoun, the well-known Indo-China explorer and pioneer, stands him in good stead in his new sphere. As we know, one of the main objects of the Company's expedition was to open up and develop Mashonaland's vast mineral resources, and in particular to search for gold. Not a moment literally was lost in carrying this fundamental portion of the programme into immediate effect. The Pioneer Corps, after completing the fort according to the terms of their contract, at once started off in all directions, mainly in the direction of Hartley Hill and the Upper Mazoe River, two districts where gold was already admittedly known to exist. There were immediately some 300 men scattered broadcast all over the country in active pursuit and search of the precious metal. From all sides, reports of the most promising and encouraging nature came in of reefs being struck and shafts being sunk, and applications were made daily for the due registration of claims under the terms of the Company's mining laws. Along with the 180 Pioneer prospectors are a considerable number of other prospectors—members of special prospecting parties allowed to enter Mashonaland with the expedition—the total number of men busily engaged in various directions in search of gold (reef and alluvial) being at once not less than 300. Among the prospectors, although the great majority are colonials and Englishmen, are found men from, or who have worked in, all the known gold territories of the world, men who have been moving on from place to place, often making their pile— sometimes big, sometimes small—and nearly as often " knocking " it down, true digger fashion. The greater number, however, are not the professional " old hands," but young Englishmen and colonials who have had some experience in the South African school, generally in the Transvaal. As soon as their discharge was obtained and permission to prospect granted, off they went, the knowing ones, or at least those who thought they were "in the know," making straight for the Umfuli and Mazoe Rivers, where very extensive old workings were known to exist. The prospecting in these two districts at first took the place very largely of "going

MR. A. R. COLQUHOUN.

for" the best known of the places where old workings were most numerous, but in a short time the prospectors spread all over the country, and the results so far are very satisfactory, large numbers of claims being pegged off. It will be interesting to give a few extracts from letters from a number of different correspondents on the gold question :—

The men who have secured claims on these old workings in the districts referred to seem to be very sanguine and jubilant over their properties. Work has been pushed on very persistently ; shafts sunk, reefs tested, the assays showing very favourable results—at least, so the claim-holders maintain. Since these claims were marked out, however, other and, according to report, richer reefs, not before known, have been discovered, the last rush being to a district some 40 or 50 miles west of Hartley Hill. On the Mazoe the finds were at first not so favourable as on the Umfuli, but latterly the prospectors working there seem to have been more fortunate, and several very good reefs have been found—so I understand. Generally speaking, the feeling of satisfaction and enthusiasm is great; but I need hardly say that, with the gold fever in a strong if not its acutest form pervading the whole community, it is necessary to receive all the glowing tales one hears with very great caution, and to place restraint on oneself against being carried away by the general enthusiasm. Still it is impossible, cautious as one may be, not to feel impressed that the consensus of opinion—so unanimous, so strong—must be right, and that in Mashonaland the Company has secured a gold territory of very great extent and value.

Already there has been ample confirmation of the hunter-stories that the natives brought gold in quills for barter. In almost every instance the tributaries of the Mazoe River yield alluvial gold, some of it of a nuggety nature, almost as coarse as gunpowder; bits of quartz have been knocked off here and there, showing good colour, and some samples taken from the vicinity of an old working are marvellously rich in visible gold.

The gold prospectors and experts accompanying the expedition pronounce the indications of reefs, examined in the neighbourhood of the Lunde and here, to be excellent. Indeed, so far as this immediate neighbourhood is concerned, they are one and all anxious to remain here. But as that is not possible, the whole force having to proceed to Mount Hampden, the objective point, they announce their intention of returning, saying that however good the Mazoe district—the one with the greatest gold-bearing reputation—may be, this is "good enough" for them. It would be premature to say much on this subject at present, for, especially with regard to gold, it is dangerous to "prophesy before you know." But all those experienced in such matters seem highly satisfied with the indications—indications in this instance not limited to a superficial examination of the lie of the country, but ascertained from actual crushings of quartz and pannings of alluvial found in the streams performed by the prospectors accompanying the expedition. Everyone seems sanguine that this part of Mashonaland, which has hitherto not been visited by a single European, except Mauch, will turn out to be a very valuable gold territory.

As far back as the Lunde River gold in alluvial deposit was distinctly traceable, and quartz reef of the most promising appearance lies at the very edge of the plateau we have now reached.

Re gold question; there is very little doubt as to the future of the Company on that point. J. and B. have already prospected and picked out half a dozen reefs in the neighbourhood of Hartley Hill. The specimens look splendid, but J. has wired all details about these. C. and C., with police prospectors,

B B

have gone in the direction of the Mazoe, and H. tells me this morning that some of his men have found extensive old workings in another direction. C. was in a couple of days ago, very secretive, and evidently has found what he wants. The police prospectors also report very favourably.

Several parties of prospectors are already at work, and in one locality large reefs have been struck, giving, to judge from the openings made through the surface stone, from 2 to 3 ozs. per ton.

Stories of the richness of the gold up at Mount Hampden and in the Manica Country are constantly reaching us, so our hopes are at "high pressure," for, as you may have heard, every man in the service of the B.S.A. Company is entitled to 10 gold claims, besides which 50 claims per troop have been given to us by Mr. Cecil Rhodes. I have heard of many offers for the "police gold rights," varying from £200 to £650 ; but I only know of two cases in which such offers have been accepted. Prospectors, with their wagons, are daily coming into the country, and everyone expects a brilliant future is in store for this country. Another shilling per diem is added to our pay on the completion of 12 months' service, a trooper in his second year receiving 5s. per diem and all found ; while up to the end of 12 months he receives 4s. per diem.

Whatever opinion may be formed of Mashonaland as a mineral country, all that is seen and learnt of it and of the Manica plateau goes to prove that the British South Africa Company and the mother country have secured a territory which, from a climatic and agricultural point of view, is beyond compare in South Africa. The fertility of the soil, the magnificent pasture, the abundance of water in the very driest season of the year, the fresh and invigorating breeze—all go to show that the long-sought, but so far unfound, White Man's Country in Central South Africa has been found. It has not only been found, it has been occupied—effectively, irrevocably. Since his return from Manica Mr. Colquhoun has organised an administration on a simple basis. The police at the forts or posts (already referred to) support the administration. Two gold diggings or fields have been opened (the Umfuli and the Mazoe) ; claim inspectors and acting mining commissioners have been appointed ; a small survey corps is hard at work, and will shortly commence the work of demarcating the claims on the diggings.

This is the site of the future township and headquarters of the administration of Mashonaland. Here we may confidently expect that at no very far distant date a busy and thriving English-speaking population will have built a substantial city, bringing with it all the old familiar sights and sounds so dear to gregarious man. It needs no great foresight to predict this. But for the next six months at least those already on the spot will have the field to themselves. In a few weeks' time the rains are due, when some of the rivers which have to be crossed on the road just opened up will attain a depth of 40 feet. . . . . We have now arrived at the edge of an undoubted gold belt, and already keen prospectors who have accompanied the column have pounced upon alluvial gold-producing streams, and have brought in wonderfully rich specimens from a quartz reef into which a 30-feet deep shaft has been sunk many years ago, nobody knows by whom. What, then, may we expect when the 170 eager pioneers and another 100 prospectors shall have been turned loose with pan, pick, and shovel ?

Says Sir John Willoughby : Gold is very plentiful, and by the 9th October, on which date I left Fort Salisbury, many valuable reefs had been located ; one in particular on the Umfuli River, at Hartley Hill, is of great extent and richness, and the reports of scientific experts speak most highly of it. It is said to average four feet in thickness, bearing three or four ounces to the ton, and many claims have been by now pegged out and shafts begun to be sunk, while samples of rich ore are on their way down country. Reports come in daily of fresh discoveries in the direction of the Amazoe River, and also between Fort Victoria and Fort Charter. Alluvial gold has not as yet claimed much attention, for as all the pioneers are entitled to fifteen reef claims and one alluvial, and the former are the most valuable, the majority of pioneers and prospectors are at present busily employed in pegging them out and doing the work of sinking shafts in accordance with the terms of the gold law. Alluvial gold has been found near Fort Victoria, and those who have visited the Amazoe River report its presence there, while gold in small quantities has been found in almost every river between Fort Charter and Fort Salisbury. Mr. Moore, who is in charge of a syndicate prospecting party, obtained in twenty-four hours, with very rude appliances, a tablespoonful of gold and one small nugget, on the Amazoe. Finally, all the experts attached to the expedition were unanimous in their opinion that Mashonaland represented one of the three great gold areas in the world, with prospects far exceeding previous anticipation. Doubtless within a few months there will be a greater rush to the country than there has ever been to any other gold field. At the time I left three hundred prospecting licences had been already issued, and on my journey down I met several well-equipped prospecting parties, hurrying up country, and a few parties of individuals on the tramp. Major Johnson, of the Pioneers, told me that he was so satisfied about the richness of the gold of Hartley Hill that he intended to obtain, at his own expense, and as soon as possible, sufficient machinery to work it. I was so impressed by what I heard and saw, that on my arrival at Kimberley I got together a small well-equipped private prospecting party, and had the satisfaction of hearing of its departure up country before I left Cape Town the following week. There is only one thing needful for the further speedy development of Mashonaland, and that is an east coast route and an outlet to the sea.

The great auriferous wealth of Mashonaland has now been placed beyond all possible doubt. The best proof of this is that some miners are clamouring for the necessary arrangements to be made to enable them to float their properties under the Company's terms. The Chartered Company has had to choose a mining expert to watch their interests, and they have selected a well-known American Mining Engineer, Mr. C. M. Rolker, to do so. That gentleman has gone to South Africa, and will soon be in Mashonaland to guide and direct the Company in this important matter. · The conditions under which the prospecting and working for gold in Mashonaland are being carried on have been drawn up under the immediate supervision and direction of Mr. Rhodes,

who has brought to bear on the subject his great knowledge
of all mining matters and his broad and liberal views. Their
chief feature is—a feature that markedly distinguishes them
from all mining conditions and regulations that have been hitherto
adopted—that the individual digger shall be entitled to half-shares
with the Company in whatever company may be floated to
work his property, in other words, the interests of the digger
and the Company are identical and one. Under this system
those objectionable elements, which seem inseparable from
every mining community—the agency of the middleman,
the flotation of bogus companies, harassing and irritating
restrictions, which have so frequently militated against and
delayed genuine mining enterprises—will to a great degree be
eliminated. Mr. Rhodes has evidently taken to heart and profited
by the lesson inculcated by the glaring grievances and inconsistencies
disclosed in the initial administration of the mining industry at
the Rand. Appendix B contains the terms upon which the
Chartered Company will permit the prospecting for minerals and
metals in Mashonaland. I need not recapitulate them here,
for no doubt they will be eagerly studied by many a prospector
and would-be prospector in South Africa and England. It will be
admitted at once, I think, that the terms are liberal. The
Company is investing an immense sum of money in opening
Mashonaland to the prospector; it has made roads of a kind, and
secured comparative safety for those who wish to follow fortune
and look for gold. There is no attempt to close the country
against private enterprise, but, on the contrary, by the payment of
one shilling for a prospector's license, any man is admitted to the
privilege gained for him by the Company. The shillings, however,
are not likely to be sufficiently numerous to repay the Company
for its enormous outlay; and in the case of all discoveries of reef
gold the Company very fairly claims one half-share of the vendor's
shares in any company floated. A strong point in favour of the
miner is that he pays nothing on his quartz claims until they were
floated into a Company. Too often the miner has to surrender his
position elsewhere because of vexatious charges on his claims in the
first instance. Again he has the unusual right of pegging twenty
quartz claims leaving him with an inalienable personal right to ten
of them. With regard to the alluvial claims, the poor man's
claims, if alluvial ground really exists, the Company claims but one
pound sterling per month, and the digger retains all the profits
of his work. There is no need to follow the memorandum through
its various clauses. A principle new to reef mining in South Africa
has been introduced—namely, that of the right to follow a reef where-
ever it may go; so that there is no danger of losing a reef owing
to its subterranean deviation. The deep level question will therefore not hinder the development of the Moshanaland Gold Fields.
For the rest, the terms are conceived and drawn up in a broad and
liberal spirit, fair to the prospectors and fair to the Company.

It was to be expected, after all that has been said and written about Mashonaland, that a number of English syndicates should be formed to follow up commercial, mining, or financial enterprise in that country. The other day the *Grantully Castle* bore away from these shores to South Africa an expedition of some importance, headed by Lord Randolph Churchill. For some months to come, at any rate, its exploits and experiences will be followed with interest. Before he left, I had the pleasure of several con-

THE RIGHT HON. LORD RANDOLPH CHURCHILL, M.P.

versations with Lord Randolph Churchill, and he discoursed interestingly on the objects of his expedition, which unquestionably is the best found of any private one which has left England for the great continent that is now so rapidly coming to the front in the esteem of the world. Even from a public point of view the departure of this exploring party to Zambesia was an event of some concern. Originally conceived to afford instructive entertainment for a long holiday, the scheme of the projectors of this visit to Golden South Africa grew in magnitude. Two well-known financial exploring Companies (the Bechuanaland Exploration Company and the Exploration Company) joined cash-forces with the cash-force at the back of Lord Randolph, contributing, I believe, £10,000 each, to be added to the £10,000 already subscribed towards the expenses of the expedition, the leading members of which were Lord Randolph Churchill, M.P., Captain Giles, R.A.—already popular in South Africa, and, perhaps, the tallest and handsomest man in the British Army—Surgeon Rayner, Grenadier Guards (who, by the special permission of His Royal Highness the Duke of Cambridge was enabled to join the party), Capt. Gwynydd Williams, son of General Owen Williams, and Mr. Henry Cleveland Perkins, the well-known mining engineer. Lord Randolph Churchill has left politics severely behind for the time, but whatever the commercial or financial results of the expedition may be, his Lordship's personally-acquired knowledge of South Africa must become useful not only to that continent, but also to the general English public. The programme of the voyaging party was a simple one. On the upward journey from Cape Town there was to be no unnecessary lingering, most of the sight-seeing being postponed till the return trek. Advantage was taken of the railway to Kimberley, where his Lordship studied the diamond industry. The party then pushed on to the interesting Witwatersrand Gold Fields. Thence they will proceed into Zambesia, following the Selous Road, to Fort Salisbury, which it is hoped will be reached by the end of July. Some months will be spent in Mashonaland, in fulfilment of the objects of the expedition. The return journey will probably be again through the Transvaal to Pretoria, where Lord Randolph hopes to have an interview with President Kruger. His Lordship will, if he carries out his present intention, pay another brief visit to Johannesburg. Old England will be reached, it is expected, in time to eat the Christmas dinner. The trip cannot fail to be of value, both to South Africa and the mother country, as it is impossible that such an intelligent publicist as Lord Randolph can travel the 20,000 miles on which he recently started without noting such observations as will prove of service to the Empire. The House of Commons is none two well supplied with those who can speak authoritatively on South African questions. Lord Randolph will study on the spot many of those matters on which even South African experts differ, and regarding which his Lordship has as yet an open mind and a very liberal feeling towards the races who occupy a great land.

It will be of general interest to state here that at a missionary meeting at the Commercial Exchange, Cape Town, on February 4, the Bishop of Bloemfontein said that about five years ago the Society for the Propagation of the Gospel gave £1,000 towards the exploration of that country which was now known as North Bechuanaland and Mashonaland. A small expedition was then fitted out, which gained the missionary information which they now had about that part of the country. A portion of the £1,000 was still left, and was being expended upon missionary operations in the country. The information then obtained and that which had been obtained since was the basis on which they were now working and on which they were framing their work for the future. Soon after the event he had mentioned the Chartered Company obtained their right to dig for minerals in Mashonaland. It was an accident, humanly speaking, that the Chartered Company and the Church should have chosen the same country for their respective purposes. Even if the Chartered Company had never thought of Mashonaland, the Church would not have given it up as a centre of missionary work. The Chartered Company was working well with the Church in this matter; £100 had just been given to pay for mission work in Mashonaland, and Mr. Rhodes had promised £500 more when missionary stations adequate for their work had been built. The Society for the Propagation of the Gospel also had voted £1,000 for seven years towards the work. Already there had been three clergymen working in the north of Bechuanaland and Mashonaland. He contended that they had a sufficient basis to go upon to consider Mashonaland as a future field of operations. The first thing that he considered ought to be done was to make one strong settlement with a strong connection with some basis of operation. It could not be decided exactly where this settlement ought to be, except that it ought to be on the top of a very high rock and as close as possible to one of the large European populations of the country. Mission stations could be formed in 20 places on certain rivers that he knew. The Chartered Company not only supported such works as these, but they excluded drink entirely. The country itself which the Church meant to occupy as its field for mission work was Mashonaland. Matabeleland would probably be included in the diocese, but Matabeleland had long been the scene of the work of the devoted London missionaries, and the kindness with which these missionaries had always looked forward to their founding a mission in Mashonaland made the Church also look forward with reciprocal good feeling. He saw no reason why in 15 months' time the Mashonaland diocese should not be founded and working. He looked for support from England. He believed that a large association could be formed in England to work the Mashonaland diocese, and that the Chartered Company would support it in the future as they were supporting it now; and what Livingstone's and Moffat's followers had been to Bechuanaland and Matabeleland, so by the grace of God the Church of England would be to Mashonaland.

The British South Africa Company has taken one more step towards the reality of its rule in the territories ceded to it by the Royal Charter. It has issued a complete set of postage and revenue stamps, specially designed for use in British Zambesia. The series embraces eleven specimens of varying value, the lowest value being a penny, and the highest ten pounds. In design the

stamps to a certain extent resemble the later Bavarian issues.
The centre is occupied by a shield.   Three ships are represented

POSTAGE AND REVENUE STAMPS.

in the centre of the shield.   On the upper part are oxen,
while the lower part is filled by a single elephant.   Over the shield

SEAL OF THE CHARTERED COMPANY.

the British lion is conspicuously placed, and above is the legend,
"British South Africa Company."   Below is the motto of the

Company, "Justice, Commerce, Freedom," and the words representing the value of the particular stamp. The four highest in value—those for one, two, five, and ten pounds—are surrounded by an engraved framework, and the whole series is, in colour and design, an admirable example of the art of the engraver.

C. H. WEATHERLEY, ESQ.

(Secretary of The British South Africa Company.)

I give facsimiles of the stamps, and also of the seal of the Company, the arms in which may be described :—

Blazon.—Gules, the chief semee of besants, the base semee of ears of wheat or ; a fesse wavy argent between two bulls passant in chief and an elephant passant in base all proper ; the fesse charged with three galleys sable.

Crest.—A Lion guardant passant, or, supporting with its dexter forepaw an ivory tusk erect proper.

Supporters.—Two Springboks proper.

Motto.—" Justice, Commerce, Freedom."

Dr. JAMIESON.   Dr. RUTHERFORD HARRIS.   Sir CHARLES METCALFE.
(South African Secretary of the
Chartered Company.)

The significance is briefly as follows : — The colour of the field, red, is the same as that in the arms of England. The besants (gold discs), in chief, refer to the gold abounding in Matabeleland, and the ears of wheat in base to the corn which has been and can be raised there in such profusion. The oxen refer to the beasts of burden employed there and to the abundance of cattle. The fesse wavy refers to the Zambesi, Limpopo, and other rivers flowing through the scene of the operations of the Company. The galleys

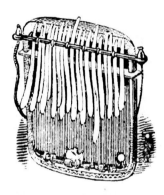

refer to the shipping which can traverse the rivers. The supporters and the crest indicate the wild animals to be found in Zambesia. The Lion also forms an allusion to the heraldic emblem of England, and the three galleys sable upon an argent field are charges borne in the arms of the Duke of Abercorn, the first President of the Company.

The Solicitors to the Company are Messrs. Hollams, Sons, Coward, and Hawksley, the well-known Mincing Lane firm. The legal business of the Company, however, falls chiefly to the share of the junior partner, Mr. Bourchier F. Hawksley, to whom, as well as to Mr. C. H. Weatherley, the courteous Secretary, I am indebted for much valuable assistance in the compilation of the facts I publish concerning the formation and object of the Company.

CHAPTER XVI.

TO enable my readers to better follow the next chapter in the history of the British South Africa Company, it will be well to remind them of the negotiations which took place last year between England and Portugal as to the delimitation of their respective frontiers in East Africa. It is unnecessary to go back to the immediate cause of these negotiations—the wanton and cruel overrunning of the Makololo for "scientific" purposes by the Portuguese. It is sufficient to recall that in August last England and Portugal were in actual agreement on the question, and nothing but the ratification of the Cortes was wanting to the indefinite perpetuation of the friendly relations which had so long subsisted between the two countries. Unfortunately for Portugal, but, as I think, fortunately for England, the Portuguese Government had reckoned without its political opponents, and had promised more than it could perform. The publication of the terms of the August Convention, with the comments of the "patriotic" press upon it, provoked a general storm of indignation, before which the Ministry went down like ninepins; the Convention was ignominiously rejected, and the breach between the two Powers became wider than ever. Yet the proposed arrangement was a very liberal one for Portugal, to which was assigned many thousands of miles more territory than it is ever likely to occupy; and, as subsequent events have proved, the Cortes, in the interests of their own country, made a grave mistake in not closing with it. By refusing the division of the Hinterland proposed, the Portuguese exposed themselves to lose the whole, for the natural effect of the rejection of the boundary treaty was to give a fresh impulse to exploration and annexation in the disputed region, where British energy and enterprise are paramount. The result was soon apparent in the extension of the sphere of operations of the British South Africa Company; and a swarm of private prospectors and pioneers rapidly spread themselves over the face of the country, naturally without any regard to the territorial claims of Portugal, which rested solely upon tradition or authority of the most shadowy character. Alarmed at this invasion, and at the prospect of the crop of conflicts and disputes to which it threatened to give rise, the new Portuguese Government approached Lord Salisbury with a view to the establishment of a *modus vivendi*, pending negotiations for a new treaty, and in November last it was announced that a provisional arrangement for six months had been concluded between the two Powers, on the basis of the rejected convention. Unfortunately for Portugal, but, as I think, fortunately for England, the news of this arrangement did not reach the interior of South Africa in time to prevent a conflict of authority between the officials of the British South Africa Company and certain Portuguese. In any case, it may be doubted if the boundaries of the respective territories of the two Powers in such hitherto remote and little-known regions could have been defined with sufficient precision and authority to prevent the "collision"; but the knowledge of the existence of an international agreement on the subject would, at all events, have moderated their rancour, and prevented in all probability such an appeal to force as that which constituted the serious feature of what became known as the Manica difficulty. In the Convention of August, the whole of the country in question, indeed, all Gazaland, was recognised as being within the sphere of Portuguese influence, though not actually in the occupation of that Power; but when the Convention was rejected, the British South Africa Company naturally felt free to push their explorations into that tempting district, where they were received with open arms by the local magnate, Umtasa. Let us now return to Fort Salisbury, the head-quarters, as we have seen, of the Chartered Company.

The first step taken by Mr. Colquhoun on assuming the administration of Mashonaland, was to proceed with a small party to Umtasa's kraal by special invitation of the Chief to make a treaty of protection with him and obtain from him for the British South Africa Company concessions for the mineral and other rights in his territory. Mr. Colquhoun, too, was desirous of obtaining some reliable information and, if possible, ocular evidence of that ever-vanishing and hitherto unknown quantity—the will-o'-the-wisp of so-called Portuguese "occupation." On their way up through Mashonaland, not a trace or vestige of the existence of the Portuguese at any time, much less of a present occupation of this country, to which they laid claim with much well-simulated indignation just a year before, could be detected, or at any rate was visible to the naked eye of the representatives of the British South Africa Company. The ruins they saw at Zimbabye, for instance, and other places could never by the wildest stretch of imagination be ascribed to Portuguese handiwork, or admitted for one moment as fulfilling their invariable contention of "ancient ruins and traditions," upon which they laid so much stress and based their chimerical rights in this part of the world. Until Mr. Colquhoun's party reached Manica there was nothing of general interest to record, beyond that they passed through some of the most charming scenery imaginable, crossing numerous streams of clear, swiftly-flowing water over rocky beds, winding their way amongst perfect wooded mountain scenery, which, if suddenly transplanted, would find its exact counterpart in favoured portions of either Scotland or Wales. Plenty of game, too, was met on the way, roan and sable antelope, tsesebe and quagga, in regard to which Mr. Selous, who accompanied Mr. Colquhoun, chief of the mission, fully sustained his reputation of being at once the mightiest and most successful of African hunters. Others of the party were Dr. Jameson, Mr. Rhodes's representative with the expeditionary force, Major Johnson, and Mr. Campbell.

On September 13 Mr. Colquhoun and his fellow travellers halted close to the objective point of the mission, the kraal of the Manica Chief, Umtasa (or Mutasa), or Mafamba-Busuko—"one who walks by night"—as he prefers to style himself, or again, Sifamba, as he is generally spoken of by the local natives. The kraal itself (at an altitude of 4300 ft. above sea level) is situated at the head of what is really a pass, completely concealed from below in mountain fastnesses and lying under a sheer massive granite bridge of rock another 500 ft. or 600 ft. high, a position, at all events in Kafir warfare, absolutely impregnable. The position is probably about 80 miles east as the crow flies and 120 by the route the party took east of the point they left the main column, at the headwaters of the Sabi.

Negotiations were at once opened and an interview arranged for the day after Mr. Colquhoun's arrival, an appointment that was punctually kept. It must be confessed that the appearance and presence of the hereditary and reigning monarch of the ancient kingdom of Manica were not quite all one would desire to see in a great ruler. No doubt the utmost resources of his wardrobe had been taxed and brought into requisition for this interview. About midday he appeared attired in a naval cocked hat, a tunic (evidently of Portuguese origin, but of ancient date, and forming perhaps some of the "ancient remains" to which the attention of the world has been so pathetically drawn), a leopard skin slung over his back, the toilette being completed by a pair of trousers that had evidently passed through many hands, or rather covered many legs, before assisting to complete the Court uniform of the "roitelet Matassa," as the Portuguese term him. He was preceded by his Court jester, who danced around him, uttering strange cries and ejaculations and singing his praises (in which Umtasa cordially joined) as "the lion or leopard who walks by night, and before whose name the Portuguese and Matabele tremble." The retinue was completed by a few girls carrying "calabashes" of Kafir beer, and by a crowd of Indunas (or counsellors) and other loyal subjects. The King was evidently anxious to satisfy himself thoroughly of the genuineness of Mr. Colquhoun's mission and the value and strength of the promises held out to him. It was not until the following day, September 14, when in the Royal Kraal a full *indaba* (or Council) of Indunas was held, and after lengthy discussion, a treaty was signed between Mr. Colquhoun, the Administrator of Mashonaland, acting on behalf of the British South Africa Company, and the King of Manica. Before signing the treaty, it was most carefully and again and again explained to Umtasa that if he had at any time granted any treaty or concession to any one else, the negotiations would be at once dropped. And it was only after his repeated assurance that such was not the case, that no treaty of any kind had ever been executed by him, and no concession ever granted to the Portuguese, that the Company's treaty with him was duly signed and formally witnessed by two of his own Indunas and some of Mr. Colquhoun's own party.

As showing Umtasa's independence and perfect freedom to enter into a treaty with the British South Africa Company, I may here quote some words of Mr. Reuben Beningfield, who, as pointed out in "Golden South Africa," was a particular friend of Umzila, the father of the present King of Gazaland. Mr. Beningfield was up the coast again quite recently, on a trip from Natal, and in describing his experiences to the *Natal Mercury*, he said :—

From Arruwangua we proceeded to Massi Kessi, in the district of Manica, where I had an interview with Baron Rezendi, the representative of the Compagnie Mozambique. From Massi Kessi we proceeded up the River Umtali, and landed at a spot 200 miles from Beira. This is the first of the gold-bearing country, and by aneroid we found that we were 4500 feet above sea level. The country is well watered, will grow almost anything, and is magnificent in the extreme. Whilst there we were requested by Umtasa, the so-called King of Manica, to pay him a visit. The King, in the first instance, sent a deputation to meet our party, stating that he would very much like to see the white man he had heard so much about, and who was so great a friend of Umzila, King of Gaza. On arriving at his royal residence, he said he wished to be friendly with me, and also with the English nation. My party was well received and most hospitably treated—indeed, I have never received better treatment from a native king. He resides in a mountain stronghold, rising in three tiers, literally covered with huge boulders, and almost impregnable. Sometimes we had to crawl through tunnels in our ascent, and on the plateaux, or tiers, where little villages are situated, massive stockades with gates, which are locked at night, surrounded them. Umtasa, or Fambaumsuka ("Go-at-night"), told me he was the independent King of Manica, and owed allegiance to no foreign power. He further said that Gunhunhama, King of the Gazas, had on two occasions sent impis to wipe him out, but had to return empty-handed, having been beaten off. After a glance at the fortress as above described, I can assure you I was not the least surprised. The country is certainly a most interesting and inviting one, and must have a very ancient history. In my rambles I came across large stones and boulders on which were some unique native paintings, all, of course, in a crude state, but well preserved as far as pigments were concerned. They must have been there for centuries. The King himself, on being asked, said he did not know who drew them, neither did his father or father's father. In the course of conversation the King told me that of late the Portuguese had put in an appearance at his place, and had made him presents. They were anxious to become friends with him, and he allowed them to come and go at will. The Baron, before mentioned, however, informed one of the party that Portugal claimed the whole of the Manica District. The King, on the other hand, asserts that he is quite independent, and is monarch of all he surveys. I remained at the royal palace a couple of days, and gave Umtasa a present of some goods which I had brought with me. The King wished me to remain longer, but this was impossible on account of the rainy season setting in, and I had a long journey before reaching the coast. Before leaving, however, he said he would make me a present. True to his word, the King sent out his indunas to collect gold dust, and his messengers overtook me on my way down, presenting me with the precious metal, along with the King's best wishes for a safe and pleasant journey. I should mention that I remained in the Manica country for two months, prospecting and making general observations, and was greatly pleased with all that I saw as regards the auriferous wealth of the district. I was very successful in bringing the horses and cattle through the fly country, which I attribute to the wonderful powers of a stuff I had with me, and with which we painted the cattle twice a day. The stuff will prove a most valuable help to future African travellers. We had very good shooting along the route, and indeed had to depend on our rifles for our meals.

Umtasa, as I say, was repeatedly asked whether at any time he had ever ceded his country, or the mineral rights of his country, either to the Portuguese Government or to the Directors of the Mozambique Company and he as repeatedly denied ever having done so, as also did his chief councillors. When questioned as to the terms he was on with the Baron de Rezende, the local representative of the Company of Mozambique at Massi Kessi, he said, " I allow him to live there. He sometimes gives me presents, but I have not given him my country, nor have I ever concluded any treaty with him." Later on he said repeatedly that the Portuguese held an assegai at his heart, and when pressed for an explanation of this statement affirmed that he was terrorised and compelled to do what the Baron required of him by the threat that if he gave any trouble Gouveia the Terrible, of whom I shall have more to say, would be called in to invade his territory with a large armed force. There is no doubt that the fear of this Portuguese executioner, ever looming in the distance, was instrumental in great measure in inducing Umtasa to conclude the treaty he did. It is true that he was evidently much impressed by the fact of a large British expedition coming through the Matabele country from the far south, and some

of its members so soon finding their way into his own dominions.
The whiteness of their skins, as opposed to the dark yellow or
black of the Portuguese half-castes, also, and their travelling with
horses and pack animals, without porters and palanquins, *à la
Portugaise*, were also a source of astonishment to him.   But the
one fact he seized upon and grasped at once was undoubtedly the
offer of protection of the British South Africa Company both for
himself and his people.   At the chief's urgent request one policeman and a native interpreter were left with him as representatives
of the Company pending the establishment later on of a regular
police post to safeguard the Company's interests in the Manica
country, and to protect Umtasa against any attack that might be
made upon him in revenge for his assertion of his independence of
Portuguese rule.

The treaty entered into between Umtasa and the British South
Africa Company is most comprehensive.   It provides that no one
can possess lands in Manica except with the consent of the
Company in writing; it concedes to the Company complete
mineral rights; it gives permission for the construction and
establishment of public works and conveniences of all kinds, such
as roads, railways, tramways, banks, &c.   On the Company's side
the King is assured of British protection both for himself and his
people, and the payment of an annual subsidy, either in money or
trading goods at the option of the King.   There is no doubt that
in concluding a treaty with the Chief of the Manica country, and
securing therein all mineral and other concessions, the Chartered
Company has become possessed of a most valuable addition and
appanage to its acquisition of Mashonaland.

Independently of Manica bringing the Company nearer to the
seaboard (to which it is of such vital importance to have access)
the Company has secured a territory of undoubted great mineral
wealth.   From time immemorial " the gold fields of Manika " have
been marked on all maps that have any pretence to accuracy of
information, and Mr. Colquhoun's party passed through three valleys
(watered by the Revue, the Umfuli, and Zambesi Rivers), and they
saw hillsides literally honeycombed with old alluvial workings for
gold; when these extensive and very numerous workings were
made it is impossible to say, but certainly centuries ago.   The
general opinion is that these shafts and pits, in places fully 70 feet
or 80 feet deep (in many of which trees of good size have grown),
were worked by gangs of slave labour under the supervision of
Jesuit priests.   Large quantities of gold must undoubtedly have
been taken out of the country.   Mr. Jeffreys, who, on behalf of a
Barberton syndicate led an expedition into Manica, described the
country in SOUTH AFRICA last July, and spoke of rich reefs near
Massi Kessi within reach of grand water and timber.   He also
referred to rich alluvial fields in the Chemeza, Revue, Mutara,
Menene, Chua, and Odzi valleys.   Another writer about the same
time said he never got a blank when he panned in a flat at the

Muza, a mile long by about half a mile broad, and he expressed his opinion that it " would pay splendidly for hydraulicing."

The " ancient kingdom of Manica," as it is called, was evidently at one time more extensive than at present, and ran right down to and included a considerable strip of the seaboard. In recent years, however, the area covered by the Manica kingdom proper seems to have undergone some shrinking process, especially on the east. Certain of Umtasa's vassals have fallen away—instigated and encouraged by the Portuguese, it is believed—from their lawful ruler. Umtasa himself, as I have shown, maintains that he has been " pressed by the assegai " of the Portuguese, and no doubt this has been the case with many others less able to take care of themselves.

The chief instrument of the Portuguese in carrying out their professions of " occupation " in these territories has been the scourge named Gouveia, whom I have referred to, and of whom a good deal was heard in connection with the Manica affair. Amongst the weak and unwarlike tribes of South-eastern Africa this Goanese adventurer, Gouveia, otherwise known as Manuel Antonio de Souza, is regarded with much the same feelings of mingled terror and detestation as two centuries ago rankled in the breasts of the pious peasantry of the Western Lowlands of Scotland against their powerful and unscrupulous oppressor, John Graham of Claverhouse. And it is surely a matter of deep reproach to a nation which makes loud boast of its enlightenment and civilisation that the terror inspired by such an agent should be the sole machinery which they possess to govern and control (and practically shut off from all the ameliorating influences of trade and commerce) many small tribes of unwarlike natives, who, powerless to resist, have groaned under oppression, and who will now welcome with open arms the influx of British settlers and miners, which will give them security of life and property. Gouveia, the worthy " Capitan-mor " of the Gorongoza province (vide map) has done considerable service for his employers. He has been, as I say, the repulsive instrument employed by them in all their " little wars," and as occasion has arisen, has been told off and commissioned to punish or (to use the expressive native term) " eat up " recalcitrant native chiefs that did not at once appreciate the blessings of being brought under Portuguese influence by jumping at the offer of their flag. This is the usual mode of establishing a footing with the simple-minded native chiefs; it is the first, and frequently the only, step in Portuguese " occupation." Gouveia is a man of considerable strength of character, and has a large force of armed blacks under his command. Being not too particular about his methods of warfare, he has inspired great dread among the various chiefs. Gouveia has been given the rank of general in the Portuguese army, and is believed to have been in receipt of a substantial subsidy from the Portuguese Government for many years past.

Gouveia, who is one of the so-called " Zambesi Princes,"

c c

and who is notorious for his tyranny and cruelty, has, by means of the annual subsidy paid him, the arms liberally supplied, and the support generally accorded him by the Portuguese, gradually gathered around him at Gouveia a body of probably as great scoundrels as that part of the world can produce. He has also, like "Colonel Ignacio de Xavier" (near Tete) and other Zambesi Princes, a very large number of slaves, and others whose servitude is hardly distinguishable from slavery. This man and the force at his disposal constituted the whole military or *quasi* military force of Portugal in interior S.E. Africa. On the coast, it is true—at Ibo, Angoche, and Chiloane and Delagoa Bay—there are small garrisons of so-called "troops" and police—at three of these places commanded by Goanese—but they are so sickly, so ill-drilled, in a word, such wretched material, that it is not an exaggeration to say that all these garrisons together could not furnish 50 men for service in the interior. At Mozambique there are some 250 men, and at Quilimane 50, the greater part quite unfit for active service through climatic disease. Delagoa Bay, the garrison of which I have described from personal observation in "Golden South Africa," requires every "man" of its available force for local protection and police duties. One fact will illustrate the strength of Portuguese force on the coast. When Quilimane was threatened in 1884 by the natives, the authorities and garrison took flight in boats, leaving the British and foreign merchants under Mr. F. Moir, of the African Lakes Company, to meet and repel the enemy, which they gallantly did near Mopea, quite unassisted by the Portuguese. At Inhambane, north of Delagoa Bay, bodies of so-called "Zulus" can be enlisted by the Portuguese. Though not really Zulus, and indifferent fighting material, they are sufficiently good for acting against the interior native tribes, wretchedly armed and, generally speaking, spiritless, peaceable agriculturists. These Zulus were employed by Serpa Pinto on his famous (or infamous) expeditions against the Makololo and on the Shiré recently, the principal object of their employment being to keep together the main body of his expedition, a slave-force drawn from the slave *prazos* in the neighbourhood of the Quilimane River. Gouveia, then, is the main support of the Portuguese in the interior, and Umtasa had very good reason, by means of diplomacy or otherwise, to avoid coming into collision with the Portuguese or bringing about one of those visits of persuasion with which Gouveia, on behalf of the Portuguese, has of late years favoured more than one independent chief—notably Makombe, not one of whose family lives to tell the tale of a terrible slaughter. Umtasa had also seen another neighbouring independent chief, Matoko—whose territory is close to what is marked as the Kaiser Wilhelm Goldfields on most maps—tackled by Gouveia; and although Matoko, who is said to have an unconquerable aversion to the Portuguese, has so well held his own that the "Guerra de Matoko" and its native equivalent are household words, Umtasa doubtless thought discretion the better part of valour. He therefore affected not to take any notice of the so-called Portuguese " occupation," and had, to use his own expression, been " sitting watching." In addition to the Baron at Massi Kessi, there have been recently several engineers employed in making reconnaissances for the much-talked-of Portuguese railway to Manica, sanctioned by royal decree in hot haste when matters were somewhat strained at Lisbon. With these exceptions, however, and one or two half-breeds living at a place on the Pungwe River close to the coast, there have been no Portuguese, either pure blood or cross-breed, south of the Zambesi, in the interior of " Portuguese" South-East Africa.

With regard to Colonel Paiva d'Andrada, who has been heard a good deal of lately, he is much superior to the ordinary Portuguese adventurer. He is well known in London geographical circles, and has done much for the exploration of Manica and the opening up of the navigation of the Pungwe River. He has been the local representative of the Mozambique Company, which has also recently come into prominence. With respect to the claims of the Ophir and other Companies working in Manica, it is to be noted that they claim under the Mozambique Company; therefore their grievance can only be against that Company, which does not give them possession of their claims. The Mozambique Company received their rights from the Portuguese Government, but unfortunately for them the Portuguese Government had no rights to give. They may claim the suzerainty over the native chiefs of Manica and Gaza, but it does not follow that they received from the chiefs any mining rights. However, I am hopeful that in any new convention entered into with Portugal, or whatever may be the fate of the Mozambique Company, all legitimate and reasonable mining rights will be confirmed to their possessors of whatever nationality, some of whom have undergone great hardship and considerable expense to acquire them.

Manica is famous in the annals of Portugal's connection with Africa. It was to obtain possession of the mines of Manica that Francisco Barreto, (whose acquaintance we made in the earlier part of this work) with a thousand men of noble birth, marched from the Zambesi in the sixteenth century, only to meet with crushing disaster. The last enterprise of Colonel Paiva d'Andrada is only the latest of a long series of attempts to take possession of Manica, not one of which has ever met with success. The name Manica is applied by the Portuguese to two areas of very different extent. On a Portuguese map of 1889, which practically gives to Portugal the whole territory, north and south of the Zambesi, which is claimed by the South Africa Company, Manica figures as a "district" of the province of Mozambique. Its boundaries extend along the Zambesi from Shupanga to near Tete; then south-west along the Mazoe and south by the Sabi River to its junction with the Odzi; then east along the Musapa and Busi to the mouth of the Pungwe. Whatever may be the grounds of

c c 2

Portugal's claim to this large area, there has been no desire on the part of the British South Africa Company to interfere with her possession of the bulk of it. The chiefship of Manica proper is a very different thing. This district is a small triangle between 18° and 19° S. lat. and 32° and 33° E. long. It is a triangle to the east of the Upper Sabi and west of the Upper Aruangua, with an altitude of from 4,000 ft. to 6,000 ft. The western limits have never been defined. In the proposed Anglo-Portuguese arrangement of August last, for some unaccountable reason, the boundary line was suddenly indented to the westwards so as to come down the Sabi. This it is stated, on good authority, was the result of a misunderstanding arising from the imperfect nature of the map used in the Foreign Office. However that may be, on the reconsideration of the arrangement, the line has been drawn directly southwards, and thus the British South Africa Company obtain nearly all that they want, although I am strongly of opinion that it would be in the interests of peace if the British South Africa Company were allowed to take Gungunhama and the whole of Gazaland under their wing. Massi Kessi has been heard a good deal about lately. It and Mutasa's kraal are separated by a distance of from twenty-five to thirty miles, the latter lying to the north-west. Both are situated on high mountainous veld, the mountains reaching a height of from 5,000 to 6,000 feet above sea-level. Between each range are extremely fertile and well-wooded valleys. To the south of Massi Kessi the country becomes less mountainous in character, and consists, for a distance of several hundred miles, of vast wooded rolling plains. The Umtali valley possesses a magnificent water-fall, the river washing in sheets of foam over 200 feet of sheer naked rock. On the ridge between the Umtali and Revue valleys a grand view is obtained of two ranges of mountains, whose summits reach to an altitude of at least 6,000 feet. A range of hills also divides the valley of the Revue from that of the Zambesi. The scenery is grand in the extreme, much resembling that of Switzerland. The country is well watered everywhere, and affords a splendid field for energy and enterprise, well directed in its future development.

Upon the conclusion of the Manica Treaty, Mr. Selous and two others of Mr. Colquhoun's mission rode on to Massi Kessi, where, it was said, some " white" men were in some manner established and settled. Could it be that the party were at last to see a " white" Portuguese? The surmise was not incorrect, as at last, after diligent search and inquiry for many weeks, one Portuguese official was found, whose dignity was all the more impressive from the solitary state of its possessor. Mr. Selous and his friends on their way to Massi Kessi met a party of East Coast blacks in charge of two Portuguese officials (one a captain in the Portuguese army, the other a civil engineer), recently arrived from the coast and bearing a letter to Mr. Colquhoun—who had remained behind in the neighbourhood of Umtasa's kraal—protesting against the presence of the representatives of the Chartered Company in Manica, as well as in Mashonaland generally. On hearing that Mr. Selous, who had informed them where they would find Mr. Colquhoun, wished to go on to Massi Kessi, they intimated their willingness to fall in with that arrangement, and Mr. Selous went on and visited the lonely Portuguese official, the Baron de Rezende. The latter may have under normal circumstances a small retinue of black "soldiers"; but these, it was understood, had been told off summarily to swell the "*cortége énorme, avec un drapeau déployé*" (as the party was afterwards described), despatched late the evening before with the letter of protest to Mr. Colquhoun. Every nerve had no doubt been strained to render the *cortége* of as imposing an appearance as possible, with the object of duly impressing Mr. Colquhoun with the solid and substantial, not to say military, nature of Portuguese occupation. Beyond, however, this one isolated official—who also acts as local representative of the Mozambique Company, and who has gone so far somewhat unwillingly, it is believed, from the seaboard on the heels of prospectors and others working under the Company, all without exception of either American or English origin—Mr. Selous failed to trace the existence of one single other resident Portuguese, either official, colonist, trader, or miner. There were certainly some two or three engineers in the neighbourhood, temporarily engaged in surveying, and there were the two recently-arrived officials from the coast already mentioned.

Contrast this with the recent occupation of Mashonaland by the Chartered Company! At Fort Salisbury—to say nothing of what has been done at the various stations below—within one month of the arrival of the expedition, 300 prospectors were scouring the country in all directions in search of gold, forts had been built, huts were springing up in every direction, and the work of administration soundly and firmly established. Postal communication, too, was punctually kept up from below, letters only taking some three weeks to reach from Cape Town, while some prospectors near Massi Kessi informed Mr. Selous that letters took two or three months to reach them, and that, too, from a seaboard only 250 miles away!

Despite his touching isolation, the Baron de Rezende was spoken of in high terms by the English prospectors who enjoy the privilege of his acquaintance—that is to say, from a personal and social point of view. Towards Mr. Selous and party his demeanour was that of frigid official courtesy. He protested (as the Portuguese are always doing, and will probably be obliged to go on doing for some time yet to come) against their presence both in Manica and Mashonaland. He pointed out that all these territories belonged to his Majesty the King of Portugal from time immemorial, that the *roitelet* of Manica was a vassal of theirs, that their authority was based either upon ancient rights or ruins (Mr. Selous could not be quite clear upon this point), and rights secured from Gungunhama,

King of the Gaza country, who recently had been induced to move with his people to the neighbourhood of Delagoa Bay, so as to enable the Portuguese to have a freer hand in Gazaland and Manica, as well as to keep in closer touch with this powerful Kafir prince. It must be admitted that the Baron de Rezende, though evidently suffering from intense irritation, played his part courteously and well. He performed with dignity and tact the exceedingly difficult, if not impossible, task of bolstering up and defending claims and pretensions to vast regions which, in legal phraseology, have no foundation either in substance or in fact. In one respect, however, he had the complete advantage over his visitors. They had gone down to Massi Kessi *inter alia* in the hope of obtaining some provisions, of which they had run terribly short, from the store of the Mozambique Company (of which the Baron, in addition to his other duties, had sole management and control), and had carefully provided themselves with the requisite funds for obtaining, it was hoped, some dainties, at any rate some of the necessaries of life. To their requests in this direction the Baron, with a shrug of his shoulders, pleaded a civil but blank *non possumus*. It says much for the versatility of Portuguese officials in these latitudes that they can be intrusted—with the full confidence of their Government, it is to be presumed—with the discharge of delicate and important political duties as well as with the disposal (at a profit, it is to be presumed) of groceries and tinned food supplies. From what has been written it must be patent to everyone that there has existed in Manica and neighbouring territories, no such thing as an effective Portuguese occupation in the proper sense of that term—viz., that these countries were being occupied, inhabited, and developed by the Portuguese themselves. The strength of the civil official staff can be judged from what has been related, and practically the only military force at their disposal south of the Zambesi and west of the Eastern littoral is that under the pretty specimen, Gouveia.

I now proceed to a fuller reference to the Manica "incident." At the beginning of November, in the absence of Lieutenant-Colonel Pennefather from Mashonaland, Major P. W. Forbes (son of Alexander C. Forbes Esq. of Whitchurch, Reading), who has been seconded from the 6th. Inniskilling Dragoons for service with the Chartered Company, was appointed to represent the Company in Manica and assume command of the police. On October 25, in consequence of reports from native sources that Colonel Paiva d'Andrada, accompanied by Gouveia with a large force of armed natives, was approaching the Manica country from the east, Sergeant-major Montgomery, with a force consisting of only ten men of the British South Africa Company's police, was despatched from Fort Salisbury to Umtasa's, and two days later Lieutenant Graham, accompanied by Sub-lieutenant Shepstone, followed to take command of this small detachment. At the same time Lieutenant the Hon. Eustace Fiennes was ordered to proceed to Umtasa's from Fort Charter with a portion of A troop of the Company's police; but owing to the difficulty that was experienced in taking wagons through a roadless country, this detachment did not reach Umtasa's until November 15. Fortunate it was that at this critical time the Company had at its disposal so efficient an officer as Major Forbes, a man with a considerable experience, for one so young, of the conditions of soldiering in South Africa; a man of clear judgment, vigorous mind, and determined character; as good a specimen of *mens sana in corpore sano* as any one would care to see. Upon his arrival at Umtasa's kraal on November 5th, Major Forbes learnt that Colonel Paiva d'Andrada, accompanied by the notorious slave-owner and captain, Gouveia, had recently arrived at Massi Kessi with from 250 to 300 so-called "bearers," the majority, be it carefully noted, being armed with rifles, sword-bayonets, and reserves of ammunition. According to the natives, the avowed object of this large armed force—as indeed it really was—was to mete out punishment to Umtasa for signing the obnoxious treaty of September 14th. Thereupon Major Forbes at once, by Lieutenant Graham and two troopers, sent a letter to Colonel Paiva d'Andrada at Massi Kessi, protesting against his entering the Manica country with a large armed force, and warning him against taking any steps which might wear the appearance of an attempt to upset the treaty concluded on 14th September, as any such action on his part would inevitably lead to serious and grave complications. Major Forbes further requested Colonel Paiva d'Andrada to withdraw his force both from Manica and from the territory of any chief with whom treaties had been concluded by the British South Africa Company. This letter, which was handed to him by Lieutenant Graham on November 6, Colonel d'Andrada declined to answer, affecting to treat the whole thing as a *mauvaise plaisanterie*. Lieutenant Graham and his two troopers were, however, treated with the greatest kindness and courtesy by Colonel d'Andrada and the Baron de Rezende.

Three days later, without any warning, Gouveia appeared at and occupied the Chief Umtasa's kraal with some seventy of his armed followers, with whom, as I have shown, he has for years been in the habit of travelling through the neighbouring country intimidating the natives, and against their wish forcing them to accept the Portuguese flag. Major Forbes, on hearing that Gouveia had established himself at the King's kraal, at once sent him a letter protesting against his presence there, and warning him that any attempt to coerce the chief into granting interviews would be in defiance of his orders, which were to prevent any outside interference with the Chief Umtasa, and these orders he was prepared, if necessary, to carry out by force. To this letter Gouveia verbally replied that he should go where he liked, and that no Englishman should stop him. At this juncture, unfortunately, the daily expected reinforcements of the Company's police had not arrived; and with only a handful of men at his disposal, Major Forbes deemed it inadvisable to attempt to eject Gouveia from Umtasa's stronghold, situated as we have seen in a mountain fastness difficult of access. It is true that Gouveia's following was only composed of a motley crew, mainly East Coast natives. Still these men, although naturally but indifferent fighting material, had to be regarded seriously, acting under the personal command of the dreaded Gouveia and the successes with which his name had

MAJOR P. W. FORBES.
(6th Inniskilling Dragoons.)

hitherto been identified. And so matters remained momentarily at a standstill. Mr. Denis Doyle, superintendent of native affairs for the Company, together with Captain Hoste and Lieutenant Biscoe, late officers of the Pioneer Corps, also reached Umtasa's just about the same time—that is, on November 15, a day after the arrival of Colonel d'Andrada and the Baron de Rezende, who, with the whole of their followers, all well armed, went inside Umtasa's stockaded kraal. But I anticipate.

The next move came from the Portuguese. In spite of Major Forbes's protest, delivered to Colonel d'Andrada at Massi Kessi on 6th November, and to Gouveia on the 8th, news reached him on the 14th that both Colonel d'Andrade and Baron de Rezende had, with over 200 armed native followers, joined Gouveia at Umtasa's kraal, the last named having persisted in remaining there with the avowed object of intimidating the chief into a repudiation of the treaty concluded on September 14th last. Major Forbes at once decided to put an end by a *coup de main* to the persistent action of the Portuguese in coercing and menacing the Company's friendly ally. Most opportunely, and in the very nick of time, Lieut. the Hon. Eustace Fiennes (second son of Lord Saye and Sele and a brother of whom served in the Zulu war) appeared on the scene with some twenty men of the Company's police, having made a forced march of 180 miles from Fort Charter to reinforce Major Forbes. The moment it arrived the little force was divided into two parties. Major Forbes, with an escort of twelve men, proceeded direct to the King's kraal, and meeting the Baron de Rezende at the threshold, informed him that he was to consider himself a prisoner. Major Forbes had received information from some of Umtasa's people that Colonel d'Andrada had given orders that if any Englishmen were seen approaching the kraal the entrances were to be blockaded, and that resistance was to be made. However, Jonas, the na-

THE HON. EUSTACE FIENNES.

tive interpreter, who had been with Trooper Trevor from the first, was able to introduce them into the kraal by a back entrance, and also to show them the huts in which Colonel d'Andrada and his officers had taken up their quarters, as also those in which the greatest number of Gouveia's followers were collected. Penetrating behind the thick palisade of rough poles among the numerous huts of the now thoroughly alarmed and excited natives (who rushed to their arms, and ran about wildly in all directions), the representatives of the Company's police proceeded in their search, and within a short time arrested Colonel d'Andrada and Gouveia (the former being highly indignant and protesting volubly), persuading them that resistance was useless and that they must proceed under escort to his camp. Meanwhile the second party, a few hundred yards off, were busy carrying out the task assigned to them, viz., of disarming the armed " bearers " of the Portuguese. The scene was an animated one. Upon the appearance of this party, and in the absence of their leader Gouveia, complete demoralisation ensued among his followers. Some gesticulated and shouted, and others scrambled out of their grass huts with all they could lay their hands on in their hurried flight; others splashed through the mountain torrent or climbed over huge granite boulders and up precipitous rocks into places of security. Owing to the nature of the ground and the smallness of the disarming party, it was found impossible to secure the whole of the now disorganised horde, but those who fell into the hands of the police speedily and without resistance gave up their arms. Thus was effected quietly, but firmly, without the firing of a shot, without the loss of a single life (although there was every element present for such an event), one of the most effective *coups de main* of modern times, and destined to have important consequences, not only as regards Manica, but South-Eastern Africa generally. The plan of campaign of this "peaceful mission" of the Portuguese through their creditable representative was to have been as follows:— Umtasa, after having been brought to a proper frame of mind by the persuasive presence of Gouveia in his kraal for some days, was, on the arrival of Colonel d'Andrada and Baron de Rezene, in full *indaba*, to have made the astounding statement that twenty years ago, in return for Gouveia's "saving his life" (in other words, in return for services rendered him by Gouveia in the shape of helping him in some war with a neighbouring chief), he had sent an " elephant's tusk full of earth " to Gouveia, with the words, "Take my country—but come and save me." But Gouveia had not reckoned on having a Major Forbes to deal with.

One incident that took place at the time of the arrests may be recorded. Colonel Paiva d'Andrada when he was discovered in one of the huts, protested indignantly against the unwarrantable intrusion of the police, drawing their attention to the fact that he could not be arrested under the Portuguese flag. He pointed theatrically to the top of the hut, where a Portuguese flag had been carefully hoisted in anticipation of the important conference to take place, but he found to his dismay that that emblem of Portuguese might (so prodigally lavished among the confiding natives of South-Eastern Africa, and as a general rule the sole evidence of Portuguese occupation) had disappeared, having a few moments before been hauled down by some enterprising trooper of the Company's police. Only a photograph taken on the spot could give any adequate idea of the expression of the Colonel's countenance, an expression betokening utter discomfiture and blank dismay.

Colonel Paiva d'Andrada protested that he was there on a peaceable mission as Director of the Mozambique Company, accompanied by his friend Gouveia, an employé of the Company, and the Baron de Rezende, the local agent; they were there to discuss certain questions in connection with the mining interests of the Company with Umtasa. Similar protests Colonel d'Andrada repeated later. These assurances, however, were hardly reconcilable with the facts that the bearers carried not only arms but side arms, that orders had actually been given to barricade the enclosure gateways, and not only offer resistance to the approach of any English to the chief's kraal, but to drive the small body of the Company's police out of Manica altogether —"peaceable" designs happily frustrated by the sudden and vigorous action taken by Major Forbes. During the whole of these proceedings Umtasa's people watched events from the tops of the huge masses of rock, some 500 or 600 feet high, below which is perched the Royal kraal, the chief himself remaining quietly in his own hut, ruminating it may be on the vicissitudes he had recently gone through, and wondering perhaps how matters would ultimately eventuate. The distinguished prisoners (for such, indeed, they must presumably be regarded, as representing the main pillars of Portuguese authority in these regions) were marched quietly off, and were soon safely and comfortably ensconced in the officer's hut at the B.S.A. Company's camp. By a strange freak of fortune the officer in charge of the prisoners bore the name of Morier, a son of Sir Robert Morier, who concluded the well-known Lorenço Marques Treaty in

LIEUT. MORIER.

his capacity as British Minister at Lisbon. Lieut. Morier, who is about seven feet high and well and proportionately built, had been specially attached to Major Forbes for political duty from his thorough knowledge of the Portuguese language. Immediately after the arrest Captain Forbes decided, with admirable judgment, to despatch Colonel d'Andrada and Gouveia, with an escort of ten men under command of Lieutenant Fiennes, to Fort Salisbury, for to have released them upon parole in the Manica country would have been a fatal mistake. Such an action would have been attributed by the natives to weakness, and would infallibly have led to a dangerous rising among Gouveia's people in the Gorongoza province ; whilst the arrest and deportation of the much-dreaded Gouveia by a handful of the B.S.A. Company's policemen could not but raise British prestige not only in Manica but throughout the whole of South-Eastern Africa. The next day Colonel d'Andrada and Gouveia were accordingly despatched as prisoners on parole to Fort Salisbury in charge of Lieutenant the Hon. E. Fiennes and an escort of ten men, arriving safely at mid-day on the 22nd. It was decided that Baron de Rezende (also a prisoner on parole) should be allowed to return to Massi Kessi, where his numerous duties, shopkeeping and otherwise, required his early and personal supervision. Meanwhile Major Forbes, leaving a representative with Umtasa, pushed forward with every man he could lay his hands on, and occupied Massi Kessi on the 19th November, quietly and without any show of resistance. He had taken with him Baron de Rezende, and also Mons. de Llamby, an engineer of the Company of Mozambique, who had accompanied the Portuguese expedition to Umtasa's kraal. On their arrival at Massi Kessi both these gentlemen were released on parole, and Massi Kessi was, as I say, temporarily occupied by a small detachment of the B.S.A. Company's forces. Massi Kessi, it may here be said, is nothing but a trading station and stockaded compound, built by the Baron de Rezende in his capacity of local representative of the Mozambique Company. There was then no Portuguese garrison there, not even one single native soldier, nor is there any large native town in the vicinity. Upon the arrival at Fort Salisbury of Colonel Paiva d'Andrada and Gouveia a prolonged interview was accorded them by the Administrator, Mr. Colquhoun, which resulted in their being sent down country in one of the Company's wagons, accompanied by Lieutenant Mundell and a small escort of police, for the instructions of the Managing Director of the Company, Mr. C. J. Rhodes, and advice and instructions of the High Commissioner, Sir Henry Loch. From first to last the prisoners were treated with scrupulous courtesy, and every consideration was shown them by the Company's officials that was possible under somewhat embarrassing circumstances. For their long journey down country by bullock wagon every provision was made that would conduce to their personal comfort—both literary and culinary—as far as the slender resources of several kind friends at Fort Salisbury, notably Mr. Borrow and Mr. Heany, would permit.

My readers will agree that the history of Major Forbes's enterprise is wholesome and welcome reading for those who would not willingly confess to themselves that we have fallen away from the traditions of our ancestors. There was no fighting and no bloodshed, and it would be absurd to congratulate those who took part in the affair on having done anything heroic. But in the promptness and the unhesitating vigour with which the blow was struck, the incident may well remind us of the series of bold strokes by which the servants of " John Company " built up the fabric of our Indian Empire. The conditions are not very dissimilar. There is the same struggle between two European influences for supremacy at the Court of a native Ruler, whose only emotion is a wish to be on the side of the stronger, and there is the same consciousness on the part of those engaged, that if anything is to be effectively done they must act on their own responsibility and initiative. The French, it must be owned, were more formidable, and perhaps more respectable, adversaries than those who represent Portugal in her African domains. Yet Colonel d'Andrada's recently expressed contempt for the interloping Britishers, who not only appropriated but colonised vast tracts of the interior, and were perpetually popping up in force at the kraal of some potentate to whose country the Portuguese, during all the centuries of their boasted sway, had never penetrated, recalls the contrast, say, between the simple Clive and the ostentatious Dupleix. Major Forbes and his companions, it appears, had the inconceivable meanness to live upon tinned provisions while they dashed from west to east, while the official who represented the dignity of Portugal and the capital of the Mozambique Company never stirred a league from the coast without having the requisites for a "Bond Street" *cuisine* in his train. Colonel d'Andrada openly expressed to the officer in charge of his escort on his way to Fort Salisbury great astonishment at the rough-and-ready style of living, and at the frugal fare on which the Company's police subsist, the officers themselves living only on tinned beef and biscuit, and cooking their own tea and coffee in their patrol tins. He regarded such fare as fit "only for slaves," and informed one of the officers (with whom, on realising the fact that it was more becoming and sensible to accept the situation than continue to indulge in impotent protestations, he became somewhat communicative) that the Portuguese never dreamed of moving about these remote regions unless accompanied by a complete *cuisine*, which, on an emergency, could turn out as good a dinner as could be obtained "in Bond Street."

As I have, I hope, given a fair, impartial statement of the Manica incident from the best available material, I need not devote much space to the Portuguese version of the affair. Needless to say, it does not quite square with what I have related. Colonel d'Andrada at Cape Town naively admitted that Manica was "worth telling some lies over." He did not say on which side the lies were being told, so my readers need not necessarily take it for granted that I have set forth any. According to the Colonel, who has published a pamphlet on the subject, there had been a great mistake about everything except that there was no doubting their villainous journey to Cape Town in a bullock wagon. The terrible slave-trader and the gallant Colonel were sent down in this very way, and the Colonel, "almost with tears in his eyes," protested that the manner of travel in ox-wagons was extremely painful to the frame. But as for anything else, Colonel d'Andrada's version simply gave the lie direct to all others. Gouveia a slave-trader? He never sold a slave in his life—is the mildest mannered of men—and though it is true that countless natives will rise at his mere word, on this particular occasion he was, fortunately or unfortunately, attended only by two or three carriers, cooks, and so forth. Armed men? There was just a fowling-piece or two to shoot game with, and, if you want to know any more, Gouveia was " travelling with an Indian lady," Donna Julia Something, a fact which stamps a character at once of respectability and peace on the whole affair. How vain, then, Umtasa's fears! Why, the pacific quality of the expedition—a sort of African Social Science Congress—is proved incontestably by the presence of a lady, the friend—(alas!)—of Gouveia. The Colonel appeared to have forgotten that love has before now ruled the camp as well as the court and the grove. As for the treaties, Umtasa would rather "cut both of his hands off at the wrist" than sign anything with the English; as for attempting politically to forestall England and the South Africa Company, Colonel d'Andrada was going up, as it might be you to me, to look after some peaceful mining works, and the presence of the Capitan Mor (with the Indian lady) was of the most uncontentious and accidental character. True, Colonel d'Andrada did hint that the explorers had just as little business in Mashonaland proper as in Manica; true, though he never heard of an English flag, he admitted that the Company's police, who were very likely indeed to have such an article with them, were there before him. But what of this? The Portugals were taken by surprise, no doubt; but they were also taken with arms in their hands which they had not time to use. " If men came up to me in Regent Street, London, and took me off so," asks the innocent Portuguese Colonel, " what could I do? " The answer to which is that *coups de main* are seldom effected in Regent Street, but do frequently occur in Africa, so that you ought to be on your guard. The prominent fact, however, remains that while in the arrest and removal of the Portuguese representatives British influence and reputation were enormously raised, at the same time the power of the most dreaded of the Capitans Mors, as well as of the most influential slave owner, south of the Zambesi, was completely broken. And as the *Times* said: " Having appealed to force and insulted the British flag, Portugal has been met by force and handsomely beaten. Upon the merits of the dispute it is difficult to form any judgment in the absence of precise information; but whatever they may be, the Portuguese are clearly in the wrong in choosing violent methods of enforcing claims which at best must be exceedingly dubious."

The Mozambique Company, and Messrs. d'Andrada, Rezende, and Llamby, recently went on the war path in England. They issued a writ out of the Queen's Bench Division against the British South Africa Company, claiming damages for actions I have been describing, and asking for an injunction to prevent the repetition of alleged annoyance. The three last-named plaintiffs also claimed damages for personal assaults which they stated had been committed upon them. The writ was served on the 13th of March last, and a preliminary argument or two have taken place. The action, however, is not likely to reach a further hearing under less than two years' time, and there is no knowing to what length after that the proceedings may be spun out. Probably the children, or the grand-children, of my readers may be in at the "finish," but I scarcely hope to be. As for the damages, I should recommend the plaintiffs to try and get something on account, for they might not enjoy them otherwise.

The larger question of the claims of Portugal to Gazaland may be also referred to here. From what I have already said the utter hollowness of any claim of Lisbon to any part of the East Coast but the fever-laden coast fringe and a few moribund seaports will have been apparent. Gazaland, of which Manica is relatively a very small portion, is a vast independent native territory situate on the South-East African littoral, being bounded on the east by the Indian Ocean for some 600 miles, on the north by the Zambesi River for some 300 miles, on the west by Mashonaland, and on the south by Tongaland, Swazieland, and the Transvaal.

At the close of the last century Gazaland, alike with all South Africa south of the Zambesi, and as far south as the Kei River district in what is now the Cape Colony, was populated by hundreds of clans or tribes of aborigines of the great Bantu race, and all speaking one or other of the dialects of the Bantu tongue. In the early part of the present century one of these many hundred native tribes, and one of the smallest numerically of them, claimed dominant power, and, partly by the commanding powers of its leader Chaka, and partly by the warlike attributes of the tribe itself, it, the Zulu tribe, grew by conquest till it had consolidated, as one large Empire, all the other hitherto independent clans and tribes within a radius of some 400 miles. Chaka's power was thus extended all over the present Colony of Natal, over a portion of the Cape Colony, over the district of Delagoa Bay, and over the Eastern portion of the Orange Free State and Transvaal. In 1820 two of Chaka's fighting captains fell into disgrace. One of these—Mosilikatse, whose career I have traced—ravaged his way to Matabeleland, and the other, Soshangane, broke to the north and settled in Gazaland, where the clans and tribes of that district accepted him as paramount chief. When Soshangane died he was succeeded by Umzila, who died in the early eighties and left a well-consolidated kingdom to his chief son, Umdungazwe (called by the Portuguese Gungunyane and Gungunhama), the present paramount chief.

Not long after Umzila died, Umdungazwe sent an embassy to the English Queen's Induna (local officer), the Governor of Natal, with the intimation that Umzila was dead, and that Umdungazwe reigned in his stead. The embassy brought with them the usual complimentary messages and also a tusk of ivory as a friendly expression, but they complained bitterly of the trouble they wer having on the coast with the Portuguese. Their statement was long, full of fact and detail, but may be summarised briefly thus :—

(a) That, whereas the Portuguese had always been friendly in their relations with the Gaza King and people, and had given them frequent gifts, they had recently been using force with some of the subsidiary Gaza tribes located on the littoral near the points tenanted by the Portuguese, that blood had been shed, that the King's treasury-house of ivory had been burnt and looted, and that the King had to take to arms, whereupon the Portuguese at once retreated to the sea again.

(b) That, while not objecting to the residing of the Portuguese on the seashore, so long as they acted as friends and made the customary presents yearly to the King, any exercise of authority in the territory or levying of war would be resented by the King and people.

(c) That the King and people had anticipated no acts of violence, the more so as the Portuguese had sent up an officer to the King's kraal, carrying gifts and expressing a wish to maintain friendly intercourse.

On the general subject of Portuguese aggression the embassy declared that there were but two classes of men who were dominant in South Africa—viz., the English and the Dutch; that the Portuguese were not white people, but a contemptible coloured race, whose chief delight was to sit on the sea sands and paddle in the water; that the Gaza King and people knew the history of the black peoples of South Africa; that they knew what had become of the Cape tribes, of the Natal tribes, of the Zulus, the Basutos, and the Bechuanas; and, knowing this, that they would have in turn to choose a white lord; that when that time came they would choose the English; but that for the present they were independent; that, as to the Portuguese on the coast, they tolerated them only, and that the two facts of the Portuguese paying tribute always, and, when trading, claiming to be subjects of the English people, made a full answer to any claim of Portuguese dominion. The Embassy was treated with scant courtesy by Sir Arthur Havelock, the Governor of Natal, but they were privately advised in a sensible manner by a leading colonist. The advice the Ambassadors returned to the Gaza King with was this :—

"Tell your King he is strong, and can therefore afford to act prudently. Tell him that, though the Portuguese who molest him are black and degenerate, they are the representatives of a white European Power, a weak Power, but still a white people. Tell him they will never overrun his country, because they are not a colonising, industrious people. Tell him, however, that he is right to resent any inroad in his own territory, or attacks on his people, and tell him his best plan is to send a definite message to the Portuguese officials, telling them that he is wishful to be at peace with them as his and their fathers were before, that the country is his for his people, that so long as they merely use the seaports for trading and come and go among the people for trading he is willing they should remain, but that they must control their people at the seaports from molesting or worrying his, the King's people."

But for their having been tolerated on the coast by the natives, no such claims as the Portuguese make nowadays could ever have been seriously preferred. The possession, however, of the only ports presently in use on the Gaza littoral allows the Portuguese to control for the moment the ingress to the country from the sea.

The Portuguese are understood to base their claims to Gazaland upon its discovery by Vasco da Gama, upon the contention that the Gaza King is their vassal, and upon the assumed existence of a treaty alleged to have been made between Gungunhama and themselves. The last-named claim may be dismissed at once. The alleged treaty proves to be a document signed at Lisbon, from which the signature of Gungunhama is absent. As regards the first-stated claim, it is a matter of history that the Portuguese did not discover the Gazaland littoral, the Zambesi, and adjacent islands. As their own records show, no one was more astonished than da Gama to find harbours, shipping, commerce, and a general refinement of manners and customs among the English and Banyan traders, a refinement which died out with the Portuguese tenancy of the coast.

Vasco da Gama found in Gazaland people clothed in textile fabrics of cotton and silk, he found gold exported to the East Indies, and diamonds imported therefrom with other products of civilization. He found the shipping there in constant trade not only with the ports to the North, but those of India. He found the compass in common use, and he gladly secured the services of Mozambique pilots to conduct him to Calicut. So pleased was he to reach civilisation once more that he called the river of Gazaland—the Zambesi—"The River of Good Signs." As to the ruins till the other day claimed by the Portuguese as proof of possession, a reference to the pages of Osirus, of Castanhede, and of Camoens and other contemporary writers of da Gama, tells against them, and that the ruins in and bordering on Gazaland were there along with the old mine workings already ancient, and their builders and workers unknown and untraceable. Juan dos Santos in his voyage published by Le Grande deals with this point in detail, but I have sufficiently dealt with it to show that whoever were responsible for the ruins they were not the Portuguese. Mozambique was a flourishing mart of that name before da Gama reached it. Ressende reported, over 300 years ago, that the Zambesi was navigable for over 200 leagues. Commodore Blanket, of H.M. Royal Navy, was stationed on the Gaza littoral at the end of the last century, and reported specially on the Mozambique shore. His reports should be at the Admiralty, and a further set of special reports were all deposited in the British Museum about that time.

Portugal has ever viewed their stations on the littoral as penal

D D

settlements and no more ; da Gama founded these by leaving a
number of capitally condemned felons there. The dire consequence of
this penal settlement view has been the existence of a low and ever-
lowering class of people on the sea coast at the points of call,
who have degraded the contiguous blacks in a terribly loathsome
manner. The result of this sort of "occupation" of Eastern
Africa has been the breeding on the coast line of a hybrid and
worthless race, who have no place in the esteem of either the
higher civilised Portuguese or the natives, but are despised alike by
both.

GUNGUNHAMA'S KRAAL.

The ultimate effect of a couple of centuries of such "occupation"
has been, so far as colonization from a European standpoint is
concerned, nil and less than nil, inasmuch as the natives near the
points tenanted by the so-called Portuguese have been shockingly
degraded. Arts, industry, and commerce alike are and have been
neglected ; the trade that is carried on is done by English and
Banyan merchants, the latter having traded there long before
Vasco da Gama cast anchor at Mozambique.

A great deal has been made of the flag question, and that
Gungunhama has allowed the Portuguese to fly a piece of bunt-
ing when on a visit to him. This has no meaning to the
native mind, and the flags left behind by the Portuguese have only
interested young women, who regarded them as welcome additions

to the limited wardrobe of the Gaza Court. When Jokane, the brother of the Gaza King, was on a short sea trip from Chiloane to Inhambane recently, he apostrophized the land in this fashion :—

" The Portuguese built on it, but it is my brother's land and my brother's trees that grow upon it. They make us angry. So angry did they make us once that we drove them into the sea and made it red with their blood. They will make us angry again, and if you (English) that we love will come to me, when they make us very angry I will lend you a hundred thousand fighting men and help you to make the sea red with their blood again, and you can take their houses, and cattle, and wives, for my brother will be glad when you come."

This is hardly the language of a vassal. When Gungunhama recently was about to make a move to his summer kraal, some Portuguese emissaries told him not to do so, as there were English prowling round to eat him up. The King angrily cried, " Am I a baby that I should be nursed and taught by you ? " His Majesty gave the Portuguese emissaries three days to clear from his sight, and, ordering Jokane to take a large number of fighting men, marched with them to his summer kraal. An obedient vassal !

If it were necessary, which it is not, to multiply evidence that the Portuguese have no real claim to remain in South Eastern Africa, excepting on the sea shore, on the sufferance of the natives, it would be easy to do so. Mr. St. Vincent Erskine, who made several trips from Natal to Gazaland nearly twenty years ago, says : " Besides this strip of country around Inhambane the Portuguese do not possess an acre that they can call their own outside the walls of any of their stations south of the Zambesi." Mr. A. A. Anderson, in his " Twenty-five Years in a Wagon in South Africa," remarks : " The Portuguese have no control over any part of Umzila's territory ; they only hold possession of narrow slips of land along parts of the coast." As Sir John Willoughby puts it :—

It seems almost a characteristic of the race to remain in lazy idleness until a temporary spurt of jealous activity is stimulated by the approach of civilisation under a more enterprising flag. Then, and only then, are the so-called Portuguese representatives stirred to the formation of nominal trading stations on the outskirts of the country to which they intend to lay claim. These stations generally consist of a few poor huts, occupied by half-bred traders and one white man, who, without the least semblance of power to enfore authority in any part of the country, assumes the title of "governor" or "commandant." The next stage is very simple, as it merely requires the Portuguese Government to lay claim to an unlimited amount of country beyond their "stations," and, by political agitation and cunning diplomacy, to wrest from others the just reward of their pluck and enterprise. By all means let the Portuguese keep what they have actually got, which is the coast line, and nothing more, if they will facilitate the civilisation of the interior by throwing their ports open to commerce without prohibitive tariffs ; but, in common justice, I trust our Government will be firm enough to resist claims which might be regarded as ridiculous were the issues involved less important to the whole question of the progress of humanity and civilisation.

And what says Capt. W. F. W. Owen, R.N., in the account of his voyages on the East Coast of Africa in the early part of the century? "Even at Mozambique the Portuguese jurisdiction and settlements do not extend ten miles in any direction, and to the southward not at all." And there is more in the same strain. Again—and I shall not go any further for similar citations— Capt. Parker Gillmore, in his "Through Gazaland," states: "The claim that Portugal has made to the possession of Gazaland is preposterous; that it be deemed the owner of Mashonaland is ridiculous. My reasons for saying so are that it has only two ports along the seaboard of the first mentioned, beyond the limits of which it dare not go; while for permission to trade at Senna, Tete, and Zumbo, stations on the Zambesi River, it annually paid to the Suzerain of Mashonaland—the Matabele King—a large subsidy, which, if not forthcoming at the stipulated date, was enforced by an army."

An important report was recently received by the British South Africa Company from their agents in Gazaland. It threw a light on the true position of the Portuguese and English in that country and might have been expected to have an influence on the negotiations between Lord Salisbury and the Government of Lisbon. It may be quoted from here. Dr. Aurel Schulz, it should perhaps be explained, is a representative of the British South Africa Company at the kraal of Gungunhama. With regard to Gungunhama himself, the Board is requested to understand that that chief is "a far more powerful prince than Lo Bengula, and that the Portuguese—who, as he says, are only black men like himself (for such almost universally are all Portuguese officials outside Portugal)—[i.e., the few officials sent from Portugal.—E.P.M.] —pay him the greatest deference and respect, and personally give him such yearly tribute as they can afford, and are positively as a fact in the country purely on sufferance as traders." At a great council of the natives, at which the Portuguese General Almedia (a black man, like Gouveia) wished the English in the person of Dr. Schulz to be turned out of the country, the King replied: " He is my friend, and the English are my friends. You and your nation have always lied to me, to my father, and to my grandfather. If you think you can turn him out of the country, you had better try. There he stands." Needless to say, the Portuguese General did not attempt to interfere with Dr. Schulz, who is a man of fine physique. The report explains that the position of Dr. Schulz at the King's kraal is most friendly; but—

So far the King has been vexed that we have not used his permission to enter the Limpopo River and convey goods to his kraal, and he was inclined to suspect Dr. Schulz's *bonâ fides*, as he cannot credit the statement that the coast line of his country is considered to belong to Portugal. He thinks this statement is a subterfuge, and an evidence that we are not willing to carry out the terms of our concession by sending the goods into the Limpopo, which has five feet of clear water over its bar. Some 40 or 50 miles up the river we are only at a distance of about 48 miles from the King's kraal. Goods could therefore be landed at his kraal from Durban in six days. It is so absurd and ridiculous to this powerful King, who collects tribute from Delagoa Bay to Beira from every race and tribe throughout the country, to be told that we cannot or dare not sail up a great river within 48 miles of his kraal because this petty race of half-caste traders will not allow us, that he refuses to believe our statements, and considers them a sign of our unwillingness to enter into an alliance with him. The Board will not forget that, as far as Gungunhama knows the Portuguese strength and power, it is represented to him by a few native officials—Goanese—and a handful of nigger soldiers. He looks with admiration on the English as a white race whose strength is everywhere, and whom both his father and his grandfather have respected. He cannot, therefore, understand any relations existing except relations between the English as a powerful race of white men and himself, as King of Gazaland. On Dr. Schulz informing him that the Portuguese claimed the coast line and would not allow us to land anywhere on his coast the lives of the Portuguese officials were in great danger; but they hastened to assure the King that this was not so. It is only when far away from Gazaland that they make their astounding statements as to their footing with the King. One thing that has impressed Gungunhama most unfavourably against the Portuguese is that the natives of Chopieland have lately revolted against him. The King sent 12,000 of his men into the country, and Dr. Schulz states that when his army returned, 7000 of them wore the death-plume, showing that each of those so distinguished had killed his man. The natives were wiped out, and the King states that he has good evidence that the Portuguese instigated this unhappy people to revolt.

So much for the Portuguese position. With regard to the English position in the country the report continues:—

The King states that he sent to the British Government on September 26, 1890, through the Shepstones, to ask for assistance and advice, stating that the Portuguese were molesting him, and he did not want them in his country, stating further that both his grandfather, father, and self had always wished to be friends with the English. Previous to this date he states that he had many times sent messages to the English Government through the Shepstones. On October 4 the King personally sent out Messrs. Kellican and Fryer to ask for British protection. His message was that the "Queen was to take him" by the hand and not to let go. Umsila, his father, had had the same wish before him. On November 2 the King declared before the whole army, just returned from the Chopie war, that he intended to become English, and, pointing to Dr. Schulz as he was surveying the army, said, "That man is my friend now, but if his nation treat us as the Portuguese have done I will kill him." On November 24 the King authorised Dr. Schulz before his Council to send the following message to the British Government:— That he had signed the paper (presumably Dr. Schulz's concession which was granted in the early part of October), before the Portuguese, in order to show the Portuguese his independence and requested that the goods, subsidy, &c., should come without delay. On December 29 he declared before the full Council of the nation, before General Almedia and party, and before Dr. Schulz's party, consisting of Mr. and Mrs. Fels, Mr. F. Colquhoun, Mr. T. M. Kellican, Mr. Barnes, and Mr. J. A. Stevens, that the Portuguese flag now flying over the Portuguese ports was there "out of politeness only." He dared the Portuguese to deny his right to pull it down and hoist the English flag whenever he liked. He instanced the three occasions on which Almedia had deceived him, and called Almedia a liar, and Almagabu a man of lies, each time repeatedly. He also challenged Almedia to speak to Dr. Schulz as the English representative. The King had authorised Dr. Schulz to be his spokesman as a white man to a white man (by courtesy). General Almedia refused to speak to Schulz, when the latter, before the whole Council, declared his mission as representing the Queen's people and the British South Africa Company, and informed the Portuguese of Gungunhama's action in sending to the Queen's Government and the British people for their alliance. Almedia then said that a conference with Schulz had no object, as the two Governments would settle the question between them. The King thereupon became furious, and broke up the Council in anger, saying, "Not without consulting me, Gungunhama, shall any question be settled concerning my affairs." According to native law, Almedia here lost his case for the Portuguese Government, whatever it may have been, by refusing to plead his cause or to challenge Dr. Schulz's credentials. Immediately after the Council the King sent to Schulz to say that Almedia had asked him to hand Dr. Schulz over as a prisoner, and that he had refused and told Almedia to go himself to Dr. Schulz. Dr. Schulz adds that Almedia never came. The King further informed Dr. Schulz that Almedia had asked him for an army to fight against the English, who, Almedia said, were encroaching on the King's ground in the north of Gazaland. The King refused.

The report concludes with a list of 10 principal indunas who are strongly in favour of the British alliance, and this proves that Gungunhama is firmly persuaded of his own right to Gazaland from the coast inward to Mashonaland, and is sincerely desirous to place himself under British protection.

It might here be suggested that if Lord Salisbury wants to get at the real truth of Gungunhama's relations to the Portuguese, and of his strong desire to come under the protection of the British, or to remain independent, the best and most expeditious way would be to send out to Gazaland a small Commission of Inquiry empowered to take evidence on the subject. Several names will at once occur to some of my readers as those of men well qualified for such a delicate task—men who are, moreover, perfectly unbiassed by any speculative or financial considerations. If this course were taken the dispute would be for ever set at rest. The expense of such a Commission would be comparatively small, but if the Government, as is usual, felt themselves unable to saddle the country with the cost, I have no doubt the British South Africa Company would be, as it has been before, very glad to come to its assistance.

The Gaza King has an army always at hand of some 15,000

men, and reserves in distant districts of double that number. All are armed with assegais and spears. Guns are almost unknown, and although the issue of any attack organized by the Portuguese on the coast would be in favour of the Gazas, yet, as the coloured felons, who would be, as heretofore, employed in such attacks are armed with Government breechloaders and led by Government officers, and as Portugal has now some presumably civilised troops in the country, bloodshed would be at once wanton and heavy. In face of these facts, as affecting the right of an independent and friendly native Power and would-be ally of England, and also in face of the fact that Gazaland is the corner which will consolidate British possessions south of the Zambesi, it is earnestly to be hoped that in any arrangement which England may make with Portugal Gungunhama will not be led to believe that he has been " thrown over " by the British. If he were to get such an idea into his head, and Portuguese adventurers were to take any advantage of the idea, there can be little doubt the results would be very serious.

At the present moment two envoys from Gungunhama are in this country to lay before the " Great White Queen " the facts I gave long ago, and now repeat as to the Gaza King's desired alliance with England, and I most sincerely trust, in the interests of the general peace of South Africa, that Lord Salisbury will allow no notions of mere present expediency to cause him to let slip a great opportunity for solidifying Britain's influence in South East Africa.

In the signing of the treaty at Umtasa's we see the " writing on the wall " in respect of Portuguese occupation in South-East Africa ; in the occupation of Umtasa's by the British South Africa Company we hear its death knell sounded. Portugal, indeed, as a colonising Power and civilising agency has, in these latter days, been " weighed in the balance and found wanting." It is high time that the truth and true facts of Portuguese "occupation" in South-East Africa should be realised. I have been endeavouring for years to obtain realisation for them. When they are fully understood at home men will cease to wonder why Englishmen in Mashonaland, and why any who know aught of the subject, consider that the days of Portuguese occupation are now numbered and that Portuguese influence in these regions is doomed. They will realise the fact that the countries from the Zambesi to the Crocodile—over which the Portuguese have hitherto exercised either a most shadowy, or, if in any degree effective, an absolutely pernicious influence ; where, as colonists, in the proper and accepted sense of the term, they have utterly and ignominiously failed—must now shortly pass into stronger, more capable, more vigorous hands.

CHAPTER XVII.

THE year 1891 will prove a fateful one for Portugal so far as
her tenure of occupation and prestige in South-Eastern
Africa are concerned; whether it will see Lisbon in the joint
possession of England and Spain, and Dom Carlos and his
family housed in a British man-of-war in the Tagus, remains to be seen.
So far the year has seen a few desperate efforts in that capital to make
the worse appear the better cause, efforts that to the placid onlooker
would appear comical if he could dismiss the reflection that they
were either on the one hand the hypocritical actions of a section
whose design is to cause the eyes of the masses to look anywhere
but at home, or the flickering ebullitions of a genuine patriotism
doomed to be sacrificed in the wreck of an expiring system of government. January saw Portugal send forth to South-East Africa, amid
pathetic demonstrations of affection, an army of nearly a thousand
officers and men, a fighting force she may yet sorely miss when
troubles overtake her nearer home. The flower of Lusitanian youth
went out not as in the days of old to perform for the world a real
and lasting service, but to do and die for a bad cause that perished
ere they had touch with the physical trials and hardships which
will prevent many from ever seeing their sunny homes again. All
the purposes for which these soldiers were to be used were not at
once apparent. It was stated that they would endeavour to com-
pel Gungunhama to recognise the Portuguese as the paramount
authority in Gazaland. For the sake of their lives I hope that the
Lisbon Government contemplate no such suicidal mission. If the
Portuguese try, as it is reported they are trying, to dispossess the
Chartered Company from territory which they rightly occupy, they
will receive the natural reward of their temerity. Should they dare
to hostilely enter Gazaland, it goes without saying that they would
rush on self-destruction. But more than this; they would raise a war
with the natives which would not only be hurtful to British prestige
locally, but might easily prove disastrous to our fellow countrymen
in Zambesia. The natives of Gazaland, from the King to the
merest herdboy, want to come under the British flag. The King

has already entered into a treaty of friendship with the British South Africa Company, and it would be a very simple thing for England to endorse that treaty. This would be the requisite signal to the Portuguese to leave, at all events, the Gazas alone. Will Lord Salisbury give that signal? If not the consequences may be very serious. Though these troops, with their stores of wine and velocipedes, do happen to dash themselves in vain against the rock of British possession, the manifestations which called them into being were, nevertheless, fruitful of mischief. For many weeks poisonous untruths invented by the so-called friends of Portugal filled the air in Lisbon and Paris (one of them that French capitalists had put a million pounds into the Mozambique Company), and the black tools and impulsive agents of Portugal on the far-away African coast were led to think that the path of insolence to the British was the way to glory. England's patience with the petulance of a senile nationality was met by brutal and ruffianly insults on her subjects at the hands of its unscrupulous hirelings, and to these a few lines may here be devoted.

At the end of February last the British steamer *Countess of Carnarvon* left Natal for the Limpopo. She went up that river to meet Dr. Jamieson and other officials of the British South Africa Company, and on her return voyage with them on board, the vessel was fired on and seized by the Portuguese steamer *Marshal MacMahon*, on a charge of smuggling, and taken to Delagoa Bay. There the British subjects on board were released, but the English steamer was detained. It was declared by the Portuguese authorities that the vessel had arms for Gungunhama on board; but this was not true. It happens to be true that the ship in question conveyed rifles to Gungunhama in accordance with a contract made with him by the British South Africa Company before the *modus vivendi* came into force; this, though, was not on the occasion when she was seized, but months before. About the same time a small hunting party of Englishmen, intending to proceed to Mashonaland by the Pungwe River, were stopped by the Portuguese at Beira. Their supplies in two boats were seized without any justification whatever, the party having declared to the customs authorities the full number of the firearms they had with them—a total armament of 24 weapons, not a very large one for a hunting party in the interior. Several members of the party, notably Messrs. Copeland and Kisch, were also subjected to personal indignities and considerable personal loss.

As before explained, the Limpopo or Crocodile River forms the northern boundary of the Transvaal, down to the point where its waters cut what the Portuguese claim as their frontier, after which it flows through territory that would have been definitely recognised as Portuguese by the Convention which Portugal foolishly rejected. Thus it is the natural highway to the sea for the Northern Transvaal on one side, and for the extensive tracts assigned to the British South Africa Company on the other. It has been proved navigable for steamers of light draught as far as the junction of the Nuanetsi, that is to say, a point between the 32nd and 33rd degrees, and consequently to the actual south-eastern border line of the Chartered Company's territory. A very little common sense should have sufficed to show the Portuguese that in these circumstances they could not hope to be allowed to close a great navigable river merely because they claim both its banks for some distance from the sea. On the contrary, a claim, however good in itself, which is pushed to so absurd and inequitable a conclusion stands a very fair chance of being swept away, and it is not to be forgotten that Gungunhama would entirely repudiate the claim. Still, had the Portuguese waited for the expiry of the *modus vivendi* before seizing a British steamer on the Limpopo, they might have acted stupidly without direct breach of engagements. As things stand, they carried out a stupid policy, in defiance of a formal agreement, actually made at their own request. By the third clause of that agreement the Portuguese Government engaged " to facilitate in every way communications between the Portuguese ports on the coast and the territories included in the sphere of action of Great Britain, especially as regards the establishment of postal and telegraphic communications and as regards the transport service." From this it follows that a British steamer was entirely within its rights in navigating that portion of the Limpopo which is claimed to be within the Portuguese sphere of influence, on its way to or from the British possessions lying inland. In the exercise of that unquestionable right, the *Countess of Carnarvon* was seized and taken as a prize into Delagoa Bay, an outrage for which the Lisbon Government had to be called to account.

The British South Africa Company will, probably know how to hold their own in the interior. If they get only a fair field and no interference, British Colonists in Matabeleland may be trusted to carry through, in defiance of Portugal, any enterprise which on commercial grounds is worth prosecuting. But as the *Times* said at the time, they cannot be expected to hold the Limpopo down to the sea, and they have a right to expect from the Queen's Government the maintenance of free navigation upon their great waterway. If, said that newspaper, Portugal carries her dog-in-the-manger policy so far in the teeth of a solemn engagement, we may imagine what she will do when she again has a free hand. The truth is that we do not negotiate upon equal terms. We are anxious to develop the country, while Portugal has been in possession of the coast for centuries, without giving a thought to the interior except as a source of supply of slaves. Portugal is content if she can thwart our policy, and does not greatly value the commercial advantages we offer to secure in return for those that we desire. But, if she adheres to this obstructive policy, measures must be taken to clear the obstruction out of our way. If she can do nothing better with the mouth of the Limpopo than simply block the way to the interior, then the mouth of the Limpopo will have to pass into other hands.

About the same time the authorities at the mouth of the Pungwe River refused admission by that route to a large party of intending passengers by a recently-established Anglo-American Pioneer Line of small river steamers and ox wagons to Fort Salisbury. This Shipping Company has organised a service of river steamers and wagons from Beira to the Mashona capital, and 250 settlers for the Mashona gold fields were to have taken advantage of it. Of course this expedition was at once magnified at Lisbon into a hostile demonstration on the part of Great Britain. The Portuguese authorities protested against the passage of armed men through territory on the flimsy pretext that Massi Kessi was in British occupation, the fact being that that little Portuguese outpost was only in the hands of a Chartered Company's trooper or two left behind to protect the goods deserted by the Portuguese themselves and being looted by the natives. As it is impossible for any settler to enter a wild country without arms, this decision applied to everyone who desired to use that route into Mashonaland, and amounted, therefore, to a virtual abrogation of the *modus vivendi*. The Pungwe River was, notwithstanding the protest of the Lisbon Government to the contrary, closed to navigation.

While demands were being made of the Lisbon Government for some satisfactory explanation of or reparation for these affairs, and while the terms of a new convention between the two countries were being discussed, there came news of the most intolerable of the long series of insults which the British have had to put up with from the half-castes who, " dressed in a little brief authority," have hitherto played their fantastic tricks with impunity. Sir John Willoughby, whom I have repeatedly mentioned, with a party of colonists proposing to settle in Mashonaland, arrived in the steamer *Norseman* at Port Beira, where they proposed to disembark. The mails for the Chartered Company's station in Mashonaland had been sent with the party. On reaching the port Sir John Willoughby applied for permission to proceed up the Pungwe River, offering at the same time payment of the duties levied by the Portuguese. No reply was vouchsafed. Sir John Willoughby says that for two whole days he tried to negotiate with the Portuguese officer in command for the passage of his steamers—that he pointed out to him the terms of the *modus vivendi*, with which he bound himself to comply—but he was met by a peremptory refusal. Upon this Sir John determined to insist upon British rights and to yield only to superior force. He thought the Portuguese would scarcely venture to fire upon the British flag. But they did fire upon it; they boarded the ships, hauled down the British flag and hoisted that of Portugal in its place, arrested the captains and crews, and sent back the rest of the party to British territory by sea. For these proceedings there was not an atom of warrant or justification. They were a gross violation of the treaty by which the navigation of the Pungwe River as of the other East Coast rivers was made free to British ships, and of a distinct pledge on the part of Portugal.

To make matters worse, there was ample ground for the belief that the action of the Portuguese was premeditated as well as deliberate. The intention of Sir John Willoughby's expedition to make for Mashonaland by way of the Pungwe was perfectly well known. No attempt had been made, and none was supposed to be necessary, to conceal the route that would be followed, and it is tolerably clear that the Portuguese laid their plans in advance to prevent the passage of the steamers up the Pungwe.

It seemed as if the gods had at last taken counsel to destroy Portugal. At all events, her representatives in South Africa were showing every symptom of preliminary madness. A perverse fate dogged Portugal, and it looked as if it would go on dogging her to her doom. Whatever might be the intentions or the good faith of Portuguese officials in Lisbon, they could not control their representatives in South Africa, among whom, as we have seen, there are many reckless scoundrels utterly incapable of appreciating an honourable understanding between two honourable nations like England and Portugal. The misfortune of the position for Portugal was, that however sincere she might be in her desire to conduct negotiations with Great Britain on a fair and reasonable basis, she could be locally tricked into having to countenance the proceedings of those who use her flag in East Africa as a cloak for atrocious offences.

The attack of the Portuguese officials on Sir John Willoughby's expedition at the mouth of the Pungwe River, brought matters in that district to a crisis. Having been brought to a crisis, if a cure had not been found by diplomatic methods in Europe it would swiftly have been found on the spot. These outrages on the British flag would have been punished by their victims long ago but for the respectful desire on the part of loyal subjects of the British Empire not to appear to interfere with England's diplomatic negotiations with a presumably friendly power. The Beira outrage, like the several other similar occurrences, will, of course, have to be heavily accounted for in the long run. The British Government recognised their duty to take some tangible apparent step which would satisfy British subjects in South Africa that the Union Jack is not to be systematically insulted with impunity even by a weakling like Portugal.

They did this somewhat tardily, and there was a natural outburst of feeling at Cape Town at the delay in making a visible sign that England had made up her mind that Portugal had at last transgressed the limits of all forbearance. But if Lord Salisbury's action was slow it was sure. He announced in the House of Lords on April 23rd that in reply to his representations to Lisbon he had been informed that the Lisbon Government had sent orders to remove (I quote from a report of his Lordship's remarks)—

Every obstacle to the passage of peaceable travellers up the waters of the Pungwe, and from that into the interior, so that if that undertaking is fulfilled we shall have, as regards the future, nothing in that respect to complain of. But the demeanour of the Portuguese officials on the East Coast of Africa has, on more than one occasion, corresponded so little with the assurances we have received from Lisbon that we thought it desirable to request that three of Her Majesty's vessels should proceed to the mouth of the Pungwe as speedily as possible. (Ministerial cheers.) They will not be large vessels, but sufficient for the purpose. The Portuguese Minister also proposed that we should place a Consular Agent of some kind at the mouth of the Pungwe, in order to see that our requirements in respect to the *modus vivendi* were complied with, and to furnish us with authentic information. That is a measure which undoubtedly ought to have been taken at a considerably earlier period during the currency of the *modus vivendi*, which has only now three or four weeks to run. It appears to be reasonable, and I hope we shall be able to do it immediately and provisionally by detailing some naval officer for that purpose. I cannot speak as to the precise steps to be taken, but I think that there is every probability that the Governments will be agreed on that measure. I hope that for the future there will be no further reason to complain of delay with respect to the passage of the Pungwe. The question which may further arise as to any reparation that may be properly required, I shall reserve until we have full and detailed accounts of the real events which have occurred. (Hear, hear.)

The prompt opening of the Pungwe River to traffic gave the Portuguese one more chance for life on the East African littoral. It soothed their *amour propre* to say that they did this because the British South Africa Company's forces had retired and left them in possession of Massi Kessi, which is now occupied by some of the Lisbon troops. As my readers will remember, the Chartered Company did not occupy Massi Kessi in the sense of taking forcible permanent possession of it, but merely detailed some troopers to guard the premises of the Mozambique Company which had been abandoned by their heroic guardians and left a prey to the looting propensities of the local natives. A step taken in the general interest was made to appear one of hostile intent towards the Portuguese. But Lord Salisbury and Englishmen in the mother country and in South Africa could afford to smile at all this; they knew that it was the readiness of England's navy on the South African coast that was the real cause of the reopening of the Pungwe River to traffic. A quotation from the *Cape Times* showing this preparedness may here be made :—

Within the past forty-eight hours probably the whole of British South Africa has turned towards Simon's Bay, anxiously awaiting events. As yet the every-day peacefulness and tranquillity of the naval station has remained undisturbed. No news "of the right sort," from Jack's point of view, no welcome telegraphic flash full of command, has been received from England or elsewhere. True, the prevailing and generally accepted rumour current points to prompt action on the part of the General commanding the British military forces in South Africa. Naval assistance under Imperial auspices is sought for. The answer may come any moment. Simon's Bay is ready. The flagship, now away cruising, is expected in port the coming week. The splendid vessel which honoured Table Bay with a visit last week, Her Majesty's ship *Magicienne*, or shall we say her full complement—every man on board looks for a speedy order to pro-

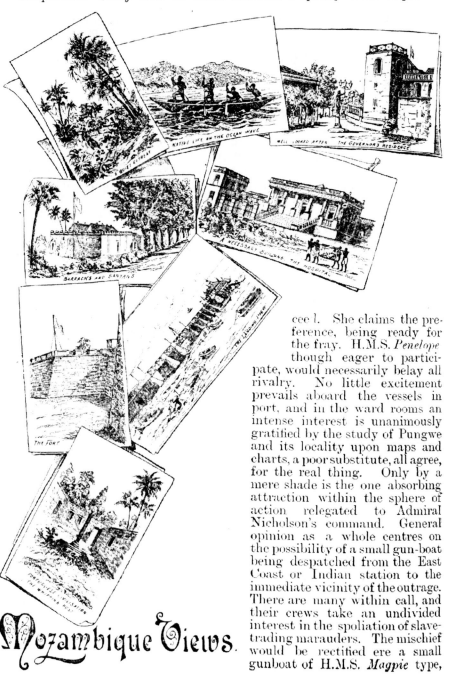

Mozambique Views.

cee l. She claims the preference, being ready for the fray. H.M.S. *Penelope* though eager to participate, would necessarily belay all rivalry. No little excitement prevails aboard the vessels in port, and in the ward rooms an intense interest is unanimously gratified by the study of Pungwe and its locality upon maps and charts, a poor substitute, all agree, for the real thing. Only by a mere shade is the one absorbing attraction within the sphere of action relegated to Admiral Nicholson's command. General opinion as a whole centres on the possibility of a small gun-boat being despatched from the East Coast or Indian station to the immediate vicinity of the outrage. There are many within call, and their crews take an undivided interest in the spoliation of slave-trading marauders. The mischief would be rectified ere a small gunboat of H.M.S. *Magpie* type, quite equal to the occasion, could arrive on the scene from Bathurst. Keen in their genuine wishes for some really good business, naval men yet dread a spell off any Portuguese hell-hole, hanging about awaiting the expiration of the *modus vivendi* or other obstacles to progress. Pungwe River may not be navigable for purposes of chastisement, but within five days from the order to sail, the rattle and boom of the *Magicienne's* big guns, so deftly handled, would scarcely harmonise with the clanking of swords and clattering spurs at Lourenço Marques of the few hundred dismounted and emasculated cavalrymen who represent the Portuguese power on the East Coast of Africa. Simon's Bay but awaits the word.

As showing a general view in the mother country at this period, this excerpt from an article in the *Saturday Review* may be given :— " But it may be plausibly contended than an ultimatum is called for, and as plausibly answered that practically the ultimatum is already before the Portuguese, and that Lord Salisbury only waits to see whether they will accept it or not before taking steps on a much larger scale than a simple demand of satisfaction for this last petulant outrage. If a solid settlement of the whole matter is probable, in the very few days which the *modus* has yet to run, insisting on Colonel Machado's head in a charger would be superfluous ; if such a settlement is again refused, we shall have to go and take things much more important than the head of Colonel Machado. The Portuguese apology is good, and English ships at the Pungwe are better. But some settlement, amicable or forcible, there must be. Eight months have now passed since Portugal refused to ratify the arrangement she had herself agreed to, and that is long enough for anything. More grace will simply breed more trouble, and once again it is time to have done with it."

Of course, as was pointed out by *The Times*, if the *modus vivendi* were allowed to lapse it was in the power of Portugal to say that she would not allow the Chartered Company to construct any route through her strip of territory to the east coast. If Portugal chooses to continue her dog-in-the manger policy by assuming such an unreasonable position, it is she that will suffer in the end, not the Chartered Company. As soon as the Company's territories are thrown open, as they certainly will be very soon, miners and settlers will flock towards the eastern plateau, and most of them will naturally take the shortest cut, which undoubtedly is from the east coast. Certainly the native chiefs will not refuse permission to pass through their territories, and what can Portugal do to prevent people landing at suitable points and making their way into the interior? Some little inconvenience might be caused at first by a policy which would be in the face of all civilized international usage. If Portugal cares to construct a railway, she will reap the advantage ; if she does not, it is certain that the railway will be made.

With regard to the Pungwe River, which has been so much talked about in this connection, it is clear that it can never be of much value as a route for heavy traffic. Even at its best it is navigable for vessels of any size only for a comparatively short distance ; and during the rainy season the current is so strong as to render navigation extremely difficult. The river may be used temporarily to M'Panda, about a hundred miles up, but Mr. Rhodes and the Company recognise that the only proper course is to construct a railway right down to the coast to Pungwe Bay. Within the next two years we may expect to see this enterprise well on the way towards accomplishment. Along the low-lying country there will be no obstacles, though precautions must be taken to prevent damage by flooding ; and there will be no great engineering difficulty in attempting to carry the railway on to the plateau. The fears expressed in certain quarters that a railway from Mashonaland to the east coast would ruin the commercial position of Cape Town, are ridiculed by those who know the real position. A glance at a good map of Africa south of the Zambesi will demonstrate the absurdity of these fears, and the necessity of railways in both directions, if the country is to be completely developed. The railway from the Cape and Port Elizabeth has now reached Vryburg, and will be rapidly pushed on to Shoshong, and ultimately even further north to the western Matabele frontier. Between that and the eastern plateau, which will be tapped by the railway to the east coast, lies a region of rugged mountains, which will certainly not be bridged by a railway for a long time to come, if, indeed, they ever will be. It is evident, then, that the railway now being pushed northwards will be the natural route for traffic from Western Matabeleland, from Khama's territory, the Western Transvaal, and Bechuanaland. In any case Beira seems destined to become an important port. A glance at the map will show its proximity to Mashonaland. Dr. Jameson and Major Johnson left Fort Salisbury on October 5th, with the object of discovering a suitable road to the coast *vià* the Pungwe River. They state that from Fort Salisbury to Pungwe Bay is a distance of about 400 miles, and that for the first 160 miles to Umtasa's Kraal, the road is good, with a gradual descent from the high to the low veld. Thence they travelled over a bad piece of ground to the Umtali River. Another ten miles, and then on to Massi Kessi, 16 miles further, all bad " going " on account of a broken range of hills ; thence 110 miles more to Sarmento by a good road, the last 30 miles through fly country, but consisting of a sandy level, easily practicable for a railway or steam tram. From Sarmento they descended the River Pungwe in a Berthen boat to Nevis Ferreira, a distance of 130 miles. For the first 60 miles the river is navigable for stern wheel steamers and boats of light draught ; the remaining 70 miles to Beira at the mouth of the river, is navigable for boats of 6 ft. or 7 ft. draught. The Pungwe is a tidal river up to 80 or 100 miles, and the mouth of the channel has been buoyed by the Portuguese. The harbourage is said to be excellent. By taking a more northerly and direct route, and avoiding Umtasa's kraal, the 26 miles of bad road can be avoided. The importance of this route to those at present engaged in opening up Mashonaland will be seen when I say that whereas the rate of transport from Cape Town to Fort Salisbury *via* Mafeking and Palapye is 60s. to 65s. per 100 lbs., by the proposed route *via* the Pungwe it will only be 10s. 8d. per 100 lbs., that is less than one-sixth of

NATIVES CHANTING THE PRAISES OF THE OCEAN.

INHAMBANE CUSTOM HOUSE.

PORTUGUESE 'DEFENCES' AT INHAMBANE.

A QUILIMANE STREET.

QUILIMANE SLAVE MARKET.

the present rate. It is not surprising, then, to learn that British commercial enterprise is finding an outlet for energy both in the direction of the Pungwe and in the direction of the Busi River, a little to the south, which is said also to be navigable for some distance inland.

A few words may here be devoted to the Portuguese towns on the East Coast. How little is done by the Portuguese to push commerce could be shown by statistics ranging over their long period of occupation of these places, but one or two of the figures referring to last year's trade as published in the consular reports just issued by the Foreign Office will suffice. The imports for 1890 at Mozambique reached £137,419, as against £141,493 in 1889, and the exports amounted to £90,374 as against £107,746 in the previous

E E

year. There is not a single British firm in Mozambique, the British mail service to the port has been dropped, and the same tale of dulness and deadness applies to the other ports. The harbour of Mozambique is formed by a deep inlet of the sea, five miles and a half broad and six long, receiving the waters of three inconsiderable rivers at its head. The wonderful fort of St. Sebastian, which is built of stone entirely brought from Portugal, was begun in 1508, and took three years to erect. It has a number of old-fashioned honey-combed guns of no service against modern artillery; indeed though the strong fortification, garrisoned by a few black soldiers, might be capable of formidable resistance, it is after all but a proud monument of a Portuguese enterprise long vanished in the past. There are some large gloomy conventual buildings, and the Custom House and Governor's palace in the town, but the streets are narrow, and the place is very unhealthy. Mozambique is reduced from its ancient wealth and vice-regal splendour to an almost forgotten seat of desolation and poverty. Other towns, such as Quilimane and Inhambane, also belong to a group in which alcohol and lust do their worst for their inhabitants and the natives.

CHAPTER XVIII.

NORTH OF THE ZAMBESI.—THE CHARTERED COMPANY'S VAST SPHERE.—THE LAKES COMPANY.—NYASSALAND.—BAROTSELAND. —A VALUABLE NEW POSSESSION.—HOW MR. SELOUS NEARLY LOST HIS LIFE.—NGAMILAND.—THE KALAHARI "DESERT."

IT will be convenient now to take a brief glance at those other countries which, though possibly at this moment beyond the sphere of the more direct operations of the British South Africa Company, are destined yet to feel the benefit of the expansion of that gigantic Corporation's enterprise. Before leaving Gazaland, or rather the Manica territory, it may be said that Mr. Selous, on behalf of the Company, has succeeded in getting a concession of Molokoland from the chief of that country. It is situated a little to the north of Manica and is a magnificent plateau, over 4000 ft. above the sea level, abundantly watered, admirably fertile, and comparatively easy of access from the coast by means of the Zambesi.

The countries lying to the north of the Zambesi which are to feel the good influence of the Chartered Company deserve more exhaustive treatment than they can at present receive at my hands. It was gratifying to note by the *London Gazette* some weeks back that the Imperial authorities continue to manifest a zealous desire to watch the interests of the Empire in that important part of the world. Mr. H. H. Johnston's nomination to the high post of Commissioner and Consul-General for the territories under British influence to the north of the Zambesi was, of course, only what might have been expected. Other selections are equally judicious, and afford every guarantee that British interests will be thoroughly well looked after. They are Mr. Lloyd William Mathews, C.M.G., to be Her Majesty's Commissioner and Consul-General in the British Sphere in

From a Photo. by]   *[Messrs. Elliott and Fry.*
MR. H. H. JOHNSTON, C.B.

E E 2

East Africa situated to the north of the German Sphere; Mr. William Algernon Churchill, to be Her Majesty's Vice-Consul at Mozambique; Mr. Alexander Carnegie Ross, to be Her Majesty's Vice-Consul for the Province of Quilimane, to reside at Quilimane; and Mr. Alfred Sharpe, to be Her Majesty's Vice-Consul at Nyassaland. These names, as I have said, indicate that the Imperial Government is fully alive to the importance of having the right men in the right place to guard their interests, and protect them from the encroachments of other nations.

The leading member of the staff of Mr. Johnston, as Commissioner, is Lieutenant Sclater, an able and promising young officer of the Royal Engineers, who has received permission from the War Office to accompany Mr. Johnston. Lieutenant Sclater, who is the son of Mr. Sclater, the well-known secretary of the Zoological Society, has taken every pains to fit himself for the varied duties which he will have to undertake. His training and experience as an engineer will be of great service to Mr. Johnston in his endeavours to open up the extensive region committed to his charge. Not only will the Stevenson Road between Nyassa and Tanganyika have to be improved, but new roads will have to be made elsewhere, and the operations connected therewith will be superintended by Lieutenant Sclater. Very careful surveys will have to be made of certain regions, and in these, again, Mr. Sclater will be able to turn his experience to account, while for general geographical observations he has taken care to specially qualify himself; and for this work the Royal Geographical Society has furnished him with instruments to the amount of £250. In addition to all this he will be commandant of the police in Nyassaland, so that Lieutenant Sclater's office will be no sinecure. His observations, combined with those of Mr. Johnston himself, Mr. Sharpe, and other members of the staff, cannot but add greatly to our knowledge of the geography of a region which so far has been explored along only a few lines. Mr. Johnston's sphere as Commissioner includes the whole region to the north of the Zambesi, to the South of the German and Congo Free States spheres, and to the east and the west of the Portuguese possessions. Its eastern boundary is Lake Nyassa, with an important section on the east of the Shiré. On the north the boundary passes some distance to the north of the Stevenson Road, includes the south end of Lake Tanganyika, the east shore of Lake Moero, the east bank of the Luapula, the whole of Lake Bangweolo, and, except the south-west corner, passes thence westwards by the undefined boundary of the Congo Free State to the Kabompo branch of the Zambesi, which it follows down so as to include the whole of the Barotse country. Here, however, the boundary cannot be regarded as definitely settled. The total area is probably not far short of 300,000 square miles; and if to this Mr. Johnston's sphere as Consul-General be added, the region committed to his charge in the interests of the Empire will cover about 600,000 square miles. It belongs to the characteristic plateau region of Central Africa.

With regard to English settlement in the country, Mr. Johnston (who left England for his post on April 10th) does not consider that the provinces of Bangweolo and Barotse are as yet suitable for what he calls " home settlement ; " that is to say, for men to take out their wives with a view to colonisation and the establishment of English homes. Roads should be opened, the country more settled, and communications more assured before this can be regarded as advisable, even in the healthy hill districts. But in Lakeland, where the climate is fairly good and settlement has now continued for upwards of twelve years, the case is different. Here there are already about 150 Europeans, and the establishment of English homes is very much to be desired. Of course none but persons of initiative and energy should contemplate such a step. For those who have these qualities there is at least abundance of food and the prospect of easy settlement. English fruit and vegetables flourish ; oranges, limes, grapes, pineapples, bananas, cucumbers, and tomatoes ripen freely in the open air. Fowls and game of all kinds abound. The red-legged partridge and the antelope are particularly good. Eggs are of course plentiful, and already tea, coffee, and sugar are produced and manufactured locally by the Scotch colonists. Potatoes and cabbages, introduced by British settlers, do very well ; onions, which were introduced by the Arabs, flourish in profusion. Sweet potatoes, peas, beans, and pumpkins are indigenous, and all kinds of grain do well. The rivers and lakes are also remarkable for good fish. Notwithstanding these natural advantages, Mr. Johnston insists very strongly on the necessity of the luxuries and decencies of life for Europeans. It is the greatest mistake, he declares, to suppose that the best settler is the man who voluntarily undergoes unnecessary privations. The tradition of the man who roughs it has gone out with a good many other copy-book maxims. For his own part, he always sleeps between sheets, and makes a rule of not dining even in the wilderness without a tablecloth and napkins, unless it is absolutely unavoidable. He takes with him always a fair supply of luxuries for the larder, in which he is not ashamed to include *paté de foie gras, caviare*, and plenty of good Huntley and Palmer's biscuits. To people who do not indulge at home in dainties of this kind he recommends marmalade, sardines, and anchovy paste. He leaves the details to choice, but insists only on the principle that half the pioneers who break down in health break down for want, not of necessaries, which are almost always obtainable, but of luxuries to which they have been accustomed ; that the waste of life thus occasioned is avoidable by exactly the same qualities of forethought and care which are exercised by every thrifty house manager at home ; and, more, that moral as well as physical well-being is maintained in the wilds by the habits of order which we have learned from civilisation. Mr. Johnston wrote a most characteristic letter from Brindisi, in which he stated he does not want to be heard of for two years, and in that time he expected to do

great things beneficial to England in Central Africa. He writes
that if he does not make some effect, " I shall deserve to be kicked
into oblivion as only one among the thousand humbugs which my
decade produces."

The Chartered Company will now work in conjunction with the
African Lakes Company in their extended and interesting sphere of
good labour. The Lakes Company was formed in Scotland in
1878, as a trading venture with the object of assisting the

UJIJI TO ZANZIBAR IN FIFTY DAYS.

This represents a party of letter-carriers. Numbers of them have now been
trained to this work, and a regular mail service has for some time been
established.

missions in the Lake districts. It has established several stations
and has steamers on the Zambesi and Lake Nyassa, but through
difficulties into which it drifted with the Arabs it was obliged
to carry on a long war, thus exhausting the whole of its
capital. At the time that the negotiations for a charter for the

British South Africa Company were proceeding the Lakes Company was depending upon outside subscriptions for support. With a view to future developments northwards, the promoters of the Chartered Company offered to assist it, and an agreement was entered into providing for its absorption into the Chartered Company should it be considered advisable to carry this into effect at any future time. The sum of £20,000 was subscribed by the Chartered Company to the capital of the Lakes Company, and the former has also undertaken to exchange the shares of the latter for its own shares at their face values, the shareholders of the Lakes Company being further accorded the privilege of subscribing for a certain amount of the capital of the British South Africa Company at par. The Chartered Company has also subsidised the Lakes Company to the extent of £9,000 a year for the purpose of maintaining law and order, and for the protection of the mission stations. For the present the African Lakes Company is left to manage its own affairs entirely, but the Chartered Company has the right, when it feels itself in a position to undertake the development of the country north of the Zambesi, to do so by indemnifying the shareholders in the African Lakes Company. At the present moment the future of these territories is receiving the careful attention of Lord Salisbury, who will, no doubt, settle upon a policy which will permit of such an administration of Northern Zambesia as will extend the blessings of civilisation still further and further towards the Mediterranean.

The legitimate sphere of the Lakes Company, it should be remembered, is not confined to Lake Nyassa. It extends westwards to Tanganyika, Lakes Moero and Bangweolo, including all that country rendered sacred by the wanderings and death of Livingstone, " the Livingstone country," *par excellence*, and down to the great bends of the Central Zambesi. The whole region now included in the sphere of the British South Africa Company's operations lies between the south end of Tanganyika, the west shores of Nyassa, the southern boundaries of the Congo Free State, the western possession of Portugal and the eastern country claimed by that nation, down, as we have seen, to the frontiers of the Bechuanaland protectorate. As to the Shiré Highlands, no doubt the great missionary work of which that is the centre, can be carried on without Portuguese interference, as Lord Salisbury assured a deputation once. But apart from that, in some part of the great region indicated, in the highlands on the west of Nyassa, in the unrivalled and richly watered Mashona plateau on the south of the Zambesi, in the lands between Nyassa and Tanganyika, other centres of missionary work can be established, the influences from which might spread over all the territory. Not only is the vast country indicated one of the richest regions in Central Africa, but by bringing it under British influence communications will be established from the Cape to the Nile. The missionaries and traders will be independent of Portugal and of the lower Zambesi, for already the railway from the Cape frontier to the Zambesi is well on its way, a means of communication much more effectual than any by the uncertain Zambesi.

Nyassaland has a history all its own. It has been told frequently and well. As the Rev. Horace Waller, formerly lay superintendent of the Universities' Mission, reminds us, it is the maturity of a scheme begun over thirty years ago. "I have opened the door," said Livingstone to the Cambridge undergraduates; "I leave it to you to see that no one closes it after me." Few are aware how that speech clung to the walls where it was uttered. Readers interested in the subject of Nyassaland ought to read Mr. Waller's vigorous little book entitled "Nyassaland: Great Britain's Case Against Portugal." The writer gives a useful list of other authorities on the subject.

HOUSE AT MANDALA BELONGING TO THE MANAGER OF THE AFRICAN LAKES COMPANY.

Mandala is situated not far from the Southern end of Lake Nyassa, and was the furthest point reached by the Portuguese in their "civilising mission." At the instance of the British Government they have now retired.

The work of the Livingstonia Mission is not proclaimed on the house-tops, but it is solid and large. From the "Third Quinquennial Narrative" which was recently issued by the Managing Committee something of the nature of that work may be gathered. It is not merely of a proselytising but also of an industrial character. Ever since the mission was started in 1875 it has been the practice to send out a stream of young artisans to make the natives carpenters and masons, blacksmiths and engineers, gardeners and printers. These artisans have a threefold occupation—to do the practical work of the mission stations and steamers, to give object lessons to the people, and to teach the children, by precept and example, what is required of a Christian. From its five centres the Livingstonia Mission extends its influence along the whole of the west of Lake Nyassa, and far beyond its northern and southern ends. However incredulous some people may be of the efficacy of "evangelisation" among the black races, not the most pessimistic can doubt the efficacy of the educative schemes which are here carried on. Even in mere life-saving, the work has been considerable, one medical missionary alone in a single year having treated 5200 cases, of which 3231 were surgical and 1969 medical. Of the industrial value of the mission good evidence can be found outside its own reports. The testimony of Mr. H. H. Johnston to the social reform evident in and around the stations is emphatic enough. He saw people who a few years ago had no knowledge of any strangers but Portuguese raiders and Arab slave-stealers, but who are now engaged in the systematic cultivation of the soil, in useful mechanical work, and even in the printing of school books and Bibles in their own language. The question of language is a difficult one for civilising agents. In the Livingstonia district no fewer than six separate languages are spoken, each of which must be mastered by those who are introducing elementary education. As knowledge of the people and their ways extends, it is hoped to fix on one dialect for the whole of Livingstonia, so as to simplify future operations. Nothing has been more remarkable in the history of missionary enterprise than the success of Dr. and Mrs. Elmslie among the wild Ugoni tribe, and nothing has been more heroic than the manner in which the missionaries in the disturbed districts held their ground and stood by their people during the late war with the Arab raiders.

One of the most interesting features of the Chartered Company's operations is the fact that by the careful policy of Mr. Rhodes a numerous company of African travellers, hunters, and traders has been gathered into the fold of the Company. Selous, Johnson, Burnett, Hoste, Joseph Thomson, and Lochner are names that will readily occur in this connection, and the fact that such a policy is pursued would seem to be one of the most potent factors in the success the Company is securing. The representative of the name set out last in the list, Mr. Frank Elliott Lochner, has been the means by which the Company has obtained a wide concession. By the efforts of Mr. Lochner, who gained considerable experience in dealing with natives as an officer in the Bechuanaland Border Police, the immense country of Barotseland, in area 225,000 square miles, has been added to the domain of the Chartered Company. Mr. Lochner was in the Barotse country seven or eight months, going up for the Chartered Company to secure an extension of a concession already got by a Mr. Ware. As far as the Zambesi River he was accompanied by friends, but parted with them there, and pursued

his journey to Barotseland alone, except for his native servants.
The Barotse people earned for themselves a somewhat unenviable
character in times past.   It was in Mashukulumbweland, which is
part of the Barotse possessions, that Mr. Selous's life was
endangered, and Dr. Holub was also attacked there by the natives.
Now, however, the Mashukulumbwe are tributary to the Barotse,
and there is comparatively greater safety.   The Barotse country
extends some hundreds of miles along the Zambesi River, in a northerly direction, the King's head place, Lialui, being about 450 miles
from the point where Mr. Lochner first struck the Zambesi.   The
first part of the country is an immense valley, which Mr. Lochner
speaks of as a hopeless fever-stricken swamp.   Europeans are
utterly unable to live there, and Mr. Lochner, himself a man of
vigorous physique, suffered from his experience of it.   The natives
themselves are unable to brave this valley, and they are
occasionally stricken by fever.   In the wet seasons, when
the valley is flooded, native canoes are used for the trans-
porting of people from kraal to kraal, and the King is anxious
for his people to leave the valley and move up higher.   This has
not hitherto been done owing to superstition, the people being
unwilling to leave the place where the bodies of their fathers have
been laid to rest.   Beyond the valley, which may be crossed safely,
though it is dangerous to remain there any considerable time, there are
high lands dry, healthy, and fertile, and it is here the Barotse
chiefly dwell.   The land is thickly populated, and the people speak
a tongue which Mr. Lochner describes as bastard Basuto.   They
are Kafirs, and picked up the language from their old masters, the
Makololo, whom they overcame years ago.   There are forty-four
tributary chiefs, who are subject to the old King of the Barotse,
Lewinika, a ruler described as intelligent but weak.   Hitherto the
country has been always more or less in a state of rebellion.   The
people are excessively suspicious, but Mr. Lochner got on amicably
with them once they fairly got to know him.   Mr. Lochner met the
King at Lialui, the great place, in the middle of the Barotse Valley
which is 2,500 to 3,000 feet above sea-level.   Beyond the valley
the country rises very rapidly towards the Congo Free State, which
is the northern boundary of the country.   The Barotse country
abounds in game, both small and large, and the people live
principally on the flesh of wild animals, in whose skins they are
clothed.   Witchcraft has existed to a horrible extent, and there
has been till lately a good deal of slavery in the country, but in
the concession the stipulation is made that the King and his
headmen will exert their influence in putting a stop to these evil
practices.   The promise, it might seem at first sight, is not worth a
great deal, but it will be borne in mind that the Company has got
a certain hold, because the people fully recognise the rights
they have bestowed upon the holders of the concession Mr.
Lochner obtained.   The concession was granted, after interviews
and explanations which took up many weeks and required

the exercise of great patience and tact, in full *pitsu*, in the presence of an assemblage which included the King, the forty-four head chiefs, and two French missionaries. These gentlemen explained, in the most careful fashion, the meaning of the Royal Charter to the King and the people, and cordial consent to the terms of the concession was signified. Mr. Lochner speaks gratefully of the kindly manner in which the missionaries dealt with him, nursing him when he was sick, and assisting him in his conferences with the King and headmen. They heard with cordial satisfaction the announcement of the Chartered Company's intentions with regard to Barotseland, and expressed the opinion that a firm and wise government of a naturally ingenious people like the Barotse would be the salvation of the country, the King himself being weak and the present Government nerveless. Regarding the physical features of the land, they resemble, in many parts, those of Mashonaland; minerals occur frequently, copper and iron predominating. In the concession a certain number of mines are reserved for native working. Gold was not searched for, but it exists in the hills, some rich specimens having been brought down. It is a magnificent pastoral country, and though the tsetse fly is met with in the forest, the open country is free from the pest. Herds of buffalo are frequently seen, especially near the Zambesi, and elephants exist in great numbers, a large trade being carried on in ivory. The Portuguese have been in Barotseland, but, for a wonder, they make no claim regarding it. Portuguese traders from the West Coast carry on business with the Barotse, but always ask permission of the King before entering his dominions. The Barotse are clever workers in ivory, and although perfect savages in many respects, are capable of much under civilizing influences. The people seemed glad to grant Mr. Lochner's request, and at the great meeting the statement was frequently made that it was time they ceased pillaging and killing each other, and live peaceably. The King keeps up great state, and has a Royal band, whose members divert the monarch from the cares of royalty by imitating the cries of animals and by beating on drums. The land is well wooded in parts, and the valuable indiarubber tree grows commonly. Mr. Lochner and the King parted in the most amicable manner, his Majesty returning the traveller's present by the gift of two fine tusks of ivory, each considerably over 100 lb. in weight, and over six feet long. These now ornament the Board Room of the British South Africa Company in their palatial office in St. Swithin's Lane. The Barotse King said he had heard of Khama, and was desirous of emulating that wise chief, for whom he expressed sincere admiration.

Mr. Lochner's expedition left Palapye early in December of 1889, and arrived towards the end of January at Kanzungulu Drift, on the Zambesi River. From this spot Mr. Lochner ascended the Zambesi to Lialui in a native canoe. The members of the expedition all suffered very much from fever in the Zambesi valley, and the ascent of the river was made under the most difficult and trying circumstances; but on July 2 last Mr. Lochner was able to inform Mr. Rhodes that at a public meeting held on the 26th of the previous month, which was attended by the Chief's headmen and people, many of whom had come from great distances, Lewinika, with the full concurrence of all present, granted to the Company, in consideration of an annual payment of £2,000, the sole and exclusive right to the minerals on his territory, exclusive of the Batoka district, which had previously been granted to Mr. Ware, subject to a royalty of 4 per cent. The Batoka district is in extent, roughly, one-fifth of the Barotse country, and this concession Mr. Rhodes has also acquired for the Chartered Company. Lewinika's concession also gives the Company the sole right to construct railways, establish banks, mints, manufactories, &c. The Barotse territory, as we have said, is, roughly speaking, some 225,000 square miles in extent, and the boundaries are, on the west, the 20th meridian east, from Lorengwe to where the Lunedji River crosses it; on the north the Lunedji and the northern watershed of the Zambesi; on the east from the confluence of the Lunge and Kafue Rivers, southwards to the Zambesi; and on the south the north-west portions of Matabeleland, the Zambesi from the Victoria Falls, and the Loenge to the 20th meridian east. If the territory in question is, as it is said to be, rich in minerals, this acquisition cannot but prove to be a most valuable addition to the Company's sphere of operations. In his concession Lewinika remarks that he gives it to " bring trade and civilize his people." A monthly postal service has been established between Lialayi and Palapye.

As I before said, it was among the Mashukulumbwe that South Africa nearly lost a valuable life, that of Mr. F. C. Selous, in 1888. In the course of a lecture at Cape Town he described a stirring incident, thus :—

They then reached the village of the Batonga Chief Monze. Livingstone had passed and stopped at this village in 1853. Monze was a very old, shrivelled-up man, but remembered Livingstone's visit quite well, and although it was thirty-five years ago, he spoke of it as if it had happened but a few years since. Monze told him how Livingstone had gone on a low hill near by, called "Owkessi-Kessi," and had used an instrument, which, from his description, was evidently a compass or a sextant. He then asked Monze about the savage tribe, the Mashukulumbwe, about whom so very little was known, and whom Livingstone had never actually visited. Dr. Holub was the only other European, besides himself, who had visited them. The former's expedition was wrecked; Oswald, the Austrian, and others of his party being killed in the attack. He never thought that they extended so far east as they actually did, and considered that by striking due north he would be able to give them a wide berth. He had to learn otherwise, however. In the beginning of July he left Monze, and in a short time came upon a small village of the dreaded Mashukulumbwe. They next came to the Rivers Magoice and Ungwessi. Dr. Livingstone marked the latter as a tributary of the Kafukwe; but this was an error, for he followed it

up, and found it flowed into the Magoice. Here they came to
another Mashukulumbwe village, the inhabitants of which assumed
a most threatening attitude. They then crossed the Ungwessi, and
reached an open tract with nothing but long grass from six to
eight feet high upon it. Suddenly they found themselves in the
midst of villages, the inhabitants of which were to all appearance
friendly; and the Chief Manga, who owned the whole district as
well as the canoes on the Kafukwe, told them to pitch their camp
near the huts. He (Mr. Selous) preferred to go to a wood some
distance off, but this was peremptorily refused. He was told that he
was a stranger, and had to pitch his camp in the open space at the
village. They accordingly pitched the camp there, constructing the
"scherm" of mealie stocks. The Chief said he (Mr. Selous) might
put his donkeys in the cattle kraal, that is to say, if they did not eat
up the cattle! Their camp was pitched in front of the
village, about 40 yards from the long grass. He desired to cross the
Kafukwe the next morning, but the Chief dissuaded him, saying that
the large canoe was some distance off, but he would send for it, and
then he (Mr. Selous) could start the morning after, spending the
next day in hunting. The shades of night were falling when the
women came down in crowds to see them and trade sweet potatoes
and other vegetables for meat. They next brought a large musical
instrument, emitting the most hideous sound, and then a grand
dance began, his own Batongas joining in it. He was lying down
about nine o'clock that evening when Manga invited him and his
two immediate attendants, Paul and Charlie, to come and drink
beer with him. He felt sleepy, and Charlie also refused, but Paul's
Zulu tastes for beer were fired and he went; luckily for them they
did not all go, for then they would have been murdered, the dance
having been specially organized to drown all noise of strife. Manga
did not, however, kill Paul, thinking it better to bide his time. A
part of the next day was spent in hunting, and the whole day their
camp was surrounded by armed natives, with their barbed assegais and
peculiar headdresses. There were three who had their hair worked up
in cones about two-and-a-half feet high, and in the apex of this cone there
was a thin slip of the horn of the sable antelope, altogether about five
or six feet above the head. He was told that when they slept they
stuck an assegai in the ground and attached the hair to it. Night
approached, and in contrast to the previous day, everything was
quite still. At about nine o'clock he lay down but could not sleep.
Then he heard one of the guides coming to tell Paul that all the
women had left the village (not a very reassuring sign). He at once
got up, put on his shoes, his cartridge belt, with but few cartridges
left in it, as he had been hunting the previous day, took up his
rifle, which was unloaded, and went to sit in front of Paul and
Charlie, who had also taken up their guns. The Kafirs had their
assegais in their hands, and looked rather uncomfortable. He
ordered them to throw ground on the fires, intending to creep round
to the back of the village. He was just reaching over to take some
cartridges out of a bag, when three guns went off in his face and
some were fired at the other side. Then the assegais came pouring
in, through and over the "scherm" by the ton! The
enemy then rushed in and all was confusion. Each one made for
the long grass as therein lay the only hope of safety. He also made
his way thither, facing them with his rifle, determined if any man
ran against it to pull the trigger and take the consequences. While

backing away thus he fell, and as he did so a body of Mashukulumbwe rushed from the grass to the camp, two falling upon the top
of him. He then turned on his hands and glided into the long grass.
For the moment he was safe, but he however determined to put a
long distance between himself and the village before daylight. He
then swam across the river Magoice, and after several hairbreadth
escapes and thrilling adventures, during which his rifle was stolen,
and an attempt was made to murder him, reached the village of
Sikabenga, whence he proceeded amidst great hardships to Pandamatenka. Here he found the remnants of his party. Paul and
Charlie had escaped unhurt, but a dozen Kafirs had been killed in
the affair at Mangas, and of those who returned five were wounded.
He himself was nearly naked, and of the donkeys he had never heard
anything since.

Still further to the North another country marked on the maps
as Msiri's Kingdom is in process of being appropriated by white
people. It has been coloured for some time as being within the
sphere of influence of the Congo Free State, and the Congo Company, by virtue of its powers, has granted a subconcession of a 99
years' lease of the mineral rights over a third of the territory to a
Brussels financial Corporation called the Katanga Company. The
capital of the Company is three millions of francs, and a considerable portion of this was subscribed by a group of English capitalists
who in recent negotiations were represented at Brussels by Commander Cameron. The Katanga Company stand on their rights
as granted by an accredited agency of the King of the Belgians
and have already despatched expeditions to occupy the country.
On the other hand, the British South Africa Company claim to
have recently entered, by their agents, Messrs. Thomson and Sharpe,
into treaties with Msiri and other chiefs by which they have the
sole right to work the minerals in the Katanga country. A very
nice point is thus raised as to which right shall stand. Possibly
an appeal to Msiri might be in favour of the Chartered Company,
but it is not to be forgotten that if the international parcelling out of
Africa by agreement in European capitals means anything at all
Katanga is within the limits of the Congo Free State. If
Belgium was using no unreasonable delay in occupying the territory
it is difficult to see that that country had not a prior right to
negotiate with the Katanga chiefs. Again if there was any unreasonable delay in occupying Katanga it was doubtless open for
the Chartered Company or anyone else to treat with the natives. A
clear case for compromise seems to have arisen, and the good sense
of the Chartered Company and the Belgian authorities will doubtless evolve some method of a joint occupation of the country.
Katanga lies to the west of Lake Bangweolo, and has for years, as I
say, been picked out on the maps of Central Africa as the Southern-
most limit of the Congo Free State. It is mainly a fine plateau
and mountainous country, is rich in copper, gold, and other
minerals, and is capable of considerable industrial development.
Msiri's capital is a great trade centre, where traders meet from all

parts of the continent from Zanzibar to Angola, and from Uganda to the Zambesi. Copper, salt, ivory, and slaves are exchanged for flint-lock guns, powder, cloth, and beads. One of the objects of the Katanga Company is to strike a blow at the slave traffic in the country to which its expeditions have started. We may trust, therefore, that a proper understanding will be come to between the *Compagnie du Katanga* and the British South Africa Company with regard to the future of Msiri's Kingdom.

When in this region the temptation is to turn the telescope on to the Congo Free State, and contrast what is being done there with the wretched state of affairs in Portuguese West Africa. But I must pass the subject over with the remark that a republic of Transvaal Boers is growing slowly but surely near Oila, possibly the most fertile and healthy district in Angolaland. Perhaps those who proposed to trek the other day into Mashonaland who are not satisfied with Mr. Rhodes' terms will go and help to build up a little state which is already causing some concern to the Portuguese. German Damaraland to the South is disappointing its German owners for the simple reason that it is but a skeleton they have got a hold of after all. Not only do the mining rights of the country and a concession to make railways in it belong to British subjects whose claims have been recognised by the Cape and English Governments, but the only port of any consequence, Walfisch Bay, is British. Not many months therefore should see that country British red on the map of South Africa, and Zambesia supplied with its proper outlet and inlet to England.

I have now pretty well described or referred to all the territories within the sphere of the control or influence of the British South Africa Company. Retracing our steps to Bechuanaland (to best understand the modern history of which readers should study the Blue Books of the past few years) perhaps a word or two should be added about the Lake 'Ngami country, and the Kalahari. The former was nearly being lost to British influence last year when the African negotiations with Germany were in progress. Fortunately, by the Anglo-German Agreement of the 1st of July of last year it was retained within the immense country now under British protection. It may be interesting to recall the facetiæ of Lord Salisbury when moving the second reading of the Anglo-German Agreement Bill in the House of Lords :—

We have in the course of the negotiations induced them to accept longitude 21, but it was accompanied by a condition to which a certain amount of exception has been taken, and that is at the very north of this Ngamiland territory they should have a strip of territory going along the Portuguese border and giving direct access to the Chobe and the Zambesi. It was not an unnatural demand, but I never was able to understand what the objections were that have been raised on several sides. Again, we are told that it would interfere with the progress of trade; but it is the last route in the world by which trade can pass. It is at the head of the waters of all the affluents of the Chobe and the

Zambesi, over an impracticable country, and leading only into the Portuguese possessions, in which, as far as I know, during the last 300 years there has been no very eager interest for trade. I think that constant study of maps is apt to disturb men's reasoning powers. Certainly the enthusiasm which has been evoked for this desolate corner of Africa has surprised me more than anything else in this controversy. We have had a fierce conflict over a lake whose name I cannot pronounce correctly, our only difficulty being that we do not know where it is. We cannot determine its position within 100 miles, certainly not within 60 miles. I am very anxious that full scope should be given to the enterprise of men who have undertaken concessions in that country from a well-affected chief; and I think that the whole country of Moremi has been retained within the British sphere. But when I hear the language that is used and the hopes that are entertained and the extraordinary reasoning as to the future placed before us, I cannot help thinking of similar language and similar hopes entertained by our ancestors some 300 years ago connected with the well-known projects for reaching the land of El Dorado. I hope that the practical sense of our countrymen will not lead them to take for absolute gospel all that has been said on the subject in this country for the last two months. I will not trouble your lordships now with one or two other arrangements or delimitations of territory which have been made in other parts of Africa. If I were to do so I believe my noble friend opposite, Lord Aberdare, would be the only person who would understand it.

Since 'Ngamiland was discovered by Livingstone in August of 1849 the country was practically unheard of until last year. It lies, as will be seen by the map, to the west of Khama's country. Its actual boundaries are :—On the west, the 20th degree; on the south, the 22nd parallel; on the east, a line drawn from the point of intersection of the Chobe River and the Zambesi, which is about fifty miles west of the Victoria Falls, through Letterboom, on the Botletli, to the 22nd parallel; and on the north, a line drawn from the same point of intersection through Andara to the 20th degree. Within the parallelogram thus described there lies one of the most fertile districts of Southern Africa. The heart of it is the point marked on the most ordinary maps as Lake 'Ngami. South of the lake the country is hilly, undulating, well-watered, and magnificently wooded. It is also supposed to be very rich in minerals, and the climate is so good that Livingstone conceived the idea of making it a health resort for Central South Africa. To the north of the lake a swampy district, full of elephants and big game, stretches for about 20 miles. Here bauze grass abounds, of which the fibre approaches silk in fineness, and has a high commercial value. The district is infested by tsetse fly, but beyond it grazing veld, upon which the finest cattle of South Africa roam in herds, stretches to the north. A deal of interesting information about 'Ngamiland and the Kalahari may be obtained from Mr. A. A. Anderson's book I have previously mentioned.

The principal lines of communication between this region and the outer world are by the River Chobe, which is at present navigable only for canoes to the Zambesi, and by the more important waterway of the Okavango, which rises in the neighbourhood of the Cunene in Portuguese territory to the north, and passing southwards by Lake 'Ngami, changes its name to the Botletli (or Zuga), and runs out into the Kari Kari lakes of Khama's country, within ten days' march of Shoshong. The country was till quite recently ruled by an enlightened chief — Moremi — to whom the tribes beyond the northern boundary were tributary. The people are a branch of the Bamangwatos; and Moremi was a cousin of Khama. He was a Christian, and had been so far educated that he could read and write his native tongue and speak a little English. He was extremely intelligent, and was reported to have two desires with regard to the development of his country. One was that he should have trading stores like those established in Khama's country, and the other that he should have mines as Johannesburg had. The people are peaceably and industriously disposed, and are at present in the habit of making yearly migrations after the fashion of Irish labourers in search of work. Great numbers have gone for this purpose to Johannesburg, and have returned with accounts of the mining operations. The superior civilisation of the 'Ngami people is attributed largely to the efforts of one man—a Mr. Strombom—who is of Swedish extraction, though an English subject. Mr. Strombom, who is now about forty years of age, has lived amongst the 'Ngami people as a minister and a trader, since he was seventeen years of age. He acquired a remarkable influence among them in his early youth, and on the death of Moremi's father, about twenty years ago, he was appointed guardian of the young chief. He had since then occupied a position which was virtually that of Prime Minister, and responsible adviser to Moremi; but news came recently that that Chief also had been gathered to his fathers. When the British Protectorate over Northern Bechuanaland was declared, and it was formally announced to Moremi that his territory fell within the sphere of British influence, he evinced the keenest satisfaction, and in August, 1889, gave within a few months substantial proof of his sentiments in the matter in the form of a concession to Mr. Strombom of all the mineral rights and certain limited grazing and timber rights in the country. Grand sport can be obtained along the Botletle River and around Lake 'Ngami.

Readers of Livingstone's "Missionary Travels" will remember the scene on Lake 'Ngami as one of the illustrations of a book which a generation ago created even greater excitement than that produced by Mr. Stanley's "Darkest Africa." Lechulathebe was the Chief at Lake 'Ngami in Livingstone's time, and Moremi, the late Chief, was his son. The name of the tribe is the same as that of Khama's people—Bamangwato; and some travellers have called the former Western, and the latter Eastern Bamangwato on the maps. Inasmuch, however, as the separation of the tribe took place under a man called Towawa, the people at the lake are also called Bechuanas, Batowana. The books which contain the fullest infor-

F F

mation on these subjects are Livingstone's "Missionary Travels
and "Researches in South Africa," Mackenzie's "Ten Years North
of the Orange River," and Dr. Emil Holub's "Seven Years in South
Africa." Need of correct information concerning these little-known
places was recently amusingly brought out by the remark of a
London paper that "the Bamangwatos are related to the Bechuanas;" that is to say, the people of Lancashire are related to the
English, or the people of Inverness to the Scotch. The Bamangwato of Khama, as well as those of Moremi, are Bechuanas; and
thus their country is surely part of Bechuanaland—a term which has
been coined by English people. Moremi was a chief who ruled his
country—and ruled it intelligently and well—by the best possible
right, the right of strength and conquest. He was anxious for
British protection and keen for British trade. English traders have
been in actual occupation for many years; trading stations have
been erected there, and the rights of English occupation have not
only been recognised by Moremi, but by Lo Bengula himself, who
paid Mr. Strombom very heavy compensation for the destruction
of his stores and houses at Lake 'Ngami during the Matabele invasion already referred to. In the neighbourhood of Lake 'Ngami are
numerous depressions, in which salt pans are formed.

Lechulathebe and his son Moremi were, as we see, friendly to the
English, and both were anxious to obtain instruction in Christianity.
Some time ago Mr. Hepburn, the missionary at Khama's town,
visited Moremi, and the work of Christian instruction was carried'
on by him with great energy, Moremi himself being one of his
disciples. Since that time the London Missionary Society has had
a native minister resident at the lake; and an English missionary,
previously residing at Shoshong, was recently announced to be on
his way to take up his abode with Moremi's people. East of
Moremi's country, on the plain of the Mababe, lie the remains of
a member of an English missionary party; while further north,
and between the Chobe River and the Zambesi, are the remains of
the Rev. Holloway Helmore and several members of his family, as
well of deceased Christian natives from South Bechuanaland—
members of the mission of which at one time Dr. Livingstone
undertook to be the leader. This sacred spot can be identified in
maps by the name Linyanti. The surviving members of this
mission — fever-stricken and helpless — were well received by
Moremi's father at the lake, and hospitably treated till their friends
reached them there. Thus the connection between Englishmen
and this part of Bechuanaland has been close and continuous
during the last 30 years.

Still further east of Moremi's country, and about 70 miles from
the Victoria Falls, is a place called Pandamatenka, an English
trading station, established there for many years with the sanction
of Khama and of his predecessors. The owner of this store, the
late Mr. Westbeech, had great influence with the natives for many
miles along the River Zambesi; and the whole trade of the region
may be said to have been in his hands.

Formerly the Kalahari "Desert" was shown as extending to the Orange River. Now a further acquaintance with the district shows it to be habitable and even capable of being made profitable. The difficulty of exploring the country has consisted of the danger in passing a wide belt of waterless country that appears to encircle a collection of depressions and pans that lie in the centre. The most important of the waters appear to be at Kang, a large native station supporting cattle belonging to the Baquenas and Bangwaketsi tribes. From Kang it is said to be easy to travel over the desert in all directions in the rainy season. There are two classes of natives living in this country—the Kalaharis or Vaalpens, and the bushmen. Both people are slaves to the tribes they acknowledge; the bushman is the lower caste and is slave to the Vaalpens. The Vaalpens own cattle, and have towns with large gardens of corn, melons, and mealies, whereas the bushman has nothing but his bow and poisoned arrows, his firesticks and ostrich egg for carrying water when he can get it.

The Vaalpens look after the cattle, receiving guns, powder, and lead with which to shoot game; in return they send to their masters the feathers and skins that are shot. Natives generally travel with pack bullocks, which are capable of travelling a great deal further without water than a wagon ox. The "desert" is still the home of crowds of game; the "desert" ostriches are noted for their unequalled plumage. The chief game are giraffe, eland, wildebeest, hartebeest, gemsbuck, and other buck that can live without water. The grass in the "desert" is of excellent quality, and there is plenty of soil admirably adapted for raising corn and mealies. Water in quantities that would make farming possible is what is required, and it would be useful if some experimental borings were made, to ascertain how far the water sinks. Plenty of water falls in the rainy season for farming purposes. A survey of the waters is also required. A curious feature appears to be the enormous elevated sand belts that stretch across the country. They are found throughout the desert up to Lake 'Ngami and to the Zambesi, and are the bugbear to South African travellers. Stretching for hundreds of miles in straight lines they are often over fifty miles wide. One may be noticed on the road between Molopolole and Shoshong. It runs east and west on the southern side of Boatlanami and Lopepe, and on the western route is nearly fifty miles wide. They appear to be formed of fine blown sand. The vegetation differs from that in the surrounding country, and except in accidental formations they are devoid of water. Bushmen live in them, and instead of drinking water eat the tuberous roots that are to be found on the surface. The desert is, generally speaking, covered with bush. There are no mountainous features in the country, but there are several large depressions. The country is said to be extremely healthy.

Recent information from a trader shows that in the Kalahari country there are plenty of cattle stations. Mr. Boyne had

F F 2

travelled and traded by a route direct west from Sechele's for about 250 miles, and then north and north-east to Lake 'Ngami. He took his ox wagons through without difficulty, and found water in a sand river south-west forty miles from Molopolole. Fifteen miles further is a pan, Metsibokluka. For the next fifty miles there were several small Vaalpens' sucking pits, and at Takatakwan a large salt pan and fresh water pit. Twenty miles further on, at Luthli, the Bakalahara had cattle of Sechele and Gaseitsewe to herd. Forty miles further on was a large pan at Rau; here there were numerous cattle. Still bearing west forty miles brings you to Lotlakani, with two large pans. Another trek of forty miles, Lohudatu is reached, where there are large pans, furnishing water for many cattle. The road or track now turns north, passing over sand hills, reaching Hukie in twenty miles, where hundreds of cattle are watered at pits. Bearing north-east for fifty miles, Takachu River is reached, a sand river running north-east, evidently to Lake 'Ngami; in the bed of this are many pits. Fifty miles further a similar river, the Okwa Lachter, is crossed, which joins the Takachu twenty miles below to the east. Thirty miles beyond this is the Ngunge Vley and river (also sand). Ghansi is reached thirty miles further on, and the road from here to the lake is known and well watered. A line of koppies is passed soon after leaving Ghansi, in which a large reef crops. The first part of this route is said to be open for some months after the rains, and from Lohudatu all the year round. The Mangwato people, Sechele, Khosi - Linche, and Gaseitswe all have cattle here; the grass is excellent and game is still abundant. The bushmen and Vaalpens are supplied with guns by their masters and shoot game and ostriches which the towns (kraal) people trade with. For generations the tribes who now have their chief towns at Molopolole and Kanje have had intercourse with the Bakalahara. In former days they used to supply them with assegais as they do now with gunpowder, and levied tribute from them. There are Bakalahara Chiefs, and formerly they possessed much cattle; but, fearing their masters, they have got rid of a great many.

It is, however, certain that this great tract, a blank upon maps, when explored will prove to be anything but the desert it has hitherto been called. Lohudatu seems the centre of all the trade, and though a few white men and Griquas have penetrated thus far, yet the natives themselves will give no information, and are very jealous and suspicious of any traders. Mr. Farini not long ago wrote in glowing terms of this country as a ranching country. He seems to have gone up from Kheis by Shelley and Orpen's old route, and on by MacCabe's, who was ten days without water. There is plenty of rain during the wet season, and if this were stored, there would be no limit to what might be made out of this vast but yet comparatively unknown district.

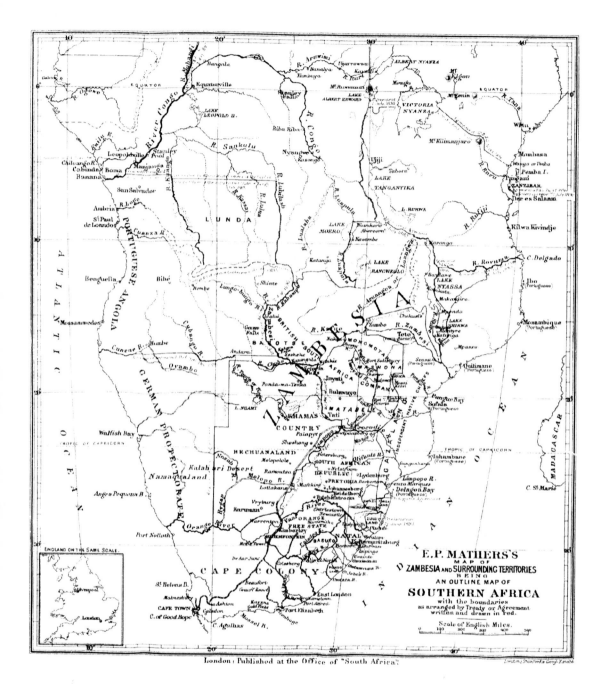

E.P. MATHERS'S
MAP OF
ZAMBESIA AND SURROUNDING TERRITORIES
BEING
AN OUTLINE MAP OF
SOUTHERN AFRICA
with the boundaries
as arranged by Treaty or Agreement
written and drawn in red.

Scale of English Miles.

ENGLAND ON THE SAME SCALE.

London: Published at the Office of "South Africa".

CHAPTER XIX.

SUMMING UP.—MR. RHODES'S POLICY.—TRADE PROSPECTS WITH
ZAMBESIA.—THE NEGOTIATIONS WITH LISBON.—PORTUGAL'S
DESTINY IN EAST AFRICA.—BRITAIN'S SHARE OF THE CONTINENT.
—ZAMBESIA'S FUTURE.—CONCLUSION.

MY laborious but well-loved task now draws to a close. My survey of a territory with a strange romantic past, a hardly less mysterious present, and having possibilities for the future unrivalled by any other in the world, is about over. Let us take stock, dear reader, of what we have done. We have dipped into remote ages and linked the golden Monomotapa of the ancients with the golden Matabeleland and Mashonaland of the sturdy moderns who have established themselves in the line of forts which stretches from the Macloutsie to beyond the headwaters of the Sabi. We have seen how the savage nation of Matabeleland was founded, and we have together observed how the foundations of a great new civilised nation have been laid above it. We have noted how the Briton in South Africa has told the Boer that as an equal he may travel northwards to the Zambesi with him, but that as a superior power he cannot. We have lingered on the most interesting sight of a South African native nation rising from the darkness of heathendom and already stretching out its arms towards a fuller civilisation, and we have been constrained to discern clearly how Portugal has had a strong hint not to quarrel with her destiny in South-East Africa, but mind her own affairs—the municipal control of a certain few unhealthy trading stations and seaports. We have glimpsed the grand Victoria Falls, which Livingstone discovered, and we have been witness how the British South Africa Company has thrown wide back the door which the great explorer opened. I shall now close with some further references to the mighty mission of the Chartered Company, and to Mr. Cecil Rhodes, its master mind.

What is Mr. Rhodes's policy? It is a question that I had thought had been answered long ago, but it appeared as if there were those in doubt on the subject when Mr. Rhodes, not long ago, added to his many cares those of the office of Prime Minister of the Cape Colony. It is now some years since Mr. Rhodes one day, pointing to a map of South Africa, and indicating what is now

Zambesia, said to a friend, "All that British! That is my dream." How soon the dream has been fulfilled we have just been watching. In a conversation with this remarkable man not long ago on the subject, and recalling earlier talks on the same theme, he said to me, with a wave of the hand towards the wall, "Yes, it is all like a picture that was at one time very dim, but has now become more and more distinct." But another dream has been dreamed, and Mr. Rhodes —a veritable modern Alexander—is sighing for other worlds to conquer. I passed the remark, "I want to see you take Colonial England through to Cairo." "Well, I have got to Tanganyika," was the slow, measured, reflecting reply. Mr. Rhodes's policy! It should be well enough known, if only by the name of the Company for which Mr. Cawston and he got a Royal Charter. It is to realise in Africa the destiny of the British race to one day colonise the Globe. He saw the Boer intriguing with the German to bar the progress of English-speaking people to the Zambesi and beyond, and he pondered deeply and successfully as to how the intrigues might be defeated; he has defined his policy as a South African policy, but that carries with it what Sir Hercules Robinson once called "The ultimate establishment of the Federal dominion of South Africa under the British flag." But while carrying on his policy, no one could have shown more tact and judgment as a reconciler of race antipathies and prejudices. The cordial satisfaction with which Mr. Rhodes' acceptance of the Premiership was received throughout the Cape Colony argued an amount of shrewd foresight and appreciation of the facts of the situation not always evinced by countries of greater pretensions. The old antagonism which brought into existence first the Orange Free State and then the Transvaal Republic, touched very nearly the heart of the Dutch population of the Cape Colony, and engendered a sense of soreness which, among a less patient and sober-minded people, might have produced lasting fruits of bitterness. But this has now passed away, and the descendants of the early settlers are found ready to co-operate loyally for the common good with an Englishman who has shown that he can sympathise with them and value their many sterling points of character, even though this involves the dissipation of the hopes and aspirations which a quarter of a century ago took form in the project of a new Netherlands in the Southern Ocean, extending from Cape Point to the Zambesi. The enthusiasm with which Mr. Rhodes was hailed as Sir Gordon Sprigg's successor found a remarkable echo in the British press, of which only one instance, that of the *Times*, may be here given :—

" Sir Gordon Sprigg's place has been taken, not by any of the prominent party leaders, but by a man of a different type, whose name is better known in this country than that of any of them. The new Premier is Mr. Cecil Rhodes, the ' Diamond King' and the moving spirit of the British South Africa Company. Mr. Rhodes is still quite a young man, but he has accomplished much, and been extraordinarily successful. After coming home to England to complete his education at Oxford, he returned to the Cape at the moment when the Diamond Fields were in the flush of their first activity. He flung himself into the search, organised and consolidated the different companies, and in so doing became a very rich man. But he looked further than Kimberley. He was fired by the ever-fresh discoveries of gold and other valuable deposits in the Transvaal and Bechuanaland; and he resolved to lay hands on the vast regions lying to the north—regions, in his belief, as rich as any that had been discovered as yet. His dealings with the diamond mines had brought him into relations not only with many native chiefs, but with many influential persons at home, and with their aid, after many voyages and much negotiations, he obtained a Royal Charter for the British South Africa Company. This success stamped him at once as, in the opinion of the world at large, the foremost man in the Cape Colony. Mr. Rhodes has also shown his diplomatic talent by bringing over all the Home parties to his side—by securing Unionist Dukes as partners in his great undertaking, by largely subscribing to Mr. Parnell's Parliamentary funds, and by making Mr. Schnadhorst a convert to Imperialism. It is, therefore, a significant and an interesting thing that he should have decided to accept office. His energy we know; his good fortune we know; it remains to be seen whether he can bring his large views of the future of South Africa into practical harmony with the thousand details, the thousand minute difficulties that arise in the government of a wide and variously peopled country. Although the Cape Parliament has rejected Sir Gordon Sprigg's railway scheme, there can be no doubt that some scheme of the kind must be taken in hand before long. Local jealousies and race antagonisms are strong in the colony; but they will be surmounted, in so far as is necessary for the passing of some measure for improving the communications of the country. Mr. Rhodes is just the man to carry such a measure."

It will be well here to place on record Mr. Rhodes's statement shortly after he met Parliament in his new *rôle*. Mr. Laing had brought forward a motion, which was, of course, negatived by a large majority :—" That in the interests of the country it is impolitic and undesirable that the official representative of the British South Africa Company should be the Prime Minister of this Colony." The mere moving of such a resolution was, however, useful, as it enabled the colonists to get the following clear statement of the new Premier's programme and ideas :—

I have to thank my honourable friend the member for Fort Beaufort, for the kindly manner in which he has referred to my efforts in the interior, but I beg to differ with him when he stated that the interests of the British South Africa Company and those of the Cape Colony would clash. I will admit that the policy of the interior and the policy of the Cape Colony might have differed if the interior had been a Crown Colony, or if there had been a division between

Portugal and Germany; but I interfered in the interior, because I wished the movement in the interior to be conducted as an expansion of the Cape Colony. I have interfered in the case of Bechuanaland, and the result is that that Colony will, in the end, belong to the Cape Colony. When there was a suspicion that the Imperial officers wished to make it a native reserve, or a reserve governed by a peculiar characteristic, namely, that "no Dutchman need apply," I interfered and claimed that Bechuanaland should be an inheritance of the Cape Colony; and it was only a development of that feeling which led me to act as I did in regard to the north. The case as it existed was that the Cape Colony had not resources such as would warrant it in itself developing the country to the north, but many of its people were most anxious to have some share in that movement. I would ask the House what my policy has been in the past. Has it been such an Imperialist policy as to be against the interests of the Cape Colony? On the contrary, my policy has been the employment of the people of this Colony, and in every way to forward their interests in regard to the interior. Because, Mr. Speaker, I am as well aware, as that I am standing here, of what is going to be the future of this Colony. I am aware that Bechuanaland is temporarily a Crown Colony, but I am also aware that the Cape Colony will in time absorb that country, and I believe that the agreement entered into between the Chartered Company and the late Government was made with that object in view. In the same way I have worked with the idea that eventually the country right up to the Zambesi should also belong to the Cape Colony, and the best guarantee that I really believe in that principle is the fact that I represent a Company whose wealth is equal to a quarter of that of the whole of the Cape Colony, and which is situated in and under the government of the Cape Colony. The diamond mines could not be dissociated from the Cape Colony, and it is the whole of my policy and object that the Cape Colony shall prosper, as through the prosperity of the Cape Colony the interests which I represent will also prosper. I felt that it was essential to the Cape Colony for the people of that Colony to be able to extend right up to the Zambesi. As they could not call upon the Cape Colony itself to step forward to undertake these responsibilities, surely it was the duty of those who had the wealth, and the foresight, and the ability to step in and save the country to the north for the Cape Colony, either from partition between two Foreign Powers, such as Germany and Portugal, or from transference to a neighbouring State, which would have weakened us in the ultimate negotiations which must end in a United South Africa. That is my argument in reference to the remarks of my honourable friend, that it was impossible to conduct the Imperial interest in touch with the Colonial interest. I claim that that might have been the case if the policy in the north had been purely that of a Crown Colony. I intended the policy of the interior to be South African. As the Colony had not been able to take the responsibilities I have referred to, and as I had the good fortune to possess the wealth and the means to seize the interior, I did so; but I did it on behalf of South Africa, and with the intention of developing a South African policy. My honourable friend has intimated that the policy of the interior must be Imperialist against South African feeling. My reply to that is that my natural desire and hope is for the prosperity of the Cape Colony. In carrying out that policy it might well be asked—Is it my intention or desire to ask the Parliament of the Cape Colony to afford me pecuniary assistance? and to that I would reply, clearly and distinctly, that it is not my intention to ask from the House one single shilling, either directly or indirectly. I have been fortunate enough to obtain a sum of money which I think is amply sufficient for my purpose; but even if it were insufficient, such is the wealth of the institutions and persons connected with the Company that I feel sure I shall be able to carry the matter to a successful issue without asking a shilling from the Cape Colony. Where the people of the Colony will benefit will be by the fact that by the agreements which have been entered into the railway lines are exclusively for the Cape Colony, the trade will be exclusively for the Cape Colony, and I have chosen for occupying the land colonists, because I thought they were most fitted to open up a new country. I have every respect for the people from Home, but it takes five years for persons to know this country, and five more to accommodate themselves to the conditions of it. I have therefore chosen people who were used to the rough life on the Border, and I believe that is the only true way to develop the land. The means in my hand are ample for my purpose. The profit rests with the Cape Colony; the responsibilities with the Chartered Company. My honourable friend has referred to an agreement made between the Colony and the Chartered Company. Well, I would say to those who object to my holding my present position on account of the agreement, that I could not have made that agreement had I been Prime Minister of the Colony at that time. In my capacity as a member of the South Africa Company I made that agreement, and there was not the slightest likelihood of my becoming Prime Minister. I think I may say that with the development of the interior devolving on me, and with the many other responsibilities I have, I would have been glad to be out of the position I now occupy; I would have been well out of it; but it resolved itself into this, that if I had also declined to undertake the responsibilities, Constitutional Government in this country would have been an admitted failure. I did not invite the late Government to enter into an agreement with me with regard to railway extension to the north. I give every credit to the late Prime Minister for the manner in which he conducted the negotiations. I worked with the idea that the Cape Colony should have such an interest in the Company that it would ultimately be brought about that the Cape Colony should absorb Bechuanaland and extend as far as Mafeking. With regard to the railway, the Prime Minister was asked to express his views, and after many negotiations an agreement was completed which gave the Cape Colony the right to take over a portion of the line. That is the only question which existed which could affect this dual capacity. I have only, in conclusion, to further assure the House that if ever such a contingency should arise —which I cannot foresee—when the interests of the Chartered Company and this Colony may clash, I shall not fail in my duty in at once placing myself in the hands of His Excellency the Governor.

A few weeks later Mr. Rhodes delivered a striking speech at Kimberley, when he was fêted there at a banquet, just as he did the other day when he was similarly entertained on his return from England. At the former demonstration he referred to the complete Customs Union he was striving for as the first step towards a United South Africa, but he left the question of the flag of this Union to be settled by the future. Just as he would not forfeit his flag they could not at once ask the Dutch Republics to forfeit theirs, and this sensible utterance led him to further references to his policy in the North. A few of his sentences on the subject may be given as they stand with the reporter's interpolations :—

"It has been my good fortune during this Session to meet from both sides of the House, and from both sections of the House, great kindness with regard to the development of the northern territory. (Cheers.) I had thought that one would meet with great opposition. I was amazed, on the proposition of the Bechuanaland railway, with the unanimity with which it was received by the House. But the people of Cape Colony felt, as a whole, that it should have a share in the development of the north. The Cape Colony felt that it had every kindly feeling towards other States, and especially the Transvaal, but it also felt that it was not going to be isolated, but that it was going to take its share of the north ; that it was not going to lie down and be cut off from the interior, and it saw that if it did not move it would be met with hostile tariffs, it would be cut off from the north, and therefore when the matter came before the House, whether it was English or Dutch, the Cape Colony was united upon it. The Parliament of the Cape of Good Hope were pleased that a mining community should have started the development to the north. They have given us every assistance ; and they wish us every success ; and I feel sure that within our lifetime the Cape will be stretched to the Zambesi. (Cheers.) Many of us are deeply interested in having relations and connections with the Pioneer Force in the north. It is a pleasure for me to tell you that I feel all risk of collision is over—(cheers)— and I believe that there will be a peaceable occupation of Mashonaland. It was an interesting fact for me to-day to receive a cession from the chief of the Barotse territory, comprising 225,000 square miles north of the Zambesi, to our Company. (Cheers.) You may think that this is an imaginative acquisition, and I might own that it may not benefit us in our lifetime ; but when the whole of the European nations had begun to paint the map red, it was judicious for the Cape Colony also to start and get some portion of this continent. (Cheers.) If nations seven thousand miles away, who spend their whole time in considering what they can take in the way of territory, start down in this part of the world to paint it for themselves, I think the descendants of those who have been here two hundred years have a right to say that they also will use the paint brush. (Laughter.) Ours is a much more practical paint brush than any of theirs—(laughter)—because we have at least sent five hundred of our citizens one thousand miles into the interior to occupy the country for us. (Cheers.) To show how great is the desire to go north, I may state that a clergyman of the Dutch Reformed Church at Colesberg recently received a call to go further north than any of the British South Africa Company's communications, beyond Barotse. I have often thought that if any of the old colonists who took this colony were told that it would extend to the Orange River and beyond it, they would have laughed at the people as madmen ; and perhaps without indulging in any too imaginative a policy, people two hundred years hence may think our present annexations are far too paltry."

With a few further personal references to Mr. Rhodes I shall take my leave of him for the present. I say for the present, for he is too commanding a personality to remain long out of any discussion of South African affairs. A writer in the *Cape Times* thus describes the Cape Premier as he appears in his place in the Cape Parliament :—

He, when he rises to address the House, presents a good upstanding appearance, being somewhere about six feet in his shoes. He is a young man, with a good physique, is a muscular-looking statesman, well shaped every way, has a pleasant, intelligent face, and is a very good type of a well-bred English gentleman. He dresses without the least consideration for fashion, and he is always unaffected and unpretending, is plain spoken, and when he is addressing the Speaker there is an apparent earnestness about him and in his mode of address which commands attention and respect apart from his position. He is not possessed of the power of oratory in the least degree, but his manner of speaking suits the House. He is an exceedingly nervous speaker, and there is a twitching about his hands, and he has a somewhat ungainly way of turning his body about, which, perhaps, he may get cured of when he has had more experience. He delivers himself of what he has to say in a very admirable tone of voice, never loud or blustering, is seldom declamatory, but his voice is clear and distinct. He is a little too apt to turn away from the Speaker, and address himself to those behind him, or to his right or left, as those he wishes to impress, correct, or refute may happen to be placed at the moment. He has no inclination to be personal, and seldom retorts upon those who have attacked him by indulging in personal reflections upon the offender. He never forgets what is due to the dignity of the high office he fills. His language is usually apt, and he has not quite what would be called the gift of eloquence, and yet an eloquence that is all his own. He is very, very seldom illogical, and he has a simple mode of convincing his audience that is very taking and serves him and his party well. He carefully avoids the use of high-flown language, never affects to be more scholarly than his surroundings, although he is immeasurably above them in that respect. In introducing a measure—that is to say, in introducing the principles of a measure—to the House on the second reading of a Bill, he is most careful in his method ; first, as a rule, giving the reasons for its introduction, then explaining the principal clauses, showing how they are adapted to meet the requirements of the case, and if any strong objections have been raised to the measure during the time of its publication, he does his best to set aside these objections, and concludes by making as clear as possible the intended operations of the measure. He is able in debate and a fair debater, sharp to detect a flaw in the argument of an opponent, and prompt to answer. Humour is not his *forte*, and when he ventures upon a joke it seems to be done rather for his own amusement than to ridicule an opponent. He takes care to master his facts perfectly, and is seldom detected in exaggerating or coining a fact, or inventing a figure, and when he makes a statement there is a disposition on the part of the House to accept it with implicit confidence in its accuracy. The honourable gentleman is careful not to abuse that confidence. Whether his vast interests in commercial and other public undertakings will encourage suspicion and tend to weaken his power and influence remains to be seen, but that at present his very substantial wealth and commercial importance gives him great political power is unquestionable, and whether if he was stripped of that wealth and importance he would have the same weight in the House, have accorded to him the same trustfulness, and be listened to with the same breathless attention, is a problem which is not likely to be solved, but it is undeniable that he would be a man of mark under any circumstance, and that in addition to the ability which has come to him from education and study, he has natural gifts of no mean order, there is no gainsaying. That he is a man of extraordinary energy is clear to everyone who takes observation of him. He is in a continued state of restlessness, whether sitting in his seat or standing on his legs. He is never still from the time he enters the House until he leaves it. When he is not addressing the House, he is for the most part either talking *sotto voce* with one of his colleagues, moving about the House, or in deep consultation with some honourable member he wants to consult, or who desires to consult him.

The policy of the British South Africa Company has been amply set forth in the preceding pages. The moral now to be drawn from all that I have set down is that a great new country—an El Dorado and a Goshen rolled into one—is being opened up for the benefit of the Anglo-Saxon emigrant and the British merchant. New markets for the products of this great insular hive of industry are ever being found in Africa as such corporations as the Chartered Company speed on their noble errand. At present Britain's share of this trade to Africa is quite 45 per cent. of the whole. But other countries, notably France, are treading close on her heels, and it is for her home merchants to grasp what is really going on in that great continent south of the Equator. Mr. Mackenzie, in his " Austral Africa," says, with reference to European trade in Matabeleland, that Manchester looms are underselling native manufactures. The Mashonas have for ages, however, smelted their own iron ore with charcoal, and their knives, razors, axes, adzes, assegais of all sorts, and battle-axes are really well made. These implements still hold the field, but it remains to be seen whether Birmingham and Sheffield might not accomplish what Manchester has already achieved in superseding local manufactures. Mr. E. A. Maund, whom I have already referred to in this connection, has done good service in spreading information about the new markets which are opening up for British goods in Zambesia. I shall quote him further, but a few words about himself may not be inappropriate. He was attached to Sir Charles Warren's staff in 1885, and was sent by him with Lieut. Haynes on a mission to Lo Bengula, with instructions to map and report on the country, which he did with much credit to himself. This mission resulted in Lo Bengula promising to respect Britain's protectorate then declared over Khama, the Bechuana chief. These gentlemen's reports were published in the Blue Book, and form the first official information of Matabeleland. On his return to England Mr. Maund, who, it may be mentioned, was educated at Peterhouse College, Cambridge, addressed the Colonial Institute on the results of his observations during this journey. After two years spent in North Africa, Mr. Maund went back, as we have seen, in 1888 to Matabeleland. Lo Bengula, finding himself beset by gold-seekers, and thinking himself threatened by Boers and Portuguese, asked Mr. Maund to take two of his Indunas to England to find out if the " White Queen " still lived, and to open relations with the Home Government, if they found England were really powerful enough to befriend them, after the stories circulated by the Boers after Majuba Hill. The mission, as we have seen, was very successful. Its results have been that Lo Bengula is loyally fulfilling his engagements; and part of his rich country is already being peaceably developed by the Chartered Company. Mr. Maund only left the King last spring, after the latter had sanctioned the opening up of Mashonaland. Though he has now returned to Mashonaland as the chief representative of a powerful syndicate of capitalists he was lately doing good work in lecturing in the mother country on Matabeleland. One of his lectures was entitled, " Trade Prospects with Zambesia," and I take a few remarks from it :—

I have pointed out the value of Mashonaland as a field for colonisation, where our congested population may find fresh breathing room and remunerative work. I have drawn attention to its grand farming capabilities, to the trade to be done in corn, rice, coffee, and sugar, and to the likely tropical products you will get for your Manchester, Leeds, and Birmingham goods. But above all these products, which require markets, and therefore vary in value according as the market be over or understocked, stands gold, which all nations by common consent have made the standard of value. That value, though arbitrary in relation to its cost of production, is practically constant and forms the highest currency. Produce your gold and you can buy anything with it, but with diamonds, copper, or even flour, by means of rings and monopolies, you may seek to limit the output, in order to command your own prices for the commodity, but after all, you must go to the market with it, and turn it into gold, before it has a buying value. Hence gold is the *summum bonum*, the philosopher's stone to seek for; the production of which from the soil of a country is the quickest means of developing that country. Free trade or protection does not affect gold, as it does other products gained by human industry from the earth. A M'Kinley tariff has few terrors for the owners of a mine from which payable gold is being extracted.

Thus, apart from corn lands and pastures and capabilities of various valuable products, the gold alone in Mashonaland is certain quickly to develop Zambesia into perhaps the richest acquisition of the empire. This is especially important at the present time when so much gold is needed for our daily increasing commerce and enterprise. These naturally must increase relatively with our population, whereas the output of gold, our standard of value, scarcely increases proportionately with our need for it—hence the greed with which we "rush" new gold regions, irrespective of dangers, climatic or human. You, gentlemen, will see a "rush" to this new colony unexampled in the history of South Africa, where the colonists have been more accustomed to the slower method of development by trekking rather than those excited rushes produced by gold. The diamond mines and the ill-managed Transvaal gold fields produced, it is true, rushes which helped to develop Griqualand West and the Transvaal. But it was fifteen years ere Kimberley was served with a railway, and the Transvaal is to-day without a mile of railway within her borders. Now in America the railways went first, and civilisation and development followed fast along their tracks.

The Chartered Company having experienced the cost of Boer methods of transport will soon be ready with a railway to supply the wants of the white population fast establishing themselves in Mashonaland. We shall soon see two systems established, one an extension of the Cape Railway from Kimberley, going possibly *via* Shoshong and Tati on to Mount Hampden. The first section of this was opened by the Company last month as far as Vryburg. A branch from this will probably diverge at Shoshong to the Victoria Falls, to tap the riches of the Barotse, who have recently asked for our protection, as well as opening the vast grazing country of Ngamiland along the Botletle River. The Transvaal system will be connected with this by a line *via* Baines Drift to Tati, or along the Matlabas to Shoshong. There are no engineering difficulties, and it would tap the rich Blauberg and Waterberg districts. The Transvaal system will consist of the High Veld line from Pretoria to Delagoa Bay, tapping Barberton, another line connecting Natal with Johannesburg and Pretoria, while there will be a direct route between Pretoria and Port Elizabeth through the Free State, *via* Bloemfontein and Colesburg. The principal traffic with the south will be along the Trunk line, *via* Tati, Mafeking, Kimberley, to Cape Town. The Transvaal will be tapped from the west by it, as there will doubtless soon be a line from Mafeking to Malmani, and thence to Johannesburg and Pretoria. We shall soon, however, hope to tap our new Colony from the East Coast. Beira, at the mouth of the Pungwe River, is scarcely more than 300 miles from the gold fields, of which Mount Hampden is at present the headquarters, for 70 miles of which the Pungwe is navigable. This route has already been roughly surveyed, as well as an alternative route by the Busi River.

It is almost useless to demonstrate the advantages of this short route over that from Cape Town, which is at least 1700 miles, of which only 750 miles is covered by railway, having, however, three faults: the gauge is too narrow, it is deficient in rolling stock, and its gradients are too steep. With nearly 1000 miles of wagon communication to Mount Hampden, the cost of freight by this route from Cape Town amounts to 60s. per 100 lbs., or £67 per ton.

Now the freight from Cape Town to Mount Hampden *via* Pungwe Bay has been tendered for at 10s. per 100 lbs., or £11 4s. per ton, or a saving of 500 per cent. To this would have to be added the Portuguese duty of 3 per cent. *ad valorem* on goods by this route, according to the terms of the Convention. The distance of Pungwe Bay from Cape Town is 1550 miles, and from Natal 800 miles. This would probably be served by the Chartered Company's ships. The distance from England *via* Cape Town to Pungwe Bay is 7500 miles, and from England *via* the Suez Canal and Zanzibar 7200 miles. Though this route is slightly shorter, and the East African Company's possessions,

Zanzibar, Mozambique, and the Lakes Company might be served, yet owing to canal dues and increased insurance, the charge would be higher. So the Pungwe route *viâ* Cape Town will probably be the favourite to Zambesia.

The Company which is now responsible for the development of Zambesia, being incorporated under royal charter, its work is necessarily of a national character, and we have therefore a guarantee that the financial blunders which have so crippled the Rand will not be repeated in Mashonaland. The history of all gold fields hitherto has been very similar in one respect. A gold fever soon follows the discovery, of which those in the know take advantage. Dangerous symptoms quickly arise of reckless flotation on worthless reports. The most wanton extravagance follows, and inevitable collapse soon supervenes. Over-speculation, not the want of payable ore, ruins the field on the markets, the necessity for economy of working entails re-organisation, then the weak things go to the wall, and it becomes soon simply a case of "the survival of the fittest." The field speedily becomes convalescent, the output increasing and expenses diminishing.

Zambesia is fast assuming the character of an organised colony under the administration of the Chartered Company. When the rush comes it will find a strong executive ready to receive and regulate it, and thus order (is wisely assured. The natives, finding well-paid employment, will cease to prey on one another, raiding will gradually cease, and slave trading, the scourge of Africa, being now checked along one of its chief arteries, the Zambesi, peace, security, and prosperity will reign over a region that has been one of the chief haunts of that accursed traffic. And civilization and Christianity will gradually thread their way thence nto the very heart of the Dark Continent.

At the time of writing, the negotiations between England and Portugal as to the recognition of the latter country as a factor in East Africa have reached no officially announced stage of finality. Certain unauthorised and speculative versions of what Mr. Rhodes and Lord Salisbury agreed to propose to Portugal have been made, but they need not be noticed here. As this page is going to press, some publication has also taken place of the presumable outlines of the new convention which the Lisbon Cortes has been asked to sanction ; but these also are incomplete and need not be discussed now. It was a primary object of these pages, subject to mechanical exigencies, to reach the public before any really permanent settlement with Portugal had been made, so that they might more clearly see how much England had sacrificed in the past, and is sacrificing in the present, in her endeavour to pacify Lisbon rowdies, and gratify the vanity of a nation, which, whatever her history in the past (and it is a noble one), can make but a poor claim to recognition as having "effectively" occupied any part of East Africa, excepting in the case of certain trading stations and sea-coast towns previously referred to. As regards the Manica country we have seen that the whole of her claim to that territory resolves itself into that which is based upon the occupation by foreigners in the name of a Portuguese Company (formed under an unsigned royal charter ceding away the inalienable rights of natives without their consent) of a very limited district in the locality of Massi Kessi. Whatever the results of the present efforts to come to an understanding with Portugal may be, they must be emphatic and final. If they are on the right lines— lines pointed out to the authorities by those who knew what they were speaking about—good and well. If they are not quite on the right lines local developments will quickly mend any inequalities. Portugal is a purely paper power in South Africa. She has fenced long enough with the crisis which was to bring this fact home to Englishmen at home, as it has long been brought home to them in that part of the world. It is monstrous that the pretensions of this Lusitanian weakling to a standing in South Africa should any longer assume the dignity of a grave international question. Not even to prop a throne may Lord Salisbury again put a blind eye to the telescope when surveying the map of Zambesia. If a European king's tenure of office hangs by such a slender thread as England's acceptance of, and recognition of the rule of a ruffian like Gouveia among the natives of East Africa, the sooner that thread snaps the better for all. It is the desire of South Africans to see everything, even their extension and territorial aggrandisement, done decently and in good order. But if Portugal thinks for one moment that the clauses of any convention will make her a power in South or East Africa, she is vastly mistaken. The facts are against her. Her own people have not the faculty to colonise, and her bastard proxies in East Africa, if they presume to thrust themselves further into the country, will be wiped out by the natives as though they had never existed, as will also her troops if they dare to try conclusions with the British or the dusky owners of the soil. The natives welcome the British everywhere and hate the half-castes who tyrannise under a flag honoured in Europe but prosti- tuted to base purposes in Africa. It is clear to my mind that if Gungunhama's petition to England for protection be spurned on any plea that he must get on the best way he can with Portugal, a rough and ready way for the extermination of Portuguese pretensions will soon become a matter of history. All may be well if it is made clear to the Gaza King that he is to regard himself as totally independent of those he calls "the yellow dogs on the coast"—not otherwise. As to the British South Africa Company and the Portuguese, the former have shown that they can pretty well take care of themselves. Mr. Rhodes has peacefully occupied Mashonaland in the teeth of odds which at one time seemed overwhelming; he is not likely to be interfered with in his big work by the mongrel bullies who cannot face an assegai poised in earnest. One result the negotiations with Lisbon must have, and that is, "The plateau all British, a route to the sea coast secured, and the opening on terms of all East Coast rivers." If the result does not come one way it will come another, because Fate has decreed that the debauching of the natives must cease, that lawless plague-spots must be gradually purified, in short, that Portugal (or what stands for her there) must notwithstanding paper permission to do otherwise, remain by the seashore and behave herself, be bought out or—go.

In the final scramble for Africa, Great Britain has managed to appropriate a very satisfactory share. South of the Zambesi she has obtained nearly all that is most worth having, and here we see in the making what in the future will become a great English-speaking nation or confederation. In the centre of the Continent, again, thanks to the public spirit of Sir William Mackinnon, her dominion extends over those great lakes which give origin to the Nile, and the magnificent plateaux with their splendid populations around them. On the other side, she has command of the Niger and the thickly populated and half-civilised countries to which that river gives access. Here she has France for her rival, and in time we may expect to see the extensive domain of French Senegambia connected by rail with her Algerian territory. As for Germany, she claims about a million square miles in East and West Africa, though whether she will be able to make anything of the enormous territory remains to be seen. It seems likely that the vast Congo basin will become a Belgian colony; while even Italy now claims suzerainty over the whole of Abyssinia and Shoa, and a great stretch of Somaliland. Except Morocco and the Central Soudan States there is really nothing left to divide; for England is supreme in Egypt, and will probably let no other power gain a footing in those upper Nile countries which are at present terrorized over by the Mahdi.

But some statistics on the subject will best show how the matter stands to-day. The partition of Africa among the Powers of Europe is so far accomplished that it is possible to take stock of the share which has fallen to the lot of each, with some approach to accuracy. In certain directions, the limits of the different claims have been laid down by international agreement; in other cases vague "spheres of influence" have been acknowledged; while in some instances only treaties with native kings or chiefs can be put forward as the bases of claims. Still, what with the recent Anglo-German and Anglo-French Agreements, the probable Anglo-Portuguese Agreement, and the arrangements made at the Berlin Congress in 1884-5, it is possible to form some idea of the areas claimed by the various Powers. Coming to Great Britain's share in the scramble, and taking the limits prescribed by the last Anglo-Portuguese proposed arrangement, we find the following results:—

BRITISH AFRICA, 1876.

	Sq. miles.		Sq. miles.
West Coast Colonies ...	15,640	Mauritius and dependencies...	900
Atlantic Islands	125		
Cape Colony and dependencies...	241,500	Total ...	279,165
Natal	21,000		

G

BRITISH AFRICA, 1890.

	Sq. miles.		Sq. miles
West Coast Colonies ...	45,000	Mauritius and depen-	
Royal Niger Company ...	400,000	dencies...	900
Atlantic Islands	125	Zanzibar and Pemba ...	760
Walfish Bay	460	British East Africa (in-	
Cape Colony, with depen-		cluding sphere of influ-	
dencies; Basutoland,		ence)	400,000
Zululand, Bechuana-		Somali Coast region ...	38,000
land, &c.	500,000	Socotra	3,000
Natal	21,000		
British South Africa Com-		Total ... 1,909,445	
pany and Nyassaland...	500,000		

Has Britain finished? Probably not, for the British East Africa Company has no northern limit to its sphere, and the English troops occupy Wady Halfa, Cairo, and Suakim. In mere area France slightly exceeds England in her share of the scramble, but in population British is a long way ahead of any of the other Africas. Again, everyone will admit that so far as value goes, England has no rival in Africa.

To sum up, the various European Powers that have joined in the scramble have apparently acquired the following areas in Africa, Turkey being excluded, and Egypt being left aside :—

	1876. Square miles.	1890. Square miles.
Portugal	612.217	774,993
Spain	3,500	210,000
France	283,450	2,300,248
Germany	—	1,035,720
Congo Free State	—	1,000,000
Italy...	—	360,000
Great Britain	279,165	1,909,445
Total	1,178,332	7,590,406

If to this we add the areas of Egypt and the Egyptian Soudan, of Tripoli, Morocco, the independent Central Soudan States, the Transvaal and Orange Free State, and patches elsewhere not yet ensphered, it will probably be found that of the 11,900,000 square miles of Africa, not more than 2,500,000 remain to be scrambled for.

But it is on the 500,000 square miles occupied by the British South Africa Company that many eyes in South Africa and England are at present turned. I have shown the great possibilities of that vast territory; how the congested labour market of the mother country will here find relief; how trade will receive an ever-growing impetus from the establishment of camps to become in time villages and large towns; and how Mr. Goschen will probably, ere long, have fewer sleepless nights when that twenty millions worth of bullion is shipped home from Mashonaland to become his second reserve. We shall then have pound and ten-shilling notes, and everybody will be happy — for the Golden Age will in verity have dawned. England and South Africa, working now as they ever must hand-in-hand, may both be congratulated on the Royal chartering of the Company that has so far pre-eminently justified its existence. Before the Charter was granted, Mr. Mandy, whom I have mentioned before, drew a picture of the prosperity which would follow in its train in Zambesia. Concluding his lecture at Cape Town, this long-time resident in Matabeleland said, and his words will bear repeating!—"The time had arrived, in his opinion, when in the interests of humanity the paramount Power in Africa should either take upon itself the government of this magnificent country or grant the charter, which was applied for by men able and willing to take upon themselves the responsibility. Then, in place of the deadly reign of terror established by the merciless Matabele, there would succeed the peaceful and benign rule of an enlightened people. The industrious and intelligent, though timid, Mashonas would emerge from their rocky fastnesses, and dwell once more secure in the open. Tens of thousands of busy, pushing white men would pour into the land, re-peopling the territories laid desolate by the savages now devastating the country. With all its rivers spanned by bridges, and a railway from the Cape to the Zambesi, civilisation would light up the land, and the continent, no longer dark and silent, would throb with ceaseless industry. The fruitful plains and valleys of Matabeleland and Mashonaland, stretching over 160,000 square miles, would teem with well-to-do agriculturists, large towns and villages would spring up, and Africa, the birthplace of a new and sturdy nation, would eventually take a prominent place amongst the nations of the world."

Yes, I believe every word of that. In Zambesia the remains of a cruel and despotic barbarism are quickly vanishing, and England's El Dorado is fast being peopled by men who will be true to the traditions of their race, and plant in the heart of Africa a nation ever rejoicing in the blessings that flow from a loyal love for the Union Jack and England's throne. It has been said that this year will see a "rush" of 10,000 people to Mashonaland. Whether this be so or not, we see history repeating itself, only that whereas in the not far past our countrymen who did not fear their fate too much, took ship for the west, they will now paraphrase the words of the song they sang a generation ago, and cheerily shout :

To the south, to the south, to the land of the free,
    Where the mighty Zambesi rolls down to the sea;
Where a man is a man, if he's willing to toil,
    And the humblest may gather the fruits of the soil.

THE END.

APPENDICES.

APPENDIX A.

THE BECHUANALAND EXPLORATION COMPANY, LIMITED.

DIRECTORS:—Chairman, Lord Gifford, V.C.; George Cawston, Esq., and Major F. I. Ricarde-Seaver, F.R.S. Edin., M.R.I., F.G.S., &c. Offices:—19, St. Swithin's Lane, E.C. Secretary:—H. K. Evans. Registered 25th April, 1888—to acquire a concession of mining rights in perpetuity over 400 square miles in Bechuanaland, South Africa, granted by Khama, Paramount Chief of the Bamangwatos. Capital originally authorised, £150,000, of which £55,000 was for working capital. A subsequent increase to £200,000 was authorised, and 37,500 shares were issued at 30s. each, the proceeds of which were applied to forming the capital of the Bechuanaland Trading Association, Limited, with a capital of £130,000, of which the Bechuanaland Exploration Company holds £110,000. The cash capital of the Trading Association is £100,000, of which £90,000 is paid up. The Bechuanaland Exploration Company, in conjunction with the members of the Board in their individual capacities, together with Mr. R. W. Murray, Mr. Edward Jones, and others, formed the Exploring Company, Limited (see below), and thus may be considered as the initiators of the Royal Chartered Company, "The British South Africa Company."

THE EXPLORING COMPANY, LIMITED.

THIS Company was registered on June 15, 1889. It had existed previously under the same name, with a capital of £12,000 for the purpose of exploring and working mines in all parts of the world. The capital was subsequently increased to £35,000, and afterwards to £70,000, in shares of £1 each. The Company sent an expedition to Matabeleland in 1888 for the purpose of obtaining a concession from Lo Bengula. Its interest in the Rudd-Rhodes concession is represented by one-fourth, together with special rights in the Mazoe and other districts. The Directors are:—Lord Gifford, V.C., Mr. Cecil Rhodes, Mr. George Cawston, Mr. Alfred Beit, and Mr. J. O. Maund. Secretary:—Mr. A. J. McPhail. Offices:—19, St. Swithin's Lane, E.C.

THE GOLD FIELDS OF SOUTH AFRICA, LIMITED.

THIS Company was registered on February 9, 1887, with a capital of £250,000, for the purpose of acquiring and dealing with certain auriferous and other mineral properties, &c., in South Africa; and also for carrying on general exploration with a view to making further investments of a similar nature. In March, 1889, the capital was increased to £370,000, divided into 230,000 fully-paid ordinary shares of one pound each, 120,000 ordinary shares of £1 with 5s. paid, and 200 founders' fully-paid shares of £100 each, making the paid-up capital £280,000. The founders' shares were allotted credited as fully-paid to the Managing Directors in payment for certain properties, and while the Company is carried on under their active management, they are entitled to about one-third of the net profits, and on retirement to one-fifth of the net

profits. In May, 1891, the capital of the Company was further increased to
£500,000 by the creation of 130,000 additional shares of £1 each. The
Directors are:—Mr. Thomas Rudd (Chairman), Mr. J. J. Hamilton, Mr. Leigh
Hoskyns, Mr. W. M. Farmer, Mr. H. E. M. Davies, and Major-General Sir
Frederick Pollock, K.C.S.I., the Managing Directors being Mr. Charles D.
Rudd, M.L.A., and Mr. C. J. Rhodes, M.L.A. Secretary:—Mr. H. D. Boyle.
Offices:—2, Gresham Buildings, E.C.

THE CENTRAL SEARCH ASSOCIATION, LIMITED.
(In Liquidation.)

THIS Company, the authorised capital of which was £120,000 (subsequently
increased to £121,000), in shares of £1 each, was registered on May 23rd,
1889. Its objects were to prospect and explore in any part of the world, to
work mines, and to execute public works of all kinds. The Directors were:—
Lord Gifford, V.C., Mr. Cecil Rhodes, Mr. George Cawston, Mr. Alfred Beit,
Mr. J. O. Maund, Mr. C. D. Rudd, and Mr. Thomas Rudd. Secretary, Mr. C.
H. Weatherley. Offices: 19, St. Swithin's Lane, E.C. The Company
liquidated and was reconstructed. It should be stated that the capital of
the Association was merely a figure adopted for the sake of apportioning the
respective shares of the parties, whose interests were "pooled" in the
Association.

THE UNITED CONCESSIONS COMPANY, LIMITED.

THIS Company is a re-construction of the Central Search Association,
Limited. Its nominal capital is £4,000,000. This figure was merely
adopted for the purpose of carrying out arrangements previously made
for satisfying various liabilities, and adjusting the shares of the
persons interested in the Rudd-Rhodes concession, which the Company
has acquired, and made over for development to the British South
Africa Company on the basis of the latter paying to the Company 50 per
cent. of the net profits. The Directors are:—Lord Gifford, V.C., the Hon. C.
J. Rhodes, Mr. George Cawston, Mr. Alfred Beit, Mr. J. O. Maund, Mr. C. D.
Rudd, and Mr. T. Rudd. Secretary:—Mr. A. J. McPhail. Offices:—19, St.
Swithin's Lane, E.C.

APPENDIX B.

THE BRITISH SOUTH AFRICA COMPANY.

MEMORANDUM of the Terms and Conditions upon which Persons are
permitted to prospect for Minerals and Metals in Mashonaland.

PROSPECTING LICENCES.

1. Any person may take out a licence on binding himself in writing to obey
the Laws of the Company and to assist in the defence and maintenance of
Law and Order, if called upon to do so by the Company—such licence to bear
a stamp of the value of one shilling.

RIGHT OF PROSPECTING HOLDERS TO PEG OFF CLAIMS.

2. Every licence-holder is free to peg off one alluvial claim and ten quartz
reef claims in block. When the claims have been marked off the same shall
be registered and the licence-holder shall receive a certificate of registration—
such certificate to bear a stamp of the value of half-a-crown.

SIZE OF CLAIMS.

3. Alluvial claims are in extent 150 feet by 150 feet. Quartz reef claims
are in extent 150 feet in the direction of the reef and 400 feet broad. The
claimholder may follow the reef in all its dips, spurs, angles, and variations.

TERMS ON WHICH QUARTZ REEF CLAIMS MAY BE HELD.

4. Every registered quartz reef claim is to be held by the prospector on joint account in equal shares with the Company, and every transfer, hypothecation, or lien of his interest in such claims is subject to the rights of the Company.

REGISTRATION OF ALLUVIAL CLAIMS.

5. Certificates of registration of an alluvial claim or portion of claim in any alluvial digging are to be covered by a stamp of £1 for each month for which such claim or portion of claim is registered, payable in advance; the Company, however, claims no rights in respect to gold won from alluvial claims.

DISCOVERIES OF ALLUVIAL DIGGINGS.

6. The discoverer of an alluvial digging, distant not less than ten miles from any known alluvial digging, shall have the right to peg out two alluvial claims in addition to his other rights.

WORK TO BE DONE ON CLAIMS.

7. Every digger shall within four months from the registration of the block of claims, under penalty of forfeiture of his claim licence, sink upon his block of quartz reef claims either a shaft of a depth of 30 feet in the reef or a shaft of at least 30 feet outside the reef with a cross-cut through the reef.

CERTIFICATE OF INSPECTION.

8. So soon as the claimholder has done the required amount of work and has given evidence that he has opened up a payable reef, he shall receive an Inspection Certificate to the effect that the required work has been done—such Certificate to bear a stamp of the value of Fifteen Shillings.

PAYMENT OF CLAIM LICENCE.

9. Prior to flotation the claimholders shall pay no licence. After flotation the licence shall be at the rate of 10s. (Ten Shillings) per Claim per month.

FLOTATION.

10. On claims being ascertained to be payable, the Company have the right to float them into either a joint stock company or into a syndicate. The Company shall therefore within a reasonable time either make a proposal or decline to do so. If the proposal is accepted by the Claimholder he shall on flotation be entitled to half the vendors' scrip in the shares of the Company so floated. If the Claimholder is not satisfied with the Company's proposals, he has the right within one year to prove to the Company that he is in a position to float on better terms, and he shall, on the flotation of the claims, give the Company half the vendors' scrip.

PEGGING OUT OF ADDITIONAL CLAIMS.

12. Any claimholder shall be at liberty to peg out a fresh block of ten (10) claims—

    (i) When he shall have given notice of abandonment of his existing block of ten claims.

    (ii) When he has received his Inspection Certificate from the Mining Commissioner. But no claimholder who has acquired his claim or claims as a prospector shall be the registered claimholder of more than two blocks of claims of 10 claims each.

AGREEMENT.

13. An agreement, binding prospectors to abide by the law of the Company under penalty of forfeiture of rights, is to be signed by all the Prospectors either at Kimberley or Tuli.

APPENDIX C.

TABLES OF DISTANCES.

The following tables will prove serviceable to the traveller in the latest discovered gold regions of South East Africa. To account for variations in some of the figures it should be stated that where the estimates or calculations as to the distances from the same points disagree, they come from different sources. It is to be remembered also that the figures may be those of travellers by post-cart, or horseback, or they may have been jotted during the more leisurely, and perhaps apparently longer journeys by ox wagon or foot. The tables have been prepared with all requisite care, and have been drawn up either from personal observation, from trustworthy notes supplied to the compiler, or from statistics published from time to time. Until surveys of the gold-fields areas and Zambesia have been effected with something approaching to scientific accuracy, such figures as are now given will remain the most reliable which can be put before the public. For all practical purposes they will be found useful, and where authorities differ perhaps it will suit the traveller to "split the difference."

ITINERARY OF ROUTE TO FORT SALISBURY.

	Distance from Mafeking about	
Mafeking		
Ramoutsa (Telegraph Station)	80	Miles.
Palla Camp (Telegraph Station—Junction of Notuani and Crocodile Rivers)..	200	,,
Elebe, on the Lotsani River	280	,,
Macloutsie Camp and Post (Macloutsie River)	320	,,
Tuli Camp and Post (Tuli and Shashi Rivers)	370	,,
Victoria Camp and Post (35 Miles North of the Lundi River)	600	,,
Charter Camp and Post (Near Mount Wedza)	750	,,
Fort Salisbury (8 Miles S.E. of Mount Hampden)	800	,,

BARKLY TO BULAWAYO.

In 1878 Mr. A. C. Bailie wrote a report of his journey from Barkly to Bulawayo, and for convenience of reference and comparison I give his table of approximate distances (obtained by trochiometer measurements) from Barkly to each of the different stations and also the distances between each station.

From	To	Miles	From	To	Miles
Barkly	Taungs	78	Taungs	Mamusa	51
,,	Mamusa	129	Mamusa	Rietfontein	98
,,	Rietfontein	227	Rietfontein	Kanya	88
,,	Kanya	315	Kanya	Molopolole	61
,,	Molopolole	376	Molopolole	Machodi	44
,,	Machodi	420	Machodi	Shoshong	166
,,	Shoshong	586	Shoshong	Gubulawayo	300
,,	Gubulawayo	886	Molopolole	Shoshong(direct)	128

Mr. Bailie made the distance from Kimberley to Gubulawayo, 910 miles by the Limpopo River and 828 by the direct road from Molopolole to Shoshong.

TO THE NORTHERN FIELDS.

The immediately following distances are from Baines' book, and although some of the stopping places may now be known no more, the tables have an interest and usefulness which warrant their republication.

Summary of distances, &c., from Port Natal to the Northern Gold Fields, Matabeleland, by Hartley's Road, viâ Bamangwato and Tati (clear of Tsetse).

	Mls.	Fur.
By rail to Durban	2	0
Pietermaritzburg	54	0
Harrismith, Orange Free State	148	6
Cross Vaal River at Lause's Drift into Transvaal	130	6
Potchefstroom, Mooi River	85	4
One mile S.E. of Rustenburg	89	4
Cross Marico River at junction with Limpopo	121	5
At cross roads, Bamangwato Hills	95	6
Cross Tati River, near Limpopo Company's store	156	3
Cross Sawpit Spruit of Mangwe River	59	4
Manyamis, outpost of Matabele	11	0
Inyati Mission Station, London Society	88	2
Cross Gwaito River over S.W. boundary	54	7
Hartley Hill, between Um Vuli and Simbo Rivers	115	3
Ganyana River, S.W. side, our N.E. boundary	37	1
	1251	6
To Maghoondas, Mashona Village, approximate	35	0
Total distance from Port Natal	1286	0

INDEPENDENT DISTANCES.

	Mls.
Hartley Hill to Umtigesi's Village	92
Hartley Hill to Willie's Grave	13
Hartley Hill down Um Vuli River	25
Hartley Hill to abandoned Gold Workings	21
Hartley Hill to Workings, resumed by Mashona, near Maghoonda's	60
Zumbo on North of Zambesi	180
Tette, Portuguese town on Zambesi	236
Thence to Quilimane River Mouth	270
Hartley Hill to Quilimane River Mouth	506
Sofala River Mouth	290

Approximate distances from Natal by the shortest route through the Gold Fields of Eersteling and Marabastadt, and through the fly country to the Northern Gold Fields; the commencement of this line is also the usual route to Lydenburg, and the Gold Fields at MacMac and Pilgrim's Rest.

	Mls.
Pietermaritzburg	54
Newcastle	159
Leathern's Drift, between Staander's and Retief's Drift, in Vaal River	64
Cross Pretoria Road a little west of Nazareth	—
Berlin Mission Station	95
Malute's Kraal	37
Eersteling, Natalia Reef, Mr. E. Button's farm. The first Quartz crushing machinery erected in the Transvaal (via Strydpoort)	68
Marabastadt (gold reefs in vicinity)	11
Pass between Blaawberg and Zoutspansberg through fly country, probably to Commando Drift, Limpopo River, enquire for safe road of Der Venage or other hunters	125

Mls.

Junction of Semotchie with Shasha River	54

From the Junction of Semotchie and Shasha to Tati Settlement, Southern, or Victoria and Albert Gold Fields is 54 miles W.N.W.

Lee's House, Mangwe (lat. and long., E. Mohr and T. Baines, crucial station)	85
Hartley Hill, my house, Northern Gold Fields	209
Ganyana River	37
Total	1078
Total *via* Hartley's Road	1249

Mr. Baines wrote:—The distance from Durban to my house at Hartley Hill, by Mr. Hartley's road, safe from fly, and healthy, is 1211 miles 7 furlongs—say

miles 7 furlongs—say	1212
By direct route, with danger of fly and fever	1078
Difference in favour of direct route	134

FROM KIMBERLEY TO DELAGOA BAY.

	m.	f.	yds.
To Christiana	57	2	0
Christiana to Bloemhof	33	1	33
Bloemhof to Klerksdorp..	90	2	90
Klerksdorp to Potchefstroom	31	2	31
Potchefstroom to Pretoria	105	4	105
Pretoria to Middleburg	88	0	0
Middleburg to Kantoor	110	0	0
Kantoor to Barberton	45	0	0
Barberton to Delagoa Bay	160	0	0
Total	720	4	39

PORT ELIZABETH TO THE TATI FIELDS.
(*Viâ Hope Town and the Diamond Fields.*)

Mls.

Port Elizabeth to Hopetown—375 to 400 miles, viz. :—	375
Kruid Fontein	25
Backhouse	18
Campbell	18
Doncé	8
Pap Kuil	16
Daniels Kuil	16
Koning (water between Daniels Kuil and Koning)	30
Kuruman, late the station of the Rev. R. Moffat (New Lattakoo) ..	22
Mathurin	16
Takoon (waters between Mathurin and Takoon)	19
Little Chuie .. ·..	19
Loharon	20
Moretimo	18
Great Chui	10
Sitlagole	18
Maritsani	16
Molopo	16
Mashuani	16
Letsa ya Motlopé	8
Malao Hills	8
Kange (Khanjie) Ba-Wangketso	18
Moshupa	16

		mls.
Moshupa River	.. ..	8
Sechelistown Ba-Kwena (they of the crocodile)	.. ..	18
Kopong	.. ..	19
Bomminigani	.. ..	24
Bo-atlanami	.. ..	21
Lepepe	.. ..	16
Moshue	.. ..	21
Kurubete	.. ..	8
Bamangwato	.. ..	20
Molachue	.. ..	24
Mitlue	.. ..	6
Tauan	.. ..	8
Chakani	.. ..	10
Limunwie	.. ..	10
Palachue	.. ..	12
Seruli River	.. ..	22
Gokwr	.. ..	20
Lotlakani	.. ..	6
Motlotsi (Maclouteie River)	.. ..	14
Shasha (Great Shasa River)	.. ..	20
Tati Settlement—Southern or Victoria and Albert Gold Fields	..	8
Ramoqueban River, N.E. boundary of Tati district	.. .. ..	20
	Total ..	1081

TO CAPE TOWN.

		Mls.
To Crocodile River (via Marais' Farm)	.. ..	24
Crocodile River to Scrobie's Farm (Grootplaats)	.. .. ..	5
Grootplaats to Hartley's	.. ..	25
Hartley's to Holfontein	.. ..	19
Holfontein to Wonderfontein	.. ..	15
Wonderfontein to Potchefstroom	.. ..	35
Potchefstroom to Klerksdorp	.. ..	31
Klerksdorp to Bloemhof	.. ..	90
Bloemhof to Christiana	.. ..	33
Christiana to Kimberley	.. ..	57
Kimberley to Cape Town (by rail)	.. ..	647
	Total ..	981

DELAGOA BAY TO PRETORIA.

		Mls.
To Barberton	.. ..	160
Kantoor	.. ..	45
Middelburg	.. ..	110
Pretoria	.. ..	88
	Total ..	403

DELAGOA BAY TO MOODIE'S.
(Viâ Swazieland.)

		Mls.
Lourenço Marquez to Pesini	.. ..	20
To Matala Poort in the Lobombo	.. ..	14
The first water on the west side of the Lobombo	.. ..	18
The Komatie River	.. ..	6

	Mls.
To The Crocodile River	16
McLachlan's	50
Moodie's	34
	158

(Viâ Spitzkop.)

	Mls.
Lourenço Marquez to Crocodile	74
To Pretorius Kop	25
Sand River	10
Spitzkop	25
Crocodile (passing Ross Hill and Wm. Palmer's Farm)	20
Entrance of Kaap Valley..	15
Moodie's (*viâ* road between Kantoor and Jamestown)	20
	189

MAJOR MACHADO'S RAILWAY SURVEY.

	Distances in		Altitudes in
	Mls.	Yds.	Eng. Ft.
From Lourenço Marquez to Komatie Poort (Lobombo)..	62	910	408
,, Frontier to Crocodile River	20	376	764
,, Crocodile to Lion's River	19	814	
,, Lion's River to Joubert's Nek	19	734	1402
,, Joubert's Nek to Nelspruit	15	722	2416
,, Nelspruit to Houtboschloop	13	434	
,, Houtboschloop to Schoeman's Farm, Sterkspruit	16	453	2503
,, Sterkspruit to Viljoen's Farm	21	742	
,, Viljoen's Farm to Minnaspoort (G. Mare).. ..	15	36	5679
,, Minnaspoort to Bergen Daal..	14	995	6437
,, Bergen Daal to Hartogh's Farm	29	299	
,, Hartogh's Farm to Middleburg	15	233	5235
,, Middleburg to Doornbult (Diedr. Muller)	32	161	
,, Doornbult to Honde River	29	692	
,, Honde River to Pretoria	28	537	4458
Total ..	348	656	

FROM TATI FIELDS.

	Mls.
To Durban	883
Port Elizabeth	1080
Pretoria	448
Eersteling	244

BECHUANALAND.

	Mls.
From Barkley to Taungs	79
,, Taungs to Vryburg	47
,, Vryburg to Sitlagoli	52
,, Sitlagoli to Mafeking	47
,, Mafeking to Kanya (Gatsibibi), by Eastern Road ..	64½
,, Mafeking to Kanya, by Western Road	49
,, Kanya to Molopolole (Sichili's)	40
,, Mafeking to Sochong (Mangwato), by Eastern Route	146½
,, Mafeking to Sochong, by Western Route along the Notuani and Marico Rivers	199½
,, Mafeking to Zeerust..	36
,, Mafeking to Malmani	30

MISCELLANEOUS DISTANCES.

	Mls.
From Potchefstroom to Witwatersrand ..	80
,, Witwatersrand to Pretoria ..	30
,, Bamangwato to Tatin ..	156
,, Tatin to Manyami (Matabele outpost) ..	70
,, Manyami to Inyati M.S. ..	88
,, Manyami to Bulawayo (Lo Bengulu's Head Kraal) ..	46
,, Fort Salisbury to Pungwe Mouth ..	400
,, ,, to Umtasa's Kraal..	160
,, Umtasa's to Umtali River ..	10
,, Umtali River to Massi Kessi ..	16
,, Massi Kessi to Sarmento ..	110
,, Sarmento to Nevis Ferreira (Pungwe Mouth) ..	130
,, Bamangwato to Victoria Falls (Mosioatanga) ..	400
,, Walfisch Bay to Victoria Falls ..	1150
,, Kimberley to Maritzburg ..	400
,, Kimberley to Bloemfontein ..	100
,, Griquatown to Bultfontein ..	60
,, Kuruman to Pitsan ..	154
,, Bamangwato to Notuani River Junction ..	55
,, Bamangwato to the Shashi River ..	163
,, Bamangwato to Makarakara ..	165
,, The Nata to Daka ..	167
,, Daka to Panda-ma-Tenka ..	18
,, Panda-ma-Tenka to Victoria Falls ..	35
,, Victoria Falls to Chobe River ..	37
,, Lake 'Ngami to Victoria Falls ..	320
,, ,, to Bamangwato ..	335
,, ,, to Sechele's ..	350
,, ,, to Walfisch Bay ..	680
,, ,, to Orange River ..	650
,, Pretoria to Pietersburg ..	180
,, Fort Tuli to Pietersburg ..	167
,, Middleburg to Pietersburg ..	140
,, Lydenburg to Pietersburg ..	110
,, Mafeking to Pietersburg ..	290
,, Valksrust to Pietersburg (via Pretoria) ..	420
,, Valksrust to Pietersburg (via Middleburg) ..	305
,, Macloutsie to Mafeking ..	440
,, Fort Tuli to Mafeking ..	489
,, Fort Victoria to Fort Tuli ..	189
,, Fort Victoria to Fort Charter ..	123
,, Fort Charter to Fort Salisbury ..	64
,, Mafeking to Fort Salisbury ..	867
,, Pretoria to Fort Salisbury ..	724
,, Middleburg to Fort Salisbury ..	684
,, Lydenburg to Fort Salisbury ..	654
,, Pietersburg to Fort Salisbury ..	544

(See also eighth, eighteenth, and other chapters.)

APPENDIX D.

ENGLAND'S AUTHORITY IN SOUTHERN ZAMBESIA.

THE following order in Council has been published in the *London Gazette* :—
At the Court at Windsor, the 9th day of May, 1891.

Present.

The Queen's Most Excellent Majesty, Lord President, Lord Steward, Earl of Coventry.

Whereas the territories of South Africa situate within the limits of this Order, as hereinafter described, are under the protection of Her Majesty the Queen :

And whereas by treaty, grant, usage, sufferance, and other lawful means Her Majesty has power and jurisdiction in the said territories.

Now, therefore, Her Majesty, by virtue and in exercise of the powers by " The Foreign Jurisdiction Act, 1890," or otherwise in Her Majesty vested, is pleased by and with the advice of Her Privy Council to order, and it is hereby ordered as follows :—

I. The limits of this Order are :—The parts of South Africa bounded by British Bechuanaland, the German Protectorate, the Rivers Chobe and Zambesi, the Portuguese Possessions, and the South African Republic.

II. The High Commissioner may on Her Majesty's behalf exercise all powers and jurisdiction which Her Majesty, at any time before or after the date of this Order, had or may have within the limits of this Order, and to that end may take or cause to be taken all such measures, and may do or cause to be done all such matters and things within the limits of this Order as are lawful, and as in the interest of Her Majesty's service he may think expedient, subject to such instructions as he may from time to time receive from Her Majesty or through a Secretary of State.

III. The High Commissioner may appoint so many fit persons as in the interest of Her Majesty's Service he may think necessary to be Deputy Commissioners, or Resident Commissioners, or Assistant Commissioners, or Judges, Magistrates, or other officers, and may define from time to time the districts within which such officers shall respectively discharge their functions.

Every such officer may exercise such powers and authorities as the High Commissioner may assign to him, subject nevertheless to such directions and instructions as the High Commissioner may from time to time think fit to give him. The appointment of such officers shall not abridge, alter, or affect the right of the High Commissioner to execute and discharge all the powers and authorities hereby conferred upon him.

The High Commissioner may remove any officer so appointed.

IV. In the exercise of the powers and authorities hereby conferred upon him, the High Commissioner may, amongst other things, from time to time by Proclamation provide for the administration of justice, the raising of revenue, and generally for the peace, order, and good government of all persons within the limits of this Order, including the prohibition and punishment of acts tending to disturb the public peace.

The High Commissioner in issuing such Proclamations shall respect any native laws or customs by which the civil relations of any native chiefs, tribes, or populations under Her Majesty's protection are now regulated, except so far as the same may be incompatible with the due exercise of Her Majesty's power and jurisdiction.

V. Every Proclamation of the High Commissioner shall be published in the *Gazette*, and shall, from and after the expiration of one month from the commencement of such publication, and thereafter until disallowed by Her Majesty or repealed or modified by any subsequent Proclamation, have effect as if contained in this Order.

VI. Her Majesty may disallow any such Proclamation wholly or in part, and may signify such disallowance through a Secretary of State, and upon such disallowance being publicly notified by the High Commissioner in the *Gazette* the provisions so disallowed shall, one month after such publication, cease to have effect, but without prejudice to anything theretofore lawfully done thereunder.

VII. The Courts of British Bechuanaland shall have in respect of matters occurring within the limits of this Order the same jurisdiction, civil and criminal, original and appellate, as they respectively possess from time to time in respect of matters occurring within British Bechuanaland, and the judgments, decrees, orders, and sentences of any such Court made or given in the exercise of the jurisdiction hereby conferred may be enforced and executed, and appeals therefrom may be had and prosecuted in the same way as if the judgment, decree, order, or sentence had been made or given under the ordinary jurisdiction of the Court.

But the jurisdiction hereby conferred shall only be exercised by such Courts, and in such manner and to such extent, as the Governor of British Bechuanaland shall by proclamation from time to time direct.

VIII. Subject to any proclamation made under this Order any jurisdiction exercisable otherwise than under this Order, whether by virtue of any Statute or Order in Council, or of any Treaty, or otherwise, and whether exercisable by Her Majesty, or by any person on Her behalf, or by any Colonial or other Court, or under any Commission, or under any Charter granted by Her Majesty, shall remain in full force.

IX. Judicial notice shall be taken of this Order, and of the commencement thereof, and of any Proclamation made under this Order, and published in the *Gazette*, and of any Treaties affecting the territories within the limits of this Order, and published in the *Gazette*, or contained in papers presented to both Houses of Parliament by command of Her Majesty.

X. This Order shall be published in the *Gazette*, and shall thereupon commence and come into operation ; and the High Commissioner shall give directions for the publication of this Order at such places, and in such manner, and for such time or times as he thinks proper for giving due publicity thereto within the limits of this Order.

XI. The Orders in Council of the twenty-seventh day of January, one thousand eight hundred and eighty-five, for the establishment of Civil and Criminal Jurisdiction in Bechuanaland, and of the thirtieth day of June, one thousand eight hundred and ninety, providing for the exercise of Her Majesty's jurisdiction in certain Territories in South Africa, shall continue in force until the commencement of this Order and be thereupon revoked, but without prejudice to anything lawfully done thereunder, and any Proclamation theretofore issued under the said Orders shall continue in operation until repealed or altered by any Proclamation of the High Commissioner under this Order.

XII. Her Majesty may from time to time revoke, alter, add to, or amend this Order.

XIII. In this Order, unless the subject or context otherwise requires,—

"Her Majesty" includes Her Majesty's heirs and successors.

"Secretary of State" means one of Her Majesty's Principal Secretaries of State.

"High Commissioner" means Her Majesty's High Commissioner for the time being for South Africa.

"Treaty" includes any existing or future Treaty, Convention, or Agreement between Her Majesty and any civilised Power, or any native tribe, people, Chief, or King, and any regulation appended to any such Treaty, Convention, or Agreement.

"Gazette" means any official Gazette published by authority of the High Commissioner, and until such Gazette is instituted, means the Cape of Good Hope Government Gazette.

C. L. PEEL.

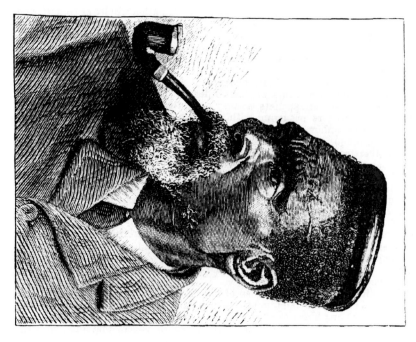

HULUHULU UMTETO.

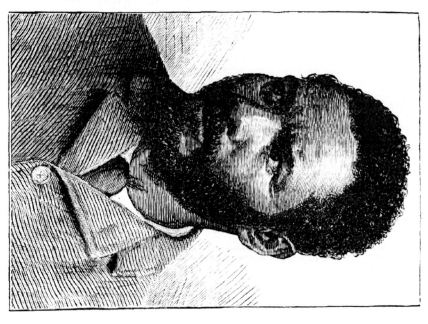

UMFETI INTENI.

APPENDIX E.

BRITISH PROTECTORATE OVER NYASSALAND.
Foreign Office, May 14, 1891.

It is hereby notified for public information that, under and by virtue of Agreements with the Native Chiefs, and by other lawful means, the territories in Africa, hereinafter referred to as the Nyassaland Districts, are under the Protectorate of Her Majesty the Queen.

The British Protectorate of the Nyassaland Districts comprises the Territories bounded on the east and south by the Portuguese Dominions; and to the west by a frontier which, starting on the south from the point where the boundary of the Portuguese Dominions is intersected by the boundary of the Conventional Free Trade zone defined in the 1st Article of the Berlin Act, follows that line northwards to the point where it meets the line of the Geographical Congo Basin, defined in the same Article, and thence follows the latter line to the point where it touches the boundary between the British and German spheres defined in the second paragraph of the 1st Article of the Agreement of the 1st July, 1890.

Measures are in course of preparation for the Administration of justice and the maintenance of peace and good order in the Nyassaland Districts.

APPENDIX F.

THE ANGLO-PORTUGUESE CONVENTION.

The text of the Convention between Great Britain and Portugal, signed at Lisbon on June 11th, and published on June 12, 1891, as a Parliamentary Paper, is as follows:—

ARTICLE I.

Great Britain agrees to recognise as within the dominion of Portugal in East Africa the territories bounded—

1. To the north by a line which follows the course of the River Rovuma from its mouth up to the confluence of the River M'Sinje, and thence westerly along the parallel of latitude of the confluence of these rivers to the shore of Lake Nyassa.

2. To the west by a line which, starting from the above-mentioned frontier on Lake Nyassa, follows the eastern shore of the lake southwards as far as the parallel of latitude 13° 30' south; thence it runs in a south-easterly direction to the eastern shore of Lake Chiuta, which it follows. Thence it runs in a direct line to the eastern shore of Lake Chilwa, or Shirwa, which it follows to the south-easternmost point; thence in a direct line to the easternmost affluent of the River Ruo, and thence follows that affluent, and subsequently, the centre of the channel of the Ruo to its confluence with the River Shiré.

From the confluence of the Ruo and Shiré the boundary will follow the centre of the channel of the latter river to the point just below Chiwanga. Thence it runs due westward until it reaches the watershed between the Zambesi and the Shiré, and follows the watershed between those rivers, and afterwards between the former river and Lake Nyassa until it reaches parallel 14° of south latitude. From thence it runs in a south-westerly direction to the point where south latitude 15° meets the River Aroangwa or Loangwa, and follows the mid-channel of that river to its junction with the Zambesi.

ARTICLE II.

To the south of the Zambesi the territories within the Portuguese sphere of influence are bounded by a line which, starting from a point opposite the mouth of the river Aroangwa or Loangwa, runs directly southwards as far as the 16th parallel of south latitude, follows that parallel to its intersection with the 31st degree of longitude east of Greenwich, thence running eastward direct to the point where the River Mazoe is intersected by the 33d degree of longitude east of Greenwich; it follows that degree southwards to its intersection by the 18° 30' parallel of south latitude; thence it follows the upper part of the eastern slope of the Manica plateau southwards to the centre of the main channel of the Sabi, follows that channel to its confluence with the Lunte, whence it strikes direct to the north-eastern point of the frontier of the South African Republic, and follows the eastern frontier of the Republic, and the frontier of Swazieland to the River Maputa.

It is understood that in tracing the frontier along the slope of the plateau no territory west of longitude 32° 30' east of Greenwich shall be comprised in the Portuguese sphere, and no territory east of longitude 33° east of Greenwich shall be comprised in the British sphere. The line shall, however, if necessary, be deflected so as to leave Mutassa in the British sphere and Massi Kessi in the Portuguese sphere.

ARTICLE III.

Great Britain engages not to make any objection to the extension of the sphere of influence of Portugal, south of Delagoa Bay, as a line following the parallel of the confluence of the River Pongola with the River Maputa to the sea-coast.

ARTICLE IV.

It is agreed that the western line of division separating the British from the Portuguese sphere of influence in Central Africa shall follow the centre of the channel of the Upper Zambesi, starting from the Katima Rapids up to the point where it reaches the territory of the Barotse kingdom. That territory shall remain within the British sphere; its limits to the westward, which will constitute the boundary between the British and Portuguese spheres of influence, being decided by a joint Anglo-Portuguese Commission, which shall have power, in case of difference of opinion, to appoint an umpire.

It is understood on both sides that nothing in this article shall affect the existing rights of any other State. Subject to this reservation, Great Britain will not oppose the extension of Portuguese administration outside the limits of the Barotse country.

ARTICLE V.

Portugal agrees to recognise as within the sphere of influence of Great Britain on the north of the Zambesi the territories extending from the line to be settled by the joint Commission mentioned in the preceding article, to Lake Nyassa, including the islands in that lake south of parallel 11° 30' south latitude, and to the territories reserved to Portugal by the line described in Article I.

ARTICLE VI.

Portugal agrees to recognise, as within the sphere of influence of Great Britain to the south of the Zambesi, the territories bounded on the east and north-east by the line described in Article II.

ARTICLE VII.

All the lines of demarcation traced in Articles I. to VI. shall be subject to rectification by agreement between the two Powers, in accordance with local requirements.

The two Powers agree that in the event of one of them proposing to part with any of the territories to the south of the Zambesi assigned by these Articles to their respective spheres of influence, the other shall be recognised as possessing a preferential right to the territories in question, or any portion of them, upon terms similar to those proposed.

ARTICLE VIII.

The two Powers engage that neither will interfere with any sphere of influence assigned to the other by Articles I. to VI. One Power will not, in the sphere of the other, make acquisitions, conclude treaties, or accept sovereign rights or protectorates.

H H

It is understood that no companies nor individuals subject to one Power can exercise sovereign rights in a sphere assigned to the other, except with the assent of the latter.

ARTICLE IX.

Commercial or mineral concessions and rights to real property possessed by companies or individuals belonging to either Power shall, if their validity is duly proved, be recognised in the sphere of the other Power.

For deciding on the validity of mineral concessions given by the legitimate authority within 30 miles of either side of the frontier south of the Zambesi a tribunal of arbitration is to be named by common agreement.

It is understood that such concessions must be worked according to local regulations and laws.

ARTICLE X.

In all territories in East and Central Africa belonging to or under the influence of either Power missionaries of both countries shall have full protection. Religious toleration and freedom for all forms of Divine worship and religious teaching are guaranteed.

ARTICLE XI.

The transit of goods across Portuguese territories situated between the East Coast and the British sphere shall not, for a period of 25 years from the ratification of this Convention, be subjected to duties in excess of 3 per cent. for imports or for exports. These duties shall in no case have a differential character, and shall not exceed the Customs dues levied on the same goods in the above-mentioned territories.

Her Majesty's Government shall have the option, within five years from the date of the signature of this agreement, to claim freedom of transit for the remainder of the period of 25 years on payment of a sum capitalizing the annual duties for that period at the rate of £30,000 a year.

Coin and precious metals of all descriptions shall be imported and exported to and from the British sphere free of transit duty.

It is understood that there shall be freedom for the passage of subjects and goods of both Powers across the Zambesi, and through the districts adjoining the left bank of the river situated above the confluence of the Shiré, and those adjoining the right bank of the Zambesi situated above the confluence of the River Luenha (Ruenga), without hindrance of any description and without payment of transit dues.

It is further understood that in the above-named districts each Power shall have the right, so far as may be reasonably required for the purpose of communication between territories under the influence of the same Power, to construct roads, railways, bridges, and telegraph lines across the district reserved to the other. The two Powers shall have the right of acquiring in these districts on reasonable conditions the land necessary for such objects, and shall receive all other requisite facilities. Portugal shall have the same rights in the British territory on the banks of the Shiré and in the British territory comprised between the Portuguese territory and the banks of Lake Nyassa. Any railway so constructed by one Power on the territory of the other shall be subject to local regulations and laws agreed upon between the two Governments, and, in case of differences of opinion, subject to arbitration as hereinafter mentioned.

The two Powers shall also be allowed facilities for constructing on the rivers within the above districts piers and landing-places for the purpose of trade and navigation.

Differences of opinion between the two Governments as to the execution of their respective obligations, incurred in accordance with the provisions of the preceding paragraph, shall be referred to the arbitration of two experts, one of whom shall be chosen on behalf of each Power. These experts shall select an umpire, whose decision, in case of difference between the arbitrators, shall be final. If the two experts cannot agree upon the choice of an umpire, this umpire shall be selected by a neutral Power to be named by the two Governments.

All materials for the construction of roads, railways, bridges, and telegraph lines shall be admitted free of charge.

ARTICLE XII.

The navigation of the Zambesi and Shiré, without excepting any of their branches and outlets, shall be entirely free for the ships of all nations.

The Portuguese Government engages to permit and to facilitate transit for all persons and goods of every description over the waterways of the Zambesi, the Shiré, the Pungwe, the Busi, the Limpopo, the Sabi, and their tributaries and also over the landways which supply means of communication where these rivers are not navigable.

ARTICLE XIII.

Merchant ships of the two Powers shall in the Zambesi, its branches, and outlets have equal freedom of navigation, whether with cargo or ballast, for the transportation of goods and passengers. In the exercise of this navigation the subjects and flags of both Powers shall be treated, in all circumstances, on a footing of perfect equality, not only for the direct navigation from the open sea to the inland ports of the Zambesi, and *vice versâ*, but for the great and small coasting trade, and for boat trade on the course of the river. Consequently on all the course and mouths of the Zambesi there will be no differential treatment of the subjects of the two Powers; and no exclusive privilege of navigation will be conceded by either to companies, corporations, or private persons.

The navigation of the Zambesi shall not be subject to any restriction or obligation based merely on the fact of navigation. It shall not be exposed to any obligation in regard to landing-station or depôt, or for breaking bulk, or for compulsory entry into port. In all the extent of the Zambesi the ships and goods in process of transit on the river shall be submitted to no transit dues, whatever their starting-place or destination. No maritime or river toll shall be levied based on the sole fact of navigation, nor any tax on goods on board of ships. There shall only be collected taxes or duties which shall be an equivalent for services rendered to navigation itself. The tariff of these taxes or duties shall not warrant any differential treatment.

The affluents of the Zambesi shall be in all respects subject to the same rules as the river of which they are tributaries.

The roads, paths, railways, or lateral canals which may be constructed with the special object of correcting the imperfections in the river route on certain sections of the course of the Zambesi, its affluents, branches, and outlets shall be considered, in their quality of means of communication, as dependencies of this river, and as equally open to the traffic of both Powers. And, as on the river itself, so there shall be collected on these roads, railways, and canals only tolls calculated on the cost of construction, maintenance, and management, and on the profits due to the promoters. As regards the tariff of these tolls, strangers and the natives of the respective territories shall be treated on a footing of perfect equality.

Portugal undertakes to apply the principles of freedom of navigation enunciated in this article on so much of the waters of the Zambesi, its affluents, branches, and outlets, as are or may be under her sovereignty, protection, or influence. The rules which she may establish for the safety and control of navigation shall be drawn up in a way to facilitate, as far as possible, the circulation of merchant ships.

Great Britain accepts, under the same reservations, and in identical terms, the obligations undertaken in the preceding articles in respect of so much of the waters of the Zambesi, its affluents, branches, and outlets as are or may be under her sovereignty, protection, or influence.

Any questions arising out of the provisions of this article shall be referred to a joint commission, and, in case of disagreement to arbitration.

Another system for the administration and control of the Zambesi may be substituted for the above arrangements by common consent of the Riverain Powers.

ARTICLE XIV.

In the interest of both Powers Portugal agrees to grant absolute freedom of passage between the British sphere of influence and Pungwe Bay for all merchandise of every description, and to give the necessary facilities for the improvement of the means of communication.

The Portuguese Government agree to construct a railway between Pungwe and the British sphere. The survey of this line shall be completed within six months, and the two Governments shall agree as to the time within which the railway shall be commenced and completed. If an agreement is not arrived at the Portuguese Government will give the construction of the railway to a company which shall be designated by a neutral Power, to be selected by the two Governments, as being in its judgment competent to undertake the work immediately. The said company shall have all requisite facilities for the acquisition of land, cutting timber, and free importation and supply of materials and labour.

The Portuguese Government shall either itself construct or shall procure the construction of a road from the highest navigable point of the Pungwe, or other river which may be agreed upon as more suitable for traffic, to the British sphere, and shall construct or procure the construction in Pungwe Bay and on the river of the necessary landing-places.

It is understood that no dues shall be levied on goods in transit by the river, the road, or the railway, exceeding the *maximum* of 3 per cent. under the conditions stipulated in Article XI.

ARTICLE XV.

Great Britain and Portugal engage to facilitate telegraphic communication in their respective spheres.

The stipulations contained in Article XIV. as regards the construction of a railway from Pungwe Bay to the interior shall be applicable in all respects to the construction of a telegraph line for communication between the coast and the British sphere south of the Zambesi. Questions as to the points of departure and termination of the line, and as to other details, if not arranged by common consent, shall be submitted to the arbitration of experts under the conditions prescribed in Article XI.

Portugal engages to maintain telegraphic service between the coast and the River Ruo, which service shall be open to the use of the subjects of the two Powers without any differential treatment.

Great Britain and Portugal engage to give every facility for the connection of telegraphic lines constructed in their respective spheres.

Details in respect to such connection, and in respect to questions relating to the settlement of through tariffs and other charges, shall, if not settled by common consent, be referred to the arbitration of experts under the conditions prescribed in Article XI.

1. A note shall be addressed to Her Majesty's Government by the Portuguese Government, undertaking to lease for 99 years to persons named by Her Majesty's Government land at the Chinde mouth of the Zambesi, to be used under regulations for the landing, storage, and transhipment of goods. Sites, price, and regulations to be arranged by three Commissioners to be named one by each of the two Governments and the third by a neutral Power to be selected by them. In case of difference of opinion among the Commissioners, the decision of the majority to be final. A note shall also be addressed to the Portuguese Government by Her Majesty's Government undertaking, on the demand of the former, to lease on similar conditions and for similar purposes to persons named by the Portuguese Government land in some spot on the south-western coast of Lake Nyassa which shall be agreed upon between the two Governments as suitable for the purpose.

2. Notes shall be exchanged between Her Majesty's Government and the Portuguese Government with regard to the traffic rates to be charged on the railway similar to those exchanged on August 20, 1890.

3. Notes shall be exchanged between the two Governments, agreeing that the importation of ardent spirits to either bank of the Zambesi and Shiré by those rivers, whether in the British or Portuguese sphere, shall be interdicted, and that the authorities of the two States shall agree upon the arrangements necessary to prevent and punish infractions of this article.

GENERAL INDEX.

ZAMBESIA
ENGLAND'S EL DORADO
IN AFRICA.
BEING A DESCRIPTION OF
MATABELELAND & MASHONALAND & AN ACCOUNT OF

THE GOLD FIELDS OF
BRITISH SOUTH AFRICA

BY

E. P. MATHERS, F.C.S. F.R.G.S.
EDITOR OF "SOUTH AFRICA"
AND AUTHOR OF
"GOLDEN SOUTH AFRICA" &C.

SOUTH AFRICA

CONDUCTED BY EDWARD P. MATHERS, F.G.S.F.R.G.S., AUTHOR OF GOLDE SOUTH AFRICA &c

A WEEKLY JOURNAL FOR ALL INTERESTED IN SOUTH AFRICA AND FINANCIAL AFFAIRS.

THE ENGLISH ORGAN OF THE SOUTH AFRICAN GOLD FIELDS

CONDUCTED BY

EDWARD P. MATHERS, F.G.S., F.R.G.S.,

Author of "Golden South Africa," "Zambesia," &c.

Unrivalled Circulation in South Africa and Europe

EVERY SATURDAY, Price

TWO EDITIONS

SOUTH AFRICAN EDITION
Weekly Mail

EUROPEAN EDITION (published on Saturday and to be had of all newsagents and from the Office).

Subscription (inclusive of postage)

"SOUTH AFRICA" is the English . . .
Letters and notes from reliable correspondents . . .
for . . . its columns. "SOUTH AFRICA" . . . features . . .
between South African import . . .
"SOUTH AFRICA" devotes . . .
matters in which South Africa . . .
Merchants, Wine and Wool Growers . . .
Diamond Dealers. Journalists, . . . an interest . . .
"SOUTH AFRICA," by reason . . . extensive journal
in England and South Africa, regarded . . . matters of interest
upon all matters pertaining to South . . .

TO ADVERTISERS.

"SOUTH AFRICA" stands unrivalled in its field of the . . .
and rapid success is without a parallel in the history of Olay and Anglo-African . . .
paper being read by all classes interested in and resident in South . . .
advantages to the shrewd Advertiser. Manufacturers of all classes of . . . export
will fail to reach the consumers they wish to secure till they advertise in . . .

THE SCALE OF ADVERTISING CHARGES WILL BE . . . ON
APPLICATION TO THE MANAGER.

Cheques (crossed "Standard Bank of South Africa,") and P.O. . . . should be
made payable to EDWARD P. MATHERS, Offices of "SOUTH AFRICA," . . . Africa

OUND

Lightning Source UK Ltd.
Milton Keynes UK
UKOW011930271011

181034UK00002B/87/P